C. R. Weaver

BASIC

Concepts and Structured Problem Solving

BASIC

Concepts and Structured Problem Solving

Michel Boillot
Pensacola Junior College

WEST PUBLISHING COMPANY
St. Paul • New York • Los Angeles • San Francisco

COMPOSITION
Carlisle Graphics

COPY EDITOR
Pamela S. McMurry

COVER PHOTO
Laser Photography by Floyd Rollefstad,
Laser Fantasy Production

50 West Kellogg Boulevard
P.O. Box 43526
St. Paul, Minnesota 55164

Printed in the United States of America

Library of Congress Cataloging in Publication Data

Boillot, Michel H.
BASIC, concepts & structured problem solving.

Includes index.
1. Basic (Computer program language) 2. Structured programming. I. Title. II. Title: BASIC, concepts and structured problem solving.
QA76.73.B3B643 1984 001.64'24 83-26036
ISBN 0-314-77843-8

1st Reprint—1984

CONTENTS

4 Flowcharting and the BASIC Statements: INPUT, GO TO, and IF 97

5 READ/DATA, Counting and Problem Solving 153

6 BASIC Functions, PRINT USING, ON GO TO, and Logical Functions 213

7 The Accumulation Process and the FOR/NEXT Statements 255

C.R. Weaver

PREFACE

People from all walks of life and from all types of backgrounds are becoming increasingly interested in computers. As more and more microcomputers find their way into homes, offices, farms, and schools, enrollments in introductory computing courses are rapidly increasing. This diversified group represents a new wave of nontraditional students for whom the traditional university-oriented BASIC text is not very well suited.

The pedagogical presentation and the organization of this text differ markedly from that of other texts. After a brief general introduction to computers in chapter 1, the student is introduced in chapter 2 to one- or two-line BASIC programs, where the emphasis is on the mechanics of typing and entering programs on a terminal: How is an instruction typed? What happens when the ENTER/RETURN key is pressed? What takes place when RUN or LIST is typed? In what way do system commands differ from BASIC instructions? The objective is to give the student confidence at the very beginning so that he or she feels in control of the computer. This important feeling of confidence continues to develop as the student becomes familiar with the operation of his or her system and is then able to predict and respond appropriately to the computer's various messages and actions.

All the chapters contain several sets of "Do It Now" exercises, which allow the student to test his or her understanding of the material just covered. Answers to these exercises are provided for immediate feedback. Although this text stresses minimal ANSI BASIC, most chapters have a short section on BASIC features generally available in most BASIC versions. The student is encouraged to try out these features. The more eager and inquisitive student may be tempted to experiment with such features as the CHR$ statement, runtime interrupts (INKEY$), various printer graphic options, and so forth. This experimentation can lead the student to discover additional intriguing and interesting features in his or her system's technical reference manual. Each chapter also contains a section entitled "My Computer Is Different," where the student can use a blank page to record special features available on his or her system; this space can also be used to jot down procedures for using specific computer peripherals.

There are many problems confronting today's instructor of an introductory course in BASIC programming, in particular, what to do about the IF THEN ELSE, pseudo code, and structured programming in general. For many, flowcharting is a tool of the past, while structured code is "in." However, many BASIC versions unlike other languages, do not support the DO WHILE or DO UNTIL constructs, which are the very ones that give legitimacy to the idea of structured programming. Yet these features should be discussed, and chapter 4 does just that. In fact, the IF THEN ELSE is used in program examples throughout the text, and even though the student's system may not support the ELSE statement, its usefulness should be understood and appreciated, since its universality is only a few years, if not only months, away. Chapter 4 also presents a case for pseudo code, which, unfortunately, cannot be put to full advantage since the DO WHILE or DO UNTIL constructs are not BASIC standards. Nevertheless, the importance of pseudo code warrants its inclusion, as well as its occasional use.

This text also differs from many other BASIC texts by discussing problem solving and program development at great length in chapter 5. How can a student learn to solve a problem on a computer? Many teachers begin solving a problem by writing the corresponding logic, either in flowchart form or in pseudo code. We find that a more successful approach is to first "warm up" the student to the right mood and level of understanding before starting the logic phase. To do this, we first try to understand the word problem by very carefully analyzing certain key words or sentences in the statement of the problem. We then reformulate the problem and try to solve it manually, without worrying about flowcharts, BASIC code, or computers. This generally requires making up a few sample input records. At this point the student usually starts participating more actively in the discussion by asking questions: What does that sentence really mean? What happens if we do this? Should this constant be part of the input record? Finally, the class arrives at an answer to the problem, and we try to determine what the output should look like: Should the report include this item? that caption? this intermediate result? Is there any information missing that a reader should know about? A sample report is then completed using the sample input records. Is the report readable, self-documenting, and attractively designed?

This discussion forces the student to understand the problem better and to set forth output objectives, and it prepares the way for the logic phase, which is the most difficult stage of the problem-solving process. This stage starts with an attempt to identify the various tools needed for the job: What variables are needed? Do we need indexes? If so, how many? What about accumulators? This process establishes an inventory of variables, which is then captured in the program through REM statements containing a data dictionary. By this time the student is conscious of what needs to be done and his or her mental muscles are nicely "warmed up"; the flowchart or pseudo code stage is about to start. The logic stage is typically the chief stumbling block for most students, but it need not be if one remembers that a program is no more than a collection of elementary tasks or techniques. The student can learn these techniques individually and then call on them to solve a particular problem.

In chapters 5 through 9, many of the most common elementary programming tasks and techniques are presented and discussed either in sections on techniques or in the programming problems. When the student has mastered these techniques, any number of them can be integrated into the fabric of a program, whenever they are needed.

All of the solved problems in the programming sections of chapters 5 through 9 follow a systematic format covering the following steps:

1. understanding the problem
2. output design
3. data dictionary
4. program development
5. testing
6. input validation (optional)

This disciplined and systematic approach to programming will give the novice programmer more insight into the problem-solving process and should assist him or her in becoming a better problem solver. The solved programs always show both the input and the output, so that the student can better relate the input and output to the various INPUT, READ, and PRINT statements in the program. All the computer output is displayed on a green background to provide quick visual access to computer-produced reports or results.

The last section in each chapter contains two sets of exercises and programming problems. The first subsection, entitled "Test Yourself," contains exercises relating to syntax as well as to programming problems. Answers to these exercises, including the BASIC code, are provided at the end of the chapter. The second subsection contains programming exercises dealing with business, mathematical, logical, physical science, and engineering problems; some of these problems require the use of random numbers.

Few successful textbooks are ever produced without the assistance and better judgments of reviewers. I would like to thank Edward Suppiger, Professor Emeritus, Princeton University, Richard L. Cowan, Robert Fincutter, Joan Ramuta, Tom Richard, Carol Rowey, and Norman Wright for their helpful comments and criticisms. I am also indebted to Eileen Entin for her superb reviews and for her many suggestions, the results of an obvious deep concern for students and how they learn. Eileen has also authored the instructor's manual for this text. Her natural teaching ability is evident in her writing and will undoubtedly be of great assistance to many teachers in the areas of testing and presentation of key concepts. I am also greatly indebted to Pamela McMurry, who has painstakingly gone through the manuscript to free it of errors. Her contribution to style and prose has made this text easier to read and to understand. Our thanks also go to the people at Carlisle Graphics, who have been so cooperative and understanding during the production phase. Not to be forgotten in this adventure are our good WEST editor and friend, Gary Woodruff, and cheerful developmental editor, Phyllis Cahoon, who made this project a reality. We would also like to thank Keith Hobbie, Tim Danielson, Renee Grevious, and the remaining silent but effective personnel at WEST.

Michel Boillot

1 COMPUTERS AND COMPUTING

1-1 The Electronic Brain

News Item: When the *Apollo 13* flight was jeopardized by unforeseen events, new flight plans were produced by computers in just 84 minutes. One person working on the problem could have performed the task in 1,040,256 years. With a desk calculator, the time could have been cut to 60,480 years.

News Item: Mathematical Application Group, Inc., has announced a commercially available animation technique called *Synthavision* that uses the computer to construct visual displays that when photographed resemble conventionally produced cartoons.

News Item: ARTRA, Inc. has announced the availability of *Housemaster,* a computer-based system that will control household lighting, heating and air conditioning, appliances, and security alarm systems, as well as provide time services and assorted entertainment programs. The system is voice-controlled; it responds to verbal commands and includes a voice synthesizer to produce spoken responses.

News Item: The U.S. Postal Service has announced the availability of an electronic mail system. Users' computers transmit mail (typically bills or advertising) to regional postal service computer centers via telephone. The computer at the regional center produces a printed version of the mail for next day home delivery.

The computers mentioned in these news items are the high-speed, internally programmed, electronic computers that have become the unseen "brain" behind most of the business transactions of everyday life. Computers have also had an incalculable influence on government, science, and the arts in the years since the first fledgling computer was invented in the mid-1940s.

Today computers are being applied to every conceivable problem. One has only to pick up any popular magazine to read about newer and larger problems being solved by computers. The computer has become an indispensable tool in all scientific and commercial endeavors and is gradually becoming an integral part of the American home as well.

1-2 Computers—*What Are They?*

Computers are automatic electronic machines that can accept data, store vast amounts of information, and perform arithmetic at high speeds to solve complex problems. Without human intervention, computers can process long sequences of instructions (called *programs* and discussed in later sections of this book) to solve a variety of problems ranging from business problems, such as payrolls, to scientific problems, such as the calculation of satellite trajectories.

1-2-1 Organization of a Computer

The computer may be thought of as a system composed of five components or subsystems, as show in Figure 1–1. These components and their functions are as follows:

1. The *input* unit feeds information from the outside world to the computer. This information includes both data[1] and instructions (programs). Input units are capable of reading information recorded on such different mediums as punched cards or magnetic tape, or from terminals. The information read from these devices is placed in appropriate memory locations.
2. The *memory* unit stores information. It holds the sequence of instructions (or program) necessary to solve a particular problem and any additional data required. The memory is divided into locations that each have an address (are *addressable*). Instructions and data are stored in these cells.
3. The *control* unit fetches the instructions and data from memory and executes the instructions one at a time with the help of either the input/output or arithmetic/logical unit. All of the other components operate as directed by the control unit.
4. The *arithmetic/logical* unit consists of the electronic circuitry that performs arithmetic operations such as addition, multiplication, subtraction, and division, and logical operations such as comparison of numbers.
5. The *output* unit can transfer or copy the contents of certain memory locations onto some external medium such as punched cards, punched paper tape, magnetic tape, a printed page produced by a teletype or line printer, or a cathode ray tube (CRT) screen for visual display.

It is quite common to refer to the memory, control, and arithmetic/logical units collectively as the *central processing unit (CPU)*. The CPU may be thought of as the seat of intelligence of the entire computer system. The input and output functions

Figure 1–1 Logical units of a computer.

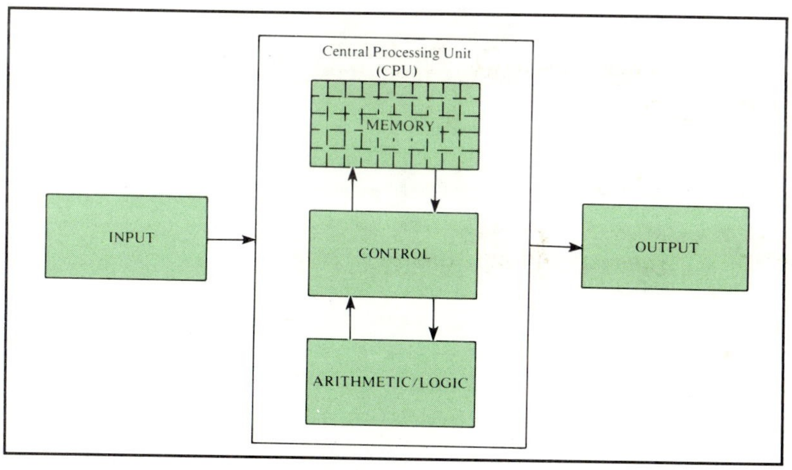

[1]Data is the information (raw facts) to be processed by a program. For example, if a program were designed to sort names into alphabetical order, then the names to be sorted would be the data for that program.

may be performed by devices located at some distance (a few feet or many miles) from the CPU.

1-2-2 Why Use a Computer?

A computer is a problem-solving machine. However, it cannot be said that the computer is suitable for solving all problems. It is sometimes more economical to solve relatively simple problems and problems that occur infrequently by mechanical methods. If, on the other hand, a problem requires the processing of a large volume of input or output, is repetitive in nature, or requires great processing speeds and accuracy, it may be worthwhile and necessary to use a computer. There are, of course, problems that cannot be solved without computers. For example, in a spacecraft-launching operation, data relayed to the ground by a spacecraft must be analyzed instantaneously to allow controllers to make on-the-spot decisions; only a computer can record and analyze the mass of data fast enough for such decisions to be practical.

1-2-3 Computer Programs

An electronic computer may be called an electronic "brain," but its function and problem-solving ability depend on the intelligence of the human beings who direct and control the machine. These people are called *programmers* and *operators* and are responsible for giving the computer a set of instructions consisting of the necessary steps required to derive a solution to a given problem and seeing that those instructions are carried out by the computer. The set of instructions that controls the computer is called a *program*.

A program can be executed by the computer only when it is stored in the computer's memory and is in machine language code. Machine language is the only language the computer can understand. It is a language in which arithmetic/logical operations are represented by machine-recognizable numeric codes and in which memory locations containing data and program instructions are represented by numeric addresses. Machine language programs are very detailed and difficult to write. Machine languages vary from one computer manufacturer to another; such languages are machine-dependent, reflecting the design of the particular computer. Other types of languages (called *high-level languages*) have been developed to allow the user to formulate problems in a much more convenient and efficient manner. Such languages are problem-oriented rather than machine-oriented. High-level languages are essentially machine-independent; programs written in such languages can be processed on any type of computer. High-level languages must ultimately be translated into machine language before they can be executed by the computer. Special programs called *language translators* or *compilers* have therefore been developed to provide this translation service. BASIC (*B*eginner's *A*ll-purpose *S*ymbolic *I*nstruction *C*ode) is an example of a high-level language.

The following example will help you understand how a language such as BASIC, instead of the machine language of the computer, is used by the programmer.

Each memory location has an *address*. Suppose we want to add the data contained in memory locations 065 and 932 and store the result in location 752. The machine instruction for this might be "43065932752." The first two digits are called the *operation code*. The operation code is used by the control unit to determine what action (add, multiply, etc.) is to be performed on the data in the specified memory locations. Following the identification of the operation, the operands are given. Operands represent the addresses of the data to be used. The data we wish to add is found in memory locations 065 and 932. We will store our result in location 752. The machine language instruction is broken down as follows:

43	065 932	752
↑	↑	↑
Operation code	Memory address of first and second operand	Address for result

In the computer, the instruction would be represented in binary (0's and 1's). In BASIC programs, arithmetic operations are indicated by the symbols:

+	addition
−	subtraction
*	multiplication
/	division
**, ↑, or ^	exponentiation.

Each memory location is assigned a symbolic name. Let us agree to call location 065 by the symbolic name P, location 932 by X, and location 752 by A. Then the BASIC instruction equivalent to the machine instruction "43065932752" would be

```
LET A = P + X
```

In practice, the high-level language programmer never needs to worry about machine addresses or operation codes. The BASIC programming system takes care of all such details, allowing the programmer to focus attention on the logic of the problem.

1-2-4 Types of Computing Systems

The very first computers required the user to prepare a program in some suitable form (usually punched cards) and submit it to the computer for processing. The computer executed each program one at a time. The user received the results, generally in printed form, at some later time. This mode of operation (known as *batch processing*) has several limitations, particularly in an educational environment. The user must wait some period of time between submitting his/her program and receiving the results. This is particularly annoying when a student is learning a new computer language and is apt to make mistakes. It may require many submissions of a program to receive an error-free output.

An alternative to batch processing is found in *interactive computing*, in which the user communicates directly with the computing system via a communication terminal (hard copy, Teletype, visual screens, etc.). The user enters the program one statement at a time. The computing system can evaluate the statement and inform the user immediately if it is not correct, allowing him/her to make any necessary changes before proceeding.[2] When a complete program has been entered, the system can then execute *(run)* the program, providing the solution almost immediately.

[2]On some systems using batch BASIC, the user must type all program statements before getting any feedback. The program is then compiled and all errors are identified to the user.

There are two types of systems providing *interactive* computing capabilities: the *microcomputing system* and the *time-sharing system*. Microcomputing systems such as the widely used Apple, Radio Shack, and IBM Personal computer systems are generally self-contained systems completely under the control of the computer user. Time-sharing systems, on the other hand, consist of a network of terminals communicating with a central computer system. The communication link between the terminal and the computer takes many forms. Telephone links are quite commonly used. To initiate communications via the telephone, the user must dial the number of the computer and place the telephone receiver in a special device (called a *modem*) that is attached to the communications terminal.

When using a microcomputing system, the user generally must enter some initial data such as the date and time. When using a time-sharing system, the user must establish his/her identity to the computer before using the computing facility. This is done to enable the system to account for the time used, to bill users accordingly, and to establish what resources are available to individual users. Before a person can make use of a time-sharing system, it is generally necessary to have an assigned account number and perhaps also a special password. After establishing the communications link, the user enters his/her account number and password. If these match a list kept by the computing system, the user is allowed to proceed; if not, the user may not have access to the computing facility. These steps, called a *sign-on procedure*, are quite specific to a particular computing system. An equally important operation is the *sign-off procedure* followed when the user is finished. Almost all systems have a command such as GOOD BYE or BYE that terminates the user's communications with the system and releases the terminal for another user. It is important that the sign-off procedure be followed after each session at a terminal. If a user does not sign off, the next person may continue without signing-on, and the time used by both persons would be charged to the first user's account, additionally stored information may also be lost.

1-2-5 Do It Now

1. What is the name of the computer you will be using?
2. Is the system batch or interactive?
3. If a batch system is to be used, how will programs be submitted?
4. If the system is interactive, is it a microcomputing or a time-sharing system?
5. If it is a microcomputing system, what procedure is needed to begin programming in BASIC?
6. If it is a time-sharing system, what is the sign-on/sign-off procedure? What commands are needed to begin entering a BASIC program?
7. If a batch system is to be used, what system control statements or job control statements (JCL) will be required to enter a BASIC program?

1-3 A Model Computer

Let us consider a very simple model computer that operates conceptually in much the same manner as its larger real-life counterparts (see Figure 1–2). The input medium is a terminal where numbers have been entered (typed). The output medium is represented by a paper pad. The memory unit consists of a group of sequentially numbered "pigeonholes." Each "hole" or location in the memory can hold one instruction or one number. Locations can be referred to either by name or by address. The arithmetic/logical unit is represented by a desk calculator capable of performing arithmetic and logical operations. The role of the control unit is played by a human operator who can fetch instructions from memory one at a time and execute them; he/she can also fetch data from or store data in various memory locations. The types of instructions the operator is capable of executing include:

1. *Input*. Read a value from the input medium and store that value in a specified memory location. For example, the instruction

   ```
   INPUT H
   ```

   will cause one value on the input medium to be read and stored in a memory location called H.

Figure 1–2 A model computer.

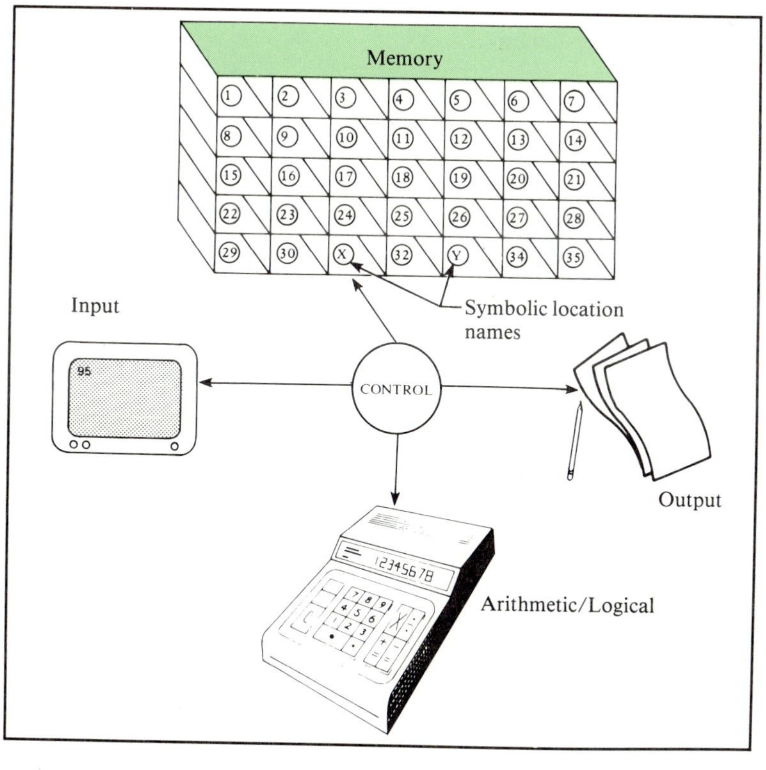

2. *Conditional branching*. Perform a comparison test between two values using the logical unit and branch to a specified memory location if the test condition is met. If the condition is not met, no transfer occurs, and the following instruction is taken from the next memory location. For example, the instruction

```
IF H < 4Ø GO TO 11
```

causes the control unit to first fetch the value H from memory and then request the logical unit to compare the value with 40. If the logical unit reports that the value of H is less than 40, the control unit fetches the next instruction from location 11. If the value of H is greater than or equal to 40, the next instruction is taken from the next sequentially numbered location. Hence a conditional transfer allows a program to process a particular instruction(s) if a certain condition is met or process another different instruction(s) if that condition is not met.

3. *Calculations*. Perform calculations using the arithmetic unit and place results in desired memory locations. For example, the instruction

```
LET P = 4*H
```

will cause the control unit to fetch the value contained in memory location H and activate the arithmetic unit to multiply that value by 4. The final result is then stored in memory location P.

4. *Unconditional branching*. Take the next instruction from a specified memory location. For example, the instruction

```
GO TO 5
```

causes the control unit to fetch the next instruction from location 5 rather than from the next sequentially numbered location. Unconditional branching, then, simply means transfer directly to a particular instruction in memory.

5. *Output*. Copy a value from a memory location onto the output medium. For example, the instruction

```
PRINT H, P
```

will cause the contents of H and P to be written out on the output pad.

6. *Termination*. Cease execution of instructions for this program and wait for a new program to be loaded into memory. For example, the instruction

```
END
```

causes the program to terminate. No more instructions in this program are executed.

To illustrate the concepts just discussed, let us write a short program to calculate and write out an amount of pay owed an employee who is paid $4 an hour with time and a half for all hours in excess of 40. The complete instructions to solve this problem might be as follows:

```
1 INPUT H              Enter number of hours worked from time card.
2 IF H > 4Ø GO TO 5    Check if number of hours is greater than 40.
3 LET P = 4*H          If not, compute regular pay,
4 GO TO 6              and go to print pay.
```

`5 LET P = 160 + 6*(H - 40)`	If hours are greater than 40, compute regular pay, which, is $160, plus overtime at rate of $6 per hour.
`6 PRINT P, H`	Print pay and number of hours.
`7 END`	Stop.

Now, suppose this program has been loaded in memory as shown in Figure 1–3. (This loading function can be performed by manually keying in the program at the terminal.)

After execution of instruction 1, the value read from the input unit (38 in this example) is placed in location H. The computer system will have automatically reserved a location for H.

In the second instruction, the logic unit will determine that the contents of location H are not greater than 40; hence, the next instruction to be executed comes from location 3.

After instruction 3 is executed, the contents of location P become 4*38 = 152.

Instruction 4 causes the control unit to take its next instruction from location 6.

The instruction at location 6 will cause the contents of location H and P to be copied onto the output medium.

Instruction 7 causes the control unit to stop and wait for the next program. The status of the model computer after execution of this program is shown in Figure 1–4.

1-3-1 Do It Now

1. What output would be produced if the input supplied to the program in Figure 1–3 were 40? 50?
2. How would the execution of the program be affected by replacing the statement in location 7 by GO TO 1? What would be the advantages and disadvantages of doing this?
3. Write a step-by-step procedure for your computing system to enter and execute the payroll program discussed in this section.

Figure 1–3 Payroll program with sample input.

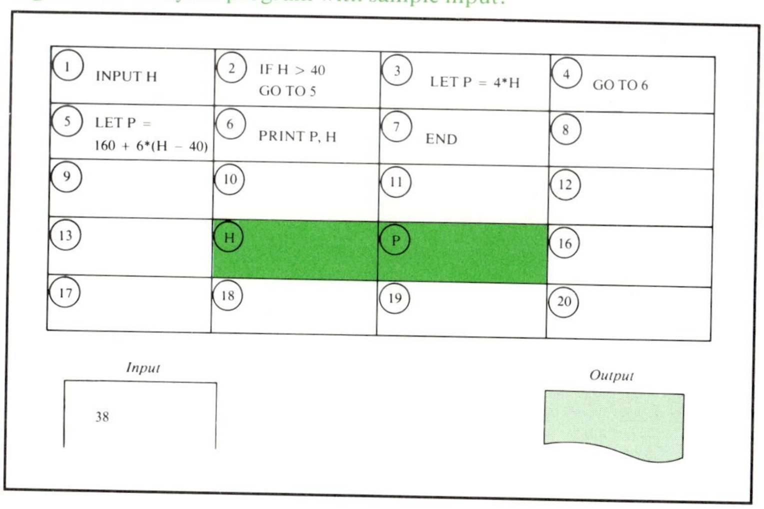

■ **Figure 1–4** Status at conclusion of payroll program.

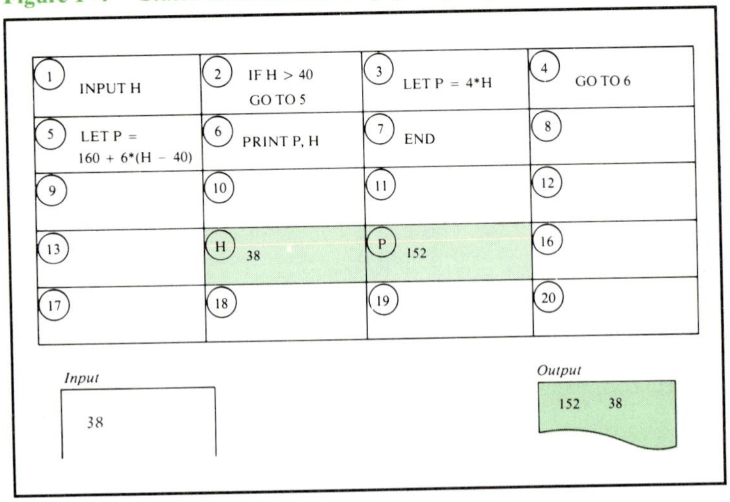

Answers

1. 160, 220
2. After processing one record, the system will input another. this is an advantange if there is more than one record (employee) to be processed; it is a disadvantage if there is only one record to be processed since it will require an extra step to terminate the program. Termination of programs that request more data is accomplished by pressing a certain key (usually the BREAK key or combination of keys, but this varies from system to system).

1-4 Computers—*What Makes Them Tick?*

1-4-1 Computer Hardware

The physical configuration (the *hardware* or machinery) used for the logical components illustrated in Figure 1–1 varies greatly from one computing system to another. Typically the memory, control, and arithmetic/logical units are grouped together and referred to as the *central processing unit (CPU)*. The CPU varies in size from a small box in a typical microcomputer (see Figure 1–5) to a fairly large unit in a typical medium-scale computer (see Figure 1–6). The internal construction of the CPU, the technology used for the memory unit, and the speed at which instructions are executed vary greatly from one computer to another. Modern systems tend to make great use of microminiaturized integrated circuits, making possible significant reduction in sizes and increase in processing speeds (see Figure 1–7).

The hardware used for input and output devices also varies greatly from one system to another. Some devices, such as the line printer, the card punch, and the graph plotter (Figure 1–8), can be used as output devices only. Other devices, such as the

■ **Figure 1-5** The Apple *IIe* personal computer (*courtesy Apple Computer, Inc.*).

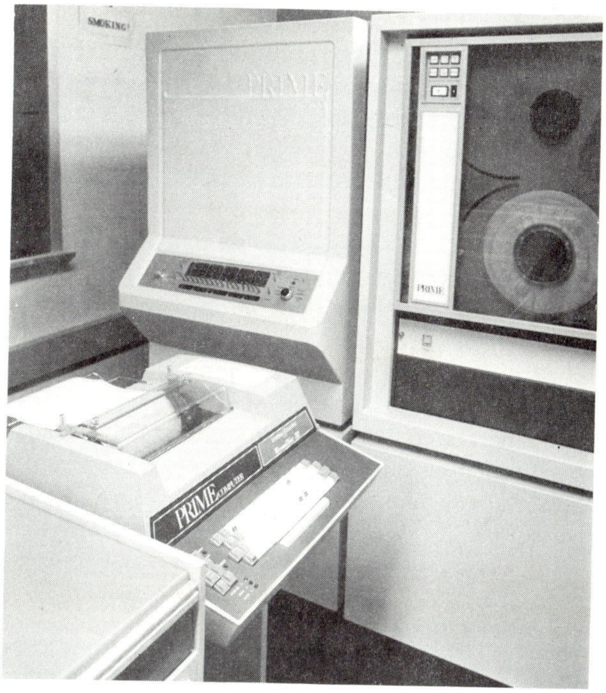

■ **Figure 1-6** The Prime computing system (*courtesy General Electric*).

■ **Figure 1-7** Magnified view of the Intel 8748 single chip microcomputer (*courtesy Intel Corporation*).

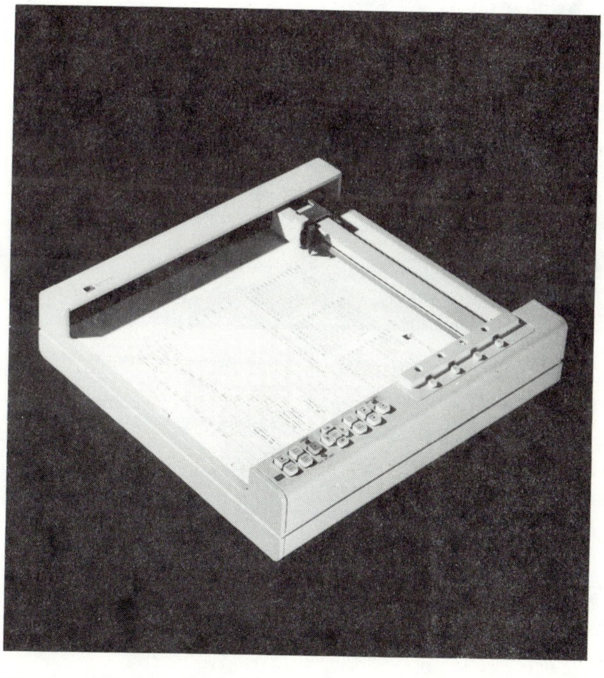

■ **Figure 1-8** A plotter (*courtesy Hewlett-Packard Company, Data Systems Division*).

punched card reader, can be used only as an input device. Some devices can be used for both input and output purposes, although generally not simultaneously. Such devices include the hard copy terminal (Figure 1–9), the CRT (cathode ray tube) console (Figure 1–10), the magnetic disk drive, and the magnetic tape drive. The latter two devices are sometimes referred to as *mass storage* devices because they are capable of storing large quantities of data and can be accessed by the CPU very rapidly.

Users of microcomputing systems generally store programs and data on a small magnetic disk known as a diskette or floppy disk. Figure 1–11 shows the user of a typical microcomputer inserting a floppy disk into the computing system. The floppy disk stores the computer's operating system, which consists of programs required to enable easy use of the computing system. The disk also stores programs and data stored by individual users. A typical diskette can store anywhere from 80,000 to 500,000 characters. The user must take good care of his/her floppy disk in order to ensure that the content of the disk is not inadvertently destroyed. The disk should not be subjected to extremes of heat or cold. The surface of the disk should not be touched at any time. With a little care, a floppy disk will provide several years of error-free service.

The input/output devices for a particular system may be located physically close to the CPU or at some distance—in an adjacent room or miles away. In the latter case, data may be transmitted to the CPU via telephone lines. This technique is called *tele-*

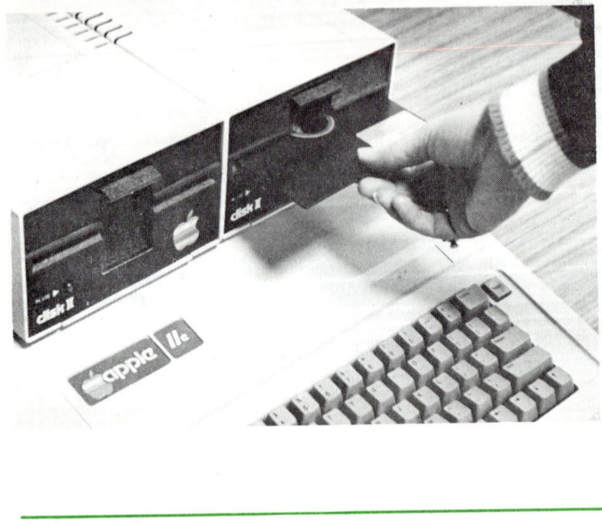

Figure 1–9 (*Top, left*) A hard copy terminal (*courtesy Hewlett-Packard Company*).

Figure 1–10 (*Top, right*) A CRT console (*courtesy Texas Instruments*).

Figure 1–11 (*Left*) Insertion of floppy disk into disk drive (*courtesy Apple Computer, Inc.*).

communication. The user may dial the computer's number to initiate communication, identify himself, transmit a program and/or data, and receive results at his/her terminal. When the user is finished, he/she can release the telephone line for another user.

A typical computing system will generally include a great variety of input/output devices. Most of these devices are electromechanical and thus operate at speeds far slower that the completely electronic CPU internal processing speeds. Therefore, if the CPU were required to wait for such devices to perform a complete operation (a data transmission from a Teletype, for example), the advantage of the tremendous internal speeds of the CPU would be greatly reduced. In most computer installations, the CPU is equipped with one or more channels. A *channel* is a special-purpose device that controls input/output operations (I/O); it relieves the CPU of the task of communicating directly with input/output devices. The CPU, for example, will instruct a channel to perform an output operation (e.g., write out results on a printer), and while the channel is busy servicing this output request, the CPU can continue processing instructions. In this way, CPU computations are carried out concurrently with input/output operations; this greatly increases the efficiency of the computer system.

Computers can be used in many different types of operating environments, each reflecting different organizational needs, hardware configurations, and economic bases. Of special interest are multiprogramming and time-sharing environments. In a multiprogramming setting, several programs are present in memory at one time. While a channel is servicing an I/O request for a particular program, the CPU can start processing a new program or resume processing a program temporarily interrupted by a previous I/O request; or each program may be interruped periodically to allow execution of other programs in memory. In a time-sharing environment, numerous terminals (Teletypes, CRT's, and so forth) are attached to the CPU by ground cables or telephone lines. These terminals allow users to communicate directly *(on line)* with the computer. Users enter their programs directly into the system via terminal stations. To the user at the terminal, it appears that he/she has the computer all to himself/herself and that only his/her program is being executed by the CPU. In reality, the CPU may be servicing several other users concurrently. This is accomplished by allowing each user a small slice of time and by processing each user's program in turn. Thus while one user is typing BASIC instructions on a terminal, the CPU may be processing another user's program. The most significant advantage of time sharing is that the user has immediate access to the computer; feedback is instantaneous. In addition, computer utilization costs can be significantly lowered by multiuser participation.

1-4-2 Software

The term *software* is generally used to describe the set of programs (written by the programmer) that causes the computer or hardware to function. There are three basic software categories:

1. Translation programs.
2. Operating system programs.
3. Applications programs.

Translation programs are programs used by the computer system to translate high-level languages or problem-oriented languages into machine language. These translation programs are generally supplied by the hardware manufacturer. There are two basic types of translation programs: *compilers* and *interpreters*. A compiler generates a completely separate translated version of the program in machine language form. The machine language program is referred to as an *object* program to distinguish it from the original version written in the high-level language (referred to as a *source* program). An interpreter, on the other hand, translates the high-level program instructions one instruction at a time and then executes the resultant code immediately. In an interpretive system there is no separate object program.

Compilers are generally useful when programs will be executed many times and when machine efficiency is important. Interpreters are useful when programs are executed infrequently and in systems where mass storage space is scarce. (There is no need to store both a source and an object program.) Many microcomputing systems utilize interpreters for BASIC, although some may offer a BASIC compiler as an optional feature.

Operating system programs are usually supplied by the computer manufacturer to assist in the overall operation of the computer system. They are used to regulate and supervise the sequence of activities going on at any time in the system. These programs minimize operator intervention in the actual operation of the computer and ensure a smooth, fast, and efficient transition among the varied tasks performed by the system. Other operating system programs aid the programmer in his/her own work; examples of such programs are utility and library programs. Some of the more important operating system programs perform the following functions:

1. Load programs into memory from mass storage.
2. Print messages for the operator and the programmer regarding the status of the program.
3. Perform job accounting by keeping track of who uses the computer and for how long.
4. Handle requests for input/output from executing programs.
5. Handle the collection of data from telecommunications lines (in a time-sharing system).
6. Schedule the slice of time to be allocated to each user's program (in a time-sharing system or multiprogramming system).
7. Perform some routine processing of data such as sorting and copying the contents of one data set onto a specified device.
8. Maintain the store of programs on the mass storage device—add programs to the store, delete those no longer needed, etc.
9. Attempt to recover from and/or correct errors that may occur in any segment of the computing system.
10. Interpret the job setup and job control instructions specified by the programmer.

At the heart of most operating systems is a program variously called the *supervisor*, the *executive*, or the *monitor*. This program is usually resident in memory at all times and performs many essential tasks such as program loading and error checking. This resident portion of the operating system loads other, less often used routines as they are required.

Applications programs are those programs written by individual users to solve particular problems. They may be written in a generalized fashion and modified as needed to fit the peculiar requirements of a particular system, or they may be constructed exactly to satisfy specific needs. For example, a company may construct its own payroll system, or it may purchase (or rent) a general set of payroll programs and modify them if necessary. Companies guard their processing programs as a very important company asset. Extensive security measures are taken to avoid the loss or theft of programs. A considerable store of programs is usually available to a computer user; in fact, the usefulness of a computer may well depend more on the variety and efficiency of the available software than on the characteristics of the hardware.

It is of interest to note that over the last decade or so computer hardware has undergone dramatic cost reductions that have not been accompanied by corresponding reductions in computer software costs. On the contrary, software development costs have soared to the point where now in a typical computer operation approximately 85% of the total computer system budget is earmarked for software costs, as opposed to only 5% in 1950.

1-4-3 Do It Now

1. List the hardware components of the computing system you will be using.
2. How much memory does the CPU of your system have? One K (1K) of memory refers to 1024 memory locations each capable of containing one character. Thus a 16 K memory means 16384 memory locations (1024 × 16).
3. Is BASIC implemented as a compiler or an interpreter on your system?
4. What is the name of the operating system you will be using?
5. Make a list of the more commonly used features of your operating system and the procedure required to make use of each feature.

1-5 You Might Want to Know

1. Just how fast do computers operate?

   Answer: The latest computers operate at speeds measured in nanoseconds (1 nanosecond-1 billionth of a second). High performance computers are capable of executing millions of instructions per second.

2. I can't conceive of how fast a nanosecond is. Can you help me?

   Answer: Yes. One nanosecond is to 1 second what 1 second is to 32 years. One nanosecond is the approximate time required for light to travel 1 foot.

3. Is there any limit to the internal speed of a computer?

Answer: Electrical signals are propagated at speeds approaching the speed of light (1 foot/nanosecond). Integrated circuits packing many thousands of transistors per square inch have been designed to minimize the length of the interconnections through which electrical signals are propagated; this reduces the time it takes a signal to travel from one transistor to another in the circuit. Figure 1–12 illustrates the size and density of an integrated single chip microprocessor.

4. Computers may be very fast and powerful devices, but aren't there problems that even the most powerful computer cannot handle?

Answer: Yes. If a computer one billion times faster than the fastest available today were to analyze all possible outcomes of the first move in a chess game, it would require on the order of 10^{100} hours (many hundreds of billions of years).

5. What computer languages are there besides machine language and BASIC?

Answer: One survey reported over 600 computer languages in more or less widespread use. Many of these were special-purpose languages oriented to a single application. Some of the better-known languages include:

FORTRAN (*FOR*mula *TRAN*slation)
COBOL (*CO*mmon *B*usiness *O*riented *L*anguage)
RPG (*R*eport *P*rogram *G*enerator)
PL/I (*P*rogramming *L*anguage *I*)
ALGOL (*ALGO*rithmic *L*anguage)
APL (*A P*rogramming *L*anguage)
Pascal (named for mathematician Blaise Pascal)

6. How many versions of BASIC are there?

Answer: Every computer manufacturer implements a BASIC system that is somewhat different from the others. BASIC systems are measured against the standard

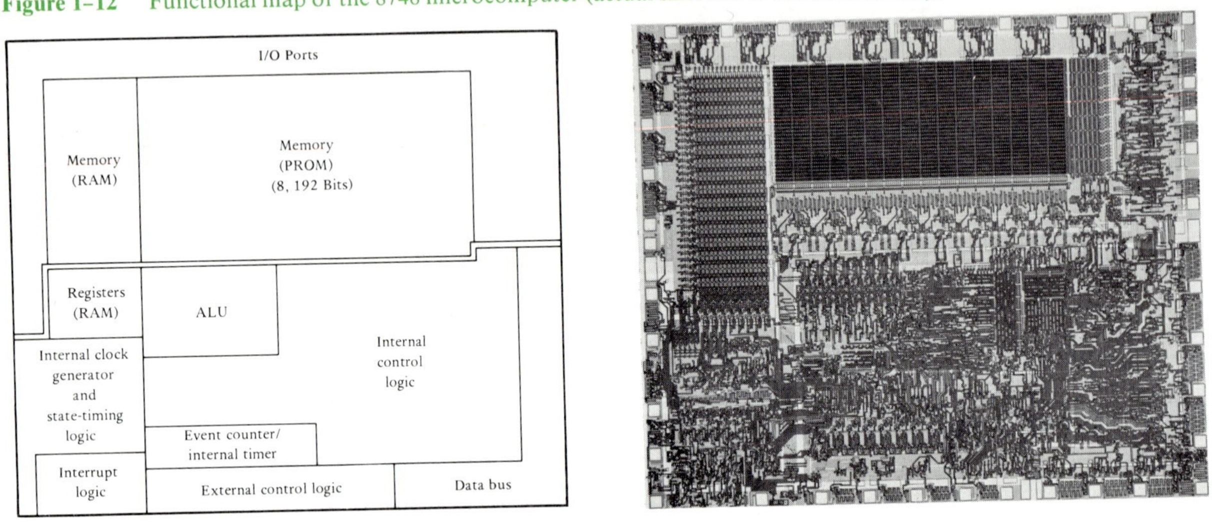

Figure 1–12 Functional map of the 8748 microcomputer (actual size: 5.6 × 6.6 millimeters).

system published by the American National Standards Institute, Inc. This standard, known as *minimal* BASIC, contains all of the most widely used features of the language. There will, however, undoubtedly be differences between minimal BASIC (which is used as a standard for BASIC as described in this text) and the version of BASIC available to you on your system. Usually, commercially available versions of BASIC will contain many enhancements—additional features and statements designed to make the task of programming easier. The manufacturer's user's guide written specifically for the BASIC at the reader's computer system is a worthwhile investment and may save hours of frustration and inconvenience. The serious student should consult a BASIC user's guide as this text is studied.

1-6 Microcomputers

A typical microcomputing system is shown in Figure 1-13. We will discuss the major components of such a system and the terminology associated with them.

1-6-1 Monitors

Monitors (TV screens, see Figure 1-14) can be color or monochrome (black/white, green/gray, etc.) and have various display sizes. Some monitors can display 16 lines of text where each line of text consists of 40 characters; other displays are 24 lines by 80 characters, and so forth.

The *resolution* of the screen refers to the number of picture elements (called *pixels*) that the screen can accommodate. These are the tiny dots that are used to create the various characters or shapes on the screen. The TRS-80 Model III has a 128 by 48 resolution, meaning 128 pixels for each of the 48 horizontal lines. The Commodore 64's resolution is 320 by 200, while the IBM's high resolution is 640 by 240. The Vectrix Corporation, which is interested in computer animation applications, manufac-

Figure 1-13 A microcomputing system.

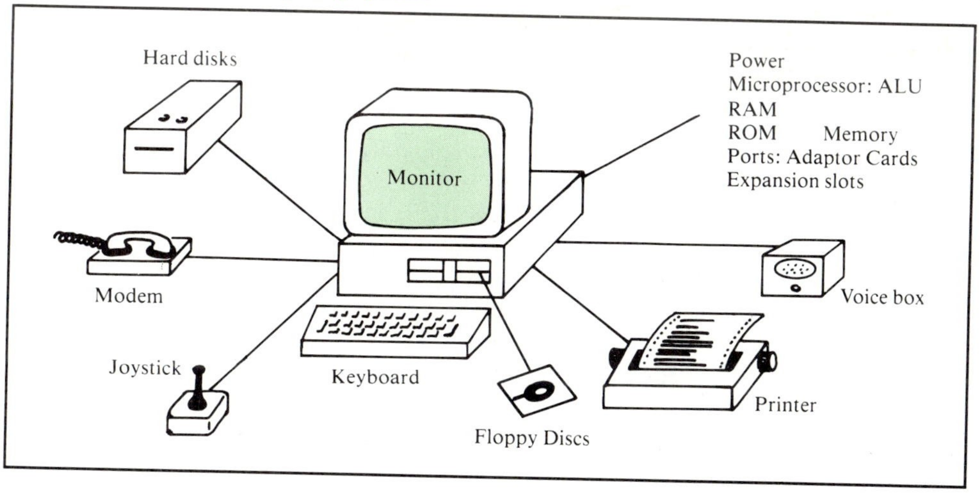

tures high resolution color display terminal systems that can be adapted to many microcomputers and have a resolution of 672 by 480 pixels, which gives an extremely crisp display.

Numerous microcomputers can handle color graphics. The DEC (Digital Equipment Company) Rainbow 100, outfitted with the color graphics option, has a dot resolution of 800 by 240 and has four displayable colors with a palette of 4096 colors to choose from. Color graphics systems generally allow for high and medium resolution, with medium resolution providing a greater variety of colors.

1-6-2 Keyboards

Chiclet keys are plastic or bubbly rubber keys that are usually smaller than the full-travel keys of regular typewriters. Standard keyboards have key layouts similar to those of typewriters, but there are some nonstandard features, such as the position of the shift keys on IBM or Atari keyboards.

Numeric keypads are extremely convenient when masses of digits need to be typed (Figure 1–15); they are becoming more and more common. Some keyboards also feature user-defined function keys, such as F1, F2, F3, ... These keys can be programmed to print a message or to execute a particular function at the touch of a key. For example, if the characters "LIST" are associated with key F1, the current program is listed when Key F1 is depressed.

1-6-3 Microprocessors and Operating Systems

The brain of the microcomputer is the microprocessor (see Figure 1–16). Many computers, such as the Apple, the Atari, and the Franklin Ace, use the 650L 8-bit microprocessor. Other low-cost computers, such as the TRS-80 Model III and the Casio, use the Z80 8-bit microprocessor. The IBM PC and the DEC Rainbow 100 use the Intel 8088 16-bit microprocessor. The current trend in home computers is toward the more powerful 16-bit microprocessor, yet most owners of 16-bit machines could do just as well with 8-bit machines.

To many users, the operating system (OS) is more important than the particular chip their computer uses. It is the operating system that gives a computer its personality. The operating system takes care of the internal housekeeping of the computer (saving, copying, editing files, etc.); it also allows the user to interact with various software such as application programs, computer games, word processing systems, and languages, all of which are dependent in one way or another on the particular operating system used.

Most computer manufacturers sell their computers with their own operating systems and with their own assortment of operating system-dependent software. For example, Radio Shack has its own TRS Disk Operating System (TRS-DOS) and myriads of business, educational, and text processing programs. Apple uses DOS or SOS operating system. Atari uses Atari OS. There are, however, software companies that specialize in designing extremely "user-friendly" operating systems that can be used on different types of computers. One well-known company, Microsoft, develops operating systems MS/DOS and a related library of programs that can be used on 16-bit machines such as the IBM PC, WANG, NEC, and DEC computers. Another equally well-known company, Digital Research, has been very successful with its CP/M operating systems and related software, which have been used by thousands of small business computing systems over the last decade. This CP/M software, due to sharp price reductions, has filtered through to home computer owners and can be used on such machines as the TRS-80, the Commodore 64, the North Star, and the Xerox and others.

1-6-4 Memory

Memory is measured in kilobytes (K) and megabytes (M). One kilobyte (one K) consists of 1024 bytes. Each byte can hold one character, such as a letter of the alphabet. A 64K machine can, then, contain approximately 64,000 (actually 64 × 1024) characters. A megabyte represents approximately one million bytes. For example, the basic unit of the Sinclair 2000 computer contains 16K of Random Access Memory (RAM) and 16K of Read Only Memory (ROM). RAM represents the programming "playground" where the user writes BASIC instructions. These instructions, however, are lost when the computer is turned off. ROM contains the system's instructions for starting up the computer when it is turned on. These instructions are factory-programmed in ROM and cannot by altered. In many microcomputers, BASIC is in ROM and the user is automatically in BASIC mode when the computer is turned on.

1-6-5 Diskettes

Diskettes, sometimes called floppy disks, are magnetically coated plastic disks stored in protective jackets (Figure 1–17). These diskettes come in 8-, 5 1/4-, and more recently in 3 1/2-inch sizes. Diskettes can be single-sided single-density type or double-sided double-density types, and other combinations are possible. Data is arranged in circular tracks. Each track is further broken down into a specific number of sectors. Data on a diskette can be located quickly by its side, track, and sector number, just as the post office can locate your home by using the town (side), street name (track), and house number (sector).

Depending on the size, density, and number of sides used, a diskette can hold anywhere from 70,000 to more than 1 million bytes. Typically, one item of information on a disk can be located in about 1/10 second. Most microcomputers have one or two disk drives into which the diskettes are inserted. The diskettes are rotated at about 2600 revolutions per second.

When using diskettes, remember the following:

1. Do not touch the exposed recording surfaces.
2. Protect the diskettes from dust, cigarette smoke, moisture, and excessive sunlight.
3. Store diskettes away from temperature extremes (a temperature range of 50°–122°F is satisfactory) and avoid magnetic sources such as calculators, scissors, and pens.
4. Use felt-tip pens when writing on labels.
5. Store diskettes in their protective covers.

Hard disks are now available to expand on-line storage capacity. They can store from 5 to 20 megabytes, depending on the particular system. Some are freestanding units, while others fit into existing disk drive slots.

1-6-6 Printers

There are two types of printers that attach very easily to microcomputers, *daisy wheel* and *dot matrix* printers (Figure 1–18). Thermal printers are especially useful for portable computers.

Daisy wheel printers resemble office typewriters and provide letter quality print. Such printers also have interchangeable elements for different typefaces. The wheel has many spokes, each of which has a character embossed towards the tip of the spoke. The wheel rotates and brings the desired character into position facing the paper, then a hammer strikes at the character causing it to imprint on the paper. These printers are generally more expensive and slower than matrix dot printers. They are capable of printing up to 65 characters per second, but they are not capable of graphic functions.

Dot matrix printers, on the other hand, are much faster and are generally less expensive than daisy wheel printers. The print element looks like a very small rectangular honeycomb where each cell contains a pin that can be fired independently of the others. Typically, the print rectangle or matrix consists of 9 rows by 8 columns of pins. A pin combination representing a particular character is then projected out of its silos to impact the printer ribbon, printing a character on the paper. Some print matrices consist of 9 by 15 pin grids which give rise to very high quality print letters rivaling daisy wheel letters. The printing head moves along each line; many dot matrix printers are bidirectional (printing takes place in a forward and backward motion) and can print up to 250 characters per second at 10, 12, or 16.7 characters per inch of paper. Many also allow for proportional spacing of characters, e.g., the letter I will use less space than the letter X, and some can be programmed to perform graphics functions.

1-6-7 Telephone Communications: Modems

Modem is a contraction for modulator-demodulator (see Figure 1–19). It is a device that allows one computer to talk to another or to share the resources of another more powerful computer by communicating through telephone or microwave systems. Computers can emit current pulses (1's and 0's); these pulses are difficult to transmit over regular carrier phone lines, so they are converted to wave form, which makes transmission much easier. The process of converting from pulse to wave form is called *modulation*. When the wave form reaches the target computer, the signals must be reconverted to pulse form (demodulated). Modems are devices that perform modulation and demodulation.

There are two types of modems: acoustic couplers and direct connect modems. In the case of the acoustic coupler (ideal for travelers!), the user dials the target computer's number, places the phone's handset on the modem's cup, and communicates with the computer. Because voice grade lines are used, there may be some loss of data due to background noises and electrical interference. Such problems can be avoided with a direct connect modem, which clips into a jack attached to the phone line.

Modems transmit data at various speeds. The transmission speed is measured in terms of bits (1's and 0's) per second. A character is typically represented by 10 bits. Voice grade lines can transmit up to 1800 bits per second. A typical home computer can receive and send 30 characters per second; special voice grade channels leased from telephone companies allow transmission speeds of up to 9600 bits per second; this means that it takes about 2 seconds to fill a 24 by 80 monitor screen.

1-6-8 Bus Architecture: Peripheral Ports and Interfaces

Bus architecture refers to a universal type of peripheral interface that allows the user to attach various types of devices to his/her system. The various types of input/output accessories that can be attached to microcomputers include printers, disk drives, joysticks, paddles, numeric keyboards, voice boxes, expansion boards to enhance memory or to upgrade a compiler to the next model, graphics boards, and modems. Microcomputers have input/output ports or peripheral ports for serial- or parallel-driven input/output devices. Other types of ports can connect solid state cartridges that contain ROM programs (games, applications programs) or for TV and video jacks.

1-6-9 Computerese Glossary

People who constantly work with computers have developed their own jargon or computer vocabulary. Among the more frequently used words and expressions are:

Hacker:	Computer fanatic; a computer enthusiast.
Frobnitz:	Any object.
Phrog:	Objectionable person.
Grok:	Understand.
Gweep:	Overwork.
Grobble:	Take a food break; to eat junk food.
Crash:	Program breaks up completely.
Gritch:	Complain.
Gronk out:	Go to sleep.
Frob(nicate):	Fiddle with the controls of a computer.
Vanilla:	Ordinary.
Real cuspy:	Very good; neat.
Flaming:	Speaking obsessively on significant and insignificant subjects.
Catatonic:	State of idleness (for the computer).

1-7 Assignments

1-7-1 Test Yourself

1. List the five components of a computer system and explain the functions of each.

2. Define the following:

a. CPU
b. CRT
c. program
d. data
e. nanosecond
f. machine language
g. unconditional branch
h. conditional branch
i. batch environment
j. conversational computing
k. compiler
l. software
m. interpreter
n. microcomputer
o. source program
p. object program

3. What values will be written by the program in Figure 1-3 if the input value is 47.5 instead of 38?

4. Determine which of the following statements are true and which are false:

a. A compiler is a program that translates machine code into a high-level language.

b. The part of a machine language instruction that tells the computer what to do is called an *operation code*.
c. Each memory location has a corresponding address.
d. Computer hardware consists of all the physical components that make up a computer system.
e. High-level languages are machine-independent.
f. The term *software* refers to such material as punched cards, paper/magnetic tape, and so forth.
g. In a batch-processing environment, the user receives an almost instantaneous response to his program.
h. Time sharing is made possible by the use of time slices.
i. Multiprogramming means that instructions from two or more programs can be processed at the same time by the CPU.

5. Modify the program in section 1–3 to read both the number of hours worked and the rate of pay from one input record. The output line should contain the pay, hours worked, and the rate. What could you do to your program to make it read more than one input record?

1-7-2 Projects

1. Enter and run the program of section 1–3 on your computing system.

2. Make a list of tasks to which computers have been applied. Pool your list with the others in your class to get a feeling for the important role the computer plays in our society.

3. List some problems that would not be suitable for solution by means of a computer. Are there any conditions that would change your assessment of the feasibility of a computer solution?

1-7-3 Answers to Test Yourself

1. *Input*: Device which reads information from some medium.
Output: Device which writes information onto some medium.
Memory: Stores program instructions and data.
Arithmetic/logical: Circuitry which performs arithmetic and decisions on the data.
Control: Executes program instructions.

2. a. CPU: Central processing unit—Memory, arithmetic/logical, and control units.
b. CRT: Cathode ray tube—Input/output visual display device.
c. Program: Instructions to solve a problem.
d. Data: Information to be processed by a program (numbers, lists of names, etc.).
e. Nanosecond: One billionth of a second.
f. Machine language: Numerical language inherent in the design of the particular computer.

g. Unconditional branch: GO TO—branch or transfer to same location each time the instruction is executed.
h. Conditional branch: IF—branch based on whether a condition is true or false.
i. Batch environment: Computing system in which programs and data are processed some period of time after submission of programs.
j. Conversational computing: Computing system in which user's instructions and data are analyzed and processed immediately.
k. Compiler: A program which translates a high-level language such as BASIC into machine language for subsequent execution.
l. Software: A set of programs that causes the computer to function.
m. Interpreter: A program which translates and executes statements in a high level language such as BASIC, one at a time.
n. Microcomputer: Small, stand-alone computing system based on a central processing unit contained on a microcircuit (chip).
o. Source program: Program written in a high-level language such as BASIC.
p. Object program: A machine language version of a source program produced by a compiler.

3. 205; 47.5

4. a. F b. T c. T d. T e. T f. F g. F h. T i. F

5. Program to process one record.

```
10 INPUT H,R
20 IF H > 40 GO TO 50
30 LET P = R*H
40 GO TO 60
50 LET P = 40*R + 1.5*R*(H - 40)
60 PRINT H,R,P
70 END
```

To process more than one record, substitute GO TO 10 for statement 70 in the above program.

Figure 1–14 A color monitor (*courtesy Radio Shack Division of Tandy Corporation*).

Figure 1–15 Calculator-type numeric keypad (*courtesy Non-Linear Systems, Inc.*).

■ **Figure 1–16** A microcomputer microprocessor (*courtesy Data Products, Inc.*).

■ **Figure 1–17** Floppy disks in 5¼″ and 3½″ sizes.

■ **Figure 1–18** A dot matrix printer (*courtesy Integral Data Systems*).

■ **Figure 1–19** A modem typically used for computer communication through the telephone system (*courtesy Hayes Microcomputer Products, Inc.*).

2 A QUICK EXPOSURE TO TERMINALS:
Getting to Know Your Work Companion

This short chapter will give you a brief introduction to what a program is, how you type a program, what type of errors you are likely to make, how you can correct errors, how you can perform input and output operations and some useful BASIC instructions. This chapter will be a very informal warm-up session before getting to the specifics of the BASIC language in chapter 3. You will learn the most from this chapter if you actually type the various programs that illustrate interactions with a computer; also be sure to answer the "Do It Now" questions and problems.

This hands-on experience will give you a quick feel for the operational aspects of a computer as well as an appreciation of some of its capabilities. This is the most important goal of the chapter. Remember, this chapter is just an overview and does not concern itself with the details of the BASIC language. You will probably raise more questions than this chapter answers; these questions will be answered in due course.

2-1 Programs

2-1-1 What Is a Program?

A program is a set of instructions identifying the steps necessary to solve a particular problem. Instructions in a program are carried out by a computer (or human being) in a particular order. In the BASIC language, all instructions are numbered and the computer executes (carries out) these instructions in ascending numerical order.

2-1-2 Writing and Carrying Out Instructions

Anyone can write a list of instructions, or specify directions! In fact, many of us who write such lists of instructions are not always the ones who eventually carry out those instructions. For example, a teacher in need of chalk could interrupt a lecture to write the following instructions on a piece of paper for a student to carry out:

1. Go to the secretary's office
2. Get a piece of chalk.
3. Return to the classroom.

} Example of a program.

Writing an instruction does *not* mean carrying out or executing the instruction the very moment the instruction is written, for example, when the teacher writes instruction 1, "Go to the secretary's office," the teacher does not go to the office! That intended action is delayed until all other instructions have been specified (stored on a piece of paper) and until the teacher gives the go ahead to a student to carry out the instructions. This program could even be written one day and executed some other day.

The same is true when you write a program on a computer. You may type all the instructions on a keyboard like those shown here.

The Macintosh keyboard
(*courtesy Apple Computer, Inc.*).

The OFIS™writer 345 keyboard
(*courtesy Burroughs Corporation*).

Each character or instruction typed on the keyboard appears on the screen or terminal. This does *not* mean that the instruction has been stored in the computer's memory. A typed instruction is stored (depending on the keyboard) in the computer's memory by pressing the ENTER or RETURN key. (Instructions are stored in the memory of the computer, just as the teacher stores instructions on a piece of paper.) When all instructions have been stored in the computer's memory, a special command is used to tell the computer to actually execute or *run* these instructions (starting with the firt one).

Let us, for example, instruct the computer to print the following message on its screen (terminal):

We need to write a little program to do this! There is an instruction in BASIC, the PRINT instruction, which tells the computer to print on the screen whatever message we want to display. The message must be enclosed in quotation marks, and each instruction should be numbered so that the computer knows the sequence in which to carry out the various instructions. (In the teacher/chalk problem, the numbers 1, 2, and 3 indicated the processing order; the numbers 10, 20, and 30 or 1, 5, and 13 could also have been used since they also indicate the correct order.) The complete BASIC instruction can be typed

```
10 PRINT "HELLO WORLD"
```

followed by pressing the ENTER or RETURN key. Typing this instruction on the screen and hitting the ENTER/RETURN key will not cause the computer to carry out the instruction, i.e., to print the message HELLO WORLD. (When the teacher writes the instruction "Go to the secretary's office," no one actually goes there; the instruction is simply stored on paper.) Depressing the ENTER key causes the computer to store what is on the terminal in the memory of the computer. To tell the computer to execute the program (instructions), we must type the system command RUN by itself (with no line number) and press the ENTER key. (An instruction or command is always completed by depressing the ENTER key.) The RUN command causes the computer to execute the program stored in its memory, starting with the instruction with the lowest line number and proceeding in ascending line number sequence. In our example the computer will print the message HELLO WORLD. The dark rectangle (■) means that the ENTER/RETURN key has been depressed.

We can illustrate this process with the following sketches:

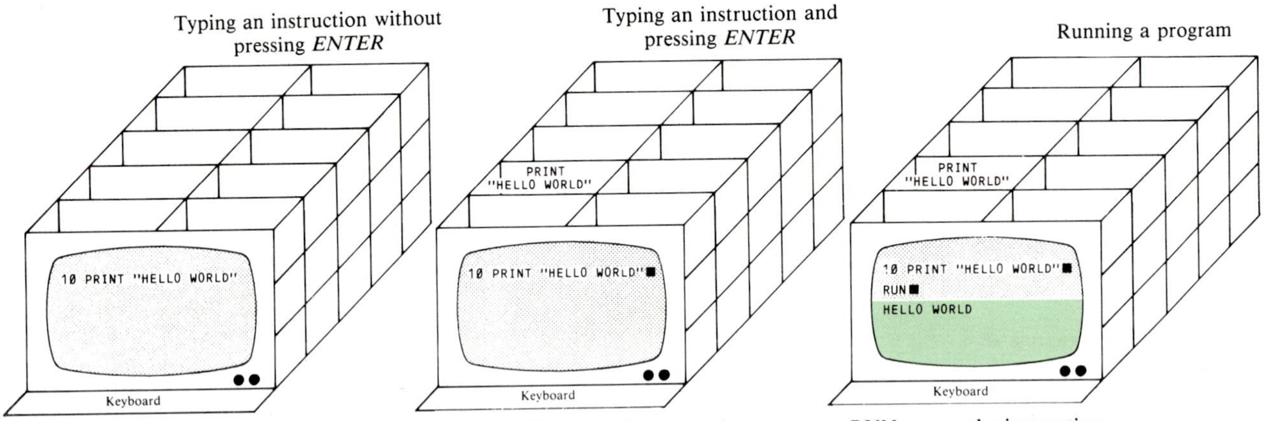

The instruction is not stored in the computer's memory.

ENTER (■) stores the instruction in the computer's memory.

RUN causes the instruction in memory to be carried out.

As a result of this human/computer interaction, the terminal has the following display:

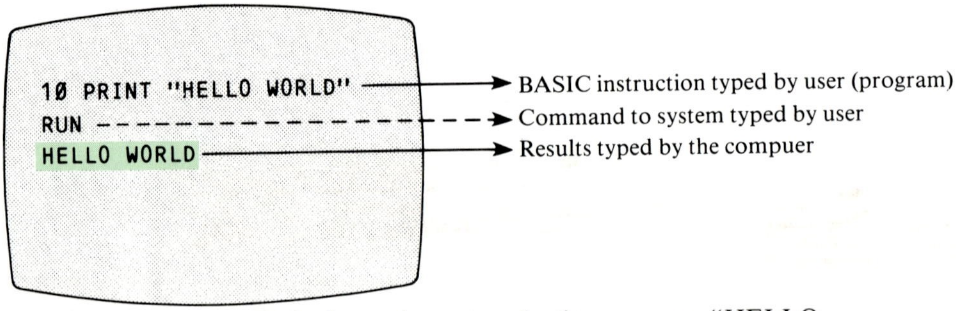

Note that if the command RUN had not been typed, the message "HELLO WORLD" would never have been printed!

This example illustrates some important points in a typical session with a computer:

1. The user writes a set of instructions coded in the BASIC language (all BASIC instructions are numbered).
2. Once all instructions have been stored in the computer's memory, the user tells the computer to carry out the instructions via the RUN command.
3. The results, called *output,* are then displayed by the computer.

2-1-3 Do It Now

1. a. How do you enter a BASIC instruction in the memory of the computer?
   b. Can a program consist of just one instruction?
   c. How do you tell the computer to carry out a program?
2. What will be printed as a result of the following instructions?

a. 1Ø PRINT "MY NAME IS JON"
RUN

b. 1Ø PRINT "WHAT'S YOUR NAME"
15 PRINT "MY NAME IS SARA-LOU"
RUN

c. 1Ø PRINT "PRINT HELLO WORLD"
RUN

d. 1Ø PRINT "!!!**><.,!"
RUN

3. In the teacher/chalk example, what meaning would RUN have? What would the "output" be?

4. Which of the following instructions are invalid to the computer? (Beware of spelling!)

a. 1Ø PRINT "THE COMPUTAH KANT SPEL"

b. 1Ø PRINT "BONJOUR MA CHERIE"

c. 15 PRIMT "THE COMPUTER CAN SPELL"

d. PRINT HELLO TOM

5. What will be the result of the following program:

1Ø PRINT "WHAT'S YOUR NAME"
15 MY NAME IS JOEL
RUN

6. What would result from the following (be as specific as you can!):

a. 1Ø PRINT "HELLOMIKE"
RUN

b. 1Ø PRINT "DOG EAT CAT
RUN

c. 1Ø PRINT "CAT EAT DOG"

d. 1Ø PRINT "MY OH MY"
15 GO TO 1Ø
RUN

(GO TO tells the computer to transfer to the indicated line number; in some BASICs it is written as one word: GOTO.)

7. How many instructions will be stored in the memory of the computer as a result of typing each of the following:

a. 1Ø PRINT ''HELLLLOOOH'' ENTER
RUN ENTER

b. 1Ø PRINT "A" ENTER
15 PRINT "B" ENTER

c. 1Ø PRINT "WELL WELL WELL" ENTER
RUN

d. 1Ø PRINT "MY NAME IS JOSE MY NAME"

e. FOR HE IS A JOLLY GOOD FELLOW! ENTER

8. Give an example of an invalid instruction for the teacher/chalk example.

Answers

1. a. Press the ENTER or RETURN key

b. Yes

c. Type RUN

2. a. MY NAME IS JON
   b. WHAT'S YOUR NAME
      MY NAME IS SARA-LOU
   c. PRINT HELLO WORLD
   d. !!!**><.,!

3. The RUN instruction would be equivalent to the teacher handing the list of instructions to a student and saying "go ahead" (carry out the instructions). The output in this case would be the physical motion of the student and the delivery of a piece of chalk.

4. a. Valid. To the computer, any character enclosed within quotes is grammatically correct. Remember, the computer does not understand English.
   b. Valid. The computer does not understand French, but that doesn't matter!
   c. Invalid. The word that the computer recognizes is misspelled, i.e., PRIMT has no meaning in the BASIC language. Expect complaints from the computer.
   d. Invalid. The message must be enclosed in quotation marks. No line number.

5. The computer understands the first instruction: it is told to print the message in quotes. In the second instruction, the word MY is not a recognized instruction such as PRINT, hence the computer views that instruction as incorrect.

6. a. HELLOMIKE will be displayed.
   b. Invalid instruction. The final quotation marks are missing.
   c. Nothing is printed, but the instruction is stored in memory if ENTER was depressed.
   d. The message MY OH MY is printed repetitively because of the GO TO instruction.

7. a. 1
   b. 2
   c. 1
   d. 0, The ENTER key was not pressed.
   e. Error. No line number!

2-2 A More Complex Problem

Let us write a computer program to compute and print an employee's pay given the number of hours he/she has worked and a particular rate of pay. If the employee has worked 20 hours at 5 dollars an hour, the program will display the number 100 on the terminal:

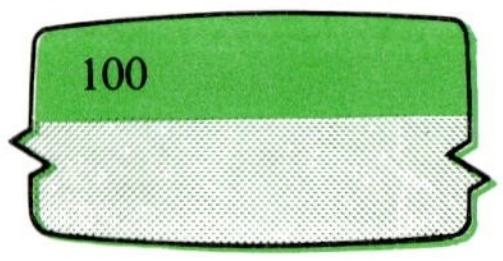

The following instructions could be used to solve the problem:

Code	*Interpretation of Code (assume RUN)*
`10 H = 20`	The number 20 is stored in memory location or memory cell H, i.e., as far as the computer is concerned H now contains the number 20. H is called a *variable name.*
`20 R = 5`	The variable R now contains the value 5, i.e., the value 5 is stored in memory cell R.
`30 P = H * R`	The expression H * R is evaluated and the result stored in memory location P. The symbol * is used to denote multiplication.
`40 PRINT P`	Since P contains the result of H * R (100) the value 100 is printed on the screen/printer.
`50 END`	The END instruction should always be the last one in a BASIC program.

This set of five instructions is an example of a program. It is *very* important to realize that these instructions do not actually get carried out as they are typed on the terminal. The instructions are simply stored in the computer's memory. The program itself is carried out only when the user types the system command RUN; this is the signal to the computer to execute whatever instructions are present in its memory, starting with the instruction with the smallest number. RUN is a system command, not a BASIC instruction.

It is important to differentiate between the program (set of instructions) and the results produced by the program. The results produced by the computer are referred to as the *output,* and the set of BASIC instructions typed by the user is called the *source* program. The output is produced only when the system command RUN has been typed, generally after the user has entered all of the BASIC instructions in the memory of the computer.

The sequence of events in the human/machine communication is illustrated in Figure 2–1.

The reader may wonder what the difference is between a system command and a BASIC instruction. They are two distinct languages, where the words used in one language are not necessarily understood by the other language. A system command is executed as soon as it is typed, whereas a BASIC instruction is stored in the memory of the computer and executed later, when the command RUN is typed. The visual difference is that BASIC instructions are numbered, while system commands are not. You will learn many other system commands such as NEW, LIST, SAVE, LOAD, etc. The NEW command (in some systems SCRATCH or CLEAR is used) tells the computing system to blank out its memory, i.e., to void its memory cells of any instruction. The user should always type NEW before typing a BASIC program, thus ensuring that BASIC instructions typed by a previous BASIC user do not interfere with the current progam. In this example, the sequence of instructions should be:

```
NEW                 Make sure all previous instructions have been erased.
10 H = 20     }
20 R = 5      }
30 P = H * R  }     New program typed in.
40 PRINT P    }
50 END        }
```

Figure 2-1 A simple BASIC program.

10 H = 20 20 R = 5 30 P = H * R 40 PRINT P 50 END	**BASIC program** The user stores these instructions in the computer's memory.	Typed by human
RUN	**system command** The user tells the computer to execute its stored instructions.	Typed by human
100	**OUTPUT** These results are produced by computer as a result of carrying out the instructions.	Typed by computer

Memory before the RUN instruction

Memory after the RUN instruction

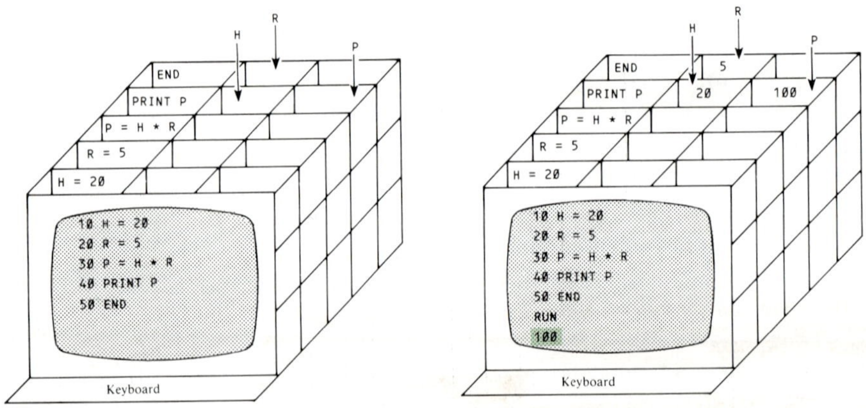

2-2-1 You Might Want to Know

1. Must line numbers start with 10 and be incremented by 10 each time?

   Answer: No, we can use 1, 2, 3, 4, 5 or 1, 11, 23, 64, 110. The numbering system tells the computer the order in which the instructions must be carried out. The order is important, not the numbers. Many people increment their lines by 5's, or 10's.

2. When I type the instruction 10 H = 20 is the number 20 stored in H the moment I depress the ENTER key?

   Answer: No, that will take place when the RUN command is typed. ENTER stores the instruction H = 20 in the memory.

3. Do I have to be careful about spaces when I type instructions, i.e, could I type 10H = 20 instead of 10 H = 20?

Answer: Blank spaces usually do not matter; some BASIC even allow you to write `PRINT` as `P R IN T`.

4. Could I have used X = 20 rather than H = 20 in the example program?

Answer: Yes, but then line 30 should be P = X * R.

5. Why can't I write HOURS = 20 instead of H = 20?

Answer: Many BASIC systems do not accept variable names that are three or more characters in length! Generally, the first character should be alphabetic followed by an optional digit, but these rules vary from one BASIC to another.

6. In the illustration of the memory in Figure 2–1, how do I tell the computer to reserve memory cells R, H, and P? Do I need to worry about where these cells are physically located in memory?

Answer: The moment you write R = *something,* the computer automatically reserves a cell for R, and you need not worry about where that cell is in memory.

2-2-2 Do It Now

1. Explain what the computer does as a result of the following code:

a.
```
15 S = 1.3          [ENTER]
```
b.
```
15 H = 35           [ENTER]
RUN
```
c.
```
10 PRINT L          [ENTER]
RUN
```

2. Determine what will take place as a result of the following code:

a.
```
10 H = 10           [ENTER]
15 R = 3            [ENTER]
20 P = H * R        [ENTER]
NEW                 [ENTER]
RUN                 [ENTER]
```
b.
```
10 H = 10           [ENTER]
20 R = 3            [ENTER]
30 P = H * R        [ENTER]
40 RUN              [ENTER]
```
c.
```
12 PRINT "WELL"     [ENTER]
11 PRINT "AM"       [ENTER]
10 PRINT "I"        [ENTER]
RUN                 [ENTER]
```

3. Since blanks do not count in BASIC, are there any differences in the following two instructions?

```
10 PRINT "ABCDE"
15 PRINT "A B C D E"
```

Answers

1. a. The instruction is stored in the computer's memory, but it is not carried out, i.e., the number 1.3 is not stored inside memory cell S.
   b. The instruction is stored, and the value 35 is stored in H.
   c. The value in memory location L (contents unknown) is printed. If L has not been defined, most systems will print a zero.
2. a. The first three instructions are stored in memory, then wiped out by the command NEW. Since there is no program in memory, there is nothing to RUN and nothing happens.
   b. The program will not run since the system command RUN has not been issued.
   c. The following message will be printed.

      ```
      I
      AM
      WELL
      ```

      BASIC executes the instructions in ascending line order.
3. Blank spaces within quotation marks do count; line 10 will print `ABCDE` while line 15 will print `A B C D E`

2-3 Errors and the Editing Process

The reader will quickly realize how easily one can make errors on a computer. Errors, commonly called bugs, come in four varieties: typographical, syntax, logical, and system errors. We will discuss each type of error and learn how errors are detected and corrected.

2-3-1 Typographical Errors

Everyone, at some time or another, mistypes characters. These errors are usually interpreted by the computer as syntax errors. Such errors are self-evident and can be minimized by concentration. A tricky error to detect is typing the letter O instead of the digit zero 0, or the lowercase l for 1. Other examples of typographical errors are:

1. You wanted to type `10 P = 1` and you typed `10 P + 1`.
2. You wanted to type `15 PRINT P` and you typed `15 PRIMT P`.

2-3-2 Syntax Errors

BASIC is a language, and like French, Arabic, or any other language it is subject to grammatical rules. BASIC instructions must be syntactically correct (syntax = physical sentence structure and grammar) if the computer is to understand (execute) the instruction properly. Recalling the teacher problem in section 2-1-2,what if the first instruction had been written as "Go to the secretary's fofice"? Obviously the instruction could not be carried out until it had been corrected.

Syntax errors include misspelled key words, unnumbered lines, faulty punctuation, mismatched parentheses, and improper word order. The computer will identify the line number where the error occurred.

Examples:

`20 X = A(B+C)`	Missing arithmetic operator after variable A
`30 PRINT "HELLO" S1 S2`	Punctuation missing before and after S1
`40 Z = (3+X*(4+T)`	Missing right parenthesis
`50 20 = H`	Improper structure; variable should be on left
`60 RUN`	RUN should not be numbered

2-3-3 Logical Errors

Logical errors are the traditional enemies of beginning and professional programmers alike. Logical errors are present in a program whenever the program does not solve the intended problem, i.e., the results produced by the computer are incorrect! Incorrect results may occur because of one silly but critical typographical error or because of incorrect reasoning or an incorrect sequence of instructions. In between these two extremes lie hundreds of other possible sources of errors.

Logical errors are the hardest ones to find in a program because generally no error messages are printed by the computer during the execution of the program. The instructions are syntactically correct (good grammar) even though they do not produce the expected results. In the context of the teacher problem in section 2-1-2, a logical error would occur if the teacher had written "Return home" instead of "Return to the classroom." This certainly would not have solved the teacher's problem even though the instruction itself would be quite clear to the one executing it. Since the computer is a "dumb machine," it will carry out whatever instruction it is given as long as the instruction is syntactically correct. The programmer is made aware of logical errors through results that are incorrect or meaningless!

Logical errors are very difficult to find since the computer doesn't really regard them as errors. If, for example, you wrote P = H + R instead of P = H * R (H = hours, R = rate) to compute a pay, the computer does not know that this is an error. After all, the grammar is correct and the computer *can* carry out the instruction! The computer has no common sense, unlike the executor of the teacher's instructions, who may question the instruction to "return home"!

Another example of a logical error can occur in the instruction 100 Y = T/N; this is a perfectly valid instruction, syntactically speaking, yet it could be a time bomb during the execution of the program if N = 0. If N = 0, the computer will stop at instruction 100, since it (like any human being) cannot divide a number by 0. (In this case an error message *will* be printed.) Somehow N should not be 0 and the programmer must play detective in order to find out why the value of N is 0 when instruction 100 is executed.

Logical errors can also be the result of careless mistakes. For example, you might want to print the result stored in memory location R but instead you write the instruction PRINT S; this yields an incorrect answer, yet as far as BASIC is concerned, this is perfectly valid since PRINT S is grammatically correct.

Thus it is important that the programmer not put blind faith in whatever the computer prints out. The fact that the computer prints out numbers does not necessarily mean that those numbers are correct! The programmer should always check and analyze computer-produced results most carefully.

2-3-4 System Errors

System errors are caused by the components of the computer system itself, such as the telephone lines, the printers, the tapes, or the diskettes. For example, a printer may not be turned on when the CPU needs it, thus generating a special error message. A system diskette may be "bad" (especially in microcomputer systems): a user diskette may not have been formatted, or an input/output failure may have occurred when saving or loading a program from tape or disk. The user should contact the lab manager or computer center personnel when system errors occur.

2-3-5 Correcting Errors

There are three stages at which errors can be caught.

1. Before pressing the ENTER key. If you type a BASIC instruction and discover a typing error before the complete instruction has been ENTERed, you can backspace (use the backspace key or the left arrow key) to the mistyped character(s), correct the error, and retype the remainder of the instruction.
2. After pressing ENTER. If you realize that the instruction just ENTERed contains an error, you simply retype the entire instruction with the same line number. The newly typed instruction replaces the old one—as long as the line numbers are the same!
3. During execution of the program. After you type RUN, the computer may stop and print an error message specifying the line number at which the error occurred. It is most likely that the error is a syntax error. You then retype the instruction as described in case 2 above.

If you want to delete a particular BASIC instruction from a program, type the line number by itself and press the ENTER key. This deletes the instruction from the program in memory even though it may still appear on the screen.

2-3-6 Listing a Program

If a program requires numerous corrections, the display of the various changes and RUN attempts on the screen (or the paper) may be quite confusing. To obtain a clean listing of a program (a line by line display of the most current version of the program), the user types the system command LIST (no line number). The computer then displays the program currently stored in its memory, i.e., the most recent version of the program, including all changes that have been made. This is illustrated in the next section.

The LIST command can be issued *any* time, while typing BASIC instructions, or before or after any RUN. If the program is not yet complete, LIST copies the portion of the program in the computer's memory onto the terminal.

2-3-7 Debugging Programs

Debugging a program means taking the bugs out of it, i.e., correcting it. Imagine that you are writing a program to calculate and print a pay, given a number of hours worked and a rate of pay:

```
NEW
10 H = 4O
15 R = 5,50
20 P = H + R
```

You type the letter O instead of zero without realizing it. Before you press the ENTER/RETURN key, you realize you typed a comma instead of a decimal point. Using the left arrow or backspace key, you backtrack to the comma and type . instead, followed by the remaining characters.

```
25 END
RUN
SYNTAX ERROR AT 10
```

You then run the program.

This is a difficult error since instruction 10 looks correct.

```
10 H = 40
```

Finally you realize that you have typed the letter O instead of zero. The most direct way to correct the error is to retype the entire instruction, i.e., retype line 10. The old line 10 will be replaced with the new line 10 just typed.

```
RUN
```

Thinking that the program is debugged, you type RUN, but no results appear.

```
22 PRINT P
```

You check the program and see that the PRINT instruction has been omitted. To insert the PRINT instruction, you type line number 22. Thus the PRINT instruction will be carried out after instruction 20 but before instruction 25.

```
RUN
45.5
```

RUN is typed again. The result printed is 45.5, which is clearly incorrect.

At this point, the screen or the printed form looks quite confusing. Many corrections to the program have been made, making it difficult to read the program. To obtain a clean listing of the most current version of the program now in memory, you type the system command LIST. Immediately an unencumbered list of the current BASIC instructions is displayed on the terminal.

```
LIST
10 H = 40
15 R = 5.50
20 P = H + R
22 PRINT P
25 END
20 P = H * R
RUN
220
```

You now examine your program clearly and see why the result (pay = 45.50) is incorrect: the plus sign at line 20 should be an asterisk for multiplication.

You then retype the instruction (H * R) and run the program to get, finally, the correct result.

220 is the result produced by the computer.

2-3-8 Do It Now

1. List all the system commands discussed so far.

2. a. The following program is supposed to compute the average of three grades G1, G2, and G3. Identify errors of syntax and logic, if any.

```
10 G1 = 30
20 G2 T 40
30 G3 = 100
40 A1 = G1 + G2 + G3 / 3
50 PRINT G1, G2, G3, A
END
RUN
```

b. The following code is supposed to compute and print the tax owed (15% of gross) on a particular gross pay. The gross pay is computed as hours times the rate plus a given bonus. Identify syntax and/or logical errors.

```
10 R = 5
12 H = 30
15 B = 10O
23 P = R * H
25 G = P + B
30 T = G * 15
35 PRINTT
40 END
```

R = rate
H = hours
B = bonus
G = gross pay
T = tax owed

3. Show what would be printed by the computer as a result of the following:

a.
```
1 H = 20
LIST
```

b.
```
1 H = 20
RUN
```

c.
```
1 H = 20
2 H = 40
5 PRINT H
```

d.
```
1 H = 20
LIST
2 PRINT H
RUN
```

e.
```
1 H = 20
2 R = 5
LIST
3 P = H * R
4 PRINT P
RUN
LIST
```

f.
```
1 H = 3
2 R = 5
RUN
4 P = H * R
RUN
RUN
5 PRINT P
```

Answers

1. NEW, LIST, RUN

2. a. Syntax error at 20; G2 = 40
Logical error at 40; only the last grade is divided by 3. Use 40 A1 = G1 + G2 + G3, 45 A = A1/3 (We will discuss the use of parentheses later.)
Logical error at 50; computer does not know what A is!
Error with END; line should be numbered.

b. Syntax error at 15; digit 0 instead of the letter O in 100
Logical error at 30; should be T = G * .15
Note that line 35 is valid, i.e., since BASIC doesn't care about blanks, PRINT T is the same as PRINTT! But you should use spaces for readability!

3. a.
```
1 H = 20
```
b. The value 20 is stored in H, but nothing is displayed on the terminal.
c. Nothing is printed since RUN was not typed.
d.
```
1 H = 20
20
```
e.
```
1 H = 20
2 R = 5
100
1 H = 20
2 R = 5
3 P = H * R
4 PRINT P
```
f. Nothing is printed.

2-3-9 MY SYSTEM IS DIFFERENT

This section is left blank for you to write any different system commands that your system uses. You may also want to list the various steps that are required to start a session with your system.

2-4 Refining a Program

2-4-1 Adding Instructions and Readability

A report produced by a computer should be self-explanatory, complete, and attractively designed as well as accurate. In the payroll program section of 2–3–7 it would be a good idea to print not only the resulting gross pay, but also the number of hours worked and the hourly rate, so that the employee or the company's controller could verify the computer-produced pay when given the report (not all people trust computers). This could be accomplished by replacing line 22 as follows:

```
22 PRINT P, H, R
RUN
22Ø     4Ø      5.5
```

The computer prints the contents of memory locations P, H, and R which contain respectively 220, 40, and 5.5. Note that the variables are separated by commas.

Note that the spacing on the paper/screen between the three values is controlled by the system. Actually, such a computer-produced report is not really meaningful to anyone other than the originator, who knows what the three numbers 220, 40, and 5.5 mean. The output should be more readable, self-documenting, and more pleasant to the eye. Three approaches, all equally acceptable, can be taken to "dress up" the output. All involve the use of captions or labels that give meaning to the numeric results.

Approach 1

Have the computer print out the following results on the terminal:

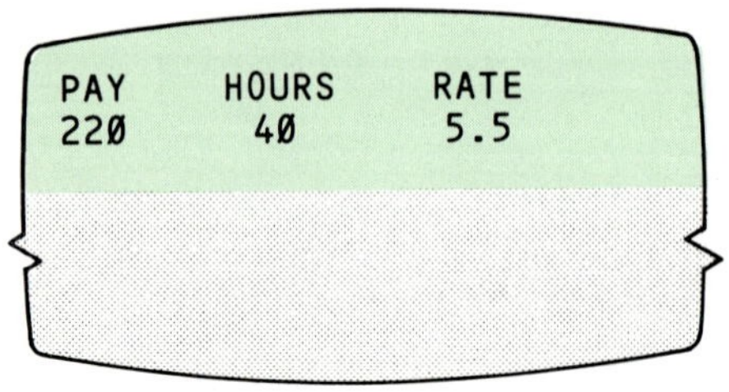

Column headings are used.

The code to produce the above printout is

```
Ø5 PRINT "PAY", "HOURS", "RATE"
1Ø H = 4Ø
15 R = 5.5
2Ø P = H * R
22 PRINT P, H, R
25 END


RUN
PAY     HOURS     RATE
22Ø      4Ø        5.5
```

Print three messages or captions separated by commas. Note that by typing line 5 on the terminal, we add another instruction to our original program.
Captions in the PRINT statement must be enclosed in quotation marks.

Approach 2

Have the computer print the results as follows:

```
PAY=220
HOURS=40
RATE=5.5
```

The code to produce this printout is

```
10 H = 40
15 R = 5.5
20 P = H * R
22 PRINT "PAY=";P
23 PRINT "HOURS=";H
24 PRINT "RATE=";R
25 END
RUN
PAY = 220
HOURS = 40
RATE = 5.5
```

Three lines are printed corresponding to the three PRINT statements. Note that our program is now two lines longer.

If the user wanted these three output lines to be displayed all by themselves on the screen, without the listing of the BASIC program, the statement 21 CLS could be added to the program. This instruction would cause the computer to clear the screen just before typing the result.

Approach 3

Have the computer print the results as follow:

```
PAY = 220        HOURS = 40        RATE = 5.5
```

The code to produce this is

The semicolon specifies compact spacing: caption "PAY = " will be printed close to the value of P.

The comma specifies distant spacing: The value of P will be printed far away from caption "HOURS = ".

```
10 H = 40
15 R = 5.5
20 P = H*R
22 PRINT "PAY="; P, "HOURS="; H, "RATE=";R
25 END
RUN
PAY= 220      HOURS= 40      RATE= 5.5
```

Note that the various items (captions, variable names) listed in the PRINT statement (line 22) must always be separated from one another by commas or semicolons. Two items separated by a semicolon in the PRINT statement will be physically close to one another (compact spacing) when printed, while two items separated by a comma will be far from one another on the output.

2-4-2 Do It Now

1. Try to predict what will occur when the following programs are run, i.e., describe what will appear on the terminal.

a.
```
10 H = 20
20 R = 5
30 P = H * R
40 PRINT P, H, R
50 PRINT "PAY", "HOURS", "RATE"
RUN
```

b.
```
10 R = 5
20 H = 20
30 P = H * R
40 PRINT "PAY", "HOURS", "RATE"
50 PRINT P, H, R
60 GO TO 10
RUN
```

2. What will be displayed on the terminal as a result of the following instructions?

```
10 H = 20
15 R = 5
20 P = H * R
RUN
25 PRINT P
LIST
RUN
```

3. Identify various types of errors (if any): (Assume H represents hours and R represents the rate.)

a.
```
10 H = 20
15 R = -5
20 PRINT HOURS=;R
25 PRINT RATE=,H
```

b.
```
10 H = 20
20 R = 5
30 PRINT "H,R"
```

c.
```
10 NEW
20 H = 20
30 PRINT "H" H
```

d.
```
10 H = 20
15 R = 5
20 P = H * R
25 PRINT P
30 PRINT P,H,R
```

4. a. If you had typed the following code and wanted to interchange lines 20 and 25 in order for the program to run correctly, what would you do?

```
10 H = 20
15 R = 5
20 PRINT P
25 P = H * R
```

b. Assume you had typed the following code, and you wanted to insert P = H * R between lines 2 and 3, what would you do?

```
1 H = 20
2 R = 5
3 PRINT P
```

Answers

1. a.

```
100        20        5
PAY        HOURS     RATE
```

b.

```
PAY        HOURS     RATE
100        20        5
PAY        HOURS     RATE
100        20        5
PAY        HOURS     RATE
 .          .         .
 .          .         .
 .          .         .
```

These two instructions will be printed over and over until the user interrupts the program.

2.

```
10 H = 20
15 R = 5
20 P = H * R
25 PRINT P
100
```

3. a. Syntax error: no quotation marks around the captions in lines 20 and 25. Logical error: line 15, R cannot be negative. Probable logical errors: lines 20 and 25, R is printed after HOURS, and H after RATE; also, the value printed after RATE will be spaced at a distance.

b. Logical error: line 30 should probably be PRINT H,R

c. Syntax error: to be effective NEW should be typed without a line number. Syntax error: punctuation missing between "H" and H at line 30

d. Possible logical error in line 25; this line could be deleted without affecting the program.

4. a. One solution would be:
Type 17 P = H * R
Type 25 to erase line 25

b. Type 3 P = H * R
Type 5 PRINT P

2-5 Program Documentation

In a real-life environment a programmer usually writes a program for a friend, a customer, or for the company for which he/she works. Thus, the program itself needs to be understood by others; indeed it may need to be revised, updated, or expanded by others. It is, therefore, very important that the program be self-documenting and that explanations be present within the program itself to help the reader understand the nature and purpose of the program. For this purpose, BASIC allows the user to intersperse *remarks* throughout the BASIC code by using the REM instruction. These help the reader understand what the program is all about. Some programmers make it a habit to start a program with a dictionary of all the variables used in the program. For example, our program could be documented as follows:

```
Ø4 REM  PAYROLL PROGRAM
Ø5 REM
Ø6 REM  H : HOURS
Ø7 REM  R : RATE
Ø8 REM  P : PAY
1Ø H = 4Ø
15 R = 5.5
17 REM  THE FOLLOWING LINE COMPUTES THE PAY
2Ø P = H * R
22 PRINT P, H, R
25 END
```

Note that the inclusion of remarks within the program does not change the output of the program. The remarks are just comments to the reader to assist him/her in understanding what the program or a particular instruction does.

The reader should understand the difference between

```
Ø4 PRINT "PAYROLL PROGRAM"
```

and

```
Ø4 REM PAYROLL PROGRAM
```

In the first case, the message "PAYROLL PROGRAM" is printed as part of the output, while in the second case PAYROLL PROGRAM is part of the BASIC program itself, not part of the output.

We will discuss REM statements in more detail in chapter 3.

2-6 The Looping Process and the INPUT Statement

What if we wanted to write a program to compute the pay for any number of employees? The program discussed so far has little usefulness since it only computes a pay for 40 hours of work at the specific rate of 5.5 dollars an hour. Yet the process for computing the pay (line 20) and the mechanics of printing it (line 22) are the same regardless of the number of hours worked or the rate, so that part of the program could be used over and over again. Of course we could proceed as follows:

```
10 H = 40
15 R = 5.5
20 P = H * R
22 PRINT P, H, R
25 END
RUN
220<-----------------1st employee's pay
10 H = 30
15 R = 4.0
RUN
120<-----------------2nd employee's pay
10 H = 60
   .
   .
   .
```

Program to compute first employee's pay for 40 hours at a rate of 5.5 dollars an hour

Program to compute second employee's pay for 30 hours at 4 dollars an hour

For every employee, we would retype lines 10 and 15 to change the hours and rates and then retype the RUN instruction to determine the corresponding pay.

A more efficient method would be to repeat the program over and over again, i.e., repeat lines 10, 15, 20, and 22 again and again for different values of H and R each time without retyping any BASIC instructions and without retyping RUN each time. This repeating process, known as *looping,* can be accomplished by using the GO TO instruction:

```
10 H = 20
15 R = 5
20 P = H * R
22 PRINT P, H, R
25 GO TO 10
RUN
```

With the GO TO statement, the computer keeps executing instructions 10, 15, 20, and 22 then 10, 15, 20, and 22 forever! This is an example of a nonterminating (infinite) loop.

There are two major problems associated with the above code:

1. The computer never stops!
2. The *same* pay is computed and printed over and over again.

We would like to give the computer a new set of values for H and R each time lines 10 and 15 are executed (for each employee). We would like the computer to pause at line 10 and cue us so that we can enter the new number of hours worked (e.g., 30) and then we would like it to pause at line 15 to prompt us to enter a new rate of pay (e.g., 4.00). Then the computer would compute and print the corresponding pay. For each employee we would need to enter just two numbers; no instructions or RUN statement necessary. The transactions on the screen would then look like the ones shown in Figure 2–2.

First the computer prints the question mark and stops. The user types the number of hours (40) the first employee worked and presses *ENTER*. (The computer stores that number in its memory.) Then the computer prints another question mark and stops. The user then enters the rate for the first employee. The computer, knowing the hours and the rate, computes and prints the pay for the first employee. The computer then automatically prints a question mark, the user enters the second employee's hours, and the same sequence of events takes place for each employee. The session could be terminated or interrupted by pressing a special key such as the BREAK key or a combination of keys (depending on the system used).

To make the computer behave in this manner, we use the INPUT instruction:

```
1Ø INPUT H
RUN
? 3Ø.5  [ENTER]
```

The numeric value is entered by the user, next to the question mark. This value is then stored in memory location H.

The question mark (prompt) is typed by the computer.

Figure 2–2 Using the same program to compute different pays.

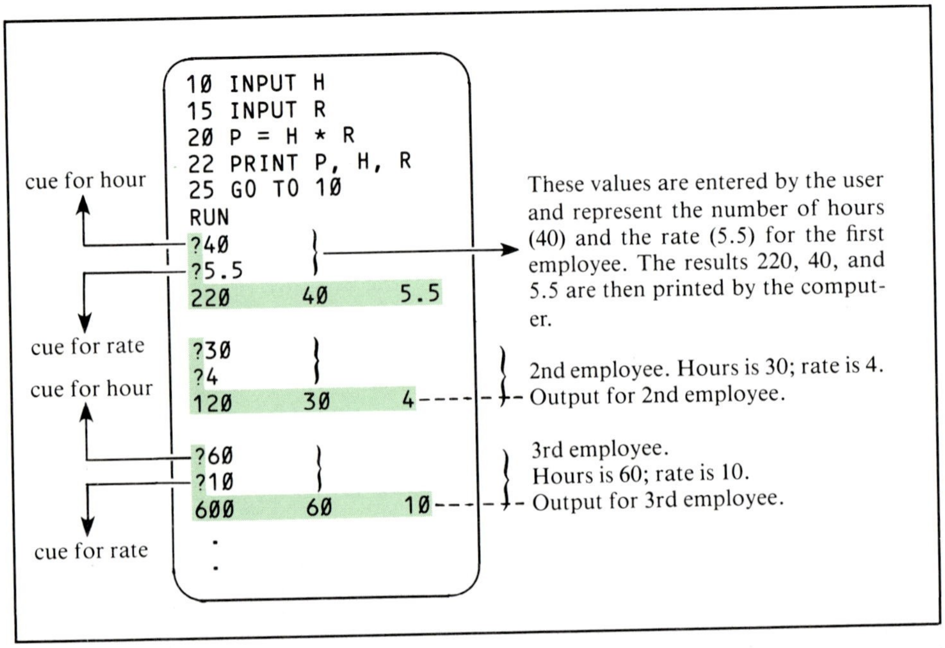

When the INPUT instruction is executed, the computer prints a question mark on the terminal and stops. This is a prompt (cue) to the user that the computer is ready to accept information from the user. The user then types a particular numeric value on the terminal and presses ENTER. The value typed by the user is stored in the memory location (variable) designated by the INPUT statement, H in this case. The computer can now process H as specified by the BASIC program instructions. In our payroll problem, we can use the INPUT statement very conveniently to communicate each employee's hours and rates as follows:

```
1Ø INPUT H              Enter the number of hours
15 INPUT R              Enter the rate of pay
2Ø P = H * R            Compute pay
22 PRINT P, H, R        Print pay, hours, and rate
25 GO TO 1Ø             Go back to repeat the above steps for each
                        employee
RUN
?3Ø
?4                      Hours and rate supplied by the user
12Ø       3Ø       4    Output for first employee
?6Ø
?1Ø                     Hours and rate supplied by the user
6ØØ       6Ø       1Ø   Output for second employee
? [BREAK]               Interrupt program to stop
```

Note that to break the loop, the user interrupts the computer by typing the BREAK key (or another type of key, depending on the system). It should be noted that ending a program in such a manner is a *bad* programming practice; more elegant and traditional methods to terminate programs will be discussed in later chapters.

2-7 The Final Program

2-7-1 Making the Program Easier to Use

The previous program is somewhat unrealistic because no names are attached to the various payroll records. To make the payroll program more realistic, employee names should also appear on the output. Let us write a program that will cause the computer to stop and ask the payroll clerk the name, the number of hours, and the rate of each employee before computing and producing the employee's payroll record. The report produced when the program is RUN should be similar to the report shown in Figure 2-3.

In Figure 2-3 notice the prompts that precede each question mark. This makes it easier for the clerk to know what information to enter when the computer stops and

■ **Figure 2-3** A complete payroll output.

```
RUN
ENTER NAME          }
?DOUGH DOUG         }
ENTER HOURS         }
?3Ø.5               }  1st employee data
ENTER RATE          }
?3.46               }
                    }----------  One blank line
NAME: DOUGH DOUG    }
HOURS: 3Ø.5         }  1st employee report
RATE: 3.46          }
PAY: 1Ø5.53         }
                    }----------  Two blank lines

ENTER NAME          }
?GOLD ERA           }
ENTER HOURS         }
?4Ø                 }
.                   }
.                   }
.                   }
```

displays a question mark on the terminal. The program to produce the output shown in Figure 2–3 is shown in Figure 2–4.

Names and other alphabetic information can be stored in memory locations in much the same way that numeric information is stored. For example, to store the number 20.5 in memory location H, we write 10 H = 20.5. To store the message "HELLO" in a memory cell, we must use a variable name that ends with a dollar sign ($), for example, 10 A$ = "HELLO". In this case, memory location A$ will contain the string of characters H, E, L, L, and O. Variables ending in a $ can be used to store any combination of letters, special characters, or digits; these are called *alphanumeric* characters.

In the program of Figure 2–4, N$ is used in the INPUT statement to "hold" the employee's name. When typing the name after the computer's prompt (?), the user does *not* need to enclose the name in quotation marks.

Also note that a blank line can be produced on the output by typing the word PRINT (lines 90, 120 and 125).

2-7-2 Do It Now

1. What results will the following program produce (make up your own input if necessary)?

a.
```
10 PRINT "WHAT'S YOUR NAME"
15 INPUT N$
20 PRINT N$;" WHAT'S YOUR AGE"
25 INPUT A
30 PRINT "WELL ";N$;" YOU SURE DONT LOOK";A;"YEARS OLD"
50 END
RUN
```

b.
```
10 A$ = "HELLO"
15 B$ = "JOHN"
20 PRINT A$;B$
30 END
RUN
```

2. Imagine you are the computer! What type of errors would you encounter in the following code:

```
10 H = 5
15 R = 20
30 P = H * R
40 PRINT "P, H, R"
50 END
RUN
```

3. Explain what happens as a result of the following.

a.
```
10 PRINT "LOOP" [ENTER]
15 GOTO 10      [ENTER]
```

b.
```
16 PRINT "A"    [ENTER]
15 PRINT "B"    [ENTER]
RUN             [ENTER]
```

■ **Figure 2–4** A complete payroll program.

```
10 REM FINAL PAYROLL PROGRAM
15 REM DATA DICTIONARY
20 REM          N$= EMPLOYEE NAME
25 REM          H = HOURLY WAGE
30 REM          R = HOURLY RATE
50 REM          P = PAY
55 PRINT "ENTER NAME"
60 INPUT N$
65 PRINT "ENTER HOURS"
70 INPUT H
75 PRINT "ENTER RATE"
80 INPUT R
85 P = H*R
90 PRINT                        PRINT by itself, prints a blank line.
100 PRINT "NAME : ";N$
105 PRINT "HOURS: ";H
110 PRINT "RATE : ";R
115 PRINT "PAY  : ";P
120 PRINT  }
125 PRINT  }                    Two blank lines are printed.
130 GOTO 55
135 END
RUN
ENTER NAME
? CLOVIS
ENTER HOURS
? 22.5
ENTER RATE
? 5.75

NAME : CLOVIS    }
HOURS:  22.5     }
RATE :  5.75     }              report for 1st employee.
PAY  :  129.375  }

ENTER NAME
? ARAMIS
ENTER HOURS
? 84
ENTER RATE
? 38.5

NAME : ARAMIS    }
HOURS:  84       }
RATE :  38.5     }              report for 2nd employee.
PAY  :  3234     }
? [BREAK]
```

Answers

1. a.
```
WHAT'S YOUR NAME
?MICHEL
WHAT'S YOUR AGE
38
WELL MICHEL YOU SURE DON'T LOOK 38 YEARS OLD
```
   b.
```
HELLOJOHN
```
   None; computer will print P, H, R

2. a. Instructions 10 and 15 will be stored in memory.
   b. B will be printed on first line followed by A on the second line.

2-8 The BASIC Clear Screen Instruction

This feature is only available on certain computers such as the TRS-80 models II, III and IV, the IBM PC, the Apple, and the Pet computers. CLS is used for the TRS-80s and the IBM PC, and we will use CLS in this section. Replace CLS with HOME if you are using an Apple or PRINT CHR$ (167) for a Pet.

When using a video screen, the results (output) appear on the screen below the source code (BASIC program). If the user wants the output to be displayed all by itself on the screen without the listing of the BASIC program, he/she can instruct the computer to clear its screen before displaying the results. This is done by inserting the clear screen instruction (CLS) just before the first PRINT statement. For our simple payroll program, the screen before and after execution would appear as:

Screen Before the Run

```
05 CLS
10 PRINT "PAY", "HOURS", "RATE"
15 H = 40
20 R = 5.5
30 P = H * R
40 PRINT P, H, R
50 END
RUN
```

Screen After Typing RUN

```
PAY          HOURS         RATE
220          40            5.5
```

Note the "clear" screen, i.e., just the results, no program.

The CLS instruction is both a BASIC instruction and a system command, i.e., if CLS is typed without a line number and the ENTER key is pressed, the entire screen will be cleared (blanked out) and the cursor will appear "home" (i.e., in the upper left corner of screen). CLS is a convenient command to use when the screen is cluttered with unsightly errata or unwanted information. Even though the screen is cleared, the BASIC program in memory is *not* wiped out, it is still stored in memory. Only the NEW command will destroy the entire BASIC program.

2-8-1 Do It Now

1. Describe what will happen and what will be displayed on the screen as a result of the following code.

a.
```
10 H = 20
20 PRINT "PAY", "HOURS", "RATE"
30 R = 5
40 P = H * R
50 CLS
60 PRINT P, H, R
RUN
```

b.
```
NEW
10 CLS
```

c.
```
10 P = 5
CLS
RUN
```

d.
```
10 CLS
CLS
RUN
```

2. Explain exactly what will happen as a result of running the following code:

a.
```
1 R = 5
2 H = 20
3 P = H*R
4 PRINT P
```

b.
```
1 R = 5
2 H = 20
3 P = H*R
4 CLS
5 PRINT P
```

c.
```
1 R = 5
2 H = 20
3 CLS
4 P = H*R
5 PRINT P
```

d.
```
1 R = 5
2 H = 20
3 P = H*R
4 CLS
5 PRINT P
6 GO TO 1
```

e.
```
1 R = 5
2 H = 20
3 P = H*R
4 CLS
5 PRINT P
6 GO TO 5
```

f.
```
1 R = 5
2 H = 20
3 P = H*R
4 CLS
5 PRINT P
6 GO TO 4
```

3. What results will the following program produce?

```
10 PRINT "WHAT'S YOUR NAME"
15 INPUT N$
17 CLS
20 PRINT N$;" WHAT'S YOUR AGE"
25 INPUT A
27 CLS
30 PRINT "WELL ";N$" YOU SURE DONT LOOK LIKE";A;"YEARS OLD"
50 END
RUN
```

Answers

1. a. The heading will appear briefly on the screen; the screen will then be blanked out and the numbers `100 20 5` will be displayed.

   b. The memory is blanked out, but the screen is not, since RUN has not been entered.

   c. The value 5 is stored in *P* and the screen is blanked out. Note that CLS in this case is a system command (no line number). When CLS is typed and then entered, the screen is immediately blanked out; but instruction 10 is still stored in memory.

d. Instruction 10 is entered into memory, the screen is then cleared. The program is then RUN, causing the screen to be blanked out again. Note that instruction 10 is still in memory.

2. a. The value 100 will be printed on the screen below the program instructions.
b. The screen will be blanked out, then the value 100 will be displayed alone on the screen.
c. Same as (b).
d. The value 100 will be blinked continuously on the screen.
e. The screen is blanked out, and the value 100 will scroll down the screen.
f. Same as (d).

3. The printed output for line 30 will appear alone on the screen.

2-9 Using the Printer

Readers who use a "hard copy" terminal (e.g., a typewriter or teletype) instead of a screen may skip this section. When working with a video screen (monitor), there will be times when the user wants to obtain a paper copy of his BASIC program.

Recall that the LIST command lists on the screen the program currently stored in the computer's memory. The LLIST command for the IBM and TRS-80 computers is identical to the LIST command, except that the current BASIC program is typed on the printer, not the screen. Note, however, that LLIST command lists *only* the BASIC program (the numbered instructions), *not* the output produced by the computer. To print the output on the printer, the BASIC instruction LPRINT should be used in the BASIC program instead of PRINT; note that the output will not appear on the screen if LPRINT is used.

Example 1:

`1 LPRINT "HELLO"`	The caption HELLO will be printed on the printer.

Example 2:

`1 PRINT "HELLO"`	The caption HELLO will be printed on the screen.

Example 3:

```
10 LPRINT "HELLO"
20 PRINT "HELLO"
```

The caption will appear on both the screen and the printer.

Using the printer can become quite involved if the user's system has a high speed printer that is shared by many other terminals. In this case, the user should consult the computer lab assistant or the instructor to find out how to create printer files, etc. The user's system may also be capable of typing (echoing) directly onto the printer whatever is typed on the screen; in this case the LLIST and LPRINT instructions are less useful, since whatever is displayed on the screen, is also typed automatically on the printer.

3 LET, REM, PRINT, TERMINATION, AND SYSTEM COMMANDS

3-1 Problem Example

Mr. Rancher owns a 198.6 by 301.5 foot rectangular plot of land in the city and some acreage in the county, the latter in the form of a perfect circle (radius 300 feet). The city lot is taxed at the rate of $0.043 per square foot, while the county land is taxed at $0.019 per square foot. Write a program to print the areas of both lots, the corresponding taxes for each lot, and the total combined taxes. The program should produce the following display on the terminal.

```
RUN
CITY AREA= 59877.9                    TAX= 2574.75
COUNTY LOT AREA= 282744               TAX= 5372.14
TOTAL TAXES= 7946.89
```

RUN implies that the user has already typed in all the BASIC instructions, i.e., these have been stored in the memory of the computer, and that now the computer is to carry out those instructions.

As you probably realize by now, there are many ways to solve a problem. A quick but tedious program using as few instructions as possible is shown in Figure 3–1. Note that the code is somewhat repetitious, i.e., to compute the tax on the city lot in line 20, we have to recompute the lot area (already done in line 10). The same area is recomputed for the third time at line 50 to compute the total tax. Note also that the code in Figure 3–1 works only for these lot dimensions stated above, i.e., if different dimensions were given, all the instructions would have to be retyped.

A better code is shown in Figure 3–2. It may seem longer and more detailed, but it is easier to read and understand (better documented) and it is more general: with a few changes, the same code could compute areas and taxes for lots with any dimensions.

Analyze carefully the BASIC instructions in Figure 3–2 and the results they produce. Note the four types of BASIC statements (all of which have line numbers):

1. The REM statements used to document the program
2. The LET replacement statement, which allows a value to be stored in a memory location
3. The PRINT statement, which causes the computer to print messages or values contained in memory locations
4. The END statement, the last statement in a BASIC program

Each BASIC instruction or system command is entered into the memory of the computer by pressing the RETURN/ENTER key.

As a precaution, the user should always type NEW before typing his/her BASIC program. This erases any BASIC session by another user at the same terminal. This applies mostly to microcomputers, i.e., stand-alone systems, and not to time-sharing or network systems requiring sign-on and sign-off procedures.

■ **Figure 3–1** First approach to a property tax problem.

```
10 PRINT "CITY LOT AREA=";     198.6 * 301.5,
20 PRINT "TAX=";               198.6 * 301.5 * .043
30 PRINT "COUNTY LOT AREA=";   300^2 * 3.14,
40 PRINT "TAX=";               300^2 * 3.14 * .019
50 PRINT "TOTAL TAXES=";       198.6*301.5*.043+ 300^2*3.14*.019
60 END
```

Compute city lot area
Compute city lot tax
Compute county lot area
Compute county lot tax
Compute sum of taxes

■ **Figure 3–2** A property tax problem.

```
NEW

10 REM PROPERTY TAX PROBLEM
14 REM
18 REM CITY LOT CALCULATIONS
22 REM
26 LET L  = 198.6
30 LET W  = 301.5
34 LET A1 = L * W
38 LET T1 = A1 * .043
42 PRINT "CITY AREA=";A1, "TAX=";T1
46 REM
50 REM COUNTY LOT CALCULATIONS
54 REM
58 LET R  = 300
62 LET A2 = 3.1416 *  R^2
66 LET T2 = A2 * .019
70 PRINT "COUNTY LOT AREA=";A2,"TAX=";T2
74 REM
78 REM CALCULATE COMBINED TAXES
82 REM
86 LET T = T1 + T2
90 PRINT "TOTAL TAXES=";T
94 END
RUN
```

NEW is a system command that erases any leftover BASIC instructions currently in memory.

The REM instruction is used for documentation. The programmer writes remarks in the program to help document it and to help explain certain instructions. A blank REM acts as a visual separator.

Store in memory location *L* the length of the city lot.

Store in memory location *W* the width of the city lot.

Compute the area of the city lot.

Compute tax for city lot area (4.3 cents/sq. ft.).

Print the captions and results. Notice their spacing on the output line. The positions of the results are controlled by the semicolon (;) for compact spacing and the comma (,) for wide spacing.

Store in memory location R the radius of the circle.

Compute the area (πR^2). Note the caret ^ in R^2.

Compute tax on circular area.

Print the captions, the area and the tax.

Add both taxes and store result in memory location *T*.

Print *T* (total taxes).

RUN is a system command telling the computer to execute the program currently in its memory (lines 10–94).

```
CITY AREA= 59877.9             TAX= 2574.75
COUNTY LOT AREA= 282744        TAX= 5372.14
TOTAL TAXES= 7946.89
```

Output of program produced by lines 42, 70, and 90.

Recall from chapter 2 that RUN is a system command that is typed by the user when all the BASIC instructions have been stored in the computer's memory. It tells the system to execute the sequence of BASIC instructions. If no errors are present in the BASIC code, the results (output) are then printed on the terminal.

Notice the output that the computer produces when the RUN system command is typed. The first semicolon in the PRINT statement at line 70 tells the system to print the contents of A2 right after the caption COUNTY LOT AREA, while the comma after A2 tells the system to skip many positions before printing the message TAX = .

This caption is followed immediately by the value of T2 (semicolon). The effect of the semicolon and comma on the spacing of the output is shown by the darkened zones:

```
70 PRINT "COUNTY LOT AREA=";A2, "TAX="; T2
.
.
RUN

COUNTY LOT AREA= 282600          TAX= 5369.4
```

Note also how squaring is accomplished in line 62. The symbol ^ (caret) is used to denote exponentiation. The same result could have been achieved by typing R * R. In many other systems, the up arrow ↑ is used for exponentiation.

** Remember **

```
15 LET...  }
.          }
.          }
55 PRINT   }
.          }  BASIC instructions
.          }
70 REM     }
.          }
.          }
80 END     }

NEW        }  System commands
RUN        }
```

3-1-1 Do It Now

1. Enter the program of Figure 3–2 on your system. To make your typing task simpler, you can omit the keyword LET. Are there any significant differences in your output?
2. Change the program of Figure 3–2 to allow for a 200 by 300 foot city lot and for a circular county lot of radius 400 feet. Would it be easier or more difficult to make the same changes to the program in Figure 3–1?
3. Change the program of Figure 3–2 to print the total area of the two lots.
4. Add the necessary code to calculate the total area of both lots in acres (1 acre = 43,560 square feet).
5. What would happen to the program if all REM instructions were removed from the program?

6. Could statements 86 and 90 be combined into one statement?

7. What would happen if the command NEW had been typed right after line 90?

Answers

2. Change lines as follows:
```
26 LET L = 200
30 LET W = 300
58 LET R = 400
```
It would be much more tedious to make the same changes on the program in Figure 3-1, since all lines of the program would have to be retyped.

3. Insert line `83 PRINT "TOTAL AREA="; A1 + A2`

4. Insert line `83 PRINT "TOTAL ACREAGE="; (A1 + A2)/43560`

5. The output would be the same, but the program would be more difficult to understand for any one other than the originator.

6. `90 PRINT "TOTAL TAXES="; T1 + T2`

7. The entire program would be wiped out of the computer's memory!

3-2 Elements of the BASIC Language

3-2-1 An Overview

As stated in chapter 2, a BASIC program is a set of instructions telling the computer what actions (operations) to carry out to solve a particular problem. There are essentially only three types of BASIC operations that the computer can carry out:

1. Arithmetic operations (add, multiply, divide, subtract, raise to a power)
2. Input/output operations (entering data from an external device into memory and printing results)
3. Comparisons (determining whether one value is less than, equal to, or greater than another value)

A BASIC instruction looks or reads very much like an English sentence. It is composed of different elements—BASIC keywords, constants, variables, arithmetic operators (+, −, . . .), relational operators (<, =, >, . . .), expressions, and so forth—that are combined together under a proper grammatical structure to yield a valid BASIC instruction.

The following examples introduce the reader to the use of those BASIC elements, which will then be discussed separately in greater detail. In the following examples of the three types of BASIC operations, the reader should identify the various BASIC elements and try to understand the context in which they are used.

Arithmetic Instructions

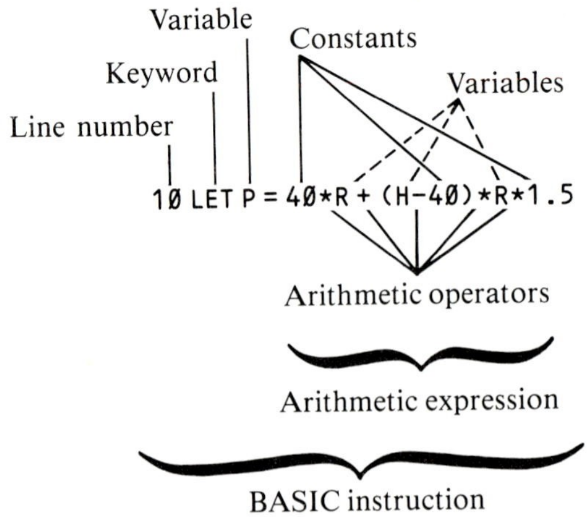

Interpretation:

> This formula is used to compute a pay for an employee who has worked overtime. H represents the number of hours, R is the rate of pay, and H – 40 is the number of hours in excess of 40. These excess hours are paid at 1½ times the rate R i.e., (H – 40) * R * 1.5. The first 40 hours are paid at the regular rate (40 * R).

The computer evaluates arithmetic expressions according to precedence rules, which will be discussed in more detail in section 3-2-6. Operations in parentheses come first, followed by multiplication/division, followed last by addition/subtraction. We can evaluate the preceding arithmetic expression (using H = 60 and R = 10) by following the precedence rules:

```
10 LET P = 40 * R + (H - 40) * R * 1.5        Parentheses
           40 * R +    20    * R * 1.5        Multiplication
           400    +    20    * R * 1.5        Multiplication
           400    +        200   * 1.5        Multiplication
           400    +            300            Addition
               700
```

Once the arithmetic expression has been evaluated to 700, that result is stored in memory location P.

Output Instructions

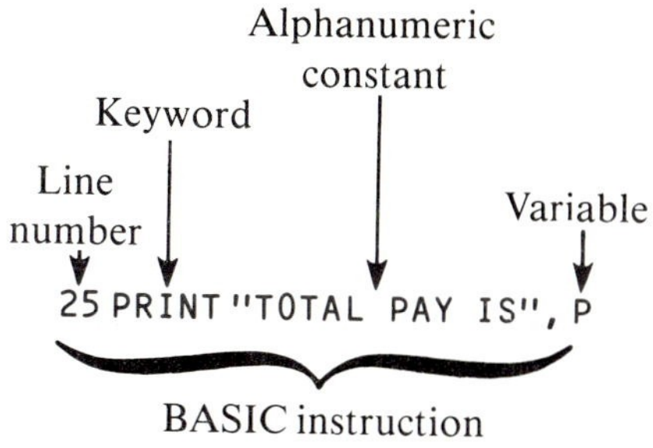

Interpretation:

The computer is told to print two items, the message TOTAL PAY IS and the contents of memory location P (whatever number is in P). The message consists of whatever characters are enclosed within the quotation marks (in this case, 12 characters including spaces).

Comparisons

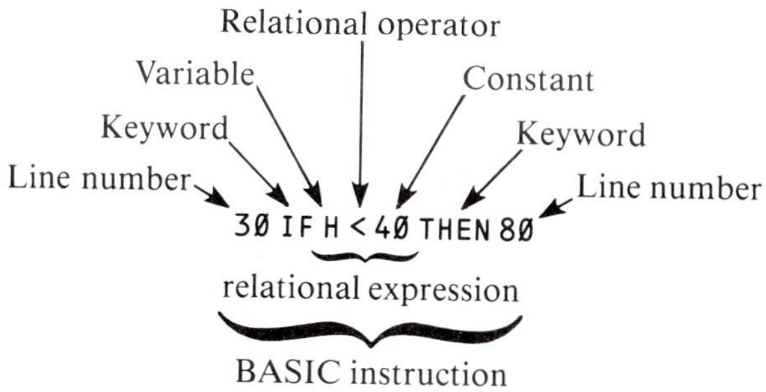

Interpretation:

If the number in H is less than 40, the computer goes to the line number specified by the THEN statement (80) and executes whatever instruction is there. If the number in H is not less than 40, the computer goes to the instruction immediately following instruction 30.

3-2-2 The Character Set

The keyboard characters that the programmer can use to type BASIC instructions are grouped into three standard classes:

1. Alphabetic
   The alphabetic characters are A, B, C, . . ., Y, Z
2. Numeric
   The numeric characters are 0, 1, 2, . . ., 8, 9

3. Special
   The special characters are . , ; " + − * / = < > ( ) ^ $ and the character "blank," which is equivalent to the space bar on the keyboard.

4. Alphanumeric characters
   Alphanumeric characters include alphabetic, numeric, and special characters, as well as other types of graphic symbols available on the keyboard, such as ? and !

Figure 3–3 illustrates a typical keyboard commonly used for BASIC.

Figure 3–3 Keyboard of a Micro Computer (Courtesy of Data Products, Inc.).

3-2-3 Constants

A constant is a quantity whose value is fixed and explicitly stated. Constants may be either numeric or alphanumeric.

Numeric Constants

Numeric constants are positive or negative numbers, with or without a decimal point. They can be added, subtracted, multiplied, divided, and raised to a power by the computer. They can also be compared to one another algebraically. A contant is made up of any of the digits 0 through 9 and may be preceded by the + or − symbol.

If the user specifies a constant with many digits (leading and trailing 0's are not counted), most BASIC systems will only retain the first 6 or 7 digits. for example, the statement 10 LET X= 123456789 will generally cause the computer to store 123457000 in memory location X, i.e., the computer retains only the first 6 significant digits and fills in zeroes for the other digits it cannot represent. This does not mean that the computer cannot store numbers of the order of the national debt (trillions, or 13 digits!). It can! For example, the statement 10 LET D = 1234567890123 will cause memory location D to contain the value $123456*10^7$. Even small computers can represent numbers with very large magnitudes (anywhere from 36 to 78 trailing zeroes). What the reader needs to understand is that the result of any arithmetic operation can only be expressed in terms of a fixed number of significant digits (6 or 7 in most small systems). For example, multiplying two 6-digit numbers yields a result that contains only 6 significant digits (the rest will be 0's).

Example 1: The following coding segments are identical in terms of the value stored in Z.

`10 LET X = 123456789`
`20 LET Y = 987654321`
`30 LET Z = X * Y`
	identical to	`10 LET X = 123457000`
		`20 LET Y = 987654000`
		`30 LET Z = X * Y`

The value stored in Z will be 121933000000000000 = 121933 × 10^{12}
whereas the true value is 121932631112635269

Example 2:

```
10 LET X = 9876
20 LET Y = 9876
30 LET Z = X * Y
```

The answer stored in Z will be 97535400, whereas the correct answer is 97535376.

For a more complete discussion on significant digits, magnitudes, and exponents, see section 3–5.

Examples of Valid Constants:

```
300      -2.31      62504.      +0.3      -123456
```

Examples of Invalid Constants:

`634,123`	No commas are allowed.
`23.24.`	Only one decimal point is allowed.
`$30.40`	Character $ is invalid.
`111-222-333`	The imbedded character – is invalid.

Alphanumeric Constants

Alphanumeric constants are generally words, messages, captions, titles, names, column headings, or digits that are enclosed in quotation marks. Actually, any combination or string of keyboard characters constitutes an alphanumeric constant. The value of the constant is the string of characters enclosed within the quotation marks. The quotation marks identify the beginning and end of the constant. For that reason, quotation marks may not be part of the constant itself.

Alphanumeric constants cannot be processed arithmetically (added, multiplied, etc.)—how could you add names or telephone numbers? They can be compared to one another, just as it is possible to compare and rearrange names in ascending or descending alphabetical order; they can also be stored in memory locations and be used in PRINT statements.

Examples of Valid Alphanumeric Constants:

`"1201 NORTH 12TH ST."`	String of 19 characters including 3 blanks.
`"1201 NORTH   12TH ST."`	This string is different from the one above; it consists of 21 characters including 5 blank spaces.
`"111-31-5444"`	A social security number, perhaps.
`"IT IS HERS"`	
`"-123"`	This constant cannot be processed arithmetically, since it is enclosed in quotes.
`"HOURS PAY BONUS"`	
`"+!!!**-<"`	This constant consists of 8 characters and has no obvious meaning!

Use of Constants in BASIC Statements

The maximum number of characters allowed in an alphanumeric string varies from system to system.[1] Constants may be used in BASIC as follows:

`LET T1 = P + (1 + I1)^N - 15`	Evaluate a formula.
`PRINT -10.36, 4.6 + 5.83, .005`	Print the numbers − 10.36, 10.43 and .005
`LET N$ = "CHARLES"`	Store the word CHARLES in memory cell N$.
`PRINT "$",A`	Print a dollar sign followed by the numeric value in A.
`IF A$ = "YES" THEN 80`	Compare the alphanumeric string in memory cell A$ with the string YES.

3-2-4 Do It Now

1. Specify which of the following are valid numeric constants. If invalid, specify the reasons.

a. `30.00.` d. `3,423,000.00` g. `-4 0 6` j. `8.000`
b. `-25.` e. `+3.25CR` h. `.0046` k. `2+2`
c. `111-22-1135` f. `10%` i. `$00321`

2. Specify which of the following are valid alphanumeric constants.

a. `"THAT'S IT"` e. `"SPELL KORRECTLY"`
b. `"ALL IN ALL` f. `IMAGE`
c. `" "` g. `"."`
d. `"020-"` h. `"2+3=6"`

3. Identify any errors:

a. `10 PRINT "HELLO`
b. `20 LET X = "11 + 22"`
c. `30 PRINT -316`

Answers

1. The following are invalid:
- a. Only one decimal point is allowed.
- c. The imbedded minus sign is not allowed.
- d. The comma is not allowed.
- e. The CR symbol is not allowed.
- f. The % character is not allowed.
- i. The $ character is not allowed.
- k. The imbedded + sign is not allowed.

2. The following are invalid:
- b. The last quotation mark is missing.
- f. There are no quotation marks.

3.
- a. The final quotation mark is missing.
- b. Alphanumeric strings must be stored in alphanumeric variables such as X$.

[1]The Apple, Pet, and IBM PC vary from 0 to 255; the TRS-80 allows 50 (or 255 by using CLEAR 255).

3-2-5 Variables

Unlike a constant, a variable may assume different values. One can think of a variable as a name given to a memory location in which a numeric or an alphanumeric item can be stored. There are two types of variables:

1. variables that contain numeric data. These can be processed arithmetically (added, subtracted, etc.) and compared to one another.
2. variables that contain alphanumeric data. These cannot be processed arithmetically, but they can be compared to one another.

The following rules for forming standard BASIC variable names can be applied to any BASIC system, although many computers have less restrictive rules:

Numeric Variables: Use a single letter of the alphabet, such as A, Z, or P, or a single letter followed by one digit (0–9), such as B9, Z1, or C0.

Alphanumeric Variables: The names are the same as those of numeric variables except that a $ is added to the variable name: A$, C1$, Z3$.

Examples:

```
10 LET X = 3.14
15 LET Y = -.14
20 LET Z = X + Y
30 LET N$ = "MOUSE"
```

The following are not valid BASIC variables because they do not conform to the rules above:

1A	Does not start with a letter
HRS	Too many letters
A.	Period is invalid
A+1	Invalid character +
AB$	A1$ would be valid
"H"	Is a constant

3-2-6 Do It Now

Which of the following are invalid variable names given the specifications described above? Why?

1. A34
2. $A
3. B%
4. "A3"
5. AZ$
6. A$$
7. 30
8. $
9. "N1$"

Answers

All are invalid.

1. Too many characters
2. $ should be last
3. % is invalid
4. Alphanumeric constant
5. Too many letters
6. Only one $ sign permitted
7. Numeric constant
8. Invalid by itself
9. Alphanumeric constant

3-2-7 Arithmetic Expressions

Recall what a BASIC expression looks like:

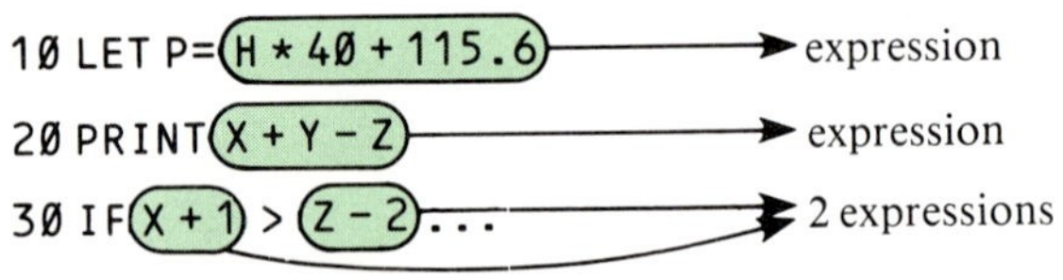

An expression may be a constant, a variable, or any combination of constants and/or variables linked by the five arithmetic operators shown below. No two arithmetic operators may be typed side by side. Parentheses may be included to denote the order of computations. The allowable arithmetic operators are:

Operator	Meaning
+	Addition
-	Subtraction
*	Multiplication
/	Division
^ or ↑ or **	Exponentiation (raising to a power)

Examples of valid expressions:

Algebraic Expression	*BASIC Expression*
$+3.5$	`3.5`
$-c$	`-C`
$a \cdot b - 30$	`A * B - 30`
$\frac{a \cdot c}{b}$	`(A/B)*C`
$ax^2 + bx + c$	`A * X^2 + B * X + C`
$(a \cdot b)^2$	`(A*B)^2`
$(-c + 1.4)d$	`(-C + 1.4)*D`
$\sqrt{x}$	`X^.5`
$\sqrt[4]{(a-b)^3}$	`((A - B)^3)^.25`
$\frac{\text{cost} - \text{salvage}}{\text{years}}$	`(C - S)/Y`
bonus + hours × rate	`B + H * R`
$\frac{1}{r_1} + \frac{1}{r_2} + \frac{1}{r_3}$	`1/R1 + 1/R2 + 1/R3`

The following errors are frequently made when writing expressions:

`3(A+B)`	Missing arithmetic operator before the first parenthesis.
`A-(B+(C*K)`	Missing right parenthesis. Parentheses should match.
`X*-3`	Invalid side-by-side operators; it should be X*(−3).

3-2-8 Precedence in Expressions

Operations within an expression are performed according to the following rules of precedence:

Operation	*Symbol*	*Precedence*
Parentheses	( )	high precedence
Exponentiation	^, **, ↑	
Multiplication, division	* or /	
Addition, subtraction	+ or −	low precedence

Operations with higher precedence are performed before operations with lower precedence. The operations addition/subtraction and multiplication/division are performed in order from left to right according to the rules of precedence. Exponentiations are also performed in order from left to right, and any operations with equal precedence are evaluated left to right. If parentheses are nested, the operation in the innermost set of parentheses is performed first.

The following example illustrates the sequence of priorities:

`3 + (2 * [2 ^ 3] / 4 + 1) - 2 / 3`	Exponentiation
`3 + ([2 * 8] / 4 + 1) - 2 / 3`	Multiplication (left to right)
`3 + ([16 / 4] + 1) - 2 / 3`	Division
`3 + [( 4 + 1)] - 2 / 3`	Add (because of parentheses)
`3 + 5 - [2 / 3]`	Division
`[3 + 5] - .666667`	Addition (left to right)
`8 - .666667`	Subtraction
`7.33333`	

Examples

1. A − B + C
   3 − 2 + 5

   B is subtracted from A, and the result is added to C.
   (3 − 2) + 5 = 1 + 5 = 6

2. A + B * C
   3 + 2 * 3

   Since multiplication has priority, B * C is computed; the result is then added to A, giving A + (B * C).
   3 + (2 * 3) = 3 + 6 = 9

3. A/B * C	Since multiplication and division have the same priority, B is first divided into A (A/B), and the result of the division is multiplied by C. This is different from A/(B * C).
9/4 * 2	(9/4) * 2 = 2.25 * 2 = 4.50
4. A/B/C	First A/B is performed, and the result is then divided by C; you will get the same answer if you calculate A/(B * C).
8/4/2	8/4 ÷ 2 = 2 ÷ 2 = 1
5. (A + B)/C * D	The parentheses indicate that the sum of A + B is to be performed first. The sum is then divided by C, and the result is multiplied by D, giving $\frac{A+B}{C} * D$ not $\frac{A+B}{C*D}$
(3 + 6)/3 * 6	9/3 * 6 = 3 * 6 = 18
6. A + B * C ^ 2	Since exponentiation has highest priority, C^2 is computed. This result is then multiplied by *B*, since multiplication has the next highest priority. Finally, this result is added to A, giving A + (B * (C ^ 2)).
3 + 3 * 2 ^ 2	3 + (3 * 2^2) = 3 + (3 * 4) = 3 + 12 = 15
7. A ^ B ^ C	Exponentiations are evaluated from left to right, therefore A is first raised to the power B, and this result is raised to the power C, giving (A ^ B) ^ C and not A ^ (B ^ C)
3 ^ 2 ^ 3	(3 ^ 2) ^ 3 = 9 ^ 3 = 729 and not 3^(2^3) = 6561

3-2-9 Do It Now

Write the BASIC expressions for:

1. $X + Y \cdot Z - 1$
2. $(A + B)^{2 \cdot X}$
3. $A + \frac{B}{3} - .5$
4. $\frac{N(1+N)}{-2}$
5. $-Y \cdot X$
6. $V.T - \frac{G \cdot T^2}{2}$
7. $X^3 - .73X + C$
8. $\frac{9}{T} - \frac{1}{(T-1)}$
9. $\frac{(X+Y)(A-B)}{(C+T)^2}$
10. $\sqrt{\frac{N(\text{SUM}) - \text{SUM}^2}{N(N-1)}}$
11. $\sqrt[6]{(-T)^5}$

Identify the order of the operations by placing an appropriate number above each arithmetic operator in the expression. For example:

```
 ⑤  ③  ⑥   ⑦    ①    ④  ②
A + 1 / 3 + B - (3 + 4) / Z ^ 2
```

12. 3 * 4 − (B − C)

13. 1 / 8 + 5 ^ 2 / 4

14. (−3 + X) * (B + C) + 3 / X + (C − 1)

15. X / A * 1 − B + (3 − Y)

Evaluate the following expressions for X = 2, Y = −2, Z = 3.

16. X / Y + Z ^ 2 * X

17. X + 2 * Y / Z + 1

18. 1 + (X ^ 2 ^ 3 − 1)

19. X / Y / Z * 2

20. X / Y * 1 − X + (3 − Y)

Answers

1. X + Y * Z − 1
2. (A + B) ^ (2 * X)
3. A + B / 3 − .5
4. (N * (1 + N)) / (−2)
5. −Y * X
6. V * T − (G * T * T) / 2
7. X ^ 3 − .73 * X + C
8. 9 / T − 1 / (T − 1)
9. (X + Y) * (A − B) / (C + T) ^ 2
10. ((N * S − S ^ 2) / (N * (N − 1))) ^ .5
11. (−T) ^ (5 / 6)
12. ②③ ①
3 * 4 − (B − C)
13. ②④①③
1 / 8 + 5 ^ 2 / 4
14. ① ④ ② ⑥⑤⑦ ③
(−3 + X) * (B + C) + 3 / X + (C − 1)
15. ②③④ ⑤ ①
X / A * 1 − B + (3 − Y)
16. 17
17. 1.666... or 1.66667
18. 64
19. −.666...
20. 2

3-3 BASIC Statements

3-3-1 The Replacement Statement LET

A replacement statement evaluates an expression and stores its value in a memory location identified by a variable name. The general form of a replacement statement is:

line number LET *variable* = *expression*

Note that a valid replacement statement *must* have the form *variable* = *expression* not *expression* = *variable.* Expressions such as X + Y = 10 or 5 = Y are invalid since they don't have a variable on the left side of the equal sign.

In most BASIC systems the key word LET is optional, it does not need to be used. When a replacement statement is executed, (RUN), the value of the *expression* (if numeric) is computed and the result is stored in the variable (memory location) specified on the left side of the equal sign.

It should be emphasized that a replacement statement is *not* an equation. When we write the statement

```
10 X = 2 * X + 1
```

we are not looking for a value of X (−1) that satisfies the equation. We are saying "find out what is in X, multiply it by 2, add 1, and store that result in memory location X." The equal sign is a replacement symbol. In this example, if memory location X contains 3, then 2 * X + 1 = 7 and the value 7 is stored in X, i.e., the old value in X (3) is replaced by 7!

Examples of valid replacement statements:

`10 LET X = - 0.07`	Store value −0.07 in X
`12 X1 = A + B / C - 1`	Evaluate the expression and store the result in X1
`14 LET C$ = "GROSS PROFIT"`	Store the string GROSS PROFIT in C$
`15 I = I + 1`	Compute I + 1 and store the result in I

Examples of invalid replacement statements:

`5 LET X + Y = 1`	This statement is incorrect for two reasons: **(1)** The left side should be a variable not an expression! **(2)** How could one store the number 1 in the sum of two memory locations?
`6 LET -3.1 = X`	One cannot store the value of X in memory location −3.1! X = −3.1 is valid, however.
`7 A1 = "PROFIT"`	One cannot store an alphanumeric constant in memory location A1 which expects numeric information. A1$ = "PROFIT" would be valid.
`9 N$ = 111 - 22 - 1348`	The expression is not an alphanumeric string. Quotation marks are needed.

3-3-2 Do It Now

1. State whether the following are constants, variables, expressions, or statements.

a. "1"
b. "2 + 3"
c. X + 1
d. X = X + X
e. Y$ = Y$
f. 1 + 2 + 3.4
g. 1 − 1
h. −.3
i. P = −H + R

2. State whether the following are constants, variables, expressions, or statements; if invalid, state the reasons.

a. 3 = 2 + 1
b. PAY = HRS + RATE
c. "A = X + 1"
d. "3 = 4"
e. X + Y = X + Y
f. 0 = 0 * 4
g. B + 3 / 2 / −4
h. A = "HELLO"
i. A$ = (X + Y) / Z
j. "A" = "C"
k. "A$" = "B$"
l. A$ = "1" * "2"

3. Determine the output produced by the following code:

```
10 LET I = 0
20 LET I = I + 1
30 PRINT I
40 GO TO 20
```

Answers

1. a. constant
b. constant
c. expression
d. statement
e. statement
f. expression
g. expression
h. constant
i. statement

2. a. Invalid statement: there should be a variable on the left side of the equal sign.
b. Invalid statement: variables contain too many characters.
c. Valid alphanumeric constant.
d. Valid alphanumeric constant.
e. Invalid statement: there is an expression (X + Y) on the left side of the equal sign.
f. Invalid statement: 0 is not a variable name.
g. Invalid expression: two operators side by side (/ −).
h. Invalid statement: the variable should be A$ instead of A.
i. Invalid statement: A$ should be A.
j. Invalid statement: there is a constant on the left side of the equal sign.
k. Invalid statement: there is a constant on the left side of the equal sign.
l. Invalid expression: one cannot multiply alphanumeric constants.

3. The numbers 1, 2, 3, 4,. . . will be printed one per line.

3-3-3 Line Numbers

Each BASIC instruction must be numbered. Line numbers must be unsigned (no plus or minus signs) integers not exceeding five digits. In most systems, statements or lines may be entered in any desired order; the system will arrange the statements in order when the program is listed or executed.

Statements will be processed by the computer in ascending line order unless a decision statement (IF) or unconditional transfer (GO TO) is encountered. These statements are discussed in chapter 4. In general, it is a good idea to number lines in increments of 5, 10, or more. This makes it easier to insert new statements between existing statements when editing a program.

For example, if you entered the following statements in the order indicated:

```
10 LET X = 3
20 PRINT C$, X, Y
15 LET Y = X ^ 3
12 LET C$ = "RESULT IS"
```

BASIC would rearrange these statements in the following order:

```
10 LET X = 3
12 LET C$ = "RESULT IS"
15 LET Y = X ^ 3
20 PRINT C$, X, Y
```

Automatic Continuation of Lines

Sometimes a BASIC instruction is too long to be typed on just one screen line (terminal line). For example, you might want to type a 70-character BASIC instruction on a system that allows 48 characters per line. In this case you should type the first 48 characters on one line and then, without pressing the ENTER/RETURN key, let the system automatically go to the next line (wrap around) and continue with the remaining characters on the second line.

If you wanted to type the following instructions on a terminal that allows 48 characters/line.

```
5 PRINT "THE TOTAL POPULATION IS "; A1; "TOTAL NUMBER OF MALES IS ";X
7 PRINT "PERCENTAGE MALES IS "; X/A1 * 100
```

you would type line 5 without worrying about when to start the next line. The terminal automatically wraps around to a new line when the 49th character has been typed. The terminal display would look like

column 48

```
5 PRINT "THE TOTAL POPULATION IS "; A1; "TOTAL N
UMBER OF MALES IS ";X
7 PRINT "PERCENTAGE MALES IS "; X / A1 * 100
```

Note:

1. No line number.
2. The ENTER/RETURN key was not pressed.

In most BASIC systems, a BASIC instruction can consist of as many as 255 characters, using several continuation lines. The number of continuation lines depends on the number of characters that can be typed on one screen line. (Terminal lines can have 48, 64, 75, or 80 characters.)

3-3-4 The REM Statement

The REM statement, which was introduced in chapter 2, is used in BASIC to make a program more understandable. The general form of the REM statement is

line number REM *literal characters*

where REM (remark) is a key word, and the literal characters are supplied by the programmer. Although the REM statement requires a line number, it is not an executable statement. Hence, when a REM statement is encountered in the program, control passes automatically to the next executable statement. Figure 3–4 illustrates the use of the REM.

■ **Figure 3–4** REM statements.

```
10 REM SOMETIMES WHEN A PROGRAM IS LENGTHY, THE PROGRAMMER MAY
20 REM FIND IT HELPFUL TO EXPLAIN WITHIN THE PROGRAM THE PURPOSE OF
30 REM ONE OR MORE BASIC STATEMENTS, THE USE OF A PARTICULAR
40 REM VARIABLE, OR THE FUNCTION OF SPECIFIC PROGRAM SEGMENTS. THE
50 REM PRACTICE OF INTERSPERSING REM STATEMENTS THROUGHOUT THE
60 REM PROGRAM CAN BE VERY HELPFUL WHEN THE PROGRAMMER AT A LATER
70 REM DATE DECIDES TO REVIEW OR MAKE REVISIONS TO PARTS OF THE
80 REM PROGRAM. FOR ANOTHER USER WHO WISHES TO USE THE PROGRAM, REM
90 REM STATEMENTS HELP TO EXPLAIN THE OVERALL PROGRAM STRUCTURE.
99 END
```

3-3-5 Do It Now

1. What would be produced by the program in Figure 3–4 if the program were RUN?
2. Do you really need to write REM for line 20 and each of the following lines in Figure 3–4? How many can you type without REM?

Answers

1. No output would be produced. The REM statements provide information for the programmer or others reading the program; they provide no information to the computer.
2. Most systems can print 255 characters in a row without pressing the ENTER/RETURN key. The program in Figure 3–4 probably needs only two or three line numbers.

3-3-6 The PRINT Statement

The general form of the PRINT statement is

line number PRINT *expression-list*

where the *expression-list* can be:

a constant	`PRINT -9.8`
a variable	`PRINT X`
an expression	`PRINT (H - 40) * R * 1.5 + 40 * R`
a character string	`PRINT "PAY HOURS RATE"`
a combination of the above, separated by commas or semicolons	`PRINT "PAY="; P, "HOURS="; H`

In many BASIC systems, output lines on a printer or screen consist of either 64 or 80 print positions (characters per line). The output line for a 64-character wide terminal is divided into 4 zones, each with 16 print positions. For a 80-character wide terminal, the output line is divided into 5 zones, each 16 characters wide. To a certain extent, the user can control the positioning of the results on the output line by selective use of the comma and the semicolon in the PRINT statement.

A comma between items in the expression-list provides wide spacing between items on the output line (each comma makes the printer skip to the next zone). A semicolon provides compact spacing between items (one or two blank spaces between numeric fields and none between character strings). A combination of commas and semicolons can also be used, as shown in Figure 3–5 (study these examples carefully). Figure 3–5 illustrates a four print zone display where X = 1, Y = −2, Z = 0.3 and N$ = "MAM".

Note the semicolon as the last character of the PRINT statement in the first line of example 11. This tells the printer to print the next item (Y) close to X (compact

Figure 3–5 Printing Zones. The comma and semicolon.

	Zone 1	Zone 2	Zone 3	Zone 4

1. `PRINT X`
`PRINT Y`
`PRINT Z`
No punctuation; 3 different lines
	1
	-2
	.3			

2. `PRINT X, Y, Z` The comma controls the zone	1	-2	.3	
3. `PRINT "HELLO";N$` No space between alphanumeric items	HELLOMAM			
4. `PRINT "HELLO ";N$` Imbedded blank within string	HELLO MAM			
5. `PRINT X;Y;Z` Compact spacing due to ;	1 -2 .3			
6. `PRINT X;Y,Z`	1 -2	.3		
7. `PRINT X,,,Z`	1			.3
8. `PRINT "HELLO";X,"HELLO",N$`	HELLO 1	HELLO	MAM	
9. `PRINT X,X,Y,Y,Z,Z` More variables than zones	1 .3	1 .3	-2	-2

10. `PRINT X,`
`PRINT Y,`
`PRINT Z`
The comma tells the system to print next item in next zone on same line if possible.
	1	-2	.3	

11. `PRINT X;`
`LET Z = .3`
`PRINT Y,`
`LET T = X + Z`
`PRINT Z`
Same as example 6
	1 -2	.3		

spacing), while the ending comma on the third line of example 11 tells the printer to print the next item (Z) one zone away from the item just printed (Y).

In the following example, PRINT statements tell the computer to skip zones, print headers, and evaluate expressions:

```
10  PRINT "ITEM", "QUANTITY", "PRICE", "COST"       <-- Printing headers
15  PRINT                                           <-- Print blank line
20  PRINT "BIT", "6", "2.98", 6 * 2.98               <-- Calculations
30  PRINT "SAWS", "8", "7.06", 8 * 7.06
35  PRINT
40  PRINT "TOTAL COST",,, 6 * 2.98 + 8 * 7.06       <-- Skipping zones
```

Running this code would produce the following output:

```
ITEM          QUANTITY      PRICE         COST

BIT           6             2.98          17.88
SAWS          8             7.06          56.48

TOTAL COST                                74.36
```

Some other examples of zones and PRINT statements for a 75-character-wide terminal are shown in Figure 3–6. Study these examples carefully.

3-3-7 Do It Now

1. Identify which of the following are invalid; state the reasons.
   a. `PRINT X Y Z`
   b. `PRINT "A"; "X; "HELLO" ;Z`
   c. `PRINT ,,,1,`
   d. `PRINT; X`
   e. `PRINT "X+Y" = ;3 + 4`
   f. `PRINT "Z;"; Z`
   g. `PRINT A^2^3 + Z;`
   h. `PRINT HELLO,A$`
   i. `PRINT ;;X`
   j. `PRINT "123";123`
   k. `PRINT "A,B;C"`
   l. `PRINT "X= ;X;"Y=";Y`
2. In what way do the statements *a* and *b* differ?
   a. `PRINT "BIT", "6", "2.98"`
   b. `PRINT "BIT", 6, 2.98`
3. Write the code to print your name in the upper middle part of your computer screen. (Assume the screen consists of 16 lines.)
4. Write the code to produce the following display. The tax is 4% of the total amount.

```
       INVENTORY ANALYSIS
  ITEM   QUANTITY   COST   TOTAL

  NUTS       58      .07     —
  BOLTS      64      .11     —

  TOTAL AMOUNT               —
  TAX                        —
```

■ **Figure 3–6** Examples of PRINT statements.

```
1Ø  LET X=Ø.2     )
15  LET Y=15      }   Initialization of constants
2Ø  LET Z=-3.9    )
25  PRINT"ØØØØØØØØØ1111111111222222222233333333";  )
3Ø  PRINT"3344444444445555555555666666666677777"   } To provide easy column
35  PRINT"1234567890123456789Ø1234567890123456 7"; } identification on output
4Ø  PRINT"89Ø123456789Ø123456789Ø123456789Ø12345"  )
45  PRINT
5Ø  PRINT X,Y,Z                      Zone spacing:     numeric              :commas
55  PRINT X;Y;Z                      Compact spacing:  numeric              :semicolons
6Ø  PRINT "HOURS","RATE","PAY"       Zone spacing:     string data          :commas
65  PRINT "HOURS";"RATE";"PAY"       Compact spacing:  string data          :semicolons
7Ø  PRINT "HOURS",Y                  Zone spacing:     numeric + string data
75  PRINT "HOURS";Y                  Compact spacing:  numeric + string data
8Ø  PRINT "X=",X,"Y=",Y      )
85  PRINT "X=";X,"Y=";Y      }       Combination commas and semicolons
9Ø  PRINT "TOTAL=";X+Y+Z     )
95  PRINT 2.34*X/Y-Z^2               Expression numeric
96  STOP
99  END

RUN
```

Column identifiers

```
ØØØØØØØØØ1111111111222222222233333333334444444444555555555566666666667777777
123456789Ø123456789Ø123456789Ø123456789Ø123456789Ø123456789Ø123456789Ø12345

 Ø.2                15                 -3.9
 Ø.2  15 -3.9
HOURS               RATE               PAY
HOURSRATEPAY
HOURS               15
HOURS 15
X=                  Ø.2                Y=                 15
X= Ø.2              Y= 15
TOTAL= 11.3
-15.1788
```

Answers

1. a. Punctuation missing between variables.
   b. Incomplete quotation marks. Should be "X"; or X;
   c. Valid
   d. Valid
   e. The equal sign cannot be recognized as such
   f. Valid
   g. Valid
   h. HELLO should be in quotes
   i. Valid
   j. Valid
   k. Valid
   l. Should be "X = ";X;...

2. The two statements differ only in the position of the results on the output.

3.
```
10 PRINT
11 PRINT
12 PRINT
13 PRINT
14 PRINT,,"MICHAEL"
```

4.
```
10 PRINT, "INVENTORY ANALYSIS"
15 PRINT "ITEM","QUANTITY","COST","TOTAL"
16 T1 = 58 * .07
19 PRINT
20 PRINT "NUTS",58, .07, T1
21 T2 = 64 * .11
25 PRINT "BOLTS",64, .11, T2
26 T = T1 + T2
28 P = .04 * T
29 PRINT
30 PRINT "TOTAL AMOUNT",,,T
35 PRINT "TAX",, P
```

3-3-8 The Termination Statements STOP and END

The last BASIC statement in a BASIC program should always be the END statement. For that reason, the END statement should always have the highest line number in your program. The END statement halts execution of your program.

The STOP statement is identical to the END instruction except that it may appear (if needed) anywhere in your program i.e., there may be more than one STOP statement in any one BASIC program, whereas in many BASIC versions the END should only appear once in your program (at the end of program). The general forms of the termination statements are

line number STOP
line number END

Any program can be written without a STOP statement. If, for example, you wish to stop execution of your program after executing a particular line number, you may transfer (using a GO TO statement) from that line number to the END statement.

3-4 Input/Output Features: LPRINT, LLIST, SAVE, LOAD

The following discussion on input/output features applies to many BASIC systems. Due to the differences among systems, section 3-4-4 is left blank for you to write the commands that work on *your* system and that are not possibly described in sections 3-4-1 and 3-4-2. You can also use this area for additional information.

3-4-1 Working with a Screen and a Printer: LPRINT, LLIST

On many BASIC systems using a video monitor and an accompanying printer, the system command LLIST, which can be executed at any time, will list the current BASIC program on the printer.

The BASIC instruction LPRINT has the same effect as PRINT, except that the output will be printed on the printer, not on the screen, when the program is run.

Example:

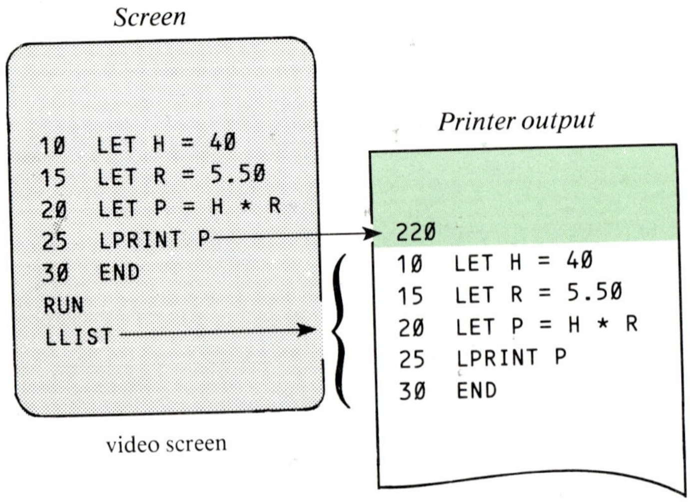

Instruction 25 causes the computer to print the result on the printer and not on the screen.

LLIST copies the current program onto the printer but not onto the screen.

In many systems, especially on microcomputing systems using a screen and a printer, it is not necessary to use the LPRINT or LLIST instructions to print results or listings. The user can activate the printer through a system command so that whatever the user or the system types on the screen is automatically printed on the printer. Another system command can also be used to deactivate the printer so that the printer is not constantly printing. The reader should consult with his/her instructor or lab manager for details or his/her technical reference manual.

3-4-2 Do It Now

1. Specify the values printed and the output device. (Assume a screen and a printer are available.) Are there any syntax errors?

```
10 X = 10
15 Y = 13
20 Z = -4
25 LPRINT X, Y, Z
LLIST
30 PRINT X, Y
```

2. Find any syntax errors.

```
10  X = 00.3
20  Y = X ^ 2
30  PRINT X ^ 2
LPRINT
```

3. The following program is supposed to find the average of scores 90, 80, and 87. Find any errors of syntax or logic.

```
10 PRINT "TEST AVERAGE"
25 LET A = 90 + 80 + 87 / 3
30 LET A = (90 + 80 + 87) / 3
40 PRINT A
50 END
```

4. Mrs. X has purchased $12,500 worth of A&L stock, which yields a 13.5% interest return. Mrs. X is in the 27% tax bracket, which means that she pays 27% of her income to the government. The program below attempts to compute and print the yearly interest on the stock, the total accumulated principal after one year, the federal tax to be paid on the interest earned, and Mrs. X's net holdings after federal income tax. Identify syntax and logical errors in the program.

```
10 S = 12,500
20 I = S * 13.5                          Compute interest
30 PRINT "YEARLY INTEREST= "I
31 REM COMPUTE TOTAL PRINCIPAL T
35 I + S = T
40 PRINT "TOTAL PRINCIPLE";T             Compute total principal
45 COMPUTE FEDERAL TAX ON INTEREST
50 F = T * .27
05 PRINT FEDERAL TAX;F
60 REM COMPUTE NET HOLDING N
70 N = 1.135 * 12500 - .135 * .27 * 12500
END
```

Answers

1. The values 10, 13, and −4 will be printed on the printer.
   Lines 10 through 25 will be listed on the printer.
   The values 10 and 13 will be printed on the screen.

2. Missing line number for LPRINT.

3. No errors of syntax or logic.

4. Syntactical errors:

   Line 10 Invalid comma; should be 12500
   Line 30 Missing punctuation before second item *I* (However, some systems don't require commas.)

Line 35 Should be T = I + S
Line 45 Missing REM statement
Line 05 Missing quotation marks; the fact that this should be line 55, not 05, is not a syntax error
END Missing line number for END

Logical errors:

Line 20 The percentage should be expressed as 0.135.
Line 50 Federal tax on interest should be I * 0.27 and not T * .27.
Line 05 At this point in the program, the value printed for F will be 0, should be 55.

After line 70 Mrs. X's net holdings are not printed.

3-4-3 SAVE and LOAD or OLD

Once you have typed a program, you may wish to save it on your central computer users' library or on your diskette, if your system is equipped with disk drives. Your program does not need to be complete to be stored on disk; you can save it as many times as you wish! Saving your program means that you can retrieve it later on using the LOAD command. The following discussion of the SAVE command uses the TRS-80 Models and the IBM PC for illustration. Your system's commands may vary (use section 3-4-4 to write them down).

To save your program in BASIC mode (assume it has been typed and is in memory) type:

	Command	
TRS-80	`SAVE "PROG :1"`	Program is stored in drive 1 under name PROG.
	`SAVE "PROG :Ø"` / `SAVE "PROG"`	Program is saved on drive 0 under name PROG.
IBM PC	`SAVE "A: PROG"` / `SAVE "PROG"`	Program is saved on drive A with name PROG.
	`SAVE "B: PROG"`	Program is saved on drive B with name PROG.

The name under which the program is saved is selected by the user; it can have at most 8 characters. In the preceding example the name PROG was chosen.

Before you save a program on a diskette, ask your instructor about formatting the diskette and about write protection.

To load the program named PROG, type (assuming the diskette is in the proper drive) the following command:

`LOAD "PROG"` or `LOAD "PROG :1"` or `LOAD "B: PROG"`

Program PROG will be retrieved from the system drive and stored in memory, erasing whatever is there. As in the examples with SAVE, the drive number can be included with the program name.

3-4-4 MY SYSTEM IS DIFFERENT

This section is left blank for you to write any different system commands that your system uses. You may also want to list the various steps that are required to start a session with your system.

3-5 Number Representation

The specifics of number representation vary from one computer to another, depending on the manufacturer. (See the computer manufacturer's reference manuals for more details.) Arithmetic operations are normally carried out in floating-point mode (system uses exponents). The range of floating-point numbers is usually approximately 10^{-76} to 10^{76}, but this depends on the computer system, and the number of significant digits varies from 6 to 15.

Constants in a BASIC program can be expressed in two different notations:

1. Decimal notation, with or without decimal points

   Examples: 45.67, -12.3, 11240, -48216, $+0.005$

2. Exponential notation, where the character E is used to represent the decimal base 10, followed by a one- or two-digit number (with or without a sign) to represent the exponent (power).

   Examples:

```
05 LET A = 9E-03
10 LET X = 3.456E+2
15 LET Y = -3.E-3
20 LET Z = 1.23E10
```

where 9E − 03 $= 9 \times 10^{-3} = .009$
where 3.456E + 2 $= 3.456 \times 10^{2} = 345.6$
where − 3.E − 3 $= -3 \times 10^{-3} = -.003$
where 1.23E10 $= 1.23 \times 10^{10} = 12300000000$

On output generated by PRINT statements, BASIC uses exponential notation for constants whose values are in a certain range, e.g., if the number is very small (between $-.01$ and $.01$) or very large (greater than 10^8 or less than -10^8). This range varies from one computer system to another. In any event, the printed value consists of n significant digits (always with one digit to the left of the decimal point) followed by the symbol E followed by the appropriate power of 10 (positive or negative). Consider the following examples where the number of significant digits is six for example:

```
10 LET A = 123456
20 LET B = 1234567
30 LET C = 123.456
40 LET D = 123456789012345
50 LET E = .01
60 LET F = .001
70 LET G = -.000324567
80 LET H = 22.1E3
90 LET I = .08E-3
95 LET K = -12.00458E6
97 PRINT "A=";A,"B=";B,"C=";C,"D=";D
98 PRINT "E=";E,"F=";F,"G=";G,"H=";H
99 PRINT "I=";I,"K=";K

RUN
A= 123456       B= 1.23457E+06     C=  123.456         D= 1.23457E+14
E= .01          F= 1E-03           G= -3.24567E-04     H= 22100
I= 8E-05        K= -1.20046E+07
```

Note that some results cannot be represented exactly in decimal notation. For example 10/3 = 3.3333.... In such cases, the first *n* digits (significant digits) are retained by the system and rounded off.

Examples (with six significant figures):

2.5645288...	would be rounded to 2.56453
2.33333...	would be rounded to 2.33333
2.55555...	would be rounded to 2.55556

3-5-1 Do It Now

1. Convert the following to exponential notation, using the notation *d.ddddd*E + *power* where *d* is a digit and where the digit to the left of the decimal point is nonzero. (Round off to six significant figures where necessary.)
   a. 3
   b. 0.1
   c. −.00000087654321
   d. 12345678
   e. 123.0034
   f. 10000.09

2. Determine the results printed by the following code. Assume 6 significant digits.

```
10 A = .05
15 B = 123
25 C = .0785423
30 D = -1345.6789
35 E = 21.45E-3
40 F = 1E-3
45 G = 100000099
50 H = .005E6
55 I = 1E30 + 9999999999999999999
60 J = 1E-30 - 1E-31
65 K = 1E15 * 2E15
70 L = E-30 + E-30
75 PRINT A,B,C,D,E,F,G,H,I,J,K,L
```

Answers

1. a. 3.E0
   b. 1.E − 1
   c. − 8.76543E − 7
   d. 1.23457E7
   e. 1.23003E2
   f. 1.00001E4

2.

```
(A)  .05          (B)  123
(C)  .0785423     (D)  -1345.68
(E)  .02145       (F)  1E-03
(G)  1E+08        (H)  5000
(I)  1E+30        (J)  9E-31
(K)  2E+30        (L)  2E-30
```

Note the loss of all 9's in the output for *I*.

3-6 Problem Examples

3-6-1 An Investment Decision

Mrs. Gabroudy would like to deposit $1,500 at a savings institution. She considers a local bank and a credit union. The credit union requires a nonrefundable membership fee of $15 (up front); deposits earn 12.75%, and interest is compounded once a year.

Deposits at the bank earn 11.75%, and interest is compounded quarterly (4 times/year). Mrs. Gabroudy will need the money in 2½ years. Which institution should Mrs. Gabroudy select? The formula to compute the value of the investment T is:

$$T = P(1 + I/J)^{N*J}$$

where T is the principal and accumulated interest
P is the principal
I is the interest rate expressed in fractional form
J is the number of times the interest is compounded
N is the duration of the investment in years

Write a program to print the total value of the investments as well as the accumulated interest for each case.

A program to solve this problem is shown in Figure 3–7. It has several features that should be noted: The interest rate (12.75%) is typed as .1275. Note that N*J1 is enclosed in parentheses for exponentiation (line 55). Finally, the accumulated interest is the difference between the final value of the investment and the original principal.

3-6-2 How Good Is Your Computer with Numbers? Finite and Infinite Sums

Consider the following three sums, S6, S7, and S8:

$$S6 = 9/10 + 9/10^2 + 9/10^3 + 9/10^4 + 9/10^5 + 9/10^6$$
$$S7 = 9/10 + 9/10^2 + 9/10^3 + 9/10^4 + 9/10^5 + 9/10^6 + 9/10^7$$
$$S8 = 9/10 + 9/10^2 + 9/10^3 + 9/10^4 + 9/10^5 + 9/10^6 + 9/10^7 + 9/10^8$$

As more terms are added to these sequences, do the successive sums get closer and closer to a particular value, or do the sums grow larger than any arbitrary value by simply adding more and more terms?

Figure 3–7 An investment decision.

```
1Ø REM INVESTMENT DECISION
15 LET P = 15ØØ                           Principal
2Ø LET I1 = .1275                         Credit union interest
25 LET J1 = 1                             Number of times interest is compounded
3Ø LET I2 = .1175                         Bank interest
35 LET J2 = 4                             Number of times interest is compounded
4Ø LET N = 2.5                            Duration of investment
45 REM
5Ø REM COMPUTE FINAL INVESTMENTS
55 LET T1 = (P-15)*(1 + I1/J1)^(N*J1)     Credit union final investment
6Ø LET T2 = P*(1 + I2/J2)^(N*J2)          Bank final investment
65 REM
7Ø PRINT "BANK AMOUNT"; T2,               Print total bank value, and on same line print
75 PRINT "BANK INTEREST"; T2-P            bank accumulated interest
8Ø PRINT "CREDIT AMOUNT"; T1,
85 PRINT "CREDIT INTEREST";T1-P           Print credit union accumulated interest
9Ø END

RUN
BANK AMOUNT 2ØØ3.67            BANK INTEREST 5Ø3.674
CREDIT AMOUNT 2ØØ4.5           CREDIT INTEREST 5Ø4.554
```

Does the infinite sum S, shown below, get closer and closer to a particular value, or does the value of the infinite sum itself become infinite?

$$S = 9/10 + 9/10^2 + 9/10^3 + \ldots + 9/10^{100} + \ldots$$

In mathematics, a sequence of numbers like this one is called a geometric progression, i.e. each new term of the sequence is equal to the preceding term multiplied by the number 1/10 (the ratio between two successive terms is constant and equal to 1/10).

The formula to compute the sum of n terms of a geometric progression is:

$$\text{Sum of } n \text{ terms} = \frac{\text{first term of sequence} * (1 - \text{ratio}^n)}{1 - \text{ratio}}$$

The formula to compute the sum of the infinite progression is:

$$\text{Sum of infinite terms} = \frac{\text{first term}}{1 - \text{ratio}}$$

Let us write a program to compute the three finite sums, S6, S7, and S8, the infinite sum S, and the difference between the infinite sum and each of the finite sums. We will assume that our computer gives six significant digits on output. The program is shown in Figure 3–8.

Note that the infinite sum S (line 45) is equal to 1. The reader should expect this result since the infinite sum S is actually

$S = 0.9 + 0.09 + 0.009 + 0.0009 + 0.00009 + \ldots = 0.9999\ldots = 1$ after an infinite number of terms.

Figure 3–8 Finite and infinite sums.

```
10 REM ERRORS INDUCED BY ARITHMETIC OPERATIONS ON SMALL NUMBERS
15 REM COMPUTE FINITE SUMS FOR 6, 7, and 8 TERMS
20 LET S6 = .9 * (1 - .1^6) / .9
25 LET S7 = .9 * (1 - .1^7) / .9
30 LET S8 = .9 * (1 - .1^8) / .9
35 REM
40 REM COMPUTE INFINITE SUM
45 LET S = .9 / (1 - .1)
50 REM
55 REM COMPUTE DIFFERENCES BETWEEN FINITE AND INFINITE SUMS
60 LET D6 = S - S6
65 LET D7 = S - S7
70 LET D8 = S - S8
75 REM
80 PRINT "S6 =";S6,, "S7 =";S7,, "S8 =";S8
85 PRINT "INFINITE SUM =";S
90 PRINT "S - S6 =";D6, "S - S7 =";D7, "S - S8 =";D8
95 END

RUN
S6 = .999999                S7 = 1              S8 = 1
INFINITE SUM = 1
S - S6 = 1.01328E-06        S - S7 = 1.19209E-07    S - S8 = 0
```

Note also that the value computed for S7 and S8 is 1. In fact, as far as the computer is concerned, all finite sums after the first seven terms are included are equal to 1. This is due to the computer's inability to work with more than six significant digits. Also notice that on the output the value printed for S − S7 = 1.19209E − 07 while S and S7 are both 1! The reason for this oddity is that internally the value stored in S7 is more accurate (more than 6 digits) than the rounded value printed for S7, when only 6 digits can be used.

3-6-3 Do It Now

Run the program in Figure 3–8 on your system and see if you obtain the same results. If D8 is not 0, compute S9 and D9 = S − S9. How many more terms do you need to add to the sum so that D*n* = S − S*n* = 0?

3-7 You Might Want to Know

1. Does it matter where I start typing my BASIC statements?

Answer: No, on most systems it does not matter. Imbedded blanks are also allowed in statements.

Example: The following statements are equivalent:

```
10 LET   X   =   C  1   +4
10LETX=C1+4
```

In an alphanumeric string, blanks do count of course, as shown below:

`PRINT "NEW YORK"`	will print 8 characters NEW YORK whereas
`PRINT " NEW YORK "`	will print 10 characters, including blanks.

2. How can I print blank lines on output?

Answer: Use the PRINT statement (or LPRINT for printed output) with no expression-list (PRINT all by itself). A blank line will be printed if the last variable in the preceding PRINT list was not followed by a comma (,) or a semicolon (;).

Example:

```
10 PRINT,,"ROLL"
15 PRINT
20 PRINT
25 PRINT,"NAME",,"TEST"
```

Two blank lines will separate the major heading "ROLL" from the subheadings NAME and TEST.

3. I am still not quite clear about significant digits. What are these exactly?

Answer: Significant digits deal with the computer's ability to represent the results of arithmetic operations using a fixed number of digits. Typically only 7 digits of a result can be stored in a particular memory location. For example, if I try to write down the national debt X = 1234567890123 the computer will store this number internally as 1234567000000. The magnitude is correct, but the computer can only capture the first seven digits! This, of course, can lead to errors (absolute errors); in the above case, $890,123! If you need more significant digits than are readily available, look up double precision numbers in your technical reference manual. It should be noted that even though the computer might be able to store the results of an arithmetic operation as a 7-digit field, that same computer might only be able to print that result as a 6-digit field (in effect rounding the number).

4. How does the computer store fractions in its memory, i.e., in what way is ⅔ stored in the memory of the computer?

Answer: All fractions are converted to decimal expressions. Since ⅔ = 0.666...6... and since the computer may only be able to print six significant digits, the result will be rounded off and printed as 0.666667.

5. I still do not quite understand the difference between alphanumeric data consisting only of digits on one hand and numeric data on the other! Could you explain?

Answer: Suppose you write the following code:

```
10  A$ = "123"
20  B  = 123
```

Certainly the number 123 can be printed by writing either PRINT A$ or PRINT B. However the variable A$ cannot participate in any arithmetic operations. Because A$ is an alphanumeric string, the digits 123 are encoded in a different way than the algebraic quantity 123. The alphanumeric characters 1,2, and 3 are encoded internally the same way as letters of the alphabet are encoded, and it certainly wouldn't make too much sense to add the characters CAT to the characters DOG! The same then hold true for the alphanumeric digits.

This does not mean, of course, that alphanumeric strings cannot be compared to one another; they can, but only one character at a time, whereas numeric data is compared as an algebraic whole, i.e., 900 < 1000 whereas "900" > "1000" since the character 9 is greater than the character 1.

6. If I forget to initialize a numeric variable to a particular value and I use that variable in an arithmetic expression or a PRINT statement, what value will be used or what value will be printed?

Answer: Most BASIC systems will initialize variables to 0 and alphanumeric variables to blanks, but to be safe you should initialize your own variables.

3-8 Getting to Know Your System Better

Section 3–8–1 deals with certain features that are available on quite a few BASIC systems. These features can be very convenient, although your instructor may wish you had never heard of them, especially item 2 in the next section. If your system does not support the features discussed, but has other similar ones, write them down in section 3–8–2.

3-8-1 Special Features

The system commands, BASIC instructions, and features discussed below are available on most BASIC systems. You may wish to make use of these convenient features when writing programs. Additional information on them can be found in your BASIC technical reference manual.

1. The AUTO system command automatically generates line numbers, i.e., you do not have to type line numbers. Every time the RETURN/ENTER is pressed, a new line number is automatically typed on the terminal.

Examples:

AUTO	generates line numbers 10, 20, 30, ...
AUTO 100,50	generates line numbers 100, 150, 200, ...

To exit from AUTO mode, press the BREAK or ESCAPE key or some other combination of keys.

2. Multiple BASIC statements can be typed on one or more lines as long as these statements are separated from one another by a colon.

Examples:

```
10 X = 1: Y = 3.1: Z = Ø
20 PRINT X,Y: Z = X + Y: PRINT Z
```

equivalent to

```
10 X = 1
20 Y = 3.1
30 Z = Ø
40 PRINT X,Y
50 Z = X + Y
60 PRINT Z
```

This practice is discouraged, however. A program written in this manner is much more difficult to read, understand, and correct.

3. The question mark (?) can be substituted for the word PRINT. When the program is LISTed, the word PRINT will replace all occurrences of the question mark.

Examples:

```
10 ? "HELLO"
20 ? "MALES=";T
```

is identical to

```
10 PRINT "HELLO"
20 PRINT "MALES=";T
```

4. If a video screen (TV) is used, the system command CLS (no line numbers) can be used to clear the screen of all characters. If a BASIC program is on the screen and CLS is typed, the screen is cleared, but the BASIC program remains intact in the memory of the computer. Only the command NEW erases the BASIC program from memory.

In a BASIC program, the BASIC instruction CLS can also be used to clear the screen during the execution of the program (RUN).

Example:

```
NEW
Ø5 CLS
10 PRINT "HELLO"
15 CLS
20 PRINT "HELLO"
25 CLS
```

When the program is executed, line 5 will clear the screen, i.e., the BASIC program will disappear from the screen. The word HELLO will be displayed in the upper left corner of the screen until line 15 is executed, at which time the screen is cleared. HELLO will reappear (line 20), and the screen will then be blanked out again. Thus the message HELLO will be blinked twice on the screen. (What would happen if instruction 20 were replaced with the instruction 20 GO TO 10?)

3-8-2 MY SYSTEM IS DIFFERENT

This section is left blank for you to write any different system commands that your system uses. You may also want to list the various steps that are required to start a session with your system.

3-9 Assignments

3-9-1 Test Yourself

1. Determine whether the following BASIC statements are valid or invalid. If invalid, explain why. Rules for valid variable names are given in section 3–2–5. (Statement numbers have been purposely omitted.)

a. `LET X = -X`
b. `LET A + B = C`
c. `LET A$ = THE CAT`
d. `LET Z19 = A + B`
e. `LET X = X + 1`
f. `LET I = C/"3"`
g. `LET B$ = "111" - "222"`
h. `LET 3X = Z`
i. `PRINT X = 4`
j. `LET Y1 = Z(Z + 1)`
k. `LET G = A/-A1`
l. `LET D * Y = -7.93`
m. `LET A1 = -(A1) + M5 - 3M`
n. `PRINT A, B, 3.2`
o. `LET 3 = 3`
p. `PRINT "X", "Y",Z`
q. `PRINT "X+Y-"`
r. `PRINT "A;",A;`
s. `X = (X + 1)`
t. `(X = X + 1)`

2. Evaluate each of the following expressions for A = 3, B = −2, J = 0 and I = 4.

a. `A ^ 2 + B`
b. `I+ 2/3`
c. `(A^B)`
d. `A * 3. + B/4`
e. `A/B * B`
f. `A/B * 3 + A`
g. `A/B/2`
h. `2 + A/B`
i. `J/I`
j. `I/J`
k. `A^2^3`
l. `J^B`
m. `A^ 1/2`
n. `A+B/B+1`

3. Translate the following algebraic expressions into BASIC.

a. $a + b \cdot c$
b. $a - 1.4 + b$
c. $-4z$
d. $-z \cdot 4$
e. $2pt^2$
f. $\frac{4}{3}ab^3$
g. $x(y+z)$
h. $2(x+y)^3$
i. $\frac{a}{xy}$
j. $(a-b)^3 + \frac{1}{x-1}$
k. $y + a^x$
l. $\frac{1}{r_1} + \frac{1}{r_2}$
m. $\sqrt{a^2+b^2}$
n. $\frac{1.4}{x+y} - \frac{z}{(x-y^4)}$
o. $\frac{p}{1-(1-\frac{n}{k})}\ a \cdot b$

4. True or false:

a. There should not be more than one END statement in a BASIC program.
b. Line numbers must be typed sequentially.
c. Syntax errors are the same as logical errors.
d. A BASIC program can have only one STOP statement.
e. SAM is a valid variable name.
f. "S1" is a valid variable name.
g. X = X + 1. is a valid BASIC expression.
h. 3/4/5 evaluates to the same as 3/(4/5)
i. 2 * 3 = 4 is a valid replacement statement.
j. S = −S is a valid replacement statement.
k. The RUN command must not be numbered.
l. The LIST command prints the results generated by a program.
m. Two instructions with the same line number will cause a syntax error.
n. Alphanumeric variables must end with a $ sign.
o. The LPRINT instruction causes all BASIC instructions (program) to be displayed on the terminal.
p. Some system commands, such as NEW or LIST, must be numbered.

q. Comments made through the REM statement are printed on the output when RUN is typed.
r. 1.3E – 4 is the same as 0.000013
s. 0.001E5 is the same as 100
t. The statement Y = 3% * X is valid.
u. "– 1,324" is a valid alphanumeric constant.
v. 1.5 * 10^3 is the same as 1.5E3
w. The statement PRINTT,B is valid.

5. Fill in the blanks appropriately.
   a. Letters of the alphabet, digits 0 through 9, and special characters are referred to as __________ characters.
   b. __________ are used to refer symbolically to memory locations.
   c. X + 3 * Y is an example of a __________.
   d. The __________ instruction causes all program instructions to be displayed on the screen.
   e. *Variable* = *expression* is an example of a __________.
   f. "AMOUNT" is an example of an __________ __________.
   g. Comparing two numbers is performed by the __________ unit of the CPU.
   h. Parentheses in an expression identify the __________ of operations.
   i. Variables in a PRINT list must be separated from one another by __________ or __________.
   j. Division by 0 is an example of a __________ error.

6. What would happen if you executed the following code?

```
10 PRINT "HELLO"
20 RUN
```

7. Which of the following are identical to A*(B + C)/D?

   a. `(B+C)*A/D`   b. `(A*(B+C))/D`   c. `(B+C)/D*A`   d. `(A/D)*(B+C)`

8. What would be the vertical spacing between HERE and THERE on the output?

a.
```
20 PRINT "HERE";
25 PRINT
35 PRINT,
40 PRINT "THERE"
```
b.
```
20 PRINT "HERE";
25 PRINT,
35 PRINT,
40 PRINT "THERE"
```
c.
```
20 PRINT "HERE";
20 PRINT,,
35 PRINT;
40 PRINT "THERE"
```

9. What values will be stored in X and Y as a result of the following?

a.
```
10 X = 9
15 Y = 4
20 Y = Y-X
```
b.
```
10 X = 9
15 Y = 3
20 X = Y
25 Y = X
```
c.
```
10 X = 9
15 Y = 10
20 T = X
25 X = Y
30 Y = T
```
d.
```
11 X = 3
14 Y = 8
13 Y = .3
```

10. Write the statements to perform the following:
    a. Double what is in C and print out result with the prefix $.
    b. Replace X by half of its square root.
    c. Add X^3 to whatever was in X.
    d. Store the characters SAM in a memory location.

11. Write a program to convert – 139.65° Fahrenheit into Centigrade. The formula is:

$$C = 5/9\,(F - 32)$$

12. Write a program to compute and print the length of the hypotenuse of a right triangle, given its two legs 0.0056 and 135.77.

13. Write a program to interchange the values contained in memory locations S and T.

14. Write a program to display a scrolling screen full of dots (periods), i.e., all lines on the video display should be filled with dots.

15. Write a program to produce the following report on the cost C of operating electrical devices:

COST ANALYSIS

WATTS	HOURS	COST/KW	COST
65	6	.087	—
100	6	.087	—

The formula is: $C = \frac{W \cdot T \cdot K}{1000}$

where W = number of watts
T = time in hours
K = cost in cents per kilowatt hours

16. Run a program to compute the following, and explain results.

a. 1/3
b. 2/3
c. 2/3 + 1/3
d. 1000000 + 99999
e. $\frac{1}{10^7} + \frac{1}{10^8}$
f. 0.7 + 0.3
g. 0.111432 + (−0.111431)
h. 100001/0.1

3-9-2 Exercises

1. Write a code to print HELLO in the middle of the screen. Then try to flash that signal by using the clear screen instruction (CLS) discussed in the computer features section.

2. Write a program to approximate the Julian date (introduced by Julius Caesar in 46 B.C.) equivalent to the calendar date given in the form month, day. The Julian date is the day of the year. January 1 has Julian date 1, February 2 has Julian date 33, December 31 has Julian date 365, etc. A formula to approximate the Julian date is (month − 1) * 30 + day. Determine the Julian dates for November 7, May 25, and March 21.

3. Write a program to print out your initials by magnifying them. For example,

```
MMM          MMM     BBBBBBB
MMMM        MMMM     BBB     B
MMMMMM    MMMMMM     BBBBBBB
MMM  MMMM  MMM       BBB     B
MMM    MM    MMM     BBBBBBB
```

4. Mr. X is a bricklayer. Last year his gross pay was $23,564.99. After deducting 6.85% for social security and 23.5% for federal income tax from his gross pay, was his net income greater than Mrs. Y's net income? Mrs. Y is a teacher who

grossed \$19,874 but had \$850.45 deducted for her income retirement plan and 16.03% of her gross income for income tax purposes. Print the salaries of Mr. X and Mrs. Y.

5. With an interest rate I of 9% and a principal P of \$1,956.45 deposited for an 11-year period in a savings account, write a program to compute a total principal T, given the formula

$$T = P(1 + I)^N$$

where N is the number of years.

6. Suppose the interest of exercise 5 is compounded daily for 11 years. Write a program to compute
   a. The total principal given by the formula

   $$T = P\left(1 + \frac{I}{J}\right)^{J*N}$$

   where J is the number of times the interest is compounded per year.

   b. The difference between total amounts when the principal is compounded once and 365 times a year. Also print the corresponding interests.
   c. What would the principal be after 11 years and 7 months?
   (Hint: Express N as total months divided by 12.)

7. A wholesaler accepts a \$5,000 promissory note at 7% in lieu of cash payment for delivered goods. Write a program to compute the maturity value of the note for a 30-, 60-, and 90-day short-term loan. The formula to compute the maturity value S is

$$S = P(1 + I * N)$$

where P is the principal, I is the interest rate, and N is the number of years (express N as number of days divided by 360).

8. Write a program to evaluate each of the formulas for the indicated values (use $\pi = 3.1416$) and print the answers with appropriate literal headings.

a. Simple interest	$i = Prt$	for $r = 4\%$ $t = 3$ $P = 100$
b. Volume of a cube	$v = c^3$	for $c = 3.167219$
c. Area of a circle	$A = \pi r^2$	for $r = 6.2$
d. Volume of a cone	$v = \frac{1}{3}\pi r^2 b$	for $r = 9.1$ $b = 4.932747$

(Expected answers: $i = 12$ $v = 31.77$ $A = 120.76$ $v = 427.76$)

9. Write a program to compute and print the area and the length (perimeter) of each of the following:

a.

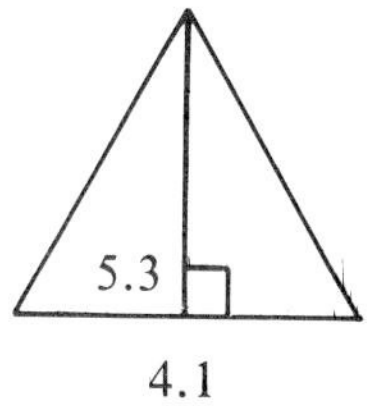

b.

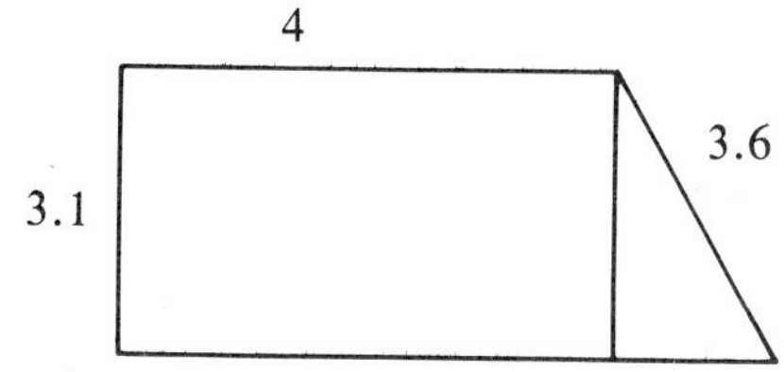

c.

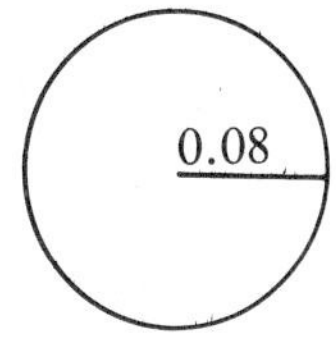

10. The truth-in-lending law requires that money-lending institutions disclose the annual interest rate charged on loans. The approximate rate is given by the formula

$$R = \frac{2 * N * I}{P(n + 1)}$$

where N is the number of payments per year, I = the total finance charge, P is the principal, and n = the number of scheduled installment payments. Write a program to determine the annual percentage rate for a loan of $5,000 for 36 months at 162.50. (Finance charge = 36 * 162.5 − 5000 = 850.)

11. (a) Miss T. drove 1050 miles in 17½ hours and spent $86.75 for gas. Her car averages 14.5 miles per gallon. Write a program to compute her average speed, number of gallons used and the average cost per gallon. The output should be as follows:

```
MILES =           1050
HOURS DRIVEN =    12.5
GAS COST =        86.75

AVERAGE SPEED =   ___
NO. GALLONS =     ___
COST/GALLON =     ___
```

(b) Miss T. estimates that she spent 12% of the travelling time on miscellaneous stops. How does this change her average speed?

12. Fifteen seconds after a stone is dropped into a well, the stone hits the surface of the water. Determine the height of the well, given the formula $d = \frac{1}{2}gt^2$ where d is the distance, g is the force of gravity (9.81 meter/s), and t is the time in seconds.

13. Write a program to compute the infinite sum of the following geometric progressions whenever possible: (use formulas in section 3–6–2).

a. `1 + 2 + 4 + 8 + 16 + ...`
b. `3 - 9 + 27 - 81 + ...`
c. `4 + 2 + 1 + 1/2 + 1/4 + ...`
d. `9/10 + 9/100 + 9/1000 + ...`

14. For four resistors R_1, R_2, R_3, and R_4 in parallel, the overall resistance R is given by

$$\frac{1}{R} = \frac{1}{R_1} + \frac{1}{R_2} + \frac{1}{R_3} + \frac{1}{R_4}$$

where R_1, R_2, R_3, and R_4 are respectively 1.5, 3, 4.5, and 6 ohms. Write a program to compute R.

15. Write a program to determine whether $x = 1.3$ is a root of the polynomial

$$\frac{17}{3}x^{17} + 4x^8 - .76x^2 - 686$$

3-9-3 Projects

1. The Sullivans would like to take a summer trip abroad in a year and a half. They estimate that their expenses will be just over $3,500. They want to start saving at a

credit union where 6.5% interest is paid on deposits. What would the Sullivans' minimum monthly deposit be in order to afford the vacation abroad? What would their deposits have to be if they made four equal deposits per year? The formula to calculate the regular deposit R is:

$$R = P\left(\frac{i/n}{(1 + i/n)^{n*y} - 1}\right)$$

where P = amount to be saved (future value), i = interest rate, n = deposits/year, and y = number of years.

2. Mary and John Soule would very much like to buy the Pitts' house. The Pitts are asking $76,000 conventional with $7,000 down, or $84,000 VA with nothing down. In either case, a 30-year mortgage is sought. Financing charges are 13.5% for VA and 14% for conventional. (Equal monthly payments will be made.) The Soules have another option: Mary's father is willing to give them $9,000 for a down payment, on the condition that they assume with him a 14.5% interest mortgage for the next 22 years and 8 months on the remainder of the conventional price, with equal payments 4 times a year. In terms of today's dollar value, what is the Soules' best financial arrangement? Identify in each case the total costs involved as well as the interest paid. The formula to compute the regular payments R (monthly, quarterly, etc.) is:

$$R = \frac{iP/n}{1 - (i/n + 1)^{ny}}$$

where P = principal, i = interest rate, n = number of payments/year, and y = number of years. (If the number of years is given in years and months, convert it to months and divide by 12.)

3. The date for any Easter Sunday can be computed as follows. (Let X be the year for which Easter Sunday is to be computed.)

   Let A be the remainder of the division of X by 19.
   Let B be the remainder of the division of X by 4.
   Let C be the remainder of the division of X by 7.
   Let D be the remainder of the division of (19A + 24) by 30.
   Let E be the remainder of the division of (2B + 4C + 6D + 5) by 7.

   The date for Easter Sunday is then March (22 + D + E). Note that this can give a date in April.

   To compute the remainder R of the division of I by J, use the BASIC statement: LET R = I − J * INT (I/J). INT is called the integer function; INT(X) finds the greatest integer not larger than X (for example, INT (9.78) = 9).

   Write a program to assign a year for the variable X and compute the date for Easter Sunday for that year using the formula March (22 + D + E).

4. Mr. Grand wants to purchase a $32,356 Jaguar. He can manage a down payment of $7,800. The trade-in allowance for his old Volvo is $2,945. Current dealer interest rates are an annual 15.6% for 2½ years. What will be Mr. Grand's monthly payment for the next 2½ years? The formula to compute the monthly payment R is:

$$R = iP\left[\frac{(1 + i)^m}{(1 + i)^m - 1}\right]$$

Where i = interest rate per month, P = principal (purchase price − down payment − trade-in allowance), and m = the number of monthly payments.

5. Write a program to generate unit-price shelf labels for a grocery store. For example, process the data:

Price	.59
Size	11.5
Item description	green beans
Standard unit size	16
Description of unit	oz.

The output should display all of the above data. The unit price is computed:

$$\text{unit price} = \frac{\text{price}}{\text{size}} \times \text{standard unit size}$$

For our example, the output should be similar to:

```
.59        GREEN BEANS       11.5 OZ.
UNIT PRICE      .82       FOR 16 OZ.
```

6. Write a program to produce a magic square. In a magic square, the sum of each row, column, and diagonal is equal. For example, the following magic square has the sum 3:

−2	2	3
6	1	−4
−1	0	4

The secret of the magic square is this: for any values of x, y, and z, a magic square can be formed from

$x-z$	$x+z-y$	$x+y$
$x+y+z$	x	$x-y-z$
$x-y$	$x+y-z$	$x+z$

In the above example, $x=1$, $y=2$, $z=3$.

3-9-4 Answers to Test Yourself

1. a. Valid.
   b. Invalid; expression is on the left side of the equal sign.
   c. Invalid; the character string must be enclosed in quotes.
   d. Invalid; Z19 is an invalid variable name (may be valid on your system).
   e. Valid.
   f. Invalid; cannot divide by an alphanumeric constant.
   g. Invalid; subtraction is an arithmetic operation not used on character strings.

h. Invalid; 3X is an invalid variable name.
i. Invalid; equal signs are not used in the PRINT statement.
j. Invalid; there must be a multiplication sign between Z and (Z + 1).
k. Invalid; the expression − A1 must be enclosed in parentheses.
l. Invalid; D * Y is an invalid variable name.
m. Invalid; 3M is an invalid variable name.
n. Valid.
o. Invalid; invalid variable on left side.
p. Valid.
q. Valid.
r. Valid.
s. Valid.
t. Invalid; (X is an invalid variable name.

2. a. 7
b. 4.66667
c. .111111
d. 8.5
e. 3
f. − 1.5
g. − .75
h. .5
i. 0
j. Invalid (division by zero).
k. 729
l. Invalid (division by zero).
m. 1.5
n. 5

3. a. A + B * C
b. A − 1.4 + B
c. − 4 * Z
d. (− Z) * 4
e. 2 * P * T * T
f. 4/3 * A * B^3
g. X * (Y + Z)
h. 2 * (X + Y)^3
i. A/(X * Y)
j. (A − B)^3 + 1/(X − 1)
k. Y + A^X
l. 1/R1 + 1/R2
m. (A^2 + B^2)^.5
n. 1.4/(X + Y) − Z/(X − Y^4)
o. P/(1 − (1 − N/K)^(A*B))

4. a. generally true
b. F
c. F
d. F
e. F on many systems
f. F (no quotation marks)
g. F (statement)
h. F
i. F
j. T
k. T (up to this point)
l. F
m. F (cannot happen!)
n. T
o. F (just output)
p. F
q. F
r. F
s. T
t. F
u. T
v. T
w. T

5. a. alphanumeric
b. variables
c. expression
d. LIST
e. replacement statement
f. alphanumeric constant
g. logical
h. hierarchy (precedence)
i. commas, semicolons
j. logical

6. In some systems RUN may not be a BASIC instruction, hence a syntax error. In systems that recognize RUN as a BASIC instruction, the program would keep printing "HELLO" forever, since after the PRINT instruction the program is run again!

7. All are identical.

8. a. HERE is on 1st line and THERE on the next line.
   b. The two words would be on the same line.
   c. The two words would be on the same line.

9. a. X = 9; Y = −5
   b. X = 3; Y = 3
   c. X = 10; Y = 9
   d. X = 3; Y = 8 (note line numbering).

10. a. `PRINT "$"; 2 * C`
    b. `X = (X^.5)/2`
    c. `X = X + X^3`
    d. `A$ = "SAM"`

11.
```
10  LET F = -139.65
20  LET C = 5/9*(F-32)
30  PRINT C
40  END
```

12.
```
10  LET A = .0056
20  LET B = 135.77
30  LET H = (A^2 + B^2)^.5
40  PRINT H
50  END
```

13.
```
10  LET X = S
20  LET S = T
30  LET T = X
```

14.
```
10  PRINT ".";
20  GO TO 10
```

15.
```
10  PRINT, "COST ANALYSIS"
15  PRINT "WATTS", "HOURS", "COST/KW", "COST"
20  PRINT "65", "6", ".087", 65*6*.087/1000
25  PRINT "100", "6", ".087", 100*6*.087/1000
```

16. The results depend on the system used. A system with six significant digits on output would give:
    a. 0.333333
    b. 0.666667
    c. 1
    d. 1.1E+6
    e. 1.1E-7
    f. 1
    g. 1.E-6
    h. 1.00001E+6

4 FLOWCHARTING AND THE BASIC STATEMENTS: INPUT, GO TO, and IF

4-1 Problem Example

Joe, the controller of the Silver Mining Company, uses a desk computer to compute each of the company's employee's gross pay. Joe does not know much about computers except the few instructions he has been told to enter on the computer's terminal. Each Friday afternoon, Joe loads the computer with the company's payroll program and types RUN. The computer asks Joe to enter the employee's name, the number of hours worked, and the rate of pay. The computer then prints out the employee's pay and asks Joe the same question about the other employees. An example of the dialogue between Joe and the computer is shown in Figure 4–1.

After Joe has typed RUN, the computer prints the first message on the terminal to tell Joe to enter the name of the employee. The computer then prints a question mark (?) on the terminal and stops. This is the signal, called a prompt or cue, that Joe is waiting for to type the employee name on the terminal. Joe types the name and then depresses the ENTER or RETURN key. This causes the computer to store the name in its memory. In the same way, Joe enters the number of hours worked and the rate of pay. The computer then calculates and prints the employee's pay. The computer continues asking the same questions about the rest of the employees. What annoys Joe is that when he is finished entering all the information concerning the employees, the

■ **Figure 4–1** A dialogue between human and computer.

RUN	Joe
ENTER NAME	Computer
?SILVERBUCK	Joe
ENTER HOURS	Computer
?40	Joe
ENTER RATE	Computer
?4	Joe
PAY TO SILVERBUCK 160	Computer
ENTER NAME	Computer
?GOLDMAN	Joe
ENTER HOURS	Computer
?60	Joe
ENTER RATE	Computer
?4.87	Joe
OVERTIME HOURS = 20	Computer
OVERTIME PAY = 146.1	Computer
PAY TO GOLDMAN 340.9	Computer
ENTER NAME	Computer
?	

computer keeps asking him to enter the name of an employee. To silence the computer, Joe hits the BREAK key (or ESC (escape) or another combination of keys). Later on we will learn how to be more civilized with the computer; terminating a program by pressing the BREAK key is "bad" programming practice!

Let us write a program to produce a payroll transaction like the one in Figure 4–1. The computer should accept an employee name, a number of hours worked, and a rate of pay. If the employee has worked more than 40 hours, the computer should print the number of overtime hours, the overtime pay, and the final pay. Hours in excess of 40 are paid at 1½ times the regular rate. If there are no overtime hours, the final pay is simply the number of hours times the rate. The computer should keep repeating this sequence of activities until the data entry clerk (controller) has processed all employees, at which time he/she presses a special key to terminate the payroll session. The program to solve this problem is shown in Figure 4–2. Note the GO TO 10 statement at line 98, which tells the computer to execute the program repeatedly. The process of repeating a sequence of instructions is called a *loop*. In this case the loop is infinite, and the only way the user can escape from it is by pressing a special key on the keyboard (see the appropriate appendix or your user's manual).

4-1-1 Do It Now

1. How could you obtain results similar to those in Figure 4–1 without the GO TO statement at line 98? (See Figure 4–2.)

Figure 4–2 Calculation of gross pay.

```
05 REM PAYROLL PROGRAM
10 PRINT "ENTER NAME"
15 INPUT N$
20 PRINT "ENTER HOURS"
25 INPUT H
30 PRINT "ENTER RATE"
35 INPUT R
40 REM
42 REM
45 IF H > 40 GO TO 65
50     LET P = H * R
55     GO TO 95
60 REM
65     LET P1 = 40 * R
70     LET V = H - 40
75     LET P2 = V * R * 1.5
80     LET P = P1 + P2
85     PRINT "OVERTIME HOURS=";V
90     PRINT "OVERTIME PAY=";P2
95 PRINT "PAY TO";N$;P
98 GO TO 10
```

The REM instruction is for documentation purposes.
The prompt message is displayed on the terminal.
When the program is RUN, the INPUT instruction at line 15 will cause the computer to stop and display a question mark (?) on the terminal; the user enters a name and presses the ENTER key. This causes the name entered on the screen to be stored in memory location N$. The hours (H) and rate (R) are likewise entered at RUN time.

If the condition is true, transfer to 65 to compute overtime, otherwise (H < = 40) the computer automatically goes to the next instruction, 50.
A transfer to line 65 is made only if H > 40 (line 45).
P1 is the first 40 hours at regular rate.
V is the overtime hours.
P2 is the overtime pay.
P is the final pay.

Line 95 is executed after line 90 or after line 55.
Process the next employee.

2. Change the program of Figure 4–2 to compute a social security deduction (6.75% of gross pay) and federal withholding tax based on a percentage entered with an INPUT statement, e.g., if the figure entered is 21.3, then the federal income tax is equal to 21.3% of gross pay. Print the employee's name, the net pay, the gross pay, and the two deductions.

Answers

1. Replace line 98 by 98 END and then retype RUN to process each employee.

2.
```
37 PRINT "ENTER PERCENTAGE FIGURE FOR FEDERAL TAXES"
39 INPUT F
95 T1 = F/1ØØ * P
96 T2 = P * .Ø675
97 N = P - T1 - T2
98 PRINT N$, "NET=";N; "GROSS=";P; "SS=";T2; "FED TAX=";T1
```

4-2 BASIC Statements

4-2-1 The INPUT Statement

So far, the only way we have assigned values to variables is by means of the replacement statement. In the program in Figure 4–2, instead of the INPUT statement at line 25, we could have specified the rate R by the statement R = 4. However, the program would then work only for R = 4, i.e., it would lack generality and its usefulness would be compromised. If we wanted to use the same program for different values of R, we would have to reset R each time, and we would need to type RUN for each employee!

A more efficient way to assign different values to a variable is to use the INPUT statement. The general form of the INPUT statement is

line number INPUT *list of variables*

where the list of variables may consist of numeric or alphanumeric variables separated from one another by commas.

When the INPUT instruction is executed (run), the computer types a question mark on the terminal and stops. The user then enters a value for each of the variables specified by the INPUT statement (commas should be typed to separate the various values). These values are stored in the computer's memory in the specified variables when the ENTER/RETURN key is pressed. Alphanumeric information can be entered with or without quotation marks. If no quotation marks are used, then the comma cannot be a part of the alphanumeric string as the comma is used to separate the various input values.

Example 1

```
10 PRINT "ENTER AGE PLEASE"
15 INPUT X
20 PRINT "YOU FIBBER, YOU ARE NOT"; X ;"YEARS OLD"
RUN
```

```
ENTER AGE PLEASE                          ⎫
? 31       (entered by user)              ⎬ Output produced
YOU FIBBER, YOU ARE NOT  31  YEARS OLD    ⎭ by above instructions
```

Note that when the INPUT X instruction is typed and the user presses the ENTER key to get to the next line (20), the computer does not display a ? and it does not stop. This only happens when RUN is typed and the program is executed.

Example 2

```
10 PRINT "WHAT'S YOUR NAME"
15 INPUT N$
20 PRINT "HELLO ";N$
```

Since an alphanumeric response is expected, the alphanumeric N$ is used to capture the name.

```
RUN
WHAT'S YOUR NAME
?SUSAN TERM
HELLO SUSAN TERM
```

The computer displays a ? and stops. The user then enters a name. That name is stored in N$ when ENTER is pressed. As a result of line 20, the computer greets Susan! The same program can of course be run again and again.

```
RUN
WHAT'S YOUR NAME
?3+4 = 11.5
HELLO 3+4 = 11.5
```

The user enters garbage. That garbage is stored in N$, replacing whatever was in N$ (SUSAN TERM), and the strange greeting message is printed.

When there is more than one item in a list of variables, the user can use either of the following methods to enter the desired list of values into the system:

1. He/she can type a list of values corresponding in number and order to the items specified in the INPUT statement's list of variables. Each value must be separated from the others by a comma. The list of values is terminated by pressing ENTER/RETURN. For example,

```
10 PRINT "ENTER HOURS,RATE,AND NAME IN THAT ORDER"
15 INPUT H, R, N$
20 PRINT "TOTAL PAY=; H * R; "BY "; N$
RUN
ENTER HOURS,RATE,AND NAME IN THAT ORDER
? 30,5,THOMPSON<------------ User-supplied values
TOTAL PAY= 150 BY THOMPSON<-- Computer printout
```

2. The user can type one value at a time, pressing the ENTER key after each value. The system replies with a question mark (?) or other message, as many times as needed to satisfy the variable list of the INPUT statement:

```
5 INPUT X, Y, Z1
7 PRINT X, Y, Z1
8 END
RUN
? 3.1
NOT ENOUGH DATA,TYPE IN MORE AT 5
?10E-4
NOT ENOUGH DATA,TYPE IN MORE AT 5
?5
3.1          .001          5
```

User-supplied values → (? 3.1, ?10E-4, ?5)

Printed results → (3.1 .001 5)

The number of allowable characters in an alphanumeric string varies among different systems, some having as few as 50 and others as many as 256. Remember that the strings can be entered with or without quotation marks, but commas must separate the input data items, as the next examples illustrate.

Example 1

```
10 PRINT "NAME, BIRTHDATE, AGE, ADDRESS?"
15 INPUT N$,B$,A,L$
20 PRINT N$;" ";L$
25 PRINT A;B$
30 END
RUN
NAME, BIRTHDATE, AGE, ADDRESS?
?DUNN, 11/08/52, 31, 18 N 17TH ST.
DUNN 18 N 17TH ST.
31 11/08/52
```

Example 2

If a comma is to be part of an alphanumeric string in response to an INPUT statement, the string should be enclosed in quotation marks.

```
10 PRINT "ENTER NAME, THEN AGE"
15 INPUT N$,A
RUN
ENTER NAME, THEN AGE
? "DOAKES, AMY",18
```

memory arrangement

N$ = | DOAKES, AMY |

A = | 18 |

If the user had typed

```
? DOAKES,AMY    ,18
```

an error message would have been printed, since the comma separating DOAKES and AMY would tell N$ to store DOAKES and A to store AMY—but A is numeric and can store only numeric data.

In BASIC programs that contain numerous INPUT statements, it is desirable to precede each INPUT statement in the program with a PRINT message (called a *prompt*) to remind the user of the nature and order of the variables to be entered at execution time. For example:

```
10 PRINT "ENTER SOCIAL SECURITY, AGE, AND SEX(1 = M, 2 = F)"
20 INPUT S,A,S1
99 END
RUN
ENTER SOCIAL SECURITY, AGE, AND SEX(1 = M, 2 = F)
?111222333,36,2
```

If the user makes a mistake while typing a response to an INPUT inquiry and the ENTER/RETURN key has not yet been pressed, he/she can backspace to the incorrect character(s), correct the mistake, and then press the ENTER/RETURN key. If the ENTER/RETURN key has already been pressed, then the incorrect data has already been stored in memory and it is too late to correct it. Rerunning the program from the beginning is the only solution!

4-2-2 The Unconditional Transfer Statement GO TO

The general form of the GO TO statement is

line number GO TO *transfer line number*

BASIC processes the statements in a BASIC program one after another in sequential order. When BASIC encounters a GO TO statement, it will transfer control to the line number specified, that is, processing will continue at the *transfer line number* statement. This allows the programmer to bypass certain instructions in the program. It can also allow the program to branch back to repeat (reprocess) certain instructions or procedures, e.g., see statement 98 in the program of Figure 4-2; this is called *looping*.

Example 1

```
   ---
   ---
┌─15 GO TO 50
│ 20 PRINT A     ⎫
│    .           ⎪
│    .           ⎬  This code is bypassed.
│    .           ⎪
│ 48 ---         ⎭
└►50 LET Y = 3 * Z
```

Example 2

```
┌►20 INPUT H,R,B
│  ---
│  ---
│  .
│  .
│  ---
└─65 GO TO 20
```

This block of code is processed repeatedly.

4-2-3 Do It Now

1. If the user enters JANE as a result of line 15, what output will be produced by the following code?

```
10 PRINT "ENTER NAME"
15 INPUT A$
20 PRINT "HELLO N$";
25 PRINT "HOW OLD ARE YOU";"N$"
```

2. Will the address and name be entered correctly?

```
10 PRINT "ENTER ADDRESS AND NAME"
15 INPUT A$,N$
RUN
ENTER ADDRESS AND NAME
? ATMORE, FL 32504,"SMITH"
```

3. What is the result of running the following coding segments:

```
a. 10 GO TO 10
b. 10 PRINT
   20 GO TO 10
```

Answers

1. The output produced is:

```
ENTER NAME
?JANE
HELLO N$HOW OLD ARE YOUN$
```

2. No. Only two strings separated by commas should be entered. To correct the error, enter "ATMORE, FL 32504",SMITH

3. a. This is the shortest infinite loop known!
   b. Blank lines are printed on the terminal forever!

4-3 Tools for Program Design: Flowcharts and Pseudo Code

In chapter 3, our programs consisted of instructions that were executed by the computer in sequential fashion. Such problems are rather simple to formulate. Generally, though, the computer will be asked to make many decisions and take appropriate actions based on the outcome of those decisions. At such a decision junction, different avenues of code may be taken and as each avenue splits up into more avenues of code, the complete traffic pattern becomes more difficult to visualize. The *flowchart* is a convenient and helpful tool for visually following the traffic pattern. A flowchart is a pictorial representation (a graphic outline) of the sequence of steps that must be taken in order to solve a particular problem.

An alternative technique for outlining the design of a program is called *pseudo* code. As the name implies, pseudo allows the programmer to write in plain English the general steps (logic) required to solve a problem. This form of free expression is not subject to the rules of the BASIC language, thus the writer can concentrate on developing the logic and the proper sequence of operations without worrying about the details of a programming language. Tasks or procedures can be expressed in a general way. For example, the pseudo code

Print headings	might imply the BASIC sentence `10 PRINT "HOURS","RATE"`
Compute pay	might mean P = H * R
Compute overtime hours	might mean V1 = (H − 40)

Pseudo code is an informal language. It does not need to be very precise, and grammatical considerations are secondary. Pseudo code focuses on the structure of the program. The structure of pseudo code is such that its conversion to BASIC is a relatively simple task, indeed easier than the conversion from a flowchart to BASIC.

In this text, both pseudo code and flowcharts are used. Historically, flowcharts were the first tools used for program design. Today, in industry and educational institutions, the trend has shifted from flowcharts to pseudo code as a result of more powerful programming languages whose control statements (e.g., IF THEN ELSE and WHILE/DO) have led to the development of structured programming designs. In the opinion of many, pseudo code captures the essence of structured design more realistically than flowcharts and is semantically closer to BASIC, permitting more straightforward conversion to program code.

The reader should try both pseudo code and flowcharting, regardless of whether or not his/her BASIC system supports such constructs as the IF THEN ELSE statement. The reader should become comfortable with both approaches, especially pseudo code, since it is becoming more and more widely used in code development.

4-3-1 Flowcharts

A *flowchart* is a pictorial representation of the logic (method) used to solve a particular problem. It is a diagram illustrating the sequence of steps that a person or machine must execute to derive the solution to a problem. A flowchart is particularly useful for visualizing paths through the logic of a problem. For example, the program of Figure 4-2 (computing pay given the number of hours worked) could be expressed in flowchart form as shown in Figure 4-3. Note that there are two paths through the flowchart; the path taken depends on the particular value of H supplied at RUN time. Since there is generally more than one correct method for solving a problem, one should expect that there might be a number of flowcharts describing various methods.

■ **Figure 4-3** A payroll flowchart.

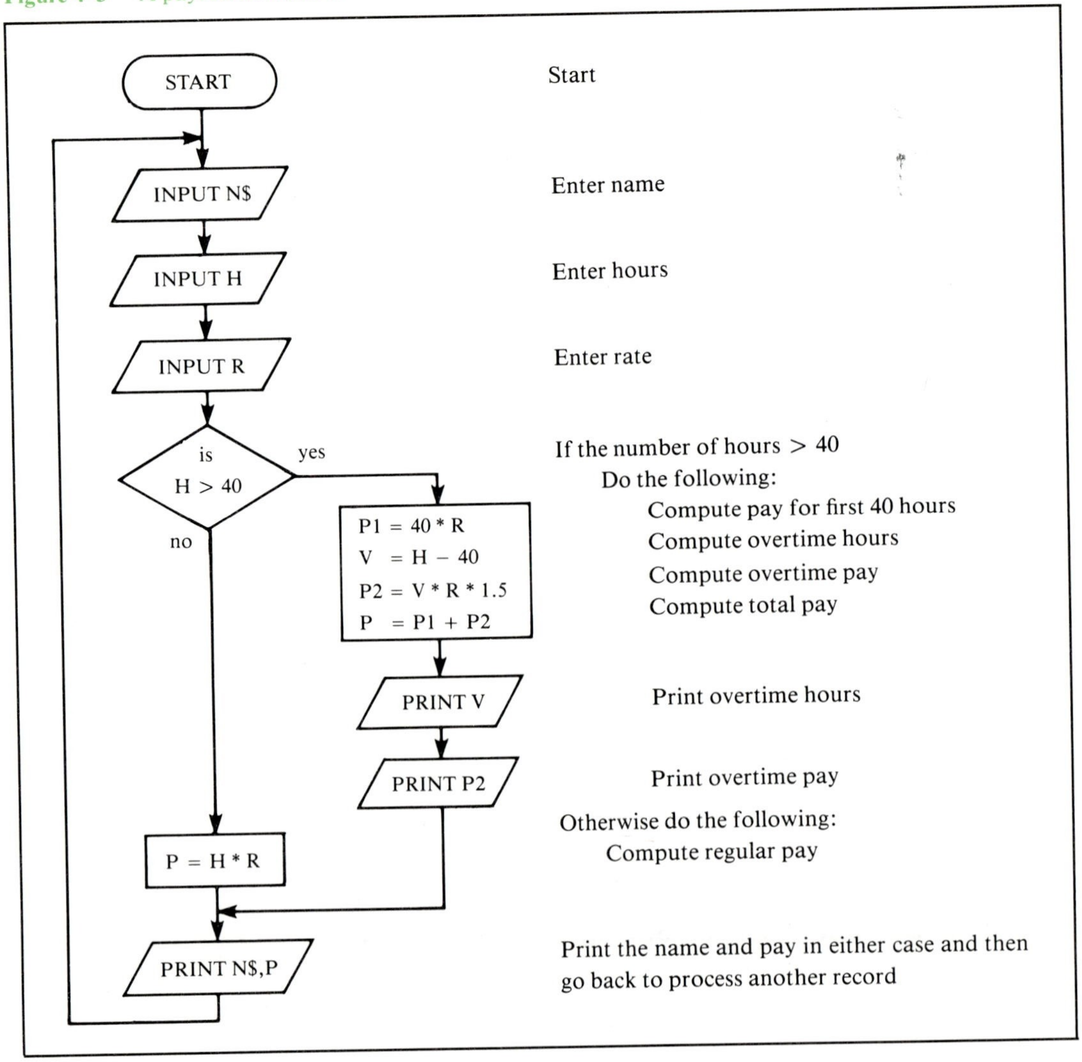

4-3-2 Flowchart Symbols

In program flowcharts, the symbols shown in Figure 4–4 are generally used. Each symbol or *block* represents a different type of operation. Written within the blocks are instructions to indicate (in general terms) what operation is to be performed. The instructions used in a flowchart block need not be written in any particular computer language; they only indicate the general functional operations to be used in the computing system. From a flowchart, it is possible to write computer programs in a number of different languages. The emphasis in a flowchart is on the logic required for solving a problem, not on the mechanics of a programming language.

Figure 4–4 Program flowchart symbols.

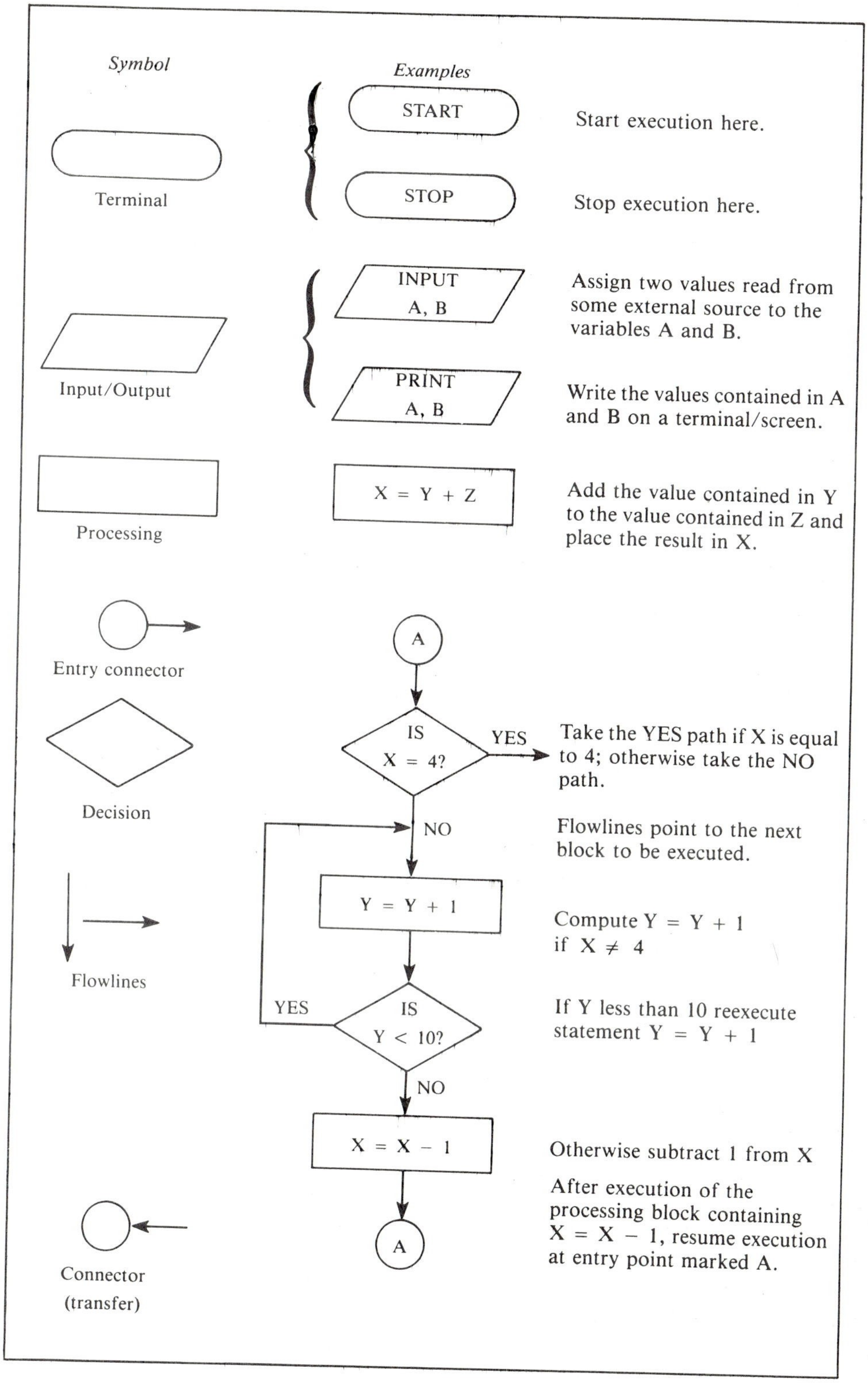

The Terminal Block

An oval ( ) is used to mark the point at which execution of instructions is to begin and end. START is used to mark the beginning point. END or STOP is used to mark the ending point. A flowchart can have only one starting point (entry point), but it may have many ending points.

The Input/Output Block

A parallelogram / / is used for input and output instructions. For an input operation, READ or INPUT, followed by a list of names (variables) separated by commas, is used. These names or variables can be thought of as symbolic names given to memory locations in which the data read will be stored. The computer, not the programmer, determines which memory cell is used to store a particular data item.

Variable names should be chosen to convey the nature of the data to be processed.[1] For example, the flowchart segment in Figure 4–5 shows that three values are to be entered from a terminal and stored in three memory locations called H (hours), R (rate), and N$ (name). Other names (such as X, Y, and Z$) could have been used instead, but judicious selection of the names H, R, and N$ identifies and documents the nature of the transaction under consideration.

For an output operation, the instruction PRINT, followed by a list of variables is used. The contents (value) of each variable are to be printed on some output device. For example, the block / PRINT P,H / indicates that values in memory cells P and H are to be displayed (written) on some device.

The Processing Block

A rectangle [ ] is used for computational instructions. The most common form for these instructions is the *replacement statement*. A replacement statement specifies the arithmetic operations to be performed on constants and/or variables and the location (variable) into which the value computed is to placed. For example, the block [P = 2 * H] specifies that the value of H is to be multiplied by 2 and the result is to be placed in P. Any sequence of operations can be performed, but there must be a single variable specified as the destination for the value calculated, i.e., there should be only one variable on the left side of the equal sign.

Figure 4–5 Meaning of the INPUT block.

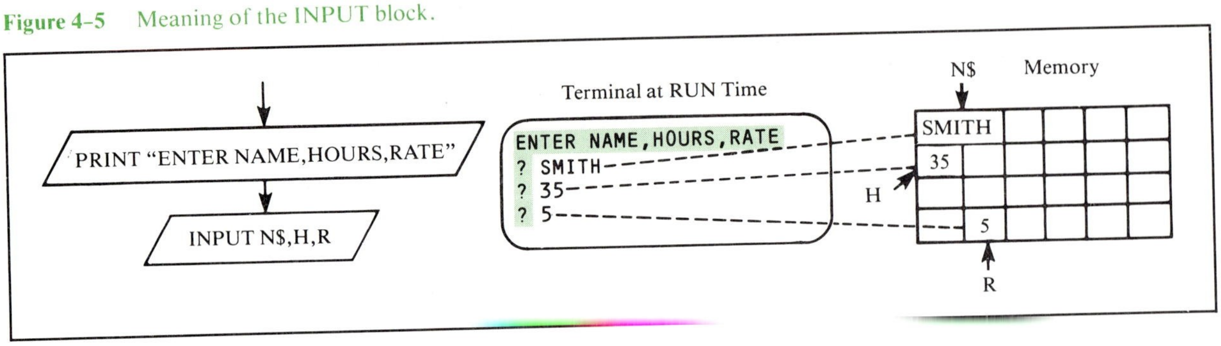

[1]Since flowcharts are independent of BASIC grammatical rules, variable names can be actual words and are not limited to a letter or a letter and a digit. You can decide what is best for you, but remember—eventually you will have to translate your flowchart to BASIC code!

The Decision Block

The diamond ◇ is used for decision making. The decision usually involves a question that can be answered *yes* or *no*. The question must involve only mathematical relations such as equal to (=), less than (<), greater than (>), less than or equal to (< =), greater than or equal to (> =), or not equal to (< >). Only two flowlines should branch out from a decision block. These flowlines indicate the paths that are to be taken for each outcome of the decision. For example, the decision block

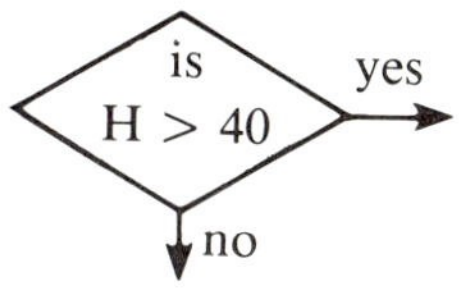

illustrates two distinct paths. The YES path is taken if H is greater than 40, otherwise (H< =40) the NO path is taken.

Flowlines

The sequence for executing the instructions in a flowchart is illustrated by straight lines with arrowheads, such as ——→ or ↓, joining one flowchart block to another. The direction of flow is in the direction pointed to by the arrowhead.

Connector Blocks

Connectors are often used when it is inconvenient to draw flowlines to connect one area of the flowchart to another. Connectors serve two purposes:

1. They identify blocks with reference labels.
2. They indicate transfer to other labeled blocks.

The symbol used for a connector is a small circle ○. A label (a number or alphabetic character) is placed in the connector block. When the flowline points away from the connector, such as ○→, the connector is an entry point, that is, a block to which transfer will be made from some point in the flowchart. When the flowline points toward the connector, as in →○, the connector is used to indicate a transfer; that is, execution resumes at an entry point with the same symbol as used in the connector at the transfer point. For example,

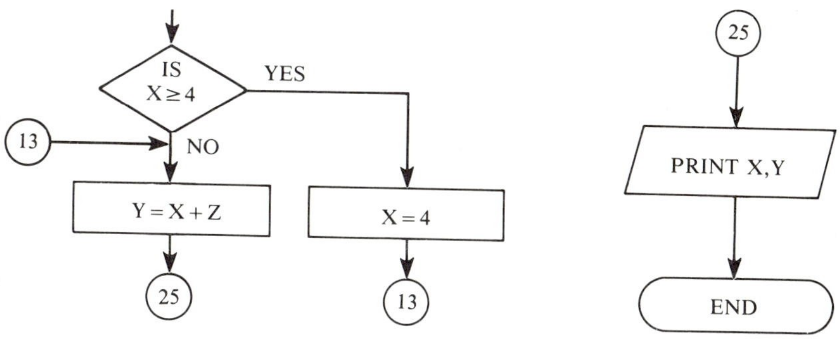

If the value of X is greater than or equal to 4, the block X = 4 is executed and a transfer is made to the entry point labeled "13." If X is not greater than or equal to 4 (i.e., X is less than 4), the block Y = X + Z is executed and transfer is made to the entry point marked "25," which contains the PRINT instruction. This flowchart is equivalent to

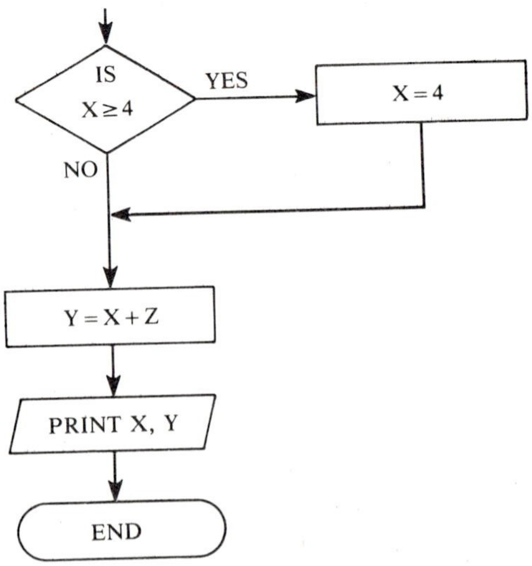

Note that in a flowchart it is possible to have many transfer connectors with the same number, such as →(48) . However, only one entry connector (48)→ may be designated in the same flowchart.

4-3-3 Do It Now

1. Determine the output produced by each of the following flowcharts.

a.

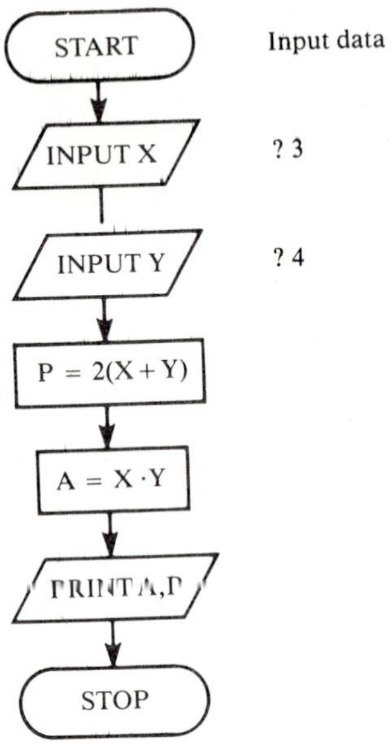

b.

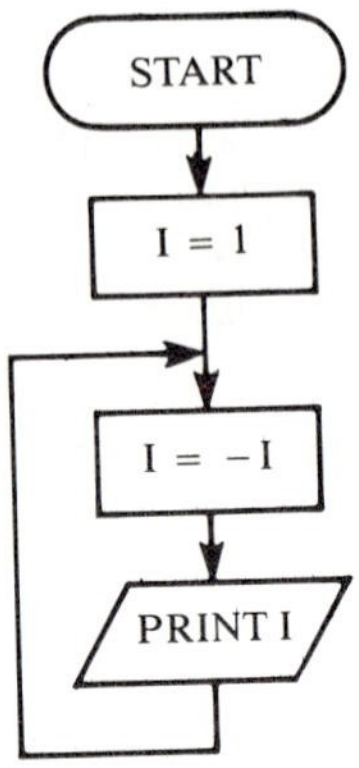

c.

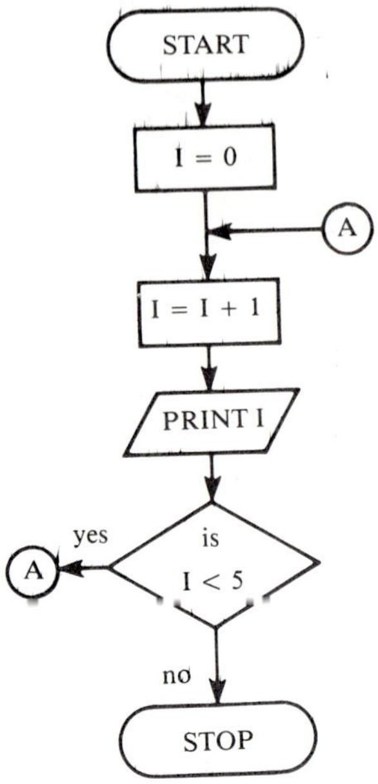

2. Do you see any flaws in the following flowcharts?

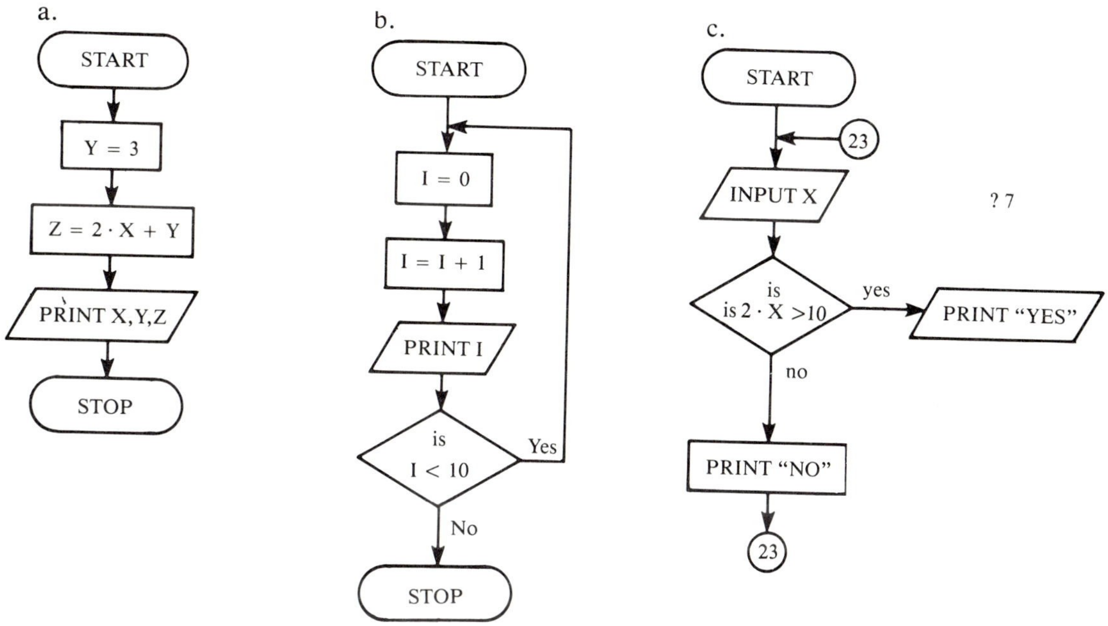

Answers

1. a. The output will be 12 and 14.
   b. The numbers −1, 1, −1, 1, . . . will be printed.
   c. The numbers 1, 2, 3, 4, and 5 will be printed.

2. a. The value of X is unknown.
   b. The number 1 will be printed indefinitely.
   c. There are no flowlines indicating what to do after "YES" has been printed. Invalid output block for PRINT "NO"

4-3-4 Pseudo Code

Pseudo code is an abbreviated form of expression that makes use of both the English language and certain programming language control words such as IF, THEN, ELSE, and END-IF. Pseudo code is semantically very close to BASIC and other programming languages. The user describes in plain English the sequence of steps necessary to solve a particular problem. Sentences are generally written one per line, and indentation is used in the IF statement to outline which actions are to be taken if a condition is true and which are to be taken if the condition is false. Such indentation makes the code more readable and clear.

Inherent to pseudo code is a natural structure that allows the reader to start reading the code at the top and proceed sequentially downwards, just like reading a paragraph from a novel! Such a top-down approach to writing code differs from flowcharts in two respects:

1. Pseudo code is self-explanatory and self-documenting since it is written in plain informal English.

   For example; the pseudo code sentence "Compute pay" means P = H * R. Any one reading pseudo code can understand what is going on in the program.

2. Pseudo code parallels the final structure of the BASIC program because it has line by line similarity to it (see Figure 4-6). Flowcharts, on the other hand, have a natural tendency to extend flowlines in all directions and thus their paths of instructions do not generally parallel the final BASIC code!

Figure 4-6 Pseudo code.

Pseudo Code	*BASIC Code*
Input the name	`10 INPUT N$`
Input the hours	`15 INPUT H`
Input the rate	`20 INPUT R`
IF the hours greater than 40	`25 IF H > 40 THEN 30 ELSE 65`
THEN	`27 REM THEN`
Compute pay for 1st 40 hours	`30      P1 = 40 * R`
Compute overtime hours	`35      V = H - 40`
Compute overtime pay	`40      P2 = V * R * 1.5`
Compute pay	`45      P = P1 + P2`
Print overtime hours	`50      PRINT V`
Print overtime pay	`55      PRINT P2`
	`60      GO TO 70`
ELSE	`62 REM ELSE`
Compute pay	`65      P = H * R`
END-IF	`70      PRINT N$,P`
Print name and pay	`75 END`

Pseudo code is a very valuable design language for writing BASIC or any other programming language, especially if the user's BASIC supports such constructs as the IF THEN ELSE and the WHILE/DO statements. It becomes less valuable if the user's BASIC supports neither of these constructs. Since most BASIC systems feature the IF THEN ELSE structure (but not necessarily the WHILE), this text will use pseudo code to solve problems with the IF THEN ELSE statement and flowcharts for those systems that do not have the IF THEN ELSE statement. It is important for the reader to use both approaches and feel comfortable with them.

The payroll flowchart of Figure 4-3 could be written in pseudo code as shown in Figure 4-6. Note the similarity between pseudo code and the BASIC code when using the IF THEN/ELSE statement.

4-4 The Decision Statement IF/THEN

4-4-1 Decisions and Conditions

Recall that the central processing unit (CPU) has a logical unit which allows the computer to compare one number to another, or one or more alphanumeric characters with others. Using this capability, the programmer can tell the computer what action to take according to the outcome of a particular comparison. If, for example, in a payroll program, the number of hours worked is greater than 40, the computer can be instructed to carry out a specific sequence of actions that differs from the sequence of actions that are to be carried out if the hours are less than or equal to 40. Hence, decisions can be made based on a condition being true or false (Hours > 40, or Hours not greater than 40). This decision-making capability is available in BASIC through the IF statement, which allows the computer to transfer to a nonsequential instruction(s).

Minimum standard BASIC supports the simple IF statement described below. Most BASIC systems, however, support the IF THEN ELSE statement which is described in section 4-4-8.

4-4-2 The Simple IF Statement

The general form of the simple IF statement is

> *line number* IF *condition* THEN *transfer line number*

where condition is an expression that can be either true or false.

In some BASIC systems you can use GO TO or THEN GO TO as well as THEN.

Action: If the condition is true, the computer takes the next instruction from *transfer line number*.
If the condition is false, the computer takes the very next sequential instruction, i.e., the one that immediately follows the IF statement.

The general form of a condition is:

{ *constant 1* / *variable 1* / *arithmetic expression 1* }	*relational operator*	{ *constant 2* / *variable 2* / *arithmetic expression 2* }

where the constant and variable can contain alphanumeric or numeric data, and the relational operator can be any of the operators described in Figure 4–7. When an alphanumeric variable is compared to an alphanumeric constant, the constant must be enclosed in quotes. It should be noted that cross-comparisons between numeric and alphanumeric data are invalid. For example IF N$ = 1.6 THEN 64 is invalid, while comparing N$ with "1.6" is valid!

Some examples of various "simple" IF statements are as follows:

```
10 IF X = 1 THEN 43
60 IF N$ = M$ THEN 440
80 IF X + Y <= Z^2 THEN 680
06 IF N$ = "FONDA" THEN 88
```

■ **Figure 4-7** BASIC relational operators.

BASIC Relational Operators	Mathematical Symbol	Meaning
=	=	Equal to
<	<	Less than
< = or = <	≤	Less than or equal to
>	>	Greater than
> = or = >	≥	Greater than or equal to
< > or > <	≠	Not equal to

4-4-3 Do It Now

1. Which of the following are valid IF statements? If invalid, specify the reason.
   a. `IF X = 1.THEN 63`
   b. `IF 3 * X ^ 2 THEN 34`
   c. `IF (X) > (4) THEN 33`
   d. `IF N$ = 3. THEN 4Ø`
   e. `IF L$ <> N$ * K$ THEN 6Ø`
   f. `IF A * X * X ^ 2 - 3.1 =< Z / 4 + T THEN 5Ø`
   g. `IF X + 1 ≤ 4.3 THEN 88`

2. Given the values A = 4, B = 2 and C = 2, indicate which statement will be executed next.
   a.
   ```
   1Ø IF A / (B + 2) = A / B + 2 THEN 6Ø
   15. . .
   ```
   b.
   ```
   1Ø IF A ^ C + 2 >= A + 14 / C THEN 6Ø
   15. . .
   ```
   c.
   ```
   1Ø IF (1.5 + B / 3) < A / 1.84621 THEN 6Ø
   15. . .
   ```

3. Is the following IF statement correct from a grammatical perspective? From a logical perspective?
   ```
   1Ø IF X + 2 * Y = 3 THEN 2Ø
   2Ø PRINT X
   ```

4. For which values of A will control be passed to 60?
   a. `IF A - 3 < Ø THEN 6Ø`
   b. `IF (A - 1) ^ 2 <= Ø THEN 6Ø`
   c. `IF (A - 3) * (4 - A) > Ø THEN 6Ø`
   d. `IF (A ^ 2 - A) = Ø THEN 6Ø`

5. True or false:
   a. Relational and arithmetic operators are one and the same.
   b. The equal sign in LET X = 4 is a relational operator.
   c. Decisions can be carried out by the arithmetic unit.
   d. For unconditional transfers THEN may be used instead of GO TO.

Answers

1. a. Valid.
   b. Invalid; no relational operator.
   c. Valid.
   d. Invalid; cross-comparison.
   e. Invalid; cannot multiply alphanumeric data.
   f. Valid.
   g. Invalid operator ≤.

2. a. 15
   b. 60
   c. 15

3. Regardless of the value of X and Y, control will always be passed to line 20. However, the instruction is syntactically valid.

4. a. A < 3.
   b. For A = 1.
   c. Any value between 3 and 4.
   d. 0,1

5. a. False.
   b. False.
   c. False.
   d. False; THEN may only be used in IF statements.

4-4-4 IF Flowcharts and Examples

The IF statement can be visualized as follows:

IF *condition* THEN 200

If the condition is false, the computer passes control to the statement immediately following the IF statement (line 60).

If the condition is true, the computer transfers to the line number specified by the THEN statement (line 200).

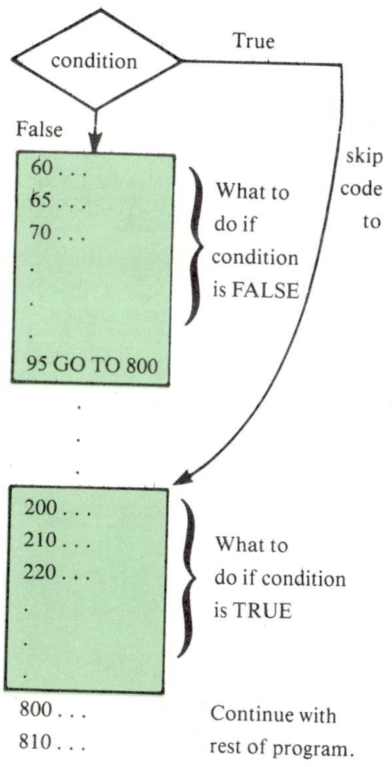

In conclusion, if the condition specified is *true*, control will be transferred to a block of code that does not immediately follow the IF statement (a skip is made). On the other hand, if the condition is *false*, the computer will always transfer to the next sequential instruction.

Example 1

Write the code to input an age, print the message "OLD" if the age is greater than 50 or print "YOUNG" if the age is less than or equal to 50, and then stop.

```
10 INPUT A
20 IF A > 50 THEN 80
30       PRINT "YOUNG"
40       GO TO 90
45 REM
80       PRINT "OLD"
90 END
```

(if no → 30; if yes → 80)

Transfer to statement 80 if age is > 50.
Otherwise, print YOUNG.
Then go to 90 to stop.

If age > 50, skip over lines 30–40 and print OLD.

Note the importance of statement 40. If line 40 had been omitted, then both messages (YOUNG and OLD) would be printed for ages less than or equal to 50.

Example 2

Write the code to input a person's name and a corresponding pay. If the name read is LUCKY, add $100 to the pay. In any event, print the person's name and the pay.

```
10 INPUT N$,P
20 IF N$ <> "LUCKY" THEN 40
30     P = P + 100
40 PRINT N$,P
```

(if no → 30; if yes → 40)

If the name is not LUCKY, print the name and pay; otherwise, if it is LUCKY, add $100 to the pay and print the results.

The reader may think that testing for "equality" of name rather than "inequality" would be more straightforward; let us see what would happen in that case:

```
10 INPUT N$,P
15 IF N$ = "LUCKY" THEN 25
20      GO TO 30
22 REM
25      P = P + 100
30 PRINT N$,P
```

If name is not LUCKY, go to 30 to print results.

In this case, coding is less efficient because of the GO TO statement at line 20. However the result is still the same.

Example 3

Write the instructions to input a code with a value of either 1 or 2. If the code is 1, compute the circumference of a circle of radius 1.34; if the code has the value of 2, compute the area of a circle of radius 3.2. Print the results.

```
     10 INPUT K
if   20 IF K = 1 THEN 50      if yes
no   25    A = 3.14 * 3.2 ^ 2
     30    PRINT "AREA=";A
     40    GO TO 90
     45 REM
     50    C = 2 * 3.14 * 1.34
     55    PRINT "CIRC=";C
     90 END
```

Line 25 is executed if K is not equal to 1.
If K = 1, compute circumference of circle (line 50).

Example 4

The line number specified by the THEN statement can precede the IF statement.

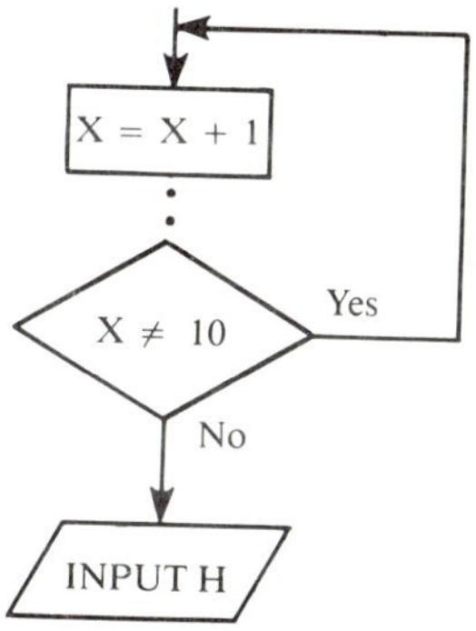


```
10 LET X = X + 1          if condition is true

20 IF X <> 10 GO TO 10

30 INPUT H                if condition is false
```

Other examples of IF statements are shown in Figure 4–8.

Figure 4–8 Examples of IF statements.

a. `1 IF X = 0 THEN 5` `3    LET A = 4`	If X = 0 transfer to statement 5; otherwise (meaning X is not equal to 0) process the next statement (3).
b. `4 IF (X - Y) ^ 2 < Z THEN 40` `8    IF Z > 2 THEN 60`	If $(X - Y)^2 < Z$ process statement 40; otherwise ($(X - Y)^2 > = Z$) fall through and execute statement 8.
c. `5 IF X ^ .5 >= 2 THEN 50` `7    PRINT X`	If $\sqrt{X} > = 2$, go to 50; if $\sqrt{X} < 2$, print X.
d. `2 IF X + Y <> J - K THEN 70` `6    INPUT A`	If $X + Y \neq J - K$, go to 70; otherwise input A.
e. `5 IF R$ = A$ THEN 30` `7    LET R$ = "DOG"`	If the two strings are equal, go to 30; otherwise store the characters DOG in R$.
f. `6 IF N$ = "YES" THEN 60` `7    PRINT N$`	If the variable N$ contains the string YES, transfer to 60; otherwise print N$.

4-4-5 Do It Now

1. Write the BASIC code for the following flowcharts

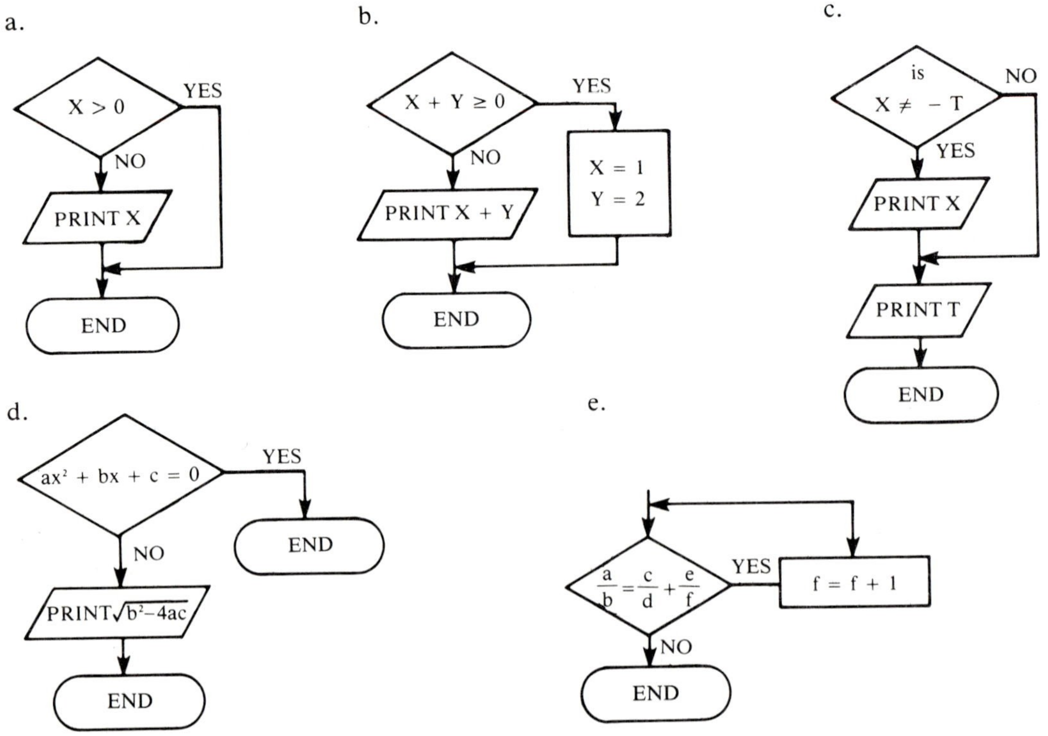

Answers

1. a.

```
10 IF X > 0 GO TO 99
20 PRINT X
99 END
```

b.

```
10 IF X+Y >= 0 GO TO 30
20 PRINT X+Y
25 GO TO 99
30 X = 1
35 Y = 2
99 END
```

c.

```
10 IF X = -T GO TO 30
20 PRINT X
30 PRINT T
99 END
```

d.

```
10 IF A*X^2+B*X+C = 0 THEN 99
20 PRINT (B^2 - 4*A*C)^.5
99 END
```

e.

```
10 IF A/B<>C/D+E/F THEN 99
25 F = F+1
30 GO TO 10
99 END
```

4-4-6 From Flowchart to BASIC Code: Tips

Drawing a flowchart to solve a problem is probably the most difficult task in writing a program. To the beginning programmer, however, translating a flowchart into BASIC code may still present some challenges, especially if numerous decision blocks are present in the flowchart. The following discussion offers advice on translating a flowchart into BASIC code.

Assume we are to accept, through the INPUT statement, the following classification code:

Code	*Meaning*
1	Freshman
2	Sophomore
3	Junior
4	Senior

and we are to write the English word corresponding to the numeric code, e.g., if K = 3, we are to print the word JUNIOR. Let us draw a flowchart to accomplish this.

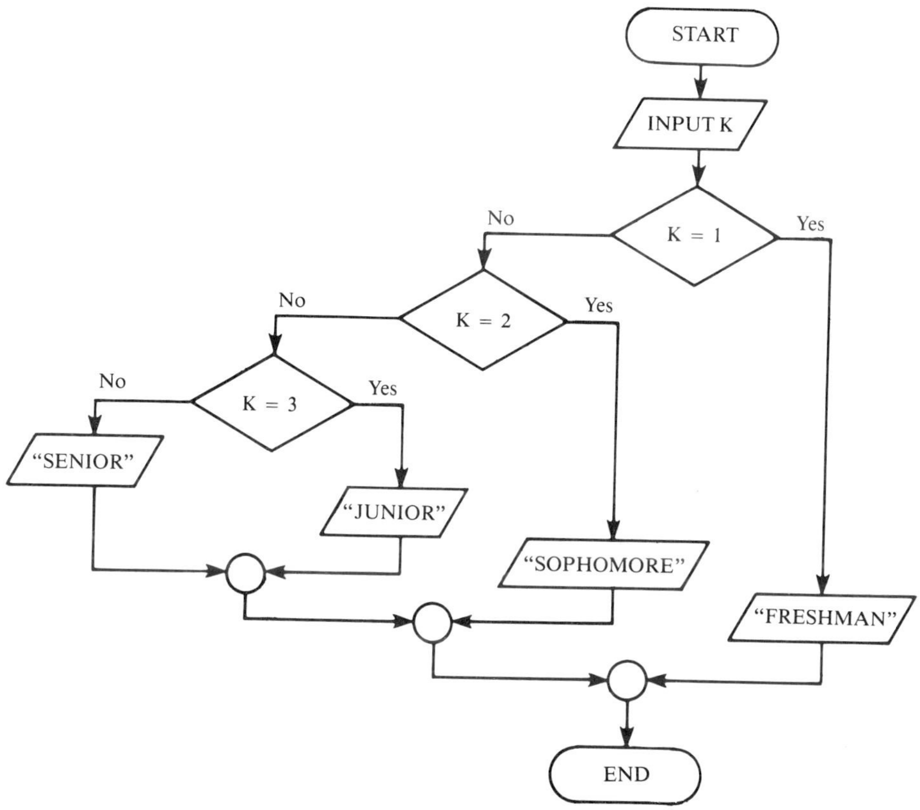

Now we must write the corresponding BASIC code. The most important point is to make sure that the flowpath in the flowchart is preserved in the BASIC code. This means, for example, that in our BASIC program the instruction that follows PRINT "FRESHMAN" should stop the program, since this is what the flowchart shows. With this in mind, we proceed to write the first two instructions:

```
10 INPUT K
20 IF K = 1 THEN ---
30
```

Since we do not know yet what line number to go to if K = 1, we draw a horizontal bar after THEN (THEN ---). This bar reminds us that we need to fill in this blank space later. Right now, though, we do know that if K is not equal to 1 we want to follow the NO branch in the flowchart. The computer will automatically proceed to line 30 if the condition K = 1 is not satisfied, so we continue as follows:

(See flowchart across on page 121)

```
10 INPUT K
20 IF K = 1 THEN ---
30     IF K = 2 THEN ---
40
```

We are now at line 40; the computer will pass control to line 40 if the condition K = 2 is not satisfied. Looking at the flowchart, we see that if K ≠ 2 we need to ask the question, is K = 3? So we type that IF statement at line 40, leaving blank the THEN statement at line 30:

```
10 INPUT K
20 IF K = 1 THEN ---
30     IF K = 2 THEN ---
40          IF K = 3 THEN ---
50
```

We know that the statement at line 50 must be PRINT "SENIOR", which must be followed by the STOP instruction as indicated in the flowchart.

```
10 INPUT K
20 IF K = 1 THEN ---
30     IF K = 2 THEN ---
40          IF K = 3 THEN ---
50               PRINT "SENIOR"
60               GO TO 99
70
```

Statement 99 will be the END statement.

At this point, we have descended through the vertical *no* paths of our flowchart and are finished with this particular logical avenue. The program, however, is not complete since no line numbers have been specified for the THEN statements at lines 20, 30, and 40. It makes no difference which THEN statement we fill in first. We could arbitrarily start with line 30 and specify 70 (PRINT "SOPHOMORE") as our THEN target. A more systematic approach would be to start at the top (line 20) and fill in, successively, the various THEN statements from the top down. Actually, a common practice is to fill in THEN "blanks" from the bottom up, i.e., start with line 40, then do line 30, and finally line 20. Using this approach we complete the code as follows:

```
10 INPUT K
20 IF K = 1 THEN ---
30     IF K = 2 THEN ---
40          IF K = 3 THEN 70
50               PRINT "SENIOR"
60               GO TO 99
70               PRINT "JUNIOR"
80               GO TO 99
```

We now specify 85 at line 30 and write two following lines:

```
85        PRINT "SOPHOMORE"
9Ø        GO TO 99
95
```

Now we fill in line 20 with THEN 95 to obtain the completed program:

```
1Ø INPUT K
2Ø IF K = 1 THEN 95
3Ø     IF K = 2 THEN 85
4Ø         IF K = 3 THEN 7Ø
5Ø             PRINT "SENIOR"
6Ø             GO TO 99
7Ø             PRINT "JUNIOR"
8Ø             GO TO 99
85          PRINT "SOPHOMORE"
9Ø          GO TO 99
95      PRINT "FRESHMAN"
99 END
```

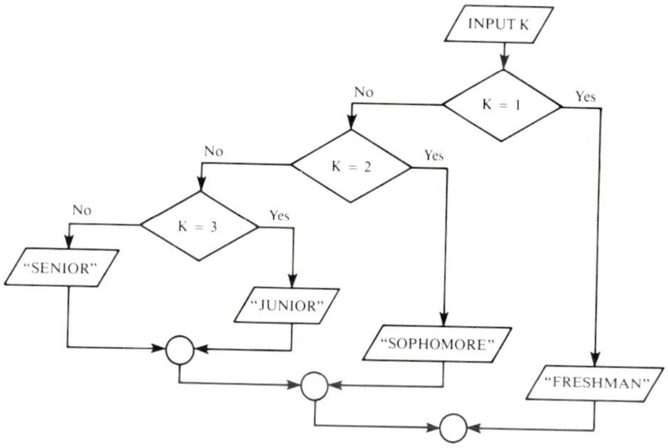

The lesson to be learned from the above process is that whenever a flowchart displays two or more consecutive decision blocks, the programmer should always write the BASIC IF statements in the order of the successive *no* paths of the decision blocks, i.e., he/she should descend the flowchart through the *no* flow lines and "stack" the corresponding IF statements.

4-4-7 Do It Now

1. Write the BASIC code corresponding to the following flowcharts.

a.

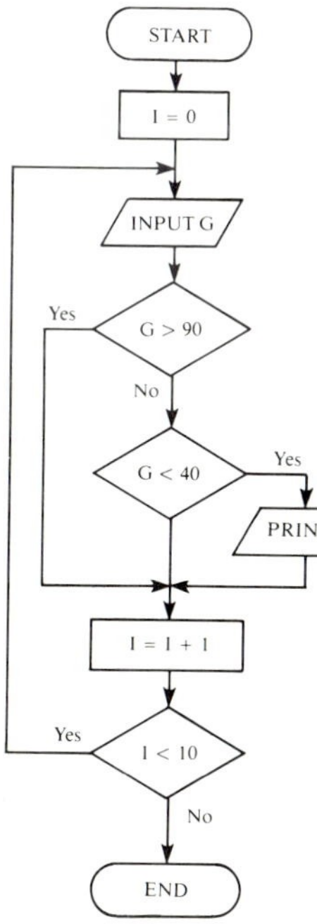

b.

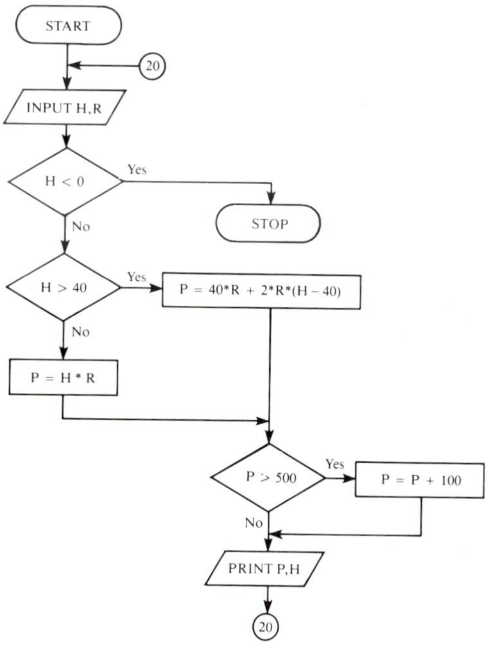

Answers

1. a.

```
10 I = 0
15 INPUT G
20 IF G > 90 THEN 30
25     IF G < 40 THEN 45
30     I = I + 1
35 IF I < 10 THEN 15
40     GO TO 55
45 PRINT G
50 GO TO 30
55 END
```

b.

```
10 INPUT H,R
15 IF H < 0 THEN 65
20     IF H > 40 THEN 55
25         P = H * R
30         IF P > 500 THEN 45
35             PRINT P,H
40             GO TO 10
45             P = P + 100
50             GO TO 35
55         P = 40 * R + 2*R*(H-40)
60         GO TO 30
65     END
```

4-4-8 The IF/THEN ELSE Statement

Most BASIC systems support the IF/THEN ELSE statement discussed in this section. It is possible, however, that this feature may not exist on the user's BASIC system. Because of the IF/THEN ELSE's importance in terms of structured design, and because of its similarity to the IF statements in other high level languages such as COBOL, FORTRAN, and PASCAL, the reader is urged to read this section carefully. In addition, the IF/THEN ELSE makes it possible for the programmer to use pseudo code as a program development language, a practice which has become universal. It should be noted that systems supporting the IF/THEN ELSE statement also support the simple IF statement discussed in section 4-4-2. The general form of the IF/THEN ELSE statement is:

line number IF *condition* THEN *true line number* ELSE *false line number*

Action: If the condition is true, transfer is made to the true line number.
If the condition is false, transfer is made to the false line number.

The following diagram illustrates the way in which the IF/THEN ELSE statement should be coded and indented. Note how the REM statements are used to separate the THEN statement actions from the ELSE statement actions; this insertion of REMarks improves both the readability and clarity of the BASIC code.

Once again, note that the THEN and ELSE words specified at lines 105 and 310 are not BASIC key words, but are just part of REMark statements to give the reader a better visual grasp of what is to be done if the condition is satisfied (lines 110–305) or if the condition is false (lines 315–800). Also note that when the ELSE statements have been executed (lines 315–800), the remainder of the program code starts at line 810. In the code the THEN statements immediately follow the IF statement; this is not necessary—the "ELSE" statements could have come first, right after the IF statement i.e., IF condition THEN 315 ELSE 110 where the true statements start at 315 and the false statements start at 110. Also note how the indentation sets off the THEN and ELSE statements.

```
100        IF condition THEN 110 ELSE 315
105   REM THEN
110        Statement 1           }
115        Statement 2           }
.          .                     }
.          .                     }  if true
.          .                     }
300        Statement n           }
305        GO TO 810             }
310   REM ELSE
315        Statement a           }
320        Statement b           }
.          .                     }
.          .                     }  if false
.          .                     }
800        Statement z           }
805   REM
810   REM END OF IF BLOCK
815
```

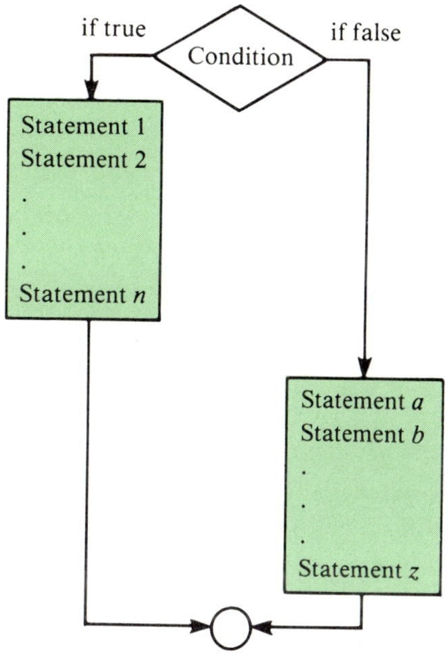

Example 1

The FHA insures home mortgages and requires a down payment as follows:

3% of the first \$25,000
5% of the remainder.

Problem:
Write the code to accept a mortgage amount and calculate and print the down payment amount.

Solution:
We will use the INPUT statement to enter the mortgage amount. If the amount is less than \$25,000, then the down payment is 0.03 times the amount. If, on the other hand, the amount exceeds \$25,000, then the mortgage amount will be 3% of \$25,000 (\$750) plus 5% of the amount in excess of \$25,000 (amount − 25,000). The pseudo code and corresponding BASIC code are shown in Figure 4–9.

- The IF statement specifies the condition.
- The statements between THEN and ELSE specify the action(s) to be carried out if the condition is true. After those statements are carried out, control is passed to the statement physically following the END-IF.
- The statements between ELSE and END-IF specify the action(s) to be carried out if the condition is false, after which control is passed to the statement after the END-IF.
- The END-IF is a visual bracket that identifies the range of the IF statement. If there were no END-IF statement, the reader might confuse the last statement

■ **Figure 4–9** A down payment problem.

Pseudo Code

```
Input mortgage amount
IF amount < $25,000
THEN
        down payment = 3% of amount
ELSE
        payment 1 = 3% of $25,000
        payment 2 = 5% of (amount – $25,000)
        down payment = payment 1 + payment 2
END-IF
Print down payment
```

BASIC Code

```
10      INPUT A
15      IF A < 25000 THEN 20 ELSE 35
20 REM THEN
25          P = .03 * A
30          GO TO 60
35 REM ELSE
40          P1 = .03 * 25000
45          P2 = .05 * (A-25000)
50          P = P1 + P2
55 REM END IF
60      PRINT "PAYMENT=";P
65      END
```

Notice the capitalized words IF, THEN, ELSE, and END-IF in the pseudo code.

(print down payment) with the ELSE statements and think that it would be carried out only if the condition were false.

Also notice the GO TO statement at line 30 in the BASIC code. This routes the *yes* branch to line 60. No GO TO statement is needed after line 50, since the next executable statement is the PRINT statement at line 60.

Example 2

Write the pseudo code and the corresponding BASIC program to compute a sales person's commission based on a graduated sales volume shown below. The sales amount is entered via the INPUT statement.

Amount Sales	*Commission (Percentage of Sales)*
Under $500	2%
$500 or more, but under $5000	5%
$5000 and over	10%

Two decisions are necessary in order to solve this problem. The first one is to determine whether the sales are less than $500 (2% of sales). If sales are greater than or equal to 500, then another decision is needed to determine if sales are below 5000. The solution, expressed in pseudo code and in BASIC, is shown in Figure 4–10.

Note in the pseudo code the use of the END – IF phrase to indicate the extent or range of the IF statement. All sentences between the THEN and ELSE key words are to be carried out if the condition specified is true, then control resumes with the first sentence following the appropriate END – IF. On the other hand, all sentences be-

■ **Figure 4–10** Salesperson's commission.

Pseudo Code

```
Input sales
IF sales less than $500
THEN
        commission = 2% of sales

ELSE
        IF sales less than $5000
        THEN
                commission = 5% of sales

        ELSE
                commission = 10% of sales
        END-IF
END-IF
Print commission
```

BASIC Code

```
10       INPUT S
15       IF S < 500 THEN 20 ELSE 35
20 REM   THEN
25            C = .02 * S
30            GO TO 70
35 REM   ELSE
40            IF S < 5000 THEN 45 ELSE 60
45 REM        THEN
50                 C = .05 * S
55                 GO TO 70
60 REM        ELSE
65                 C = .10 * S
70 REM        END IF
75 REM   END IF
80       PRINT "COMMISSION=";C
85       END
```

tween the ELSE and END – IF key words will be carried out if the specified condition is false, then control is passed to the sentence immediately following the appropriate END – IF.

4-4-9 Do It Now

1. Write the BASIC code to input three scores (0 to 100) and print the message FAIL if the average is less than 80 and PASS otherwise.
2. Write the code to input a temperature and print the message WARM if the temperature is anywhere between 70 and 90 (inclusive). Otherwise stop.
3. Write the program of Figure 4–10 (salesperson commission) using simple IF statements.

Answers

1.

```
10 INPUT T1,T2,T3
20 A =(T1 + T2 + T3)/3
30 IF A > 80 THEN 40 ELSE 60
40      PRINT "PASS"
50      GO TO 70
60      PRINT "FAIL"
70 END
```

Note that lines 20 and 30 could have been combined:

```
IF (T1 + T2 + T3)/3 > 80 THEN 40 ELSE 60
```

2.
```
10 INPUT T
15 IF T >= 70 THEN 20 ELSE 30
20      IF T <= 90 THEN 25 ELSE 30
25           PRINT "WARM"
30 END
```

3.
```
10 INPUT S
15 IF S < 500 THEN 45
20      IF S < 5000 THEN 35
25           C = .1 * S
30           GO TO 50
35           C = .05 * S
40           GO TO 50
45      C = .02 * S
50 PRINT "COMMISSION=";C
```

4-4-10 The IF Statement Revisited

Another extension of the IF statement available on most systems is:

> *line number* IF *condition* THEN *single statement*

where the *single statement* can be only one input/output statement, one replacement statement, or a STOP statement.

Action: If the condition is true, the *single statement* is executed, after which control falls through to the next statement. If the condition is false, the next statement is executed.

This form of the IF statement can be visualized as follows:

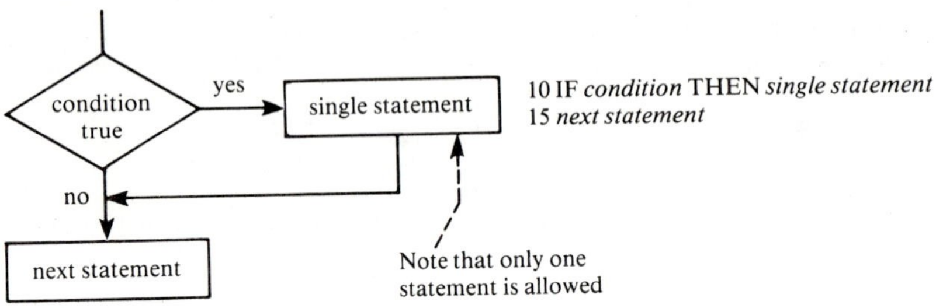

Example 1

Given a number of hours worked and a rate of pay, write the code to give those employees who have worked in excess of 65 hours a bonus of $100.00. Assume all hours are paid at regular time (no overtime).

```
10 INPUT H,R
15 P = H * R
20 IF H > 65 THEN P = P + 100
25 PRINT "PAY=";P
```

Example 2

Write the necessary instructions to read a marital status code. If the code is 1, print SINGLE; if the code is 2, print MARRIED; if the code is 3, print DIVORCED; if the code if 4, print WIDOWED.

```
1Ø INPUT C
15 IF C = 1 THEN PRINT "SINGLE"
2Ø IF C = 2 THEN PRINT "MARRIED"
25 IF C = 3 THEN PRINT "DIVORCED"
3Ø IF C = 4 THEN PRINT "WIDOWED"
```

Could we have replaced line 30 with the statement 30 PRINT "WIDOWED"? No—regardless of what C was, the message WIDOWED would always be printed!

Example 3

Note the proper code for the following flowchart:

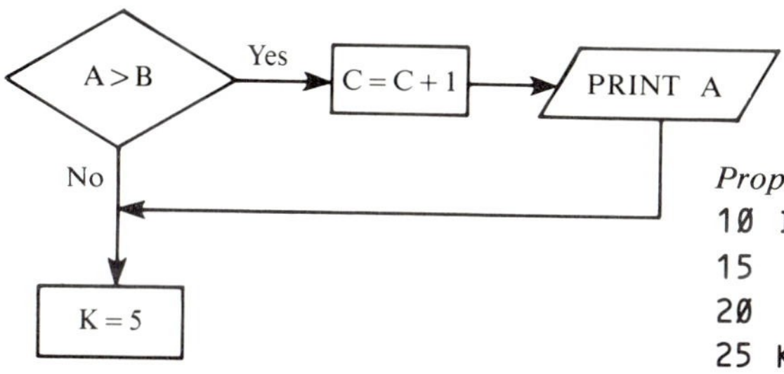

Proper Code

```
1Ø IF A <= B THEN 25
15     C = C + 1
2Ø     PRINT A
25 K = 5
```

Improper code

```
1Ø IF A > B THEN C = C + 1
15 PRINT A
2Ø K = 5
```

In the improper code, PRINT A is always executed which is *not* what is intended. You need to be very careful when using this particular version of the IF statement.

Example 4

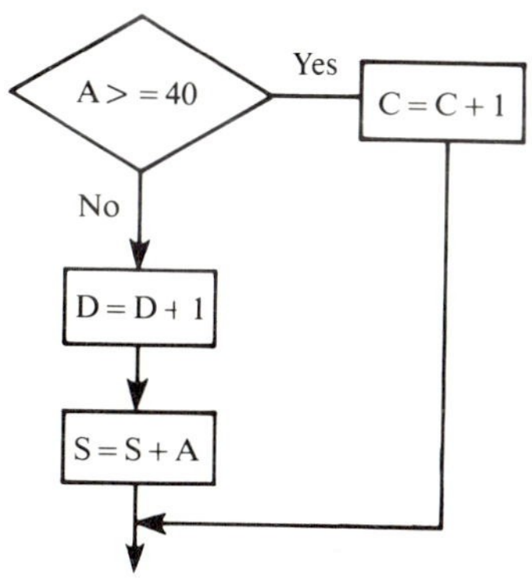

Incorrect Code

```
1Ø IF A >= 4Ø THEN C = C + 1
2Ø D = D + 1
3Ø S = S + A
.
.
.
```

Correct Code

```
1Ø IF A >= 4Ø THEN 5Ø
2Ø D = D + 1
3Ø S = S + A
4Ø GO TO 6Ø
5Ø C = C + 1
6Ø statement
```

Note that in the incorrect version, the statements C = C + 1, D = D + 1, and S = S + A would be executed in sequence if A > = 40 is true. This clearly does not reflect the logic of the flowchart.

4-5 You Might Want to Know

1. Can I write a statement such as PRINT (G1 + G2 + G3)/3?

   Answer: Yes. Any arithmetic expression can be specified in the PRINT statement.

2. What can I do to stop the system when my program is caught in a loop?

   Example:

```
 5 INPUT N
10 PRINT N
15 PRINT "OH AM I IN TROUBLE"
20 GO TO 5
```

   infinite loop

   Answer: In many systems, you can press the ESC (escape) or BREAK key and then change the logic of your program. In some other systems, a combination of keys is needed. Therefore you should consult ahead of time with your computer center staff to determine the correct procedures.

3. Suppose that I key in a wrong value while providing data for an INPUT statement and I realize my error before pressing the RETURN key. What do I do?

   Answer: Backspace over the mistyped characters, correct the error, and transmit. Once an incorrect numerical value has been entered, there is no way to alter that value other than to RUN the program again!

4. Suppose that I have entered an illegal value (special characters) or alphabetic data as a result of an INPUT statement. What do I do?

   Answer: The system will print an error message and allow you to retype the value.

   Example:

```
 5  INPUT N
10  PRINT N * N
15  END
RUN
? I
 ILLEGAL INPUT,RETYPE INPUT AT 5
? 12
 144
```

   An alphanumeric value is entered instead of a number.

5. My friend wrote the following coding segment; can that code be simplified?

```
35  LET L = N3
40  GO TO 55
45  IF N1 < N3 THEN 70
.
55
.
70      GO TO 35
```

   Answer: Yes. Replace line 45 by IF N1 < N3 THEN 35 and delete line 70.

6. Is this the best way to code this flowchart?

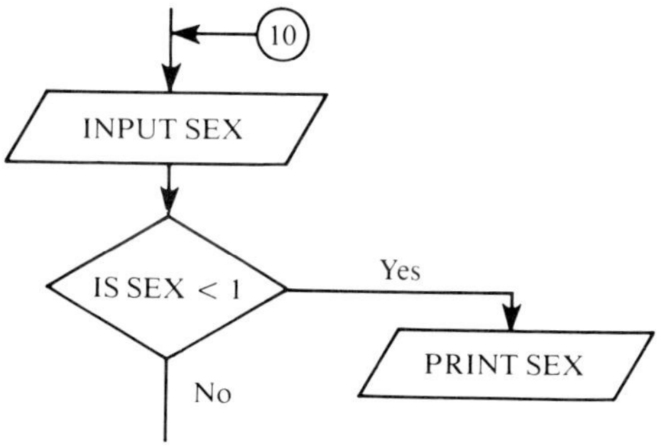


```
10 INPUT S
15 IF S < 1 THEN 30
20 GO TO 10
30 PRINT S
```

Note

Answer: The code is correct. However, in most cases there is *no* need for a GO TO statement to follow an IF statement. The decision block could be rewritten more elegantly in this manner:

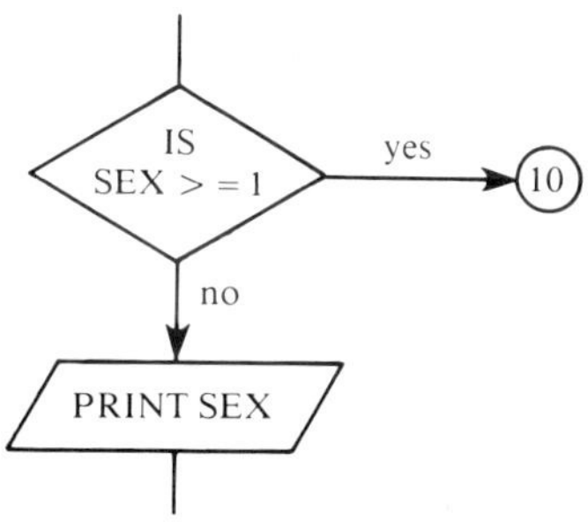


```
10 INPUT S
15 IF S >= 1 THEN 10
20 PRINT S
```

7. In this chapter, all IF statements in the flowcharts are illustrated with the *yes* branch extending horizontally and the *no* branch vertically. Can I draw my flowcharts as follows?

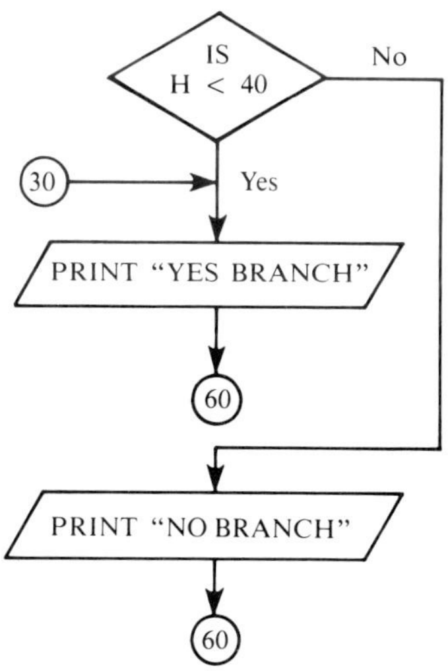


```
10 IF H < 40 THEN 30
15 PRINT "NO BRANCH"
17 GO TO 60
30 PRINT "YES BRANCH"
35 GO TO 60
```

Answer: Certainly. For the beginning student, it may be easier to have the YES branch extending out horizontally; otherwise there is no one-to-one match be-the flowchart blocks and BASIC statements. In any event, many students may not wish to draw their flowcharts in vertical fashion as shown in this text, but may wish to spread out all over right and left—and that's all right!

8. What happens if I GO TO a REM statement or transfer to one as a result of an IF statement?

Answer: REM is not an executable statement, i.e., the computer cannot carry out a remark! Hence control is passed to the first instruction that the computer can carry out. It is a good idea to pass control to a REM statement in the following cases:

```
10      IF X = 3 THEN 20 ELSE 35
20 REM THEN
25            PRINT A
30            GO TO 45
35 REM ELSE
40            PRINT B
45 REM END IF
```

This practice improves readability and documentation in a program.

9. Are program flowcharts of any use once a program has been written?

Answer: Yes, program flowcharts serve as documentation of the logic used in the program. Any changes that need to be made to a program can be visualized more easily by referring to the flowchart rather than to the actual program.

10. Often computer output consists of alphabetic as well as numeric characters. How can this be indicated on a flowchart?

Answer: A common means of indicating alphabetic or *literal* data to be written on an output device is to use quotations around the desired characters in an output block. For example, the block /"PAY = ",P/ would indicate that the characters PAY = are to be printed, followed by the value in location P.

4-6 Programming Examples

4-6-1 Finding the Largest of Three Numbers

Let us write a program that will accept three numbers and print the largest of the three values. If the three numbers are equal, it should print one of the values. The flowchart, pseudo code, and the corresponding BASIC codes for this problem are shown in Figure 4–11.

Figure 4–11 Finding largest of three numbers.

Pseudo Code

INPUT first, second, and third number
IF first is greater than second
THEN
    IF first is greater than third
    THEN print first
    ELSE print third
    END – IF
ELSE
    IF second is less than third
    THEN print third
    ELSE print second
    END – IF
END-IF

Flowchart

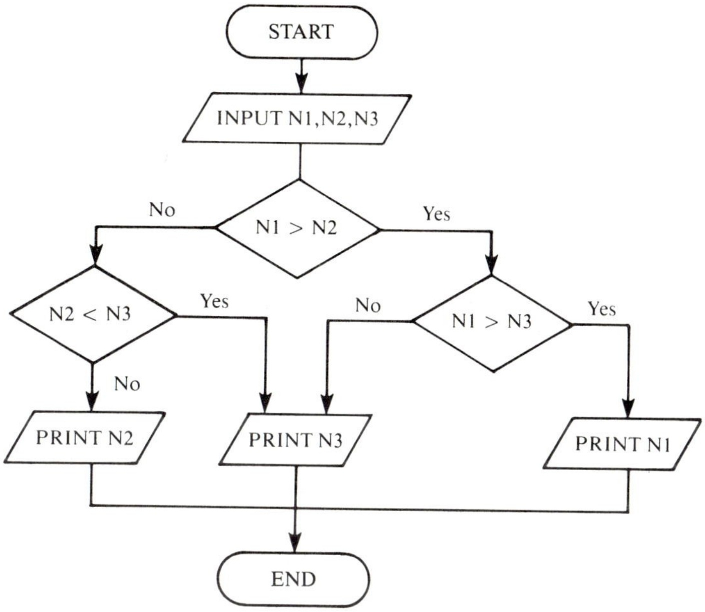

BASIC Code: IF/THEN/ELSE

```
10 REM LARGEST OF 3 NUMBERS
20     INPUT N1,N2,N3
25     IF N1 > N2 THEN 30 ELSE 75
30 REM    THEN
35          IF N1 > N3 THEN 45 ELSE 55
40 REM         THEN
45                PRINT N1
50                GO TO 99
55 REM         ELSE
60                PRINT N3
65                GO TO 99
70 REM    ELSE
75          IF N2 < N3 THEN 80 ELSE 95
80 REM         THEN
85                PRINT N3
90                GO TO 99
95 REM         ELSE
97                PRINT N2
99      END
```

Basic Code: Simple IF

```
10 REM LARGEST OF 3 NUMBERS
12 INPUT N1,N2,N3
20 IF N1 > N2 THEN 40
25    IF N2 < N3 THEN 45
30       PRINT N2
35       GO TO 60
40    IF N1 > N3 THEN 55
45       PRINT N3
50       GO TO 60
55       PRINT N1
60 END
```

Note that lines 55–65 could be omitted by changing line 35 as follows:

```
IF N1 > N3 THEN 45 ELSE 85
```

4-6-2 Do It Now

1. Can you rewrite the program of Figure 4–11 using only two IF statements? Draw the flowchart and the corresponding BASIC code.
2. Change the BASIC code of Figure 4–11 so that a message is printed if all three numbers are equal.

Answers

1.

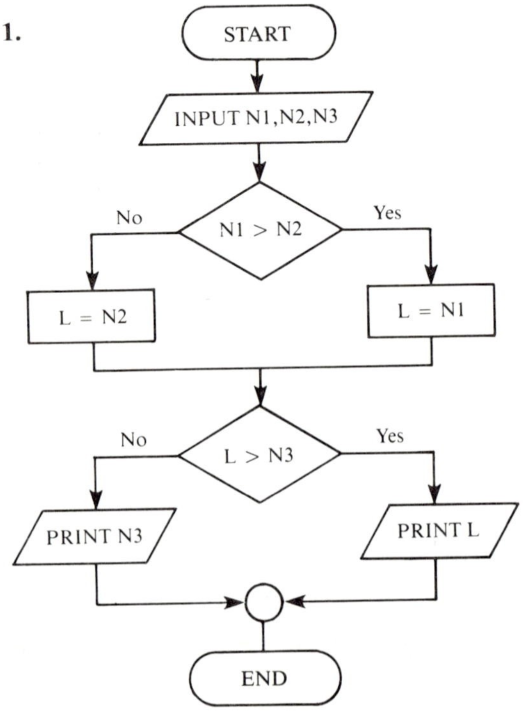


```
10 INPUT N1,N2,N3
15 IF N1 > N2 THEN 30
20     L = N2
25     GO TO 35
30     L = N1
35 IF L > N3 THEN 50
40    PRINT N3
45    GO TO 99
50 PRINT L
99 END
```

2. Add lines

```
13 IF N1 >< N2 THEN 20
15     IF N2 >< N3 THEN 20
17         PRINT "NUMBERS ARE EQUAL"
19         GOTO 60
```

4-6-3 Solution of a Quadratic Equation

Let us write a program to determine the roots of the quadratic equation $ax^2 + bx + c$ The three constants a, b, and c are entered at run time.

If there are no real roots, print the message	NO REAL ROOTS
If the roots are equal, print the message	EQUAL ROOTS = XX
If the roots are unequal, print the message	ROOT1 = XX ROOT2 = XX

Figure 4–12 Quadratic equation.

Program

```
2 REM  SOLVING A QUADRATIC EQUATION
4 REM
6 REM  DATA DICTIONARY
8 REM  A,B,C, = COEFFICIENTS
10 REM D = DISCRIMINANT
12 REM X1,X2 = ROOTS
14 REM
18     INPUT A,B,C
20 REM COMPUTE DISCRIMINANT
22     LET D = B * B - 4 * A * C
25     IF D < 0 THEN 70
28 REM COMPUTE ONE ROOT
30         LET X1 = (-B + D ^ .5)/(2 * A)
35         IF D = 0 THEN 55
37 REM COMPUTE SECOND ROOT
40             LET X2 = (-B - D ^ .5)/(2 * A)
44             PRINT "ROOT 1 ="; X1
46             PRINT "ROOT 2 ="; X2
50             GO TO 75
52 REM ROOTS ARE EQUAL (D = 0)
55         PRINT "EQUAL ROOTS"; X1
60         GO TO 75
62 REM ROOTS ARE IMAGINARY
70     PRINT "NO REAL ROOTS"
75     END
```

Output

Example 1: $X^2 + X - 2 = 0$

```
RUN
?1, 1, -2
ROOT 1 = 1
ROOT 2 = -2
```

Example 2: $X^2 + 1 = 0$

```
RUN
?1, 0, 1
NO REAL ROOTS
```

Example 3: $X^2 - 3.2X + 2.56 = 0$

```
RUN
?1, -3.2, 2.56
EQUAL ROOTS 1.6
```

Recall that the formula to compute the roots of a quadratic equation is:

$$x_1 = \frac{-b + \sqrt{b^2 - 4ac}}{2a} \quad \text{and} \quad x_2 = \frac{-b - \sqrt{b^2 - 4ac}}{2a}$$

If $b^2 - 4ac < 0$, roots are imaginary.
If $b^2 - 4ac = 0$, roots are equal.

A program to solve this problem is shown in Figure 4–12.

4-6-4 Year-end Bonus

Employees at Sarah's Style Shop are to receive a year-end bonus. The amount of the bonus depends on the employee's weekly pay, position code, and number of years with the store. Each employee is assigned a bonus based on the following rules:

Position Code	*Bonus*
1	One week's pay
2	Two week's pay; maximum of $700
3	One and a half week's pay

Employees with more than 10 years' experience are to receive an additional $100.

Employees with fewer than 2 year's experience are to receive half the usual bonus.

Problem:

Input an employee number, a weekly pay, a position code, and a number of years, compute and print the employee's bonus.

Solution:

The best way to solve such a problem is to first work out a few examples manually, without thinking about computers or flowcharting. Make up artificial entries (pay, code, years) and figure out the answers to warm up for the flowchart/pseudo code phase. For example, assume that the weekly pay is $200, the position code is 3, and the employee has 15 years' experience. The position code tells us that the bonus is 1½ weeks' pay ($200 + $100 = $300). Since this employee has been with the company more than 10 years, add $100 to the bonus ($300 + $100 = $400). Now we have figured out the bonus for one particular employee.

Let's look at another case where the weekly pay is $500, the position code is 2, and the employee has 1 year of experience. In this case, the bonus is 2 weeks' pay ($1,000); however, since the problem states that the maximum bonus is $700, the bonus is set to $700. (Had the weekly pay been $300, the bonus would have been 2 × $300 = $600; and the limitation would not apply.) Since the employee has less than 2 years' experience, the final bonus is cut in half ($350).

Now that we have some ideas about how to solve the problem, we start writing them down, using either a flowchart or pseudo code. These, as well as the BASIC code, are shown in Figure 4–13.

4-7 Getting to Know Your System Better

As in previous chapters, this section deals with system and BASIC features available in most BASIC systems. Since these features do vary from one particular system to the next, you may want to include your system's version in section 4–7–7, which is left blank for your convenience.

4-7-1 Variable Names: More Meaningful Names

Most systems will allow a variable name to start with *at least* two letters of the alphabet. This option gives more flexibility in naming variables and makes programs more readable and self-documenting.

Examples: SS, SS1, AM$ are valid variable names.
Of course *some* systems only look at the first two characters, in which case PEN refers to the same variable as PET! The IBM PC allows any length, but only the first 40 characters are significant!

Figure 4–13 A year-end bonus.

Pseudo Code

```
INPUT employee number, pay,
      position code and years

IF position code = 1
THEN
      set bonus to 1 week's pay
ELSE
      IF position code = 2
      THEN
            IF 2 weeks pay > 700
            THEN
                  Set bonus to 700
            ELSE
                  Set bonus to 2 week's pay
            END-IF
      ELSE
            Set bonus to 1.5 weeks' pay
      END-IF
END-IF
IF years greater than 10
THEN
      Add 100 to bonus
ELSE
      IF years less than 2
      THEN
            Cut bonus in half
      ELSE
            Bonus stays the same
      END-IF
END-IF
PRINT employee number and bonus
```

Flowchart

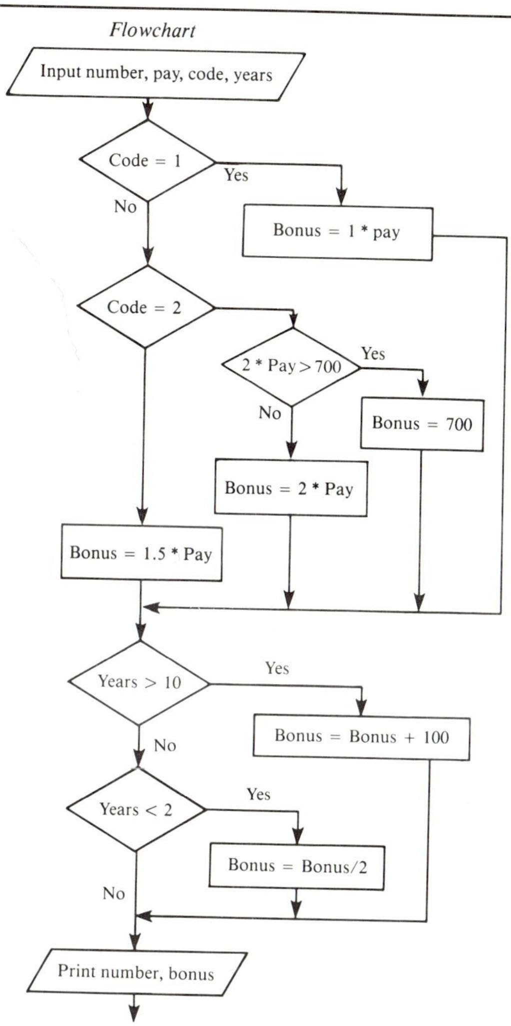

BASIC Code: IF THEN ELSE

```
10 INPUT N, P, C, Y
15 IF C = 1 THEN 20 ELSE 30
20     B = P
25     GO TO 65
30     IF C = 2 THEN 35 ELSE 60
35         IF 2 * P > 700 THEN 40 ELSE 50
40             B = 700
45             GO TO 65
50             B = 2 * P
55             GO TO 65
60         B = 1.5 * P
65 IF Y > 10 THEN 70 ELSE 80
70     B = B + 100
75     GO TO 90
80     IF Y < 2 THEN 85 ELSE 90
85         B = B/2
90 PRINT N, "BONUS=";B
99 END
```

BASIC Code: Simple IF

```
10 READ  N, P, C, Y
15 IF C = 1 THEN 60
20    IF C = 2 THEN 35
25        B = 1.5 * P
30        GO TO 65
35    IF 2 * P > 700 THEN 50
40        B = 2 * P
45        GO TO 65
50    B = 700
55    GO TO 65
60 B = P
65 IF Y > 10 THEN 85
70    IF Y >= 2 THEN 90
75        B = B/2
80        GO TO 90
85 B = B + 100
90 PRINT N, "BONUS=";B
95 END
```

4-7-2 RENUM/RESEQUENCE: Renumber or Resequence Line Numbers

Suppose you run the 3-line BASIC program

```
10 INPUT X
14 ...
15 ...
```

and then realize that you want to insert a line between 14 and 15. Most systems allow you to renumber the lines so that this can be done. The commands may vary from one system to another, but typically there is a command such as RENUM or RESEQUENCE which does the following:

Code	*Command*	*Result*

`10 IF X = 0 THEN 15`
`14 ...`
`15 ...`
	RENUM	`100 IF X = 0 THEN 300`
		`200 ...`
		`300 ...`

`10 IF X = 0 THEN 16`
`14 ...`
`15 ...`
`16 ...`
	RENUM 20, 15, 10
	Start renumbering at line 15. The first renumbered line becomes 20. Use increments of 10.
		`10 IF X = 0 THEN 30`
		`14 ...`
		`20 ...`
		`30 ...`

`10 IF X = 0 THEN 15`
`14 ...`
`15 ...`
	RENUM 30,, 6
	Renumber entire code. The first line becomes 30. Use increments of 6.
		`30 IF X = 0 THEN 42`
		`36 ...`
		`42 ...`

Notice that the original line numbers designated by the THEN statement are also changed to reflect the new numbering sequence.

4-7-3 LIST: Partial Listing of Program

Sometimes you may want a partial listing of a program. You can list one line or a part of a program by using the following features:

`LIST`	The entire program is listed.
`LIST 80`	Line 80 is displayed.
`LIST 10-80`	List lines 10 through 80 inclusive.
`LIST -75`	List all lines up to and including line 75.
`LIST 100-`	List line 100 to last line inclusive.

When listing a long program on a video monitor, you can interrupt the scrolling process by pressing a BREAK key, an ESCAPE key, or a combination of keys such as the shift key and the S key (or other particular keys). To resume scrolling, any key can be pressed. Check with your system reference manual since each BASIC system may have a different procedure.

4-7-4 DELete Command to Delete Lines

A line can be deleted by entering the desired line number and pressing the ENTER/RETURN key. One or more consecutive lines can also be deleted using the command DELETE or DEL, as follows:

`DELETE 5Ø`	Deletes line 50.
`DELETE 35-85`	Deletes lines 35 through 85 inclusive.
`DELETE -6Ø`	Deletes all lines up to and including 60.

4-7-5 INPUT *"Prompt Message", List of Variables*

Instead of preceding an INPUT statement with a PRINT statement telling the user what to do when the question mark is printed on the screen at run time, the prompt or cue can be part of the INPUT statement itself:

```
1Ø INPUT "ENTER 3 SCORES", T1, T2, T3
15 INPUT "WHAT'S YOUR NAME", N$
RUN
ENTER 3 SCORES? 8Ø, 4Ø, 7Ø
WHAT'S YOUR NAME? DONKEY DONG
```

4-7-6 The SPC Space Function

If you want specific spacing between titles or data items on your output, for example, AGE*bbbb*SEX*bbb*STATUS*bb*CODE (where *b* represents a blank space), you can use

```
PRINT "AGE";SPC(4);"SEX";SPC(3);"STATUS";SPC(2);"CODE"
```

↓ gives four spaces between AGE and SEX

↓ separates STATUS from CODE by two spaces

4-7-7 MY SYSTEM IS DIFFERENT

This section is left blank for you to write any different system commands that your system uses. You may also want to list the various steps that are required to start a session with your system.

4-7-7 MY SYSTEM IS DIFFERENT

4-8 Assignments

4-8-1 Test Yourself

1. In flowcharting, the decision symbol can be expressed in a more powerful way than the way shown in this text. It is possible to write a three-way decision block:

Symbol | *Meaning*

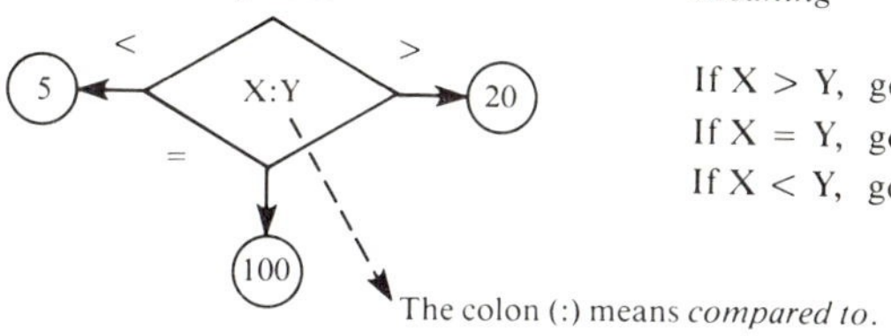

If X > Y, go to 20.
If X = Y, go to 100.
If X < Y, go to 5.

Write the BASIC IF statements for each of the following cases:

a.

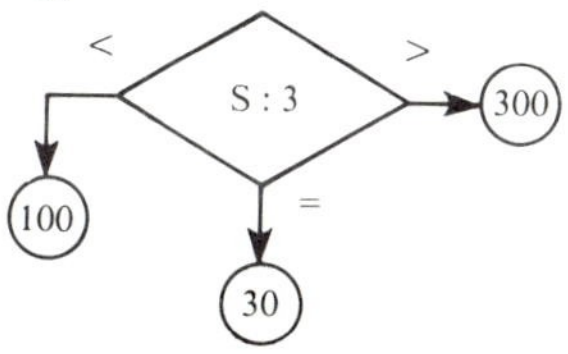

b.

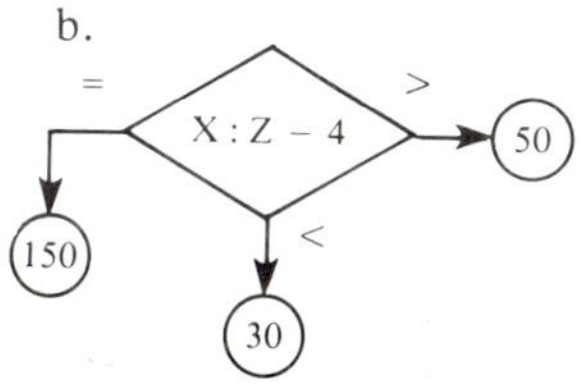

c.

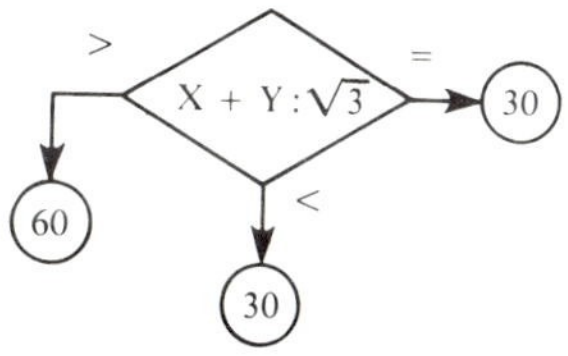

2. Write the BASIC code for the following flowcharts:

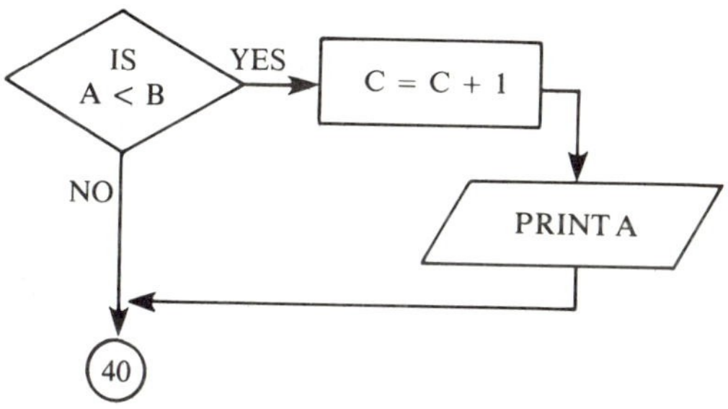

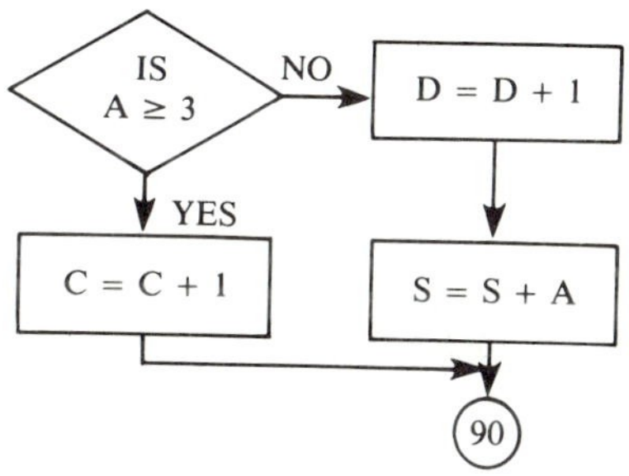

3. Convert the following pseudo code into flowchart and BASIC code.

```
INPUT amount due
INPUT amount received
IF amount due < amount received
THEN compute credit owed
        PRINT credit
ELSE IF amount due = amount received
       THEN PRINT "nothing owed"
       ELSE compute a 2% service charge of the unpaid balance
               PRINT new amount due
       END-IF
END-IF
END
```

4. Write the BASIC code using the IF THEN ELSE for the following flowcharts. Eliminate redundancy, if any.

a.

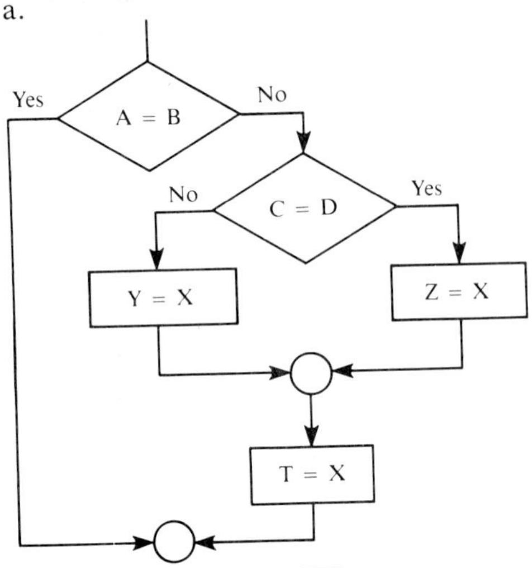

b.

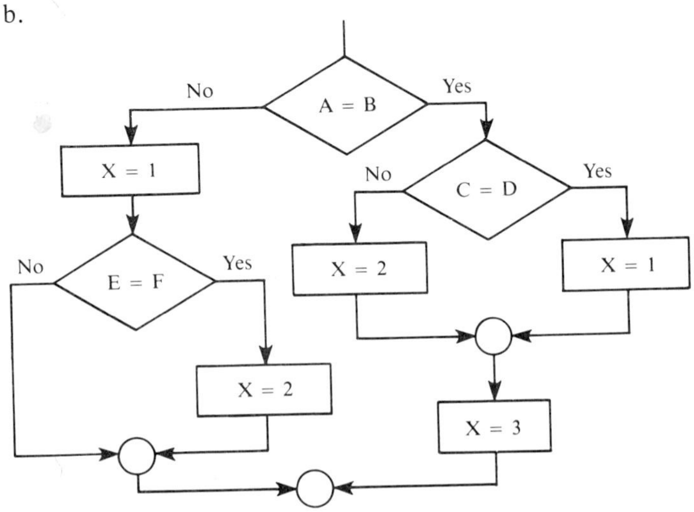

5. What will be the result of each of the following IF statements, for each of the two given cases?

Case 1: A = 3 B = −2 C = 2
Case 2: A = −4 B = −4 C = 1

a.
```
10 IF B * B <= 4 * A * C THEN 40
15 R = 1
.
.
40 R = 2
```

b.
```
10 IF A > B THEN PRINT A
15 STOP
```

c.
```
10 IF A <= 0 THEN A = -A
15 PRINT A
```

d.
```
10 IF B >= C - 4 THEN STOP
15 C = 0
20 PRINT C
```

e.
```
10 IF A ^ 1/2 <> C * 3 THEN PRINT C
15 PRINT A
```

6. Identify errors in the following flowcharts.

a.

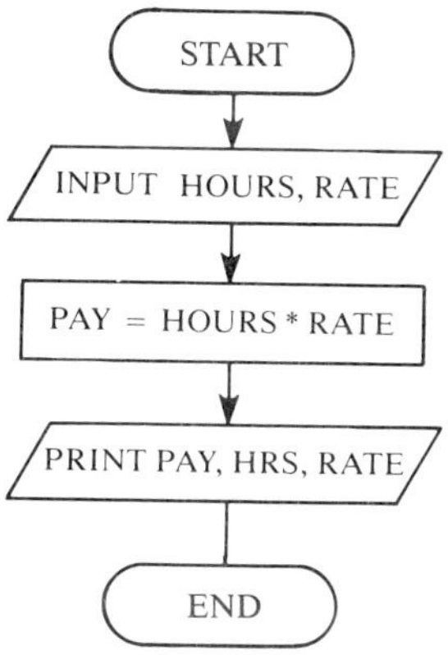

b.

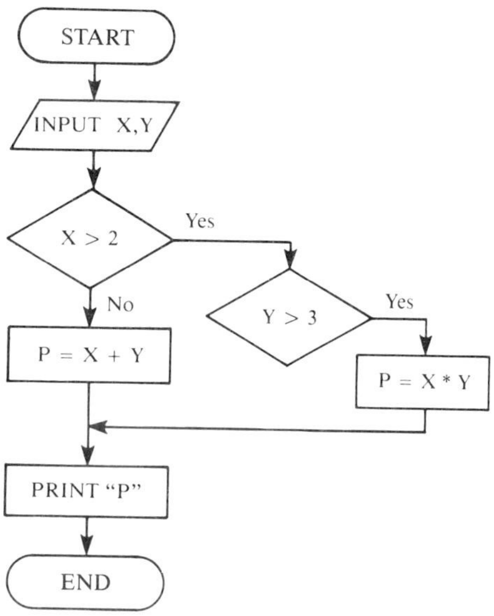

c.

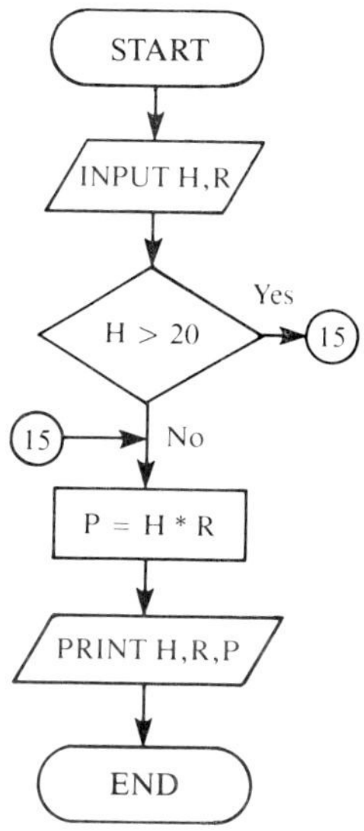

7. Write the pseudo code for the following flowchart segment.

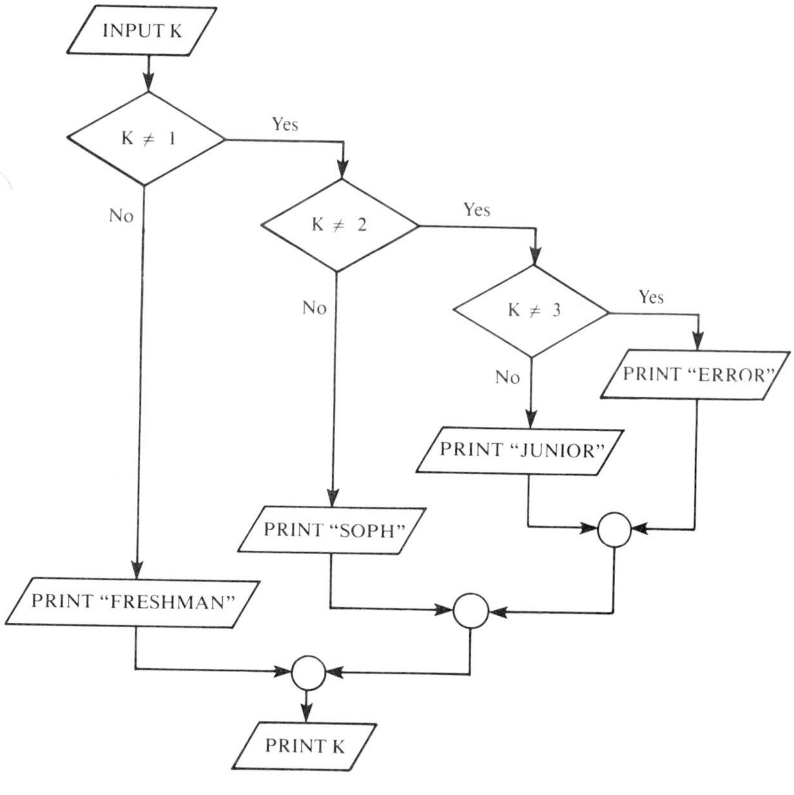

8. Write the BASIC code for the following flowcharts.

a.

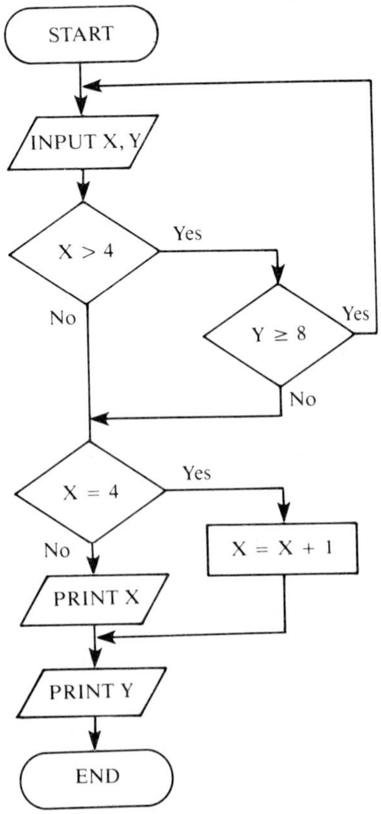

b.

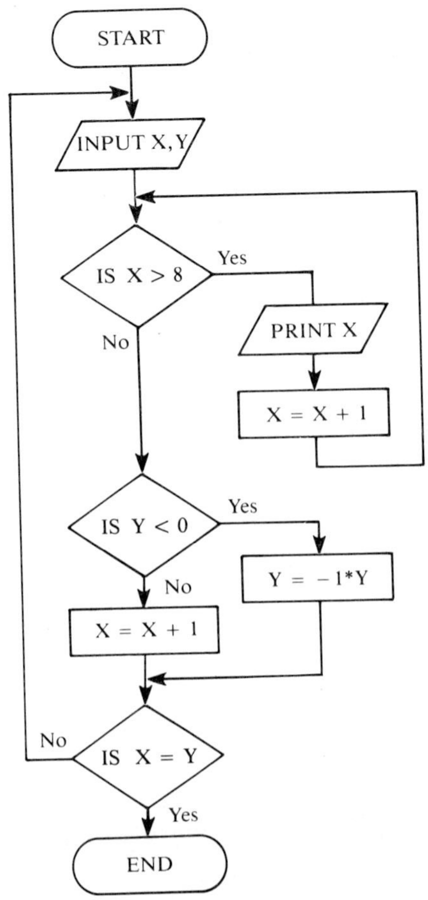

9. Write a program to input a number of feet and a numeric code (1 = centimeters, 2 = inches, 3 = yards) and convert the number of feet into the units specified by the numeric code (1 foot = 30.48 cms.).

10. Write flowcharts and BASIC statements for each of the following:
   a. If B is larger than or equal to 60, increase C by 1, then go to statement 1; otherwise go directly to statement 1.
   b. If X is larger than M, assign this value to M; otherwise continue.
   c. If H is greater than 40, compute the wage as 1.5 * H * R;
      if H is equal to 40, compute wages as 1.02 * H * R;
      if H is less than 40, compute wage as H * R.
   d. If X is greater than 0 but less than 3 * A, go to 7.
   e. If both A and B lie between 1 and 8 inclusive, go to 8; otherwise go to 4.
   f. If X exceeds 4 while Y is less than 5, or if X is less than 5 while Y is greater than 4, go to 100; otherwise stop.

11. Input a number of inches and convert it to a number of yards, feet, and inches. For example, 140 inches = 3 yards, 2 feet, and 8 inches. (Hint: Use the INT function described in project 3, section 3-9-3.)

12. Assume code is a numeric code representing a student classification (1 = Freshman, 2 = Sophomore, 3 = Junior, Other = Error). Will the following pseudo code print the English word corresponding to the numeric code?

```
IF code = 1
THEN write word Freshman
END-IF
IF code = 2
THEN write word Sophomore
END-IF
IF code = 3
THEN write word Junior
ELSE write error
END-IF
```

4-8-2 Exercises

1. Final grades in a course are determined by adding scores obtained on three tests T1, T2, and T3. Students get a PASS grade if the sum of the three scores is above 186 and a FAIL otherwise. Write a program to enter three scores and determine the grade. Print the input scores, the average, and the final grade.

2. A salesperson receives a commission of 10% on all sales if he/she has sold at least $10,000 worth of merchandise in a pay period, but only 8.5% if his/her sales are below $10,000. Write a program to input an amount of sales, compute the commission, and print the commission earned.

3. Change the program of Figure 4–11 (finding the largest three numbers) to print a message if any two numbers (but not three numbers) are equal.

4. An income tax agent is checking a file of wage earners in the income bracket $20,000 to $30,000. Each record contains the federal tax paid and gross earnings. If taxes paid are below 27.5% of gross earnings, compute the amount due and print a stern message to the wage earner specifying the amount due. (Assume that taxes are 27.5% of gross earnings in this tax bracket.) If the amount due is over $5,000, add a penalty charge of 1.5% of the amount due. Reject entries with incomes outside the range $20,000–$30,000. Produce a self-explanatory report.

5. The FMT Corporation provides home mortgages up to $70,000. The down payment schedule is as follows:

   3% of the first $30,000
   10% of the next $22,000
   20% of the remainder

   Enter a mortgage amount and print the down payment required. Reject any application for an amount over $70,000.

6. Input a student name and three test scores. The student's average is based on his/her two best scores. Write the code to print the student's name and average on one line and the three test scores on another line as follow:

   ```
   NAME: EDSEL JOHN AVERAGE = 88.5
   TESTS   62   100   77
   ```

   Process at lest three records to test for all possibilities.

7. Enter an amount in cents between 0 and 100. Write a program to break down the amount read into the least number of quarters, nickels, and pennies possible. For example, 76 cents = 3 quarters and 1 penny.

8. The metric system is upon us! Some simple approximation rules for metric conversions are:

   Fahrenheit to centigrade: Take half and subtract 15.
   (86°F.: 86/2 = 43 − 15 = 28°C.)

   Inches to centimeters: Double, then add half.
   (40 inches: 40 * 2 + 20 = 100 cms.)

   Miles to kilometers: Add 60 percent
   (100 miles: 100 + 60% of 100 = 160 kms.)

   Pounds to kilograms: Take half and then subtract 10%
   (60 lbs.: 60/2 = 30 − 10% of 30 = 27 kgs.)

   a. Write a program to enter a Fahrenheit temperature, a number of inches, a number of miles, or a number of pounds and convert to corresponding metric measures. Identify all results with appropriate headers.
   b. Write a program to convert metric measurements to Fahrenheit, inches, etc.

9. The Gull Power Electric Company charges supermarkets and small businesses for electricity according to the following scale:

Kilowatt Consumption	*Cost*
0 - 300	$5
301 - 1000	$5 + 6.113 cents for each kwh over 300 (June thru Oct.) $5 + 5.545 cents for each kwh over 300 (other months)
over 1000	Previous rate up to 1000 kwh and 98% of either 5.545 or 6.113 cents for each kwh over 1000, depending on season

Write a program to accept a date (month, day, and year), an account number, a current meter reading, and a previous meter reading and produce invoices similar to the one shown. Run program at least three different times to test various data combinations.

```
RUN
DATE? Ø4,25,83
METER READINGS? 2335,1998
ACCOUNT? SAE558

--------------------------------------------------------------
ACCOUNT NUMBER                METER NUMBER        DATE
12300                         SAE558              Ø4/25/83

  METER READING               KW HOURS            AMOUNT
PRESENT      PREVIOUS           USED            WINTER RATE
2335         1998               337               $7.Ø5
--------------------------------------------------------------
```

#10

10. Write a program to accept a grade between 0 and 100 and print out the appropriate letter grade according to the following table:

Grades	*Letter Grade*
0–49	F
50–59	D
60–79	C
80–89	B
90–100	A

11. Consider the polynomial $P(x) = x^2 - 1.596x + .266$, which has a root between 1.3 and 1.4. Find by trial and error an approximation r to that root such that $|P(r)| < .001$. (Recall that a root s of $P(x)$ is such that $P(s) = 0$.)

12. Write a program to compute and print the absolute value of x; x is entered via an INPUT statement. Recall that $|x| = x$ if $x >= 0$ and $x = -x$ if $x < 0$.

13. Input three values and determine whether they represent the three sides of a right triangle.

14. Write a program to compute the area of a triangle given three sides a, b, and c using the formula:

$$\text{where } s = \frac{a + b + c}{2} \qquad \text{area} = \sqrt{s(s-a)(s-b)(s-c)}$$

(*Caution*: Not all possible values of a, b, and c represent a triangle. How could your program detect such values?)

15. In baseball, a batting average is computed by dividing the total number of hits by the total number of times at bat. The slugging average is computed by dividing the total number of bases by the total number of times at bat. For this computation, a single is counted as one base, a double as two bases, etc. Write a program that will accept as input the number of singles, doubles, triples, and home runs and the total number of times at bat for a player. Compute and print the batting average and the slugging average. Use the following test data:

Player	*Singles*	*Doubles*	*Triples*	*Home Runs*	*At Bat*
1	5	3	1	2	70
2	3	0	2	1	15
3	10	5	3	0	30

The expected output is:

```
PLAYER   BATTING AVERAGE   SLUGGING AVERAGE
  1           .157               .314
  2           .400               .867
  3           .600               .967
```

16. The present value of an investment P invested at interest rate R for T years with interest compounded N times a year is given by the formula:

$$A = P(1 + \frac{R}{N})^{T*N}$$

a. Enter P, R, and T and determine the difference between compounding once a year and 365 times a year.
b. Enter a principal and an interest rate and, by trial and error, determine the number of years it will take before the original principal is doubled.

17. Write a program to compute the total number of coins and the value of the coins when the number of half dollars, quarters, dimes, nickels, and pennies is input to the program. Your program should have appropriate prompts to tell the user what data to enter.

18. Salaries at the XYZ Corporation are based on job classification, years of service, education, and merit rating. The base pay for all employees is the same; percentage of the base pay is added according to the following schedule:

Job Classification	*Percentage of Base Pay*	*Education*	*Percentage of Base Pay*
1	0	1 (high school)	0
2	5	2 (junior college)	10
3	15	3 (college)	25
4	25	4 (graduate degree)	50
5	50	5 (special training)	15

Merit Rating	*Percentage of Base Pay*	*Years of Service*	*Percentage of Base Pay*
0 (poor)	0	0–10 years	5
1 (good)	10	each additional year	4
2 (excellent)	25		

Write a program to accept numerical codes for each of the four variables and calculate the employee's salary as a percentage of a base pay.

19. Write a program to make daily weather reports. Input nine integer values giving the following information: current month, day, and year; high temperature for the day, low temperature for the day; year in which the record high for this day was set, record high temperature; year of record low for this day, record low temperature. After entering an input record, print a message of one of the following three types, depending on the data:

a.
```
10/23/84    HIGH TODAY    52
            LOW TODAY     23
```

b.
```
10/24/84    HIGH TODAY    71 *
            LOW TODAY     38

* (BEATS RECORD OF 70 SET IN 1906)
```

c.
```
10/25/84    HIGH TODAY    73 *
            LOW TODAY    -10 **

 * (BEATS RECORD OF 68 SET IN 1938)
** (BEATS RECORD OF -8 SET IN 1918)
```

Input at least three records so that the three output reports are produced.

20. Write the BASIC code to simulate a conversation between a physician and yourself. The physician should introduce himself/herself to you and ask your name, age, and what problems you have had lately. You should respond to those questions and possibly also ask him/her some questions.

21. Systems of equations can be solved by iterative techniques. For example, the system

$$\begin{cases} 2x + y = 3 \\ x - 3y = 2 \end{cases}$$

can be solved by solving for x in terms of y in the first equation, and for y in terms of x in the second equation, to obtain:

$$\begin{cases} x = (3 - y)/2 \\ y = (x - 2)/3 \end{cases}$$

Starting with an initial approximate solution $x = y = 0$, we refine this approximation by computing a new x and y as follows:

$$\begin{cases} x = (3 - y)/2 = (3 - 0)/2 \quad = 1.5 \\ y = (x - 2)/3 = (1.5 - 2)/3 = -.1666 \end{cases}$$

This procedure is repeated by computing new values for x and y in terms of the values x and y just computed until the following sets of equations are satisfied.

$$\begin{cases} 2x + y \simeq 3 \\ x - 3y \simeq 2 \end{cases} \text{ or } \begin{cases} 2x + y - 3 \simeq 0 \\ x - 3y - 2 \simeq 0 \end{cases} \text{ or } \begin{cases} |2x + y - 3| < \epsilon \\ |x - 3y - 2| < \epsilon \end{cases}$$

where ϵ is a prescribed degree of accuracy ($\epsilon = 0.01, 0.0001$, etc.)

Write a program to solve the following system of equations using this iterative technique with $\epsilon = .01$

$$\begin{cases} 2.56x - .034y = -.56 \\ 3.14x + 1.32y = 50.76 \end{cases}$$

22. Write a program to solve the following system of three equations in three unknowns using the approach in exercise 21. Initially set $x = y = z = 0$, and set $\epsilon = 0.1$

$$\begin{aligned} 3.1x - \quad y + \quad 2z &= -.4 \\ x - 10y - 1.3z &= 10 \\ -2.1x - \quad 3y + \quad 10z &= -103.2 \end{aligned}$$

23. The square root of a number A can be computed by successive approximations using the iterative formula $x_{n+1} = \frac{1}{2}(x_n + \frac{A}{X_n})$. This formula can be expressed in BASIC as $X = .5*(X + A/X)$. Starting with an initial approximation $X = 1$, a new approximation X is computed using the above formula. This new approximation, in turn, can be substituted in the iterative formula to compute a newer approximation X. This process can be continued until the square of the new approximation x is close to A within a prescribed degree of accuracy ϵ (where $\epsilon =$ 0.1,0.01,0.001, etc., depending on the accuracy needed); that is,

$$|X^2 - A| < \epsilon.$$

Write a program to read A and ϵ and compute $\sqrt{A}$. Write an error message if $A < 0$. For example, to compute the square root of 24 we start as follows:

$$x_1 = \frac{1}{2}\left(x_0 + \frac{24}{x_0}\right) = \frac{1}{2}\left(1 + \frac{24}{1}\right) = 12.5$$

$$x_2 = \left(\frac{1}{2} x_1 + \frac{24}{x_1}\right) = \frac{1}{2}\left(12.5 + \frac{24}{12.5}\right) = 7.21$$

$$x_3 = \left(\frac{1}{2} x_2 + \frac{24}{x_2}\right) = \ldots$$

4-8-3 Answers to Test Yourself

1. a.
```
10 IF S < 3 THEN 100
20 IF S > 3 THEN 300
30
.
.
```

b.
```
10 IF X = Z - 4 THEN 150
20 IF X > Z - 4 THEN 50
30
.
.
```

c.
```
20 IF X + Y > 3 ^ .5 THEN 60
30
.
```

2. a.
```
10 IF A >= B THEN 40
20 LET C = C + 1
30 PRINT A
40 ...
```

b.
```
10 IF A >= 3 THEN 40
20 LET D = D + 1
30 LET S = S + A
35 GO TO 90
40 LET C = C + 1
45 GO TO 90
.
```

3.

```
10 INPUT D
15 INPUT R
20 IF D < R THEN 55
30 IF D = R THEN 50
35 A = 1.02 * (D - R)
40 PRINT A
45 GO TO 99
50 PRINT "NOTHING OWED"
52 GO TO 99
55 C = R - D
60 PRINT C
99 END
```

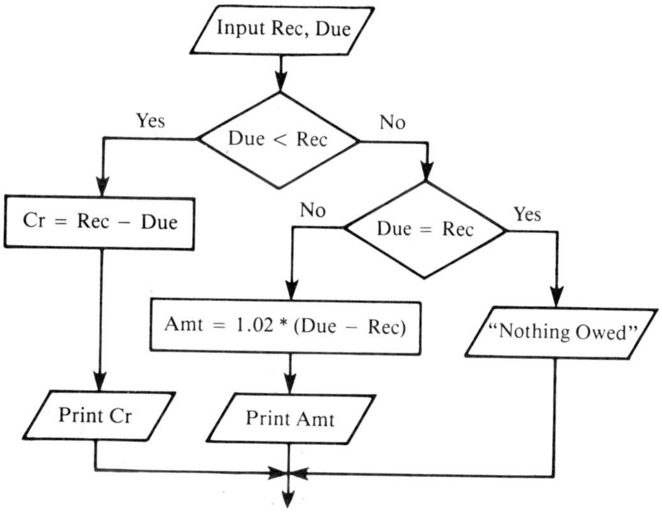

4. a.
```
10 IF A = B THEN 99 ELSE 15
15     T = X
20     IF C = D THEN 25 ELSE 35
25         Z = X
30         GO TO 99
35         Y = X
99
```

b.
```
10 IF A = B THEN 15 ELSE 25
15     X = 3
20     GO TO 99
25     X = 1
30     IF E = F THEN X = 2
99
```

5. a. Case 1: R = 2
Case 2: R = 1

b. Case 1: 3 is written
Case 2: Nothing is written

c. Case 1: 3 is written
Case 2: 4 is written

d. Case 1: STOP
Case 2: 0 is written

e. Case 1: 2 and 3 are written
Case 2: 1 and −4 are written

6. a. Since this is a flowchart, there are no rules concerning variable names, e.g., HOURS is a valid variable name. This is a valid flowchart.
b. There is no NO branch on the Y > 3 decision block. Invalid PRINT block.
c. This is a valid flowchart, although the decision block is useless.

7.
```
INPUT K
IF K ≠ 1
THEN IF K ≠ 2
          THEN IF K ≠ 3
                    THEN print error
                    ELSE print junior
                    END-IF
          ELSE  print sophomore
          END-IF
ELSE print freshman
END-IF
PRINT K
```

8. a.
```
10 INPUT X, Y
15 IF X > 4 THEN 40
20      IF X = 4 THEN 50
25      PRINT X
30      GO TO 55
40 IF Y >= 8 THEN 10
45      GO TO 20
50      X = X + 1
55      PRINT Y
99 END
```

b.
```
10 INPUT X, Y
15 IF X > 8 THEN 40
20      IF Y < 0 THEN 55
25           X = X + 1
30           IF X <> Y THEN 10
35                GO TO 99
40 PRINT X
45 X = X + 1
50 GO TO 15
55 Y = -Y
60 GO TO 30
99 END
```

9.
```
10 INPUT F, C
15 IF C = 1 THEN PRINT F * 30.48
20 IF C = 2 THEN PRINT F * 12
25 IF C = 3 THEN PRINT F/3
30 GO TO 10
```

10.

a.

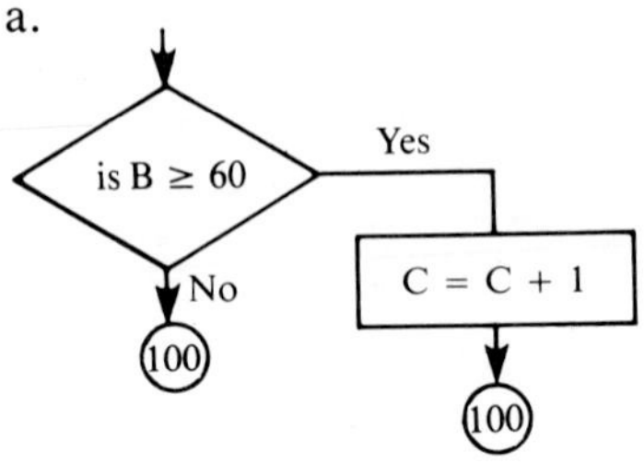


```
10 IF B < 60 THEN 100
20      C = C + 1
30      GO TO 100
```
or
```
10 IF B >= 60 THEN C=C+1
20 GO TO 100
```

b.

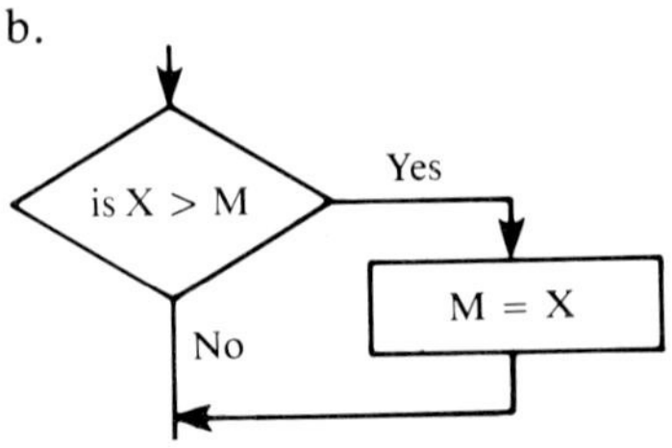


```
10 IF X < = M THEN 30
20      M = X
30      . . .
```
or
```
10 IF X > M THEN M=X
```

c.

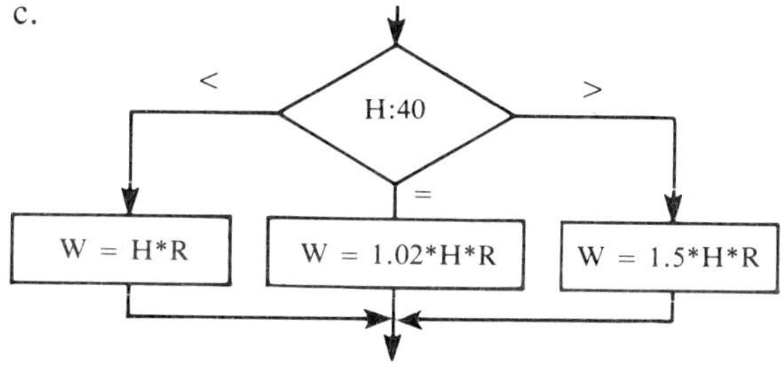


```
10 IF H < 40 THEN 50
20     IF H > 40 THEN 70
30         W = 1.02*H*R
40         GO TO 80
50 W = H*R
60 GO TO 80
70 W = 1.5*H*R
80 . . .
```

d.

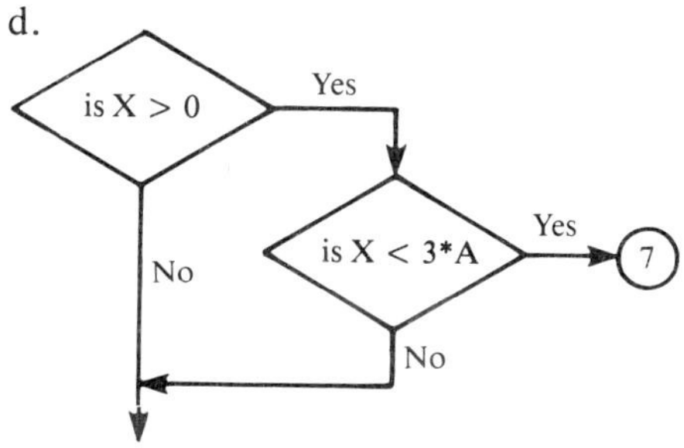


```
10 IF X > 0 THEN 30
20 GO TO 40
30 IF X < 3*A THEN 70
40 . . .
```

e.

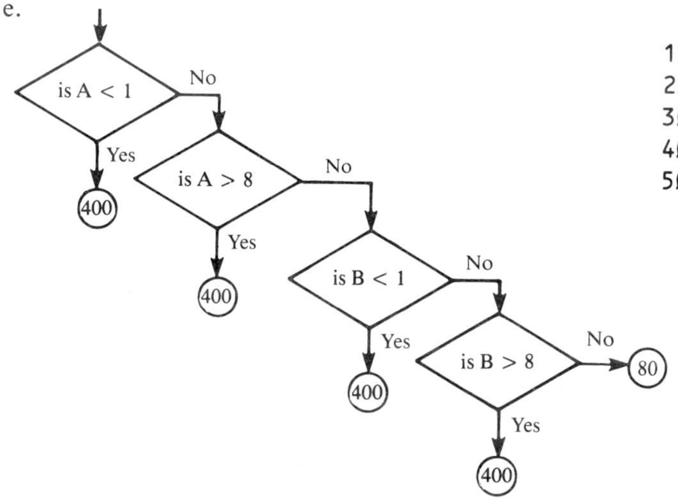


```
10 IF A < 1 THEN 400
20 IF A > 8 THEN 400
30 IF B < 1 THEN 400
40 IF B > 8 THEN 400
50 GO TO 80
```

f.

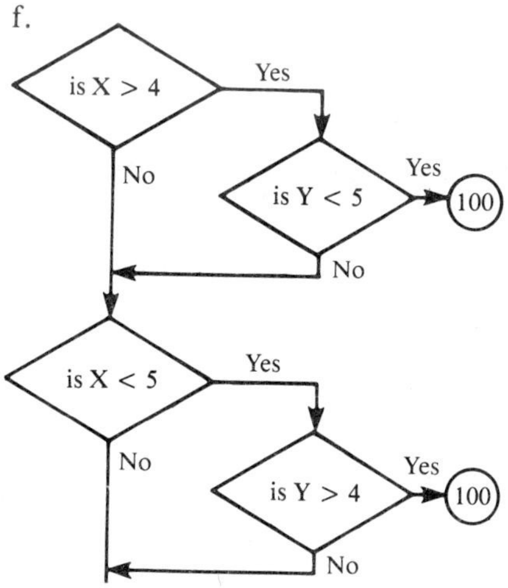


```
10 IF X > 4 THEN 40
20 IF X < 5 THEN 60
30 STOP
40 IF Y < 5 THEN 100
50 GO TO 20
60 IF Y > 4 THEN 100
70 STOP
```

11.
```
10 INPUT I
20 Y = INT(I/36)
30 R1 = I - 36 * Y
40 F = INT(R1/12)
50 N = R1 - 12 * F
60 PRINT "YARDS=" ;Y
70 PRINT "FEET=" ;F
80 PRINT "INCHES=" ;N
90 GO TO 10
```

12. No; IF code is 1 or 2, error will also be written.

5 READ/DATA, COUNTING AND PROBLEM SOLVING

5-1 Problem Example: An Opinion Poll

A poll was conducted at a college to determine students' feelings about a nuclear freeze. The code used to record the students' opinions was:

Code	*Meaning*
1	In favor of nuclear freeze
2	Opposed to nuclear freeze
3	Undecided

All responses were collected in list form as follows: 1, 1, 2, 3, 1, 1, 2, 1, 1, 2, 3, 3, ..., 2, 1, −4. A negative number was purposefully put at the end of the list to indicate the end of the data.

Let us write a program to read this list of codes and analyze the outcome of the poll in total counts. The program should produce a summary report similar to the following (codes that are neither 1, 2, or 3 are identified on the output as unrecognizable codes):

```
            POLL RESULTS

UNRECOGNIZABLE CODE 5
UNRECOGNIZABLE CODE 7

FOR NUCLEAR FREEZE 2742
AGAINST NUCLEAR FREEZE 21ØØ
UNDECIDED 35Ø
```

This problem deals with two concepts, reading and counting. Reading lists of items or values is done in BASIC through the READ statement in conjunction with the DATA statement (list of values), as explained in the next sections. Counting on the other hand is simply a programming technique where ordinary variables are used as *counters* to count the occurrence of certain events. In the above problem we need to read a code and then determine whether that code is a 1, 2, or 3. If the code read is 1, then we need to add 1 to the count of those favoring nuclear freeze; if the code is 2, we add 1 to the count of those "against," and so forth. An important issue here is how long to keep reading and counting, i.e. when do we tell the computer to stop reading? The answer is fairly simple—we use a negative number (e.g., −4) to tell the computer that we have reached the end of the list, i.e. all response codes have been read! We then tell the computer to print the final value of each of the three counts.

Counting, in this case, implies that we use a different variable to keep track of each count: i.e., we will use F for those in favor of a freeze, A for those against, and U for those who are undecided. We set these variables to 0 before reading the data. Then, every time we read a code equal to 1, we add 1 to F; likewise, when we read a code equal to 2, we increment A by 1, and so forth.

If the computer is to read a list of codes, then the list must be typed by the programmer and placed somewhere in the program. This is done with a DATA statement:

```
1Ø DATA 1, 1, 2, 3, 1, 1, ..., 2, 1, -4
```

■ **Figure 5–1** Counting: An opinion poll.

```
10 REM POLL ANALYSIS
12    PRINT TAB(12);"POLL RESULTS"
14    PRINT
16 REM INITIALIZE COUNTERS TO 0'S
18    F = 0
20    U = 0
22    A = 0
24 REM
26    READ C
28    IF C < 0 THEN 56
30    IF C = 1 THEN 50
32    IF C = 2 THEN 46
34    IF C = 3 THEN 42
36 REM CODE IS NEITHER 1,2 OR 3 HENCE ERROR
38    PRINT "UNRECOGNIZABLE CODE";C
40    GOTO 26
42    A = A + 1
44    GOTO 26
46    U = U + 1
48    GOTO 26
50    F = F + 1
52    GOTO 26
54 REM PRINT RESULTS
56    PRINT
58    PRINT "FOR NUCLEAR FREEZE";F
60    PRINT "UNDECIDED          ";U
62    PRINT "AGAINST FREEZE     ";A
64 REM
66 REM FOLLOWING IS THE LIST OF CODES
68    DATA 1,1,2,3,2,3,1,1,3,2,2,1,1,1,3
70    DATA 2,3,3,2,2,1,1,1,3,3,2,5,6,1,-4
72    END
RUN
```

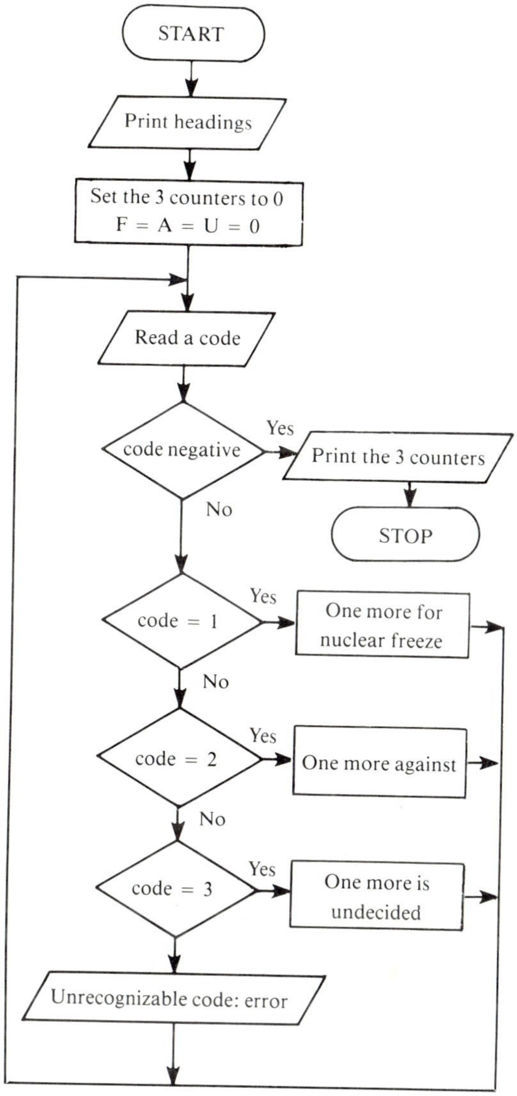


```
            POLL RESULTS

UNRECOGNIZABLE CODE 5
UNRECOGNIZABLE CODE 6

FOR NUCLEAR FREEZE 11
UNDECIDED          8
AGAINST FREEZE     8
```

DATA is a BASIC keyword. It is followed by a list of values separated by commas. These values can be read by the computer through the keyword READ. The first time the READ C instruction is carried out, the computer reads the first value in the DATA list and stores that value in memory location C. The second time READ C is executed, the second value is read into C, destroying whatever previous value was there. The negative number will be the last one read into C.

Even though many READ operations will be carried out, only one READ instruction needs to be specified in the BASIC program—that instruction is executed repeatedly. Each time the computer reads C, it tests C for 1, 2, or 3 and increments the appropriate counter. When it encounters a negative code, it prints the final values of the three counters. The entire process is shown in flowchart form and as BASIC code in Figure 5-1.

5-2 BASIC Statements

5-2-1 The DATA Statement

The INPUT statement is one way to enter information into a memory location. However, the INPUT statement can be very unwieldy in many situations. Suppose, for example, that one wanted to count the number of grades over 90 in a class of 100 students. If we used the INPUT statement to enter the grades one at time with statement INPUT G, then at execution time the computer would stop 100 times to print a question mark, and the user would need to enter 100 grades. This would be very time consuming, and the output would be very bulky and unsightly with all those question marks on the screen or the printer. A much more convenient and elegant way to read those grades is through the DATA statement, which the user can prepare ahead of time, before the program is run. The DATA statement lists all the grades (separated from one another by commas) on one or more lines, as follows:

```
10 DATA 80, 60, 40, 20, 80, 40, 90, 76, 84, 76, 99, ...
```

These grades can then be read by the computer by means of the READ instruction. READ G will read the first grade and store 80 in G; if the READ instruction is carried out again, 60 will be stored in G. By executing the READ instruction repeatedly, all the grades in the DATA list can be read and processed.

The general form of the DATA statement is:

line number DATA *list of constants*

where *list of constants* can be numeric or character constants. These constants must be separated from each other by commas. Alphanumeric and special character constants can be specified with or without quotation marks.

Example 1:	*Memory Storage*
`15 DATA 1, -1, 3.Ø21` `2Ø READ X, Y, Z`	`X = 1, Y = -1, Z = 3.Ø21`

Example 2:	

`1Ø READ N1$, N2$, N3$`
`15 DOE J, COORS L, "ARMSTRONG L,II"`
	`N1$ = DOE J`
	`N2$ = COORS L`
	`N3$ = ARMSTRONG L,II`

Example 3:	

`1Ø DATA BURNS JOHN, 48.5, "NOV.8,1968"`
`2Ø READ N$, A, D$`
	`N$ = BURNS JOHN`
	`A  = 48.5`
	`D$ = NOV.8,1968`

Notice the quotation marks around the third items in examples 2 and 3. If no quotation marks were present, N3$ would have been read as ARMSTRONG L since the comma after the L would indicate a new element.

DATA statements can be placed *anywhere* before the END statement in the BASIC program. For orderliness and readability, DATA statements are generally grouped either at the "top" or the "bottom" of the program.

The DATA statement informs the BASIC system that the numbers specified in its constant list are to be stored in memory until the user decides to process them during program execution. BASIC collects all numbers or string literals specified in all the DATA statements of the program and stores them in a memory area (a DATA block) in the order in which the DATA statements are physically encountered in the program. The values in the DATA block can be retrieved only by READ statements.

In the three following examples, notice the different DATA statement arrangements in the BASIC code. These give rise to the same memory block and same output.

Example 1:

```
1Ø DATA 3
15 DATA 5
2Ø DATA 1Ø
25 READ A, B, C
3Ø PRINT A, B, C
```

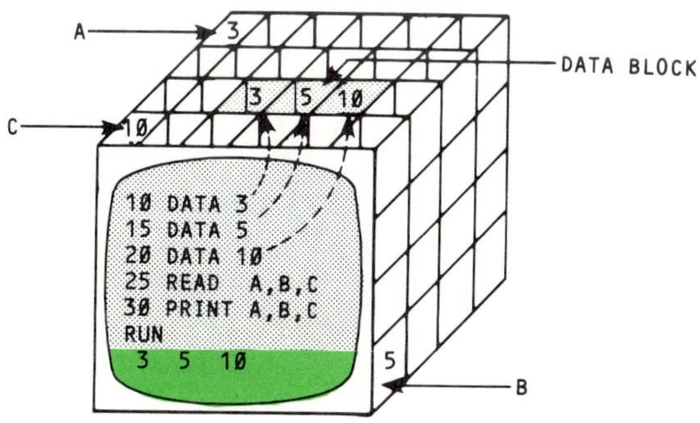

Example 2:

```
10 DATA 3, 5, 10
15 READ A, B, C
20 PRINT A, B, C
```

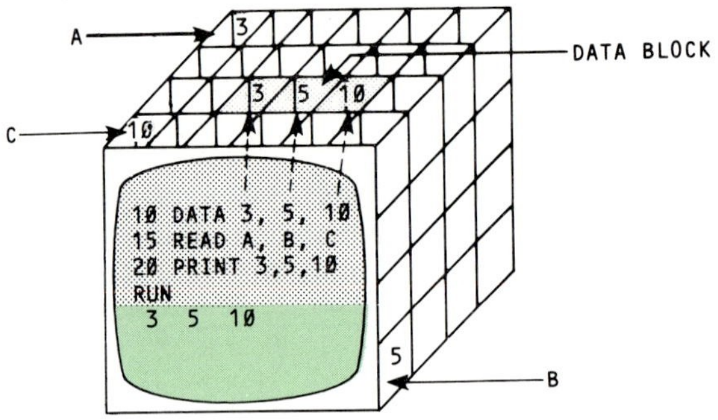

Example 3:

```
10 DATA 3
15 READ A, B, C
20 DATA 5
30 PRINT A, B, C
35 DATA 10
```

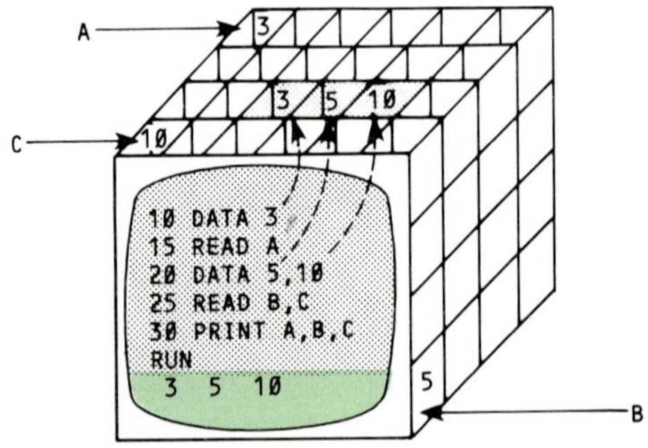

In the following example, the DATA block contains alphanumeric and numeric values. Note that in this example the DATA statement at line 20 has not been read! Note once more that even though the DATA values are stored in memory (in the DATA block), these are accessible to the user only through the READ statement.

Example 4:

```
10 DATA DOE, 4, 50
15 DATA LAD, 3, 60
20 DATA HOT, 3.5, 70
25 READ N$, R, H
30 PRINT N$, R * H
35 READ N$, R, H
40 PRINT N$, R * H
```

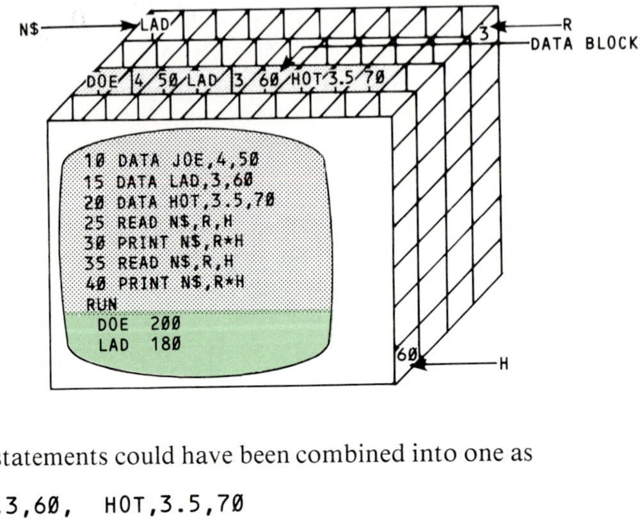

Also notice that the above DATA statements could have been combined into one as

```
10 DATA DOE,4,50,  LAD,3,60,  HOT,3.5,70
```

with the same results.

DATA statements can be continued on several lines if the entire DATA statement does not exceed 255 characters, for example:

```
DATA 36, 43, 64, 73, 48, 70, 80, 90, 100, -3.45, 76, 84.2, 40,
20, 30, 66, 48, 64, 74, 48, 64
```

If masses and masses of constants are to be listed, several DATA statements may be needed, as follows:

```
10 DATA 36, 40, 64, 48, 70, 80, 60, -1.3, 70, 80, 40, 20, 70
15 DATA 48, 66, 47, 33, 93, 77, 52, 75, 32, 96, 58, 49, 18
20 DATA 12, 23, 64, -48, 93, 111, 98, 47, 86, 88, 29, 43, 4.7
```

In that case (more than one DATA statement), each DATA statement must *not* end with a comma. Example:

```
DATA 3, 4, -7, 8, 10.5, 4,<--Invalid because of comma.
DATA 2, 1
```

However, the following statement is valid:

```
DATA 3, 4, -7, 8, 10.5, 4,<--Comma is valid because
     2, 1                   the line continues.
```

5-2-2 READ Statement

The general form of the READ statement is

> *line number* READ *list of variables*

where READ is a keyword. The list of variables consists of variables separated from one another by commas.

The READ statement causes as many values to be fetched from the DATA block as there are variables in the READ list. The assignment of values to variables is made in the order in which variables appear in the READ list. Consider the following example and note assignments of values to variables:

```
5  READ X, Y
10 DATA 1,3
15 READ Z$
20 DATA "WE", 4, 6
25 READ W
```

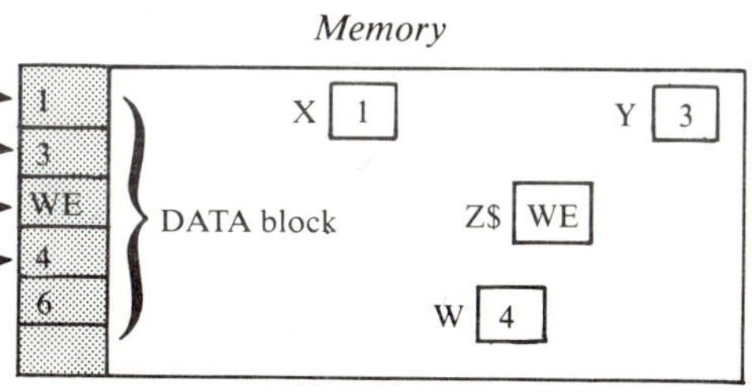

If an attempt is made to read more variables than there are values in the DATA block, an "out of data" error message will be printed, pointing to the READ statement for which not enough data was available, for example,

```
10 DATA 3, 4, 6
15 READ X, Y, Z, (W)—— no data for W
RUN
END OF DATA AT 15
```

The values 3, 4, and 6 are stored respectively in variables X, Y, and Z. Since there is no corresponding value in the DATA statement for W, the computer prints an error message.

CAUTION: Alphanumeric values in a DATA statement must be read by alphanumeric variables in the READ statement, and numeric variables in the READ statement must read numeric values in the DATA statement.

```
10 DATA DOE, 3, 4
15 READ X, Y, Z
```

This is invalid since X can only read a numeric value. X should be X$.

However the following is valid:

```
10 READ X$
15 DATA -3
```

X$ will contain the characters minus and 3, not to be confused with the signed number negative 3!

5-2-3 Do It Now

1. Discuss the following coding segments in terms of values read, DATA blocks, and errors. Indicate output.

a.
```
10 DATA 3,4
15 INPUT X
20 PRINT X ^ 2
```

b.
```
10 DATA 2
15 DATA 3
20 INPUT Y
25 READ X, X
30 PRINT Y ^ X
```

c.
```
10 READ X$, B
15 DATA 3.1, DOE
20 PRINT B, X$
```

d.
```
10 READ N$
15 DATA 3.1, -4
20 READ C
25 PRINT N$, C
```

e.
```
10 DATA 1, 2, 3
15 READ X
20 PRINT X
25 GO TO 10
```

f.
```
10 DATA "JOE, M",N. 10 ST., 4
15 READ N$, A$, K
20 PRINT N$, A$, K
```

g.
```
10 DATA DOE M, NOV 8, 1984
15 READ A$,B$
20 PRINT A$, B$
```

h.
```
10 DATA "MIKE", 3.5, 50
15 PRINT "NAME"; N$
20 PRINT "RATE"; R
25 PRINT "HOURS"; H
```

i.
```
10 DATA 3.1
15 DATA DOE
20 READ X, Y
25 PRINT X, Y
```

j.
```
10 DATA 3, 43, 23,,6, 8
15 READ A, B, C, D, E
20 PRINT A, B, C, D, E
```

k.
```
10 DATA 3, 2, -1, 4, 2
15 READ X
20 IF X > 0 THEN 15
25 PRINT X
30 END
```

l.
```
10 READ X, Y, Z
15 DATA 10, 15
20 DATA 21, 33, 41
25 READ X
```

Answers

a. If X is 2, the value 4 is printed; the DATA list is not used!

b. If Y is 4 (Y is typed in response to the INPUT statement), then the value 64 is printed; the last value for X is 3.

c. Invalid READ operation. Variable B expects a numeric value.

d. The values 3.1 and − 4 are printed. Note that 3.1 is an alphanumeric string of 3 characters: the 3, the period, and the 1.
e. The values 1, 2, and 3 will be printed. An out-of-data error message will then be printed, since the computer is asked to continue reading values when there are no more in the DATA statement.
f. The values JOE, M and N. 10 ST. and 4 are printed.
g. The values DOE M, and NOV 8 are printed.
h. The values for N$, R and H have not been defined, hence the output is unpredictable.
i. READ error for Y; Y expects a numeric value.
j. The values 3, 43, 23, 0 and 6 are printed. Note the two consecutive commas in the DATA statement causing a zero value to be read for D.
k. The value − 1 is printed; the code looks for the first negative value.
l. X = 33, Y = 15, and Z = 21, but there is no printed output.

5-3 Counting

Counting is an essential technique in programming. Counting can be used to control the reading of a specified number of data items from a DATA list, to repeat a procedure a certain number of times, to count the occurrence of specific events, or to generate sequences of numbers for computational uses. The computer cannot count by itself. The programmer must tell it how! Counting techniques are best described by illustration as in the following examples.

5-3-1 Counting for Loop Control

Suppose we have a DATA statement consisting of five grades and we want to write a program to print them. Any of the following three methods could be used.

1.

```
10 DATA 10,86,44,65,85
15 READ G  }
20 PRINT G }  one time
25 READ G  }
30 PRINT G }  two times
.
.
.
60 READ G  }
65 PRINT G }  five times
```

2.

```
10 DATA 10,86,44,65,85
15 READ A, B, C, D, E
20 PRINT A, B, C, D, E
```

3.

```
10 DATA 10,86,44,65,85
15 READ G
20 PRINT G
30 GO TO 10
```

Method 1 is very long! Method 2 would be all right, but what would happen if we had 300 grades? Method 3 looks fine, but an error message would be printed when the READ statement runs out of data!

What we need to do is write something like method 3 and tell the computer to stop when it has read and printed the fifth grade. One way to do that is to count the number of times that we read and print a grade , i.e., we set up a counter so that each time we read a grade the computer adds 1 to the previous count. As long as this counter is less than five, we go back and read another grade. We check the count to make sure there are still some grades left in the DATA statement so that the program does not stop. Initially we set the counter to 0 before the first grade is read.

A counter in BASIC is simply a variable that assumes numeric values. The counting process is illustrated in the following flowchart:

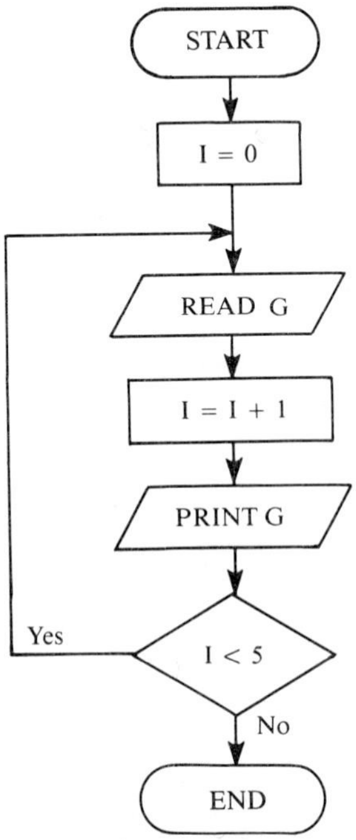

I is the counter to count the grades. Initially it is set to 0.

A grade is read.

The counter I is incremented by 1; the first time through the loop I = 0 + 1 = 1, meaning that one grade has been read so far. The second time through, I = I + 1 = 1 + 1 = 2, reflecting the fact that a second grade has been read.
The grade read is also printed.

As long as I is less than five, fewer than five grades have been read, so we can go back and safely read another grade from the DATA statement.

Note that the DATA statement is not shown in the flowchart. We never depict the DATA statements in flowcharts or pseudo code; we assume that when an INPUT or READ instruction is executed, the user will enter a response on the terminal or a DATA statement(s) will be present in the BASIC code.

The statement I = I + 1 is of such paramount importance that we reemphasize its meaning:

I = I + 1 means add 1 to I and call this the new value *I* (or the new value for I is equal to its old value plus 1).

This of course, destroys the value that was previously stored in I.

The above flowchart can be translated into BASIC as follows:

```
05 DATA 50, 60, 70, 80, 90
10 I = 0
15 READ G
20 I = I + 1
25 PRINT G
30 IF I < 5 THEN 15
35 END
```

Tabulation Process

G	I
	0
50	1
60	2
70	3
80	4
90	5

Altogether five grades are read and printed.

Statements 15 through 30 constitute a loop—these statements are executed repeatedly until I is no longer less than 5. To visualize the loop process, we can trace through the flowchart and record the values taken on by *I* and *G* for each cycle through the loop. A table of values shown above can then be constructed. After the fifth grade is read, I is 5. The fifth grade is then printed and the program stops, since 5 is not less than 5 at line 30.

5-3-2 Do It Now

1. How many grades will be read by each of the following flowcharts? Assume that the READ statements refer to 10 DATA 50, 60, 70, 80, 90.

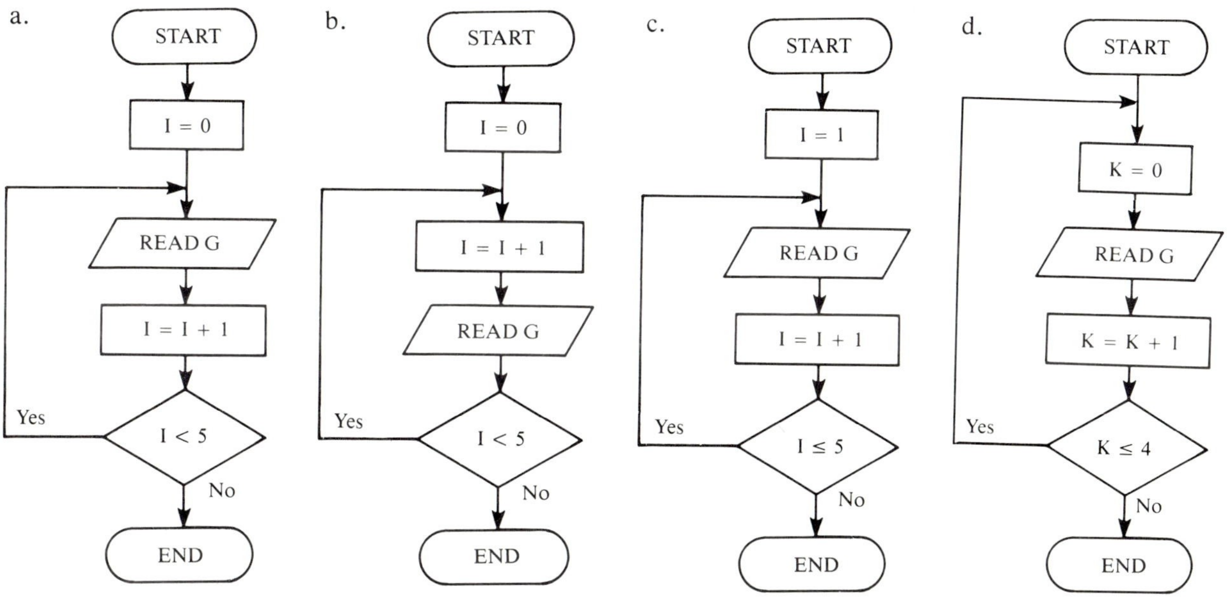

2. a. Explain in accurate English prose what the following program does:

```
10 DATA 98, 60, 89, 80, 90
15 K = 0
20 READ G
25 K = K + 1
30 IF G < 90 THEN 40
35 PRINT G
40 IF K < 5 THEN 20
50 END
```

b. Explain what would happen if line 40 were changed to IF K < 5 THEN 25.

c. Explain what the following does:

```
10 DATA 50, 60, 70, 80, 90, 66, 48
15 J = 5
20 READ X
25 PRINT X
27 J = J - 1
30 IF J > 0 THEN 20
35 END
```

3. The Personpower Company must pay ten workers for a special project. Each of the ten employee records (DATA statements) contains the hours worked, the rate of pay, and the amount to be withheld. Write a program to prepare a payroll report showing all input data and the amount of each paycheck. There is no overtime pay.

Answers

1. a. The computer will read five grades and stop.
   b. The computer will read five grades and stop. Notice that counting takes place before reading. The end result is the same as reading and then counting. Just as in real life, it you know you are going to do something, you can do it and then count it or you can count it and then do it!
   c. Five grades will be read, since the program starts with I = 1 and tests for the condition I less than or equal to 5.
   d. An error message will be printed when the READ instruction tries to read the sixth grade, since there is no sixth grade. This is an example of an infinite loop. On each cycle through the loop the value of K is reset to 0 at the top of the flowchart. The only values taken on by K are 0 and 1; hence the condition $K \leq 4$ is always satisfied and the program, runs out of data.

2. a. The program will print any grade equal to or greater than 90. In this case, the values 98 and 90 will be printed.
   b. The grade 98 will be printed five times, then program will stop.
   c. This program will print the first five grades read. The counter is initially set to five and decreased by one each time the READ statement is executed.

3.

```
Ø5 DATA 4Ø, 5, 25  )
1Ø DATA 6Ø, 3, 2Ø  |
.                  } 10 DATA statements
.                  |
.                  )
4Ø I = Ø
45 READ H, R, W
5Ø P = H * R - W
6Ø PRINT H, R, W, P
65 I = I + 1
7Ø IF I < 1Ø THEN 45
8Ø END
```

5-3-3 Counting for Number Generation

Another important application of counting is number generation. To generate the even positive integers 2, 4, 6, 8 ..., the statement I = I + 2 is repeatedly processed with I set initially to 0. To generate the odd positive numbers, the same formula could be used with I set initially to 1.

Example: Let us write a program to print out the N's multiplication table where N is accepted from input. If N = 8 then we print the 8's multiplication table:

```
WHICH TABLE
? 8
8 × 1 = 8
8 × 2 = 16
.
.
.
8 × 12 = 96
```

We need to print 12 lines for the multiplication table. Each line actually consists of five items: the number 8, the multiplication symbol ×, the number I (which will vary from 1 to 12), the equal sign, and the product I * 8. The counter I is used to print the numbers 1 through 12 and also as a test variable to tell the computer when to stop printing (when I = 12).

The pseudo and BASIC codes to print the multiplication tables are:

Pseudo Code	*BASIC Code*
	10 REM MULTIPLICATION TABLES
	15 PRINT "WHICH TABLE"
INPUT a value for N	20 INPUT N
	25 REM I IS THE COUNTER
Set counter I to 0	30 I = 0
→ Add 1 to counter	35 I = I + 1
Compute product = N * counter	40 P = N * I
PRINT N, counter and product	50 PRINT N; "X"; I; "="; P
	55 REM 12 LINES WRITTEN?
IF counter < 12 reexecute loop	60 IF I < 12 THEN 35
END	65 END

```
N   I   P = N * I
↓   ↓   ↓
8 × 1 = 8
8 × 2 = 16
.
.
.
8 × 11 = 88
8 × 12 = 96
```

5-3-4 Do It Now

1. What numbers will be printed by the following flowcharts?

a.

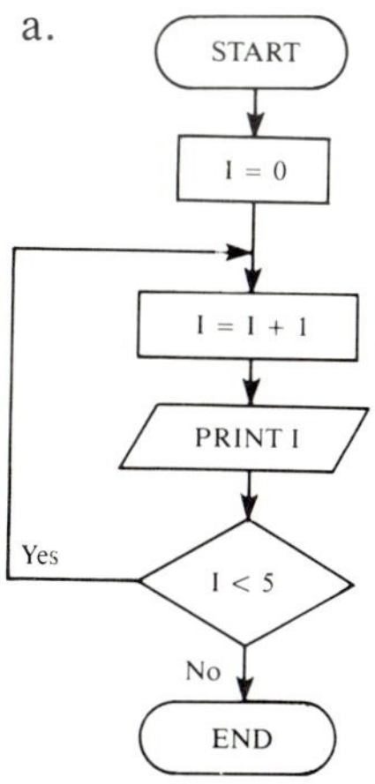

b.

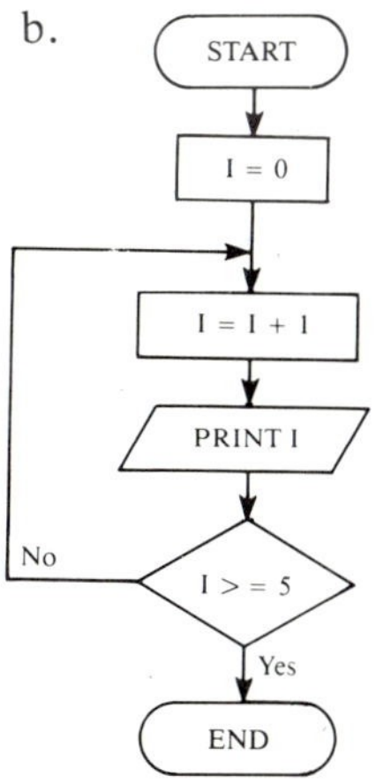

c.

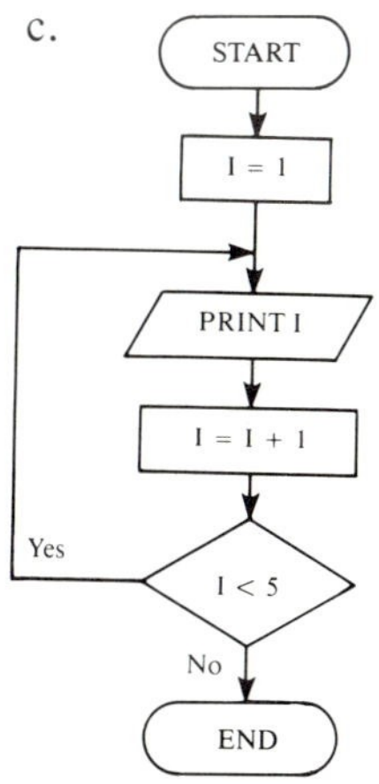

d.

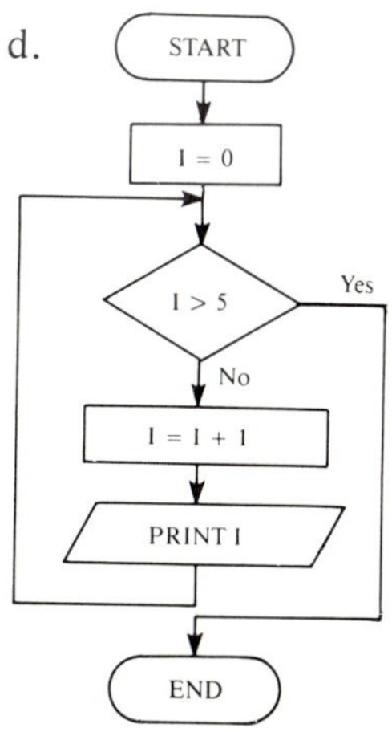

2. Write the code to print the following sequences of numbers.

   a. 1, 3, 5, 7, ..., 227
   b. 20, 19, 18, ..., 2, 1
   c. 2, 4, 8, 16, 32, ..., 512
   d. − 1, 1, − 1, 1, ... (20 terms)

Answers

1. Flowcharts a and b will print the numbers 1 through 5, flowchart c will print 1 through 4, and flowchart d will print 1 through 6.

2. a.
```
10 I = 1
15 PRINT I;
20 I = I + 2
25 IF I <= 227 THEN 15
30 END
```

b.
```
10 I = 21
15 I = I - 1
20 PRINT I;
25 IF I > 1 THEN 15
30 END
```

c.
```
10 N = 2
15 PRINT N
20 N = 2 * N
30 IF I <= 512 THEN 15
35 END
```

d.
```
10 I = 1
15 PRINT (-1) ^ I
20 I = I + 1
25 IF I <= 20 THEN 15
30 END
```

5-3-5 Counting for Certain Events and for Loop Control

Suppose that a DATA statement consists of eight grades. Let us write a program to read these eight grades and count and print those scores above 90.

Solution: To solve this problem, we need two counters: one counter I to count all of the grades so that we can tell the computer when to stop reading and another counter C to count the grades over 90. Every time a grade is read it will be tested against 90; if it exceeds 90, then C will be incremented by 1. The counter C will be printed *only* when all the grades have been processed, not every time such a grade is found. The solution process can be visualized in Figure 5–2.

5-4 DATA Files and End-of-File Checking

DATA statements consist of data items, i.e., numeric or alphanumeric items separated from one another by a comma. One or more data items may form what we call a record. A *record* is a collection of related items that together describe a particular entity, for example, an employee record might consist of a name, a sex code, an age, and an address item. A student record could consist of a name and three test scores. A *file*

Figure 5–2 Counting grades over 90.

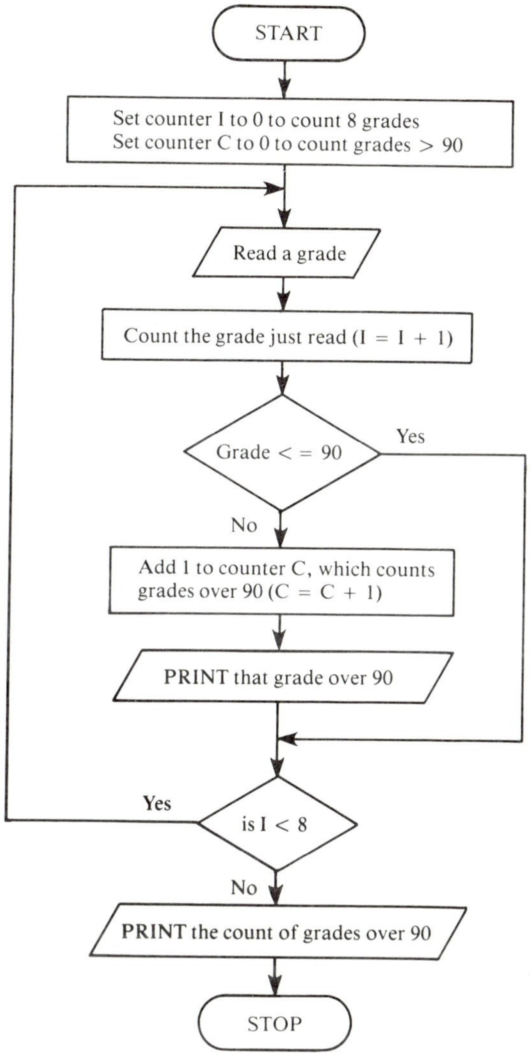


```
10 REM I COUNTS ALL SCORES
12 REM G IS THE GRADE READ
15 REM C COUNTS GRADES > 90
20      I = 0
25      C = 0
30      READ G
35      I = I + 1
40      IF G <= 90 THEN 55
45      C = C + 1
50      PRINT G
55      IF I < 8 THEN 30
60      PRINT "NO. GRADES > 90 =";C
70 DATA 10,20,98,40,90,95,60,91
80 END
```

Tabulation

G	I	C
	0	0
10	1	
20	2	
98	3	1
40	4	
90	5	
95	6	2
60	7	
91	8	3

Output

```
98
95
91
NO. GRADES > 90 = 3
```

is a collection of related records; for example, the employee records of a particular company constitute the company's personnel file. Some examples of data items, records, and files follow.

Example 1: A DATA file consisting of scores obtained by different students, where each student record consists of only one score:

```
10 DATA 84, 66, 74, 88, 76, 98, 48
```

Score DATA file consisting of 7 records (84: score data item (student record); 98: score data item (student record))

Example 2: DATA file consisting of 4 records, where each record consists of 3 data items:

```
      Name      Age     Social Security
      item      item    item
        ↓        ↓        ↓
10 DATA TODD L, 21, 222112222 )
15 DATA DOE J,  18, 111223333 |  DATA file consisting
20 DATA SIMS K, 24, 111441111 |  of 4 records
25 DATA LARK S, 20, 212335555 )
        \_____________________/
        1 record consisting of 3 items
```

Note that the above DATA file could be rewritten as:

```
10 DATA TODD L, 21, 222112222, DOE J, 18, 111223333,...
        \___________________/  \____________________/  \__________/
              record #1              record #2          record #3
```

When one reads a DATA file, it is important not to attempt to read more records than are present in the file, since trying to read a data item from an exhausted DATA list results in an error message. Thus, some methods to avoid reading records indefinitely are necessary. We have discussed a method based on counting that can be used when the number of records is known, but in most cases it is impractical to count the number of records a file contains before processing them. A commonly used technique to take care of such a situation is the last-record check, which is also called the *trip record* method.

5-4-1 The Trip Record Method

Assume the computer is to read an input file consisting of an unknown number of records, where each record consists of just one grade. How do we tell the computer when to stop reading the file, i.e., how does the computer know it has read the last record so that it does not try to read another record? If the computer had eyes, we could color the last grade red and then instruct the computer to stop reading after the red grade. A conceptually similar but more realistic end-of-file technique is to type an "unusual" grade (for example a negative grade) as the last data record in the DATA list. Every time the computer reads a grade, we ask it if the grade just read is negative—if it is, the end of file has been reached!

Of course, precautions must be taken so as not to process the negative grade. We must not, for example, include it in an average of grades or count it as part of the count of all grades, since it is not a real grade. If, on the other hand, the grade read is not negative, it is a real grade and we can process it (add it, print it, and so forth). The unusual grade or end-of-file item is often referred to as a *trip* or *trigger* code, since the computer is meant to trip on such a code, and since it should trigger a very special response on the part of the computer. In the example of reading grades, other trip codes could have been chosen, such as a grade above 100, if it were known that the grades ranged from 0 to 100.

The important point to keep in mind when selecting a trip code is to choose a data item that is not part of the original data file, one that cannot possibly occur in the original DATA list. In the above example, it would be silly to use 0 or 67 as trip codes (even if these numbers do not actually appear in the user's particular DATA list) since such values could conceivably show up in the input file as valid grades. Hence an out-of-range grade is used as a trip code.

The final input file for the above example could then be constructed as follows:

original list of grades — Trip or trigger code

```
10 DATA 70, 80, 64, ..., 84, 98, -8
```

The trip code is the last data item in the list.

When reading a file with an unknown number of records, the user should always append a trip record to the DATA file.

Alphanumeric and Numeric Trip Codes

Suppose that our data file consists solely of alphanumeric characters, such as names. What type of trip code should we use? We could use any string of characters that is "unexpected," i.e., any string that is purposefully different from every other data item in the DATA list. If names are read, then a name trip might be XXXX or *** or 0!

What if the DATA list consists of temperatures that can be either positive or negative? Can we use a negative number as a trip? Yes, as long as that trip value is known to be less than all other values in the DATA list. A very large positive trip value could also be used. The key point is to select a trip value that is outside the known range of the DATA values.

Number of Trip Codes

Often a record consists of more than one data item, for example, a record might consist of a name, a sex code, and an age. The trip record *must* contain as many items as are present in the input record: if three items are to be read each time, as in our example, then the trip record should also contain three items. The user has a choice of trips—the trip could be the name (XXXX), the sex (use a value that is neither a 1 nor a 2), or the age (a negative age or an age > 200). Any of the following would be satisfactory trips:

```
DATA ***, 1, 21      Trip on name
DATA SUE, -1, 29     Trip on sex
DATA JON, 1, 340     Trip on age
DATA 0, 0, 0         Trip on any item
```

However, under no circumstances should the trip record contain fewer than three items, since the READ statement that is repeatedly executed (READ N$, S, A) will always require three items from the DATA list. If fewer than three items are present in the last record, then the computer will run out of data and produce an error message:

```
1   DATA SLIM, 1, 38
2   DATA JIM, 2, 6
.
.
8   DATA SUE, 2, 18
9   DATA ***
         ↑    ↑  ↑
10 READ N$, S, A
.
.
60 GO TO 10
RUN
OUT OF DATA AT LINE 10
```

Trip record chosen by user.

Since there are no values specified for S and A for the last READ operation, a READ error message is printed and the computer stops.

Where to Test for the Trip Code

Any time the trip code method is used, the test for the trip value should *always* be made *immediately after* the READ statement:

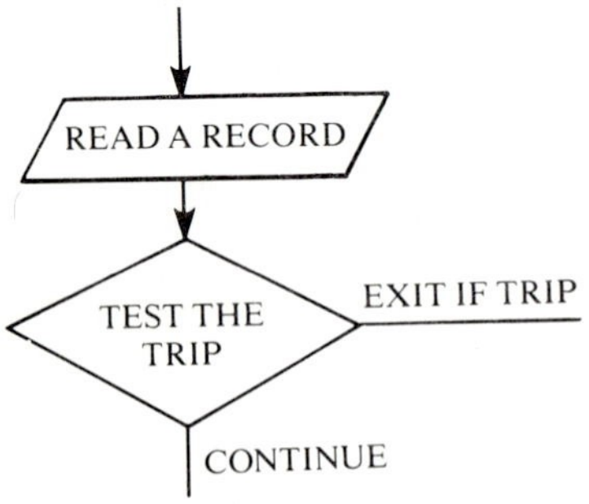

TEST TRIP RIGHT AFTER READ.

Placing the test somewhere other than right after the READ statement will usually cause logical errors. Testing the trip means checking the item just read to see if it is real or artificial. If it is artificial, then the program should obviously not process that item like a real item. The following flowcharts indicate the proper versus improper placement of trip tests.

Proper

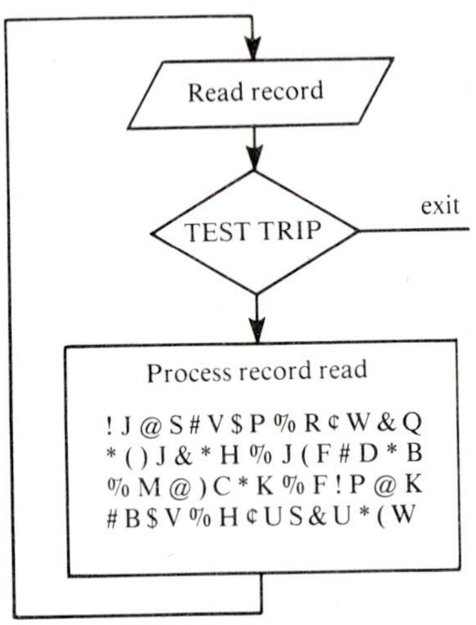

The trip is not processed as a real item.

Improper

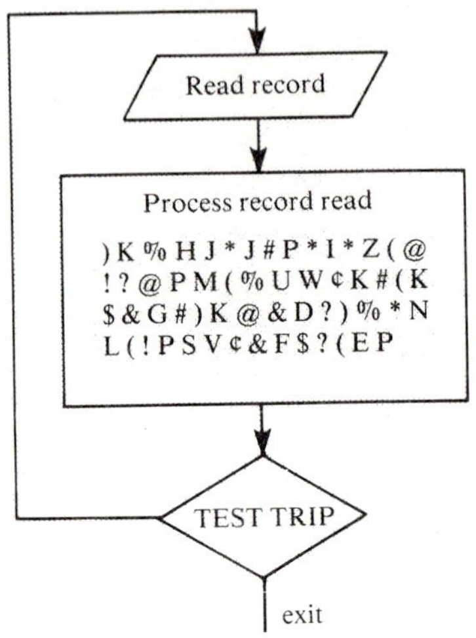

The trip is processed as if it were a real item.

5-4-2 Do It Now

1. A DATA statement contains exactly five grades. (Grades may vary from 0 to 100.) Which of the following programs will print those five scores? Specify the output produced by each program and indicate any error that might occur.

a.
```
1 DATA 3,5,8,9,6
2 I = Ø
3 IF I > 5 THEN 9
4 READ G
5 PRINT G
6 I = I + 1
7 GO TO 3
9 END
```

b.
```
1 DATA 3,5,8,9,6,END
2 READ G
3 IF G = "END" THEN 9
4 PRINT G
5 GO TO 2
9 END
```

c.
```
1 DATA 3,5,8,9,6,-3
2 READ G
3 PRINT G
4 IF G < Ø THEN 9
5 GO TO 2
9 END
```

d.
```
1 DATA 3,5,8,9,6
2 I = 1
3 IF I > 5 THEN 9
4 READ G
5 I = I + 1
6 PRINT G
7 GO TO 3
9 END
```

e.
```
1 DATA 3,5,8,9,6
2 I = Ø
3 READ G
4 IF I > 5 THEN 9
5 PRINT G
6 I = I + 1
7 GO TO 3
9 END
```

f.
```
1 DATA 3,5,8,9,6
2 READ G
3 IF G < Ø THEN 9
4 IF G > 1ØØ THEN 9
5 PRINT G
6 GO TO 2
9 END
```

2. A DATA list contains an unknown number of records. Each record contains a name and a sex code (1 = male, 2 = female). Write the code to print the number of records in the DATA file.

Answers

1. a. An "out of data" error message will be printed by the system, since the code forces the computer to read six records.
   b. Error at line 2: the variable G cannot read alphanumeric data END.
   c. Invalid: the program will print six scores, including the trip of -3.
   d. Program will read and print the 5 grades.
   e. Program will print 5 grades but will run out of data when I = 6.
   f. An "out of data" error message will be printed. No trip was appended to the DATA list.

2.
```
1  DATA SUE, 1
.
.
8  DATA JOE, 2
9  DATA *, Ø
1Ø I = Ø
12 READ N$, S
15 IF N$ = "*" THEN 8Ø
2Ø I = I + 1
25 GO TO 12
8Ø PRINT I
99 END
```

5-5 Problem Solving

Learning the BASIC language *per se* is not a formidable undertaking. Mastering its rules, syntax, and operations requires little creativity, imagination, or "thinking" skills. Writing a program of BASIC instructions that satisfy a stated problem however is another matter. Problem solving is more mental and less technical; some might even say it is an art form.

The purpose of this section is to teach some fundamental steps of the problem-solving process. By using these steps, we can outline a systematic approach to the art of programming. We will establish a list of tasks that need to be addressed during the various stages of the problem-solving process. Applying them will give the beginning programmer more insight into the problem-solving process and will assist him/her in becoming a better problem solver and programmer.

5-5-1 Steps in Problem Solving and Programming

The six steps of problem solving and programming are:

1. Understanding the problem. You should first try to solve the problem without the use of the computer, i.e. figure out some of the answers manually.
2. Designing a layout for the output. What results are to be printed and where are they to be printed on the output form?
3. Constructing a dictionary of variables that will be needed by the program.
4. Identifying the programming techniques required to solve the problem.
5. Testing the program. Choose or invent data to test each path in the program, and make sure the results are correct.
6. Input data validation. Make sure that the program is able to screen invalid entries and take corrective or appropriate measures, such as reaccepting improperly typed data or printing out error messages.

If these six steps are systematically covered every time a program is coded and run, confusion is less likely to arise, and your task is much simpler. These six steps are discussed in greater detail in the following sections.

Understanding the Problem

Many beginning programmers start to write out the BASIC code right away, before they even understand what the problem is all about. Some read the problem so quickly that their resulting code does not solve the intended problem. Others are confused by the wording of the problem itself—understanding the problem becomes the primary obstacle!

Temptations to code a problem in a hurry or difficulties in understanding a problem can be taken care of by reading the statement of the problem slowly and carefully, underlining the key words, and then trying to solve the problem manually with pencil and paper for a particular set of data. No flowcharts should be drawn at this stage and no BASIC code should be written—don't worry about the computer yet! To solve the problem manually, you may need to make up some dummy (artificial) data so that you can figure out an answer, especially if the problem requires input data.

Let's look at an example: Write the code to accept a value for N and compute the sum of the first N odd integers.

What does this mean? One easy way to make some sense out of this problem is to give a value to N and then rephrase the problem:

"Write the code to accept the value 5 and compute the sum of the first 5 odd integers." This makes a little more sense. The problem can then be decomposed into elementary parts:

What are the first 5 odd integers? *Answer*: 1, 3, 5, 7, 9,

What is the sum of the first 5 odd integers? *Answer*: 1 + 3 + 5 + 7 + 9 = 25

Hence the answer to the problem is 25 if N has the value 5. At this point you have analyzed the problem and have found an answer.

Output Design

Finding a particular solution to the problem is the first step. Perhaps you have scribbled down the answer or answers on a piece of paper. Now you need to arrange the results into an attractive report (neat and clear) that can be produced by the computer. Captions or header labels should be used to make the report readable, self-explanatory, and self-documenting. Designing the layout of the output is very important, as it forces you to set up definite goals. As you proceed to write the code, you will know exactly what to aim for.

Example:

> A DATA statement contains an employee name, the number of hours worked, and the rate of pay. Write a program to compute the employee's pay and give a bonus of 10% of the amount earned to any employee who worked more than 50 hours.

If the problem itself does not specify any particular output layout, you should design a complete report that is self-explanatory and that enables its reader to verify the correctness of the results. Printing the employee name and his/her pay is not sufficient, since the pay amount cannot be verified. In general, it is a good practice to print out any information or data that is read by the program. For this example, the following format might be used: (No overtime rate)

PAYROLL REPORT

NAME	HOURS	RATE	BONUS	PAY
S. MART	40	10	0	400.00
T. LING	60	7	42	462.00

Headings and subheadings should be part of any report even though they require extra typing effort on your part. You should remember that in real life, programs are for other people (teacher, supervisor, contractor, and so forth) to look at and analyze. Hence the output should be attractive, easy to read, and self-explanatory.

Data Dictionary

You have probably heard the term *structured programming*. Languages such as COBOL and PASCAL are examples of languages where structured programming is practiced. The programmer must identify, at the start of the program, all the variables that will be used in the program. This forces the programmer to determine ahead of time the number of variables needed and the roles they will play. This practice of inventorying variables leads to a more disciplined approach to programming and results in better thought-out code. Each variable is accounted for, thus the user does not whimsically create a new variable in the midst of a program. In this structured and documented environment, all variables are spoken for through an identification section and a type of data dictionary. In BASIC, the same thing can be accomplished through the REM statement.

Let's develop a data dictionary for the example in step 1:

Write the code to input a value for N and compute the sum of the first N odd integers. Remembering the way we solved the problem manually, we know that the program must:

1. generate the odd integers 1, 3, 5, 7 ... (K)
2. accumulate the sum of the odd integers 1 + 3 + 5 + 7 + ... (S)
3. count the number of odd integers to be added, i.e., count 1, 2, ...,N (I)

From the above decomposition of the problem, we see that four variables will be needed: N, which is to be accepted from INPUT; the counter K to generate the odd integers; the counter I to keep track of the number of odd numbers that have been summed up; and finally S to accumulate the sum of the odd numbers. These can be identified at the start of the BASIC program:

```
10 REM   DATA DICTIONARY
12 REM
15 REM   N: NUMBER OF ODD NUMBERS TO PROCESS
20 REM   K: GENERATES ODD NUMBERS
25 REM   I: COUNTS FROM 1 TO N
30 REM   S: ACCUMULATES SUM OF ODD NUMBERS
35
```

You should now be ready for the next stage, development of the program logic.

Program Development, the Logic and Documentation Stage

No attempt should be made to write the BASIC code right away. You should first draw a general outline of the logic using a flowchart or pseudo code. In a very general way, most problems look alike; most require that you print headers, read data, process the data read, and print the data and the results. In general, you can "steal" parts of one problem to solve another, if not physically (line by line) at least conceptually. Of course, processing the data in one program may be quite different from processing the data in another program, but in many programs you will have to count records, count the number of times a specific event takes place, perform arithmetic operations, determine the highest value in a list, accumulate sums of numbers, and so forth.

Each program will probably make use of a number of these techniques. You can learn how to use each of them individually, then integrate any combination of them into a program. This book discusses each of these programming techniques in detail, and you can assemble these "prefabricated" coding components to form a program. Flowcharts or pseudo code offer a very convenient way to link or assemble these components together.

Example:

Every time a meal is sold at the Elite Diner's Club, a record is prepared with the cost of the order and the meal code: 1 = breakfast, 2 = lunch, 3 = dinner. At the end of the day, the meal transaction file is to be read by the system to produce the following information:

a. the total sales for the day
b. the average cost of breakfasts
c. the minimum dinner cost

We can immediately see that the program to perform these tasks must have the following components:

a. Reading a file with an unknown number of records; this procedure uses the trip record technique (section 5–4–1).
b. Accumulating sales for the day; the accumulation technique (chapter 7) does this.
c. Average breakfast cost. This is done by the counting technique (counting breakfasts) and the accumulation technique (sum of breakfast costs).
d. Minimum dinner cost. This is found through the minimum/maximum search technique (section 5–7–2).

Thus the problem can be decomposed into four subtasks, all of which will be familiar to the student. You should now be able to draw the flowchart or write the pseudo code from which the BASIC code is then derived.

The Testing Phase

This phase is probably the most crucial phase in the program development process, since the fate of the real-life programmer is determined by the correctness of his/her computer-generated results. In an environment where managers and corporate executives increasingly make decisions based on computer-produced reports, a programmer whose program results are faulty has a dismal job outlook. Yet many beginning (and some not-so-beginning) programmers put blind trust in whatever output is produced by their programs arguing that since no errors showed up during the RUN phase and since captions and numeric values were printed, the results must be correct. Nothing, of course, could be further from the truth. Computer-generated results are often incorrect—the numbers simply do not add up!

The remedy to this problem is to check your results to make sure that they are correct. This, of course, may require a great deal of time. The best way to proceed is to manufacture hypothetical data that will force the program to test each and every path that can be taken during execution of the program. (In a parallel context, if you built a lawn-watering system with numerous cut-off valves, you would want to check that no particular line or pipe was obstructed, i.e., that water would flow through each and every line. Checking just one particular circuit or one component of the pipeline and observing that it worked would not imply that the other lines also worked!) In a programming environment, different types of input values may need to be "invented" so that the action of the program on these dummy values can be observed and checked out. This process is known as *tracing* through a program, a flowchart, or pseudo code. You must follow and record what happens to each experimental input item as it travels through the network of instructions until the end of the program is reached. (See Figure 5-3.) You should manufacture as many experimental items as there are paths in the flowchart and you should follow each item through the entire network.

Example:

> Assume that we are to test the program logic of the Elite Diner's Club where each DATA statement consists of two entries, a meal cost and a meal code (1 = breakfast, 2 = lunch, 3 = dinner), and where it is desired to compute the day's total sales, the average breakfast meal cost, and the minimum dinner cost.

Figure 5-3 Valid versus invalid testing.

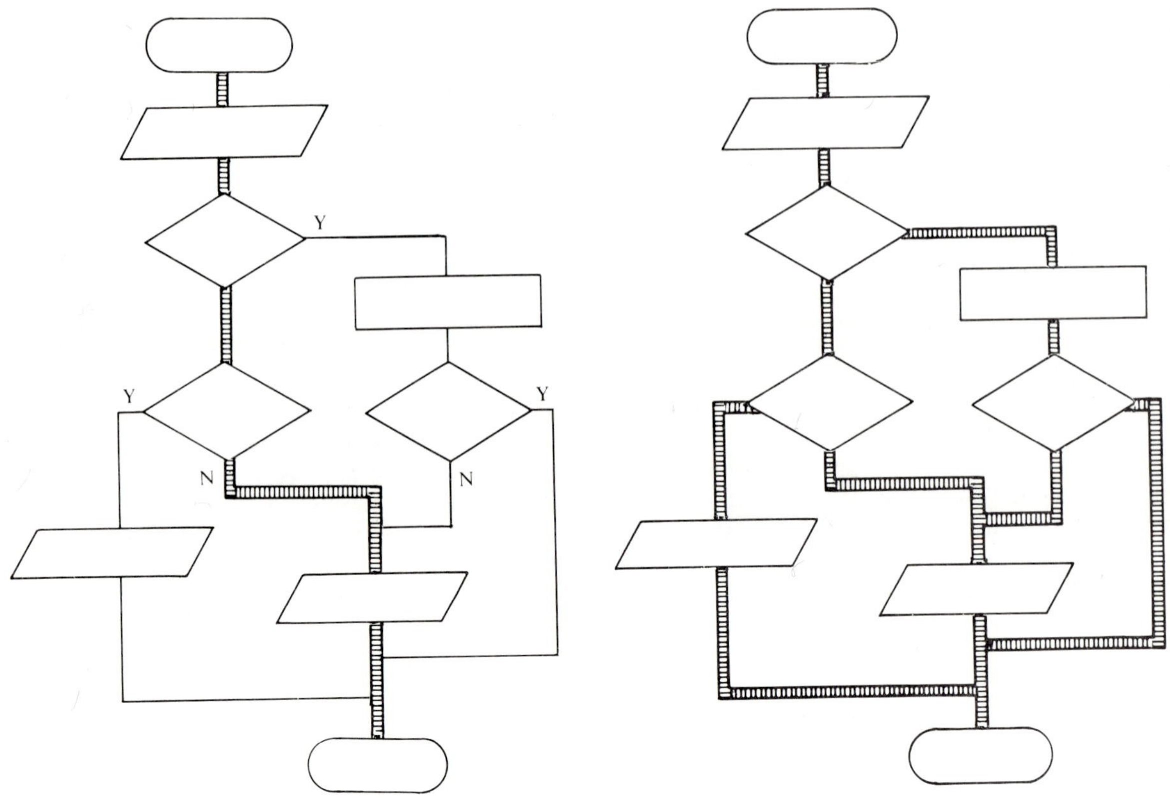

User checks only one out of four paths.
Invalid testing

User checks all possible paths with different data items.
Valid testing.

We must ask what minimum number of data records is required to test the program for all possible different paths (outcome)? To test for the minimum dinner cost, we should have at least two dinner entries with different meal costs; we should also have one lunch entry, and one (two would be better) breakfast entries. Altogether a minimum of four DATA records should be used.

Input Data Validation

Even though a program may be perfect in the sense that it contains no syntax or logical errors, it can be less than perfect in the hands of others who try to use it. For example, what would a program do at RUN time if the user were asked to enter a value of 1 or 2 for a particular variable X, and the user inadvertently entered the value 3? Theoretically, the program should inform the user that the value entered is incorrect, and ask him to please reenter a 1 or 2! This means that the program cannot assume that the value for X will always be a 1 or 2; in fact, when dealing with humans, the value entered could be a 1, a 2, or any other character on the keyboard! Hence, the program should test X for the value 1, and then, if X is not 1, test for the value 2. If X is not 2, then the human goofed! An appropriate action should be taken by the computer.

In the same context, consider the case of the Elite Diner's Club, where all the DATA statements have been prerecorded and where this file is processed by the READ statement. Each record consists of a meal cost item and a meal code item 1, 2, or 3. What should the program do if a meal code of 5 is incorrectly typed in the DATA statement? Should the system stop at RUN time and ask a clerk to check and reenter a different value on the terminal? What if the clerk does not know what is going on or there is no clerk? Or should the system ignore that invalid record, print an error message, and continue processing the remaining records, making the day's total sales inaccurate? Or should the program immediately be aborted? A more insidious dilemma might be: what if a breakfast cost entry in a particular record were recorded as 1000? Could a breakfast cost that much? (A famished sheik?) And should the program include this amount in its computation of the average breakfast cost? Should the computer screen unrealistic figures?

Testing every input item for every imaginable (or unimaginable) value can soon become a programmer's nightmare, and adding the extra code to take care of the input validation process can swell a "skinny" program into the obese league in no time at all!

Yet, theoretically, a program should be written in such a way that it is "human-goof-proof" and such that the program would remain unperturbed even if a kitten were to pounce on the computer's keyboard.

For the reasons cited above, the input validation process is a very important part of the problem-solving process. Its importance becomes even more critical during application of the program or system.

5-5-2 Do It Now

Write the code to solve the following problems. Take care of the input data validation process.

1. Input two grades; compute and print the average of these grades. The grades lie in the interval (0, 100).

2. An input file consists of an unknown number of records where each record supposedly contains an item name description, an item quantity, and a cost per item. No item quantity is supposed to exceed 90. Examples of invalidly transcribed input files are shown in cases 1 through 6:

		Record #1	*Record #2*	*Record #3*	
	DATA	CHAIR,3,5Ø.7,	DESK,1Ø,1ØØ.75,	LAMP,3,15	Correct original file
Case 1:	DATA	CHAIR,3,5Ø.7,	DESK,1ØØ,1ØØ.75,	LAMP,3,15	Invalid quantity entry
Case 2:	DATA	CHAIR,3,5Ø.7,	DESK,1Ø,Ø,2ØØØ,	LAMP,3,15	Invalid cost entry
Case 3:	DATA	CHAIR,3,5Ø.7,	DESK,1ØØ,2ØØØ,	LAMP,3,15	Invalid cost and quantity entries
Case 4:	DATA	CHAIR,3,5Ø.7,	13Ø,1Ø,1ØØ.75,	LAMP,3,15	Invalid desk name
Case 5:	DATA	CHAIR,3,5Ø.7,	DESH,1Ø,1ØØ.75,	LAMP,3,15	DESK misspelled
Case 6:	DATA	CHAIR,3,5Ø.7,	DESK,1Ø,	LAMP,3,15	Missing item for DESK

Write a program to produce the following type of output:

```
ITEM      QUANTITY    COST      VALUE

CHAIR         3        5Ø.7     152.1Ø
DESK         1Ø       1ØØ.75   1ØØ7.5Ø
LAMP          3        15.       45.ØØ
```

In this problem, the system should identify errors on the terminal and allow the clerk to correct these errors; if the clerk enters invalid data, these should also be corrected. The system should then continue processing the remaining records. The output transaction for the input file described in case 3 above might look as follows:

```
                                  ITEM      QUANTITY     COST     VALUE

                                  CHAIR         3         5Ø.7    152.1
INCORRECT DESK QUANTITY: 1ØØ
ENTER NUMBER
? 98
INCORRECT DESK QUANTITY: 98
ENTER NUMBER
? 1Ø
INCORRECT DESK COST: 2ØØØ
ENTER COST
? 1ØØ9
INCORRECT DESK COST: 1ØØ9
ENTER COST
? 1ØØ
                                  DESK         1Ø         1ØØ      1ØØØ
                                  LAMP          3          15        45
```

Answers

1.
```
05 REM N1: 1ST GRADE  N2: 2ND GRADE
10 INPUT N1
12 IF N1<0 THEN 20
14 IF N1>100 THEN 20
16 GOTO 30
20 PRINT "INVALID GRADE; PLEASE REENTER"
25 GOTO 10
30 INPUT N2
32 IF N2<0 THEN 40
34 IF N2>100 THEN 40
36 GOTO 50
40 PRINT "INVALID GRADE; PLEASE REENTER"
45 GOTO 30
50 PRINT (N1 + N2)/2
55 END
RUN
? 108
INVALID GRADE; PLEASE REENTER
? 10
? 200
INVALID GRADE; PLEASE REENTER
? 20
 15
```

2.
```
05 REM N$: ITEM NAME   Q:QUANTITY   C:COST   V:VALUE
10 PRINT TAB(34);"ITEM";TAB(41);"QUANTITY";TAB(52);"COST";TAB(60);"VALUE"
15 DATA CHAIR,3,50.7
20 DATA DESK ,100,2000
25 DATA LAMP ,3,15
27 DATA -3,-3,-3
30 READ N$,Q,C
35 IF C < 0 THEN 105
40 IF Q > 90 THEN 65
45 IF C > 1000 THEN 85
50 V = C * Q
55 PRINT TAB(34);N$;TAB(43);Q;TAB(51);C;TAB(59);V
60 GOTO 30
65 PRINT "INCORRECT ";N$;"QUANTITY:";Q
70 PRINT "ENTER NUMBER"
75 INPUT Q
80 GOTO 40
85 PRINT "INCORRECT ";N$;"COST:";C
90 PRINT "ENTER COST"
95 INPUT C
100 GOTO 45
105 END
```

5-6 Programming Examples

5-6-1 Computing a Percentage of Passing Grades

An input file consists of several sets of records, each containing grades obtained by different class sections of an introduction to management course (see illustration below). Each set is identified by a header record specifying the number of scores for a particular section and the section number. Write a program to determine the number and percentage of passing scores for each section. Passing scores are those scores above 70. The program should list each section's scores and the output should be similar to the one shown below:

Number of Scores in Packet that Follows — *Section Number*

```
DATA 3, 102
DATA 78     } Packet #1
DATA 82     } 3 scores
DATA 80

DATA 20, 105
DATA 68     } Packet #2
DATA 60     } 20 scores
.
.
.
DATA  90
DATA  -4, -4 <-- Trip record
```

```
        SECTION 102
          SCORES

            78
            82
            80

NUMBER OF SCORES = 3
PASSING SCORES = 3
PASSING PERCENTAGE = 100%

        SECTION 105
          SCORES

            68
            60
            .
            .
            .
            90

NUMBER OF SCORES = 20
PASSING SCORES = 10
PASSING PERCENTAGE = 50%
```

Understanding the Problem

To understand the problem, we manufacture some "dummy" input data like that shown above, and we then try to solve the problem manually. The header record tells us how many scores we need to process, and what the class section number is. The section number is important because we need to print it out. The number of scores tells us how many more data items we need to read before we encounter the next packet of information. For the first packet in the example, we need to read three scores: 78, 82, and 80. Since they all exceed 70, the percentage of passing grades is 100 percent and the count of passing scores is 3. Since we have read the three scores, we know that the next record will be a header record and we will need to process the 20 scores of section 105. We will eventually encounter a negative number of scores, which will signify the end of the input file.

Output Design

In this case, the design is already specified.

Data Dictionary

Since the header record contains two items, we will use N to capture the number of scores and S to capture the section number. In addition, we will need a counter I to count N scores in each set, and another counter C to count the number of scores above 70. Finally, G will read the scores, and P will be the percentage of passing scores.

Program Development

The first READ statement must read the number of scores N and the section number S. Since we need to read N scores, we need a counter to count 1, 2, 3, ... up to N, so we use the counting technique to read N scores. We know that a header record awaits us after we have read N scores. Every time we read a header record, we test for the trip record (the first item on the header record). The entire logic can be visualized in pseudo code as follows:

```
──►Initialize counter of all scores (I) and counter of scores above 70 (C) to 0
   READ number of scores N and section number S
   IF number of scores N is < 0
   THEN stop
   ELSE   PRINT section number S
          PRINT caption "SCORES"
          READ score G ◄──────────────────────────────────────┐
          add 1 to score counter I                             │
          PRINT score G                                        │
          IF score G < = 70                                    │
          THEN go and test if more scores to read - - - - - ┐  │
          ELSE add 1 to counter that counts scores over 70 (C) ¦  │
          END-IF                                         ¦  │
          IF we haven't read all N scores ◄- - - - - - - - ┘  │
          THEN go back and read more ─────────────────────────►┘
          ELSE   compute percentage of passing grades P = C/N * 100
                 PRINT number of scores, passing scores C, and percentage passing
                 scores
◄─────────────── and go back and read the next header
          END-IF
   END-IF
END
```

The program to solve this problem is shown in Figure 5–4 in minimal and IF/THEN/ELSE BASIC versions.

Testing

For the testing phase, we "manufacture" two packets of data to make sure the logic works for two sections. We make sure that some of the scores are below 70 and some are above 70.

Figure 5–4 Percentage of passing grades.

```
10 REM PERCENTAGE PASSING GRADES
14 REM DATA DICTIONARY
16 REM N: NUMBER OF SCORES PER SECTION
18 REM S: SECTION NUMBER
20 REM I: COUNT SCORES IN EACH SECTION
22 REM G: NAME USED TO READ SCORES
24 REM P: PERCENTAGE OF SCORES OVER 70
25 REM C: COUNT OF SCORES ABOVE 70
28 C = 0
30 I = 0
32 READ N, S
34 IF N < 0 THEN 82
36 PRINT TAB(8);"SECTION";S
38 PRINT TAB(11);"SCORES"
40 PRINT
42 READ G
44 I = I + 1
46 PRINT TAB(12);G
48 IF G <= 70 THEN 52
50 C = C + 1
52 IF I < N THEN 42
54 P = C * 100 / I
56 PRINT
57 PRINT "NUMBER OF SCORES=";N
58 PRINT "PASSING SCORES =";C
60 PRINT "PASSING PERCENTAGE =";P;"%"
62 PRINT
64 GOTO 28
68 REM  TEST DATA
72 DATA 3,102
74 DATA 78,82,80
76 DATA 4,104
78 DATA 58,84,71,42
80 DATA -3,-3
82 END
```

```
10 REM PERCENTAGE PASSING GRADES
14 REM DATA DICTIONARY
16 REM N: NUMBER OF SCORES PER SECTION
18 REM S: SECTION NUMBER
20 REM I: COUNT SCORES IN EACH SECTION
22 REM G: NAME USED TO READ SCORES
24 REM P: PERCENTAGE OF SCORES OVER 70
25 REM C: COUNT OF SCORES ABOVE 70
28 C = 0
30 I = 0
32 READ N, S
34 IF N > 0 THEN 36 ELSE 72
36   PRINT "SECTION";S
37   PRINT "SCORES"
38   PRINT
40   READ G
42   I = I + 1
44   PRINT G
46   IF G > 70 THEN 48 ELSE 50
48     C = C + 1
50     IF I < N THEN 40 ELSE 52
52       P = C * 100 / I
53       PRINT "NUMBER OF SCORES =";N
54       PRINT "PASSING SCORES =";C
56       PRINT "PASSING PERCENTAGE =";P
58       PRINT
60       GOTO 28
62 DATA 3,102
64 DATA 78,82,80
66 DATA 4,104
68 DATA 58,84,71,42
70 DATA -3,-3
72 END
RUN
```

```
          SECTION 102
             SCORES

               78
               82
               80

NUMBER OF SCORES = 3
PASSING SCORES = 3
PASSING PERCENTAGE = 100 %
          SECTION 104
             SCORES

               58
               84
               71
               42

NUMBER OF SCORES = 4
PASSING SCORES = 2
PASSING PERCENTAGE = 50 %
```

5-6-2 Impact of Interest Rates on Monthly Payments—Nested Loops

A good friend of yours has been looking at 60, 70, 80, and 90 thousand dollar homes. She knows you have a computer and has asked you to figure out the monthly payments that she would have to make on such homes given 30-year mortgage rates of 11.5, 12.5, and 13.5%. She states the problem rather vaguely, "Can you print out the monthly payments for all the different rates and costs? I'd also like to know the total mortgage payments over 30 years for the four prices of homes."

Solving the Problem

First, to understand and to solve the problem, you need the formula to compute the monthly payment amount, based on the mortgage amount A, the duration time D in years, and the interest rate I. That formula is

$$\text{Monthly payment} = \frac{A \cdot \dfrac{I}{12}}{1 - \left(\dfrac{1}{1 + \dfrac{T}{12}}\right)^{D \cdot 12}}$$

To get a feel for the problem, work out an example with A = \$60,000, an interest rate of 11.5%, and a duration D of 30 years (write the interest rate in decimal form):

$$\text{Monthly payment} = \frac{60000 \times (0.115/12)}{1 - (1 / (1 + .0115/12))^{30*12}}$$

To get the total payments over 30 years, you need to multiply the monthly payment by the number of months in 30 years (30 * 12). You also need to compute monthly payments for the 70, 80, and 90 thousand dollar homes at the three interest rates, as well as doing the calculations for the 60 thousand dollar home at the other interest rates. You can see that you will have to print a lot of results, so you must design an output that your friend will be able to understand. The output design is very important in this case because it will also help you organize the steps you will need to take in your program.

Output Design

For an attractive design and a column arrangement of figures, you choose the following:

MORTGAGE DURATION 30 YEARS

Amount	*Interest Rate*	*Monthly Payment*	*Total Payment*
60000	11.5	XXX.XX	XXX.XX
60000	12.5	.	.
60000	13.5	.	.
70000	11.5	.	.
70000	12.5	.	.
70000	13.5	.	.
.	.	.	.
.	.	.	.

Data Dictionary

You will need the following variables:

- D: duration of the mortgage, 30 years.
- I: the interest rate, expressed in the formula in decimal form (.115 instead of 11.5%).
- A: the mortgage amount, initially 60000. That amount is incremented by 10000 until it reaches 90000.
- M: the monthly payment calculated by the formula.
- T: the total payment over the entire 30-year mortgage.

Program Development

Looking at the output, you can see that you will need two loops. In fact, one loop will be part of another loop (a *nested* loop). When A is 60000, you will need to run the interest rate from 11.5 to 13.5% in increments of 1%. Then A will become 70000 and the interest rate will run through its cycle again. Hence an outer loop will control A in increments of 10000, and an inner loop will control I in increments of 1%. The results need to be rounded off to two digits to the right of the decimal point. You can now outline the logic chart as follows:

```
Initialize the amount A to 60,000
Set the rate I to 11.5 percent
Compute monthly payment M
Compute total payment T over 30 years
PRINT amount, interest rate, monthly amount, total payment
Increment interest rate I by 1 %
IF interest rate I ≤ 13.5
THEN go back and compute monthly payment M
ELSE Increment amount A by 10,000
        IF amount A ≤ 90,000
        THEN go back to reset rate I to 11.5 percent
        ELSE stop
        END IF
END IF
```

The program is then coded as shown in Figure 5–5.

Testing

In this case, there is no data to be read—all the data is generated by the program. The results really cannot be verified by hand (some of the results could be checked with a hand calculator) hence you need to triple-check the formula to make sure parentheses are where they are supposed to be, especially for the exponent D*12 at line 40.

Figure 5–5 A mortgage problem.

```
10 REM MORTGAGE PAYMENT
12 REM D:  MORTGAGE TIME DURATION
14 REM I:  INTEREST RATE
16 REM A:  MORTGAGE AMOUNT
18 REM M:  MONTHLY PAYMENT
20 REM T:  TOTAL PAYMENT
22 INPUT "MORTGAGE DURATION";D
24 PRINT "MORTGAGE DURATION";D;"YEARS"
26 PRINT
28 PRINT "AMOUNT","INTEREST ","MONTHLY "," TOTAL "
30 PRINT "      "," RATE   ","PAYMENT ","PAYMENT"
32 A = 60000
34 I = .115
38 PRINT
40 M = (A * I / 12)/(1 - (1/(1 + I/12))^(D * 12))
42 T = 12 * D * M
44 REM ROUND OFF MONTHLY AND TOTAL PAYMENTS
46 M = INT((M + 0.005) * 100)/100
48 T = INT((T + 0.005) * 100)/100
50 PRINT A,I * 100, M, T
52 I = I + .01
54 IF I <= .135 THEN 40
56 PRINT
58 A = A + 10000
60 IF A <= 90000  THEN 34
62 END

RUN
MORTGAGE DURATION? 30
MORTGAGE DURATION 30 YEARS

AMOUNT      INTEREST    MONTHLY    TOTAL
              RATE      PAYMENT    PAYMENT

 60000        11.5       594.17    213902.9
 60000        12.5       640.36    230527.8
 60000        13.5       687.25    247409

 70000        11.5       693.2     249553.4
 70000        12.5       747.08    268949.1
 70000        13.5       801.79    288643.9

 80000        11.5       792.23    285203.9
 80000        12.5       853.81    307370.4
 80000        13.5       916.33    329878.7
```

5-6-3 A Car Rental Problem

The cost of rental cars at Acme Rental is based on the type of car, the insurance purchased, the miles driven and number of days of rental. The company leases three types of cars:

Type	*Daily Rental*	*Mileage Charge*
1	$ 40.00	$ 0.06
2	$ 45.00	$ 0.08
3	$ 50.00	$ 0.12

The company offers two insurance plans:

Plan	*Cost*
1	5 % of the combined daily and mileage charges, $10 minimum
2	$ 6 per day of use

Write a program to read records that contain the type of car, the insurance plan selected (1 or 2), the mileage, and the number of days and print a report that will display this information as well as the total charge. Print an error message if the code for the car type is unrecognized.

Solving the Problem

To get a good feel for the problem, let's work out a few examples and see if we can come up with some answers without the computer's help. Let us look at a type 1 car, used for 2 days, driven 100 miles, and having insurance plan 2. The rental charge is 2 times $40 ($80). To that we must add the mileage charge, 100 miles at 6 cents/mile ($6). The total daily charges then are $80 + $6 = $86. The insurance cost is 2 days at $6 ($12). Hence the final bill will be the total daily charges of $86 plus $12 insurance, or $98 altogether. If insurance plan 1 had been selected, the insurance cost would either be 5% of total daily charges (0.05 * 86 = $4.30) or $10. Since $4.30 is less than the $10 minimum, the insurance cost would be $10, and the total bill would be 86 + 10 = $96.

Output Design

In this problem, many minor results are computed, such as the mileage charge, the insurance cost, and the daily charges. These could be printed along with the input items such as the type of car and the insurance plan code. Since most BASIC systems allow a maximum of only 5 result fields (zones) per line with the comma, we will print the type of car, the insurance plan, the miles driven, the number of days, and the final bill on the first trial run. Later, when the program is run and debugged, we could refine the report to include additional minor results by using the TAB function discussed in chapter 6. For now, we will use the following design:

```
TYPE CAR   INS. PLAN    MILEAGE    DAYS    BILL

  1           2           100        2      62
  1           1           100        2      32
  .           .            .         .       .
  .           .            .         .       .
  .           .            .         .       .
```

Data Dictionary

We will use the following variables in our program:

- T: Type of car (1, 2, or 3)
- I: Insurance plan (1 or 2)
- M: Miles driven by customer
- D: Number of days customer rents car
- D1: Daily rental charge: number of days times daily charge
- M1: Mileage cost: miles driven * mileage charge
- C: Total daily charges = M1 + D1
- I1: Insurance cost, either $10 or 5% of C
- F: Final charge = total daily charges + insurance; C + I1

Program Development

Many approaches can be taken to solve this problem. One approach is as follows:

1. We do not need to compute and store the daily rental charge and mileage charge separately, since we can compute the daily charges directly:

   C = 40 * D + .06 * M for a type 1 car
   C = 45 * D + .08 * M for a type 2 car
   C = 50 * D + .12 * M for a type 3 car

   In the program, however, we break these formulas into two parts, in case we later decide to print the mileage cost and the daily rental charge separately. Since there are three types of cars, three tests are needed to specify which formula to use. If the car type is not 1, 2, or 3, it is invalid and an error message is printed.

2. After the total daily charges have been computed, we deal with the insurance plan. If the insurance plan code is 1, the insurance cost is 5 % of the total daily charges, but if that figure is less than $10, the insurance cost is the $10 minimum. (Another way to say this is: The insurance cost is the larger of two figures—5 % of the total daily charges or $10.) If the insurance plan code is 2 the insurance cost is simply 6 * D.

3. The final total charge is the sum of the insurance cost and the total daily charges.

This logic is captured in flowchart form in Figure 5–6, which also displays the BASIC program.

Testing

It is very important in this program that we test all possible paths that our program will take. Looking at the flowchart in Figure 5–6, we see that we need at least 10 DATA statements (lines 325–364) to correspond to all the possible flowchart paths.

■ **Figure 5–6** A car rental problem.

```
100  REM DATA DICTIONARY
105  REM  T : TYPE OF CAR
110  REM  M : MILEAGE
115  REM  M1: MILEAGE COST
120  REM  D : DAYS RENTED
125  REM  D1: DAYS*TYPE COST
130  REM  I : INSURANCE PLAN
135  REM  I1: INS. PLAN COST
140  REM  C : TOTAL DAILY CHARGE
145  REM  F : FINAL BILL
150  REM
155  PRINT "TYPE CAR","INS. PLAN",
160  PRINT "MILEAGE","DAYS","BILL"
165  PRINT
170  READ T,I,M,D
175  IF T < 0 THEN 370
180  IF T <> 1 THEN 205
185            D1 = 40 * D
190            M1 = .06 * M
195            GOTO 265
200  REM
205  IF T <> 2 THEN 230
210            D1 = 45 * D
215            M1 = .08 * M
220            GOTO 265
225  REM
230  IF T <> 3 THEN 255
235            D1 = 50 * D
240            M1 = .12 * M
245            GOTO 265
250  REM
255  PRINT "CHECK CAR TYPE ";T
260  GOTO 170
265  C = D1 + M1
270  REM COMPUTING INSURANCE COST
275  IF I <> 2 THEN 290
280            I1 = 6 * D
285            GOTO 305
290  I1 = .05 * C
295  IF I1 >= 10 THEN 305
300            I1 = 10
305  F = I1 + C
310  PRINT T,I,M,D,F
315  GOTO 170
320  REM
325  DATA 1 , 1, 500 , 1
330  DATA 1 , 2, 500 , 4
335  DATA 2 , 1, 100 , 2
340  DATA 2 , 2, 100 , 2
345  DATA 3 , 1, 100 , 2
350  DATA 3 , 2, 100 , 2
355  DATA 5 , 2, 100 , 1
360  DATA 1 , 1, 10  , 1
362  DATA 3 , 1, 900 , 4
364  DATA 1 , 2, 500 , 1
365  DATA -3, 0, 000 , 0
370  END
RUN
TYPE CAR       INS. PLAN      MILEAGE       DAYS          BILL
 1              1              500           1             80
 1              2              500           4             214
 2              1              100           2             108
 2              2              100           2             110
 3              1              100           2             122
 3              2              100           2             124
CHECK CAR TYPE  5
 1              1              10            1             50.6
 3              1              900           4             323.4
 1              2              500           1             76
```

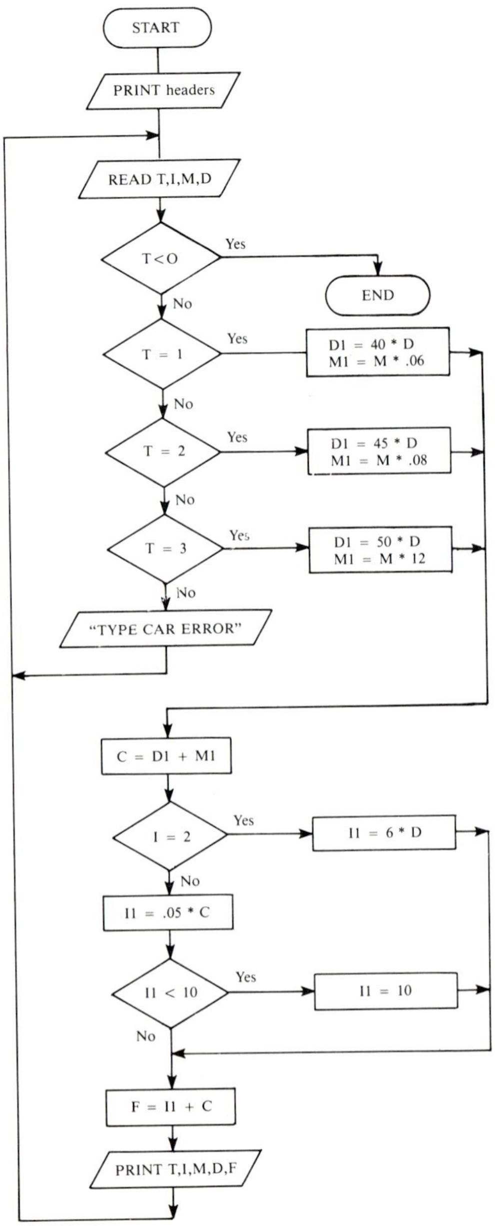

5-7 Programming Techniques

5-7-1 Counting for Loop Control

It is often necessary to repeat a set of instructions a certain number of times, for example, you may need to read exactly 10 records or print last week's daily sales (7 entries). There are standard techniques for doing a particular procedure a certain number of times. In the following discussion we will represent the procedure to be carried out more than once by a rectangle ▭.

In many cases, repeating a task more than once implies counting. Counting, in turn implies using a counter and initializing, incrementing, and testing the counter. These three tasks (initialization, incrementing, and testing) must be carried out in a particular order. Two approaches are given here, and they can be used systematically whenever you want to repeat a procedure a fixed number of times. In the following presentation, we will use the variable N to identify the number of times the procedure is to be carried out.

Technique 1

1. Before entering the procedure (loop), initialize the counter to 0.
2. Increment counter by 1.
3. Test counter. If counter > N, go to step 6; otherwise, proceed with step 4.
4. Carry out the procedure (set of instructions).
5. Go back to step 2.
6. Continue with the program.

This technique can be flowcharted as follows:

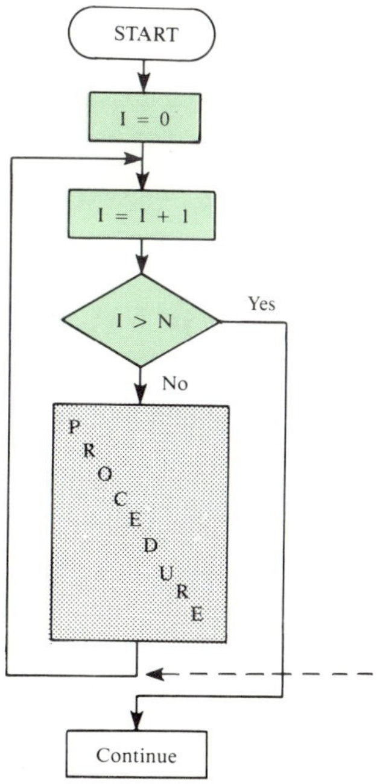

Initialize counter to 0.

Add 1 to counter.

Have we gone through the loop N times? (Is the counter > N?) If this is the case, bypass the procedure. If on the other hand, the counter is ≤ N, then we keep carrying out the procedure until the counter is > N.

Another time through the procedure; go back and count.

For example, if N were 3, the above flowchart could be tabulated as follows:

I	N	Checking number of times procedure is carried out
~~0~~	3	
~~1~~		✓
~~2~~		✓ } Procedure is carried out 3 times
~~3~~		✓
4		

Technique 2

1. Initialize counter to 0.
2. Carry out the procedure.
3. Increment counter by 1.
4. Test counter. As long as counter < N, go back to step (2); otherwise take step 5.
5. Continue with program.

This approach can be flowcharted as follows:

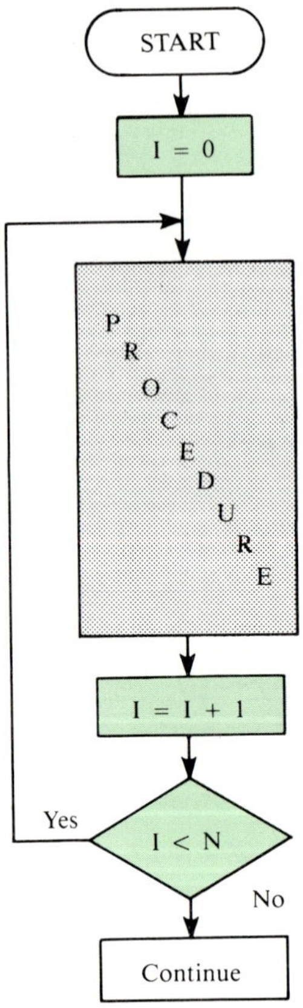

Initialize counter to 0.

Carry out procedure.

Increment counter by 1, since procedure has been carried out.

As long as counter is less than N, keep repeating the procedure. At some point, the value of the counter will equal N, and the test "is N < N" will be false—exit from the loop and continue.

Example: Using both techniques, write programs to read exactly 10 grades from a DATA statement and print all grades read and the count of grades over 90.

Technique 1

```
10 I = 0
15 C = 0
20 I = I + 1
25 IF I > 10 THEN 55
30 READ G
35 PRINT G
40 IF G <=90 THEN 50
45 C = C + 1
50 GO TO 20
55 PRINT C
60 END
```

(Lines 30–45: procedure to be carried out 10 times)

Technique 2

```
10 I = 0
15 C = 0
20 READ G
25 PRINT G
30 IF G <= 90 THEN 40
35 C = C + 1
40 I = I + 1
45 IF I < 10 THEN 20
50 PRINT C
55 END
```

(Lines 20–35: procedure to be carried out 10 times)

5-7-2 Search for a Maximum/Minimum

It is often necessary to go through a list of values to identify the largest or smallest value in that list. To illustrate such a search technique, consider the following problem:

A DATA statement consists of an unknown number of scores ranging from 0 to 100.

Write the code to read these scores and print the highest score.

Solution

To determine the highest score we must compare each new score with the highest score found so far (use the variable name MAX for highest score). If MAX is less than the score read, we replace MAX with the score just read; otherwise, we keep on reading scores until we find one that is larger than MAX (if there is one). When the end-of-file is encountered, MAX is the highest score.

To start the comparison between MAX and the other scores, we read the first score in a separate READ statement and call that value MAX. (After all, if there were only one score, then MAX would be that score). All other scores are then read by a different READ statement. This method is shown in the following codes:

Pseudo Code

```
READ max-score
READ score
IF end of file
THEN PRINT max-score
        Stop
ELSE
        IF max-score < score
        THEN set max-score equal to score
        ENDIF
ENDIF
Go back and read another score
END
```

BASIC Code

```
10 READ M
15 READ S
20 IF S < 0 THEN 25 ELSE 35
25      PRINT M
30      GO TO 50
35      IF M < S THEN 40 ELSE 15
40      M = S
45      GO TO 15
47 DATA 25, 14, 68, 94, 78, -1
50 END
```

To simplify the coding, we could arbitrarily set MAX to 0, i.e. replace line 10 by 10 M = 0. This way, when we read the first score S at line 15 and compare it with MAX at line 35, MAX will be less than S, and MAX in effect becomes initialized to the first score read. In the above example, MAX would become 25 as a result of executing line 40 for the first time.

To find the minimum score, change line 35 to IF M > S instead of IF M < S, and arbitrarily set M to any number over 100 at line 10!

5-7-3 Sequence Check

In many instances, a programmer will need to process lists of names or numbers that are supposed to be arranged in a particular order (ascending or descending). It is conceivable, though, that some of these items might be out of order. Thus, when processing the list, it may be necessary to perform a *sequence check* and flag (identify) those elements that are out of sequence. Consider the following problem:

Problem:

> A DATA statement contains a list of scores supposedly arranged in ascending order. Write the code to verify that the list is indeed in ascending order. Print all scores and place an asterisk by those that are out of sequence.

To get a preliminary feel for this problem, let us look at a few examples:

```
a. 10 DATA 1,3,21,46            All scores are in sequence.
b. 10 DATA 8,1,2,3,4,5
              └───────────── All these scores are out of sequence since
                              they are all less than 8! Note that the first
                              score determines the starting point of the
                              sequence.
c. 10 DATA 15,18,13,21
                 └────────── Out of sequence, since 13 is less than 18.
d. 10 DATA 15,18,12,15,60
                 └──┼─────── Out of sequence, since 12 < 18.
                    └─────── Out of sequence, since 15 < 18.
```

Note that in example *d* the score 15 is out of sequence even though it is in sequence compared to 12. The point is that 12 is out of sequence and hence should *not* be used in determining whether or not the next score is in sequence.

Solution

To determine whether the scores are in ascending order, we check whether the score just read (let's call it NEW) is larger than the previous score (called OLD). Clearly, this process needs to be repeated for every new score read. If NEW is greater than OLD, then the two scores are in sequence; otherwise NEW is out of sequence. To understand what happens next, consider the following specific example:

```
      OLD  NEW
       ↓    ↓
... 15,  18,  20, ...
```

In this case, NEW is greater than OLD, so 15 and 18 are in sequence. What we want to do now is read the next score 20 (which becomes the new NEW!) and ask whether that NEW score is greater than the one we were calling NEW for the previous comparison, i.e., the old NEW, which was 18. However, by reading the next score (20) into NEW, we have destroyed the old NEW (18)! Hence, before we read NEW (20), we need to save the current NEW, i.e., save 18 into OLD! Then, on the next go-round, we will be comparing NEW with OLD or 20 with 18, which is just what we want to do:

```
          OLD   NEW
           ↓     ↓
... 15,   18,   2Ø, ...
```

If we did not set OLD to NEW before reading the next score, the value of OLD would never change, and thus we would always compare a new score with the same OLD score (in this case 15)!

What happens now if NEW is less than OLD? For example,

```
    OLD   NEW
     ↓     ↓
... 15,   12,   14, ...
```

In this case, NEW is less than OLD, so 12 is out of sequence! Before we read the next NEW score (14), we do *not* save 12 into OLD (If we did, then on the next go-round, NEW (14) would be greater than OLD (12), which would imply that 14 is in sequence. This is clearly not the case, since any new score read must be greater than the last score in sequence (15)). When a score is out of order, we leave OLD unchanged.

To begin the comparison between NEW and OLD, we read the first score independently of all others and assign that value to OLD. We then use a different READ statement to read all remaining NEW scores. The entire process is shown in flowchart form and in BASIC code in Figure 5–7.

Figure 5–7 A sequence check.

```
1Ø REM SEQUENCE CHECK
12 REM
15 REM     A: PREVIOUS SCORE
2Ø REM     N: NEW SCORE
25 READ A
3Ø PRINT A
35 READ N
4Ø IF N < Ø THEN 99
45 IF N > A THEN 6Ø
5Ø PRINT N,"*"
55 GO TO 35
6Ø A = N
65 PRINT N
7Ø GO TO 35
75 DATA 1Ø, 15, 12, 14, 18, -4
99 END
```

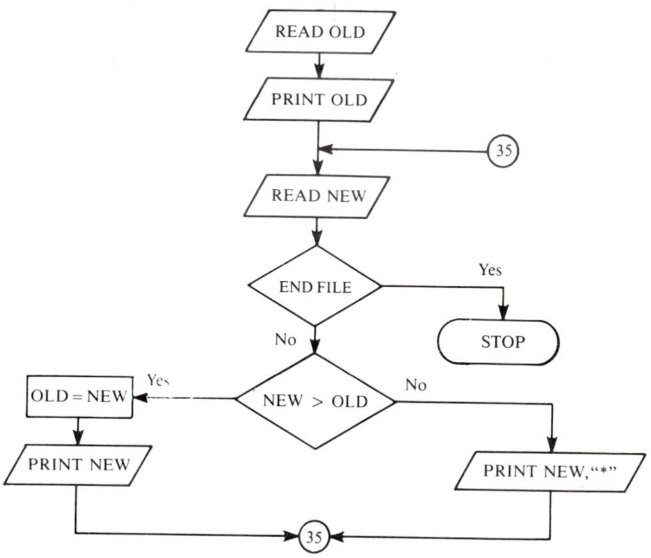

5-8 Assignments

5-8-1 Test Yourself

1. How many records will be read by the following flowcharts?

a.

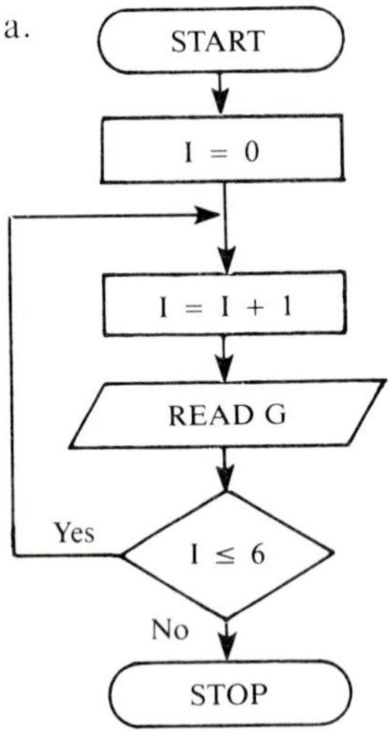

b.

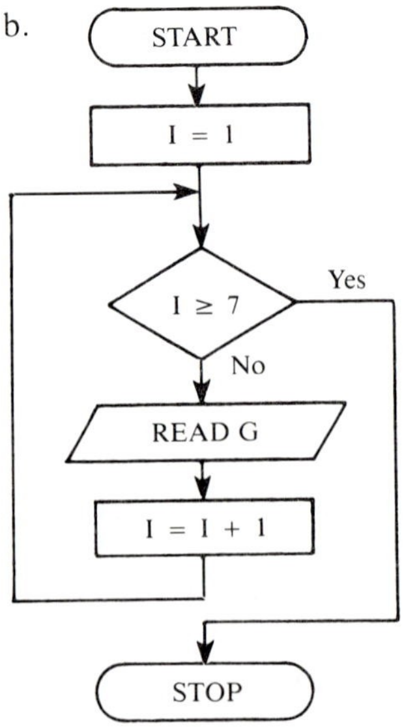

c.

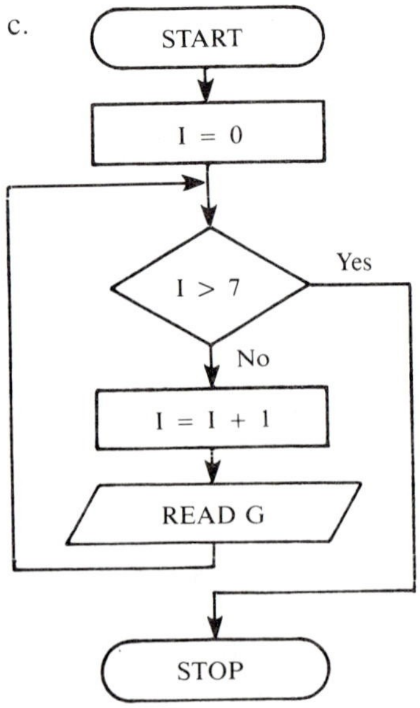

d.

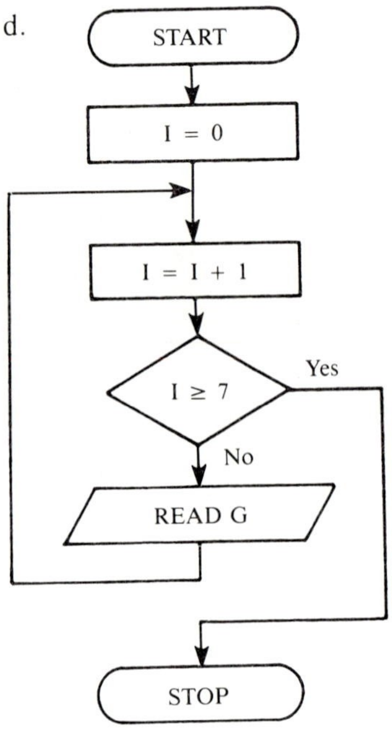

e.

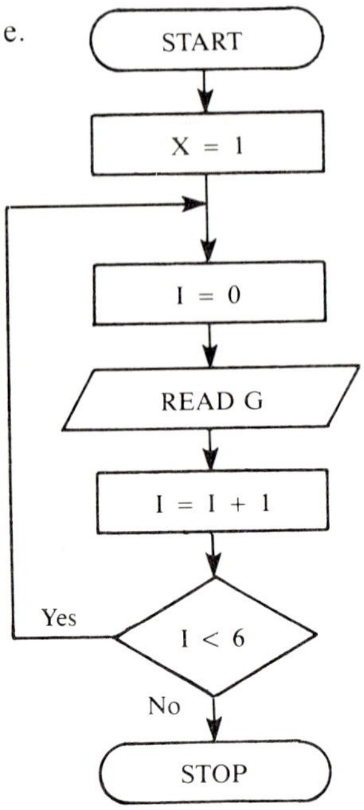

f.

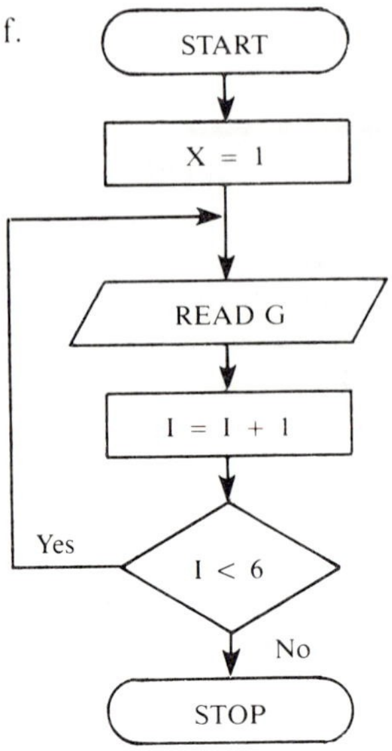

g.

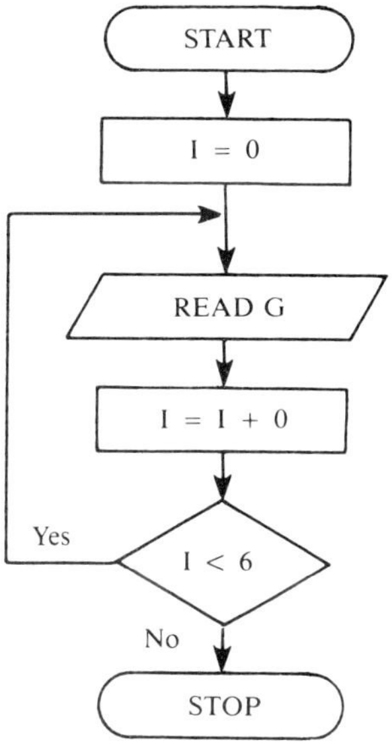

h.

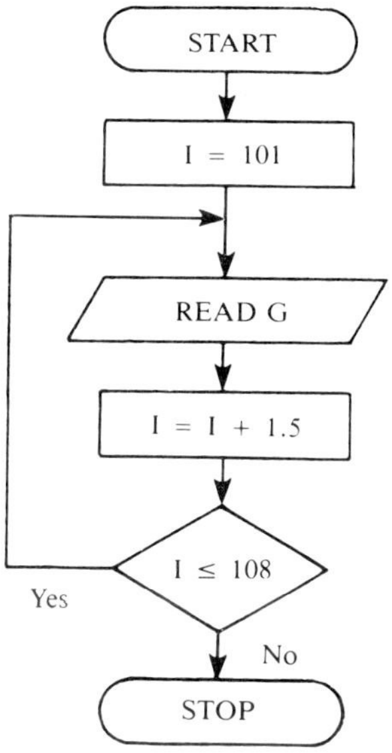

2. A certain file contains 10 data records. Which of the following flowcharts will read 10 and only 10 data records?

a.

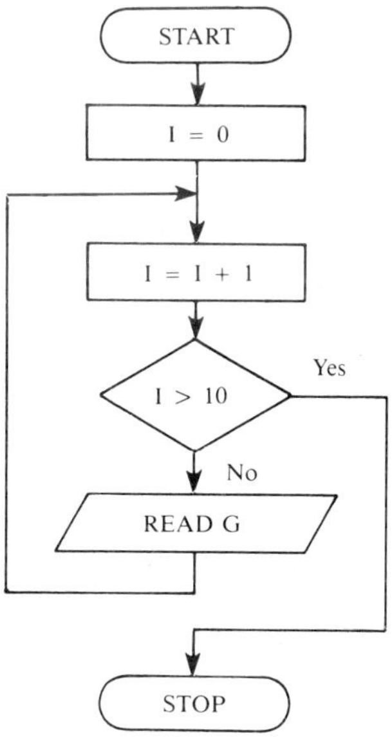

b.

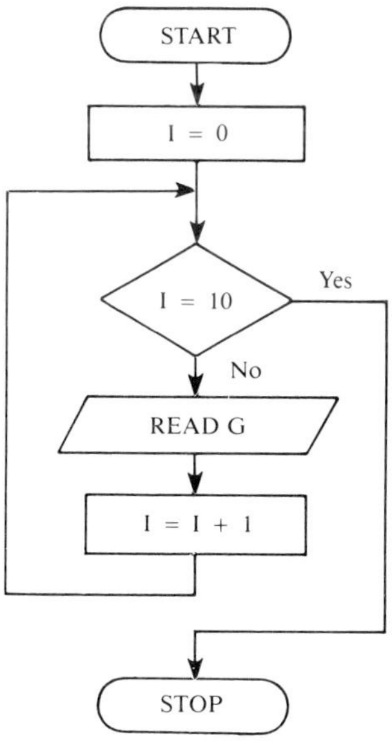

c.

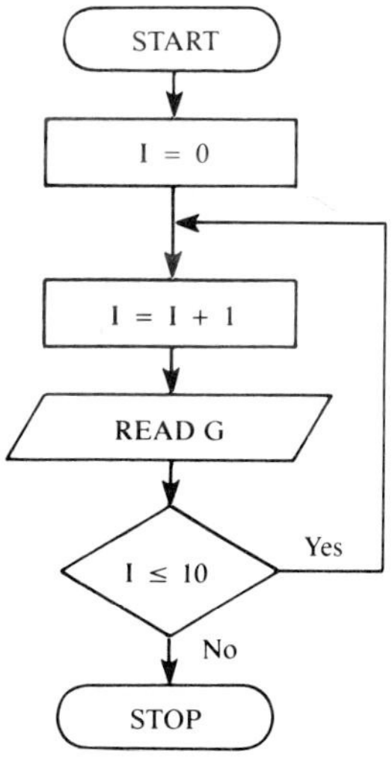

d.

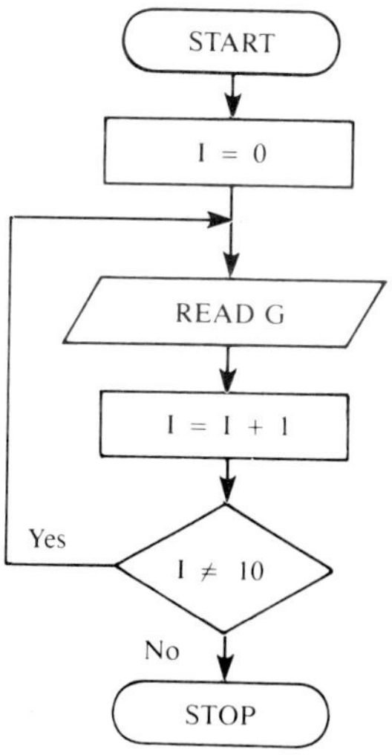

3. Complete each IF statement so that the program will read 10 data items.

a.
```
10 LET I = 0
15 READ J
20 IF I[    ]THEN 99
25 LET I = I + 1
30 GO TO 15
99 END
```

b.
```
10 LET I = 0
15 LET I = I + 1
20 READ J
25 IF I[    ]THEN 15
99 END
```

c.
```
10 LET I = 0
15 READ J
20 IF I[    ]THEN 30
25 GO TO 99
30 LET I = I + 1
35 GO TO 15
99 END
```

d.
```
10 LET I = 0
15 IF I[    ]THEN 99
20 READ G
25 LET I = I + 1
30 GO TO 15
99 END
```

e.
```
10 LET I = 10
15 IF I[    ]THEN 99
20 READ T
25 LET I = I - 1
30 GO TO 15
99 END
```

f.
```
10 LET I = 10
15 LET I = I - 1
20 READ J
25 IF I[    ]THEN 15
99 END
```

4. Write down any six positive numbers (less than 100), one per record, and determine the action of the following flowcharts on the six numbers (each READ reads one number per record).

a.

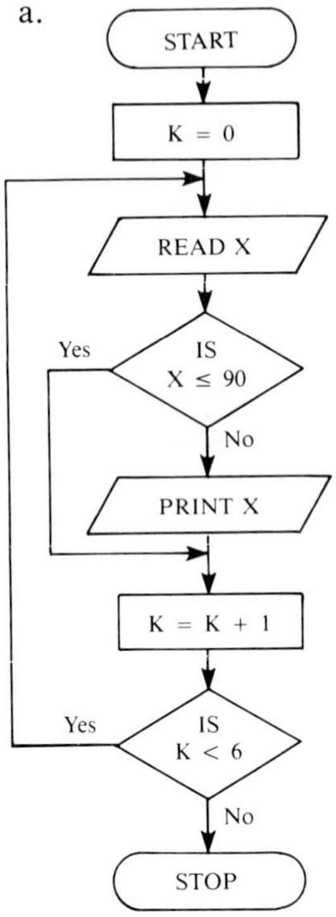

b.

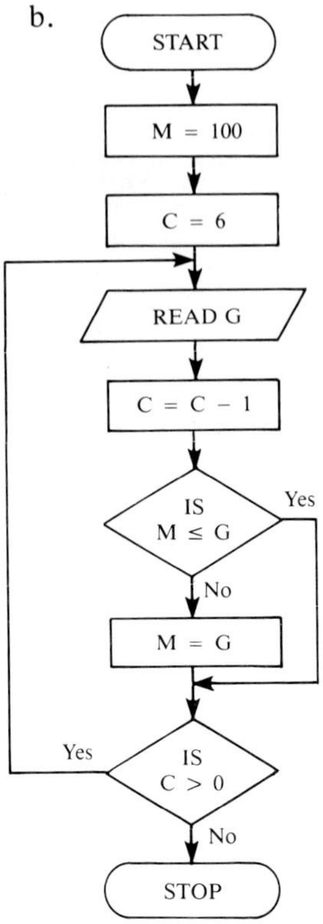

c.

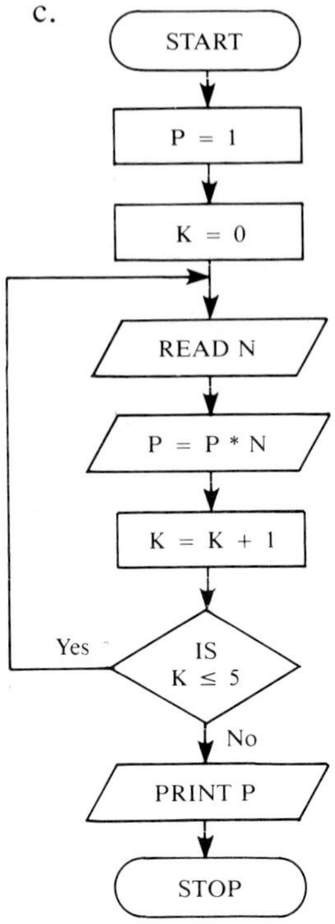

5. Fill in the blanks.
   a. Two examples of nonexecutable statements are __________ and __________.
   b. Items in a DATA block are accessed by the __________ statement.
   c. Tabulation for a program or flowchart is useful for __________.
   d. Some tasks accomplished by counting include __________.
   e. A trip record is used to __________.

6. Write programs to produce the following sequences:
   a. 0, 5, 10, 15, 20,..., 100
   b. 1, 2, 4, 8, 16,...,4096
   c. 1, −2, 4, −8, 16,...N for N accepted from input.
   d. N, N − 1,...,4, 3, 2, 1 for N accepted from input.

5-8-2 Exercises

1. A file consists of an unknown number of records; each record contains a Social Security number, a sex code (1 = male, 2 = female), and earnings. Write a program using the sex as a trip record to count the number of males earning above $30,000 and to list the females, by Social Security numbers, earning less than $35,000.

2. A DATA statement contains numbers supposedly arranged in numerical ascending order. Write a program to print the message "IN ORDER" if they are in order and message "OUT OF ORDER" if they are not. All records must be read.

3. A DATA statement contains 10 pairs of grades. 1) Write a program to print each pair and its sum. 2) Now the first number in the DATA statement is a number that tells how many pairs of grades follow that first number. Write a program to process this file and print the same information as in case 1.

4. A DATA statement contains an unknown number of positive and negative numbers varying from − 1,000 to + 1,000. Write a program to determine how many positive numbers, how many negative numbers, and how many zeros there are in the DATA statement.

5. Each data record in a file contains two items: an age and a code for marital status (1 = single, 2 = married, 3 = divorced, 4 = widowed). There are an unknown number of data records. A code of 9 in the marital status field indicates that it is the last record. Write one program to compute and print:
   a. The percentage of people over 30 years of age
   b. The number of people who are either widowed or divorced
   c. The number of people who are over 50 or less than 30 and who are not married

6. Write a program to print out multiplication tables from 2 to 10 as follows:

```
MULTIPLICATION TABLES

 2 ×  1 =  2
 2 ×  2 =  4
      .
      .
      .
 2 × 10 = 20

 3 ×  1 =  3
 3 ×  2 =  6
      .
      .
      .
 3 × 10 = 30
      .
      .
      .
10 ×  1 = 10
10 ×  2 = 20
      .
      .
      .
10 × 10 = 100
```

Note blank lines between tables.

7. Write a program to compute how much a person would weigh on the following planets based on the following table:

Planet	*Percentage of Earth Weight*
Moon	16
Jupiter	264
Venus	85
Mars	38

Create a table with weights ranging from 50 to 250 pounds in steps of 50 pounds. The same program should generate both of the following outputs:

a.

Earth	*Moon*	*Jupiter*	*Venus*	*Mars*
50	XXX	XXX	XXX	XXX
100	.	.	.	.
.				
.				
250	XXX	XXX	XXX	XXX

b.

Planet Number	Earth Weight	Planet Weight
1	50	XXX
	100	XXX
	.	.
	.	.
	250	XXX
2	50	XXX
	100	XXX
	.	.
	.	.
	250	XXX
.		
.		
.		
4	50	XXX
	100	XXX
	.	.
	.	.
	250	XXX

On output b, the planets are represented by numerical codes 1, 2, 3, and 4. A blank line should separate the two tables from one another.

8. Make your family a temperature conversion chart that displays the temperatures in Fahrenheit and centigrade starting at $-35°F$ and going up to $125°F$. The formula is ($F = 9/5*C + 32$).

9. Write a program to print out the following board (exactly):

```
.............................
.    .    .    .    .    .   .
.    .    .    .    .    .   .
.    .    .    .    .    .   .
.............................
.    .    .    .    .    .   .
.    .    .    .    .    .   .
.    .    .    .    .    .   .
.............................
.    .    .    .    .    .   .
.    .    .    .    .    .   .
.    .    .    .    .    .   .
.............................
.    .    .    .    .    .   .
.    .    .    .    .    .   .
.    .    .    .    .    .   .
.............................
```

10. The formula to compute a simple interest I on a loan of P dollars at an interest rate R (for example R = .135: 13.5%) for T days is:

```
I = P * R * T/360
```

Write a program to read a dollar amount and an interest rate and produce a table showing the interest to be paid at the end of each month for a period of 12 months (assume each month is 30 days).

11. Write a program to draw a flag as shown below. No alphanumeric string should contain more than 1 asterisk or more than 1 hyphen or minus sign symbol.

```
* * * * * * ----------------------------------
* * * * *
* * * * * * ----------------------------------
* * * * *
* * * * * * ----------------------------------
* * * * *
* * * * * * ----------------------------------
* * * * *
* * * * * * ----------------------------------
----------------------------------------------
----------------------------------------------
----------------------------------------------
```

12. Mrs. X has just invested \$9,000 at 13.5% yearly interest rate. She has decided to withdraw the accumulated interest as soon as that interest has exceeded \$11,000.00. How many years will Mrs. X have to wait before she can withdraw at least \$11,000 of accumulated interest? Could you be more specific and identify the number of years and months?

13. Each DATA statement contains a name, a sex code, and earnings. Write a program to read an unknown number of such records to provide the average male earning and to specify by word (male or female) the gender of the person with the highest individual earnings, i.e., there could be two different types of outputs as follows:

```
AVE MALE EARNING = XXXXX
HIGHEST EARNINGS OBTAINED BY MALE
```

```
AVE MALE EARNING = XXXXX
HIGHEST EARNINGS OBTAINED BY FEMALE
```

14. A data file consists of records containing an employee number, a number of hours worked, and an hourly rate of pay. Overtime is time and a half for each hour over 40. Federal and state taxes are 18 and 5% of gross earnings respectively. Social security deductions are 6.74% of gross pay up to \$34,000 and 0% beyond that amount. Write a program to produce an output with the following headings:

```
                         PAYROLL REPORT

EMPLOYEE    GROSS    SOC. SEC.    FED. AND ST.    NET PAY
                     DEDUCTION       TAXES
```

15. Write a program to simulate octal counting up to 27_8, that is, print the numbers 1, 2,..., 7, 10, 11,..., 17, 20, 21,...,27. Can you generalize your program for counting in octal up to any number?

16. Write a program to input a positive value for J and print:
    a. The even integers from 0 to J.
    b. The first J odd positive integers.
    c. A message if J is a prime number.

17. A data file consists of 14 positive or negative numbers. Write a program to stop reading the file whenever two numbers of the opposite sign follow one another. Print the number of items read up to this point.

18. Data for a store shows daily sales for corresponding days of succeeding years. The first value on the record is the amount of sales for a given day in the first year: the second value is the amount of sales for the corresponding day in the second year. Find the number of days in which the second year's daily sales exceeded the first year's daily sales by more than 10% of the first year's sales. The output should be similar to the following:

Sample DATA

```
DATA 500,550
DATA 400,441
DATA 300,500
DATA 600,448
```

Sample Output

```
FIRST YEAR          SECOND YEAR
  500                  550
  400                  441 **
  300                  500 **
  600                  448
NUMBER OF SUPERIOR SALES DAYS 2
```

(Note that ** identifies those records for which the second year's daily sales exceeds the first year's daily sales by more than 10%.)

19. A wholesaler accepts a $5,000 promissory note from a retailer at 15% in lieu of cash payment for delivered goods. Write a program to compute the maturity value of the note for a 30-, 60-, and 90-day short-term loan. (Formula for maturity value is $S = P(1 + I \cdot N)$. S is the maturity value, P is principal, I is interest rate, and N is the number of years, or if less than 1 year, number of days/360.)

20. Each employee working at Personpower, Inc., is paid at a regular hourly rate of $5.00 for the first 40 hours. The overtime rate is 1.5 times the regular rate. The number of hours worked by each employee is entered on DATA statements.

    a. Write a program to read the number of hours worked by each employee and compute each employee's pay. The output should be similar to the following:

```
HOURS    RATE   OVERTIME HOURS    PAY
10.00    5.00          0          50.00
50.00    5.00         10         275.00
  .        .           .            .
  .        .           .            .
  .        .           .            .
```

    b. Write a program similar to the one in part a, but read both the number of hours and the rate of pay from DATA statements. Also, deduct 6.1% of each employee's pay for the first 30 hours for a pension plan. The output should be similar to

```
HOURS    RATE   PENSION PLAN    PAY
50.00   10.00      18.30      531.70
  .       .          .           .
  .       .          .           .
  .       .          .           .
```

c. Write a program similar to the one in part b; now the DATA statement contains a bonus amount in addition to the hours and rate of pay for each employee. If the employee's pay exceeds $500, the bonus is added to the employee's pay: otherwise the bonus field is left blank on the output (the bonus is not included in the pay):

```
HOURS    RATE     PENSION PLAN    BONUS     PAY

5Ø.ØØ    1Ø.ØØ          18.3Ø      1ØØ    631.7Ø
1Ø.ØØ     5.ØØ           3.Ø5             46.95
  .        .              .          .       .
  .        .              .          .       .
  .        .              .          .       .
```

Note the blank field for the second entry

21. A simulated well problem: In parts a, b, and c that follow we will assume the well is dry (no water).

a. Write a program to input an integer value for N and draw a well N meters deep. Use upper case I to draw the walls of the well and the minus sign for the base of the well. One meter is the equivalent of the graphic symbol I.

Examples:

```
    N = 5            N = 7           N = 1
I       I        I       I        I-------I
I       I        I       I
I       I        I       I
I       I        I       I
I-------I        I       I
                 I       I
                 I-------I
```

b. Expand your program to simulate dropping a stone into a well *N* meters deep by graphing its linear trajectory with a sequence of dots:

```
N = 5     I   .   I
          I   .   I    trajectory of stone
          I   .   I
          I   .   I
          I---.---I    Stone hits bottom of well
```

c. Ten seconds after a stone has been thrown into a well, it hits the bottom of the well. Write the code to draw the well and the dropping stone, as in part b, also print the depth of the well and the time it takes the stone to reach the bottom, as shown in the examples. The distance traveled (assume no air resistance) is:

$$d = \frac{1}{2}gt^2$$

where t is the time expressed in seconds and g is the force of gravity (9.81 meters/second^2). Round the distance to the nearest meter.

Examples:

```
                           t=1 second              t=1.2 seconds
                                ↓                       ↓
                           I    .    I            I     .     I
                           I    .    I            I     .     I
Depth = 5 meters           I    .    I            I     .     I     Depth = 7 meters
                           I    .    I            I     .     I
                           I---.---I              I     .     I
                                                  I     .     I
                                                  I---.---I
```

d. Now imagine that the well contains water and is infinitely deep! Start the game by inputting an arbitrary depth (D) for the well (define the depth as the distance from the ground surface to the water level). We will develop a game in which you tell the computer how many seconds you think it will take a dropped stone to reach the water surface. The computer should then produce a graphic display of what happens in that time interval (the time duration you guessed)—either the stone does not reach the water, or it just hits the water, of it falls below the water level. (To make the program simpler, use $d = 1/2\, gt^2$ to compute the distance the stone travels under water.)

For example, if you specified $D = 8$ meters and you guessed 1 second for the stone to hit the surface of the water, the computer should produce the following display (the message SHORT is printed alongside the well):

```
                I    .    I
5 meters to     I    .    I     The stone travels 5 meters
water level     I    .    I     in 1 second
surface         I    .    I
                I    .    I        SHORT
                I         I
                I         I
                I-------I
```

Since the player guessed short, he/she now guesses 1.4 seconds. This time the stone travels under water for a total distance of 9.6 meters, rounded off to 10. The computer then displays the following results (the caption LONG is printed alongside the well):

```
                    I    .    I
                    I    .    I
                    I    .    I
8 meters to         I    .    I
water level         I    .    I     In 1.4 seconds the stone
surface             I    .    I     has traveled 10 meters.
water surface       I    .    I
               ---> I---.---I       LONG
                    I    .    I
                    I    .    I
```

The display shows how many more meters the stone travels after hitting the water.

The player then guesses 1.3 seconds. With this guess, the distance traveled is 8.2 meters, which is sufficiently close to the water level to be a hit or a win! The computer then prints

```
I   .   I
I   .   I
I   .   I
I   .   I
I   .   I
I   .   I
I   .   I
I---.---I        YOU MADE A HIT!
```

We shall agree that if the distance traveled is within one-half meter of the surface (above/below) a win occurs. This implies:

If the distance traveled < D − .5, the guess is short (increase guess next time).

If the distance traveled > D + .5, the guess is long (decrease guess next time).

If neither above conditions are satisfied, the player wins!

Write a program for the game described in this section. A complete example of an output is shown in Figure 5–8.

22. The simple discount is the amount deducted from the maturity value S of an obligation when the latter is sold before its date of maturity. The formula is $SD = S \,.\, D \,.\, N$, where SD = simple discount, S = maturity value, D = discount rate, and N = term of loan, that is, time remaining before maturity.

A wholesaler received a $10,500 promissory note for goods sold to a retailer. The note matures in N months and bears an I percent interest rate. One month later, the wholesaler sells his note to a bank at 9% discount rate. Write a program to compute:

a. The maturity value of the note for N = 30, 60, and 90 days with an interest rate of I = 4%, 5%, and 6%. That is, N = 30 for I = 4%, 5%, and 6%; N = 60 for I = 4%, 5%, and 6%, and so forth.

b. The proceeds received by the wholesaler as a result of selling the note to the bank for N = 30, 60, and 90 days with an interest rate of 4%, 5%, and 6%.

23. Mr. Small is thinking of borrowing $5,000 for N months at 8% simple discount rate to purchase a new automobile. Write a program to compute the proceeds of this loan for the following values of N: 6 months, 1 year, 2 years, and 3 years. The proceeds (P) is the sum remaining after the discount is deducted: $P = S(1 - D - N)$.

24. Lurnlot University in Florida recognizes four student classifications for billing purposes: in-state full time, out-of-state full time, and in-state part time, and out-of-state part time. A student who enrolls for less than 12 hours of courses is

■ **Figure 5–8** Depth-finding game.

```
ENTER DISTANCE TO WATER
? 5
ENTER GUESS IN SECONDS FOR STONE TO HIT WATER
? .5
                  I    .    I
                  I    .    I       SHORT
                  I         I
                  I         I
                  I---------I
ENTER GUESS IN SECONDS FOR STONE TO HIT WATER
? 1.2
                  I    .    I
                  I    .    I
                  I    .    I
                  I    .    I
                  I----.----I
                  I    .    I
                  I    .    I       LONG
ENTER GUESS IN SECONDS FOR STONE TO HIT WATER
? 1
                  I    .    I
                  I    .    I
                  I    .    I
                  I    .    I
                  I----.----I       YOU WIN
DO YOU WANT TO PLAY ANOTHER GAME
? YES
ENTER DISTANCE TO WATER FOR STONE TO HIT WATER
? 100
ENTER GUESS IN SECONDS
? 6
```

considered to be a part-time student. The schedule of charges for each classification is summarized in the following table:

SCHEDULE OF CHARGES

	full time		*part time*	
	in-state	*out-of-state*	*in-state*	*out-of-state*
Tuition & Fees	$545	$1,184	$44/hour	$94/hour
Fixed Fee	$60			
Board	$425			

The university needs a computer program to compute student bills. The input to the program consists of a file of student records where each record contains the student's:

a. name
b. residence status: state abbreviation, FL if in-state
c. scheduled hours
d. request for board: *yes* if requested, *no* otherwise.

Write a program to list each student's name and total bill. For example:

Input

```
DATA EDMUND SC, 10, YES
DATA LITTLE SC, 20, YES
DATA ZONE   SC, 10, NO
DATA HUGHES SC, 20, NO
DATA DANGER FL, 09, YES
DATA RANT   FL, 09, NO
DATA DOE    FL, 15, YES
DATA MIGHT  FL, 15, NO
```

Output

```
NAME     STATE  HOURS  BOARD    BILL

EDMUND   SC      10     YES   1425.00
LITTLE   SC      20     YES   1669.00
ZONE     SC      10     NO    1000.00
HUGHES   SC      20     NO    1244.00
DANGER   FL       9     YES    881.00
RANT     FL       9     NO     456.00
DOE      FL      15     YES   1030.00
MIGHT    FL      15     NO     605.00
```

25. The Kiddie Up Company manufactures toys for adults. The company expects fixed costs for the next year to be around $180,000. With the demand for adult toys increasing, the company is looking for sales of $900,000 in the year to come. The variable costs are expected to run at about 74% of sales.

a. Write a program to determine the break-even point (BEP) (the dollar amount of sales that must be made to incur neither a profit nor a loss) and compute the expected profit. The formula to compute the BEP is:

$$\text{BEP} = \frac{\text{total fixed costs}}{1 - \dfrac{\text{variable costs}}{\text{sales}}}$$

b. The Kiddie Up Company management is arguing that, with the current rate of inflation, variable costs will run higher for the next year—probably any-

```
                    KIDDIE UP COMPANY
             1984 OPERATIONS FORECAST (1984)

PROJECTED SALES: 900,000
FIXED COSTS:     180,000

VARIABLE     VARIABLE COST     BREAK EVEN     PROFIT     DEFICIT
 COSTS        PERCENTAGE          POINT

675000            75             720000       180000       ***
   .               .                .            .           .
   .               .                .            .           .
   .               .                .            .           .
747000            83            1058823        ***       205882
```

where from 75 to 83% of sales. With sales still projected at $900,000, the management directs its data processing staff to generate the following report to determine the break-even point and the profits and losses for different variable costs. Sales and fixed costs remain constant.
Write a program to complete this report. Place three stars (***) in the profit column if there is no profit. Do the same for deficit.

c. The company employees have just won a new contract. As a result, variable costs are expected to reach 81 or 82% of next year's projected $900,000 sales. A recent internal study carried out by the company on the various aspects of the manufacturing operations disclosed production inefficiencies. Corrective measures could significantly lower fixed costs. Project a range of fixed costs to show a company profit of anywhere from 50 to 100,000 dollars, given that variable costs are expected to reach 81 or 82% of sales next year.

26. A store is planning a sale to sell slow-moving items from its computerized inventory. The first DATA statement in a set of DATA statements contains the current date. Each succeeding DATA statement contains the item number and description, the date of the last time an item was sold, the number of items on hand, the cost per item, and the regular selling price for the item. The store needs a program to produce a report showing recommended sale prices:

If item has not been sold in the last 30 days, the discount should be 10%.
If item has not been sold in the last 60 days, the discount should be 20%.
If item has not been sold in the last 90 days, the discount should be 40%.

However, any item that has sold in the last 30 days is not to be placed on sale. Also, if there is only one item left in stock, it should not be placed on sale, no matter what the last date of sale. The amount of discount allowed should never be such that sales price is lower than cost. Write a program to produce the report.

27. One method for calculating depreciation is to subtract a fixed percentage of the original value of the item each year. Thus, a $100 item depreciated at 10% would be valued at $90 at the end of the first year, $80 at the end of the second, and so forth. Another method for calculating depreciation is to subtract a fixed percentage of the present value of the item. A $100 item depreciated at 10% would be valued at $90 at the end of the first year, $90 − .1 × 90 = $81 at the end of the second year, and so forth. Write a program to accept as input the original value *(V)*, the depreciation rate *(R)*, and a number of years *(N)*, and produce a table showing the value of the items for the first, second, third,..., *N*th year using both depreciation methods.

28. The number e can be defined as the limit of $(1 + 1/n)^n$ as n (integer) gets larger and larger. Write a program to approximate a value for e. Stop when the difference between two successive approximations is less than .001. Print out the values for e and n.

For example:

$$e_1 = (1 + \frac{1}{1})^1 = 2$$

$$e_2 = (1 + \frac{1}{2})^2 = 2.25$$

$$e_3 = (1 + \frac{1}{3})^3 = 2.37$$

The difference between e_3 and e_2 is still greater than .001; hence new values for e have to be computed until $e_{n+1} - e_n < .001$.

29. The Fibonacci sequence is formed by assigning the value 1 to the first two terms and then computing each successive term as the sum of the two preceding terms. Thus $a_1 = 1$, $a_2 = 1$, $a_3 = a_1 + a_2 = 1 + 1 = 2$, $a_4 = a_2 + a_3 = 1 + 2 = 3$, and so on. The first few terms of the Fibonacci sequence are 1,1,2,3,5,8,13,21,34,55,...

    a. Write a program to generate the first 20 terms of the Fibonacci sequence.
    b. A number is said to be a Fibonacci number if it occurs as a term of the Fibonacci sequence. Write a program to read a number and determine if it is a Fibonacci number. (Assume number is less than 100,000.)

30. The golden mean was used by ancient Roman architects in the design of structures. A building in which the ratio of the length to the width equalled the golden mean (which is approximately equal to 1.618) was believed to be most pleasing aesthetically. It can be shown that the limit of the ratio of successive terms of the Fibonacci sequence is equal to the golden mean. Write a program to compute terms of the Fibonacci sequence and the ratio of each term to its predecessor. How many terms are required before the difference between successive ratios is less than 0.01? 0.0001? How many terms are required before successive ratios are equal? (The answers to these questions depend on the data representation of the computer is use; the ratios should become equal in fewer than 100 terms.)

31. The following formula provides an approximation for the nth term in the Fibonacci sequence:

$$0.447264 \times (1.61803)^{n-1}$$

Write a program to generate the actual terms of the Fibonacci sequence, the approximation, the absolute difference between the actual term and the approximation, and the relative error (difference divided by actual value). What happens to the values of relative error for successively larger values of n? How "good" is the approximation? Can you improve on the approximation formula?

32. Mortgages are generally amortized with a fixed monthly payment that will pay off the loan in a specified amount of time. The formula for the monthly payment is given in problem 34. In many instances the original holder of the mortgage sells it to a third party at a discount. The third party will then receive payments in the same way as the original mortgage holder. For example, suppose $50,000 is to be amortized at 14% for 25 years. The monthly payment would be $601.88. Suppose further that the mortgage is sold to a third party at a 10% discount. The third party receives the $50,000 mortgage at a net cost of $45,000. What is the effective interest rate to the third party? In this case, it is necessary to compute the interest rate given the new principal ($45,000), time (25 years), and monthly payment ($601.88). The algorithm shown below uses an iterative method to approximate the interest rate:

P = Principal
T = Time
MP = Monthly payment

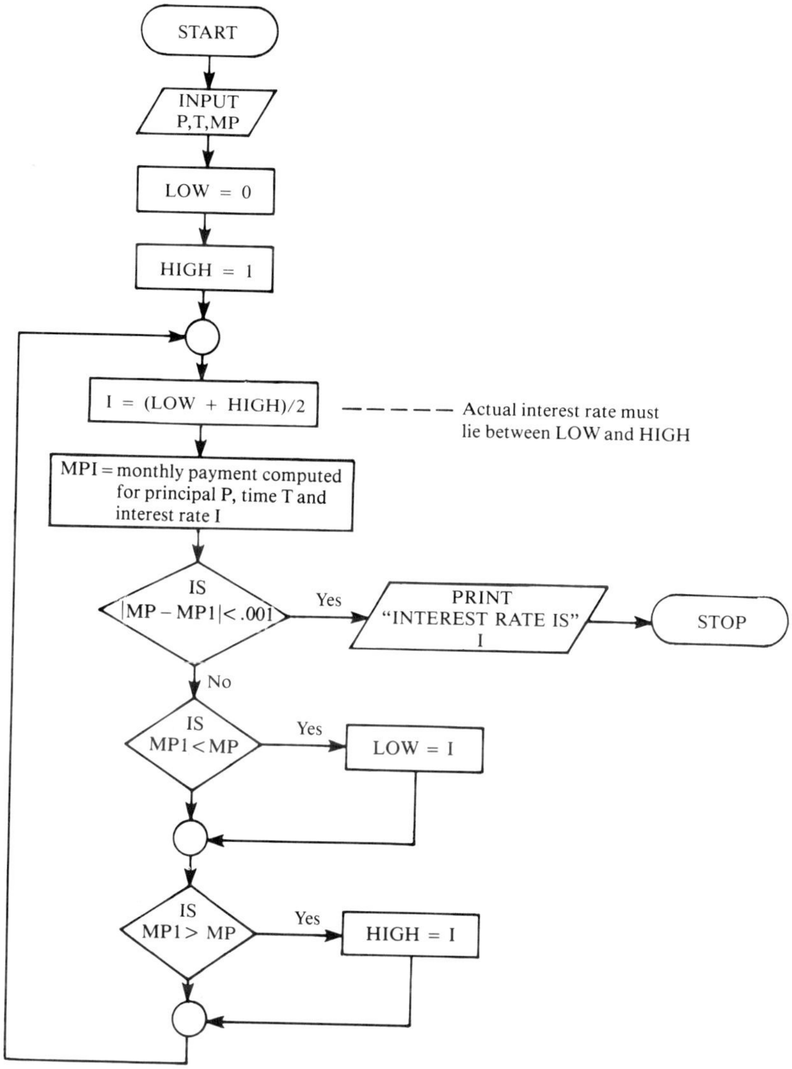

Write a program based on this method. For the example given above, the effective interest rate for the third party is approximately 15.7%.

33. You have been hired by E. Naddor, Inc., a world-famous firm specializing in inventory control problems, to write a computer program for one of Naddor's largest customers, the Shopping Basket. This firm would like to computerize part of its reordering system to cut down on the cost of replenishing inventories.

Each Friday at the close of business, the ending inventory of each product is compared to the fixed reorder point for that product. If the ending inventory is equal to or below the reorder point for that product, the Shopping Basket orders enough of the item to bring the amount on hand up to a predetermined order level (any order placed on Friday is delivered over the weekend so that the company can begin a new week of business with well-stocked shelves). It is possible for the ending inventory to be negative, indicating that demand exceeded supply during the week and some orders were not filled. Shopping Basket policy is to order enough to cover this backordered demand.

To aid you in your task, you have been given some old records that illustrate how the reorder system works.

Item number / *Description*	*15202* *Tuna fish*	*67180* *Charcoal lighter*	*51435* *Mouthwash*	*49415* *Pizza mix*	*24361* *Asparagus*
Unit price (per case)	4.27	8.48	12.29	9.27	15.32
Order level (cases)	30	25	55	75	15
Reorder point (cases)	5	8	10	25	2
Ending inventory (cases)	9	5	7	−10	6

Your task is to write a program to read five data records (using the sample data in the above inventory summary) to determine which items must be ordered and the respective quantities to be ordered for each item. The program should also calculate the cost of such orders and the total cost for all items ordered. The sample input and output are shown below:

INPUT LAYOUT

Positions	*Field Description*
1	Item number
2	Unit price (dollars and cents)
3	Order level (cases)
4	Reorder point (cases)
5	Ending inventory

For example, the data record corresponding to the tuna fish would be:

DATA	15202,	427,	30,	5,	9
	↓ Item number	↓ Unit price	↓ Order level	↓ Reorder point	↓ Ending inventory

A sample output for the records given above would be:

Sample Output

```
                    THE SHOPPING BASKET
                       ORDER REPORT

ITEM     UNIT     ORDER   REORDER    ENDING
NUMBER   PRICE    LEVEL    POINT    INVENTORY   ORDER     COST
15202    4.27      30        5          9         0       0.00
67180    8.48      25        8          5        20     169.60
51435   12.29      55       10          7        48     589.92
49415    9.27      75       25         10        85     787.95
24361   15.32      15        2          6         0       0.00
                                         TOTAL COST $1547.47
```

Some helpful rules are:

a. Order an item only if ending inventory is less than or equal to the reorder point for the item.
b. Amount to order = order-level − ending inventory.
c. Cost of ordering an item = amount ordered * unit price.

34. Compute the monthly payment for a $45,000 loan at interest rates varying from 12.00% to 16.00% in increments of 0.25% for 15-, 20-, 25- and 30-year mortgages. The output should be similar to the following:

```
PRINCIPAL: 45ØØØ

INTEREST   DURATION   MONTHLY PAYMENT
 12.ØØ        15          54Ø.Ø8
              2Ø          495.49
              25          473.95
              3Ø          462.88

 12.25        15          547.34
              2Ø          5Ø3.36
              25          482.29
              3Ø          471.55

 12.5Ø        15          554.64
              2Ø          511.27
              25          49Ø.66
              3Ø          48Ø.27
   .           .             .
   .           .             .
```

The formula to compute the monthly payment is: $\text{MP} = \dfrac{i \cdot P/12}{1 - (i/12 + 1)^{12 \cdot T}}$

where i and P are interest and principal, and T is the time in years.

35. Each record of an input file contains a last name and a final test score. Names are supposed to be in reversed alphabetical order (Z to A). Write a program to identify those that are not in sequence by name. If all names are in order, print the message NAMES ARE IN ORDER.

Example:

```
DATA WOE,8Ø, SAME,32, TOON,22, HIRAM,34, POT,23, TANNER,23
```

The output produced would be:

```
3 TOON          The number identifies the position
5 POT           of the name in the list
6 TANNER
```

5-8-3 Answers to Test Yourself

1. a. 7 b. 6 c. 8 d. 6
e. infinite f. *I* not defined g. infinite h. 5

2. a,b,d

3. a. I = 9 b. I < 10 c. I < 9 d. I = 10 e. I = 0 f. I > 0
Note: Other answers may also be correct.

4. a. Prints values for *X* that are larger than 90.
b. *M* will store the smallest value of *G*.
c. Value of *P* will be the product of the six values of *N*.

5. a. DATA, REM
b. READ
c. understanding how the procedure represented in the program/flowchart is carried out
d. determining how many items in a set meet a criterion, loop control, and number generation
e. detect end-of-file

6. a.

```
10 LET I = 0
20 PRINT I
30 LET I = I + 5
40 IF I < = 100 THEN 20
50 END
```

b.

```
10 LET I = 0
20 PRINT 2 ^ I
30 LET I = I + 1
40 IF 2 ^ I =< 4096 THEN 20
50 END
```

c.

```
10 INPUT N
20 LET M = 1
30 LET C = 1
40 PRINT M*C
50 LET C = C * 2
60 LET M = -M
70 IF C < = N THEN 40
80 END
```

d.

```
10 INPUT N
20 PRINT N
30 LET N = N - 1
40 IF N > 0 THEN 20
50 END
```

6 BASIC FUNCTIONS, PRINT USING, ON GO TO, AND LOGICAL FUNCTIONS

6-1 BASIC Functions

6-1-1 Definitions

You are probably already familiar with many mathematical functions, such as the square root, and the exponential and trigonometric functions. Let's look at an example using the trigonometric function *tangent*. An observer on shore sights a ship one mile away. This ship is moving along a line perpendicular to the observer's line of sight. One hour later, the observer sights the ship and finds an angle of 25° between the two sightings. How far has the ship traveled? Using trigonometry, it can be shown that the distance traveled is $x = \tan 25°$. The code to perform this computation would be:

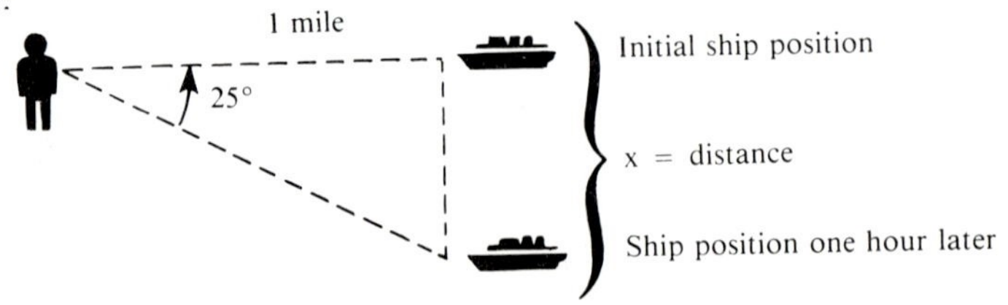


```
10 X=TAN(25./57.296)
15 PRINT X
20 END
   RUN
   .4663
```

The program uses the function TAN; the programmer does not have to write a routine to evaluate the tangent function. Note that the argument of the function TAN must be expressed in radians. One radian is equivalent to 57.296° (180° = π radians), hence 25° = 25/57.296 radians.

Trigonometric functions and other functions are available in BASIC through libraries provided by the computer system. BASIC also allows you to define and code your own functions through the DEF statement (see chapter 10).

A *function* is a correspondence between one set of numbers called *arguments* and another number called the value of the function. For example, let's look at the square root function:

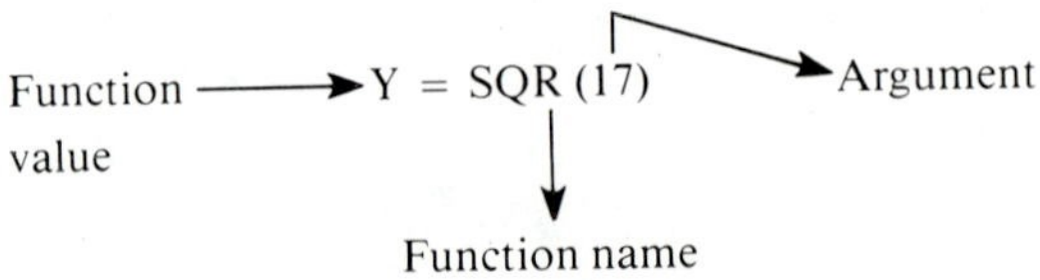

The following code illustrates the correspondence between functional values and arguments for the square root function:

```
05 I = 1
10 PRINT "ARGUMENT", "VALUE"
15 I = I + 1
20 PRINT I, SQR(I)
25 IF I < 4 THEN 15
RUN
ARGUMENT    VALUE
   1        1
   2        1.414
   3        1.732
   4        2
```

In BASIC, a function reference may be included as a part of any arithmetic expression. The general form of a function reference is:

function name (argument expression)

All BASIC functions require an *argument expression* enclosed in parentheses after the function name. The *argument expression* may take the form of a constant, a variable, another function reference, or an expression containing constants, variables, arithmetic operations, and function references. The expression is evaluated to a single value, which is then passed to the function as an argument. Logically, we can think of the function as being evaluated when it is called. Internally, a function consists of a series of statements that calculate the value of the function based on the value of the argument. A function returns control to the point at which it is called.

6-1-2 Mathematical Functions

Common mathematical functions supplied with BASIC are shown in Figure 6-1. Note that there are restrictions on the range of values acceptable as arguments for some functions. For example, the natural logarithm (LOG) function requires an argument greater than zero. If an invalid argument is given to a function, an error message will be printed.

Figure 6-1 BASIC supplied mathematical functions.

Function	*Argument*[1]	*Value*
SIN(x)	Must be expressed in radians	The sine of x
COS(x)	Must be expressed in radians	The cosine of x
TAN(x)	Must be expressed in radians	The tangent of x
ATN(x)	Must be expressed in radians	Arctangent of x ($-\pi/2 < \text{ATN}(x) \leq \pi/2$)
EXP(x)	A real number	The value of e^x ($e = 2.718...$)
LOG(x)	A positive real number	The natural iogarithm of x

[1]Argument may be any arithmetic expression and may contain one or more function references

Examples:

`I=COS(X)^2+C*EXP(-SIN(X))`	Evaluates to $\cos^2 x + c\,e^{-\sin x}$.
`IF LOG(R) > 31.6 THEN...`	The natural logarithm (base e) is computed. If R is negative, an error message will be printed, since logarithms of negative numbers are not defined.

6-1-3 Do It Now

Write BASIC statements for each of the following:

1. $\sin x + \cos x$
2. $\sin^2 x + \cos^2 x$
3. $\tan^{-1} x$
4. $\ln (x + y)$
5. $(\tan x)^{-1}$
6. $\dfrac{1}{\sin x^2 + \cos x^2}$
7. $e^x + e^{-x}$

Answers

1. SIN(X) + COS(X)
2. SIN(X)^2 + COS(X)^2
3. ATN(X)
4. LOG(X+Y)
5. (TAN(X))^(−1) or 1/TAN(X)
6. 1/(SIN(X^2) + COS(X^2))
7. EXP(X) + EXP(−X)

6-1-4 Other BASIC-Supplied Functions

Certain other functions, shown in Figure 6–2, are also included in BASIC.

The Square Root Function

The square root of a positive number can be computed with the SQR function.

Examples:

`10 Y = SQR(16)`	$y = 4$
`15 T = SQR(X)`	$t = \sqrt{x}$
`20 Z = SQR((A * X^2)/(C - 1))`	$z = \sqrt{\dfrac{ax^2}{c-1}}$
`25 PRINT SQR(-X^2 - 1)`	Invalid since $-x^2 - 1$ is negative
`30 T = SQR(SQR(17))`	$t = 2.03054$

Note that SQR(X) is the same as X^.5 (raising a number to the one-half power is the same as taking the square root).

Figure 6–2 BASIC functions.

Function	*Argument*[1]	*Value*
ABS(X)	A real number	The absolute value of X ($\|X\| = X$ if $X \geq 0$ $\|X\| = -X$ if $X < 0$)
SQR(X)	A positive real number	The square root of X
INT(X)	A real number	Greatest integer less than or equal to X
SGN(X)	A real number	$\begin{cases} -1 \text{ if } X < 0 \\ 0 \text{ if } X = 0 \\ 1 \text{ if } X > 0 \end{cases}$
RND(X)	May or may not be required	In many BASICs a random number between 0 and 1, i.e., 0 < RND(X) < 1. In other BASICs, an integer between 1 and X.
TAB(X)	A real number	Identifies column position on output

[1]Argument may be any arithmetic expression and may contain one or more function references.

The INT or INTeger Function

The INT function truncates (snips off) the fractional part of a number. To be more precise, the INTeger value of *X* is equal to the largest whole number less than or equal to *X*. We can see this on the real line, where INT (*number*) gives the first integer to the left of *number* (unless the number is an integer):

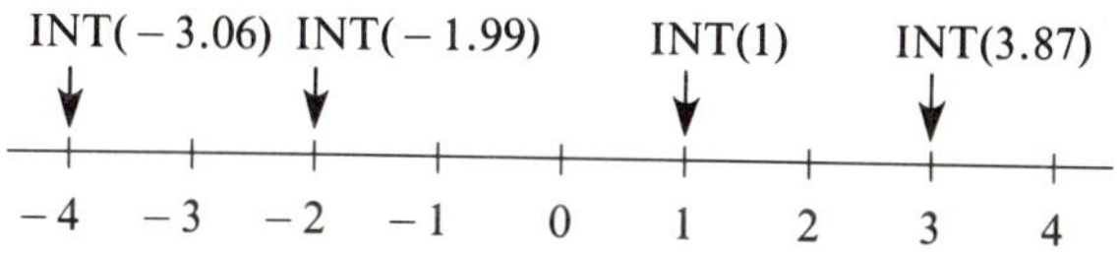

Examples:

`10 Y = INT(1.8)`	Since 1 is largest integer ≤ 1.8, the value 1 is stored in Y.
`15 Y = INT(-1.1)`	Since −2 is largest integer ≤ −1.1, −2 is stored in Y.
`20 PRINT INT(-2.55)`	−3 will be printed.
`25 Y = INT(-4)`	−4 is stored in Y.
`30 Y = INT(X + 1)`	If X = −.6, then 0 will be stored in Y.

In some applications (see exercise 16 in this chapter), it may be important to compute the remainder of a division. For example, the remainder of 14/3 is 2 since

$$\frac{14}{3} = 4 + \frac{(2)}{3} \quad \rightarrow \text{remainder}$$

In general, the remainder of A divided by B is:

$$\text{remainder of } (A/B) = A - \text{INT}(A/B) * B$$
$$\text{remainder of } 14/3 = 14 - \text{INT}(4.666\ldots) * 3 = 14 - 4 * 3 = 2$$

The INT function can also be very useful to truncate or round off numbers to a specified number of fractional digits (decimal positions). Numerical computations are carried out internally to at least six digits on most computer systems, yet often no more than two or three decimal places (fractional digits) are needed for the computed result. For example, suppose that internally X = 32.4562 and we wished to truncate the last two digits (retain two fractional digits). We could use the following method:

1. Multiply X by 100 to obtain 3245.62 `(LET X = 100*X)`
2. Take the integer part to obtain 3245. `(LET X = INT(X))`
3. Divide by 100 to obtain 32.45. `(LET X = X/100)`

To be even more precise, we could round off the second fractional digit by adding .005 to X to get

$$\begin{array}{r} 32.4562 \\ \underline{.005} \\ 32.4612 \end{array}$$

We then truncate X using steps just described. We can write the entire round-off procedure in one step, as follows:

```
10 LET X = INT((X + .005)*100)/100
```

Examples using INT to round to the nearest integer are shown in Figure 6–3.

The integer function can also be used to determine if certain numbers can be divided evenly into another number. For example, the number X is divisible by 2 if INT(X/2)*2 = X; the number Y is divisible by 17 if INT(Y/17)*17 = Y.

The Sign Function

The sign function (SGN) gives the sign of a number: −1 if the number is negative, 1 if the number is positive, or 0 if the number is zero. Examples are shown in Figure 6–3.

The Random Number Function RND

In most systems, the random number function RND does not require any arguments (a few systems require integer arguments, while others permit arguments for specific purposes described later). The result given by RND is a number from a uniform distribution in the open interval (0,1), meaning that any number between 0 and 1 (but neither 0 nor 1) is as likely to come up as any other. Consider the following program, for example:

```
10 PRINT RND
11 PRINT RND
12 PRINT RND
13 PRINT RND
14 PRINT RND
RUN
 .263884          close to .3
 .708429          close to .7
 .197174          close to .2
 .79064           close to .8
2.5235E - 3       close to 0
```

■ **Figure 6–3** Sample values of INT and SGN.

```
Ø1 PRINT
Ø5 PRINT "X", "INT(X)","INT(X + .5)","SGN(X)"
1Ø INPUT X
2Ø PRINT X, INT(X) ,INT(X + .5) ,SGN(X)
3Ø GO TO 1Ø
4Ø END
RUN
 X                    INT(X)       INT(X + .5)       SGN(X)
? 3                     3              3               1
? 3.4                   3              3               1
? 3.5                   3              4               1
? 3.99                  3              4               1
? Ø                     Ø              Ø               Ø
? -3                   -3             -3              -1
? -3.4                 -4             -3              -1
? -3.5                 -4             -3              -1
? -3.99                -4             -4              -1
```

One of the interesting aspects of RND is that if the above program were run again, the same sequence of numbers would be printed again! See what happens when you run the following code repeatedly:

```
1Ø PRINT RND
RUN
.263884
RUN
.263884
RUN
.263884
```

Every time the program is run, the same sequence of numbers is generated.

This can be both an advantage and a disadvantage. It is a definite advantage if you are trying to debug a program in which RND is used, since the results will always be the same, i.e. the random numbers will not change unexpectedly. On the other hand, it is a disadvantage when the program is debugged and run and the same sequence of events always take place. In the case of a game with the computer, you quickly learn its responses!

To take care of this problem, most systems will allow you to start with a different set of random numbers every time you type RUN if you include the statement RANDOMIZE at the beginning of your program. For example,

```
1Ø RANDOMIZE
15 PRINT RND
RUN
.37421Ø
RUN
.9Ø8721
```

The sequence of numbers changes with each different RUN because of the RANDOMIZE statement.

The random number function can be very useful in computer applications dealing with simulation of random events or in games where the computer is one of the players. However, the fractional numbers generated by RND are not too convenient in that form. Suppose, for example, that we wished to pick integer random numbers between 1 and 6 to simulate the throw of a dice. How do we go from a fractional number in the interval (0,1) to the integer interval (1,6)? The following sequence of transformations illustrates the way in which this can be accomplished.

	Value of RND Case 1	Value of RND Case 2	Value of RND Case 3
`10 T1 = RND`	.000001	.501234	.999999
`15 T2 = RND * 6`	.000006	3.007404	5.999994
`20 T3 = RND * 6 + 1`	1.000006	4.007404	6.999994
`25 T = INT(RND * 6 + 1)`	1	4	6

Hence the statement T = INT(RND * 6 + 1) transforms the set of random fractional numbers between 0 and 1 into the set of random integers 1, 2, 3, 4, 5, and 6.

In general, to generate real or integer numbers between L (low) and H (high) inclusive of L and H, the following formulas can be used:

Real values between L and H : `10 X = RND * (H - L) + L`

Integer values between L and H : `10 X = INT(RND * (H - L + 1) + L)`

In some BASIC systems, such as the TRS-80 Models II, III, and IV, the statement Y = RND(6) will generate integer values between 1 and 6 (inclusive of 1 and 6). In general, for those systems, RND(N) will generate integer random numbers between 1 and N.

Some versions of BASIC that do not have the RANDOMIZE statement require that RND have an argument such as 0, or 1, or even negative values, or a variable, as in RND(X). In these versions, changing the values of the argument generates different sequences of random numbers.

Programming Example: A Guessing Game

Let us write a program to do the following:

> The computer picks a random number between 1 and 10 and a player must guess the number picked by the computer. The dialogue between computer and player should be similar to

```
RUN
MY NAME IS ZEN. WHAT'S YOUR NAME?
? AMY
AMY I'M GOING TO CHOOSE A NUMBER BETWEEN 1 AND 10. PLEASE GUESS IT
ENTER GUESS
? 7
NO, TRY AGAIN
? 2
NO, TRY AGAIN
? 9
TERRIFIC AMY! WOULD YOU LIKE TO PLAY ANOTHER GAME?
? YES
ENTER GUESS
? 3
NO, TRY AGAIN
? 6
```

```
TERRIFIC AMY! WOULD YOU LIKE TO PLAY ANOTHER GAME?
? NO
THANK YOU AMY FOR PLAYING WITH ME
```

Solution to the problem:

The computer picks a random number by using the random function RND, which is available on all BASIC systems. However, the way in which RND is used may differ from one system to another. On many systems it is possible to use the formula RND(10) to return any random integer value between 1 and 10:

`10 K = RND(10)` This code will pick an integer between 1 and 10 and stores that number in K.

Other systems might require a statement like: `K = INT(10 * RND + 1)`
or: `K = INT(RND(X) * 10 + 1)`

where X is any positive or negative number.

In Figure 6–4 the random number picked by the computer is K. The number picked by the user is X (line 65). The two numbers are compared. If they are different, then the player makes another guess at line 65. If they match, the player has won, a congratulatory message is printed, and the computer asks the player if she/he wants to play another game (line 95).

Figure 6–4 A guessing game.

```
10 REM GUESSING GAME
15 REM          K = RANDOM NUMBER
20 REM          X = NUMBER OF PLAYER
25 REM          N$ = NAME OF PLAYER
30 REM          A$ = YES OR NO
35 PRINT "MY NAME IS ZEN. WHAT'S YOUR NAME?"
40 INPUT N$
45 PRINT N$,"I'M GOING TO CHOOSE A NUMBER";
50 PRINT " BETWEEN 1 AND 10. PLEASE GUESS IT"
55 K = INT(RND * 10 + 1)
60 PRINT "ENTER GUESS"
65 INPUT X
70 IF X = K THEN  90
75    PRINT "NO, TRY AGAIN"
80    GO TO 65
85 REM
90    PRINT "TERRIFIC ";N$;"! WOULD YOU ";
95    PRINT "LIKE TO PLAY ANOTHER GAME?"
100   INPUT A$
105   IF A$ = "YES" THEN 55
110   PRINT "THANK YOU ";N$;
115   PRINT " FOR PLAYING WITH ME"
120 END
```

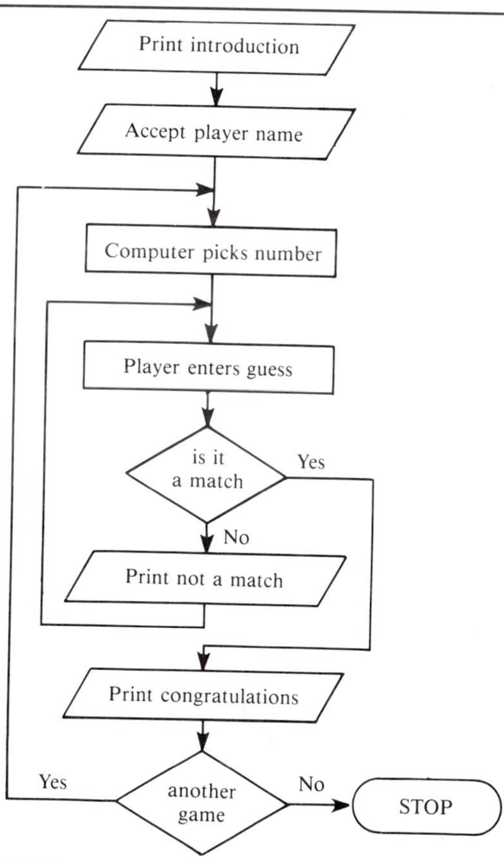

The ABS or ABSolute Value Function

Recall that the absolute value of X is equal to X if X is positive but is equal to $-X$ if X is negative; the absolute value function does not change positive values, but it strips the negative sign from negative values.

Examples:

`10 Y = ABS(-10)`	The value 10 is stored in Y.
`15 PRINT ABS(X)`	If $X = -3$, the number 3 is printed. If $X = 0$, the number 0 is printed.
`20 Y = ABS(X-1)`	$Y = X-1$ if $X-1 >= 0$, i.e., if $X > 1$ $Y = -X+1$ if $X-1 < 0$, i.e., if $X < 1$

The absolute value function often deals with the idea of distance, i.e., how close one number X is to another number Y. For example, if we say that the distance separating X from Y is 3, this means that X is 3 units either to the right or to the left of Y. We express this distance as $|X-Y| = 3$. Suppose that we wish to determine whether X lies in the interval $Y + 1.5$ to $Y - 1.5$ (the interval AB).

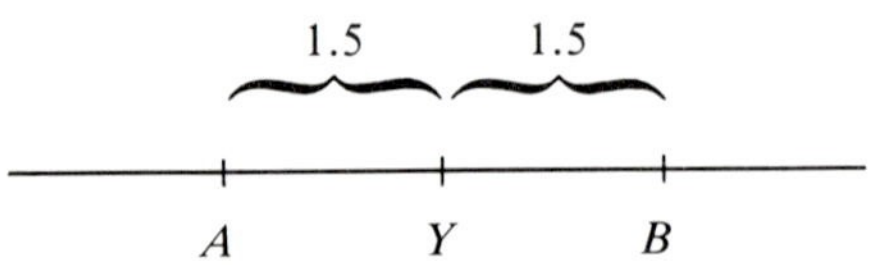

We could ask "Is $|X-Y|$ less than 1.5?" If this is true, then X is either between A and Y or between Y or B.

The TAB Function

One of the advantages of BASIC over many other programming languages is that you do not need to be concerned about the details of output formatting. If values for X, Y, and Z are to be printed, you just write PRINT X, Y, Z and the computer places these values on the output line the way it wants to! However, this can be a problem when headings and subheadings must be neatly arranged on the page/screen and when columns of numeric data must be centered beneath the headings. Free format, in such instances, is not very desirable, since output fields cannot be positioned exactly where desired on the output line when they are controlled by the comma or semicolon.

Output can be positioned more precisely by using the TAB function, which allows you to specify a starting column position for a particular output field. If, for example, you want to print three captions at positions 10, 25, and 40 on the output line, you can communicate those starting positions to the terminal.

The general form of the TAB function is:

> TAB (*expression*); *output item*

where *expression* is evaluated to an integer value, i.e., TAB(3.9) is the same as TAB(3). On some systems the value of the expression may be 0 in which case TAB(0) refers to the first column on the printer or terminal; in other systems the value of the expression must be 1 or more in which case TAB(1) refers to the 1st column on the output device. This integer value tells the printer the exact column position where the next alphanumeric character is to be printed (if the next item to be printed is an alphanumeric string). If the next item is a number, TAB gives the starting column of the numeric field; the first digit of the number may not be printed at that exact position (see line 30 of following exercises). (To print a numeric digit at an exact column position, use the PRINT USING statement discussed in section 6–2.)

Example 1:

```
10 PRINT "1234567890123456789012"
20 PRINT TAB(7);"HELLO"
30 PRINT TAB(7);3
40 PRINT TAB(7);.001
50 PRINT TAB(7);-123.567
60 PRINT TAB(7);-123.567;TAB(15);-123.567
70 PRINT TAB(0);4.1;TAB(7);"HI"
80 PRINT TAB(2);"HELLO";TAB(4);"DANG"
90 PRINT "HELLO",TAB(6);"DOG"
95 PRINT "0123456789012345678901 2"
```

Output

```
RUN
0123456789012345678901 2
       HELLO
        3
        1E-03
       -123.567
       -123.567 -123.567
 4.1   HI
  HELLODANG
HELLO               DOG
0123456789012345678901 2
```

These fields (3 and 1E-03) start in Column 8 and not 7 because of the sign.

Notice that it is not easy to pinpoint a starting position for the first digit of a numeric item, as shown in lines 30 through 60.

Note, also, that TAB(7) really means "start at column position 8" since the first position on the screen/printer is labelled as 0! (This is true for systems which permit TAB(0)).

Finally, note the effect of the comma at line 90, which propels the printer head beyond the sixth position, into the second zone. In such a case, the TAB function is ignored. On some systems this also happens in the case of overlapping fields, as shown at line 80.

Example 2:

The TAB function can be used to move characters around the screen/printer and is very useful for graphing functions (see chapter 10).

```
10 LET I = 1
20 PRINT TAB(I);"*"
25 I = I + 1
30 IF I < 5 THEN 20
50 END
```

Output

```
RUN
*
 *
  *
   *
```

Example 3:

The TAB function is also very useful for dressing up a report, as shown in Figure 6–5. Notice that the TAB function does not allow the terminal to backspace. For example, the statement

```
10 PRINT TAB(11);"CHARLIE";TAB(1);"HI"
```

does not print HI CHARLIE. Instead it may print CHARLIE HI on one line or on two lines as follows:

```
           CHARLIE
HI
```

Figure 6–5 Use of the TAB feature.

```
10 PRINT"00000000001111111111222222222233333333334444444444445";
30 PRINT"01234567890123456789012345678901234567890123456789O"
55 PRINT
60 PRINT TAB(18);"COMMUNITY TELEVISIONS"
70 PRINT TAB(22);"BALANCE SHEET"
80 PRINT TAB(21);"AUGUST 31, 1984"
90 PRINT TAB(9);" ASSETS";TAB(41);"LIABILITIES"
RUN
0000000000111111111122222222223333333333444444444445
01234567890123456789012345678901234567890123456789O

                   COMMUNITY TELEVISIONS
                       BALANCE SHEET
                      AUGUST 31, 1984
          ASSETS                         LIABILITIES
```

6-1-5 Do It Now

1. a. What would happen to the game in Figure 6–4 if line 105 specified THEN 60 instead of THEN 55?
   b. What would happen if line 70 is changed to IF X = K THEN 75?
   c. What happens if line 80 says GO TO 55?

2. Determine the values of the following expressions:
   a. `SQR (3 ^ 2 + 4 ^ 2)`
   b. `INT (67 / 4)`
   c. `SQR (ABS (-16))`
   d. `SQR (12 - SQR (4))`
   e. `ABS (INT (-5 / 4))`
   f. `41 - 10 * INT (41 / 10)`

3. Explain the effect of the following statement:
   a. `Z = A/B - INT (A/B)` (if A and B have the same sign)
   b. `Z = A/B - INT (A/B)-1` (if A and B have opposite signs)

c. `Z = INT (3.666 + .5)`

d. `Z = INT (3.666 * 10 + .5)/10`

e. `Z = INT (3.666 * 100 + .5)/100`

4. Determine whether A = B in the following code.

```
10 X = 9999.002
15 A = SQR(X)
20 B = X ^ .5
```

5. Using RND to generate random numbers between 0 and 1,
   a. Write the formula to generate random integer numbers between 5 and 10.
   b. Write the formula to generate random numbers 1, 11, 21, 31, ..., 101.

6. Using RND(X) to generate random integer numbers between 1 and X,
   a. Write the formula to pick random integer values between 5 and 30.
   b. Write the formula to pick random integer values 1, 11, 21, 31, ..., 101.
   c. Write the formula to pick random integer values between − 10, and + 10.

7. Consider the following graphs:

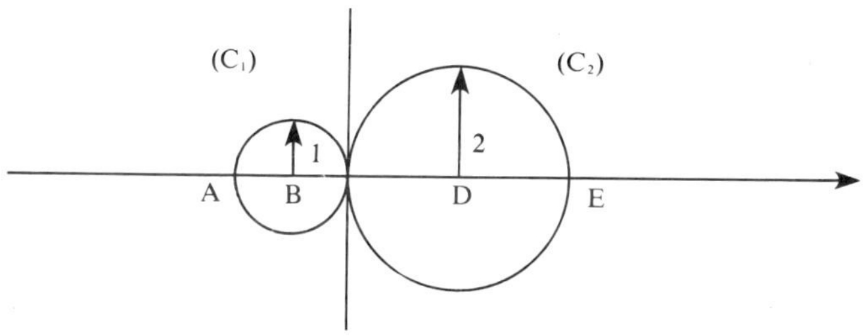

Using the absolute function ABS, write the conditions under which a point P would be

   a. in circle C_2 of radius 2
   b. in circle C_1 of radius 1

8. Write the code to drill a student on the multiplication tables 0 through 12. The student is allowed three tries, after which the program prints the correct result and presents a new multiplication problem.

Display the first six lines printed by the following coding segments:

9. a.

```
10 I = 1
15 PRINT TAB(64-I);"*"
20 I = I + 1
25 GO TO 15
```

b.

```
10 K = 6
15 I = 1
20 PRINT TAB(I);"*";TAB(K);"*"
25 I = I + 1
30 K = K - 1
35 IF I <= K THEN 20
40 PRINT TAB(K);"*";TAB(I);"*"
45 GO TO 25
```

Answers

1. a. The computer will play with the same number every time.
   b. The computer is a cheat!
   c. The computer changes its guess every time, making it more difficult for the player to guess the right number.

2. a. 5   d. 3.16228
   b. 16   e. 2
   c. 4   f. 1

3. a. The remainder (fractional part) is computed.
   b. The remainder (fractional part) is computed.
   c. 3.666 is rounded off to 4.
   d. 3.666 is rounded off to one decimal position, giving 3.7.
   e. 3.666 is rounded off to two decimal positions, giving 3.67.

4. $A = 99.99501$ $B = 99.99499$ on some systems.

5. a. `K = INT (RND * 6) + 5`
   b. `K = INT (11 * RND) * 10 + 1`

6. a. `K = RND(26) + 4`
   b. `K = RND(11) * 10 - 9`
   c. `K = RND(21) - 11`

7. a. `ABS(P-D)` less than 2
   b. `ABS(P-B)` less than 1

8.

```
 02 RANDOMIZE                             To start each session with a different multipli-
 05 LET X = 0                             cation operation.
 10 LET M1 = INT(RND(0)*13)               Select two random numbers between 0 and 12.
 20 LET M2 = INT(RND(0)*13)
 30 PRINT M1;"*";M2;"=";
 40 INPUT P                               Enter answer.
 50 IF M1*M2 = P THEN 140
 60 LET X = X + 1                         If the response is incorrect on third try, the pro-
 70 IF X = 3 THEN 100                     gram types the correct answer.
 80      PRINT "INCORRECT TRY AGAIN"
 90 GO TO 30
100 PRINT "INCORRECT ANSWER";M1;"*";M2;"=";M1*M2;
110 PRINT "LETS TRY ANOTHER PROBLEM"
120 GO TO 5
140 PRINT "CORRECT"
150 GO TO 5
999 END
```

9. a.

```
     *
    *
   *
  *
 *
*
```

b.

```
*    *
 *  *
  **
  **
 *  *
*    *
```

6-2 The PRINT USING Statements

Generating an elegant output with titles, headings, and subheadings and aligning numeric fields properly under headings requires a great deal of counting print positions with the TAB statement; and this still does not ensure decimal point alignment for columns of numbers! However, very attractive reports (Figure 6–6, for example) can be designed with the editing features of the PRINT USING instruction.

There are two different types of PRINT USING statements. Main frame and minicomputers generally support type 1 PRINT USING statements, while smaller and microcomputer systems support type 2 PRINT USING statements.

Type 1 (for smaller systems and microcomputers):

1Ø PRINT USING "*image*", [*items*]

Type 2 (for main frame and minicomputers):

1Ø PRINT USING *image line number*, [*items*]
2Ø : *image*

Type 2 statements generally require two BASIC instructions: one identifying the list of items to be printed (line 10), and another instruction (the image line, line 20) specifying the way in which the various items are to be printed on the line. Type 1 state-

■ **Figure 6–6** An inventory evaluation.

G. SIMS APPAREL COMPANY
INVENTORY EVALUATION
Ø5/Ø6/84

		UNIT COST		EXTENDED		
	QUANTITY	COST	MARKET	COST	MARKET	LOWER COST
MENS DEPT						
SUITS	3ØØ	$1ØØ	$ 92	$ 3Ø,ØØØ	$ 27,6ØØ	
COATS	2ØØ	6Ø	65	12,ØØØ	13,ØØØ	
SHOES	5Ø	4Ø	42	2,ØØØ	3,ØØØ	
SHIRTS	1ØØØ	12	13	12,ØØØ	13,ØØØ	
TOTAL				$ 56,ØØØ	$ 56,6ØØ	$ 56,ØØØ
LADIES DEPT						
DRESSES	4ØØ	$ 6Ø	$ 65	$ 24,ØØØ	$ 26,ØØØ	
COATS	185	184	2ØØ	34,Ø4Ø	37,ØØØ	
SHOES	6ØØ	4Ø	3Ø	24,ØØØ	18,ØØØ	
LINGERIE	5ØØ	36	3Ø	18,ØØØ	15,ØØØ	
TOTAL				$1ØØ,Ø4Ø	$ 96,ØØØ	$ 96,ØØØ
INVENTORY AT LOWER COST/MARKET						$152,ØØØ

ments require only one line; both the image (format) and the list of items are specified on the same line. To determine the type used on your system, try running both of the following codes:

Type 1

```
10 X = 23.44
15 PRINT USING "TYPE 1 ##.##";X
RUN

TYPE 1 23.44
```

Type 2

```
10 X = 23.44
15 PRINT USING 20,X
20 :TYPE 2 ##.##
RUN
TYPE 2 23.44
```

Only one will run! After determining which PRINT USING statement your system supports, go on to section 6–2–1 if your system uses type 1, or section 6–2–2 for type 2.

6-2-1 Type 1 PRINT USING

The general form of the type 1 PRINT USING is

line number PRINT USING { *"format"* / F$ } ; *expression list*

where the *format* describes how the items in the expression list are to be arranged (edited) and printed. The *expression list* consists of a sequence of constants, variables, or expressions, with the items separated by commas; it is similar to the expression list found in any PRINT statement. Note the semi colon separating the expression list from the "format."

Another option is to store the format in an alphanumeric string (F$), which is then referred to by the PRINT USING statement.

Format control characters are used in the format to edit numeric and alphanumeric results. They can be used to prefix numeric fields with $ signs or leading asterisks, insert commas in numeric fields, or print columns of numbers with the decimal points aligned. Standard format control characters and their meanings are shown in Figure 6–7. The user should check his/her technical reference manual for other nonstandard control characters for his/her system.

By analyzing the examples in Figure 6–8, you can see how the PRINT USING statement can be used to improve the physical appearance of computer-generated results. Notice the last example of Figure 6–8, which illustrates storage of the format in an alphanumeric string. More examples are shown in Figure 6–9. All the examples should be analyzed carefully.

The following three examples illustrate the most valuable use of the PRINT USING statement.

Example 1: Printing Headers and Columns of Numeric Data

Consider the very attractive arrangement of the following report:

Figure 6–7 Format control characters.

Format Control Character	*Meaning*	*Format*	*Data Items to Be Edited*	*Edited Field*
#	Numeric position	`"###";`	23	b̸23
.	Decimal point	`"##.#";`	1.6	b̸1.6
,	Comma	`"#,###";`	1234	1,234
–	Trailing – sign	`"###-";`	-109	109-
$	Leading $ sign	`"$##.##";`	3.45	$b̸3.45
$$	Floating $ sign	`"$$#.##";`	3.45	b̸$3.45
*	Check protection	`"**#.##";`	3.45	**3.45
↑ or ^	E notation	`"#.#^^^^";`	19	1.9E101

In the next example, *caption* refers to a string of characters (e.g., names) enclosed by two backslashes \\ (or % in other systems). The backslashes are format-control characters and count for two positions on the output field. The caption will be left-justified in the resulting output field, with the first character starting at the first backslash.

caption\\ % %	Character replacement	`"\b̸b̸b̸b̸b̸\";` `"\b̸\\b̸b̸b̸\";`	"SUSAN" "JO","SUE"	SUSANb̸b̸ JOb̸SUEb̸b̸
Fixed characters in format		`"b̸\b̸\AT b̸b̸#.#\b̸b̸b̸\.";`	"JO",3.3,"SUE"	b̸JOb̸ATb̸b̸3.3SUEb̸b̸.

```
                      PAN AMERICAN APPAREL COMPANY
                          INVENTORY EVALUATION

                          UNIT COST                    EXTENDED
            QUANTITY   COST        MARKET          COST           MARKET
MENS DEPT
SUITS            300   100.92       92.99      30,276.00       27,897.00
COATS            200    60.87       65.78      12,174.00       13,156.00
SHOES             50    40.53       42.77       2,026.50        2,138.50
SHIRTS          1000    12.25       13.05      12,250.00       13,050.00
```

We can use the PRINT USING statement with alphanumeric strings to capture the design of the entire report without resorting to the inconvenient TAB function. As we see in lines 10 through 20 in Figure 6-10, the arrangement of the various headings and column captions is simulated by the alphanumeric strings F1$, F2$,..., F6$. Thus the various headers and captions can be effortlessly positioned to produce a visually pleasant arrangement. After the headers have been constructed one line at a time and properly arranged, the numeric line A$ for the detailed entries is constructed. The numeric entries, identified by the appropriate string of format control characters, are placed under their respective headings as shown by line 22.

The program first prints the first six header lines and then reads the DATA records, which consist of an item description, quantity, store cost, and market value (retail price). Each time a record is read, the total inventory list figure and the total inventory market value for that item are computed.

Figure 6–8 Examples of PRINT USING statements.

BASIC Instructions	*Printed Results*
1Ø X = 2345.8572 15 Y = 1.5 2Ø PRINT USING "####.##";X 25 PRINT USING "##.##";Y,.3,2 3Ø PRINT USING "##.";8	 2345.86 Note rounding off. b̸1.5Øb̸Ø.3Øb̸2.ØØ repeated image. b̸8.
1Ø PRINT USING "RESULTb̸=b̸###.##"; 345.6	RESULTb̸=b̸345.6Ø
1Ø X = 3456.76 15 Z = 1.75 2Ø PRINT USING "$#,###.##";X 25 PRINT USING "$$,###.##";X 3Ø PRINT USING "$#,###.##";Z 35 PRINT USING "$$,###.##";Z 4Ø PRINT USING "**,###.##";Z	 $3,456.76 $3,456.76 $b̸b̸b̸b̸1.75 b̸b̸b̸b̸$1.75 *****1.75
1Ø PRINT USING "WEb̸AMb̸US!"	WE AM US!
1Ø X = 1 3Ø Z = 3.8 4Ø PRINT USING "b̸b̸SEXb̸b̸AMOUNT" 5Ø PRINT USING "b̸b̸b̸#b̸b̸b̸b̸#.#b̸b̸";X,Z	 b̸b̸SEXb̸b̸AMOUNT b̸b̸b̸1b̸b̸b̸b̸3.8b̸b̸
1Ø N$ = "MONA" 15 PRINT USING "b̸HIb̸\b̸b̸b̸\,\b̸\.";N$,"JOE"	 b̸HIb̸MONAb̸,JOE.
1Ø INPUT N$ 15 A = 23 2Ø PRINT USING "\b̸b̸b̸b̸\ARE YOU##YEARS?";N$,A	?MIKE MIKEb̸b̸ARE YOU23YEARS?
15 F$ = "PAY TO \b̸b̸b̸b̸b̸\b̸$###.##b̸TODAY" 2Ø READ N$,P 25 PRINT USING F$,N$,P 3Ø DATA CANTER, 98.76	 PAY TO CANTERb̸b̸$b̸98.76b̸TODAY

■ **Figure 6–9** More PRINT USING statements.

Format Strings	*Values to Be Edited*	*Edited Results*
`10 PRINT USING "##.##";`	1.24	` 1.24`
`12 PRINT USING "##.##";`	17.876	`17.88`
`14 PRINT USING "###.##";`	123.45	`123.45`
`16 PRINT USING "### ";`	3, 978, 42.3	`  3 978  42`
`18 PRINT USING "###";`	1.5	`  2`
`20 PRINT USING "##.#";`	3 * 2.4	` 7.2`
`22 PRINT USING "##";`	123	`%123`
`24 PRINT USING "#,###.##";`	3421.7	`3,421.70`
`26 PRINT USING " ##.## BUCKS";`	24.47	` 24.47 BUCKS`
`28 PRINT USING "$###.##";`	13.15	`$ 13.15`
`30 PRINT USING "**##";`	9	`***9`
`32 PRINT USING "$$###.##";`	13.15	`  $13.15`
`34 PRINT USING "**$###.##";`	13.15	`***$13.15`
`36 PRINT USING "PLUS ##.##+";`	17.346	`PLUS 17.35+`
`38 PRINT USING "##.#   +###   #.#";`	-8, -4, 2	`-8.0    -4  2.0`
`40 PRINT USING "+## ##.#- $**";`	2, -3, 2.34	` +2  3.0- $*2`
`42 PRINT USING "##.##^^^^  ";`	234.56, 8.759999E-03	` 2.35E+02   8.76E-03`
`44 PRINT USING "##.####^^^^";`	234.56	` 2.3456E+02`
`46 LET A$="SUE": LET B$="JO"`		
`48 PRINT USING "! "; A$, B$`		`S J`
`50 PRINT USING "HELLO\   \";`	A$	`HELLO SUE`
`52 PRINT USING "HELLO\   \ AND \\ ";`	A$, B$	`HELLO SUE  AND JO`
`54 PRINT USING "\  \";`	"MICHAEL"	`MICH`
`56 PRINT USING "PAY TO \  \ $$.# DOLLARS";`	A$, 2.59	`PAY TO SUE $2.6 DOLLARS`

```
58 REM
60 REM
62 REM
64 REM
66 REM
68 REM
```

Format strings can be read or inputted, and used in the PRINT USING statement (see lines 70, and 74). The 3 variables F$,L$ and A are edited by the format string T$ read at line 70.

```
70 READ T$
72 READ F$, L$, A
74 PRINT USING T$; F$, L$, A
76 GOTO 72
78 DATA "PAY TO !. \      \ #,###.## DOLLARS"
80 DATA JIM   , GREEN , 1000.38
82 DATA LINDA, TURMAN, 423
```

Edited results:

```
PAY TO J. GREEN   1,000.38 DOLLARS
PAY TO L. TURMAN    423.00 DOLLARS
```

Note how the initials of the first names are produced through the format string character! in lines 48 and 78. The period after the initial is printed by line 78 since it is physically present in the format string.

■ **Figure 6–10** Report layout.

```
10 F1$="                          PAN AMERICAN APPAREL COMPANY                            "
12 F2$="                              INVENTORY EVALUATION                                "
14 F3$="                                                                                  "
16 F4$="                               UNIT COST                        EXTENDED          "
18 F5$="                QUANTITY    COST       MARKET            COST             MARKET "
20 F6$="MENS DEPT                                                                         "
22 A$ ="\           \    ####      ###.##       ###.##         ##,###.##      ##,###.##"
23 REM
24 PRINT F1$
26 PRINT F2$
28 PRINT F3$
30 PRINT F4$
32 PRINT F5$
34 PRINT F6$
35 PRINT
36 READ C$, Q, C, M
40 IF C$ = "END" THEN STOP
44 C1 = Q * C
48 M1 = Q * M
52 PRINT USING A$; C$, Q, C, M, C1, M1
56 GOTO 36
60 DATA SUITS  , 300,  100.92, 92.99
64 DATA COATS  , 200,   60.87, 65.78
68 DATA SHOES  ,  50,   40.53, 42.77
72 DATA SHIRTS, 1000,   12.25, 13.05
76 DATA END    , 0000,  00000, 00000
RUN
                       PAN AMERICAN APPAREL COMPANY
                           INVENTORY EVALUATION

                           UNIT COST                      EXTENDED
            QUANTITY    COST       MARKET            COST              MARKET
MENS DEPT

SUITS          300     100.92       92.99        30,276.00         27,897.00
COATS          200      60.87       65.78        12,174.00         13,156.00
SHOES           50      40.53       42.77         2,026.50          2,138.50
SHIRTS        1000      12.25       13.05        12,250.00         13,050.00
```

Example 2: Combination of Literal Text and Numeric Fields

A customer company name (N$), a current date (D$), a balance (B), an exchange (E), a collection fee (C), and an insufficient fund (N) amounts are to be read from a DATA record. A program is to be written to produce a bank reconciliation statement similar to the one shown below. The report should identify the name of the company and the date and should compute the adjusted balance given by the formula A = B − E − C − N.

```
                     M.C. HOOTEN COMPANY
                     BANK RECONCILIATION
                         JUNE 27 1984

BALANCE PER BOOKS..................................$3,290.37
DEDUCT BANK'S CHARGES NOT ON THE BOOKS:
  EXCHANGE.............................$ 0.10
  COLLECTION...........................  0.25
  N.S.F. CHECK T. MARTIN............... 63.95
ADJUSTED BALANCE...................................$3,226.07
```

Just as in example 1, the entire output layout is captured in alphanumeric strings (see lines 10 through 26 of Figure 6–11) where the format control characters are specified. The pair of backslashes in lines 10 and 14 specify where the name of the company and the date are to be printed on the output line.

Example 3: Multiple Variable Alphanumeric Fields

You may need to write programs to print multilevel headers or captions or organizational charts such as

```
                          BOARD OF TRUSTEES
     INTERNAL AUDITOR          PRESIDENT        ASSISTANT TO PRESIDENT
                            VICE PRESIDENT
          DEAN 1                DEAN 2                  DEAN 3
```

where names might later be substituted for position titles.

The program shown in Figure 6–12 can be used to produce the above chart. As in the preceding examples, the entire output is set up by alphanumeric strings (lines 10 through 16); in this case only backslash format control characters are used. The three pairs of backslashes in line 12 specify where the internal auditor, the president, and the assistant to the president are to be placed on the output. (The dots below are shown for positional purposes only.)

Internal Auditor (line 12) — Board of Trustees (line 10) — Assistant to President (line 12)

```
10 F1$="                     \.................\                        "
12 F2$=" \...............\       \........\       \.....................\"
14 F3$="                      \.............\                           "
16 F4$="      \.....\            \.....\                 \.......\      "
```

The PRINT USING statement at line 24 actually prints the three titles, while the PRINT USING at line 38 substitutes names for the titles.

■ **Figure 6–11** PRINT USING: literal text and numeric fields.

```
10 F1$ = "                    \              \                   "
12 F2$ = "                    BANK RECONCILIATION                "
14 F3$ = "                      \         \                      "
16 F4$ = "BALANCE PER BOOKS...............................$#,###.## "
18 F5$ = "DEDUCT BANK'S CHARGES NOT ON THE BOOKS:                  "
20 F6$ = "  EXCHANGE...............................$##.##          "
22 F7$ = "  COLLECTION............................. ##.##          "
24 F8$ = "  N.S.F. CHECK T. MARTIN................. ##.##          "
26 F9$ = "ADJUSTED BALANCE................................$#,###.## "
30 REM
32 READ N$,D$,B,E,C,N
34 A = B - (E + C + N)
36 PRINT USING F1$; N$
38 PRINT            F2$
40 PRINT USING F3$; D$
42 PRINT
44 PRINT USING F4$; B
46 PRINT            F5$
48 PRINT USING F6$; E
50 PRINT USING F7$; C
52 PRINT USING F8$; N
53 PRINT USING F9$; A
54 DATA M.C. HOOTEN COMPANY, JUNE 27 1984
56 DATA 3290.37, .10, .25, 63.95

RUN
                    M.C. HOOTEN COMPANY
                    BANK RECONCILIATION
                        JUNE 27 1984

BALANCE PER BOOKS...............................$3,290.37
DEDUCT BANK'S CHARGES NOT ON THE BOOKS:
  EXCHANGE...............................$ 0.10
  COLLECTION.............................  0.25
  N.S.F. CHECK T. MARTIN................. 63.95
ADJUSTED BALANCE................................$3,226.07
```

6-2-2 Type 2 PRINT USING

The general form of the PRINT USING is

line number PRINT USING { *image line number* | F$ (alphanumeric variable) } [*expression list*]

Image line number: *image* (not used if F$ is used)

■ **Figure 6–12** Organizational charts.

```
10 F1$="                          \                    \                          "
12 F2$="\                  \         \        \          \                      \"
14 F3$="                          \                  \                            "
16 F4$="    \      \                \        \                \        \          "
18 REM
20 B$ = "BOARD OF TRUSTEES"
22 PRINT USING F1$;B$
24 PRINT USING F2$;"INTERNAL AUDITOR","PRESIDENT","ASSISTANT TO PRESIDENT"
26 PRINT USING F3$;"VICE PRESIDENT"
28 PRINT USING F4$;"DEAN 1","DEAN 2","DEAN 3"
30 PRINT
32 PRINT
34 READ  A1$, A2$, A3$, A4$, A5$, A6$, A7$
36 PRINT USING F1$; B$
38 PRINT USING F2$; A1$, A2$, A3$
40 PRINT USING F3$; A4$
42 PRINT USING F4$, A5$, A6$, A7$
44 DATA  DELLABRAVOURA M., DENTON K., SANTADELLAROSARINO J., SOMMERSET M.
46 DATA  COOPER T., KEY C., LINUS B.

RUN
                        BOARD OF TRUSTEES
INTERNAL AUDITOR            PRESIDENT             ASSISTANT TO PRESIDENT
                          VICE PRESIDENT
     DEAN 1                 DEAN 2                     DEAN 3


                        BOARD OF TRUSTEES
DELLABRAVOURA M.            DENTON K.             SANTADELLAROSARINO J.
                          SOMMERSET M.
     COOPER                  KEY C.                    LINUS B.
```

where the *image line number* is the number of a BASIC statement that describes the format (image, layout) of the data items (*expression list*) to be printed.

The *expression list* consists of a sequence of constants, variables, and/or expressions, with the items separated by commas; it is similar to the expression list in any ordinary PRINT statement.

Image describes the way in which the items in the expression list are to be edited and arranged on the output line.

Image control characters are used in the image to edit numeric and alphanumeric results. They can be used to prefix numeric fields with a dollar sign or with leading asterisks, to insert commas in the numeric field itself, and for many other nice editing features. Some common image control characters are shown in Figure 6–13. Other control characters, not shown in this figure, may be available on your system (check the reference manual).

An alternative method is to store the image as an alphanumeric string in a variable (F$); in this case no image line number is typed. One advantage of this method is that images can be read from DATA lists.

Figure 6–13 Image control characters.

Format Control Character	*Meaning*	*Image*	*Data Items to Be Edited*	*Edited Output*
#	Numeric position	:###	23	ƀ23
.	Decimal point	:##.#	1.6	ƀ1.6
,	Comma	:#,###	1234	1,234
–	Trailing – sign	:###–	–109	109–
$	Leading $ sign	:$##.##	3.45	$b3.45
$$	Floating $ sign	:$$#.##	3.45	ƀ$3.45
*	Check protection	:**#.##	3.45	**3.45
↑,^	E notation	:#.#^^^^	19	1.9E+01
'	The image control characters L, C, R are used to place alphanumeric data (names, addresses, etc.) in predetermined positions on the output line. The single quote (apostrophe) must precede any of the L, C, or R character fields; it is counted in the length of the output field.			
C	Centered character	:'CCCC	"HI"	ƀHIƀƀ
R	Right-justified	:'RRR	"AT"	ƀƀAT
L	Left-justified	:'LLLLL	"TOM"	TOMƀƀƀ
C,L,R	Combination	:'LL'RR	"LO","VE"	LOƀƀVE
Fixed characters in image	:ƀHE'RRRƀIS##.#FOOT		"MAN",8.1	ƀHEƀMANƀISƀ8.1FOOT

By analyzing the examples in Figure 6–14, you can readily see how the PRINT USING statement can be used to improve the physical appearance of computer-generated results.

To better understand the application of the PRINT USING feature, consider the following problem examples:

Example 1: Numeric, Alphabetic, and Literal Images: The L and # Image Control Characters.

Let's write a payroll program to read employee names, their rate of pay, and hours worked to produce a report similar to the following one. (The dots are not part of the output but are purposefully typed to indicate the exact position of the various fields.)

```
NAME........RATE OF PAY......HOURS......GROSS PAY
JONES P.        36.45         84.00       3061.80
ARDAMAN J.      98.00         37.00       3626.00
GRIZZI M          .50           .50           .25
```

Note that the first line consists solely of literal data (headings) and can be produced by executing statement 10 in Figure 6–15. The following lines are produced by statement 25, using image line 55. This image is used to print alphabetic and numeric data.

Figure 6–14 Samples of PRINT USINGs.

```
10 X = 8345.868
15 Y = 1.078
20 PRINT USING 30,X
25 PRINT USING 30,Y
28 PRINT USING 30,2*X
30 :####.##
```

Printed Output

```
8345.87
ƀƀ1.08
&16691.74
```

Note rounding of 7

If number exceeds length of field an ampersand or asterisk precedes leftmost position. Correct result if printed.

```
10 PRINT USING 30,134
30 :RESULTƀ=ƀ###.#
```

```
RESULTƀ=ƀ134.0
```

```
10 X = 3456.76
15 Z = 1.75
20 PRINT USING 80,X
25 PRINT USING 85,X
30 PRINT USING 80,Z
35 PRINT USING 85,Z
40 PRINT USING 90,Z
80 :$#,###.##
85 :$$,###.##
90 :**,###.##
```

```
$3,456.76
$3,456.76
$     1.75
     $1.75
*****1.75
```

```
10 PRINT USING 20
20 :WEƀAMƀUS.
```

```
WE AM US.
```

```
10 X = 1
30 Z = 3.8
40 PRINT USING 60
45 PRINT USING 70,X,Z
60 :ƀƀSEXƀƀAMOUNT
70 :ƀƀƀ#ƀƀƀƀ#.#
```

```
ƀƀSEXƀƀAMOUNT
   1     3.8
```

```
10 N$ = "MONA"
15 PRINT USING 50,N$
20 PRINT USING 55,N$
30 PRINT USING 60,N$
50 :HI'LLLLLLLbDEAR
55 :HI'CCCCCCCbDEAR
60 :HI'RRRRRRRbDEAR
```

```
HIMONA      DEAR
HI  MONA    DEAR
HI      MONA DEAR
```

Note that the single quote (') occupies a print position on the output.

```
10 PRINT USING 20,"1234","1234","1234"
20 :'LL'CC'RR
```

```
'LL'CC'RR
↓  ↓  ↓
123123234
```

Note the truncation.

```
10 INPUT N$
15 A = 23
20 PRINT USING 60,N$,A
60 :'LLLLLbAREbYOUb##bYEARSbOLD?
```

```
?MIKE

MIKE   ARE YOU 23 YEARS OLD?
```

```
10 F$ = "PAYbTOb'LLLLLb$###.##bTODAY"
20 READ N$,P
30 PRINT USING F$,N$,P
40 DATA SMITH,99.56
```

Note that F$ could have been read from a DATA statement

```
PAY TO SMITH   $ 99.56 TODAY
```

■ **Figure 6–15** Output design with PRINT USING.

```
10 PRINT USING 50
15 READ N$,R,H
16 IF N4 = "END" THEN STOP
20 P = R * H
25 PRINT USING 55,N$,R,H,P
30 GOTO 15
35 DATA JONES P.    ,36.45, 84
40 DATA ARDAMAN J. ,98.00, 37
45 DATA GRIZZI M.   ,00.50, .5
46 DATA END         ,00.00,  0
48 REM
50 :NAME          RATE OF PAY       HOURS        GROSS PAY
55 :'LLLLLLLLLLbbbb##.##bbbbbbbbb##.##bbbbbbb####.##
```

Name field consisting of a maximum of 11 alphanumeric characters. The image control character L is reserved for alphanumeric characters. The 10 L characters will be replaced by left-justified name when PRINT USING 55 is processed. Note the apostrophe before the first L, which also acts as an L control character.

Pay field consisting of a maximum of 7 print positions (including the decimal point). The image control character # is reserved for numerical data. The . is used to align all decimal points. The image field specifies two fractional and two whole digits.

```
RUN
NAMEbbbbbbbbbRATE OF PAYbbbbbbHOURSbbbbbbGROSS PAY
JONES P.        36.45          84.00         3061.80
ARDAMAN J.      98.00          37.00         3626.00
GRIZZI M.         .50            .50             .25
```

Note the *b*'s (blanks) are not really part of output.

The image control character L is used for alphanumeric data, and the pound sign (#) is used for numeric data. At RUN time, the field of L's and fields of #'s will be replaced by the values to be printed. The apostrophe preceding the L field also acts as an L character, i.e., the output length for the left-justified field is actually 11 positions long (see line 55).

Note that image line 50 just specifies headings. The image consists only of literal data and there are no image control characters.

With the PRINT USING statement, the final layout of the report can easily be constructed by first positioning the headings (line 50), and then placing the corresponding numeric fields (line 55) under them. Thus the entire design of the report is set up by lines 50 and 55.

Example 2: The $ and C Image Control Characters.

In many financial statements, a leading $ is required at the beginning of the dollar amount field. In BASIC, the image control character $ is placed at the beginning of the numeric image field (# characters) to print the dollar sign at the print position where the $ is typed. For example, see statements 30, 40 and 55 in Figure 6–16.

Subheadings can automatically be centered beneath other headings with the image control character C. A field of C's is typed in the image statement, causing the character string printed in that field to be centered. For example, see statements 15 and 25 of Figure 6–16 and note the apostrophe before the first C which also acts as a C character.

Figure 6–16 computes an adjusted balance for a bank reconciliation statement. A customer company name (N$), a current date (D$), a balance (B), an exchange (E), a collection (C), and an insufficient fund (N) amount are read. An adjusted balance A (A = B − E − C − N) is computed.

Figure 6–16 The $ and C image control characters.

```
15 :b̸b̸b̸b̸b̸b̸b̸b̸b̸b̸b̸b̸b̸b̸b̸b̸b̸b̸b̸b̸b̸'CCCCCCCCCCCCCCCCCCC
20 :                     'BANK RECONCILIATION
25 :                     'CCCCCCCCCCCCCCCCCCC
30 :BALANCE PER BOOKS..................................$####.##
35 :DEDUCT BANK'S CHARGES NOT ON THE BOOKS:
40 :  EXCHANGE.................................$##.##
45 :  COLLECTION..............................  ##.##
50 :  N.S.F. CHECK SUE LIN....................  ##.##
55 :ADJUSTED BALANCE...................................$####.##
56 REM
60 READ N$,D$,B,E,C,N
65 LET A=B-(E+C+N)
70 PRINT USING 15,N$
75 PRINT USING 20
80 PRINT USING 25,D$
82 PRINT
85 PRINT USING 30,B
90 PRINT USING 35
95 PRINT USING 40,E
100 PRINT USING 45,C
105 PRINT USING 50,N
110 PRINT USING 55,A
115 DATA "M.C. HOOTEN COMPANY","JUNE 27 1984"
120 DATA 3290.37,.10,.25,63.95
130 END
RUN
                     M.C. HOOTEN COMPANY
                     BANK RECONCILIATION
                        JUNE 27 1984

BALANCE PER BOOKS..................................$3290.37
DEDUCT BANK'S CHARGES NOT ON THE BOOKS:
  EXCHANGE.................................$ 0.10
  COLLECTION..............................   0.25
  N.S.F. CHECK SUE LIN.................... 63.95
ADJUSTED BALANCE...................................$3226.07
```

Example 3: Multiple Variable Alphanumeric Fields.

You may need to write programs to print multilevel headers or captions or organizational charts such as:

```
                    BOARD OF TRUSTEES
INTERNAL AUDITOR        PRESIDENT        ASSISTANT TO PRESIDENT
                     VICE PRESIDENT
     DEAN 1               DEAN 2                 DEAN 3
```

where names might later be substituted for position titles.

The program shown in Figure 6-17 can be used to produce the above chart. As in the case of the preceding examples, the entire output is set up by lines 10 through 16;

Figure 6–17 Organizational charts.

```
10 :                     'CCCCCCCCCCCCCCCCC
12 :'LLLLLLLLLLLLLLLLLLLL'CCCCCCCCCCCCCCCCC'RRRRRRRRRRRRRRRRRRRRR
14 :                     'CCCCCCCCCCCCCCCCC
16 :'CCCCCCCCCCCCCCCCCCCC'CCCCCCCCCCCCCCCCC'CCCCCCCCCCCCCCCCCCCCC
18 REM
20 B$ = "BOARD OF TRUSTEES"
22 PRINT USING F1$;B$
24 PRINT USING F2$;"INTERNAL AUDITOR","PRESIDENT","ASSISTANT TO PRESIDENT"
26 PRINT USING F3$;"VICE PRESIDENT"
28 PRINT USING F4$;"DEAN 1","DEAN 2","DEAN 3"
30 PRINT
32 PRINT
34 READ  A1$, A2$, A3$, A4$, A5$, A6$, A7$
36 PRINT USING F1$; B$
38 PRINT USING F2$; A1$, A2$, A3$
40 PRINT USING F3$; A4$
42 PRINT USING F4$, A5$, A6$, A7$
44 DATA  DELLABRAVOURA M., DENTON K., SANTADELLAROSARINO J., SOMMERSET M.
46 DATA  COOPER T., KEY C., LINUS B.

RUN
                      BOARD OF TRUSTEES
INTERNAL AUDITOR          PRESIDENT           ASSISTANT TO PRESIDENT
                       VICE PRESIDENT
      DEAN 1                DEAN 2                    DEAN 3


                      BOARD OF TRUSTEES
DELLABRAVOURA M.          DENTON K.           SANTADELLAROSARINO J.
                        SOMMERSET M.
      COOPER T.               KEY C.                   LINUS B.
```

in this case the C, L, and R format control characters are used. The string of L's, C's and R's at line 12 specify where the internal auditor, the president and the assistant to the president are to be placed on the output line.

Internal Auditor (line 12) — Board of Trustees (line 10) — Assistant to President (line 12)

```
10 :                     'CCCCCCCCCCCCCCCCC
12 :'LLLLLLLLLLLLLLLLLLLLL'CCCCCCCCCCCCCCCCC'RRRRRRRRRRRRRRRRRRRRR
14 :                     'CCCCCCCCCCCCCCCCC
16 :'CCCCCCCCCCCCCCCCCCCCC'CCCCCCCCCCCCCCCCC'CCCCCCCCCCCCCCCCCCCCC
```

The PRINT USING statement at line 24 actually prints three titles, while the PRINT USING at line 38 substitutes names for the titles.

6-3 A Deeper Look

6-3-1 Compound Logical Functions AND, OR, XOR, and NOT

Compounding of logical functions is possible on most BASIC systems, as shown in the following examples:

```
10  IF  A < 40 AND S = 1 THEN 43 ELSE 74
20  IF  NOT S = 1 OR NOT (A > 40 AND S < 2) THEN 30
```

Most BASIC allows the use of *compound conditions*, i.e., connecting one or more conditions with the logical operators NOT, AND, OR, and XOR (exclusive OR). The meaning of those operators is illustrated as follows:

`15 IF` *condition 1* `AND` *condition 2* `THEN 40` `20 ...`	Transfer to 40 if both conditions are true; otherwise take line 20.
`15 IF` *condition 1* `OR` *condition 2* `THEN 40` `20 ...`	If one or the other or both conditions are true, transfer to 40; otherwise fall through to line 20.
`15 IF` *condition 1* `XOR` *condition 2* `THEN 40` `20 ...`	Transfer to 40 if one condition is true and the other one is false; otherwise fall through to line 20.
`15 IF NOT` *condition* `THEN 40`	Transfer to 40 if the condition is NOT true; otherwise fall through.

Logical operators are also governed by rules of precedence, which tell which operations are to be considered first. They are illustrated as follows:

Operations	*Precedence*
Grouping (parentheses)	Highest
Arithmetic operations:	
^ or ** or ↑	
* /	
+ −	
Conditions:	
< > = and so forth	
Logical operators:	
NOT	
AND	
OR	
XOR	Lowest

Example 1:

To determine whether an age lies between 18 and 30 inclusive, the following statement could be used:

```
IF A >= 18 AND A <= 3Ø THEN PRINT "YES"
```

Example 2:

Assume $X = 30$, $Y = 40$, and $A = 10$.

IF

Arithmetic expressions are evaluated first.

Relations are evaluated next.

Logical operations are evaluated last.

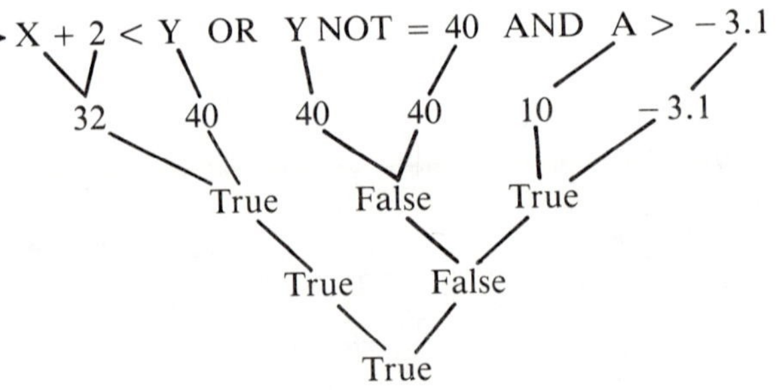

6-3-2 The ON GO TO Statement

The ON GO TO statement is a very convenient statement that allows the user to branch to different points in a program depending on the outcome of a particular condition. The general form of the statement is:

> *line number* ON *expression* GO TO *line number 1*, *line number 2*, ..., *line number n*

where the *expression* is evaluated to an integer value (3.8 becomes 3) and *line number 1*, ... are line numbers in the program. The mechanics of the ON GO TO are as follows:

If the value of the expression is 1, control is transferred to *line number 1.*
If the value of the expression is 2, control is transferred to *line number 2.*

If the value of the expression is n, control is transferred to *line number n.*

If the value of the expression is 0, negative, or equal to an integer value that exceeds the number of line numbers specified in the ON GO TO statement, the ON GO TO statement is ignored and control is passed to the statement immediately following the ON GO TO.

Example 1:

```
30 I = I + 1
.
.
100 INPUT N
110 ON N GO TO 30, 170, 200
115
.
.
170 PRINT R
.
.
200 IF X = 1 THEN 300
```

First N is evaluated to an integer value, i.e., if N = 3.8, then the value is 3.
If N is 1, control is passed to the first statement, line 30.
If N is 2, control is passed to the 2nd statement i.e., 170
If N is 3, control is passed to the 3rd statement i.e., 200
If N is any value other than 1, 2, or 3, then control is passed to statement 115.

Example 2:

```
20 ON J - 2 * K GO TO 30,10      IF J – 2*K = 1, tranfer to line 30.
25                               IF J – 2*K = 2, transfer to line 10.
```

Example 3: Lottery Simulation

A player picks any number between 1 and 10. Lucky numbers 3, 5, and 6 receive 10 dollars, but number 4 means that the player must pay 15 dollars.

```
10 N = RND(10)                      Player picks a number (1 – 10)
15 ON N GO TO 20,20,40,50,40,40
20 PRINT "YOU LOSE"                 Player picked a 1 or 2 or 7 thru 10
25 GO TO 99
40 PRINT "YOU WIN 10 DOLLARS"
45 GO TO 99
50 PRINT "PAY 15 DOLLARS, BUSTER"
99 END
```

Note that if the player picks a number greater than 6, control is passed to line 20.

6-3-3 The RESTORE Statement

In general, elements from a DATA list are read by a READ statement only once, i.e., when all the DATA statements have been exhausted and the user tries to read another item, the error message "out of data" will be displayed on the terminal. If the user wishes to reread all elements starting with the very first element, he/she can use the RESTORE instruction, which will cause the next READ instruction to start at the "top" (the very first item of very first DATA statement) of the DATA block. Here are some examples illustrating the mechanics of the RESTORE statement:

Example 1:

```
10 DATA 80, 70, 90
15 READ G1, G2, G3           Read 80, 70, and 90.
20 PRINT G1 + G2 + G3        240 is printed.
25 RESTORE                   The next READ will start at line 10.
30 READ X, Y, Z              X = 80, Y = 70, Z = 90.
35 PRINT X * Y               5600 will be printed.
40 PRINT G1 + Z              G1 = 80, Z = 90, hence 170 is printed.
```

Note that if the RESTORE statement had been omitted, a READ error would have occurred at line 30 (no more data).

Example 2:

```
10 DATA ANDY
15 DATA 60, 70
20 READ G$                   Read ANDY.
25 PRINT G$                  Print ANDY.
30 RESTORE
35 READ N$, X                Read ANDY and 60.
40 RESTORE
45 READ L$                   Read ANDY.
50 READ X, Y                 X = 60, Y = 70.
```

RESTORE can be very convenient when it is necessary to process items in DATA statements more than once, although arrays (see chapter 8) are more convenient. To illustrate the use of the RESTORE statement, consider the following problem:

Problem:

The final grades for an introduction to management class have already been recorded on DATA statements in descending order. The instructor is allowed to give 10 percent of the class A's. Write a program to list all A scores for that class. A fractional percentage should be rounded up to the next whole percentage figure, i.e., 9.1% becomes 10%.

Solution:

Using the trip method to read all the scores, we determine the number of scores N. We then compute 10% of N. Using the RESTORE statement, we reread and print the first 10% of the scores. The program to solve this problem is shown in Figure 6-18. Note how the counting process at line 90 rounds up the 10% calculated at line 65.

Figure 6–18 Rereading a list of scores: RESTORE.

```
10 REM  REREADING A DATA LIST: RESTORE
12 REM
15 REM  N:  COUNTS TOTAL NUMBER SCORES
20 REM  P:  NUMBER OF A'S
25 REM  S:  READS THE SCORES
30 N = 0
35 READ S
40 IF S < 0 THEN 60
45       PRINT S;
50       N = N + 1
55       GO TO 35
60 PRINT
65 P = N/10
70 RESTORE
75 READ S
80 PRINT S;
85 P = P - 1
90 IF P > 0 THEN 75
95 DATA 98,86,85,78,76,72,60,40,20,9,8,-1
99 END
RUN
98 86 85 78 76 72 60 40 20 9 8
98 86
```

Lines 40–55: Determine number of scores in DATA list.

Line 65: Number of A's allowed.

Line 70: Go back to first score on DATA list.

Lines 75–90: Print 10% of grades (A's).

6-4 A Simulation/Game Problem: Moles and Mazes

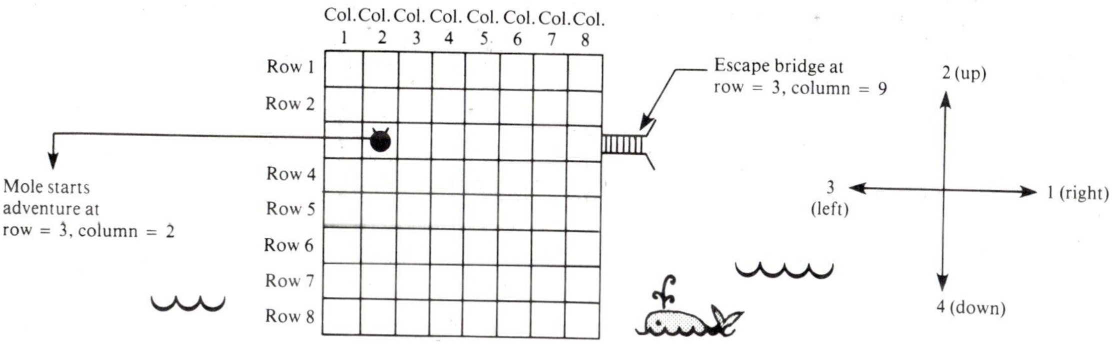

The above diagram represents an island surrounded by water. The island can be thought of as a square grid divided into 8 rows and 8 columns. One bridge leads out of the island at row 3 and column 9. Let us place an imaginary mole at the black square (row - 3, column - 2). The mole moves one square at a time in one of 4 directions: right, up, left, and down. A random number between 1 and 4 tells the mole what direction to take before making a move, i.e., we arbitrarily associate the right-hand direction with the number 1, the up direction with the number 2, and so forth. The mole keeps moving from one square to the next until it either hits the water and drowns or gets to the bridge and escapes. Write a program to determine the mole's chances of escape. Express this result as a percentage figure, for example 1.8%.

In this problem the sequence of moves that lead the mole to either an escape or a drowning is called a mole adventure. Adventures may last anywhere from 2 moves (shortest distance to water) to hundreds of moves.

One Short, Sad Adventure
2 Moves: Drown

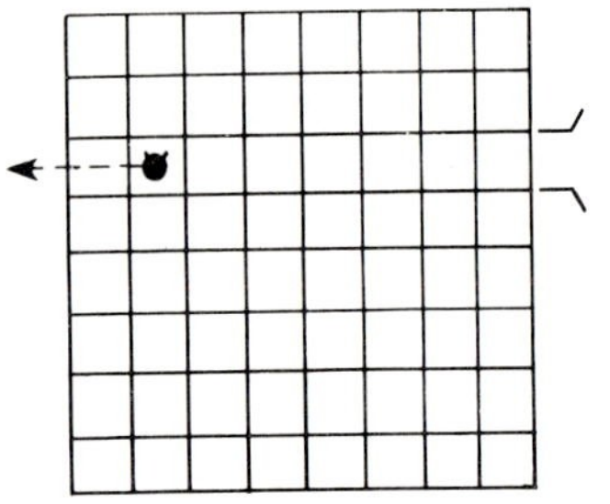

One Long, Happy Adventure
23 Moves: Escape

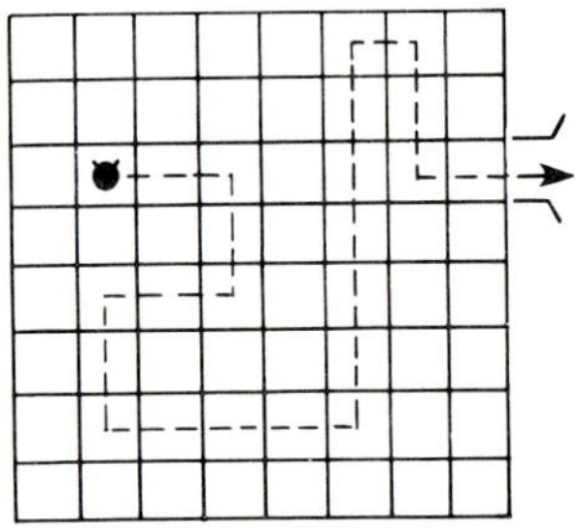

Obviously, 10 or even 50 such adventures may not be enough to determine the mole's chances of escape. The mole may never escape in its first 50 adventures. For the results to be meaningful, let us give the mole 500 distinct adventures, i.e., we will restart the mole in the starting block 500 times and count the number of times the mole escapes or drowns.

So that the programmer can see the progress of the mole on the terminal let us print the letter A or E every time a drowning accident or an escape occurs. Five hundred such letters should be printed as shown below. E identifies the times the mole escaped.

```
AAAAAAAAAAAAAAAAAAAAAAAAAEAAAAAAAAAAAAAAAAAAAAAAAAAAAAAAAAAAAAAAAAAAAAAAEAAAAAAAAAAAAAAA
AAAAAAAAEAAAAAAAAAEAAAAAAAAAAAAAAAAAAAAAAAAAAEAAAAAAAAAAAAAAAAAAAAAAAAAAAAAAAAAAAAAAAAAA
AAAAAAAAAAAAAAAAAAAAAAAAAAAAAAAAAAAAAEAAAAAAAAAAAAAAAAAAAAAAAAAAAAAAAAAAAAAAAAAAAAAAAAAA
AAAAAAAAAAAAAAAAAAAAAAAAAAAAAAAAAAAAAAAAAAAAAAAAAAAAAAAAAAAAAAAAAAAAAAAAAAAAAAAAAAAAAAAA
AAAAAAAAAAAAAAAAAAAAAAAAAAAAAAAAAAAAAAAAAAAAAAAAAAAAAAAEAAAAAAAAAAAAAAAAAAAAAAAAAAAAAAAA
AAAAEAAA
```

Understanding the Problem

To solve this problem with pencil and paper could require a long, long time! Nevertheless, we could proceed as follows:

> Draw an 8 row by 8 column grid, and place pieces of paper numbered 1, 2, 3, and 4 in a hat.
>
> We then position a mole at row 3 and column 2 and draw a number from the hat.
>
> If the number picked is a 2, we move the mole up one square, i.e., we stay in the same column, but we move from row 3 to row 2. (If the number picked is a 3, we move one square left. If the number picked is a 4, we move one square down. If the number picked is a 1, we move one square right.)
>
> Once the mole has been moved, we replace the first number and draw another number from the hat to determine our next move. We then move the mole appropriately, and we keep repeating this same sequence of steps until we move outside the grid for either a drowning or an escape. For an escape, we add 1 to our escape counter; otherwise we add 1 to our accident counter.
>
> Once the first adventure is completed, we reposition our mole at row 3 and column 2 to start our second adventure. We continue in this manner for 500 adventures altogether. Since, on the average, a particular adventure lasts 30 moves, we may need to draw 15,000 numbers from the hat!

Output Design

The output design is already specified in the statement of the problem: every time a mole drowns we print an A and every time a mole escapes we print an E. This way we can visually track what happens to the mole during the execution of the program. The percentage of escapes is the number of escapes divided by 500 and multiplied by 100, or simply E/5.

Data Dictionary

To keep track of the position of the mole, we need two variables R and C to reflect the current row and column position of the mole. Thus, at any given time the mole will be located at the intersection of row R and column C.

A variable, E is needed to count the occurrences of escapes.
The variable K is used to generate the random numbers 1, 2, 3, and 4.
The variable I is used to count the 500 adventures.

Program Development

There are two key questions in this problem: How do we move the mole around, and how do we know when the mole drowns or escapes?

Initially we position the mole at row 3 and column 2 by writing R = 3 and C = 2. We then generate a random number K between 1 and 4 (K = RND(4), for example) to tell us what direction to take (1 = right, 2 = up, 3 = left, 4 = down).

If K has value 2, we move the mole up one square, from row 3 to row 2. Hence we subtract 1 from the current value of R (R = R − 1).

Assume before the move that
R = 3 and C = 2

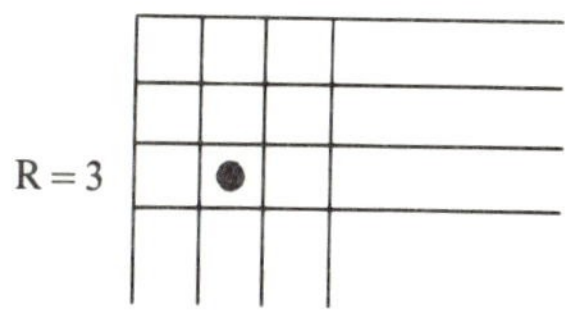

after the move If K = 2, then
R = 2 and C = 2

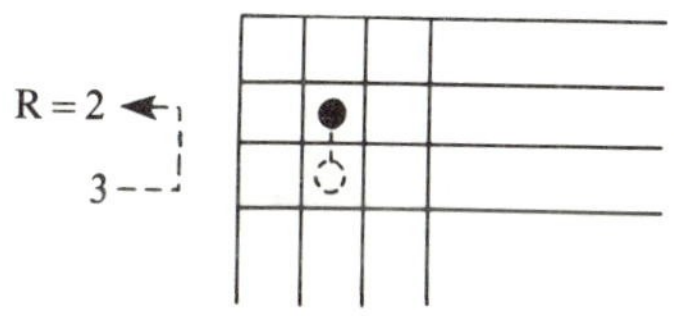

Note that when moving in an upward direction, the column C does not change.

If K has value 3, and we are initially at R = 3 and C = 2, we move the mole from column 2 to column 1 (C = C − 1). If K has value 4, we need to add 1 to R (R = R + 1). If K has value 1, we need to add 1 to C (C = C + 1).

Each time we move the mole to its new position, we must check to see if it has hit the water (R = 0, R = 9, C = 0, or C = 9) or escaped (R = 3, C = 9). It is fairly evident that when the mole is moving in an upward direction, the only bad thing that can happen is drowning at row 0! When moving up, the mole cannot drown to the left, to the right, or backwards! Similarly, if the mole moves left (K = 3), we need to check whether column C is 0; obviously we do not need to check for R = 0, C = 9, or R = 9 when moving in a leftward direction.

When moving down, we should check whether R = 9 (drown), and when moving to the right we should check whether C = 9. If C = 9, the mole can escape if R = 3. Hence, when moving right, we should check for C = 9 *and* R = 3. If both these conditions are satisfied, we increment the escape counter by 1 and print the letter E on the terminal to advertise the mole's escape. If C = 9 but R ≠ 3, the mole has drowned. If

$C \neq 9$, the mole is still on the island, and we go to the random number generator for its next move.

An adventure ends when the mole either drowns or escapes. At that time, we print an A or an E on the terminal to inform the user of the outcome of the adventure. Before we start a new adventure by repositioning the mole at its starting block (R = 3 and C = 2), we must determine whether we have gone through 500 adventures. If we have completed 500 adventures, we compute the percentage of escapes by computing E * 100/500 or E/5.

The flowchart outlining the logic to solve this problem is shown in Figure 6–19, which also displays the BASIC code.

Testing

A simulation problem such as this one is extremely difficult to test since the user has no idea what the results are supposed to look like. The user should carefully examine all instructions and make sure the logic is correct!

6-5 Exercises

6-5-1 Test Yourself

1. Write the following in BASIC.
   a. $|a + b|$
   b. $\sqrt{a + b}$
   c. $\sqrt{\sin^2 x + \cos^2 x}$
   d. $|a - b|\,|x - y|$

2. What is the value of each of the following if A = −3 and B = 4?
   a. INT(A/B)
   b. SGN(A*B)
   c. ABS(A+B)
   d. SQR(B)
   e. ABS(INT(B/A))
   f. SGN(A)*SGN(B)
   g. LOG (EXP(B))

3. Under what conditions will a marriage proposal letter be written as a result of the following code?

   `IF H$="BLACK"  AND  H>5.8  OR  E>10000` *then write letter*
   where H$ is the hair color H is a height and E is an earning.

4. Assume X = 30, Y = 40, A = 1, and B = 4. Is the following statement true or false?

```
NOT (X + Y < 100 OR A = 1) AND B > 3
```

5. Assume X = 3, Y = 2, and Z = −1. Which of the following statements are valid?
   a. `IF (X + Y) ^ 2 < -1 AND Y > Z ...`
   b. `IF X - Y = 0 OR Z AND X = 0 ...`
   c. `IF -3 < Z OR 1 = X ...`
   d. `IF X + 1 OR Y + Z > 3 ...`
   e. `IF X NOT > 4 ...`
   f. `IF NOT (Y >< -1) ...`

6. Let the computer pick a number between 1 and 10 using the random number function. Draw a flowchart and write the code to give a player three chances to guess the computer's number.

7. Modify the code in exercise 6 to flash the message GENIUS ten times in the middle of the screen when the number is guessed.

Figure 6–19 Moles and mazes.

```
100 REM MOLE PROJECT
105 REM
110 REM DATA DICTIONARY
115 REM R: KEEPS TRACK OF ROW POSITION
120 REM C: KEEPS TRACK OF COLUMN POSITION
125 REM E: COUNTS NUMBER OF ESCAPES
135 REM I: COUNTS NUMBER OF ADVENTURES
140 REM K: DIRECTION FOR MOLE TO TAKE
145 REM     1=RIGHT; 2=UP; 3=LEFT; 4=DOWN
155 E = 0
160 I = 0
165 I = I + 1
170 REM 500 ADVENTURES COMPLETED?
175 IF I > 500 THEN 371
180 REM POSITION MOLE AT ROW=3 & COL=2
185 REM AFTER EACH ESCAPE OR DROWNING
190 R = 3
195 C = 2
200 REM MOVE THE MOLE RANDOMLY
205 K = INT(RND(1) * 4 + 1)
210 REM MOLE MOVES UP
215 IF K = 2   THEN 290
220 REM MOLE MOVES LEFT
225 IF K = 3   THEN 305
230 REM MOLE MOVES DOWN
235 IF K = 4   THEN 320
240 REM MOLE MOVES RIGHT
245    C = C + 1
250 IF C = 9   THEN 265
255    GOTO 205
260 REM HAS MOLE ESCAPED? R=3 C=9
265 IF R<> 3   THEN 340
270    E = E + 1
275 REM START NEW ADVENTURE
280    PRINT "E";
285    GOTO 165
290    R = R - 1
295 IF R = 0   THEN 340
300    GOTO 205
305    C = C - 1
310 IF C = 0   THEN 340
315 GOTO 205
320    R = R + 1
325 IF R = 9   THEN 340
330    GOTO 205
340 REM MOLE HAS DROWNED
345 PRINT "A";
350 REM START NEW ADVENTURE
355 GOTO 165
371 PRINT "PERCENT ESCAPES  ="; E/5
375 END
RUN
```

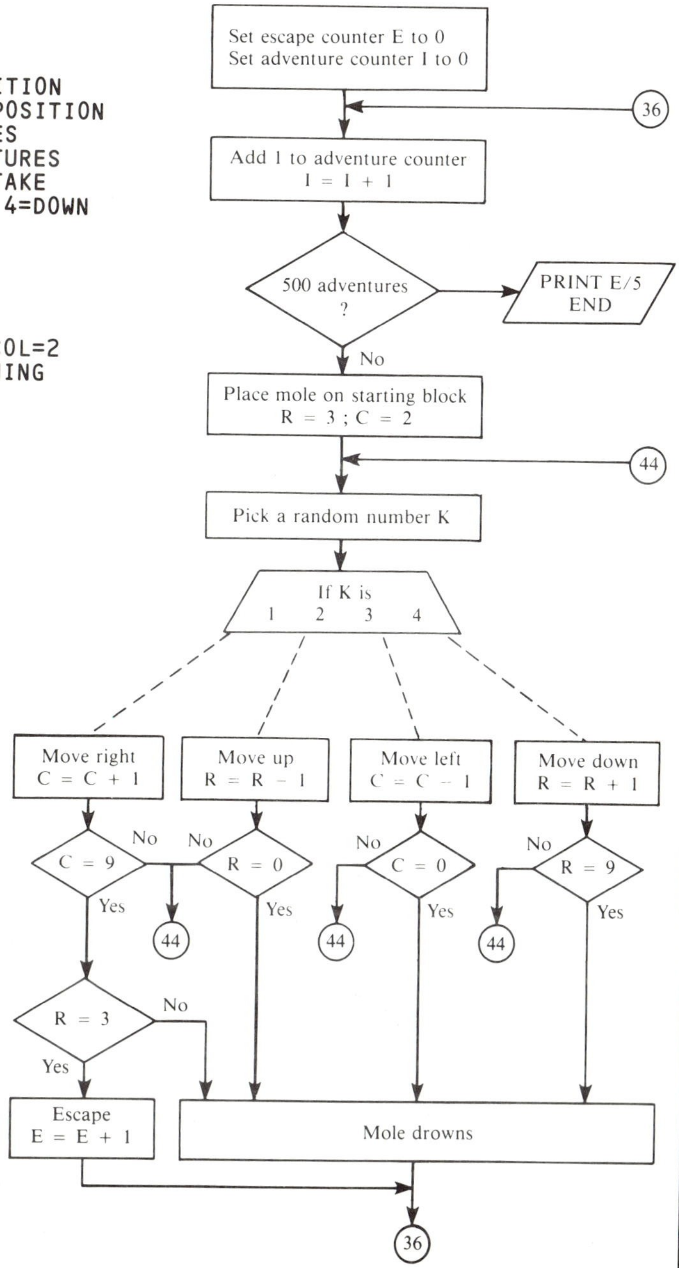


```
AAAAAAAAAAAAAAAAAAAAAAEAAAAAAAAAAAAAAAAAAAEEAAAAAAAAAAAAAAAAAAAAAAAAAAAAAAAAAAAA
AAAAAAAAAAAAAAAAAAAAAAAAAAAAAAAAAAAAAAAAAAAAAAAAAAAAAAAAAAAAAAAAAAAAAAAAAAAAAAAA
AAAAAAAAAAAAAAAAAAAAAAAAAAAAAAAAAAAAAAAAAAAAAAAAAAAAAAAAAAAAAAAAAAAAAAAAAAAAAAAA
AAAAAAAAAAAAAAAAAAAAAAAAAAAAAAAAAAAAAAAAAAAAAAAAAAAAAAAAAAAAAAAAAAAAAAAAAAAAAAAA
AAAAAAAAAAAAAAAAAAAAAAAAAAAAAAAAAAAAAAAAAAAAAAAAAAAAAAAAAAAAAAAAAAAAAAAAAAAAAAAA
AAAAAAAAAAAAAAAAAAAAAAAAAAAAAAAAAAAAAAAAAAAAAAAAAAAAAAAAAAAAAAAAAAAAAAAAAAAAAAAA
AAAAAAAAAAAAAAAAAAAAAAAAAAAAAAAAAAAAAAAAAAAAAAAAAAAAAAEAAAAAAAAAAAAAAAAAAAAAAAAA
AAAEAAAAAAAAAAAAAAAA
PERCENT ESCAPES     = 1
```

6-5-2 Programming Exercises

1. Write a program to play a guessing game with the computer, as follows:
   a. The computer thinks of a number between 1 and 10, and you have to guess its number by entering your guess at the terminal. If you guess it, the computer should print a complimentary remark. At the end of the game the computer should ask you whether you desire to play another game.
   b. To make the game more entertaining, print out random messages such as "TOO BAD, TOM, TRY AGAIN" or "WHAT'S THE MATTER WITH YOU, TOM" or "YOU'RE NOT IN MY LEAGUE", and so forth, when the player enters an incorrect guess. Print suitable random messages when the player wins.
   c. To make the game more exciting and to help the player guess the number more quickly, print out messages such as YOU'RE HOT or YOU'RE COLD.

2. Simulate a dice game. The computer throws two dice for itself and then throws two for you. The one who wins is the one who throws the first pair. A congratulatory message should be addressed to the winner. To simulate the throw of a die, use the statement LET K = INT(RND(1) *6) + 1 or LET K = RND(6).

3. Draw a starry summer night on the screen by printing a period in a random position on each line. Fill the screen or page with such lines, and you will be amazed at how well the result simulates the heavens on a cloudless night.

4. Write a program to input an amount in cents (up to one dollar) and break that amount into half dollars, quarters, dimes, nickels, and pennies. Use the INT function and the remainder formula discussed in section 6-1-3. For example: 78 cents = 1 half dollar, 1 quarter, and 3 pennies.

   (*Hint:* Divide amount by 50 and compute the remainder, then divide that remainder by 25 and compute another remainder, then divide the new remainder by 10 and so forth. If you can't think of a way to use the remainder ask the question "is amount greater than 50." If it is, you have a half dollar; you then compute a new amount = amount − 50. . . . If the amount from the first question is not greater than 50, ask the question "is amount greater than 25." If it is, you have a quarter; you then compute amount = amount −25 and ask if amount is greater than 10 (dimes) etc. [Draw a flowchart first.])

5. Read *N* grades already sorted in ascending order (N is accepted from input) and compute the median. The median is the mark that divides a distribution of scores in two equal parts. (To determine whether N is even or odd, evaluate 2*INT(N/2) − N.)

   `1Ø, 11, 12, 13, 14, 15, 16` The median is 13.

   `1Ø, 11, 12, 13` The median is $\frac{11 + 12}{2} = 11.5$

6. Write a program to check the "honesty" of your random number generator by generating randomly a whole number between 1 and 4 and counting the occurrence of each of the numbers (use the ON/GO TO if you have that feature).

7. Write a program to create modern art: Associate with the number 1 a line consisting of, say, 10 consecutive stars (asterisks), with the number 2 a line with 15 consecutive stars, and so on up to the number 6. Then generate a random number be-

tween 1 and 6 and print out its corresponding pictorial representation (line of stars). Repeat the process 10 or 15 times. You may want to experiment with symbols other than asterisks for the graphic display.

8. A dog is lost in a tunnel at node 0 (see diagram). It can move one node at one time in either direction right or left with equal probability (1 = right, 2 = left). When the dog hits node L_2, however, a force of nature always propels him directly to node L_4. The dog escapes from the tunnel when he either hits L_5 or R_4. Write a program to determine:

a. Whether the dog has a better chance to exit from the right or the left: in fact, what are the odds that he will exit from R_4?

b. How long, on the average, the dog stays in the tunnel (each node takes one minute to cover).

c. Whether he might stay in the tunnel forever.

Restart the dog at node 0 a thousand times and count the number of times he escapes through R_4 or L_5.

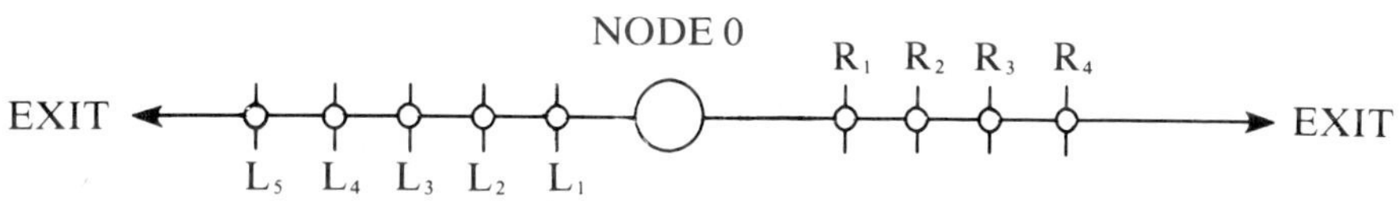

9. Do the same problem as exercise 8, but let node L_2 propel the dog to L_4 only when traveling in a left direction. If node L_2 is reached when traveling to the right, the node L_2 has no effect.

10. Marc and Laura each toss a die. What is the chance that they each toss the same number? (Simulate 100 throws.)

11. Sue and Tom each toss a pair of dice. What is the chance that both toss out a 2, (i.e., a pair of 1's each)? a 3? a 4 (2 and 2 or 3 and 1)? a 5? a 12? Express the chance as "so many" out of 100.

12. Charlie tosses a pair of dice. What number (sum of the face values of both dice) is most likely to be thrown? (A 2 is the sum of 1 and 1; a 7 is a combination of 4 and 3, 5 and 2, or 6 and 1; and so forth.)

13. Write a second-grade level computer-assisted instructional unit on addition and subtraction of numbers ranging from 1 to 10. Subtraction should not give rise to negative numbers. The CAI unit should consist of 10 questions. Numbers as well as the operations should occur in random fashion. Print the percentage of correct answers; if the user cannot get the right answer in three attempts, print a message with the correct answer.

14. A method that can be used to find random numbers is to begin with any two-digit number and square it. The middle two digits of the product will be a random number. A new random number can be computed by repeating the process using the random number just computed. Write a program to generate 50 random numbers using this method.

(*Hint*: To extract the digit 3 from X = 834, look at R = INT(X/10) then compute R/10 − INT(R/10) and multiply by 10 to get 3.)

15. A submarine has been trapped in an enemy bay with only one escape channel leading out of the bay. The bay is surrounded by mines as shown below. All navigating equipment is malfunctioning, and the blind submarine is now moving randomly in any of the four cardinal directions one square at a time. If the sub hits any of the mines, it is instantly destroyed. Write a program to determine the sub's escape chances from its present position of row 4 and column 2. The sub escapes when it reaches row 2 column 5.

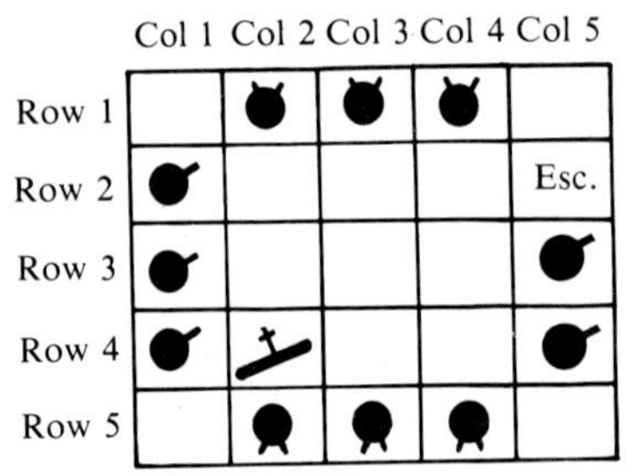

16. The following flowchart calculates the exact date for Easter given any year after 1583. Write a program to compute the Easter date for any given year.

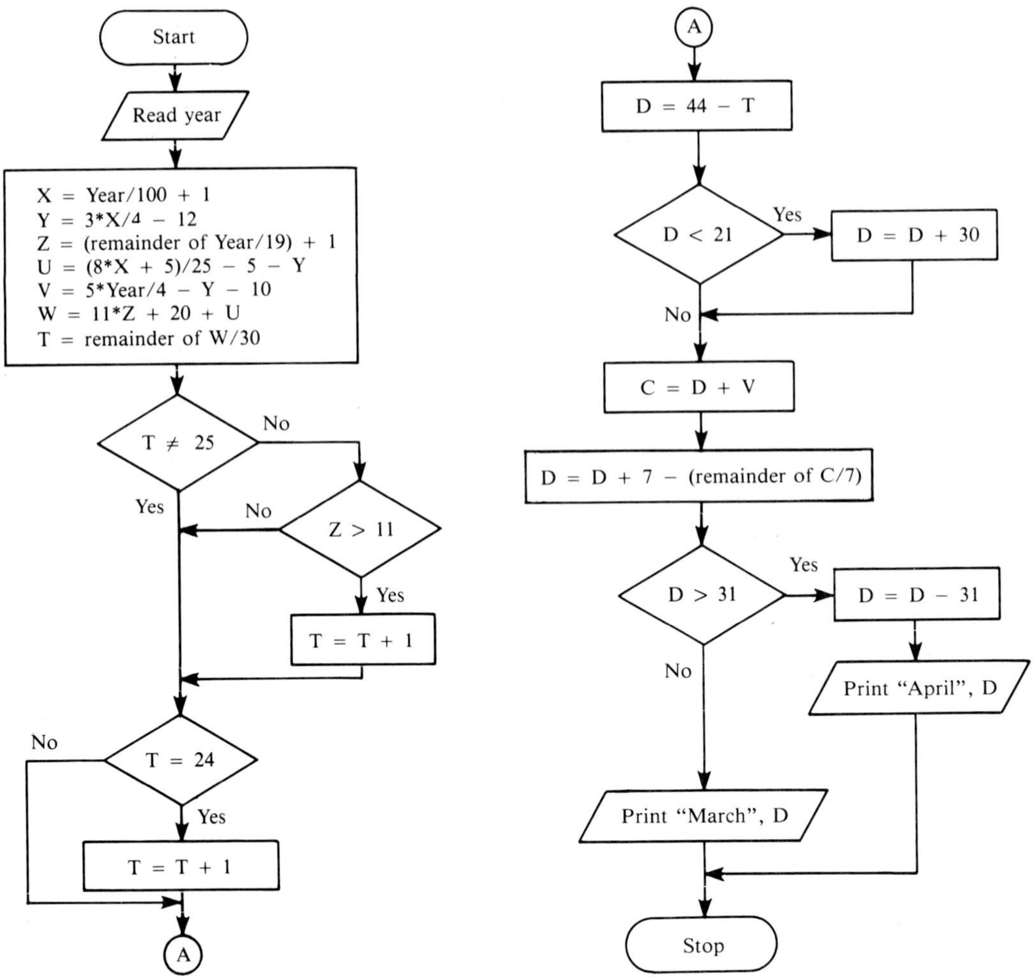

17. Write a program using the PRINT USING to read check amounts (negative values) and deposit amounts to produce a bank statement similar to the following (note the check amounts are positive numbers in the report):

M.H. GUNSON **STATEMENT OF ACCOUNT**
146 N.E. 35 ST. **POUREMS STATE BANK**
CHICAGO, ILLINOIS

CHECKS	*DEPOSITS*	*DATE*	*BALANCES*
		May 31,1983	4,000.00
	100.00	June 1, 1983	4,100.00
	200.00	June 2, 1983	4,300.00
	300.00	June 3, 1983	4,600.00
	400.00	June 4, 1983	5,000.00
	500.00	June 5, 1983	5,500.00
600.50		June 6, 1983	4,899.50

18. Write a program using PRINT USING to design checks and read dollar amounts to write out the checks.

19. You have probably cut out, completed, and sent off coupons as shown below. Write a program using the PRINT USING to design such a form and then input the necessary data to fill the form.

CAMCOT
CAMOUFLAGE COMPANY, INC.
1715 N.W. ST., MIDDLAND, NY 11797

______ Please send me the CAMCOT KIT @ $2.95 per kit

______ Please have a representative call me

Name ______________________________ Phone ________

Organization ______________________________

Address ______________________________

City/State ______________________________ Zip _____

Number of Kits _____ Amount enclosed $________

20. The following is an organizational chart of a major corporation. Names of executive officers are shown in parentheses. Write a program using the PRINT USING to design such a chart and read a list of names that are to replace the current names of the executive officers.

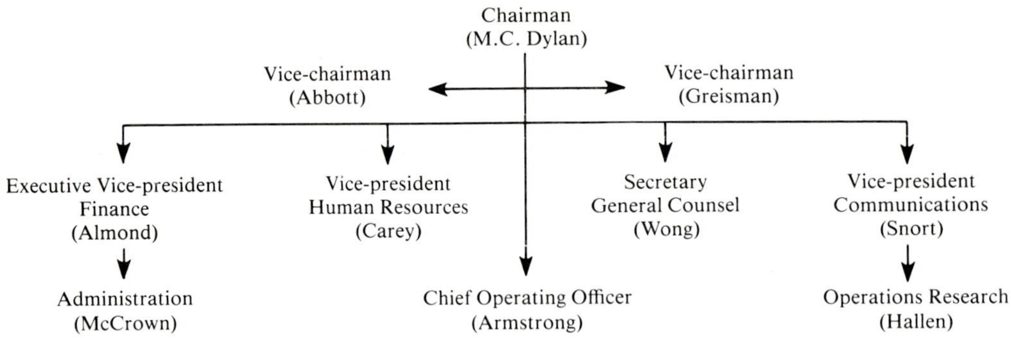

6-5-3 Answers to Test Yourself

1. a. ABS(A + B)
   b. SQR (A + B)
   c. SQR(SIN(X)^2 + COS(X)^2)
   d. ABS(A – B)*ABS(X – Y)

2. a. –1
   b. –1
   c. 1
   d. 2
   e. 2
   f. –1
   g. 4

3. A marriage proposal letter will be written if either of the following conditions is true:
   a. If earnings > 100,000
   b. If hair is black and height is at least 5 foot 8 inches.

4. False

5. a. Valid
   b. Invalid "Z and X" (Z or X are not logical values.)
   c. Valid
   d. Invalid use of the OR
   e. Invalid (NOT >)
   f. Valid

6.
```
10 K = INT (RND * 10 + 1)
```

7.
```
15 I = 0
20 INPUT X
25 I = I + 1
30 IF X = K THEN 45
35 IF I < 3 THEN 20
40 STOP
45 I = 0
46 PRINT
47 I = I + 1
48 IF I < 12 THEN 46
49 I = 0
50 PRINT TAB (38);"GENIUS"
55 CLS
60 I = I + 1
65 IF I < 10 THEN 45
70 END
```

Flowchart for Part 1

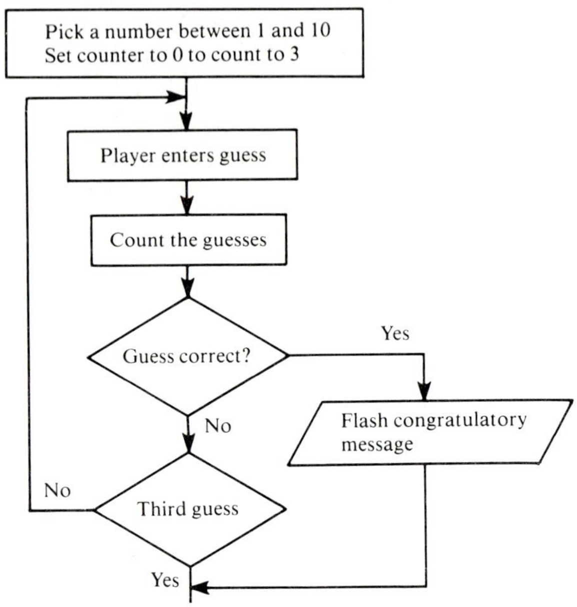

7 THE ACCUMULATION PROCESS AND THE FOR/NEXT STATEMENTS

7-1 Problem Example

Let us write a program to compute the weight of a house cat on the moon, on Jupiter, and on Venus (see the table below) for weights varying from 1 to 5 pounds in increments of 1 pound. The output should be similar to:

EARTH	MOON	JUPITER	VENUS
1	.16	2.64	.85
2	.32	5.28	1.7
3	.48	7.92	2.55
4	.64	10.56	3.4
5	.8	13.2	4.25

Celestial bodies	Percentage of Earth Weight
Moon	16
Jupiter	264
Venus	85

This problem requires us to carry out a procedure five times, i.e., 5 different sets of weights need to be computed and printed. When a procedure needs to be carried out a fixed number of times, the programmer can always use the FOR/NEXT statements. The block of code to be repeated is simply placed between the FOR and NEXT statements (see Figure 7–1). The FOR statement tells BASIC how many times the block of code is to be repeated; it simulates counting by initializing, incrementing, and testing a counter in just one statement. This simplifies the programmer's task, as he/she no longer needs to ponder where to increment and test the counter. Figure 7–1 displays this automatic loop control.

Figure 7–1 Use of the FOR/NEXT statements.

```
10 REM PLANETARY CAT WEIGHTS
15 REM     M: MOON WEIGHT
20 REM     J: JUPITER WEIGHT
25 REM     V: VENUS WEIGHT
30 REM     C: CAT WEIGHT ON EARTH
35 PRINT "EARTH", "MOON",
37 PRINT "JUPITER", "VENUS"
40 FOR C = 1 TO 5
45     M =  .16 * C
50     J = 2.64 * C
55     V =  .85 * C
60     PRINT C, M, J, V
65 NEXT C
70 END
```

Process the lines between FOR and NEXT five times, as C goes from 1 to 5 in steps of 1. The first time through the loop, C = 1 and the three weights are computed; the second time C = 2 and the three weights are computed again, and so forth. The last three weights are computed when C = 5. At this point NEXT C causes an exit from the loop.

7-2 Elements of the BASIC Language

7-2-1 FOR/NEXT Statements

The statements FOR/NEXT represent no new programming concepts; in fact, any BASIC program can be written without the FOR/NEXT statements. The purpose of these two statements is strictly convenience to the programmer. They are used primarily for loop control. The usual procedure for loop control is to initialize a counter to a certain value, then increment that counter by a constant, and finally compare the counter to a terminal value for loop exiting. With the FOR/NEXT statements, the user specifies in the FOR statement the initial, incremental, and test values of the counter (index) and identifies the range of the loop by making the NEXT statement the last statement of the procedure to be repeated.

The general form of the FOR statement is

line number FOR *index* = e_1 TO e_2 STEP e_3

statement 1
statement 2
.
. } body
.
statement n

line number NEXT *index*

where FOR, TO, and STEP are key words, and the *index* must be a variable name. e_1, e_2, and e_3 are expressions that (when evaluated) specify the *initial, test,* and *incremental* values of the index respectively. The STEP phrase is optional; if it is omitted, the incremental value is assumed to be 1. *Statement 1, statement 2, . . . , statement n* constitute the body of the loop, the statements that are to be repeated. NEXT is a key word, and its *index* is a variable name that must be the same as the index in the corresponding FOR statement. A NEXT statement is used to denote the physical end of a loop initiated by a FOR statement; it is a visual bracket that identifies the end of the loop.

Internally, the action taken by BASIC on encountering the following code

```
10 FOR I = E1 TO E2 STEP E3
        Body
          of
            the
              loop
90 NEXT I
```

can be interpreted as follows:

Case 1:

The incremental value E3 is positive.

Step 1: The two expressions E1 and E2 are evaluated and the value E1 is assigned to the index I.

Step 2: The index I is compared to the value of E2. If the index is greater than E2, control is passed to the statement following the NEXT statement, otherwise the body of the loop is executed.

Step 3: When the NEXT I statement is reached, the value of the index is incremented by E3 and control is passed to step 2.

Case 2:

The incremental value E3 is negative.

The same steps are taken as in Case 1, except that in step 2 control is passed to the statement following the NEXT statement if the index is less than E2.

The following flowchart shows the symbol for the FOR/NEXT loop (assume the incremental value E3 is positive):

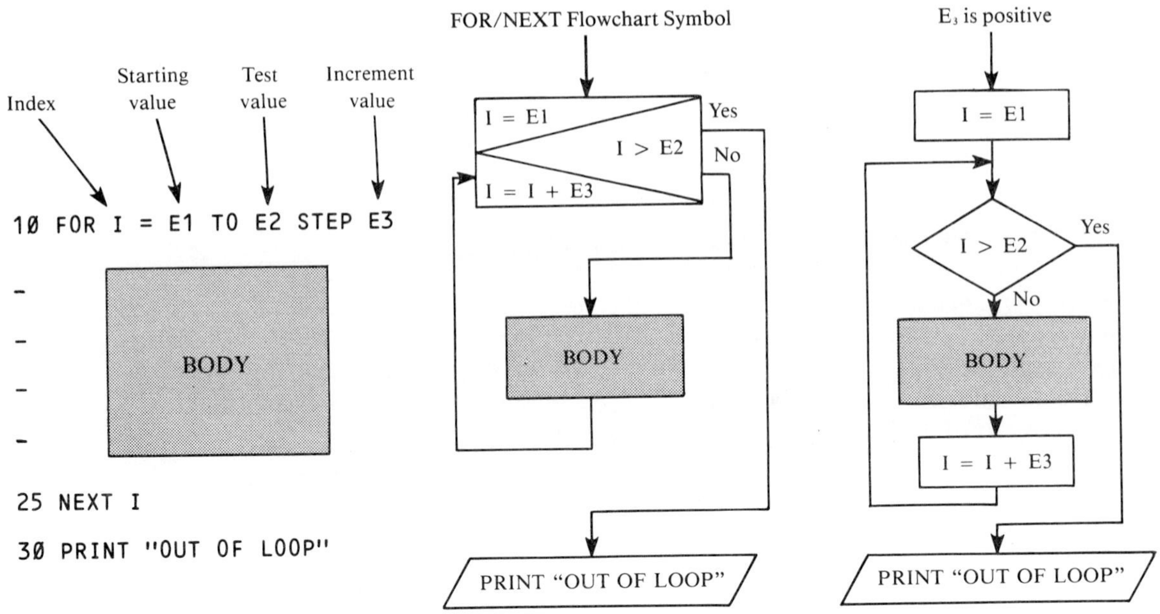

If the increment E3 is negative, then the condition I > E2 would be replaced by I < E2 in the flowchart.

To improve the readability of the program, it is helpful to indent all statements in the body of the loop.

Examples of FOR/NEXT Loops

a.
```
FOR I = 2 TO 1Ø STEP 2

NEXT I
```
The body of the loop will be carried out five times, and the values for I within the loop, will be 2, 4, 6, 8, and 10.

b.
```
FOR J = 5 TO 1 STEP -1

NEXT J
```
The body of the loop will be carried out 5 times, and the values for J within the loop will be 5, 4, 3, 2, and 1.

c.
```
FOR X = 2 TO 1

NEXT X
```
Since the intial value exceeds the test value, the body of the loop is bypassed. (On some nonstandard BASICs, the body will be executed once.)

d.
```
FOR I = -2 TO 2.3 STEP .5

NEXT I
```
Note, the negative starting value of index and the fractional value for increment. The values assumed by the index I are −2, −1.5, −1, −.5, 0, .5, 1, 1.5, and 2; hence the statements in the body of the loop will be executed nine times.

It is often convenient to express the intital, test, or increment value of a FOR/NEXT loop as a variable, as in examples (e) and (f):

e.
```
INPUT N
FOR K = 1 TO N

NEXT K
```
Repeat the body of the loop N times.

f.
```
READ L,K
FOR M = L+1 TO 2Ø STEP L/K

NEXT M
```
The initial, test, and incremental expressions are evaluated and the loop is carried out.

CAUTION:

Generally speaking one should *not* change the value of the index or values dealing with the initial, test, or increment variables while in the loop. None of these variables should be specified to the left of the equal sign during the looping process. Avoid these common pitfalls:

```
 5 FOR J = K TO 1Ø
1Ø    READ X, J
15 NEXT J
```
The index J is redefined by the READ statement.

```
 5 FOR I = 1 TO L
1Ø    LET L = L+1
15 NEXT I
```
The value of L should generally remain fixed within the loop.

This, of course, does not mean that the index cannot be used in an expression on the right side of the equal sign; it can, as shown in Figure 7–1.

7-2-2 Do It Now

1. Determine whether the following FOR/NEXT loops are syntactically correct. Give reasons if incorrect.

a.
```
1 FOR I = -1 TO 3
3     PRINT I
4 NEXT
```
b.
```
1 FOR K = 2 TO 1
3     X = K
5 NEXT X
```
c.
```
1 FOR L = N TO M STEP .5
2 PRINT "CAUGHT IN LOOP"
5 PRINT L^2
7 STOP
```

2. What output is produced by the following FOR/NEXT loops?

a.
```
1 FOR L = 1 TO 4
3     PRINT L, L^2, L^.5
5 NEXT L
```
b.
```
1 FOR L = 2 TO 21 STEP 3
3     PRINT L;
5 NEXT L
```
c.
```
1 FOR T = 3 TO 1
3     PRINT T+1
5 NEXT T
```
d.
```
1 FOR I = 1 TO -1 STEP -.5
3     PRINT 10-I
5 NEXT I
```

3. Write BASIC codes using FOR/NEXT statements to generate the following sequences of numbers:

a. 1, 3, 5, 7, ..., 51
b. $-10, -9, -8, \ldots, -1$
c. 25, 36, 49, ..., 441 ($5^2, 6^2, 7^2, \ldots, 21^2$)
d. 1, 1/2, 1/3, ..., 1/99 (1, .5, .3333.., .25, ...)

Answers

1. a. Invalid: line 4 should be NEXT I.
   b. Invalid: Index for NEXT must be same as index for FOR.
   c. Invalid: NEXT statement is missing.

2. a.

1	1	1
2	4	1.414
3	9	1.732
4	16	2

   b. 2, 5, 8, 11, 14, 17, 20
   c. Nothing is printed, since the starting value of the index is greater than the terminal value.
   d. 9, 9.5, 10, 10.5, 11

3. a.
```
10 FOR I = 1 TO 51 STEP 2
20     PRINT I;
30 NEXT I
```
b.
```
10 FOR K = -10 TO -1
20     PRINT K;
30 NEXT K
```
c.
```
10 FOR I = 5 TO 21
15     PRINT I^2;
20 NEXT I
```
d.
```
10 FOR I = 1 TO 99
15     PRINT 1/I;
20 NEXT I
```

7-2-3 The Accumulation Process

We have already counted in BASIC by repeated execution of statements such as I = I + 1, after setting an initial value for I. Counting can be thought of as "accumulating a count." The main difference between *counting* and *accumulating* is that, instead of repetitively adding a constant (1, for example) to a counter, a variable is repetitively added to (or sometimes multiplied by) an accumulator, which is a special variable used to keep track of running sums, partial sums, products, and so forth. See Figure 7–2.

Figure 7–2 Counting versus accumulating.

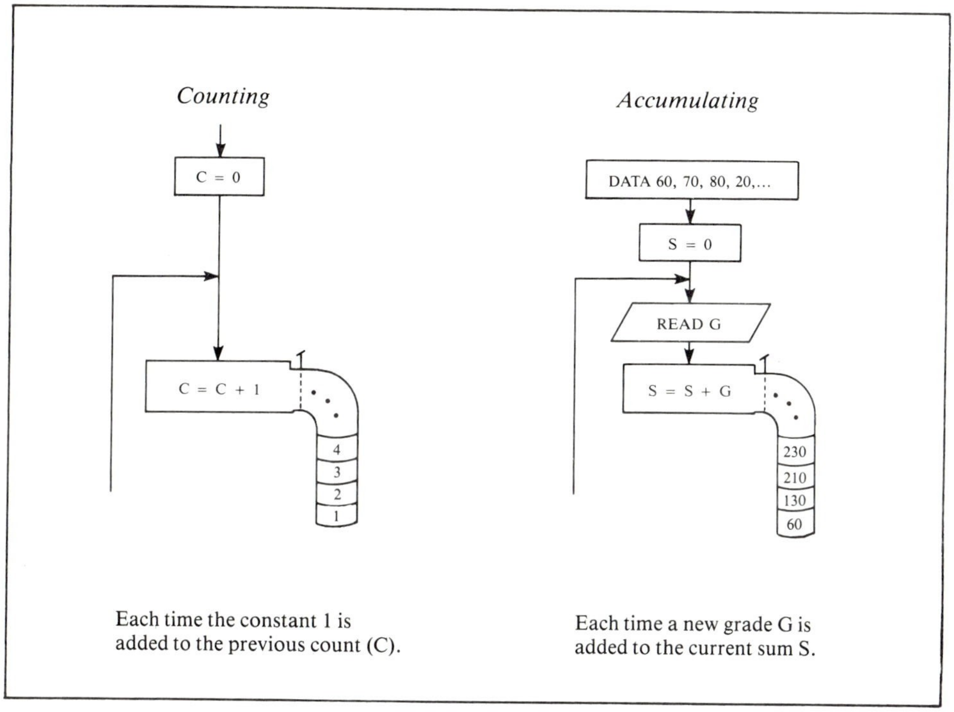

The following two examples illustrate the accumulation process.

Example 1: A Grade Average Computation

An input file consists of five scores. Write the code to print the five scores and compute the average score. The output should be similar to the following:

```
  SCORES
    60
    90
    70
    20
    10

AVERAGE = 50
```

This caption is printed once, outside the loop.

As each score is read, it is printed.

Every time a score is read, it is added to the previous score to form a sum of scores. When five scores have been summed, the sum is divided by five to give the average.

The program to solve this problem is shown in Figure 7-3. Analyze the accumulation process carefully (line 60) to see how the sum of all the scores is obtained.

■ **Figure 7–3** Computing an average of scores.

```
10 REM COMPUTING AN AVERAGE
15 REM     S: SUM OF SCORES
20 REM     I: COUNTER
25 REM
27 DATA 60, 90, 70, 20, 10
30 S = 0
35 PRINT "SCORES"
40 FOR I = 1 TO 5
50    READ G
55    PRINT G
60    S = S + G
70 NEXT I
75 A = S/5
80 PRINT "AVERAGE=";A
85 END
```

Line 30: Initialize sum of scores to 0 outside loop.

Line 40: Process statements 50 through 60 five times.

1st time	2nd time	3rd time	4th time	5th time
60	90	70	20	10
↓	↓	↓	↓	↓
S = 0 + 60	S = 60 + 90	S = 150 + 70	S = 220 + 20	S = 240 + 10

Lines 75–85: When the loop has gone through its cycle five times, the average is computed and printed.

Note the importance of setting the accumulator S to 0 outside the loop. Every time a new score is read, it is immediately added to the current sum of scores at line 60; this is shown in Figure 7–3.

Example 2: Computation of the Sum of the First 100 Integers

Let us write a program to compute SUM = 1 + 2 + 3 + ... + 100. In this program we need:
an accumulator S to keep adding the numbers 1, 2, 3, ... and
a counter I to generate the numbers 1, 2, 3, ... Thus, every time we generate a new number for I, we will immediately add that number (I) to S to get the new sum (current sum).

One easy way to generate the numbers 1, 2, 3, ... is to use a FOR/NEXT loop. Then the problem can be solved as follows:

```
10 S = 0                Initialize sum to 0 outside loop.
15 FOR I = 1 to 100     Generate the numbers 1, 2, 3, ... and as these numbers are generated,
20     S = S + I        keep adding them to the sum.
30 NEXT I               When the loop has gone through its complete cycle, print the sum.
40 PRINT S
```

7-2-4 Do It Now

1. Write the code to compute:
   a. 5 + 10 + 15 + ... + 675
   b. 1 * 2 * 3 * 4 * ... * 17
   c. 1 + 1/2 + 1/3 + ... + 1/100

2. What output would you expect from the following programs?

a.
```
Ø5 S = Ø
1Ø FOR K = 1 to 1Ø
15 S = S - (-1) ^ K * K
2Ø NEXT K
25 PRINT S
```

b.
```
1Ø DATA 2Ø, 4Ø, 7Ø, 9Ø
15 LET A = Ø
2Ø FOR I = 1 TO 4
3Ø   READ X
4Ø   LET A = A - X
5Ø NEXT I
6Ø PRINT A
7Ø END
```

Answers

1. a.
```
1Ø S = Ø
15 FOR K = 5 TO 675 STEP 5
2Ø     S = S + K
25 NEXT K
```

b.
```
1Ø P = 1
15 FOR J = 1 TO 17
2Ø     P = P * J
25 NEXT J
```

c.
```
1Ø S = Ø
15 FOR I = 1 TO 1ØØ
2Ø     S = S + 1/I
25 NEXT I
```

2. a. S = 1 - 2 + 3 - 4 + ... +9 - 1Ø = 5

b.

A	I	X
Ø	1	2Ø
-2Ø	2	4Ø
-6Ø	3	7Ø
-13Ø	4	9Ø
-22Ø	5	

Expected output: −220

7-2-5 Transfer Into and Out of Loops

As common sense would dictate, transfer from a statement outside of a loop to a statement within the body of the loop is not permitted, since the index of the loop in the FOR statement would not be initialized properly. Similarly, no transfer should be made from a statement within the body of a loop to the FOR statement, as an infinite loop would occur since the index would be reinitialized. Study the following examples carefully.

1. *Example*

```
10 IF X > 1 THEN 50
.
.
.
50 FOR I = 1 TO 66
.
.
.
35 NEXT I
```

Transfer to a FOR/NEXT loop is permissible as long as the transfer target is the FOR statement.

2. *Example*

```
10 FOR T = 1 TO 17
.
.
.
35     IF X < 3 THEN 65
.
.
.
65     PRINT "RES=";X^2
.
.
.
98 NEXT T
```

Transfer can be made from one statement to another within the loop.

3. *Example*

```
05 INPUT N
10 FOR   K = 1 TO 30
15     PRINT K^2
.
.
.
40     IF N < 2 * K THEN 95
.
.
.
95 NEXT K
```

It is permissible to stay in the loop, but bypass the block of code between 40 and 95.

If N = 3, statements 15 through 40 will be carried out 30 times, while the statements between 40 and 95 will only be carried out once, when K = 1.

Transferring to the NEXT statement either causes the loop process to continue or causes an exit from the loop.

4. *Example*

```
10 FOR K = 1 TO 30
.
.
.
35    IF Y = 6 THEN 95
.
.
.
75 NEXT K
.
.
.
95 PRINT K
```

Transfer can be made from a statement within a loop to a statement outside the loop which is not necessarily the NEXT statement.

The value of the index will be printed.

5. *Example*

This is a typical beginner's attempt to transfer out of a loop to perform a particular task and then come back into the loop after completing that task. This practice is to be avoided. The task to be performed should be coded within the loop as follows:

Bad Practice: Task Outside Loop

```
10   FOR I = 1 TO N
.
.
.
35      IF X > L THEN 95
38      PRINT S
.
.
.
70   NEXT I
.
.
.
95      Task to be
96      performed
97
98 GO TO 70
```

Good Practice: Task Within Loop

```
10   FOR I = 1 TO N
.
.
.
35      IF X > L THEN 57
38      PRINT S
.
.
.
55      GO TO 70
57
          Task to be
.         completed
.
.
70   NEXT I
```

6. *Example*

Transfer Within a Loop to the NEXT statement

Let us read an input file consisting of 10 records, each containing an age and a sex code (1 = male, 2 = female), and write the code to compute and print the average male and female age.

```
1Ø DATA 23,1  \
11 DATA 46,2   |
.              |  Input file consisting of exactly 10 records.
.              |
.              |
19 DATA 24,1  /
25 REM   INITIALIZATION OF COUNTERS AND ACCUMULATORS
3Ø M  = Ø                        M counts the number of males.
32 A1 = Ø                        A1 sums the ages of all males.
34 F  = Ø                        F counts the number of females.
36 A2 = Ø                        A2 sums the ages of all females.
38 FOR I = 1 TO 1Ø               Process 10 records.
4Ø        READ A,S               Read a record.
42        IF S = 1 THEN 62       If a male, transfer to process males.
5Ø           A2 = A2 + A         Accumulate ages of females.
52           F  = F + 1          Count the females.
54           GO TO 66            Continue the loop process.
6Ø REM
62           A1 = A1 + A         Accumulate ages of males.
64           M = M + 1           Count the males.
66 NEXT I                        Keep processing the remaining records.
68 PRINT "MALE AVG=";A1/M
7Ø PRINT "FEM AVG="; A2/F
72 END
```

Note the importance of statement 54, which transfers to the NEXT statement and which causes proper incrementing of the index of the FOR/NEXT loop. It would have been incorrect to say GO TO 38 instead of GO TO 66, since this would start the loop over from the beginning (I = 1).

7-2-6 Do It Now

1. Which of the following coding segments are invalid? State your reasons.

a.
```
1Ø IF X = 4 GO TO 68
:
68 FOR I = 1 TO N
:
78     PRINT S
79     IF I > 6 THEN 98
:
84 NEXT I
:
9Ø GO TO 68
:
98
```

b.
```
1Ø IF X = 4 GO TO 68
:
45 FOR K = 1 TO N
:
68     S = S + L
7Ø NEXT K
```

c.
```
 5 FOR I = 1 TO 1Ø
1Ø     LET X = I^2 - 7*I + 12
15     IF X <> Ø THEN 5
2Ø     PRINT I
25 NEXT I
```

2. a. If we replace line 54 in Example 6 with 54 GO TO 40 what would the computer do?
   b. Add the code to Example 6 to print an error message if the sex code is neither a 1 nor a 2.

3. Write the code to fill up your screen with asterisks. Only one PRINT statement and only one asterisk should be specified in the PRINT statement.

4. Write the BASIC code to print the first integer value of X in the range 1 to 10 to satisfy the condition

$$X^2 - X - 6 = 0$$

If there are no such values, print an appropriate message.

Answers

1. a. Valid
   b. Invalid: the transfer to 68 is to the middle of a loop.
   c. Invalid: line 15 causes an infinite loop.

2. a. The loop will not read 10 records since the index I will not be incremented properly. If the records were all female records, the final value of the index I would be 1 and an out-of-data error message at line 40 would be printed.
   b. Add the following code:

```
44 IF S = 2 THEN 50
45    PRINT "INVALID SEX"
46    GO TO 66
```

3. (enter the character width of your output device)

```
10 INPUT N
15 FOR I = 1 TO N
20     PRINT "*";
25 NEXT I
30 GO TO 15
```

4.

```
10 FOR X = 1 TO 10
20    IF X ^ 2 - X - 6 = 0 THEN 60
30 NEXT X
40 PRINT "NO VALUES OF X SATISFY THE CONDITION"
50 STOP
60 PRINT X; "SATISFIES THE CONDITION"
70 END
```

7-2-7 Nested Loops

When writing programs, it is often necessary to repeat an entire loop a certain number of times. This is an example of a loop within a loop, where a complete loop is part of the body of another loop. In such cases, each pass in the outer loop causes the inner loop to run through its complete cycle. The following code illustrates the mechanism of the so-called nested loop.

Outer Loop

Since I varies from 1 to 3, the inner loop will be processed 3 times.

```
10 FOR I = 1 TO 3
15       FOR J = 1 TO 4
20             PRINT I, J
25       NEXT J
30 NEXT I
```

Inner Loop

The inner loop is processed 4 times. Since the other loop is processed 3 times, the PRINT statement will be processed 12 times altogether.

The results produced by the above code is:

```
I   J

1   1  )
1   2  }  First time through the inner loop (outer loop index I = 1)
1   3  }
1   4  )
2   1  )
2   2  }  Second time through the inner loop (outer loop index I = 2)
2   3  }
2   4  )
3   1  )
3   2  }  Third time through the inner loop (outer loop index I = 3)
3   3  }
3   4  )
```

When using nested loops, it is important to remember that each loop must have a different index and that each nested loop must lie totally within the body of the outer loop. Consider the following illustrations of valid and invalid nested loops:

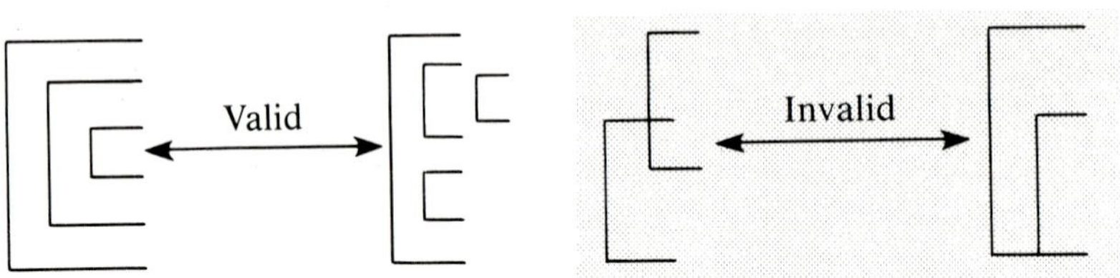

The following examples show nested FOR/NEXT loops:

Example 1: First Five Multiplication Tables for 1 through 6

```
10 FOR J = 1 TO 6
50    FOR K = 1 TO 5
60       PRINT K;"X";J;"=";K*J,
70    NEXT K
75    PRINT
80    NEXT J
```

The innermost loop controls the horizontal lines; it will print
1 × J = —   2 × J = —   . . .   6 × J = —
six times for values of J ranging from 1 to 6

The output is shown on the next page.

```
RUN
1 × 1 = 1       2 × 1 = 2       3 × 1 = 3       4 × 1 = 4       5 × 1 = 5
1 × 2 = 2       2 × 2 = 4       3 × 2 = 6       4 × 2 = 8       5 × 2 = 1Ø
1 × 3 = 3       2 × 3 = 6       3 × 3 = 9       4 × 3 = 12      5 × 3 = 15
1 × 4 = 4       2 × 4 = 8       3 × 4 = 12      4 × 4 = 16      5 × 4 = 2Ø
1 × 5 = 5       2 × 5 = 1Ø      3 × 5 = 15      4 × 5 = 2Ø      5 × 5 = 25
1 × 6 = 6       2 × 6 = 12      3 × 6 = 18      4 × 6 = 24      5 × 6 = 3Ø
```

Example 2: Printing Diagonal Tables

To print the two tables shown below the following code could be used:

```
1Ø FOR K = 1 TO 6
15    FOR J = 1 TO 7-K                    J takes on values 1 through 6.
2Ø       PRINT J;                         Print first part of first table.
25    NEXT J
3Ø    PRINT TAB(2Ø + 3*K);                Start 2nd table at position 23.
35    FOR L = 7-K  TO 1 STEP -1           L takes on values 6 through 1.
4Ø       PRINT L;                         Start printing second table.
45    NEXT L
5Ø    PRINT                               Start at beginning of new line.
55 NEXT K
```

```
RUN
1  2  3  4  5  6       6  5  4  3  2  1
1  2  3  4  5             5  4  3  2  1
1  2  3  4                   4  3  2  1
1  2  3                         3  2  1
1  2                               2  1
1                                     1
```

Produced by lines 15 through 25 (left table); Produced by lines 35 thru 45 (right table)

The FOR statement at line 10 controls the number of times a complete line is printed. The loop starting at line 15 prints the first (left) table, while the loop starting at line 35 prints the second (right) table (6 5 4 3 2 1). The TAB at line 30 separates the first table from the second, and offsets each new table entry by 3 positions to the right (3*K) on each succeeding line. The PRINT at line 50 forces the beginning of each new line.

7-2-8 Do It Now

1. Write the code to reproduce the following rectangle exactly (width = 40, length = 6).

```
****************************************
*                                      *
*                                      *
*                                      *
*                                      *
****************************************
```

2. Write the code to produce the following tables:

a.
```
5
5  4
5  4  3
5  4  3  2
5  4  3  2  1
```

b.
```
            5
         4  5
      3  4  5
   2  3  4  5
1  2  3  4  5
```

3. How many times will the PRINT statement in the following codes be executed?

a.
```
FOR I = 2 TO 3
FOR J = 1 TO 4
FOR K = 0 TO 2
    PRINT K
NEXT K
NEXT J
NEXT I
```

b.
```
FOR J = 40 TO 60
FOR K = 1 TO 3
    PRINT J
NEXT K
NEXT J
```

c.
```
FOR I = 2 TO 8 STEP 2
FOR J = 1 TO 4
FOR K = 1 TO 4 STEP 2
    PRINT K
NEXT K
NEXT J
NEXT I
```

Answers

1.
```
10 FOR I = 1 TO 40
20     PRINT "*";
30 NEXT I
40 PRINT
50 FOR I = 1 TO 4
60     PRINT "*";TAB(40);"*"
70 NEXT I
80 FOR I = 1 TO 40
90     PRINT"*";
100 NEXT I
```

2. a.
```
10 FOR I = 5 TO 1 STEP -1
20 FOR J = 5 TO I STEP -1
30     PRINT J;
40 NEXT J
45 PRINT
50 NEXT I
```

b.
```
10 FOR I = 5 TO 1 STEP -1
15 PRINT TAB(3*I);
20 FOR J = I TO 5
25     PRINT J;
40 NEXT J
45 PRINT
50 NEXT I
```

3. a. 24 $(2 \times 4 \times 3)$
b. 63 (21×3)
c. 32 $(4 \times 4 \times 2)$

7-3 Programming Examples

7-3-1 An Amortization Schedule

Suppose you take out a loan of $1,000 at a yearly interest rate of 12%, and you intend to repay that loan at $200 (including the interest payment) per month until the loan is fully repaid. You would like an amortization schedule similar to this:

```
                 AMORTIZATION TABLE
      PRINCIPAL  $1,000.00    INTEREST    12.00%
                REGULAR PAYMENT   $  200.00

NO.   INTEREST    AMORTIZED     BALANCE    INTEREST TO DATE
 1     10.00        190.00       810.00         10.00
 2      8.10        191.90       618.10         18.10
 3      6.18        193.82       424.28         24.28
 4      4.24        195.76       228.52         28.52
 5      2.29        197.71        30.81         30.81
 6      0.31         30.81         0.00         31.12

LAST PAYMENT = $ 31.11713
```

Write a program to input a loan principal, an interest rate, and a monthly repayment amount to generate a similar table.

Understanding the Problem

If no interest were charged, it would take 5 months to repay a $1,000 loan at $200 per month. When interest is charged, the $200 monthly payment must take care of the repayment of the capital (paying back the 1,000 dollars) and the interest on the outstanding balance of the loan. The part of the monthly payment that goes to repay the capital is called the amortized amount. The interest amount taken from the monthly payment is the interest on the unpaid balance; this amount represents the cost of borrowing money.

In the above problem, a 12% yearly interest rate means a 1% monthly interest rate, i.e.,

the interest for month 1 is	$1,000 * 0.01	= $ 10
the payment to capital is	$200 − 10	= $190
the remaining balance is	$1,000 − 190	= $810
the interest for month 2 is	$810 * 0.01	= $ 8.10
the payment to capital is	$200 − 8.10	= $191.90
the remaining balance is	$810 − 191.90	= $618.10

This process continues until the remaining balance is less than or equal to $200 ($30.81, in this example). Since that amount will be paid at the end of the month, an interest of 1% is computed on that amount (31 cents), so the last payment is \$30.81 + .31 = \$31.12. At that point the remaining balance is set to 0. (The accumulated interest is \$31.12; if the borrower had made just one interest payment at the end of six months, the interest would have been 1000 * 6% = 60 dollars.)

Output Design

The statement of the problem dictates the output design. Because there are many columns of information in the report and because the result entries represent dollar amounts, the PRINT USING statement is used to round off all figures and to center the entries under the various column captions.

Data Dictionary

The following variables will be used in the program:

- P initially represents the loan amount; subsequently P is used to represent the various monthly balances on the loan.
- I is the interest rate. In the program, the interest rate I is first divided by 100 to express it as a percentage; then that figure is divided by 12 to obtain the monthly interest rate.
- N computes the interest on the outstanding balance.
- D accumulates the monthly interest charges.
- M is the monthly payment for the loan; it is a fixed amount except (possibly) for the last payment.
- A is the amount amortized monthly, i.e., the amount the borrower pays toward the capital every month. Note that this amount increases from month to month, since the balance and the interest payment decrease every month.
- K counts the number of payments.

Program Development

This problem requires two programming techniques:

- *Counting*: Counting the number of payments through the variable K.
- *Accumulating*: Every month the new balance is equal to the old balance minus the payment to the capital, while the payment to capital is equal to the monthly payment minus the interest on the remaining balance.

The logic of the problem can be visualized in pseudo code as follows:

```
Print headers
Input principal (old balance), interest rate, monthly payment
Set counter to compute number of payments to 0 (K)
Set accumulator to accumulate interest payments to 0 (D)
```

```
Add 1 to counter of payments <-----------------------+
Compute interest on balance (N)                      |
Add that interest N to interest accumulator          |
Compute amortized amount: monthly payment - interest |
Compute (new) balance: (old) balance - amortized amount
Print various results                                |
IF (new) balance > = 200 return to ------------------+
ELSE
          Add 1 to the counter that counts monthly payments
          Compute interest on last balance
          Set the amortized amount to the last balance figure
          Set the balance to 0
          Print the last results
END-IF
```

This process is captured in BASIC code in Figure 7-4.

Testing

Testing in this case is difficult, since the results cannot be readily verified. To see if the results seem reasonable, we could take P = \$1,000, I = 12% (1% per month), and monthly payment = \$200. Without the interest payment, the repayment schedule should take 5 months, i.e., K = 5; hence with an interest charge, we would expect K to be about 6 months. Looking at the total accumulated interest, a ballpark figure can be computed by noting that if the borrower had waited six months before paying the \$1,000 plus the interest, he/she would have had to pay \$60; hence we would expect a lesser amount if the interest is payed every month, so \$31.12 seems like a reasonable amount.

7-3-2 Do It Now

1. Run the amortization program for P = \$5,000, I = 12%, and monthly payment of \$200. In the report, skip a line when 12 payments have been made (1 year), and start the next year with month numbers 1, 2, 3, ... rather than 13, 14, 15.
2. Change the program of exercise 1 for quarterly payments, i.e., \$600 is paid every 3 months.
3. Determine how much "faster" the payment schedule would be if, at the end of each month, the borrower paid the interest for the next month in advance.

7-3-3 Charlie's Eatery

Whenever a meal is sold at Charlie's Eatery, the cost of the order and a corresponding meal code (1 = breakfast, 2 = lunch, 3 = dinner) are recorded on a terminal. At the end of the day, Charlie would like to obtain the following information: the day's total sales, the average breakfast cost, and the lowest dinner cost.

■ **Figure 7–4** An amortization schedule.

```
100 REM  AMORTIZATION PROBLEM
105 REM  DATA DICTIONARY
110 REM    P: PRINCIPAL (ALSO THE BALANCE)
115 REM    I: INTEREST RATE (12%)
120 REM    M: MONTHLY PAYMENT
125 REM    K: COUNTS THE PAYMENTS
130 REM    D: ACCUMULATES INTEREST
135 REM    A: MONTHLY AMORTIZED AMOUNT
140 REM
145 F1$ = "                          AMORTIZATION TABLE                    "
150 F2$ = "            PRINCIPAL   $#,###.##   INTEREST  ##.##%            "
155 F3$ = "                  REGULAR PAYMENT   $#,###.##                   "
160 F4$ = "NO.   INTEREST  AMORTIZED    BALANCE     INTEREST TO DATE       "
165 F5$ = " #      ###.##   #,###.##     #,###.##          ###.##          "
170 F6$ = "LAST PAYMENT = $###.##                                          "
175 REM
180 PRINT "ENTER PRINCIPAL, INTEREST RATE, MONTHLY PAYMENT"
185 INPUT P, I , M
190 PRINT F1$
195 PRINT USING F2$; P,I
200 PRINT USING F3$; M
205 PRINT
210 PRINT F4$
215 I = I/100/12         Convert interest to monthly decimal form
220 K = 0                K counts the number of payments
225 D = 0                D accumulates the monthly interest
230 K = K + 1
235 N = I * P            N computes the interest on current balance
240 D = D + N            Sum up the interests
245 A = M - N            Amortized amount = monthly payment - interest
250 P = P - A            The new balance P = old balance - amortized amount
255 PRINT USING F5$;K, N, A, P, D
260 IF P >= M THEN 230     Exit from the loop when balance < monthly payment
265 K = K + 1              Count the last payment
270 N = I * P              Compute interest on last payment
275 D = D + N              Add this last interest to accumulated interest
280 A = P                  Amortized amount equals last balance
285 P = 0                  Balance is set to 0; loan has been repaid
290 PRINT USING F5$; K, N, A, P, D
295 PRINT
300 PRINT USING F6$; A + N      add monthly interest to last balance
305 END
```

```
RUN
ENTER PRINCIPAL, INTEREST RATE, MONTHLY PAYMENT
? 1000,12,200
                      AMORTIZATION TABLE
          PRINCIPAL  $1,000.00   INTEREST  12.00%
              REGULAR PAYMENT  $  200.00

NO.   INTEREST   AMORTIZED    BALANCE    INTEREST TO DATE
 1      10.00     190.00       810.00          10.00
 2       8.10     191.90       618.10          18.10
 3       6.18     193.82       424.28          24.28
 4       4.24     195.76       228.52          28.52
 5       2.29     197.71        30.81          30.81
 6       0.31      30.81         0.00          31.12

LAST PAYMENT = $ 31.12
```

Write a program to read an input file where each record consists of a meal cost and a meal code and produce a report similar to the following:

```
COST                CODE

7.36                 1
6.78                 2
9.87                 3
4                    1
2.78                 3

TOTAL SALES = 3Ø.79
AVERAGE BREAKFAST COST = 5.68
MINIMUM DINNER COST = 2.78
```

Understanding the Problem

To compute the daily total sales, the program simply accumulates the various meal costs as they are read. To compute the average breakfast cost, the program must count the number of breakfasts and accumulate all breakfast costs. For the minimum dinner cost the user can arbitrarily set the minimum cost to an unrealistic figure, say $1000, so that when that "minimum" is compared to a first dinner cost, that dinner cost will obviously be less than $1000 and will become the new minimum.

Output Design

Note that all the input data items are listed on the output. This allows the user to verify the results easily.

Data Dictionary

The following variables are used in the program of Figure 7–5:

- S accumulates the sum of all meal costs (7.36 + 6.78 + 9.87 + 4 + 2.78).
- B accumulates all breakfast costs (7.36 + 4).
- K counts all breakfasts (2).
- M keeps track of the current minimum dinner cost. Initially it is set to 1000, which is immediately replaced by the first dinner cost.

A and C are the two variables used to read the cost and meal code from each input record.

Program Development

This program requires three techniques: (1) counting (breakfast), (2) accumulating (total sales and breakfast sales), and (3) finding a minimum value (minimum dinner cost). The entire logic of the problem is shown here in flowchart form and in Figure 7–5 in BASIC code.

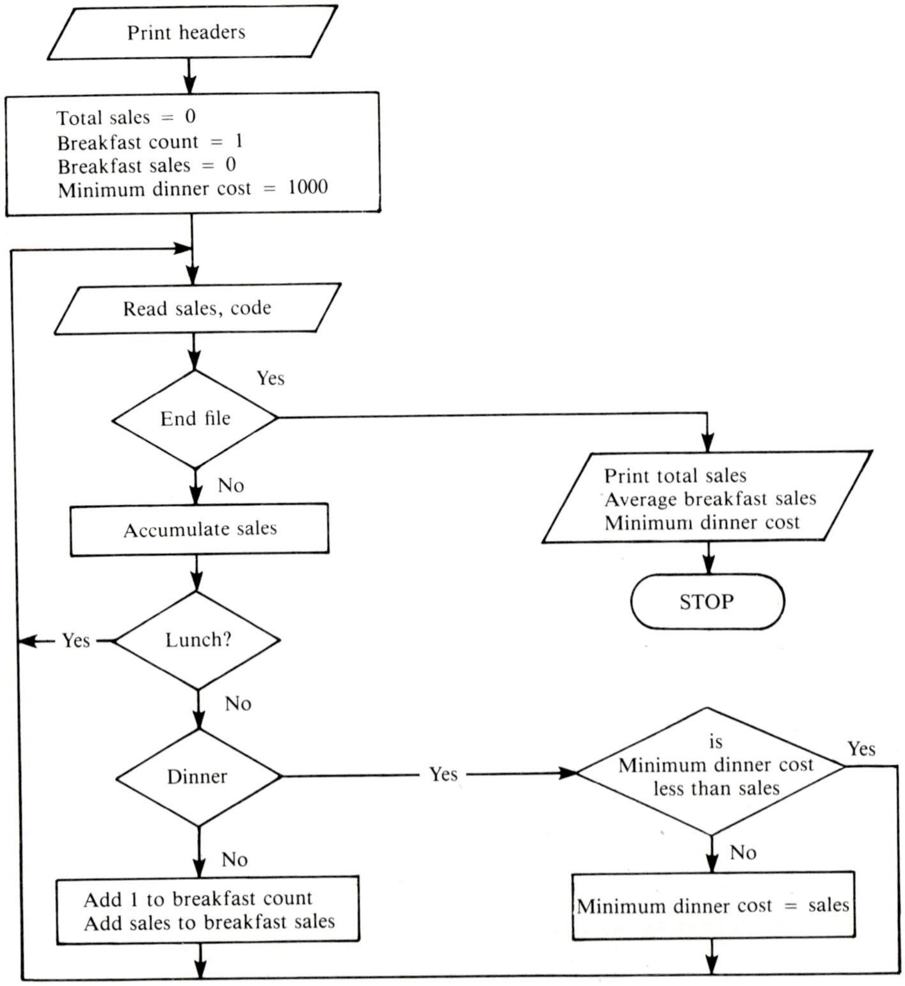

Testing

A minimum of five input records is needed: at least two dinner records (for the minimum cost), at least two breakfast records (for the breakfast average), and one lunch record.

7-3-4 Do It Now

1. What would happen to the minimum dinner cost if no dinner records were present in the input file? Change the program to respond appropriately.
2. What would happen to the program if no breakfasts were served? Change the code appropriately.
3. Rewrite the program in Figure 7–5 using the ON/GO TO statement. Also print error messages if the meal code is invalid or if any meal cost exceeds $1,000.
4. Print BREAKFAST, LUNCH, and DINNER in the report instead of codes 1, 2, and 3.

Figure 7–5 Charlie's eatery.

```
10 REM CHARLIE'S EATERY PROBLEM
12 REM
14 REM DATA DICTIONARY
16 REM        S: ACCUMULATES ALL MEAL COSTS
18 REM        B: ACCUMULATES BREAKFAST COSTS
20 REM        K: COUNTS ALL BREAKFASTS
22 REM        M: REPRESENTS MINIMUM DINNER COST
24 REM        A: VARIABLE USED TO READ MEAL COST
26 REM        C: VARIABLE USED TO READ MEAL CODE
28 REM            1=BREAKFAST 2=LUNCH 3=DINNER
30 REM
32 PRINT " COST", "CODE"
34 PRINT
36 S = 0                    }
38 B = 0                    }  Initialize counters and accumulators
40 K = 0                    }
42 M = 1000                    Set minimum to $1,000
44 READ A, C                   Read meal cost and meal code
46 IF A < 0 THEN 68            If end of file print results
48 S = S + A                   Accumulate all sales
50 PRINT A, C                  Print meal cost and meal cost
52 IF C = 2 THEN 44            Lunches don't require any action
54 IF C = 3 THEN 62            Take care of dinner at line 62
56    K = K + 1                Count breakfasts
58    B = B + A                Accumulate breakfast sales
60    GOTO 44                  Read next record
62 IF A >= M THEN 44           Don't change minimum if amount > minimum
64    M = A                    Have found a new minimum (A < M)
66    GOTO 44                  Go read the next record
68 PRINT
70 PRINT "TOTAL SALES ="; S                  }
72 PRINT "AVERAGE BREAKFAST COST ="; B/K     }  Print results
74 PRINT "MINIMUM DINNER COST ="; M          }
76 REM
78 DATA 7.36, 1   }
80 DATA 6.78, 2   }
82 DATA 9.87, 3   }  Input data file
84 DATA 4.00, 1   }
86 DATA 2.78, 3   }
88 DATA -3.0, 0   }
90 END

RUN
 COST          CODE

 7.36          1
 6.78          2
 9.87          3
 4             1
 2.78          3

TOTAL SALES = 30.79
AVERAGE BREAKFAST COST = 5.68
MINIMUM DINNER COST = 2.78
```

7-3-5 Standard Deviation

The general formula to compute the standard deviation for n grades $x_1, x_2, x_3, \ldots, x_n$ is:

$$SD = \sqrt{\frac{n(x_1^2 + x_2^2 + x_3^2 + \ldots + x_n^2) - (x_1 + x_2 + x_3 + \ldots + x_n)^2}{n(n - 1)}}$$

Write a program to input n grades and compute the average grade and the standard deviation. A negative grade indicates the end of the list of grades.

Understanding the Problem

If you are unsure about the meaning of the standard deviation, consider this illustration. The following tables show the final scores obtained in two introduction to computers classes taught by two different instructors.

Class A	*Class B*
40	90
55	20
60	80
45	10

At the end of the semester, the two instructors discuss how well their classes did that semester. Both recall that their class average was 50, whereupon both express surprise at this coincidence. Little do they realize how different their ranges of scores are. The average does not reflect this difference. In Class A, all the scores are close together, while in Class B the scores spread out considerably; yet the averages are identical. If the average does not capture the spread of the scores, what mathematical measure does? Answer: the standard deviation.

The standard deviation gives us a feel for the distribution of scores. In Class A the "distance" between the outermost scores and the average is 10, while in Class B that distance is 40 (90 – 50, or 10 – 50). In general, the standard deviation gives an indication of how much the scores deviate from the average. A small deviation implies that most of the scores are clustered, while a large deviation implies a large spread among the scores. A deviation of 0 means that all the scores are the same. If the standard deviation is 15 and the score average is 70, then this means that the great majority of scores fall in the interval 70 + 15 and 70 – 15 (between 85 and 55).

To understand the mechanics involved, let's compute the standard deviation for Class A, where x_1, x_2, x_3 and x_4 are 40, 55, 60, and 45, and $n = 4$.

Sum of the squares of each score ↑ (points to $4(40^2 + 55^2 + 60^2 + 45^2)$)

Sum of the scores times itself ↑ (points to $(40 + 55 + 60 + 45)^2$)

$$\text{Standard Deviation} = \sqrt{\frac{4(40^2 + 55^2 + 60^2 + 45^2) - (40 + 55 + 60 + 45)^2}{4(3)}} = 9.13$$

Note that the numerator is simply n (sum of all scores^2) – (sum of scores)^2

Understanding the Problem

Altogether, seven lines are to be printed, with each line consisting of three items: the day number, the sales amount, and a set of asterisks equal to the sales amount. If the amount of sales is three, then three asterisks need to be printed. If no sales occur that day, then no asterisks should be printed. In general, if S is the amount of sales read, then S asterisks are to be printed. Two loops will be required: an outer loop to read each day's sales, and an inner loop to print one asterisk at a time until the number of asterisks equals the sales amount for that day.

Output Design

This is described in the statement of the problem.

Data Dictionary

The following variables will be used:

- D Index of the external loop, which counts the days from 1 to 7.
- S The sales amount, which is used as the terminal value of the inner loop to control the number of asterisks printed.

Program Development

Two loops are needed: one outer loop to control the number of days, and an inner loop to print the appropriate number of asterisks. The logic of the problem, as well as the BASIC code, is illustrated in Figure 7–7. Note the comma at line 50, which forces the asterisks to be printed on the same line as the day number and the sales amount; the semicolon in line 60 keeps the printer on the same line. Note also that if S is 0, the inner loop is bypassed (lines 60 and 65); this may not be true for nonstandard BASICs. Finally, note the importance of the PRINT statement at line 70, which ends the line on which the asterisks were printed. The logic of the program is shown in Figure 7–7.

Testing

The user should obviously test 7 sales entries, one of which should be 0. These entries should all be less than the number of printable printer/screen columns.

7-3-7 Do It Now

Write a program to draw a bar graph to represent average daily temperatures for a week; the readings vary from −10 to +10 degrees. Given, for example −3, 2, 6, 8, −2, −5, 1, the output should be similar to

```
TEMPERATURE                  |
                             |
     -3                   ***|
      2                      |**
      6                      |******
      8                      |********
     -2                    **|
     -5                 *****|
      1                      |*
```

■ **Figure 7–7** A bar graph.

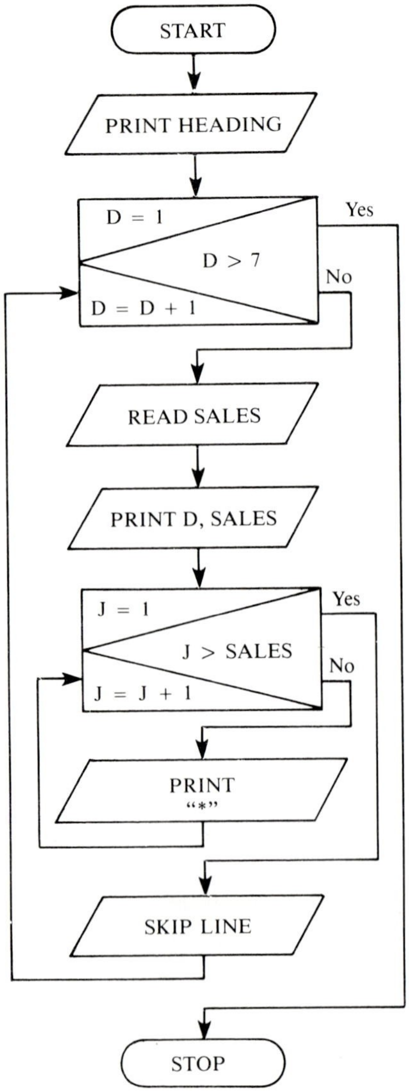


```
10 REM BAR GRAPH PROBLEM
15 REM DATA DICTIONARY
20 REM      S: AMOUNT OF SALES
25 REM      D: DAY NUMBER 1...7
30 PRINT" DAY", "SALES"
35 PRINT
40 FOR D = 1 TO 7
45     READ S                    Read the sales.
50     PRINT D; S,
55     FOR J = 1 TO S            Print the asterisks.
60         PRINT "*";
65     NEXT J
70     PRINT                     Skip to next line.
75 NEXT D
80 DATA 5,11,14,0,2,25,11
85 END
```

```
RUN
 DAY            SALES

 1  5           *****
 2  11          ***********
 3  14          **************
 4  0
 5  2           **
 6  25          *************************
 7  11          ***********
```

7-3-8 An Approximation to the Sine Function

The general formula to compute an approximation for the sine of x, where x is any angle measured in radians, is:

$$\sin x = \frac{x^1}{1!} - \frac{x^3}{3!} + \frac{x^5}{5!} - \dots - \frac{x^{11}}{11!} + \dots$$

Write a program to read a value for x to compute and print the sine of x using the first six terms of the formula. Recall that 5! (read as 5 factorial) is equal to 1*2*3*4*5.

Understanding the Problem

The reader may recall that the sine of 90° ($\pi/2$) is 1, or that the sine of 30° ($\pi/6$) is 1/2, while the sine of 0 is 0. The above formula can be used to compute an approximation of the sine of an angle. This approximation becomes more accurate as more terms of the formula are computed. Let us, for example, compute the sine of $\pi/2$ (which is exactly equal to 1) using the first 3 terms of the formula. Note that $\pi/2 \simeq$ 1.57080.

$$\text{sine}\,(1.57080) = 1.57080 - \frac{(1.57080)^3}{3!} + \frac{(1.57080)^5}{5!}$$

$$= 1.57080 - 0.64597 + 0.07969 = 1.00452$$

This result is fairly accurate, since the real answer is supposed to be 1.

Program Development

Computing the sine of x requires the following steps:

1. Read x
2. Keep accumulating a product of integers (PRODUCT) in such a way that PRODUCT is first 1
   then 1*2*3
   then 1*2*3*4*5
   and so forth
   PRODUCT serves as the denominator in the terms of the formula.
3. Accumulate the terms
   $\frac{x}{\text{PRODUCT}}, \frac{x^3}{\text{PRODUCT}}, \frac{x^5}{\text{PRODUCT}}, \ldots$ as each new PRODUCT is computed.
4. Capture x^1, x^3, x^5, ... through the use of x^i where i is initially set to 1 and incremented by 2's to obtain odd powers of x.
5. Generate the oscillating sequence of terms: $x, -x^3, x^5, -x^7, \ldots$
   To do that, we note that $(x)^1, (-x)^3, (x)^5, (-x)^7$ gives rise to x, $-x^3$, x^5, and $-x^7$. Hence we replace x by $-x$ to generate successive terms of the sequence.

The entire logic of the program is displayed in semi-BASIC code as follows:

`READ X`	
`PRODUCT = 1`	Used to compute 1, then 1*2*3, then 1*2*3*4*5, etc.
`SUM = Ø`	Used to accumulate X, $\frac{-X^3}{3!}, \frac{X^5}{5!}$
`FOR I = 1 TO 11 STEP 2`	I is used for the exponent and the PRODUCT.
`SUM = SUM + X^I/PRODUCT`	$\frac{X^1}{1}, X^1 - \frac{X^3}{1\cdot2\cdot3}, X^1 - \frac{X^3}{1\cdot2\cdot3} + \frac{X^5}{1\cdot2\cdot3\cdot4\cdot5}$
`PRODUCT = PRODUCT*(I+1)*(I+2)`	Generates 1*2*3, then 1*2*3*4*5,
`X = -X`	Generates the oscillating sequence −, +, −, +,...
`NEXT I`	

The complete BASIC program is shown in Figure 7–8.

Figure 7–8 A sine approximation.

```
10 REM COMPUTATION OF SINE(X)
15 REM DATA DICTIONARY
20 REM     X: VALUE IN RADIANS
25 REM     P: COMPUTES THE VARIOUS PRODUCTS
30 REM     S: ACCUMULATES TERMS OF FORMULA
35 REM     I: EXPONENT OF X; USED IN PRODUCTS
40 READ X
45 P = 1
50 S = 0
55 FOR I = 1 TO 11 STEP 2              I is the exponent for X
60      S = S + (X^I)/P                Accumulate all terms
65      P = P * (I + 1) * (I + 2)      Compute the products 1*2, 1*2*3,...
70      X = -X                         Switch from - to +
75 NEXT I
80 PRINT "ANGLE =; X, "SINE ="; S
82 DATA 1.57                           :1.57 is π/2: hence sine (1.57) should be
85 END                                 close to 1

RUN
ANGLE = 1.57  SINE = .9999996
```

7-3-9 Do It Now

How many terms of the approximation formula would you need to accumulate to compute sine of 1.57 before the difference between any two successive approximations was less than 0.0001 in absolute value? Would computing the sine of 3.14 require as many terms to get the same difference between two approximations (.0001)?

Answer

Six approximations for 1.57 and 8 for 3.14.

7-4 Reports and Control Breaks

The observation that computer-produced reports should be easy to read, easy to understand, and attractively designed appears so evident that one might feel this subject warrants no further comment. Yet the physical appearance of a report is of dramatic importance. Decisions are made daily by people of all walks of life based on computer-produced reports—detailed reports, summarized reports, and so forth.

A good report is self-explanatory (and accurate, obviously), self-contained, and organized in a way that allows the reader to capture the essence of the report as well as the detail. These characteristics should be reflected in a design that is neat, clear, and pleasant to the eye. It is impossible to list all the ingredients that comprise an ideal report; a partial list, however, follows:

1. Major or documentary headings: identification of the purpose of the report, date of the report or transaction and identification of the company, agency, or other producer or subject of the report.
2. Subheadings: titles or labels should be provided for each column of information listed (in some cases underlining might improve the appearance of the report).
3. Summary or intermediate results should be printed whenever necessary to provide subtotals for groups of entries that are similar in nature, for example, sales subtotals for a given salesperson in a sales report, or item subtotals in an inventory.
4. Overall or grand totals reflecting sums of subtotals. An accompanying descriptive explanation should precede numerical results.

7-4-1 A Control Break Example

Let us look at a file in which each record contains a salesperson number, and an amount of sales, where all records for a given salesperson occur in a group. Note that in the sample file shown below, the number of records for a given sales person is variable; for example, salesperson 400 has made two sales, while salesperson 200 has made one sale. Let us write a program to produce a report that will summarize the sales for each salesperson and also show the total for all the salespeople.The input and output would look like:

Input File

```
10 DATA 100,50
15 DATA 100,60
20 DATA 300,34
25 DATA 200,40
30 DATA 400,80
35 DATA 400,15
40 DATA -8,0
```

```
    NUMBER      SALES     SUBTOTALS

    100         50
    100         60
                          110
    300         34
                          34
    200         40
                          40
    400         80
    400         15
                          95

  TOTAL SALES             279
```

For this type of report, the program keeps accumulating a salesperson's total sales (minor total) until a change occurs in the salesperson number. When the record pertains to the same salesperson as the preceding record, the sales amount is added to the current minor total. If the record read is for a new salesperson, a *control break* has been found. At this point the minor total for the previous salesperson is printed and the accumulator for the new minor total is set to 0 (see Figure 7-9). When the salesperson number read belongs to a new salesperson, we store that number in OLD; then when we read the NEW salesperson number, we compare NEW with OLD. If we fail to change OLD, we would always be comparing NEW with the very first salesperson number. To start the comparison between OLD and NEW, we read the first record with a separate READ statement.

Figure 7–9 shows the flowchart for this problem, while Figure 7–10 illustrates the BASIC code.

■ **Figure 7–9** A control break problem.

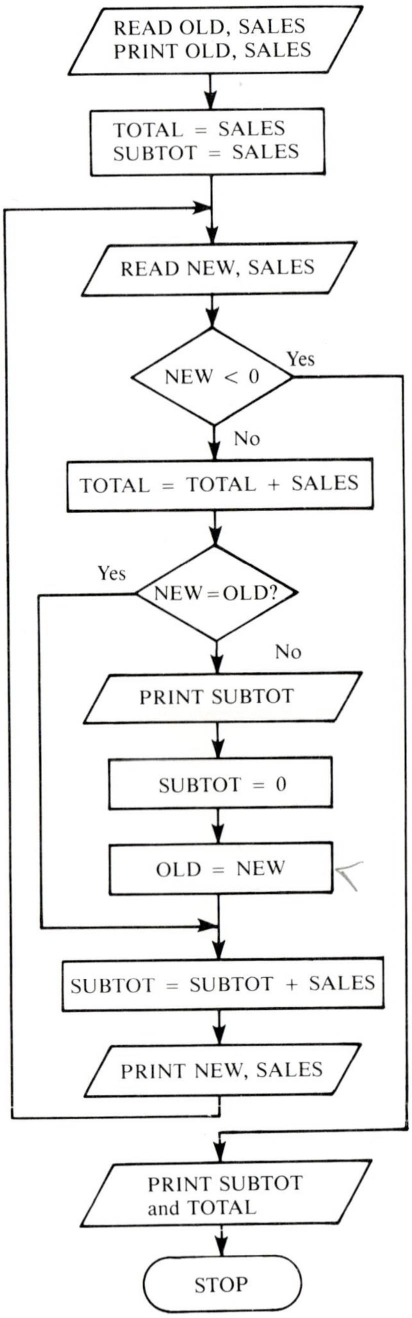

Read a salesperson number and call it OLD. Print the first number and the first sales.

TOTAL accumulates the sum of all sales. SUBTOT accumulates the totals for each salesperson.

Read the next salesperson number and sales.

Have we reached the end of the file?

Accumulate the sales just read into TOTAL.

Is it the same salesperson?

If it is not the same number, then we have encountered a new salesperson and we must print the previous salesperson's subtotal.

We also need to reset SUBTOT to 0 to start accumulating new subtotals for the new salesperson.

We also reset OLD to NEW, since we need to compare it with the next salesperson number to be read.

Add sales just read to the current subtotal.

Print salesperson number and sales.

When the end-of-file is reached, print the last salesperson's subtotals. Then print the total sales.

■ **Figure 7–10** A control break problem.

```
10 REM CONTROL BREAK PROBLEM
12 REM DATA DICTIONARY
14 REM       N1: OLD SALESPERSON NUMBER
16 REM       N2: NEW SALESPERSON NUMBER
18 REM       T1: TOTAL SALES
20 REM       T2: SUBTOTAL SALES
22 REM       S:  SALES AMOUNT READ
24 PRINT "NUMBER", "SALES","SUBTOTALS"
25 PRINT
26 READ  N1, S                Read first record.
28 PRINT N1, S
30 T1 = S                     Set total sales to sales just read.
32 T2 = S                     Set subtotal to sales just read.
34 READ N2, S
36 IF N2 < 0 THEN 54
38    T1 = T1 + S             Accumulate all sales.
40    IF N1 = N2 THEN 48      Check for identical salesperson.
42       PRINT ,, T2          If different, print subtotal of previous salesperson.  }
44       T2 = 0               Reset subtotal to 0.                                   } control break
46       N1 = N2              Set old salesperson number to salesperson number       }
48       T2 = T2 + S          just read. Accumulate subtotal.
50       PRINT N2, S
52       GOTO 34
54    PRINT,,T2               At end-of-file, print last subtotal.
55    PRINT
56    PRINT "TOTAL SALES",, T1
58 DATA 100, 50   }
60 DATA 100, 60   }
62 DATA 200, 34   }
64 DATA 300, 40   }  Input data file
66 DATA 400, 80   }
67 DATA 400, 15   }
68 DATA -5,  00   }
70 END

RUN
NUMBER              SALES             SUBTOTALS

 100                 50
 100                 60
                                       110
 200                 34
                                       34
 300                 40
                                       40
 400                 80
 400                 15
                                       95

TOTAL SALES                            279
```

7-4-2 Do It Now

Study flowcharts 1 and 2 carefully and determine whether the logic illustrated will create the salesperson report discussed in section 7–4 and displayed in Figure 7–10.

1.

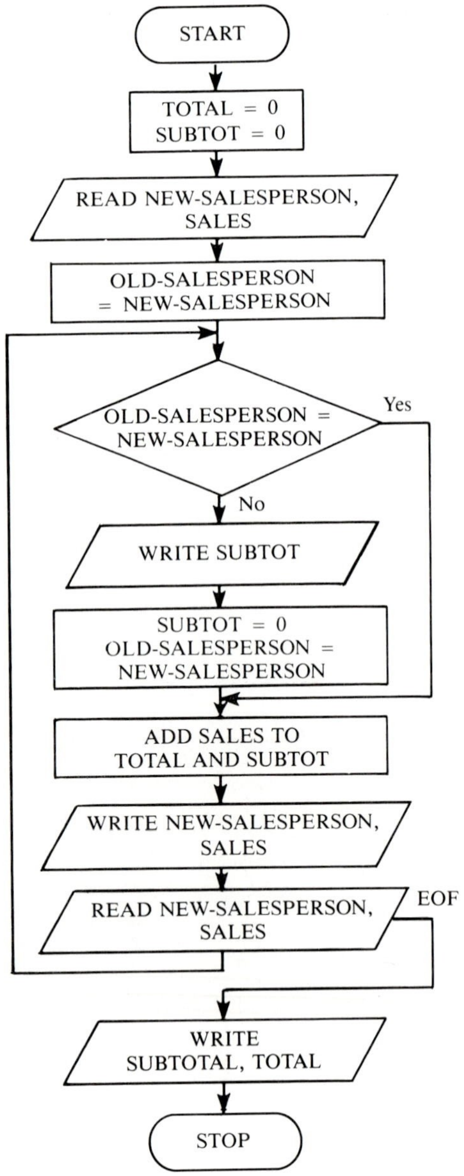

2.

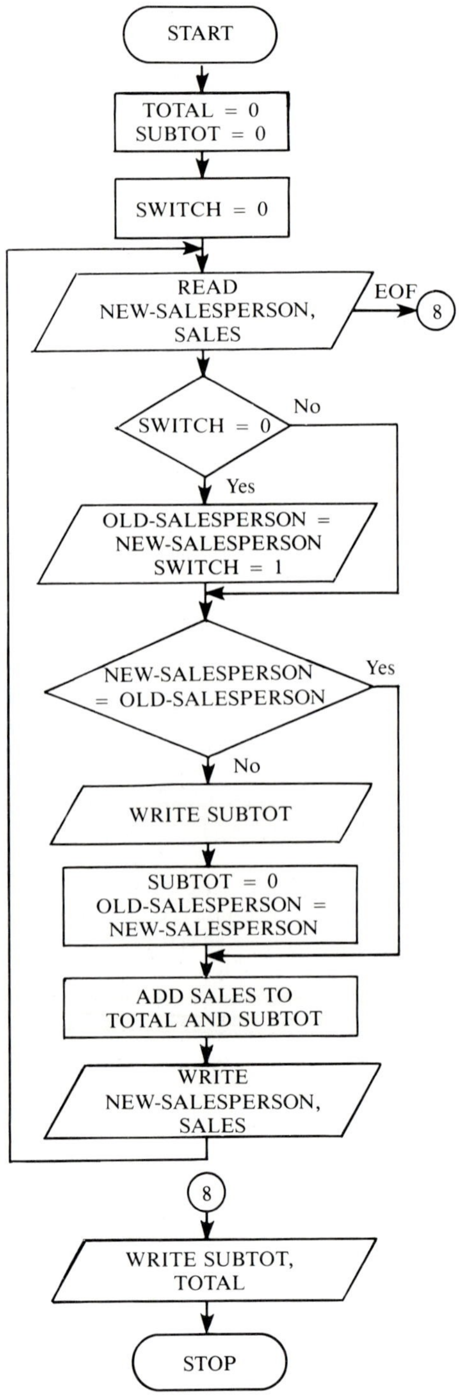

Answers

1. yes
2. yes

7-5 You Might Want to Know

1. To what depth or level can loops be nested?

   Answer: It depends on the manufacturer's BASIC. It is safe to assume that all BASIC systems will allow a depth of three nested loops. (Check with your BASIC technical reference manual.)

2. What happens to the FOR/NEXT loop in the following cases?
   a. FOR I = 5 TO 5
   b. FOR J = 100 TO 1
   c. FOR K = 2 TO 10 STEP − 1

   In most systems the following actions will be taken:

   Case a: The loop is executed only once.

   Case b: The loop is not executed and control is passed to the statement following the NEXT statement. In nonstandard BASICs the loop is executed once.

   Case c: Same as case *b* since the value of K is less than the test value and the increment is negative.

3. Can the programmer count on the value of the index to be the same as the terminal value specified in the FOR/NEXT statement when exiting out of the loop through the NEXT statement?

   Answer: No. If that value is desired, use another variable in the loop to keep track of it. However, the value of the index is preserved if transfer out of the loop is made before the loop has run its full cycle.

4. Is there a formula that can tell me how many times a FOR/NEXT loop will be executed depending on the value of the parameters?

   Answer: Given positive *integer values* for the initial value (I), step value (S), and terminal value (T) of the FOR/NEXT statement, the formula to compute the number of times (NT) the loop will be executed is given by

   $NT = \frac{T - I}{S} + 1$ Here, only the integer result of the division is kept.

   Example:

```
                 I    T      S
                 ↓    ↓      ↓
        FOR K =  3 TO 10 STEP 2
```

   The number of times the body of the loop is executed is given by

$$NT = \frac{10 - 3}{2} + 1 = \frac{7}{2} + 1 = 3 + 1 = 4.$$

7-6 Know Your System Better: Intrigue and Fun

As in similar previous sections, some of the following features may not be available on your system. Section 7–6–5 is left open for variations of your system's features.

7-6-1 Debugging Feature TRON and TROFF

The TRON (TRace ON) and the TROFF (TRace OFF) feature can be a very powerful and useful tool during program debugging. TRON forces the computer to list all line numbers corresponding to the instructions carried out by the computer during run time. In this way the user can follow the footsteps of a program and play detective: which sets of instructions did the computer repeat? how many times? what transfers were made as a result of IF or GOTO statements? and so forth. The line numbers produced by TRON are listed horizontally with brackets. Other results from the program's PRINT statements are also displayed.

TRON and TROFF can be used in system command mode as well as in BASIC mode, as shown in the following two examples.

System Command

```
TRON
1Ø DATA 2Ø,3Ø,4Ø,63,78.5
15 S=Ø
2Ø FOR I = 1 TO 4
25     READ G
3Ø     S = S + G
32     PRINT I
35 NEXT I
4Ø IF S > 15Ø THEN 55
45     PRINT "FAIL"
5Ø     GOTO 6Ø
55   PRINT "PASS"
6Ø END
RUN
[1Ø][15][2Ø][25][3Ø][32] 1
[35][25][3Ø][32] 2
[35][25][3Ø][32] 3
[35][25][3Ø][32] 4
[35][4Ø][55]PASS
[6Ø]
TROFF
```

produced by line 55 (PASS); produced by line 32 (1, 2, 3, 4)

BASIC Mode

```
1Ø DATA 2Ø,3Ø,5Ø,63,78.4
15 S= Ø
2Ø FOR I = 1 TO 4
22     TRON            Set the automatic trace on.
25     READ G
3Ø     S = S + G
32     PRINT I
33     TROFF           Turn off the trace.
35 NEXT I
4Ø IF S > 15Ø THEN 52
45     PRINT "FAIL"
5Ø     GOTO 6Ø
52     TRON            Turn the trace back on.
55     PRINT "PASS"
56     TROFF           Turn it off.
6Ø END

RUN
[25][3Ø][32] 1
[33][25][3Ø][32] 2  }
[33][25][3Ø][32] 3  }  Trace produced by computer
[33][25][3Ø][32] 4  }
[33][55]PASS
[56]
```

Note that in the BASIC mode example, TRON and TROFF can be placed at preselected positions in the program. This is very convenient when TRON generates large volumes of line numbers that are not particularly useful to the programmer.

7-6-2 The CHR$ Function (for screen and printer users)

Generally speaking, you can display all keyboard characters (graphic symbols) on the screen or on the printer simply by depressing the corresponding keyboard key. These characters are common to the screen and printer and include the letters of the alphabet, the digits 0 through 9, and the special characters such as the comma, the period, and so forth. There are, however, many other graphic symbols (fancy characters) that can be displayed on the screen and on the printer but are not shown on the keyboard. These unusual symbols can be displayed by means of the CHR$ function, if one knows the internal codes for these graphic symbols. The internal code (ASCII character codes) for these symbols are shown in the appendix of the user's video monitor and printer technical reference manuals. Unfortunately, these codes will not only vary from one printer model to another and from one video monitor to the next, but also from one manufacturer to the next! Consider the following examples:

	ASCII Character Code	*Graphic Symbol*
IBM MONOCHROME VIDEO	CHR$(1)	☺
	CHR$(14)	♫
	CHR$(172)	¼
	CHR$(219)	■
	CHR$(251)	√
	CHR$(7)	Video beep 1/4 second
TRS-80 MODEL II VIDEO	CHR$(25)	Sets black on white screen instead of white on black
	CHR$(31)	Sets 40 character mode i.e., all characters are twice as large
	CHR$(158)	■
	CHR$(160)	ƀ
	CHR$(127)	±
TRS-80 DMP 400 PRINTER	CHR$(161)	á
	CHR$(173)	¾
	CHR$(191)	ƒ
	CHR$(237)	▙
EPSON MX GRAFTRAX PRINTER	CHR$(7)	Beep sound on printer
	CHR$(129)	£
	CHR$(253)	}
	CHR$(254)	~

You can determine the set of graphic symbols available on your video screen by typing the following code:

```
10 FOR I = 0 TO 255
15    PRINT CHR$(I)
20 NEXT I
```

The codes for the printer graphic symbols will be different than the codes for the video graphic symbols (except for the digits, special characters, and letters of the alphabet). You can determine what your printer graphics symbols look like by running the same program with LPRINT replacing PRINT. The output produced by a DMP 400 printer was:

```
!"#$%&'()*+,-./Ø123456789:;<=>?@ABCDEFGHIJKLMNOPQRSTUVWXYZ[/]^_'abcdefghijk
lmnopqrstuvwxyz{:}~XXXXXXXXXX
XXXXXXXXXXXXXXXXXX àç£µ°'†ss
   XXXXXXXXXXXXXXXXXXXXXXXXXXXXXXXX
```

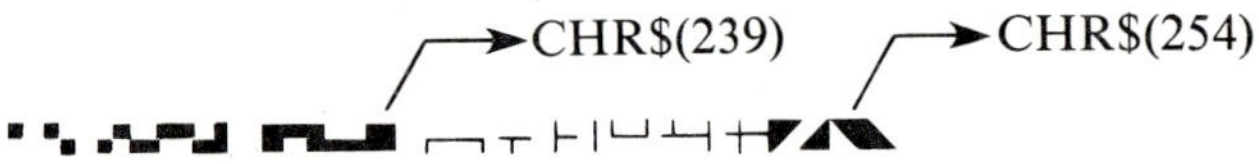

Once again, the reader should understand that many video graphic symbols may not exist on the printer and vice versa. Furthermore, graphic symbols common to both the screen and printer will generally not have the same code, i.e. the dotted square ■ for the IBM video screen is CHR$(219), while the same graphic symbol on the DMP 400 printer is CHR$(239)! This means that an attractive graphics design drawn on the screen cannot be copied onto the printer as such. To draw graphic symbols on the printer, the user must find out what the printer's graphic symbol codes are, then use those numeric codes with the LPRINT instruction and the CHR$ function to produce black-on-white graphic symbols.

7-6-3 Do It Now

1. What output will be produced by the following on an IBM Monochrome Video?

```
10 FOR I = 1 TO 40
15    PRINT CHR$(219);
20 NEXT I
25 PRINT CHR$(219),TAB(40);CHR$(219)
30 GO TO 10
```

2. What output will be produced by the Mx Graftrax Printer?

```
10 PRINT "DO YOU HEAR THE BIRD?"
15 FOR I = 1 TO 10
20    LPRINT CHR$(7);          Note the LPRINT instruction to the printer
25 NEXT I
```

3. What output will be produced on your screen and/or printer as a result of

```
1 FOR I = Ø TO 255
4    PRINT CHR$(I) (or LPRINT)
8 NEXT I
```

Answers

1.

2. DO YOU HEAR THE BIRD?
The printer will then beep for 3 or 4 seconds.

7-6-4 Error Trapping: Automatic End-of-File

When the computer encounters any type of errors during execution of a program, the system generally prints an error message and then stops. Typical errors are: running out of data, syntax errors,division by 0, not turning on the printer, and so forth. Most systems allow you to use the ON ERROR GO TO statement to specify what action is to be taken if any such errors occur.

For example, if you run out of data, you can tell the program to resume execution at a particular instruction (then the end-of-file techniques discussed in Chapter 4 are no longer needed—no more trip records). Or, if the printer is off, you can print a message TURN ON PRINTER and continue execution of the program.

If you expect more than one type of error, you can ask the system what type of error occurred (through the ERR statement) and, as a result, take appropriate action.

The following examples illustrate the use of the ON ERROR GO TO and the ERR statement:

Example 1. Automatic End-of-File Technique: A Grade Average Computation

```
10 DATA 20,30,40,50,60
15 ON ERROR GO TO 50         When an out-of-data condition occurs,
                             transfer to line 50.
20 S = 0                     Initialize counter and accumulator.
25 C = 0
30 READ G                    Read a grade. If no more grades, go to 50.
35 S = S + G                 Accumulate grades.
40 C = C + 1                 Count grades,
45 GO TO 30                  and keep reading grades.
50 PRINT "AVE=";S/C          When no more grades, print the average.
```

The only problem with this code is that if any other type of error occurs, control will automatically be passed to line 50, i.e., if a syntax error occurs, then line 50 will be executed! To differentiate among various types of errors, you can ask the system what type of error was committed! The ERR instruction is used for this purpose, as follows:

```
IF ERR = 4 RESUME 86      Error code 4 means out of data—resume control at line
                          86
IF ERR = 11 RESUME 46     Error code 11 means divide by 0—resume at line 46
```

The list of error codes is standard among different machines (for standard errors!). The appendix of your system reference manual will identify these various codes.

As an example, consider the program shown on the next page, which is supposed to compute an average of scores even though it runs out of data and even though the printer is off initially! Note the message printed by the computer at line 70 because of a division by 0.

Program	Explanation
`1Ø DATA 1Ø,2Ø,3Ø,4Ø,5Ø`	
`15 ON ERROR GOTO 8Ø`	Transfer to line 80 if any errors occur during execution of program.
`2Ø S=Ø`	
`25 C=Ø`	
`3Ø READ G`	When out of data, transfer to 50.
`35 S = S + G`	Accumulate all scores.
`4Ø C=C+1`	Count all scores.
`45 GOTO 3Ø`	
`5Ø LPRINT "AVE =";S/K`	K should be C; division by 0 occurs.
`55 STOP`	
`6Ø PRINT "TURN ON PRINTER"`	Print message if printer is off, and try to print again.
`65 GOTO 5Ø`	
`7Ø PRINT "DIVISION BY Ø AT LINE 5Ø"`	Print message if division by 0.
`75 STOP`	Line 80 is executed as result of line 15.
`8Ø IF ERR = 4  THEN RESUME 5Ø`	If out of data continue at 50.
`85 IF ERR = 11 THEN RESUME 7Ø`	If division by 0, go to 70.
`9Ø IF ERR = 24 THEN RESUME 6Ø`	If printer is off, alert user at 60.
`95 ON ERROR GOTO Ø`	If it is neither a 4, 11, or 24 error type, system takes care of error message and terminates.
`.`	
`.`	

```
RUN
TURN ON PRINTER
DIVISION BY Ø AT LINE 5Ø
```

7-6-5 MY SYSTEM IS DIFFERENT

This section is left blank for you to write any different system commands that your system uses. You may also want to list the various steps that are required to start a session with your system.

MY SYSTEM IS DIFFERENT

7-7 Assignments

7-7-1 Test Yourself

1. Using FOR/NEXT loops, write the codes to print the values corresponding to the following sequence of numbers:
   a. 1,3,5,9, ...,99
   b. − 1, 1, − 1, 1, ... (25 terms)
   c. 1/2/3/4/ ... /N where N is an INPUT value
   d. N, N − 2, N − 4, ... 0 where N is an even positive number
   e. 1/9, 1/99, 1/999, ..., 1/9999999

2. Trace through the following flowchart and record all values taken on by the variables K, A, and B in the table below. The first few values are already recorded in the table. The values to be read are recorded on the DATA statements.

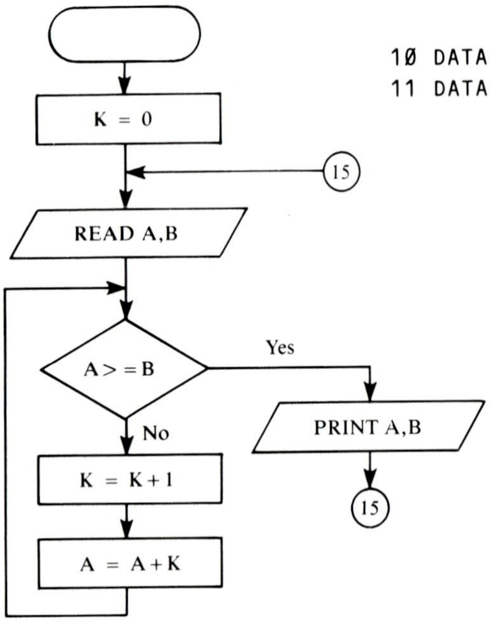


```
1Ø DATA 3,9
11 DATA Ø,1Ø
```

K	A	B
Ø	3	9

Display values for A & B

3. Write the code to accumulate and print the following:
   a. $1^2 + 2^2 + 3^2 + \ldots + 10^2$
   b. $2 + 4 + 8 + 16 + \ldots + 1024$
   c. $1 - 2 + 3 - 4 + \ldots - 1000$
   d. $1 + (1*2) + (1*2*3) + (1*2*3*4) + \ldots + (1*2*3 \ldots * 100)$
   e. $1 + 1/3 + 1/5 + \ldots + 1/77$

4. State whether the following are valid or invalid FOR/NEXT loops; if invalid, explain why. (Assume there are line numbers for each statement.)

a.
```
FOR K = K TO 5.6
.
.
NEXT K
```

b.
```
FOR I+1 = 1 TO -9 STEP -1
.
.
NEXT I+1
```

c.
```
FOR J = 1 TO 10 STEP -1
X = X*I+1
NEXT I
```

d.
```
FOR K = 1 TO 6
READ K1,K
S = S + K1
NEXT K
```

e.
```
FOR J = 1 TO 3
PRINT
FOR I = 1 TO 2
J = I^2+1
NEXT I
PRINT
NEXT J
```

f.
```
FOR K2 = -3 TO 2
FOR K = 2 TO 15
PRINT K^2
PRINT K + K2
NEXT K2
PRINT
NEXT K
```

g.
```
FOR I = 1 TO 4
PRINT I+1
NEXT I
I = 4
FOR I = 2 TO 10
PRINT I-2
NEXT I
```

h.
```
10 FOR I = 1 TO L
.
.
45 IF Q = 6 GO TO 51
.
.
51 FOR K = 1 TO 10
.
.
60 NEXT K
65 L = L-1
70 NEXT I
```

5. How many times will the statement LET X = 1 be processed?

a.
```
FOR I = 1 TO 3
FOR J = 1 TO 4
FOR K = 1 TO 10
LET X = 1
NEXT K
NEXT J
NEXT I
```

b.
```
FOR I = 10 TO 20
FOR J = 3 TO 17 STEP 5
LET X = 1
NEXT J
NEXT I
```

c.
```
FOR I = 1 TO 8 STEP 2
FOR J = I TO 10
LET X = 1
NEXT J
NEXT I
```

d.
```
FOR K = 1 TO 6 STEP 2
FOR I = 1 TO K
S = S + I
NEXT I
NEXT K
```

6. Will the following code segments compute the average (A) of 10 grades?

a.
```
LET S = 0
FOR I = 1 TO 10
READ G
LET S = S + G
NEXT I
LET A = S/I
PRINT A
```

b.
```
LET S = 0
FOR I = 1 TO 10
READ G
LET S = S + G
LET A = S/I
NEXT I
PRINT A
```

7. To determine how "good" your random number generator, write a program to generate 1000 random numbers between 1 and 4 and count their occurrence. Use the FOR/NEXT.

8. Write a BASIC program to read ten values and determine if the values are in ascending sequence (each value greater than or equal to its predecessor).

9. Does the following flowchart solve the control break problem of Figure 7–9 section 7–4.

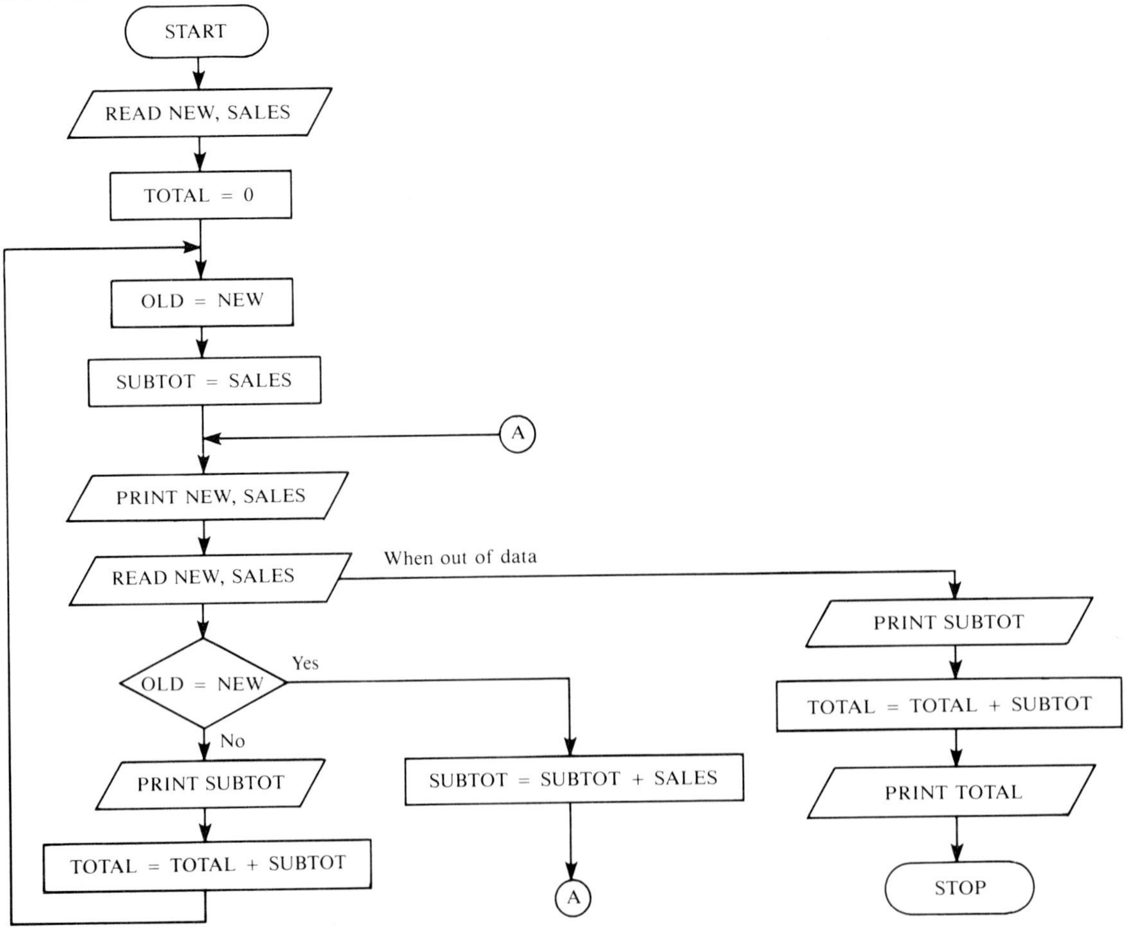

10. Using no more than 5 asterisks per PRINT statement and only one such PRINT statement, write the code to produce.

```
*****     *****     *****     *****     *****
*****     *****     *****     *****     *****
*****     *****     *****     *****     *****
*****     *****     *****     *****     *****
*****     *****     *****     *****     *****
     *****     *****     *****     *****     *****
     *****     *****     *****     *****     *****
     *****     *****     *****     *****     *****
     *****     *****     *****     *****     *****
     *****     *****     *****     *****     *****
*****     *****     *****     *****     *****
*****     *****     *****     *****     *****
*****     *****     *****     *****     *****
*****     *****     *****     *****     *****
*****     *****     *****     *****     *****
     *****     *****     *****     *****     *****
     *****     *****     *****     *****     *****
     *****     *****     *****     *****     *****
     *****     *****     *****     *****     *****
     *****     *****     *****     *****     *****
*****     *****     *****     *****     *****
*****     *****     *****     *****     *****
*****     *****     *****     *****     *****
*****     *****     *****     *****     *****
*****     *****     *****     *****     *****
```

11. Write a program without using the INT function to input a value in cents less than or equal to a dollar and express it in the least number of quarters, dimes, nickels and pennies. For example, 93 cents = 3Q + 1D + 1N + 3P.

(*Hint*: Subtract 50, then 25, then 10, etc.)

7-7-2 Exercises

1. Write the code to print the following sequence of numbers and stop when the corresponding sum exceeds 1000.

$$1, 1, 2, 3, 5, 8, 13, \ldots$$

(*Hint*: Each term is equal to the sum of the two preceding terms.)

2. A data statement contains a list of positive and negative numbers varying from −100 to +100. The last item on the list is a special code 999. Write a program to compute the sum of the positive values and the sum of the negative values (exclusive of the special code). Print both sums.

3. Grades are recorded on a DATA statement. A special code of 999 terminates the list. Write a program using FOR/NEXT to determine the largest and smallest grade. Print both these grades and an appropriate message if the highest score was obtained by more than one student.

4. Mr. SLY convinced his employees to work for them for 30 days as follows: The first day Mr. SLY get paid 1 cent, the second day 2 cents, the third day 4 cents, the fourth day 8 cents, and so forth (each day's pay is twice the previous day's pay). Print a table showing Mr. SLY's earnings during the last 10 days. (Make sure these earnings are displayed in dollar figures.)

5. For a first class letter, the Post Office charges 20 cents for the first ounce or part thereof and 17 cents for each additional ounce or part thereof. Write a program to accept letter weights in ounces and print the required postage.

6. The *mode* of a set of scores is the score that occurs most frequently. For example, in the set

   13,13,15,20,20,31,31,46,46,46,50

   the mode is 46. Write a program to read a set of scores already arranged in numerical ascending order and print the scores and the mode.

7. Mrs. Spander is spending her money faster than she earns it. She has now decided to keep track of all her expenses. For every purchase or expense, she enters on her home computer the expense description, the amount, and an expense category code (1 = household, 2 = medical, 3 = recreation, 4 = utilities). Then every Sunday night she runs her budget program to obtain the following analysis:

BUDGET ANALYSIS

	HOUSEHOLD EXPENSES	MEDICAL EXPENSES	RECREATION EXPENSES	UTILITY BILLS
PLANTS	12.33			
MOVIES			6.50	
MORTGAGE	389.75			
DENTIST		154.25		
GAS				99.66
VACATION			1156.56	
SUBTOTALS	402.08	154.25	1163.06	99.66

TOTAL EXPENSES $1819.05

Write a program to oblige Mrs. Spander.

8. You are the owner of a bookstore that sells both paperback and hardback books. For every book you sell, you have a record with two numbers: the amount the book cost and either a 0 or a 1 (0 if the book is a paperback, 1 if the book is hardback). Write a program to obtain the following information.
   a. Total amount taken in
   b. Total number of books sold
   c. Average price per book
   d. Minimum price of a hardback book
   e. Average price of a paperback book

9. A data file consists of records, each containing the following information about items produced at the XYZ manufacturing plant: a department number, an item number, a quantity, and a cost per item. Assume the file has been sorted into order by ascending department number. Write a program to produce a summary report as follows:

DEPARTMENT	ITEM	QUANTITY	COST/ITEM	VALUE	TOTALS
15	1389	4	3.2Ø	12.8Ø	
15	3821	2	7.ØØ	14.ØØ	
					26.8Ø
16	Ø122	8	2.5Ø	2Ø.ØØ	
					2Ø.ØØ
19	1244	1ØØ	.Ø3	3.ØØ	
19	1245	2Ø	4.ØØ	8Ø.ØØ	
19	2469	4	16.ØØ	64.ØØ	
					147.ØØ
				GRAND TOTAL	193.8Ø

Could you alter the program to write each subtotal on the same line as the last transaction line of each department? Make up your own data file.

10. A large clothing store keeps track of its inventory by department (1 = men's wear, 2 = ladies' wear, 3 = girls' wear, and 4 = boys' wear). The store's inventory file consists of four packets of data, each packet representing a particular department. A typical input file is shown below, where each record consists of a department number, an item of clothing, an item quantity, a cost figure, and a market figure (cost to the customer).
    a. Write a program to process the input file to compute the store's inventory at lower cost (the lesser of cost or market value for each whole department).

    The output should be similar to the one on the following page.

Dept. no. | Quantity | Cost to Store | Cost to Customer

```
1,SUITS,     3ØØ,1ØØ, 92
1,COATS,     2ØØ, 6Ø, 65
1,SHIRTS,   1ØØØ, 12, 13
2,DRESSES,   4ØØ, 6Ø, 65
2,COATS,     185,184,2ØØ
2,SHOES,     6ØØ, 4Ø, 3Ø
3,JEANS,     2ØØ, 4Ø, 35
3,SHOES,     2ØØ, 3Ø, 34
4,JEANS,     3ØØ, 42, 43
```

```
                      PAN AMERICAN APPAREL COMPANY
                         INVENTORY EVALUATION
                               Ø5/Ø6/84

                               UNIT COST                  EXTENDED
                 QUANTITY    COST    MARKET        COST               MARKET     LOWER COST
MENS DEPT

 SUITS             3ØØ        1ØØ      92         3Ø,ØØØ             27,6ØØ
 COATS             2ØØ         6Ø      65         12,ØØØ             13,ØØØ
 SHIRTS           1ØØØ         12      13         12,ØØØ             13,ØØØ
  TOTAL                                         $ 54,ØØØ           $ 53,6ØØ     $ 53,6ØØ
LADIES DEPT

 DRESSES           4ØØ         6Ø      65         24,ØØØ             26,ØØØ
 COATS             185        184     2ØØ         34,Ø4Ø             37,ØØØ
 SHOES             6ØØ         4Ø      3Ø         24,ØØØ             18,ØØØ
  TOTAL                                         $ 82,Ø4Ø           $ 81,ØØØ     $ 81,ØØØ
GIRLS DEPT

 JEANS             2ØØ         4Ø      35          8,ØØØ              7,ØØØ
 SHOES             2ØØ         3Ø      34          6,ØØØ              6,8ØØ
  TOTAL                                         $ 14,ØØØ           $ 13,8ØØ     $ 13,8ØØ
BOYS DEPT

 JEANS             3ØØ         42      43         12,6ØØ             12,9ØØ
  TOTAL                                         $ 12,6ØØ           $ 12,9ØØ     $ 12,6ØØ

           INVENTORY AT LOWER COST                                              $161,ØØØ
```

Note the various subtotals for each of the four departments, as well as the grand total.

b. Compute the lower cost inventory line by line instead of for the whole department. For example, for the men's department the cost inventory is: 27,600 + 12,000 + 12,000 = 51,600

11. Write a program to accept an input value for N and draw the following axis graduated in units of 5:

```
If N = 31        ----5----0----5----0----5----0-
If N =  7        ----5--
If N =  3        ---
```

Apply the above to the bar graph problem of section 7-3-6. The last graduation symbol should reflect the maximum sales for the week, as shown in the following example:

```
DAY  SALES

1     15      ***************
2     19      *******************
3     23      **********************[*]
4     16      ****************          |
5     21      *********************     |
6     12      ************              |
7     15      ***************           |
              ----5----Ø----5----Ø--V
```

graduated axis

12. *Straight line fitting*: Imagine that you are running an experiment for a physics or a biology project, and you obtain six points with coordinates x and y that you graph carefully as shown. The points seem to fit a straight line, and you would like to find the equation of the line that best fits these points. The equation could then be used to find corresponding y values for points on the x-axis—these points could be between x_1 and x_6 or they could be outside the experimental range.

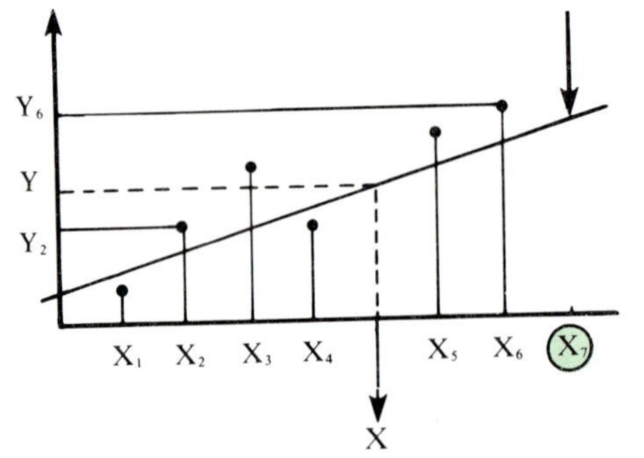

The least squares method can be used to find the equation of the straight line that best fits the experimental points. In this example, we will fit six experimental points $(x_1,y_1), (x_2,y_2),\ldots,(x_6, y_6)$ to the straight line:

$$y = m * x + b$$

where m (the slope) and b (the y intersect) are given by the following formulas:

$$m = \frac{N * SUM_{xy} - SUM_x * SUM_y}{N * SUM_{x2} - (SUM_x)^2}$$

$$b = \frac{SUM_{x2} * SUM_y - SUM_x * SUM_{xy}}{N * SUM_{x2} - (SUM_x)^2}$$

Notice that the two denominators are the same. The meanings associated with the above variables are

N	is the total number of points, six in this case.
SUM_{xy}	is the sum of the $x*y$ product for each point: $x_1*y_1 + x_2*y_2 + \ldots + x_6*y_6$
SUM_y	is the sum of the y's, i.e., $y_1 + y_2 + \ldots + y_6$
SUM_x	is the sum of the x's, i.e., $x_1 + x_2 + \ldots + x_6$
SUM_{x2}	is the sum of all the x's squared, i.e., $x_1^2 + x_2^2 + \ldots + x_6^2$

Write a program to compute m and b for the following two sets of experimental data:.

Experiment 1	x	5	29.7	48.4	73	98	8.2
6 points	y	6.883	−51.13	−94.02	−150	−208.6	0.03

Experiment 2	x	0.43	0.28	0.39	0.62	0.36	0.7	0.67	0.62	0.23	0.59
10 points	y	0.0047	0.0027	0.0036	0.0065	0.0035	0.007	0.0064	0.0056	0.0021	0.0064

Then, using the RESTORE statement, compute the difference between each experimental y value and the corresponding y value obtained from the least squares straight line.
Identify the experimental point that seems to be the least accurate in terms of its relationship with the least squares straight line and the other experimental points.

13. Write a program to convert binary numbers to decimal. One method that can be used is applied to 1011_2 in the following example:

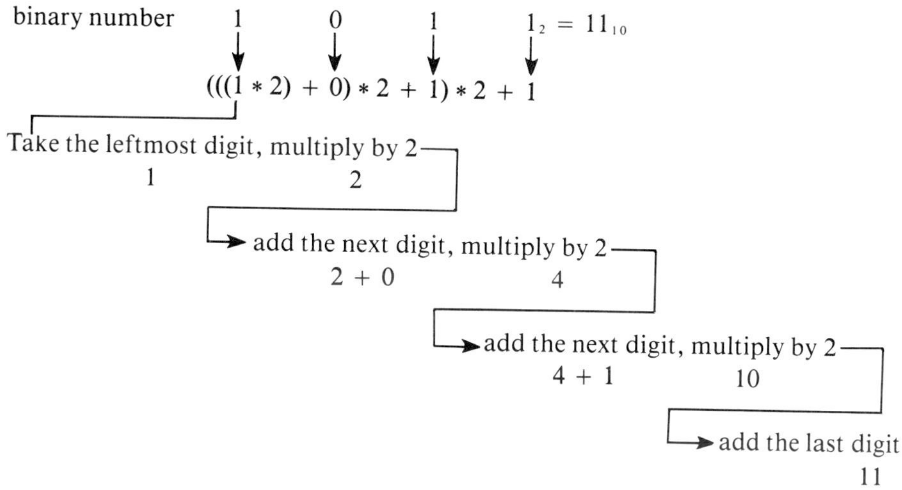

This method requires us to decompose a binary number into separate digits. Let's look at a method of decomposition for decimal numbers. To decompose a number into distinct digits, e.g., 143 into 3 digits (1, 4, 3), consider the following:

```
FIRST  =   INT(143/100)          =  (1)
RMDER  =   143 - 100 * FIRST     =  43      143
SECOND =   INT(RMDER/10)         =  (4)
THIRD  =   RMDER - SECOND * 10   =  (3)
```

A similar technique can be used to decompose 1011_2 into successive digits.

14. Assume each of four variables (I, J, K, and L) contains a digit. Write the code to fuse these 4 digits into the variable X, i.e., if I = 2, J = 8, K = 3, and L = 6, then X = IJKL = 2836, a numeric variable equal to 2836!

(*Hint*: See the first part of problem 13, but in the conversion process multiply by 10 instead of by 2.)

15. Given a 6-digit number such as X = 134578, decompose X into 6 variables in such a way that I = 1, J = 3, K = 4, L = 5, M = 7, N = 8.

(*Hint*: See the second part of problem 13.)

16. The greatest common factor (gcf) for two integers is the largest interger that will divide both numbers evenly. For example, the greatest common factor of 9 and 12 is 3, since 3 is the largest number that divides evenly into 9 and 12. The gcf of 8 and 9 is 1; the gcf of 27 and 18 is 9. An interesting algorithm (attributed to the mathematician Euclid) for computing the greatest common factor is shown in flowchart form below.

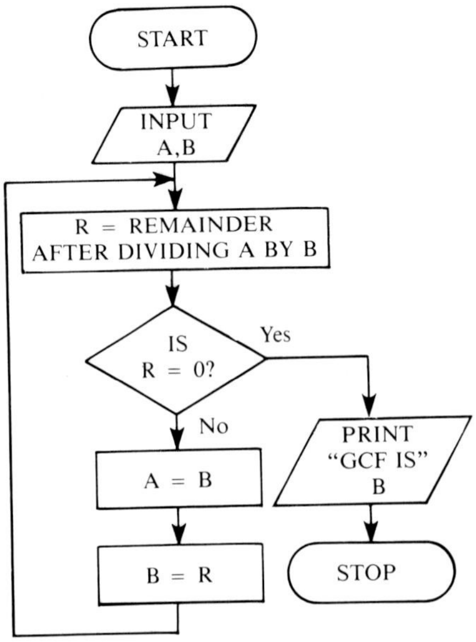

Write a program to find greatest common factors using the Euclidian algorithm. Can you explain why it works?

17. Write a program to compute the following sequences of sums:

$S_1 = 1$

$S_2 = 1 + 1/2$

$S_3 = 1 + 1/2 + 1/3$

$S_4 = 1 + 1/2 + 1/3 + 1/4$

How many different sums would you have to compute before the sum exceeds 3.9?

18. The number e can be approximated by the formula

$$e_4 = 1 + \frac{1}{1}\left(1 + \frac{1}{2}\left(1 + \frac{1}{3}\left(1 + \frac{1}{4}\right)\right)\right)$$

however, a better approximation would be

$$e_{100} = 1 + \frac{1}{1}\left(1 + \frac{1}{2}\left(1 + \frac{1}{3}\left(1 + \frac{1}{4}\left(1 + \frac{1}{5}\left(1 + \frac{1}{6}\left(\ldots + \frac{1}{99}\left(1 + \frac{1}{100}\right)\right)\ldots\right)\right)\right)\right)\right)$$

Write a program to compute e_{100}.

19. It can be shown that the irrational number $e = 2.71828\ldots$ can be approximated by taking as many terms as desired in the relation

$$e = 1 + 1/1! + 1/2! + 1/3! + 1/4! + \ldots$$

Draw a flowchart for a program to approximate the value of e using this method. Stop when successive approximations differ by less than 0.001.

For example: 1st approximation is 1
2nd approximation is $1 + 1/1! = 2$
3rd approximation is $1 + 1/1! + 1/2! = 2.5$
4th approximation is $1 + 1/1! + 1/2! + 1/3! = 2.666$

20. Write a program to compute the value of $\pi/4$ using the following formula:

$$\frac{\pi}{4} = 1 - \frac{1}{3} + \frac{1}{5} - \frac{1}{7} + \frac{1}{9} - \ldots$$

1st approximation is $\pi/4 = 1$;
2nd approximation is $\pi/4 = 1 - 1/3$;
3rd approximation is $\pi/4 = 1 - 1/3 + 1/5$

Stop when the difference between two successive approximations is less than 0.01.

21. Write a program to convert decimal numbers to binary. A method that can be used is to divide the number by 2 keeping track of the integer quotient and the remainder. The first remainder is the 1's digit of the binary numeral. The remainder obtained by dividing the quotient by 2 is the 2's digit; the process is repeated until the quotient is zero.

Example: Convert 28 to binary

28	2		
14	0	$28 \div 2 = 14$	remainder 0
7	0	$14 \div 2 = 7$	remainder 0
3	1	$7 \div 2 = 3$	remainder 1
1	1	$3 \div 2 = 1$	remainder 1
0	1	$1 \div 2 = 0$	remainder 1

The result is read from the bottom up: $28_{10} = 11100_2$

Thus $28_{10} = 1\,1\,1\,0\,0_2$. This is verified by multiplying each binary digit by its place value:

$$1 \times 16 + 1 \times 8 + 1 \times 4 + 0 \times 2 + 0 \times 1 =$$

$$16 + 8 + 4 + 0 + 0 = 28$$

Make sure that your output lists the binary digits in proper sequence from left to right—from most significant digit to least significant digit.

22. A prime number is any number which can be divided only by itself and 1. Write a program to input a number $N \leq 5000$ and determine whether N is prime.

7-7-3 Exercises Requiring Use of Random Numbers

1. Write a program to determine the least number of random numbers between 1 and 100 that must be generated so that the average of these numbers lies in the interval 47 to 53.

2. John Jones has $200,000 to invest in speculative gold stock. The gold mines are of such a nature that they either go broke, leaving stock worthless, or strike gold and make the stockowners wealthy. Mr. Jones's goal is to retire with $2,000,000. He plans to invest $100,000 at a time. He estimates that the probability of losing each $100,000 investment is 75% while the probability of making $1,000,000 from the same investment is 25%. In either case, he will sell the stock and make further $100,000 investments of the same nature

a. What is the probability of Mr. Jones's retiring with $2,000,000? [Hint: Simulate the 75%/25% lose/win probability by generating integer random numbers in the range 1 to 4. Arbitrarily choose one number to represent a loss. The probability of getting any value in this range is 1/4 = 25%.] Simulate 100 such investment sequences and count the wins (makes $2,000,000) and losses (goes broke); from these figures, determine the probability for a successful retirement.

b. Determine whether, in the course of the 100 investment trials, Mr. Jones ever won $1,000,000 only to lose it, i.e., did it ever happen that after winning $1,000,000, he failed to retire with $2,000,000?

c. Instead of a return of $1,000,000 for a $100,000 investment, suppose that the return was only $500,000. How would this change Mr. Jones's chances of success? Experiment with returns varying from $300,000 to $3,000,000 in steps of $100,000, and see how the odds for successful retirement change.

3. You are now at the famous Monte Carlo casino and you have $1,000 to burn. You are not a sophisticated roulette player, so you decide to place bets on the even or odd. The roulette ball lands on any of 37 numbers (0–36). The number 30 is the house's lucky number, and the croupier rakes in everything on the board (i.e., you lose your bet). Correct bets on even or odd squares double your input bet. A correct bet on any of the numbers 1 through 36 gives you 20 times the original amount you bet. Write a program to continuously accept bets, and print your remaining balance. The game should go on till you have either run out of cash or doubled your initial investment. Play 10 such games and keep track of how many you win and how many you lose. What are your chances of doubling your initial investment?

4. A submarine has been trapped into an enemy bay with only one escape channel leading out of the bay. The bay is surrounded by mines as shown below. All navigating equipment is malfunctioning, and the blind submarine is now moving randomly in any of the four cardinal directions one square at a time. If the sub hits any of the mines, it is instantly destroyed. The sub escapes when it reaches row 2 column 5.

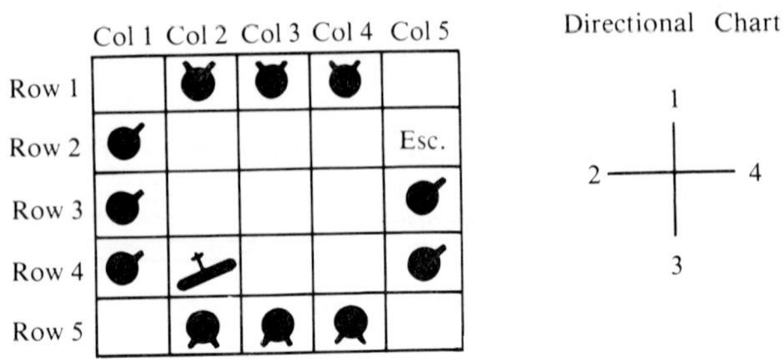

a. Write a program to determine the sub's escape chances from its present position of row 4 and column 2.

b. Compute the submarine's chances of escape for each of the squares in the above grid.

c. Allow the submarine to restart at row 4, column 2, 10,000 times. In those 10,000 attempts, determine the least number of steps the submarine took to escape. Do you think the answer will be 5?

d. Assume there is another moving blind submarine in row 3, column 4. What are the chances of the submarines' colliding with each other? Take into account the fact that both submarines can escape!

e. Change the program to allow the submarine to travel in any diagonal direction. Do you expect the sub's chances of escape are improved with the sub's increased versatility?

5. Refer to the mole problem of chapter 6, section 6–4 for this problem:

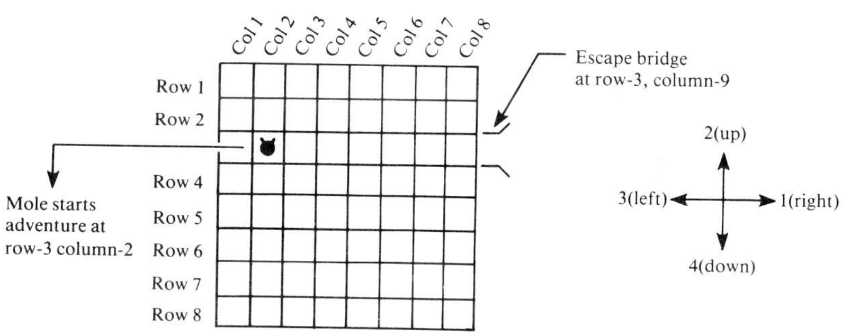

a. Compute the average number of moves the mole takes before it either drowns or escapes.
b. In the course of its 1000 adventures, record the maximum number of steps taken by the mole before it escapes.
c. The above island (maze) has now been transformed into a closed arena from which no mole can escape. One mole is placed in row 1, column 1 and another mole in row 6, column 6. Moles move about the arena as described in part a above. Upon hitting a wall, a mole bounces back to the position it occupied prior to hitting the wall. Both moles move at the same time. Write a computer program to determine, on the average, how many mole moves are made before a mole collision occurs. (*Hint:* After any collision, restart the moles back in R = 1, C = 1 and R = 6, C = 6 one thousand times.)

6. Write a program to compute the area under a curve $y = f(x)$:

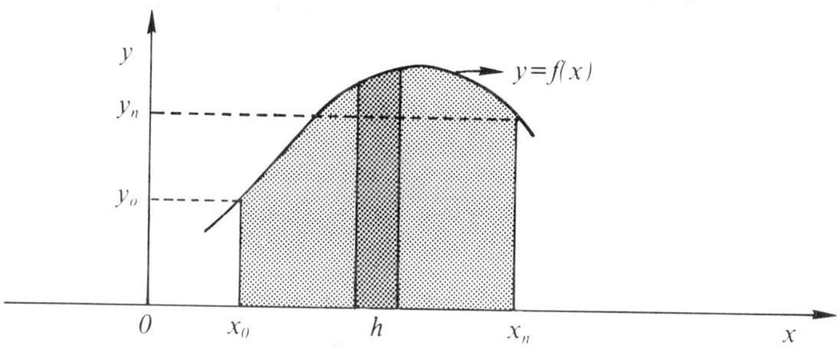

The darkened area under a curve $y = f(x)$ can be approximated by breaking the interval (x_o, x_n) into n equals interval of size

$$h = \frac{x_n - x_o}{n}$$

and computing the sum of the n areas of the trapezoids with base h. The smaller the interval h, the closer the approximation is to the exact area. The formula to compute the sum of the areas of the n trapezoids is

$$A = \frac{h}{2}\left(y_0 + 2y_1 + 2y_2 + \dots + 2y_{n-1} + y_n\right)$$

where $y_0, y_1, y_2, \dots y_n$ are the values of the function at the points $x_0, x_1, x_2, \dots, x_n$. Your program should approximate the area under the curve $y = e^{-x^2/2}$ for x between 1 and 2 for three different values of h: 0.1, 0.01, 0.001. (This is equivalent to obtaining an approximation for $\int_1^2 e^{-x^2/2}$.)

7. A study was conducted to determine whether different computer communication modes could affect a student's attitude toward programming. In a computer-related course, thirteen students used the batch processing mode to solve problems on the computer while twelve other students used the conversational mode to solve the same problems. The following entries reflect the average score obtained by each student across all the twenty questions of the Attitude Test Toward Programming (ATTP) given at the end of the semester:

Mode of Communication	
Batch Processing	*Conversational*
2.75	4.15
2.95	3.70
3.00	3.55
3.10	4.45
4.50	4.20
4.75	3.95
2.50	3.80
3.35	4.00
4.00	3.00
3.05	3.65
2.00	4.00
3.35	4.35
4.10	

Students using the conversational approach had a higher average score than students using the batch processing approach. Write a program to determine if this difference is significant. The difference is significant if $t > 2.069$, where t is given by the following formula:

$$t = \frac{X_c - X_b}{\dfrac{(N_c - 1)\,S_c^2 + (N_b - 1)S_b^2}{(N_c + N_b - 2)} \cdot \dfrac{N_c + N_b}{N_c \cdot N_b}}$$

where: X_c and X_b are the averages of the conversational and batch scores respectively

S_c and S_b are the standard deviations for conversational and batch modes respectively (See Section 5–3–2 for the programming example of a standard deviation)

N_c and N_b are the number of scores for conversational and batch processing respectively

7-7-4 Answers to Test Yourself

1. a.
```
FOR I = 1 TO 99 STEP 2
    PRINT I
NEXT I
```

b.
```
FOR I = 1 TO 25
        PRINT (-1)^I
NEXT I
```

c.
```
INPUT N
R = 1
FOR I = 1 TO N
    R = R/I
NEXT I
PRINT R
```

d.
```
FOR I = N TO 0 STEP -2
    PRINT I
NEXT I
```

e.
```
FOR I = 1 TO 7
    PRINT 1/(10^I - 1)
NEXT I
```

2.

K	A	B
0	3	9
1	4	
2	6	
3	9	
4	0	10
5	4	
6	9	
	15	

```
 9    9
15   10
```

3. a.
```
S = 0
FOR I = 1 TO 10
    S = S + I * I
NEXT I
PRINT S
```

b.
```
10 S = 0
20 I = 2
30 S = S + I
40 I = I * 2
50 IF I <= 1024 THEN 30
60 PRINT S
```

c.
```
S = 0
FOR I = 1 TO 1000
S = S - (-1)^I * I
NEXT I
PRINT S
```

d.
```
P = 1
S = 0
FOR I = 1 to 100
P = P * I
S = S + P
NEXT I
PRINT S
```

e.
```
S = 0
FOR I = 1 TO 77 STEP 2
S = S + 1/I
NEXT I
PRINT S
```

4. a. Invalid: index K is used as starting value.
b. Invalid index I + 1.
c. Invalid NEXT statement: should be NEXT J.
d. May cause problem: index K is redefined in the loop by the READ statement.
e. Invalid: index J is redefined in the loop.
f. Invalid indexes in NEXT statement; index mismatch.
g. Valid.
h. May cause problem: test value L is redefined at line 65.

5. a. 120 times
b. 33 times
c. 28 times
d. 9 times

6. a. Not necessarily; it depends on the last value of the index I.
b. Yes.

7.
```
K1 = 0
K2 = 0
K3 = 0
K4 = 0
FOR I = 1 TO 1000
    L = RND(4)
    IF L = 1 THEN K1 = K1 + 1
    IF L = 2 THEN K2 = K2 + 1
    IF L = 3 THEN K3 = K3 + 1
    IF L = 4 THEN K4 = K4 + 1
NEXT I
PRINT K1,K2,K3,K4
```

8.
```
 10 DATA ...
 20 READ X
 30 FOR I = 1 TO 9
 40   READ Y
 50   IF X >= Y THEN 100
 60   LET X = Y
 70 NEXT I
 80 PRINT "VALUES ARE IN SEQUENCE"
 90 STOP
100 PRINT "VALUES ARE OUT OF SEQUENCE"
110 END
```

9. Yes

10.
```
10 A$ = "*****"
15 B$ = "     "
20 FOR L = 1 TO 5
25    FOR J = 1 TO 5
30       FOR I = 1 TO 5
35         PRINT A$;B$;
40       NEXT I
45       PRINT
50    NEXT J
55    T$=A$
60    A$ = B$
65    B$=T$
70 NEXT L
```

11.

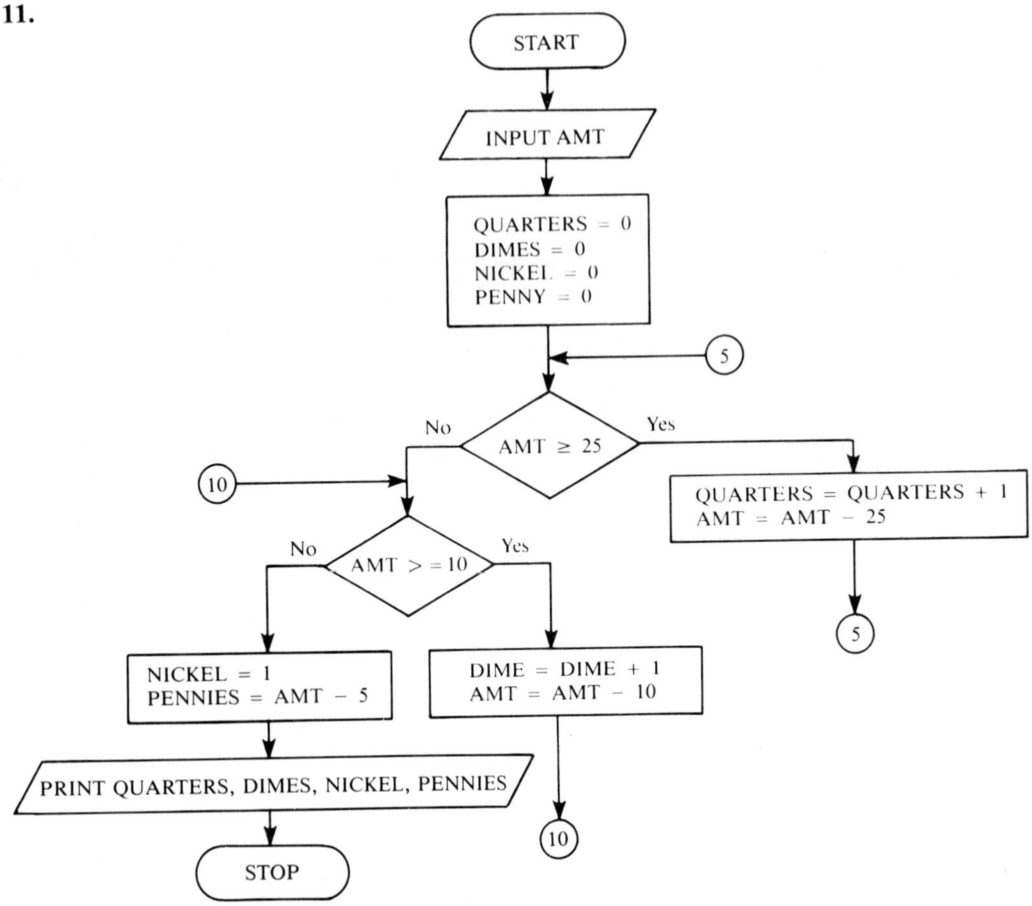

8 ONE-DIMENSIONAL ARRAYS AND THE DIM STATEMENT

8-1 Arrays

8-1-1 Why Do We Need Arrays?

Is life possible without arrays? Consider the following two examples:

Example 1

Suppose an input file consists of five records, where each record contains a grade. We want to print the difference between each grade and the average. Computing the average of grades poses no problem: Each time a grade G is read, it can be accumulated into a variable S through the statement S = S + G. But a problem arises once the average has been computed and it is time to determine the difference between each grade and the average. By this time all the grades read are no longer in memory, since only one variable G was used to successively store all the grades read. Determining the difference between each grade and the average requires the computer to remember (store) the grades as they are read, so that after the average is computed, the computer can remember (retrieve) each grade one at a time and compute the difference between it and the average. The only way the computer can remember these grades is to store them in different memory locations, i.e., provide each grade with a separate name, as shown in Figure 8–1. The code in Figure 8–1 is laborious and impractical because each grade is individually processed; what would happen if the input file consisted of 100 grades or, even worse, an unknown number of grades?

A more convenient approach would be to design a system or a notation that could create a table of five scores, store the table in the memory of the computer, and then be able to refer to any grade in the table by its position in the table (i.e., the first one, the second one, and so forth). For example, we could designate G(3) to mean the third grade in the table G, or G(I) to be the 4th grade if I were set to 4. With this capability, we could then index the table, allowing us to access successive entries to the table simply by manipulating the index I (adding 1 to I, for example, to "get to" the next table element). With such an indexing mechanism, a word problem such as "Giv-

Figure 8–1 Average and deviation without arrays.

```
10 REM DEVIATION OF FIVE GRADES WITHOUT AN ARRAY
15 READ G1, G2, G3, G4, G5
20 LET A = (G1+G2+G3+G4+G5)/5
25 PRINT G1, G1 - A
30 PRINT G2, G2 - A
35 PRINT G3, G3 - A
40 PRINT G4, G4 - A
50 PRINT G5, G5 - A
60 DATA 56,78,89,45,80
99 END
```

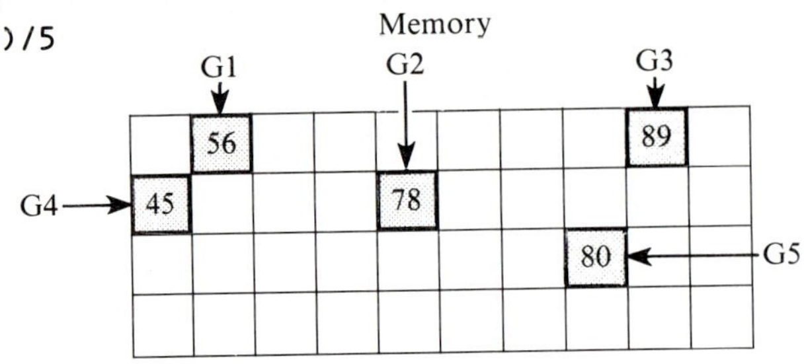

en a table of 100 grades, determine the number of grades in that table that exceed 90" could be restated as "Determine the number of times G(I)>90 as I varies from 1 to 100"; this statement is very close to the actual BASIC statement.

Example 2

Another problem that is difficult to solve without tables is this: Given the tax table shown in Figure 8–2, write a program to compute the amount of tax owed on an adjusted gross income read from an input record.

The problem is, how can the computer compute the tax if it doesn't have the tax tables in its memory? This type of problem obviously requires a data structure different from any we have encountered so far. One approach would be to create and use an amount table (*A*), a tax table (*T*), and an adjust table (*V*), as shown in Figure 8–3. For example, if these three tables were stored in memory, we could compute the tax on an adjusted income of $9,800 by successively comparing $9,800 with the 1st, 2nd, 3rd, ... entry of Table A until an entry is found that is larger than 9800—in this case, the 6th entry of table amount or A(6). The tax due on $9,800 would then be:

Due = $1,380 + 22% over $8,000

Due = 5th entry of Tax + 5th entry of Percent Over * (9800 − 5th entry of amount)

D = T(5) + V(5) * (9800 − A(5))

The last statement is actually the correct BASIC expression to compute the tax due.

Figure 8–2 A tax table.

Adjusted Income	*But Not Over—*	*Tax*	*Of the Amount Over—*
$1,000	$2,000	$140 + 15%	$1,000
$2,000	$3,000	$290 + 16%	$2,000
$3,000	$4,000	$450 + 17%	$3,000
$4,000	$8,000	$620 + 19%	$4,000
$8,000	$12,000	$1,380 + 22%	$8,000
$12,000	$16,000	$2,260 + 25%	$12,000
$16,000	$20,000	$3,260 + 28%	$16,000
$20,000	$24,000	$4,380 + 32%	$20,000
$24,000	$28,000	$5,660 + 36%	$24,000
$28,000	$32,000	$7,100 + 39%	$28,000
$32,000	$36,000	$8,660 + 42%	$32,000
$36,000	$40,000	$10,340 + 45%	$36,000
$40,000	$44,000	$12,140 + 48%	$40,000
$44,000	$52,000	$14,060 + 50%	$44,000
$52,000	$64,000	$18,060 + 53%	$52,000
$64,000	$76,000	$24,420 + 55%	$64,000
$76,000	$88,000	$31,020 + 58%	$76,000
$88,000	$100,000	$37,980 + 60%	$88,000
$100,000	$120,000	$45,180 + 62%	$100,000
$120,000	$140,000	$57,580 + 64%	$120,000
$140,000	$160,000	$70,380 + 66%	$140,000
$160,000	$180,000	$83,580 + 68%	$160,000
$180,000	$200,000	$97,180 + 69%	$180,000
$200,000	.....	$110,980 + 70%	$200,000

■ **Figure 8–3** Tables A, T and V.

Adjusted Income	*But Not Over—*	*Tax*	*Of the Amount Over—*
$1,000	$2,000	$140 + 15%	$1,000
$2,000	$3,000	$290 + 16%	$2,000
$3,000	$4,000	$450 + 17%	$3,000
$4,000	$8,000	$620 + 19%	$4,000
$8,000	$12,000	$1,380 + 22%	$8,000
$12,000	$16,000	$2,260 + 25%	$12,000
$16,000	$20,000	$3,260 + 28%	$16,000
$20,000	$24,000	$4,380 + 32%	$20,000
$24,000	$28,000	$5,660 + 36%	$24,000
$28,000	$32,000	$7,100 + 39%	$28,000
$32,000	$36,000	$8,660 + 42%	$32,000
⋮	⋮		

	Amount (A)	*Tax (T)*	*Over (V)*	
A(5)	$1,000	$140	.15	
	$2,000	$290	.16	
	$3,000	$450	.17	
	$4,000	$620	.19	
$9,800	$8,000	**$1,380** ← T(5)	**.22**	← V(5)
gross	$12,000	$2,260	.25	
	$16,000	$3,260	.28	
	$20,000	$4,380	.32	
	$24,000	$5,660	.36	
	$28,000	$7,100	.39	
	⋮	⋮	⋮	

The examples just described require the use of tables. In BASIC and in most nonbusiness programming languages, tables are called *arrays*.

8-1-2 How Do Arrays Work?

An array is a sequence of consecutive memory locations in which entries (numbers or alphanumeric data[1]) can be stored. In essence, it is a chunk of memory that can be sliced into a certain number of memory locations by means of the DIM statement, which specifies the name of the array and the number of entries in the array. For example, DIM G(5) means: reserve five consecutive memory locations called G(1), G(2), G(3), G(4), and G(5).

Internally, these five locations are equal in length. In fact, there is no internal difference between G(2), which is called a *subscripted* variable, and a variable such as X, which is just called a variable. Both are the same size. Both can hold the same number, i.e., we can write G(2) = −1.4 and X = −1.4. The important difference in terms of memory arrangement is that we know what item precedes G(2) (item G(1))

[1]Some BASIC systems do not allow alphanumeric data to be stored in arrays.

and what item follows it (G(3)). In contrast, we do not know what follows or precedes X. Such an indexing structure gives rise to the notion of a list, which is something very important in life! So far, we have been able to process only one item of information at a time (a variable). Now, with arrays, we can process a list of items of information.

In example 1, the array of grades might be called G. The problem of Figure 8–1 can be solved with or without the use of arrays. Both methods make use of the same number of memory locations (see Figure 8–4). If we call the array G, a block of five sequential memory locations (G(1), G(2), ..., G(5)) is reserved for the five grades, and each element of the array can be referred to by specifying the name of the array and its position (subscript). Five memory locations are also used in the case of the individualized labeling of each grade G1, G2, G3, ... What makes the array concept different and powerful is that elements within the array can be indexed with a subscript, thereby greatly simplifying the task of manipulating array elements for processing and for input/output considerations.

The grade problem in example 1 can be broken into the following three tasks:

1. Reading the grades from the DATA statement into the array G.
2. Accumulating the grades in the array and computing the average.
3. Printing the grades and the deviations (grade – average).

Some of these tasks could be consolidated, but let us illustrate these three tasks independently of one another.

Task 1: Reading the 5 grades into the array G

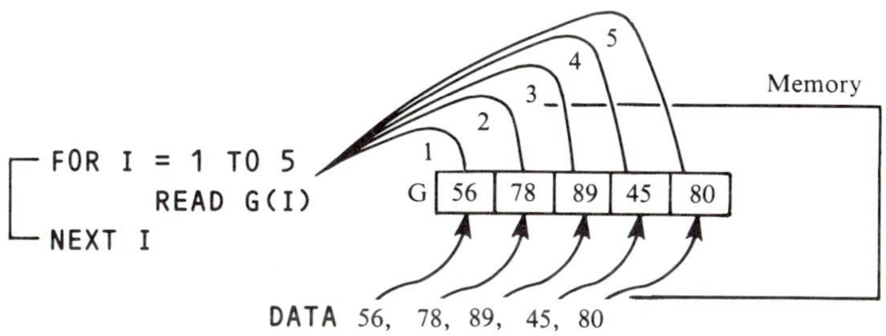

Figure 8–4 Individual labeling of grades versus array.

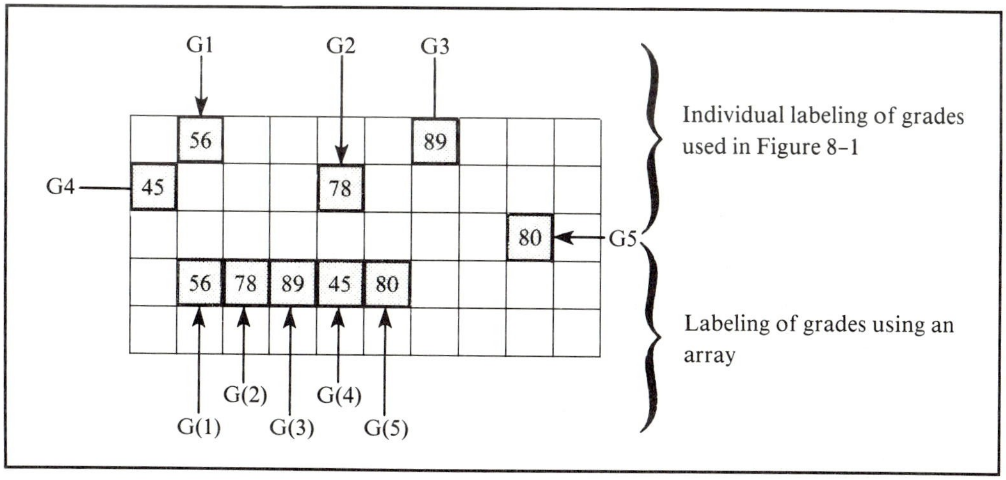

Note that the READ G(I) statement is processed five times as I takes on values 1 to 5. I is the subscript (it is also used as the index of the FOR loop.) Initially I is 1, so that the first time the statement READ G(I) is executed, G(I) will refer to G(1), and hence the value read from the DATA statement will be stored in G(1); the second time, I is 2, G(I) will identify G(2), and a new grade will be stored in G(2). Eventually, I will be 5, G(I) will refer to G(5), and the last grade will be read into G(5). The task of reading the grades into the array is now completed.

Task 2: Accumulating the grades in the array and computing the average

```
S=Ø
FOR I = 1 TO 5
    S = S + G(I)
NEXT I
A = S/5
```

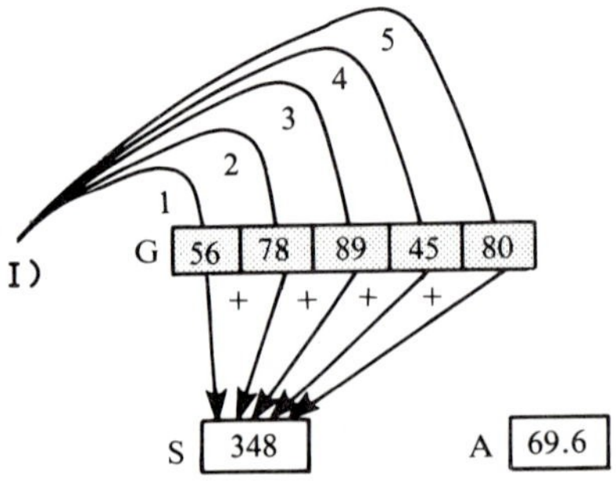

The 1st time (I = 1) through the loop, S = S + G(I) = 0 + G(1) = 56
The 2nd time (I = 2) through the loop, S = 56 + G(I) = 56 + G(2) = 56 + 78 = 134
The 3rd time (I = 3) through the loop, S = 134 + G(I) = 134 + G(3) = 134 + 89 = 223
The 4th time (I = 4) through the loop, S = 223 + G(I) = 223 + G(4) = 223 + 45 = 268
The 5th time (I = 5) through the loop, S = 268 + G(I) = 268 + G(5) = 268 + 80 = 348

Note that the grades are *not* read from the array through the READ statement, but are simply retrieved or accessed by their very own names, such as G(I). (READ can be used only to read data from DATA statements.)

Task 3: Printing the elements of array G

```
FOR I = 1 TO 5
    PRINT G(I),G(I)-A
NEXT I
```

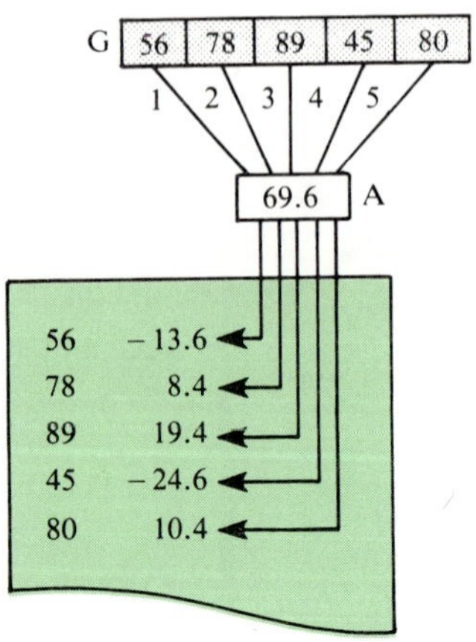

The 1st time through the loop, I = 1, and G(1) and G(1) – A are printed. By varying the subscript from 1 to 5, all the elements of the array and their difference from the average are thus printed.

The entire program is illustrated in Figure 8–5.

Figure 8-5 Computing deviation of grades.

```
10 REM GRADE DEVIATION USING ARRAYS
12 REM DATA DICTIONARY
14 REM          G: ARRAY TO HOLD GRADES
16 REM          S: TO ACCUMULATE SUM OF GRADES
18 REM          I: SUBSCRIPT FOR ARRAY G
20 REM          A: COMPUTES GRADE AVERAGE
21 REM
22 DIM G(5)                             Reserve 5 memory locations for array G.
24 PRINT "GRADES", "DEVIATION"
26 FOR I = 1 TO 5                       Read all grades into array; when I = 1
28      READ G(I)                       G(I) is G(1) and 56 is read into G(1).
30 NEXT I                               Do the same thing for I = 2, 3, 4, and 5.
32 S = 0                                Initialize grade accumulator to 0.
34 FOR I = 1 TO 5                       Add all the grades one at a time to
36      S = S + G(I)                    the accumulator S.
38 NEXT I
40 A = S/5                              Compute the average of grades.
42 FOR I = 1 TO 5
44      PRINT G(I), G(I) - A            Print each grade and the difference.
46 NEXT I
48 DATA 56, 78, 89, 45, 80
50 END
RUN
GRADES        DEVIATION
 56           -13.6
 78            8.400001
 89            19.4
 45           -24.6
 80            10.4
```

8-1-3 Do It Now

1. Could the grades have been accumulated at the same time they were read into the array?
2. How would the program of Figure 8-5 handle 97 grades?
3. Think of a problem that you could not handle without arrays.

Answers

1. Yes. Insert line 36 after statement 28, and delete lines 34 and 38. Move line 32 (S = 0) to a position preceding the loop at line 26.
2. Specify DIM G(97), change FOR I = 1 TO 5 to FOR I = 1 TO 97 throughout the program, and change line 40 to A = S/97.
3. Sorting grades.

8-2 BASIC Statements

Since many BASIC systems do not allow alphanumeric data (character strings) to be stored into arrays, discussion of arrays for character data is deferred until Section 8–6. The following sections refer to numeric arrays only.

8-2-1 DIM Statement

The general form of the DIM[2] statement is

> *line number* DIM *variable*$_1$ (*limit*$_1$) [,*variable*$_2$(*limit*$_2$) ...]

where DIM is a BASIC keyword, *variable*$_1$, *variable*$_2$, ... are names of the various arrays (any valid variable name), and *limit*$_1$, *limit*$_2$, ... are unsigned integer constants representing the number of memory locations to be reserved for each array.

This does not mean that all reserved locations must be used when processing the array. Array subscripts may vary from 1 to the limit declared in the DIM statement and may not exceed that limit. Any array used in a program must first be declared in a DIM statement.[3] Any number of arrays may be declared in a DIM list. For example, the statements

```
10 DIM X(1Ø), Z1(2Ø), J(1Ø7)
15 DIM K(3)
```

declares X, Z1, J and K, as arrays. The array X may contain up to 10 elements, the array Z1 up to 20 elements, the array J up to 107 values, and the array K up to 3 values. One might visualize the elements of X, Z, J, and K as shown in Figure 8–6.

Figure 8–6 Representation of one-dimensional arrays.

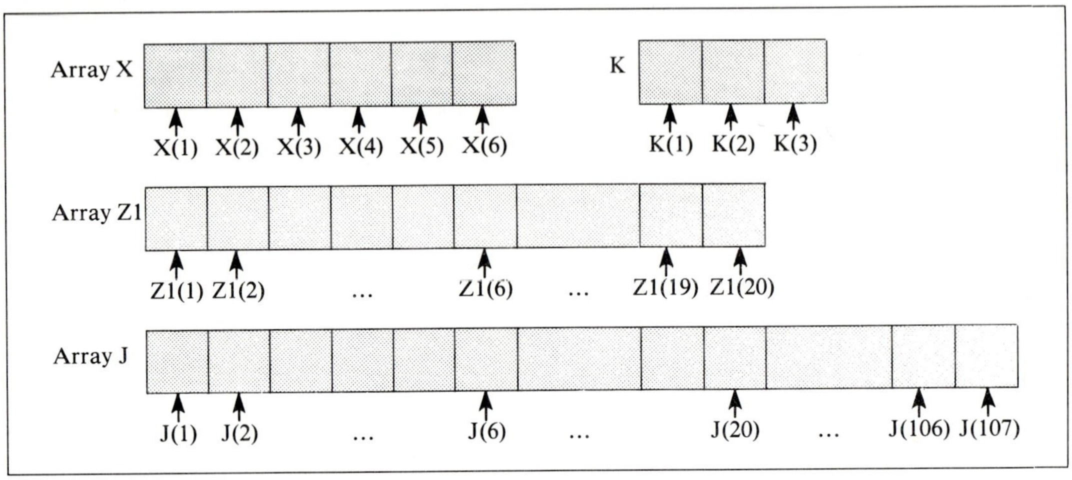

[2]On most BASIC systems the lower limit may be 0, i.e., the subscript can vary from 0 to limit$_1$.

[3]The DIM statement is not necessary if the size of the array is not to exceed 10 array entries, but it is good programming practice to declare all arrays.

Note that the DIM statement does *not* initialize the array elements to any value; it simply reserves memory locations.

DIM statements should appear in the program prior to the first executable statement (replacement, input/output, IF, or GO TO statements). A simple practice is to place the DIM statement at the very beginning of the program. Array names are ordinary variable names that must be declared in a DIM statement. The maximum size of an array (i.e., the maximum limit that can be specified) may depend on the size of the memory of the particular computer used.

8-2-2 Subscripts

Subscripts are used with array names to locate specific elements of an array. The subscript is an expression enclosed in parentheses following the array name. For example,

X(4), Z(I), X(I + 3), Z(R*W), Z(A(2)^2), and X (ABS(Y) + RND(4))

are all valid references to elements of arrays X and Z. Note that the subscript can be a single constant, a single variable, or an arithmetic expression. Since subscripts identify the position of an element in an array, it is important that no subscripts evaluate to a negative number; for example, J(−3) is invalid. Note also that J(I/3) where I = 5 refers to the same element as J(1). The result of a subscript division is an integer, that is, the resulting digits to the right of the decimal are discarded.

It is important to differentiate between the subscript value and the corresponding array element value. The value of A(3) generally has nothing to do with the number 3; for instance, A(3) could well be equal to 0.0076. Also, the same subscript can be used to refer to two different array elements; for example, A(I) and B(I).

Suppose, for example, that the array A and variables I and R contain the following data:

Array A	1.3	4.	8.9	−2.9	2.9	0.
	A(1)	A(2)	A(3)	A(4)	A(5)	A(6)

I	R
1.	5.

The following examples illustrate the use and meaning of the subscripts:

Subscript Form	*Example*	*Meaning*
Constant	A(4)	The value of the fourth location is −2.9.
Constant	A(3.7)	The fractional part is dropped. A(3.7) refers then to A(3) or 8.9.
Variable	A(I)	The subscript is evaluated first. Since I = 1, this means A(I) refers to the first element of A, i.e., 1.3
Expression	A(24/R − 2.3)	The expression evaluates to 4.8 − 2.3 = 2.5. This is truncated to 2 hence A(24/R − 2.3) = A(2) = 4.
Subscripted variable	A(A(2))	Since A(2) = 4 the variable becomes A(4), which is −2.9.
Function	A(INT(A(4) + 4))	A(4) + 4 = 1.1. The integer part evaluates to 1. Hence the variable refers to A(1) = 1.3.
Expression	(A(2*I + 1) − A(R))/2	Becomes (A(3) − A(5))/2 = 6/2 = 3.

CAUTION

1. When you have dimensioned an array to a particular size, say DIM X(33), you must make sure that any subscripts used in conjunction with array X do not exceed 33. This is easier said than done! If, in your program, you refer to X(I) on the left or right of the equal sign in a replacement statement or in an input or output statement, the value of I *must* be less or equal to 33; if this is not the case, an error message specifying "invalid index" will be printed. After all, what would you do if you had a list of 10 names and someone asked you "What is the name of the 15th person on your list?"!

2. When declaring an array through the DIM statement, make sure you specify the size of the array with an integer constant. Now, if some program written for a particular application requires that array X be large enough to contain 10 elements one day and 100 elements another day, *don't* write the following:

```
1Ø DIM X(N)
15 INPUT N          Decide on the size depending on the application
```

   This will *not* work. Simply use the statement DIM X(100) and don't fret about the fact that you may not be using array X efficiently.

8-2-3 Do It Now

1. Write DIM statement(s) to create an array Q containing 10 elements and an array R containing 25 elements.

2. Suppose an array X has the following content:

Array X	X(1)	X(2)	X(3)	X(4)	X(5)	X(6)	X(7)
	−3.	2.3	0.	3.	−2.	6.	10.

   and suppose I = 3 and J = 2. Evaluate each of the following expressions:

   a. X(3)
   b. X(1 + 4)
   c. X(1) + X(4)
   d. X(I)
   e. X(I − J)
   f. X(I) − X(J)
   g. X(X(4))
   h. (X(7) − 3) / X(4)
   i. X(ABS(X(I/J))^.5 + 1)/2
   j. X(2*I + 1) − X(J/I)

Answers

1.

```
1Ø DIM Q(1Ø), R(25)
```

or

```
1Ø DIM Q(1Ø)
2Ø DIM R(25)
```

2. a. 0
   b. −2
   c. −3 + 3 = 0
   d. 0
   e. −3
   f. 0 − 2.3 = −2.3
   g. X(3) = 0
   h. 2.333333...
   i. 1.366025
   j. X(0) is undefined

8-2-4 Array Manipulation

When working with arrays, it is often necessary to initialize arrays to certain values, create duplicate arrays, interchange elements within arrays, merge two or more arrays into one, search or accumulate array entries, sort arrays, and so forth. This section illustrates some of the commonly used array manipulation techniques so that the reader can become more familiar with the array index mechanism. In the following examples, it is assumed that values have already been stored in the various arrays.

Array Initialization and Duplication

The following code sets all elements of array A to zeroes, sets each element of array B to the variable X, sets C(1) = 1, C(2) = 2, ..., C(10) = 10, and creates a copy of array D in array S. (Assume D has been loaded with appropriate data.)

```
10 DIM A(10),B(10),C(10)
15 DIM S(10),D(10)
50 INPUT X
55 FOR I = 1 TO 10
60     A(I) = 0
65     B(I) = X
70     C(I) = I
75     S(I) = D(I)
80 NEXT I
```

As I varies from 1 to 10,
A(1), A(2), ..., A(10) are set to 0 one at a time,
B(1), B(2), ..., B(10) are set to the value X,
C(1) = 1, C(2) = 2, ..., C(10) = 10, and
S(1) = D(1), S(2) = D(2), ..., S(10) = D(10).

Sometimes it may be necessary to set an array C equal to the sum of two other arrays A and B in such a way that C(1) = A(1) + B(1), C(2) = A(2) + B(2), . . ., C(100) = A(100) + B(100). The following code could be used:

A→	3	−1	2	5	. . .	8	10
B→	−1	2	3	17	. . .	6	9
C→	2	1	5	22	. . .	14	19

```
10 DIM A(100), B(100), C(100)
 .
 .
 .
50 FOR I = 1 TO 100
55     C(I) = A(I) + B(I)
60 NEXT I
```

Suppose you want to initialize two arrays A and B, as follows:

A(1) = B(10) = 1
A(2) = B(9) = 2
A(3) = B(8) = 3
.
.
.
A(10) = B(1) = 10

The code on the right could be used:

```
10 DIM A(10),B(10)
15 FOR I = 1 TO 10
20     LET A(I) = I
25     LET K = 10-I+1
30     LET B(K) = I
35 NEXT I
```

The variable K generates the numbers 10,9,8,...,1 as I ranges from 1 to 10. If I ranged from 1 to N, the formula K = N − I + 1 would generate the numbers N,N − 1, N − 2,...,3,2,1.

The same results could have been achieved with the following code:

```
15 FOR I = 10 TO 1 STEP -1
20     B(I) = 11-I
25     A(11-I) = B(I)
30 NEXT I
```

Reversing Arrays

Suppose A is an array of size N, where N has been defined previously, and we want to reverse the array, i.e., interchange A(1) with A(N), A(2) with A(N − 1), A(3) with A(N − 2), and so forth. The following code could be used:

```
10 DIM A(100)
15 INPUT N                 Array has N elements (N <= 100).
50 FOR I = 1 TO N/2        Interchange N/2 pairs of elements.
55     T = A(I)            Save elements to be replaced in T.
60     K = N-I+1           K= N, N-1, N-2, ..., N/2+1
65     A(I) = A(K)         Insert A(K) in vacated position.
70     A(K) = T            Set A(K) to saved value.
75 NEXT I
```

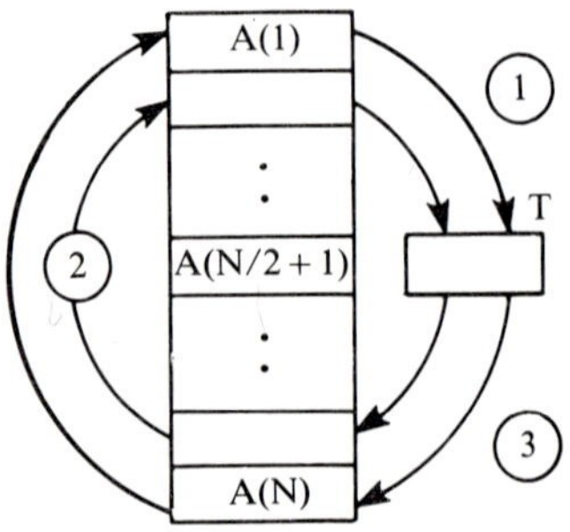

Since each interchange step involves a pair of elements

(A_1,A_N), (A_2,A_{N-1}), ... the interchange process needs to be repeated only N/2 times. If N is odd, the middle element remains the same. T is a temporary location needed to save A(1) before we move A(10) into A(1) etc. If we simply wrote A(1) = A(10), the value of A(1) would be lost.

Accumulation of Array Elements

To compute the product of the elements of the array A = | 10 | 20 | 30 | 40 | 50 | , the following code could be used:

```
10 LET P = 1           P is initially set to 1 before the loop is entered.
15 FOR K = 1 TO 5      The first time through the loop, P = P*A(1)=1*10=10.
20     LET P = P*A(K)  The second time through the loop, P = P*A(2) =
25 NEXT K              10*20 = 200, and so forth.
```

To compute the sum of two arrays S = A(1) + B(1) + A(2) + B(2) + ... + A(50) + B(50), we could use

```
10 LET S = 0
15 FOR K = 1 TO 50
20     LET S = S + A(K) + B(K)
25 NEXT K
```

Assume a store keeps track of its inventory as follows: array C identifies the cost of each of 100 different items that the store retails, and array Q identifies the corresponding item quantities.

C(1) = 4.5	Item 1 costs \$4.50.		Q(1) = 40	There are 40 of item 1.	
C(2) = 3.74	Item 2 costs \$3.74.		Q(2) = 60	There are 60 of item 2.	
⋮	⋮		⋮	⋮	
C(100) = 1.76	Item 100 costs \$1.76.		Q(100) = 48	There are 48 of item 100.	

The store wishes to determine its market value inventory. The inventory value is simply:

$$C(1) * Q(1) + C(2) * Q(2) + \ldots + C(100) * Q(100)$$

In BASIC, the code for the inventory computation would be

```
10 I = 0                          Set inventory to 0.
15 FOR J = 1 TO 100
20    I = I + C(J) * Q(J)
25 NEXT J
```

Array Merge

Suppose A and B are two arrays of size 10 and we want the array C to contain the data

$$A_1, B_1, A_2, B_2, \ldots, A_{10}, B_{10}$$

arranged in that order. Any of the following codes could be used:

1.
```
10 LET K = 1
15 FOR I = 1 TO 10
20      C(K) = A(I)
25      K = K + 1
30      C(K) = B(I)
35      K = K + 1
40 NEXT I
```

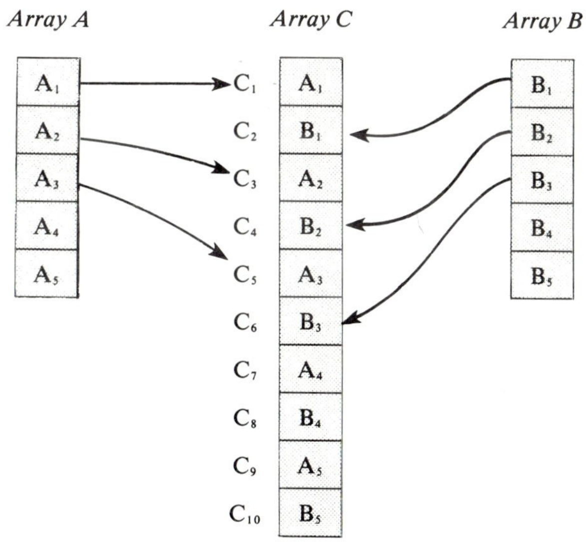

2.
```
10 LET K = 1
15 FOR I = 1 TO 20 STEP 2
20    LET C(I) = A(K)
25    LET C(I + 1) = B(K)
30    LET K = K + 1
35 NEXT I
```

3.
```
10 FOR I = 1 TO 10
15    LET C(2*I - 1) = A(I)     2*I – 1 generates the odd entries of C.
20    LET C(2*I)     = B(I)     2*I generates the even entries of C.
25 NEXT I
```

Array Searches

Assume array A contains 100 grades, and we want to know the number of grades over 60. The following code could be used:

```
10 LET K = 0
15 FOR I = 1 TO 100
20     IF A(I) <= 60 THEN 30
25     LET K = K + 1
30 NEXT I
```

K is used to count grades over 60.

If A(I) < = 60, skip the counting of grades over 60, but stay in the loop by connecting to the NEXT I statement.

Assume array A contains N scores that are supposed to be in ascending order. Write the code to perform a sequence check and write an error message if the scores are out of sequence. If the scores are in sequence, write an appropriate message. Stop as soon as the first out-of-sequence score is detected.

```
10 FOR L = 1 TO N-1
15     IF A(L+1) < A(L) THEN 35
20 NEXT L
25 PRINT "NOS. IN SEQUENCE"
30 STOP
35 PRINT A(L+1);"IS OUT OF SEQUENCE"
```

Assume an array G contains 10 scores and you want to determine the highest score. One way to do this is to use a variable L to contain the current highest score and keep comparing L with the next score. If the next score is larger than L, then L is set to that score: otherwise L is compared to the following scores. Initially, L is set to the first score.

```
20 LET L = G(1)
30 FOR I = 2 TO 10
40     IF L >= G(I) THEN 50
45     LET L = G(I)
50 NEXT I
60 PRINT "LARGEST VALUE", L
```

Set L initially to the first grade.
Start comparing L with the second entry.
If the largest grade (L) so far is less than the new grade G(I), replace L by new grade G(I).
Otherwise, look at the next grade.

This code does not, however, indicate the position of the largest element of the array G, i.e., it does not show whether the largest number was found at the 5th or 7th position, for example. One way to do that would be to insert the following two lines in the above code:

```
15 P = 1        Assume position of largest element is at position 1.
46 P = I        Store in P the position of current largest number.
60 PRINT "POSITION OF LARGEST GRADE IS"; P
```

Line 15 is required in the event the largest number is at position 1!
Notice that if the largest score is found at position P of the array G, then the value of the largest score is G(P).

8-2-5 Do It Now

1. What values will array Y contain?

```
10 DIM Y(10)
20 LET Y(1) = 1
30 LET Y(2) = 1
40 FOR I = 3 TO 10
50     LET Y(I) = Y(I-1) + Y(I-2)
60 NEXT I
```

2. The statements:

```
30 FOR I = 2 TO 6 STEP 2
35   X(I-1) = I
30   X(I) = -I
45 NEXT I
```

will put values into locations:

a. X(1), X(2), X(3)
b. X(2), X(4), X(6)
c. X(1), X(3), X(5)
d. X(1), X(2), X(3), X(4), X(5), X(6)

3. If I = 3, J = 5, X(I) = 10 and X(J) = 20, the statement:

```
30 X(I+J) = X(I) + X(J)
```

will set:

a. X(8) = 8
b. X(8) = 30
c. X(30) = 8
d. X(30) = 30

4. Write the code to fill successive elements of an array with the values 5, 7, 9, 11, ... 225, do not use a READ or INPUT statement.

5. Assume array X has 50 elements. Write the code to compute the sum of the squares of the elements of A.

6. Array C with N elements is supposed to be in ascending order. Write the code to perform a sequence check. Print all numbers that are out of sequence.

7. Array C contains 17 elements. Find the element in C whose value is closest to 5.37; print that element and identify its position, i.e., was that number the 1st, 2nd, 3rd, 14th?

8. Would the following code print the position of the highest score and the highest score itself, given an array G containing 5 scores?

```
10 LET K = 1
15 FOR I = 2 TO 5
20     IF G(K) >= G(I) THEN 30
25     K = I
30 NEXT I
35 PRINT "POSITION HIGHEST SCORE IS";K,
       "HIGHEST SCORE IS",G(K)
```

Answers

1.

1	1	2	3	5	8	13	21	34	55
Y(1)	Y(2)	Y(3)	Y(4)	Y(5)	Y(6)	Y(7)	Y(8)	Y(9)	Y(10)

2. b

3. d

4.
```
10 DIM A(150)
12 K = 1
15 FOR I = 5 TO 225 STEP 2
20    A(K) = I
22    K = K + 1
25 NEXT I
```

5.
```
10 S = 0
15 FOR I = 1 TO 50
20    S = S + X(I) ^ 2
25 NEXT I
```

6.
```
10 M = C(1)
15 FOR I = 2 TO N
20    IF M < C(I) THEN 35
25    PRINT C(I)
30    GO TO 40
35    M = C(I)
40 NEXT I
```

7.
```
05 K = 1
10 M = ABS(C(1) - 5.37)
15 FOR I = 2 TO 17
20    D = ABS(C(I) - 5.37)
25    IF D > M THEN 40
30    M = D
35    K = I
40 NEXT I
45 PRINT "POSITION IS";K;"NUMBER IS";C(K)
```

8. Yes, K identifies the position of the highest score, while G(K) is the highest score.

8-3 Input/Output of Arrays

The FOR/NEXT loop can be used conveniently when one knows exactly how many records are to be read. Consider the following data files that are to be read into arrays.

Example 1

A DATA file consists of 5 scores: DATA 31,42,61,66,48
To read these scores into array G, the following code could be used:

```
1 DIM G(5)
2 FOR I = 1 TO 5
4     READ G(I)
6 NEXT I
8 DATA 31,42,61,66,48
```

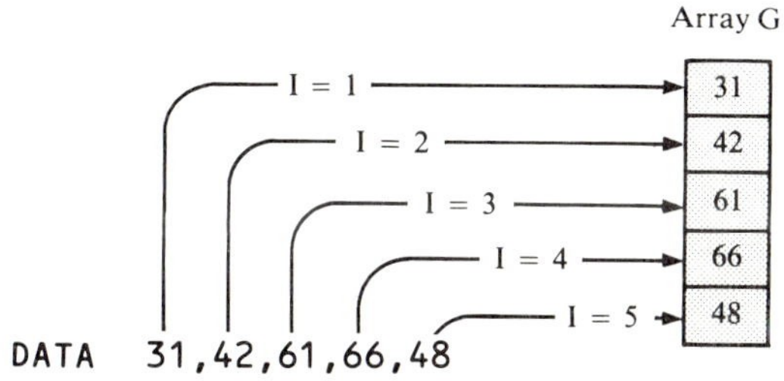

The first time through the loop, I is 1 and 31 is read from the DATA statement and stored in G(1). The second time through the loop, I is 2 and the next data item (42) is read and stored into G(2), and so forth. Finally, I is 5 and the 5th data item is read into G(5).

Example 2

A DATA file consists of 100 DATA records, where each record consists of a student ID and the student's final scores in management and algebra classes.

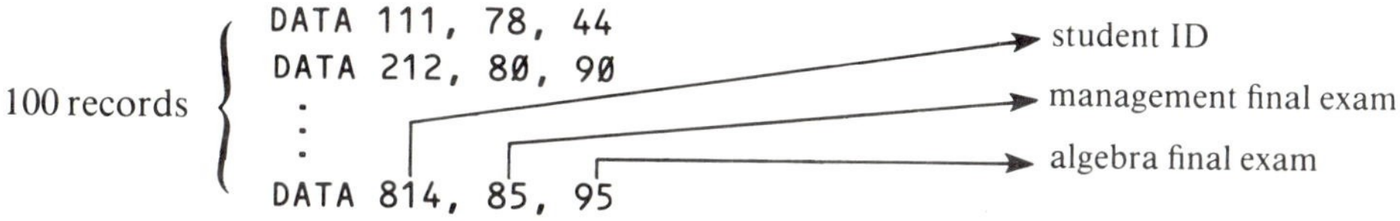

Write the code to load all management scores into array M and all algebra final exams in array A.

```
10 DIM  M(100), A(100)
15 FOR K = 1 TO 100
20     READ I, M(K), A(K)
25 NEXT K
```

Read the ID but don't store it. Read M(1), A(1), M(2), A(2),...into the two arrays.

Example 3

Assume that each element of array S contains a daily sales amount and that you want to print the daily sales with each corresponding day. The following code could be used:

```
05 DIM S(7)
10 PRINT "DAYS", "SALES"
15 FOR I = 1 TO 7
20     PRINT I, S(I)
25 NEXT I
```

Output

DAYS	SALES
1	101.0
2	200.0
3	50.5
4	35.5
5	100.0
6	300.0
7	50.0

Note that I represents the day and S(I) represents sales for the corresponding day, i.e., S(I) is the sales for the Ith day.

Example 4

Suppose the correct answers to a multiple choice test (maximum of 25 questions) are recorded on a DATA statement, with the first entry of the statement indicating the number of test questions that follow. For example:

```
DATA        7,              4, 3, 1, 1, 2, 2, 2
            ↓               ⏟
        number of        seven answers to
      test questions      test questions
```

The following code first reads the number of test questions (7) into N and then reads the N answers to the test questions in array A:

```
5 DIM A(25)
10 READ N
15 FOR I = 1 TO N
20     READ A(I)
25     PRINT A(I);
30 NEXT I
```

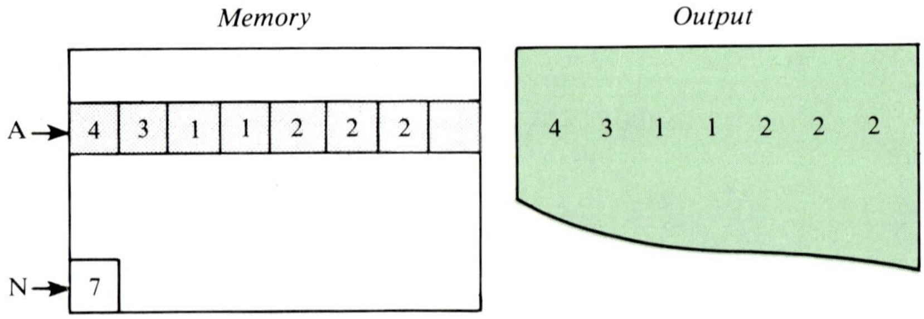

End-of-File Conditions

More often than not, an input file consists of an unknown number of records. In such a case, how do we know how many entries to reserve for a particular array if the input data is to be read into that array? The DIM statement requires an integer constant for the size of the array, i.e., the user cannot specify a variable size for the array such as DIM X(N) where N varies from one application to the next. One way to take care of this problem is to estimate a maximum size. The particular problem will often specify the maximum number of records to be processed, so use that maximum! Remember, not all reserved array entries have to be used. Consider the following example:

Example: An input file consists of an unknown number of scores, terminated by a negative number. Write the code to determine the number of scores below the average. Assume there are no more than 100 scores. The code is shown in Figure 8–7.

8-3-1 Do It Now

1. Could you have used a FOR/NEXT loop in Figure 8–7 to load the grades in array G?
2. A data file is broken down into packets of scores. The first packet contains final scores obtained by an algebra class, while the second packet contains scores

Figure 8–7 Loading an array with an unknown number of records

```
10 DIM G(100)              Reserve a maximum of 100 entries.
15 T = 0                   T is used to accumulate the scores.
20 I = 0                   I is used as an index for the score array G.
25 READ S                  Read a score.
30 IF S < 0 THEN 55        If it is not the trip code,
35 I = I + 1               increment the index by 1 and
40 G(I) = S                store the scores in successive array locations.
45 T = T + S               Add to the sum of scores.
50 GO TO 25                Go read another record.
55 A = T/I                 Compute average.
60 K = 0                   K counts number of scores less than the average.
65 FOR L = 1 TO I          Altogether there were I scores.
70    IF G(L) > A THEN 80  Compare each score with the average.
75    K = K + 1            Count number of scores less than the average.
80 NEXT L
85 PRINT K                 Print number of scores less than the average.
90 END
```

obtained by an accounting class. Each packet ends with a negative number. Write a program to read the scores into two arrays and print the number of scores in each packet. The DATA file can be visualized as follows:

DATA 10, 80, 64, 86, 44, 28, −3, 43, 74, 86, 94, 21, −7

10, 80, 64, 86, 44, 28	43, 74, 86, 94, 21
Algebra scores At most 100 scores	Accounting scores At most 50 scores

3. Suppose the correct answers (1,2,3, or 4) to a multiple choice test of 10 questions are recorded on the first record of an input file. Succeeding records contain the name of a student and the student's 10 answers. Write the code to compute each student's final score (each question is worth 10 points). The input and output look like:

correct answers to test (first DATA line)

```
DATA  1,1,2,3,1,4,2,4,3,3
DATA JONES  1,1,2,3,1,4,2,4,3,3
DATA HILL   1,1,2,3,1,1,1,3,2,4
DATA CLAM   4,1,2,3,1,4,2,4,3,2
```

```
NAME          SCORES           GRADE

JONES   1 1 2 3 1 4 2 4 3 3     100
HILL    1 1 2 3 1 1 1 3 2 4      50
CLAM    4 1 2 3 1 4 2 4 3 2      80
```

Answers

1. Yes, as follows:

```
10 DIM G(101)
15 T = 0
20 FOR I = 1 TO 101
25     READ G(I)
30     IF G(I) < 0 THEN 45
35     T = T + G(I)
40 NEXT I
45 A = T/(I-1)
50 K = 0
55 FOR L = 1 TO I-1
60
 .
 .
 .
```

The reason for using 101 instead of 100 at lines 10 and 20 is this: If we had written FOR I = 1 TO 100 and there had been exactly 100 scores, then exit from the loop would have occured at line 40 and not at line 30 (since the trip would be the 101st value). This means that the loop would have gone through its complete cycle, and in such a case the value of the index I is undetermined (it could be 101, 102, or some other value). To avoid this situation we force an exit out of the loop before it has gone through its complete cycle; this will preserve the value of the index I. Note that the final value of I reflects the count of all scores plus the trip value, hence I – 1 is used at lines 45 and 55.

2.

```
10 DIM A(100),T(50)
15 K = 0                        K counts the algebra scores
20 READ G
25 IF G < 0 THEN 45
30     K = K+1
35     A(K) = G
40     GO TO 20
45 L = 0                        L counts the accounting scores
50 READ G
55 IF G < 0 THEN 75
60     L = L+1
65     T(L) = G
70     GO TO 50
75 PRINT "ALGEBRA";K,"ACCOUNTING";L
```

3.

```
10 DIM C(10)
12 PRINT "NAME",,"ANSWERS","SCORE"
15 FOR I = 1 TO 10 )
20     READ C(I)     }     Read correct answers in array C.
25 NEXT I          )
27 L = 0                   L counts the number of correct answers.
30 READ N$
35 IF N$ = "XXX" THEN 99        If end of file, terminate.
37 PRINT N$;
40 FOR I = 1 TO 10
```

```
45       READ A                      Read a student answer.
50       IF A >< C(I) THEN 60
55       L = L + 10                  Each time an answer is correct, add 10 points.
60       PRINT A;
65  NEXT I
70  PRINT, L                         Print student's score.
75  GO TO 27
99  END
```

8-4 Programming Examples

8-4-1 Inventory-Update Program

Problem:

An input file consists of two sets of records:

1. The first set of records is the master file which reflects an item inventory at the start of the business day. Each master file record contains a part number and a corresponding item stock quantity. The end of the master file is identified by a record containing negative entries. The master file contains no more than 100 records.
2. The second set of records, which follows the master file, reflects the transactions for each of the various items during that day. Transaction records have the same format as the master file records; they contain the item number and the corresponding total number of items sold that day.

Write a program to update the master file against the transaction file to produce the new master file at the end of the day. A reorder notice should accompany any item number for which fewer than 10 items remain in stock. A list of invalid item numbers, if any, should be printed before the final master file is printed. Invalid items correspond to incorrectly recorded items in the transaction file for which there are no corresponding items in the master file.

Input and output should be similar to:

Input

```
       Item No.  Quantity
          ↑         ↑
DATA   444,      40  }
DATA   111,      30  }
DATA   222,      15  }  Master file
DATA   134,      20  }
DATA   353,       5  }
DATA    -3,      -4     End of master file
DATA   134,       3  }
DATA   111,      29  }
DATA   112,       9  }
DATA   353,       2  }  Transaction file
DATA   352,      12  }
DATA   222,      10  }
DATA    -3,      -4
```

Output

```
CURRENT INVENTORY
ITEM NO.    QUANTITY

 444            40
 111            30
 222            15
 134            20
 353             5

UPDATED INVENTORY
ITEM NO     QUANTITY
                         INVALID ITEM 112
                         INVALID ITEM 352
 444            40
 111             1       RE-ORDER
 222             5       RE-ORDER
 134            17
 353             3       RE-ORDER
```

Understanding the Problem

In the above input file example, the master file consists of five items that represent the inventory at the beginning of the business day. Sales are reflected in the master file by subtracting the number of units sold for each item from the corresponding master item quantity. For example, originally there are 20 of item 134; 3 of these are sold during the day, hence the updated master file quantity for item 134 should be 17 (20 − 3).

First, we read the master file into two arrays: one contains the master item numbers (in this case there are five), and the other contains the corresponding item quantities.

We then read the transaction file one record at a time; every time an item is read (sold) the master file is updated to reflect the current number of items on the shelf. This requires a search of the master table to identify which master file item number is to be updated. In the transaction for item 134, we look for an entry equal to 134 in the master item table; in this case it is the 4th entry of the table. We then subtract the item quantity (3) from the 4th element of the master file quantity table.

If there is an incorrect item number in the transaction file, there will be no corresponding match in the master item table. If this should happen, we print the invalid item and read the next record. By the time all transaction records have been read, the master file is updated. Then the master file is printed, two entries at a time. If the item quantity is less than 10, a reorder message is printed. The process can be visualized as follows:

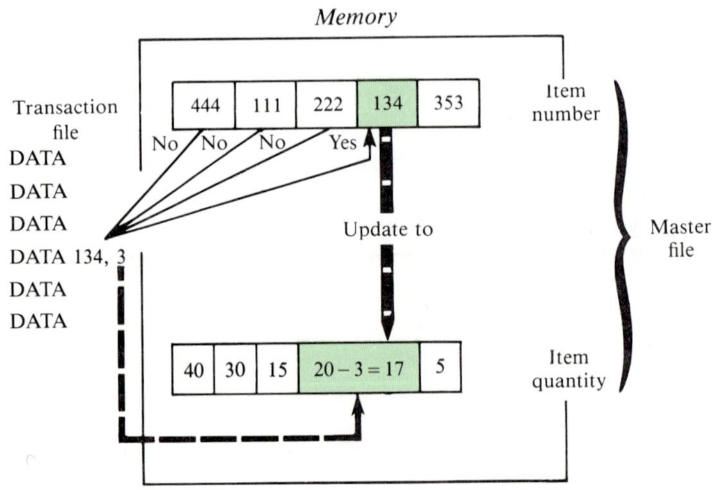

Data Dictionary

We will need 2 arrays:

N to hold the item numbers, and
Q to hold the item quantity.

N1 and Q1 will be the variables used to read the item number and the quantity from both the master and transaction records.

I is the counter used to count the number of items in the master file.

Program Development

Three techniques will be used to solve the problem.

1. The arrays N and Q are loaded into memory by using an independent subscript I (which also counts the number of records read). The first negative values encountered in the input file terminate the loading process.
2. A transaction record is read, and a search is made for a match between the transaction item number and the item numbers in the array. If no match exists, the transaction number is invalid and an error message is printed; otherwise, the transaction quantity is subtracted from the array quantity entry for the corresponding item.
3. The item and quantity arrays are printed with one entry from each array per line; a reorder message is added if the quantity is below 10.

The logic of the problem can be seen in the BASIC code in Figure 8–8.

8-4-2 Array Input/Output

Each record of an input file (no more than 100 records) contains a candidate's ID number and his/her score on the CTC examination. An applicant whose board score is 70 or more becomes certified. Write a program to print all the ID numbers of the candidates who passed (three per line) and then the numbers of those who failed (one per line). For example, given the input file shown below the program should produce the following output.

Input

```
DATA 111, 84
DATA 222, 91
DATA 333, 4Ø
DATA 444, 71
DATA 555, 52
DATA 666, 48
DATA 777, 72
DATA 888, 69
DATA 999, 8Ø
```

Output

```
PASSING:  111   222   444
          777   999

          FAILING
           333
           555
           666
           888
```

Understanding the Problem

Since the scores have to be broken down into two groups, those above 70 and those below, we need an array P to store the numbers of those candidates who passed and another array F for those who failed. Every time we read a score, we store the corresponding candidate's number in either the next available slot in array P or the next available slot in array F. To do this we need two independent subscripts, P1 and F1, to tell us the next free position in array P or in array F, respectively. Initially, P1 is set to 0; every time we need to store an applicant's number in P, we add 1 to P1 and *then* store the applicant's number in P(P1). Thus P1 also keeps a count of passing scores.

■ **Figure 8–8** An inventory update program.

```
10 REM INVENTORY UPDATE PROBLEM
12 REM DATA DICTIONARY
14 REM    N : ARRAY FOR ITEM NUMBERS
16 REM    Q : ARRAY FOR ITEM QUANTITIES
18 REM    N1: USED TO READ ITEM NUMBER
20 REM    Q1: USED TO READ ITEM QUANTITY
22 REM    I : COUNTS NUMBER MASTER RECORDS
23 REM
24 DIM N(100), Q(100)
26 PRINT "   CURRENT INVENTORY"
28 PRINT "ITEM NO", "QUANTITY"
30 I = 0
32 READ N1, Q1                  Read a master record.
34 IF N1 < 0 THEN 46
36    PRINT N1,Q1               Print the record read.
38    I = I + 1                 Count the number of master records.
40    N(I) = N1                 Store the item number read in array N.
42    Q(I) = Q1                 Store the quantity read in array Q.
44    GOTO 32                   Go back and read another master record.
46 PRINT
48 PRINT "   UPDATED INVENTORY"
50 PRINT "ITEM NO", "QUANTITY"
51 REM
52 READ N1, Q1                           Read a master record.
54 IF N1 < 0 THEN 70
56 FOR K = 1 TO I                        Search master file for transaction item number.
58    IF N1 < > N(K) THEN 64             If no match, keep searching.
60       Q(K) = Q(K) - Q1                If a match, update corresponding item quantity,
62       GOTO 52                         then go and read the next transaction record.
64 NEXT K                                If the loop runs through its complete cycle,
66 PRINT,, "INVALID ITEM"; N1            this means that no match was found. Print
68 GOTO 52                               error message and read next transaction record.
70 FOR K = 1 TO I                        Print new master file.
72    IF Q(K) < 10 THEN 78               If the quantity is less than 10, print a reorder message;
74       PRINT N(K), Q(K)                otherwise just print item and quantity.
76       GOTO 80
78       PRINT N(K), Q(K); "REORDER"
80 NEXT K
82 DATA 444, 40  \
83 DATA 111, 30   |
84 DATA 222, 15   |  Master file
85 DATA 134, 20   |
86 DATA 353,  5  /
87 DATA -30, -2
88 DATA 134,  3  \
89 DATA 111, 29   |
90 DATA 112,  9   |  Transaction
91 DATA 353,  2   |  file
92 DATA 352, 12   |
93 DATA 222, 10  /
94 DATA -30, -3
95 END
```

```
   CURRENT INVENTORY
ITEM NO        QUANTITY
 444            40
 111            30
 222            15
 134            20
 353            5

   UPDATED INVENTORY
ITEM NO        QUANTITY
                              INVALID ITEM 112
                              INVALID ITEM 352
 444            40
 111            1 REORDER
 222            5 REORDER
 134            17
 353            3 REORDER
```

F1 is used in a similar way. To better visualize the movement of information, consider the following diagram:

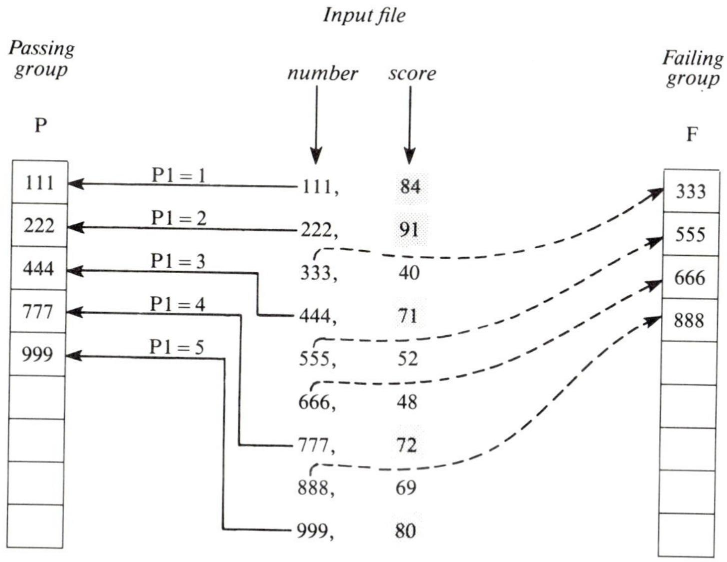

Data Dictionary

We will need two arrays:

P to store the numbers of the passing candidates
F to store the numbers of the failing candidates

To index both arrays and to keep track of the successive entries into which candidates' names are to be moved, we use P1 for array P and F1 for array F. To print the three numbers per line, we use the counter K to count from 1 to 3. Every time K is 3, we go to the next line.

N and G are used to read each candidate's number and score.

Program Development

Candidates' numbers are stored either in array P or in array F. When the end-of-file is encountered, there are P1 passing candidates and F1 failing candidates.

Printing the array of passing candidates with three entries per line requires a little bit of counting gymnastics—we set up a counter so the computer will skip to the next line that when three numbers have been written per line. Since P1 represents the count of the passing candidates, we need to print the first P1 entries of array P.

The logic of the program is displayed along with the output in Figure 8–9.

8-4-3 Do It Now

Will the program in Figure 8–9 print the correct results if either all candidates pass or all candidates fail?

Answer:

Write the code on your system and observe what happens.

Figure 8–9 An array input/output problem.

```
10 REM ARRAY INPUT OUTPUT PROBLEM
12 REM DATA DICTIONARY
14 REM      P:  PASSING GROUP
15 REM      F:  FAILING GROUP
16 REM      P1: INDEX TO IDENTIFY NEXT FREE POSITION IN P
17 REM      F1: INDEX TO IDENTIFY NEXT FREE POSITION IN F
18 REM      K:  COUNTER USED TO PRINT 3 NUMBERS PER LINE
19 REM      N:  USED TO READ ID NUMBERS
20 REM      G:  USED TO READ SCORES
23 DIM N(100), G(100)
24 P1 = 0
26 F1 = 0
28 READ N, G
30 IF G < 0 THEN 46
32    IF G < 70 THEN 40
34       P1    = P1 + 1
36       P(P1) = N
38       GOTO 28
40       F1    = F1 + 1
42       F(F1) = N
44       GOTO 28
46    PRINT "PASSING:",
48    K = 0
50    FOR J = 1 TO P1
52        K = K + 1
54        PRINT P(J);
56        IF K < > 3 THEN 64
58           K = 0
60           PRINT
62           PRINT,
64    NEXT J
66    PRINT
67    PRINT
68    PRINT, "FAILING"
70    FOR I = 1 TO F1
72        PRINT, F(I)
74    NEXT I
76 DATA 111, 84
78 DATA 222, 91
80 DATA 333, 40
82 DATA 444, 71
84 DATA 555, 52
86 DATA 666, 48
88 DATA 777, 72
90 DATA 888, 69
92 DATA 999, 80
93 DATA -99, -9
94 END
```

Line 28: Read a candidate number and a score.

Lines 34–36: If passing, identify the next available slot in array P where we can store the number just read.

Lines 40–42: If failing, identify the next available slot in array F where we can store the number just read.

Lines 48–62: K is used to print three entries per line. Print all passing candidate's numbers. Count the entries per line (no more than 3). Print passing candidate's number. Determine whether 3 entries have been printed. If three numbers have been printed, reset counter K to 0, and restart printing on a new line.

Lines 70–72: Print all the numbers of the candidates who failed.

Lines 76–93: Each record consists of a candidate's number and score.

```
RUN
PASSING:          111  222  444
                  777  999

                 FAILING
                  333
                  555
                  666
                  888
```

8-4-4 Frequency Distribution Problem

An input file contains an unknown number of records. Each record contains a score. Write a program to determine the number of times each score occurs.

Understanding the Problem

Given a list of scores in the range 1 to 100 we must determine how many times score 1 appears, how many times score 2 appears, and so forth. It is possible that many of these scores will not appear in the input list at all.

Since we do not know what scores will appear, we need 100 different counters to count all possible score occurrences. Also, since it would be quite impractical to have 100 differently labeled variables to count the occurrence of each score, we will use 100 array elements as counters to count all possible score occurrences. We need to choose which of the array elements will count which scores. Let us decide on the following:

K(1) will count the occurrence of score 1
K(2) will count the occurrence of score 2
.
.
.
K(36) will count the occurrence of score 36, and
K(S) will count the number of times the score S appears in the input list.

Thus every time we read a score S we will use that S as the subscript of K to designate which counter to increment. The process can be diagrammed as follows:

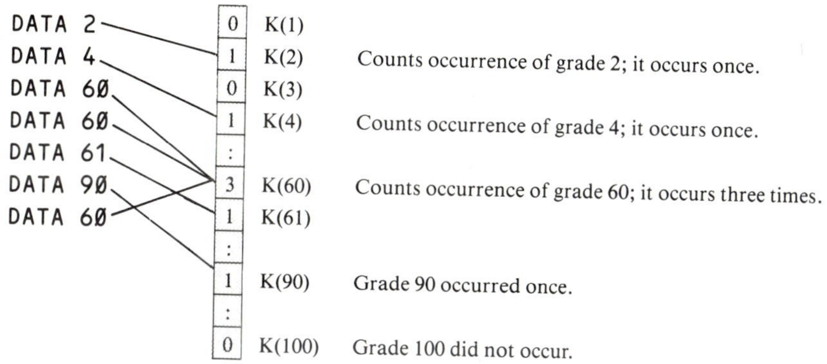

Output Design

We will list the various scores and their corresponding frequencies as follows:

Score	*Frequency*
2	1
4	1
60	3
61	1
90	1

Data Dictionary and Program Development

The 100 elements of array K will be used as counters. Every time we read a score S, we will add 1 to the counter that counts the score S by using the statement K(S) = K(S) + 1, i.e., if S = 80 then K(80) = K(80) + 1, meaning that the count of score 80 is equal to the old count of score 80 plus 1. Obviously K(80) and all the other counters must be initialized to 0.

When all the scores have been read, we will print all those scores whose frequency counts are nonzero! This means that we must to through the array of counters K, starting with K(1), and ask the question: Is K(1) = 0? If K(1) = 0, this means that there were no scores equal to 1 so we will not print the score 1. If, on the other hand, K(1) = 3, this means that the score 1 occurred three times in the list and so we write the score 1 and its corresponding frequency (3). In general, if the answer to the question "Is K(I) = 0?" is *yes*, then the score I is *not* printed; if the answer is *no*, score I and the frequency count K(I) are printed.

The BASIC code is shown in Figure 8–10.

8-4-5 Do It Now

1. Modify the program in Figure 8–10 to accommodate scores in the range 0 to 100.
2. Modify the program in Figure 8–10 to accommodate scores with one digit to the right of the decimal point, for example, 89.5 of 56.4.
3. Modify the program of Figure 8–10 to produce a sorted list of scores, i.e., if score 64 occurs 3 times, print 64,64,64.

Answers

1. Change line 45 to FOR I = 0 TO 100
   Change line 80 to FOR I = 0 TO 100
2. Essentially, multiply each score by 10 and use the same logic.

```
35 DIM K(1000)
45 FOR I = 1 TO 1000
70 K(S*10) = K(S*10) + 1
80 FOR I = 1 TO 1000
90 PRINT I/10,K(I)
```

3. Insert the following lines:

```
86 FOR J = 1 TO K(I)
88     PRINT I
89 NEXT J
```

and delete line 90.

8-4-6 Table Look-Up

Table look-up is a fast and efficient method to access data in a table directly without any search of the table elements, something like looking up your taxes in the tax table (fast and painful!). Consider the following example:

United Package Service operates under a cost delivery system based on article weight and destination zone. The rate table per pound is as follows:

Zone code	*Cost per pound*	*Meaning*
1	$ .55	The cost to ship 1 pound to zone 1 is $ .55.
2	$ .80	.
3	$1.03	The cost to ship 1 pound to zone 3 is $1.03.
4	$1.30	.
5	$1.75	.
6	$2.01	.

Let us write a program that will read an input file where each record contains two entries: a destination zone and a shipment weight. The program will print the destination zone, the weight, and the corresponding shipping cost.

■ **Figure 8–10** A frequency distribution program.

```
10 REM FREQUENCY DISTRIBUTION PROBLEM
20 REM DATA DICTIONARY
25 REM       K: ARRAY USED FOR THE 100 COUNTERS
30 REM       S: REPRESENTS THE VARIOUS SCORES READ
35 DIM K(100)
40 PRINT "SCORE", "FREQUENCY"
45 FOR I = 1 TO 100
50     K(I) = 0                 Zero out array counter.
55 NEXT I
60 READ S                       Read a score.
65 IF S < 0 THEN 80
70     K(S) = K(S) + 1          Increment the counter corresponding to score S
75     GOTO 60                  (If S = 68 then K(68) = K(68) + 1).
80 FOR I = 1 TO 100             Print all scores for which the corresponding
85     IF K(I) = 0 THEN 95      frequency count is nonzero.
90     PRINT I, K(I)
95 NEXT I
100 DATA 12, 23, 45, 12, 98, 12, 98, 98, 23, 98, -3
105 END

RUN

SCORE      FREQUENCY
 12          3
 23          2
 45          1
 98          4
```

Understanding the Problem and Output Design

To understand the problem, let us look at the following example. Suppose we wanted to send a 2-pound parcel to zone 6. We would look up the zone 6 and identify the corresponding cost per pound entry, which is $2.01. Since the parcel is 2 pounds, the total cost would be 2 * 2.01 = 4.02. An attractive output design might be:

ZONE	WEIGHT	COST
6	2.0	4.02
2	3.5	2.80

Data Dictionary and Program Development

A convenient way to look up the cost associated with a particular zone is to create an array R such that R(1) = $.55, R(2) = $.80, ..., R(6) = $2.01. In this way, if the zone is 6, for example, we can immediately look up the 6th entry of R, which is $2.01. In general, if the zone is Z, the cost associated with zone Z is simply R(Z). Hence if we read a zone Z and a weight W, the shipment cost is R(Z) * W.

The program in Figure 8-11 first loads the cost table R with the 6 cost entries, then inputs a zone Z and a weight W, and finally prints the zone Z, the weight W, and the resulting cost R(Z) * W.

Figure 8–11 A table look-up problem.

```
10 REM TABLE LOOK-UP PROBLEM
15 REM DATA DICTIONARY
20 REM        R: ARRAY IN WHICH THE 6 COSTS ARE STORED
25 REM        Z: REPRESENTS THE ZONE READ FROM RECORD
30 REM        W: REPRESENTS THE WEIGHT READ FROM RECORD
35 REM
40 DIM R(6)                    Cost per pound table.
45 FOR I = 1 TO 6              Read the costs in the table.
50 READ R(I)
55 NEXT I
60 PRINT,, "ZONE","WEIGHT", "COST"
65 REM
70 INPUT; Z, W                            Enter a zone and a weight.
75 IF Z < 0 THEN 95
80    PRINT,,Z, W, R(Z) * W               Compute corresponding cost.
85    GOTO 70
90 DATA 0.55, 0.80, 1.03, 1.30, 1.75, 2.01
95 END

RUN
                    ZONE        WEIGHT        COST

? 5,10              5           10            17.50
? 4,5               4           5             6.50
? 1,3               1           3             1.65
? -1, -1
```

8-5 Sorting

Given a list of any type of unprocessed or raw information, such as a list of names or employee numbers, one's first impulse is, generally, to sort out these items into some particular order (descending or ascending) so that looking them up will be a great deal easier. Hence it should come as no surprise that sorting is one of the most practiced forms of data processing (for directories, tax tables, book retrieval, identifications, and so forth). Arrays obviously lend themselves to this type of manipulation.

There are many clever and sophisticated ways to sort arrays (one is shown in Exercise 30 of section 8–8–2). Two traditional methods are presented in this section: the *bubble sort* and the *mini/max* methods. Although these two methods may not be used often in a real-life environment, they will give you some insight into the sorting process as well as an appreciation of array indexing.

8-5-1 The Bubble Sort

Assume the following list of numbers is to be sorted into ascending sequence:

4 5 3 2

One systematic approach begins by comparing the first pair of numbers and interchanging the first number with the second number if the first number is greater than the second number. Then we move on to the next pair, 5 and 3, and do the same thing—this time we interchange 5 and 3. Then move on to the next pair, 5 and 2, and perform an interchange if necessary (in this case we interchange 2 and 5). In this way we ensure that the largest number is continuously moved to the right. At the end of this first pass through the list, the numbers are

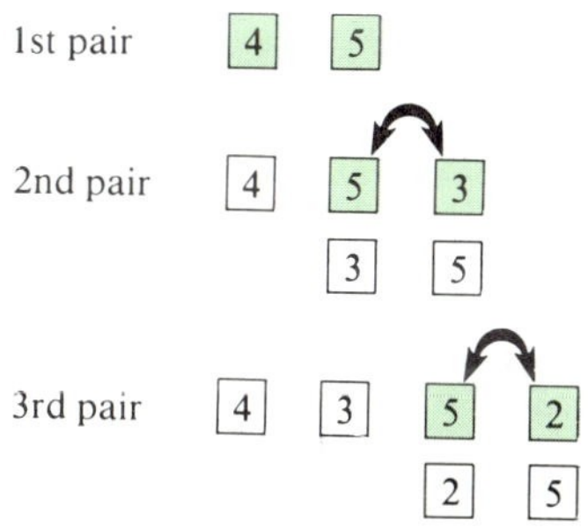

4 3 2 5

The largest number is now in the right-most position

We now repeat the procedure:

Compare the first pair 4, 3 and obtain 3, 4.

Compare the second pair 4, 2 and obtain 2, 4.

Compare the third pair 4, 5 and obtain 4, 5.

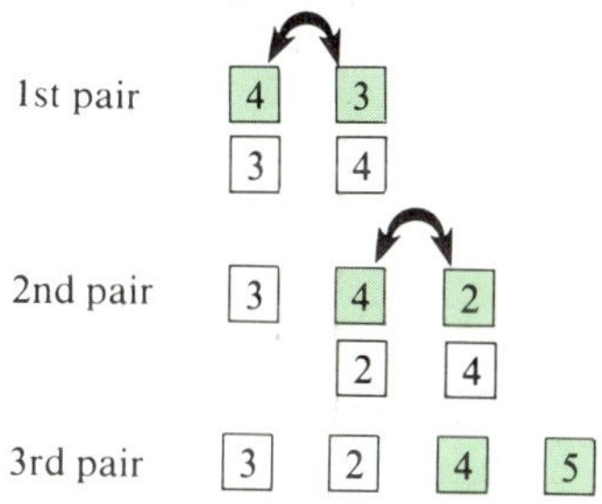

Actually we do not need to process the third pair since we already know that the largest number is in the last position. At the end of this second pass, the second largest number is in the second-to-last position and the numbers are now:

3 2 4 5

We now carry out the same procedure for the third time.

Compare the first pair 3, 2 and obtain 2, 3.

Compare the second pair 3, 4 and obtain 3, 4.

Compare the third pair 4, 5 and obtain 4, 5.

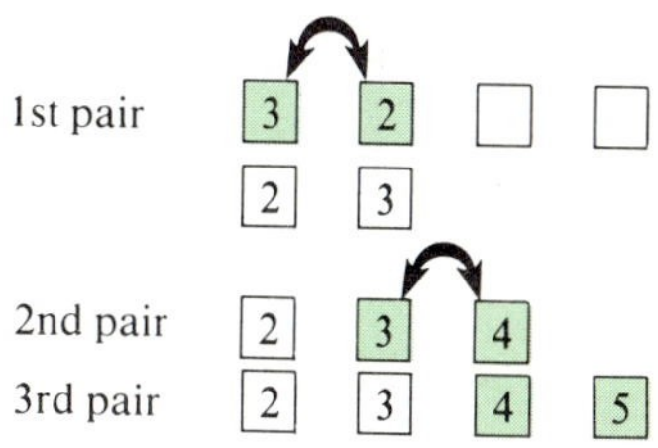

Actually, we only needed to compare the first pair of numbers, since we know the last two numbers are already in order.

By the end of the third pass, all the numbers are sorted. We note, then, that if four numbers have to be sorted, only three passes are needed. In general, if N numbers are to be sorted, N − 1 passes are needed.

Let us write the BASIC code for the first pass (moving the largest number to the right most position):

```
10 DIM G(4)
15 FOR I = 1 TO 3
20     IF G(I) < G(I+1) THEN 40
25     T = G(I)
30     G(I) = G(I+1)
35     G(I+1) = T
40 NEXT I
```

The upper limit for I is 3, so that when I is 3 we will be comparing G(3) with G(4), which is G(I + 1).

G(I) and G(I + 1) are interchanged if G(I + 1) is less than G(I). The interchange cycle requires three steps:

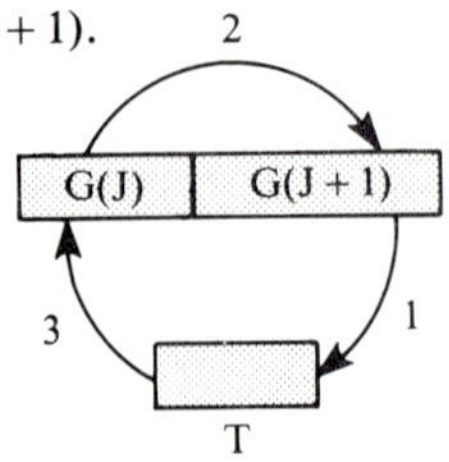

This code will move the largest number in the array G into the right-most position. To sort the entire array, we need to make three passes through the list. Hence we will carry out the above procedure three times by using the following code:

```
10 DIM G(4)
12 FOR J = 1 TO 3
15     FOR I = 1 TO 3
20         IF G(I) < G(I+1) THEN 40
25             T = G(I)
30             G(I) = G(I+1)
35             G(I+1) = T
40     NEXT I
45 NEXT J
```

This code will sort all elements of the array. You might find this code easy to remember at the expense of efficiency—on the second pass, the code compares G(3) with G(4), although we already know that G(4) is the largest. This is also the case on the third pass: G(2) is compared with G(3), although G(3) is already larger than G(2). It would be better to stop at G(2) for the third pass, i.e., we would like the limit of the index I at line 15 to be 3 for the 1st pass, 2 for the second pass and finally 1 for the third pass. To do that, we replace FOR I = 1 TO 3 by FOR I = 1 TO 4 − J, since 4 − J will generate the numbers 3, 2, and 1. The complete code to sort an array G of size N is shown in Figure 8–12.

8-5-2 Interchange Minimum/Maximum (Mini/Max) Sort

Another method that can be used to sort an array of numbers in ascending order is to determine the location (position) of the smallest element in the array and interchange that element with the first element of the array (see Figure 8–13). At the end of this

■ **Figure 8–12** The bubble sort.

```
10 REM BUBBLE SORT PROGRAM
12 REM DATA DICTIONARY
14 REM       G: ARRAY OF GRADES TO BE SORTED
16 REM       N: TOTAL NUMBER OF GRADES
17 REM       P: REPRESENTS NUMBER OF PASSES (N - 1)
18 REM       T: TEMPORARY LOCATION FOR INTERCHANGING TWO GRADES
19 REM
20 DIM G(100)
21 PRINT "UNSORTED GRADES";
22 FOR I = 1 TO 100
24     READ G(I)
26     IF   G(I) < 0 THEN 34
28     PRINT G(I);
30     N = I
32 NEXT I
34 P = N - 1
36 FOR L = 1 TO P
38     FOR J = 1 TO N - L
40         IF G(J) < G(J+1) THEN 48
42            T      = G(J+1)
44            G(J+1) = G(J)
46            G(J)   = T
48     NEXT J
50 NEXT L
52 PRINT
54 PRINT "SORTED GRADES  ";
56 FOR I = 1 TO N
58     PRINT G(I);
60 NEXT I
62 DATA 42,65,36,48,92,78,50,-2
64 END

RUN
UNSORTED GRADES 42  65  36  48  92  78  50
SORTED GRADES   36  42  48  50  65  78  92
```

Read the input file. (line 22)

N is the final number of scores. (line 30)

P is the number of passes. (line 34)

Controls number of passes. The first pass shifts highest grade in right-most position (G(N)); the second pass shifts the second-highest grade into next-to-last position (G(N – 1)), and so forth. (line 36)

N – L represents the size of the ever shrinking array as it gets smaller with each pass. J is used to index the interchange procedure to keep moving the largest numbers to the right. (line 46)

Print the sorted numbers. (line 58)

first search pass, the smallest element is in the first position. The array is then searched for the next smallest element, with the search starting at position 2 of the array; the smallest element is then swapped with the number in position 2 of the array. At the end of the second search pass, the first two elements of the array are in ascending sequence order. The search for the next smallest number starts in position 3, and the same search and interchange process is repeated until the last two (rightmost) array elements are processed. Using this sorting procedure, an array of N elements requires N – 1 passes for the search and interchange procedure. The search for the smallest number involves comparing N numbers during the first pass, N – 1 numbers during the second pass, and two numbers during the last pass. Figure 8–13 illustrates the sorting process with an array G containing 4 numbers:

Figure 8–13 Mini/max sorting process.

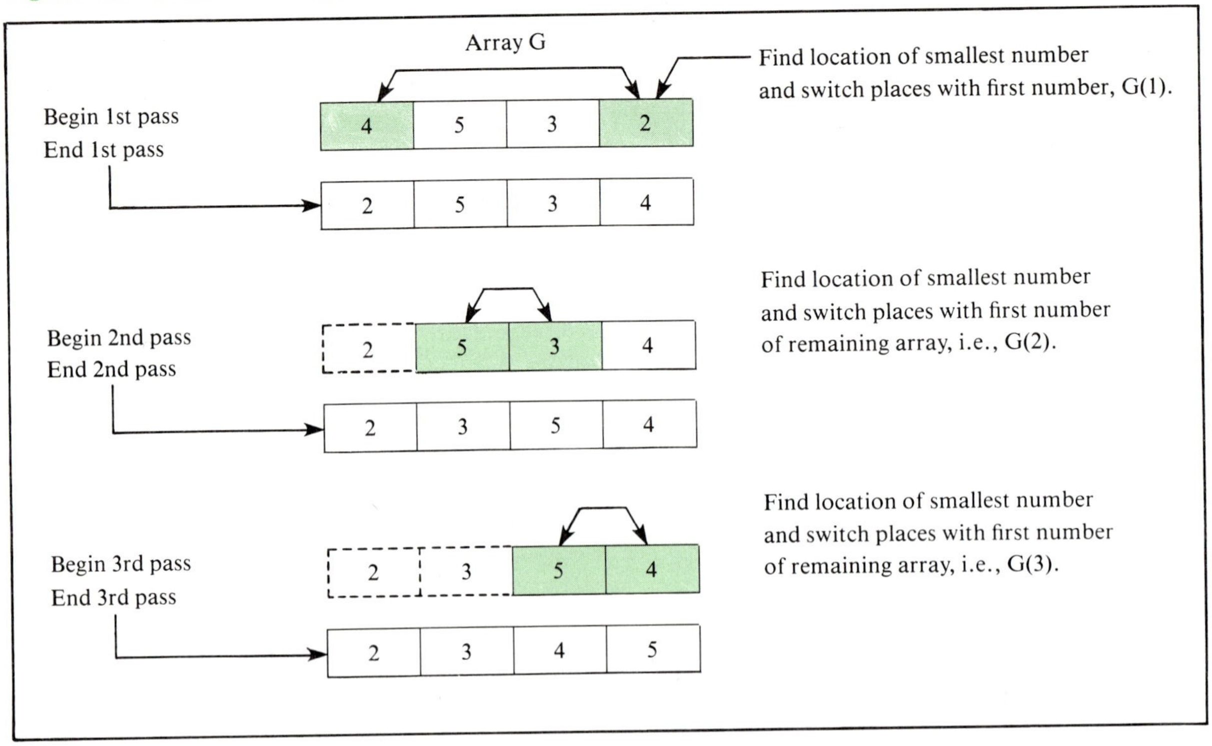

To understand the process better, let us write the code for just the first pass, which determines the position of the smallest element of the array and interchanges the smallest number with the number in the first position of the array. Assume the array G contains four elements.

```
10 S = G(1)
15 S1 = 1
20 FOR J = 2 TO 4
25     IF S =< G(J) THEN 40
30         S = G(J)
35         S1 = J
40 NEXT J
45 T = G(S1)
50 G(S1) = G(1)
55 G(1) = T
```

Start by assuming that the smallest element is G(1) in position 1 (S1), subject to later change.
Start comparing S with the remaining elements.
If S <= G(J), then S is still the smallest element so S and its position S1 do not change.
If S > G(J), then the new smallest number is G(J) at location J so we set S1 equal to J and we reset S to G(J) to keep track of current smallest number.
After the loop is completed, we switch the smallest number G(S1) with the number in the first position.

This code illustrates the first pass. At the end of the first pass, the smallest element is in position 1, so we start looking for the next smallest number at position 2 of the array. Hence, prior to the second pass, we set S to G(2) and S1 to 2. At the conclusion of the second pass, we interchange the smallest number (in position S1) with the number in the second position; the same process is continued until sorting is complete. The entire BASIC code is shown in Figure 8–14.

Figure 8–14 The mini/max sort.

```
10 REM MINI MAX SORT PROGRAM
12 REM DATA DICTIONARY
14 REM       G: ARRAY OF GRADES TO BE SORTED
16 REM       N: TOTAL NUMBER OF GRADES
17 REM       P: REPRESENTS NUMBER OF PASSES (N - 1)
18 REM       T: TEMPORARY LOCATION FOR INTERCHANGING TWO GRADES
19 REM       S: SMALLEST SCORE
20 REM       S1: LOCATION OF SMALLEST SCORE
22 REM
24 DIM G(100)
26 PRINT "UNSORTED GRADES";
28 FOR I = 1 TO 100                 Read the scores into array G.
30     READ  G(I)
32     IF    G(I) < 0 THEN 40
34     PRINT G(I);
36     N = I                        N keeps track of the number of scores.
38 NEXT I
40 P = N - 1                        P is the number of passes.
42 FOR L = 1 TO P                   L controls the number of passes.
44     S  = G(L)                    Before starting a pass, assume S = G(L) is
46     S1 = L                       the smallest score and that its location is
48     FOR J = L+1 TO N             S1 = L.
50         IF S =< G(J) THEN 56     Find the real smallest score S and its location
52         S    = G(J)              S1, then place the smallest score in G(L).
54         S1   = J
56     NEXT J                       Lines 56–60 interchange the smallest
58     T      = G(S1)               score found during the 1st pass with the
60     G(S1) = G(L)                 1st element, then the smallest score
62     G(L)  = T                    found during the 2nd pass with the sec-
64 NEXT L                           ond element, and so forth.
66 PRINT
68 PRINT "SORTED GRADES  ";
70 FOR I = 1 TO N
72     PRINT G(I);                  Print the sorted numbers.
74 NEXT I
76 DATA 42,65,36,48,92,78,50,-2
78 END

RUN
UNSORTED GRADES 42  65  36  48  92  78  50
SORTED GRADES   36  42  48  50  65  78  92
```

8-5-3 Do It Now

1. Tabulate the Bubble sort program in Figure 8–12 for the following DATA file (i.e., list the values taken on by all the variables):

```
DATA  5,  1,  2,  3,  -2
```

2. In the Bubble sort program of Figure 8–12, can you stop the sort process if all numbers are sorted before all passes are completed?
3. Tabulate the Mini/max sort program of Figure 8–14 for the following DATA file:

```
DATA   5,  3,  2,  -2
```

Answers

1.

I	G(1)	G(2)	G(3)	G(4)	G(5)	N	P	L	J	T
1	~~5~~	~~4~~	~~2~~	~~3~~	−2	4	3	~~1~~	~~1~~	~~1~~
2	1	~~5~~	~~5~~	5					~~2~~	~~2~~
3		2	3						~~3~~	3
4								~~2~~	~~1~~	
5									~~2~~	
								3	1	

2. The sort process can be terminated as soon as it is discovered that no elements are interchanged during any one pass. If the numbers are all in sequence, lines 42 to 46 are not executed. Hence, before any given pass, we will set a variable to 0, and reset that variable to 1 if lines 42 to 46 are executed. If the variable is still 0 at the end of a pass, the sort process is stopped. This is done by adding the code:

```
37 S = Ø
47 S = 1
49 IF S = Ø THEN 52
```

3.

I	G(1)	G(2)	G(3)	G(4)	N	P	L	S	S1	J	T
1	~~5~~	~~3~~	~~2~~	−2	3	2	~~1~~	~~5~~	~~1~~	~~2~~	
2								~~3~~	~~2~~		
3	~~2~~		5					~~2~~	~~3~~	~~3~~	~~2~~
4		~~3~~					2	3	2	3	
		3									3

8-6 Character Strings

8-6-1 Introduction

Many times it may be convenient or necessary to process alphabetic or alphanumeric information. Recall that alphanumeric data is defined as a sequence of letters, digits, and/or special characters. For example, "1102 NORTH 12 AVE." is a string of 18 characters consisting of 6 digits, 3 blanks, 8 letters, and a period; it is commonly referred to as a character string or a literal string. Zip codes, telephone numbers, social security numbers, names, and addresses are examples of character strings.

As might be expected, computers can process alphabetic or alphanumeric data as easily as numeric data. The following points should be remembered when working with character strings:

1. Character string names are formed by adding a $ to a variable name:

   A$, Z$, A1$, Z9$.

2. Most systems allow storage of up to 256 characters per memory cell (variable).
3. Character strings may not participate in arithmetic operations. (How could you add "1102 NORTH 12 AVE." to "3214 SCENIC DRIVE"?)
4. Character strings may be compared to one another by using an IF statement.
5. Character strings must be enclosed in quotation marks in a PRINT, replacement, or IF statement. Quotation marks around the string are optional in a DATA statement or in a response to an INPUT statement.

The following examples illustrate the ways in which character strings can be used in a BASIC program.

```
10 G$ = "246 ACACIA DR."
15 A$ = "1130"
20 READ X$,Y$,Z$
25 DATA "111-23-4114",SUSAN,"A,B,C"
30 IF A$ = "YES" THEN 50
35 INPUT G$,A$
     ?230,JOHN
```

X$ contains	1	1	1	–	2	3	–	4	1	1	4
Y$ contains	S	U	S	A	N						
Z$ contains	A	,	B	,	C						
G$ contains	2	3	0								
A$ contains	J	O	H	N							

8-6-2 Character String Comparisons

Since the internal code to represent character data is different from the code used to represent signed numbers, no meaningful comparisons can be made between numeric and character data. In fact, an error message will be printed if such an attempt is made, i.e., the character string 123 cannot be compared to the signed number 123. However, it is possible to compare two character strings to each other. Such a comparison is performed one character at a time according to the following collating sequence:

$$\text{blank} < A < B < C < \ldots < Y < Z$$

and

$$0 < 1 < 2 < \ldots < 8 < 9$$

(For the collation sequence for special characters, check your technical reference manual under ASCII or EBCDIC code.)

In the event that the two operands to be compared are unequal in length, the shorter operand is padded with blanks to the right, to make up the difference.

Examples:

D E A N	<	D E E M	since A < E
D A D	>	C	since D > C
D A D	=	D A D ␣	A trailing blank is provided for 1st operand, hence equality.
N E W ␣ Y O R K	>	N E W ␣ ␣ ␣ ␣	4 trailing blanks are provided to 2nd operand. Y > blank.
T H E	>	␣ ␣ ␣ ␣	Since T > blank, result holds.
4 1	>	3 9 9	41 > 399 since 4 > 3 ! (for character fields)

8-6-3 Do It Now

1. Using your particular system, determine whether digits are "less" than letters of the alphabet.

2. Determine the contents of the following variables. (Specify errors, if any.)

a.
```
READ X$,Y$,Z$
DATA 1,2,3
```
b.
```
READ X$,Y$,Z$
DATA "1,2,3"
```
c.
```
READ A$,B$
DATA A$,A$
```
d.
```
READ X,Y
DATA +34.,+2.
```
e.
```
READ A$,B$
DATA +34,-33
```
f.
```
READ B$,C$
DATA 1<3,.
```

3. Determine line numbers to which transfer will be made.

a.
```
1Ø G$ = "13Ø"
15 IF "14" > G$ THEN 4Ø
2Ø
```
b.
```
1Ø INPUT G$ (?1Ø)
15 IF G$ = 1Ø THEN 6Ø
2Ø
```
c.
```
1Ø READ N$
15 IF "TOM" > N$ THEN 6Ø
2Ø
8Ø DATA T,O,M
```
d.
```
1Ø INPUT A$ (?NO)
15 IF A$ = NO THEN 6Ø
2Ø
```

Answers

1. Most BASIC systems use the ASCII code to encode character data. Using the ASCII code, the digits 0 through 9 are "less" than the letters of the alphabet. If the EBCDIC code is used, the reverse is true. To find out which code is used on your system, type:

```
1Ø IF "A" > "1" THEN 25
15 PRINT "EBCDIC"
2Ø STOP
25 PRINT "ASCII"
STOP
```

2. a. X$ = 1; Y$ = 2; Z$ = 3
   b. X$ = 1 , 2 , 3; out of data
   c. A$ = A$; B$ = A$
   d. X = 34; Y = 2
   e. A$ = +34; B$ = −33
   f. B$ = 1<3; C$ = .

3. a. Transfer to 40.
   b. Invalid comparison; line 15 should be IF G$ = "10".
   c. Transfer to 60 since TOM > T.
   d. Invalid IF statement; line 15 should be IF A$ = "NO".

8-6-4 Character Strings and Arrays

Many BASIC systems do not allow the user to store character strings in arrays. To determine whether your system allows character arrays or not, type the following:

```
10 DIM A$(5)
15 A$(5) = "TOM"
20 PRINT A$(5)
RUN
TOM
```

If RUN is typed and a system error occurs at line 15, then you may *not* use arrays to store character strings on your system. If TOM is printed, your system supports character arrays.

If your system does not support character arrays, type the following code to make sure your system supports one-dimensional character strings:

```
10 DIM A$(5)
15 A$ = "TOM"
20 PRINT A$(3)
RUN
M
```

If RUN is typed and the third letter of the string (M) is printed, your system supports one-dimensional character strings.

Note that only *one* of the above features (or none) is supported by any one BASIC system. If your system does *not* support character arrays skip to section 8-6-8.

Character arrays are manipulated in the same way as numeric arrays; the maximum number of characters that each array entry can contain varies from 15 to 256 characters, depending on the BASIC system used. The following examples illustrate various uses of character arrays. Once again if your system does not support character arrays skip to section 8-6-8.

Example 1: A Computer Drill Program

Let us write the code to drill grade school students on addition, subtraction, multiplication, and division of numbers between 1 and 100. For division problems, the numbers should divide evenly. Random congratulatory messages should be printed whenever the student's response is correct; otherwise the student should keep working on the same problem. The output should be similar to the one shown in Figure 8-15.

To solve this problem, we store different congratulatory messages in the first four entries of array M$. Whenever the student's response is correct, we pick a ran-

■ **Figure 8–15** A computer drill program.

```
10 REM BASIC ARITHMETIC DRILL
12 REM DATA DICTIONARY
14 REM       M$: ARRAY CONTAINING CONGRATULATORY MESSAGES
16 REM       T$: ARRAY SPECIFYING ARITHMETIC OPERATIONS
18 REM       K : RANDOM NUMBER BETWEEN 1 AND 1ØØ
2Ø REM       L : RANDOM NUMBER BETWEEN 1 AND 1ØØ
22 REM       I : RANDOM NUMBER (1-4) SELECTS OPERATION
24 DIM M$(5), T$(5)
26 T$(1) = "+"
28 T$(2) = "-"
3Ø T$(3) = "X"
32 T$(4) = "/"
34 M$(1) = "FANTASTIC"
36 M$(2) = "UNBELIEVABLE"
38 M$(3) = "ELECTRIFYING"
4Ø M$(4) = "UNREAL"
42 K = INT(RND*1ØØ + 1)
44 L = INT(RND*1ØØ + 1)
46 I = INT(RND*4 + 1)
48 REM
5Ø IF I < > 4 THEN 6Ø
52     IF K/L = INT(K/L) THEN 6Ø
54         K = INT(RND*1ØØ + 1)
56         L = INT(RND*1ØØ + 1)
58         GOTO 52
6Ø PRINT "WHAT IS"; K; T$(I); L
62 INPUT A
64 ON I GOTO 7Ø, 74, 78
65 REM
66 IF K / L >< A THEN 6Ø
68 GOTO 8Ø
7Ø IF K + L <> A THEN 6Ø
72 GOTO 8Ø
74 IF K - L <> A THEN 6Ø
76 GOTO 8Ø
78 IF K * L <> A THEN 6Ø
8Ø PRINT M$(INT(RND*4 + 1))
82 INPUT "WANT TO STOP";N$
84 IF N$ = "NO" GOTO 42
86 END
RUN
WHAT IS 38 + 51
? 89
UNBELIEVABLE
WANT TO STOP? NO
WHAT IS 92 / 46
? 3
WHAT IS 92 / 46
? 2
ELECTRIFYING
WANT TO STOP? NO
WHAT IS 7Ø - 7
? 63
FANTASTIC
WANT TO STOP? NO
WHAT IS 18 / 2
? 9
UNREAL
WANT TO STOP? NO
WHAT IS 88 X 14
? 1232
UNBELIEVABLE
WANT TO STOP? YES
```

Array T$ contains arithmetic symbols.

Array M$ contains congratulatory messages.

The computer picks two random numbers between 1 and 100.
I identifies the operation:
1 = add; 2 = subtract; 3 = multiply; 4 = divide.

Check the numbers for division:
If the two numbers don't divide evenly,
keep picking K and L until they divide evenly.

Give user the arithmetic problem.
User answers.
If division, go to 66; go to 70, 74, or 78 for addition, subtraction, or multiplication respectively.
Numbers divided correctly? If not, repeat the question.
If correct, print congratulations.
Numbers added correctly?

Numbers subtracted correctly?

Numbers multiplied correctly?

Continue or stop?

dom number between 1 and 4 and print the corresponding congratulatory message (see line 80). For example, if the random number is 2, then M$(2) is printed (unbelievable!). Similarly, the array T$ is used to store the 4 arithmetic symbols for the 4 different types of operations that the student will be practicing with. A particular arithmetic operation is randomly selected through the statement T$(I) where I is a random number between 1 and 4 (see lines 46 and 60); I = 1 indicates addition, 2 is subtraction, 3 is multiplication, and 4 is division. The computer checks whether the student's answer is correct (line 66).

For division problems, the program makes sure that the two numbers divide evenly; if this is not the case, i.e., if the integer part of K divided by L is not equal to K/L, new random numbers K and L are chosen so that they do in fact divide evenly (lines 52–58). The program to solve this problem is shown in Figure 8–15.

Example 2: A File Update Program

Dr. X is an information science teacher. A file consisting of his students' names and the respective grades is stored in memory as follows:

Student	*Grade 1*	*Grade 2*	*Average*
BOILLOT	91	56	?
GLEASON	40	50	?
HORN	50	65	?
MONISH	70	70	?
.	.	.	.
.	.	.	.
.	.	.	.
XXX	0	0	

The last entry of the name table is XXX. Let us write the code to compute and store all students' averages in an array. The program should also allow Dr. X to correct his file in case grades are listed incorrectly. Grades can be changed as follows:

ENTER GRADE CHANGE? *student name, grade 1, grade 2*

If one of the student's does not need to be changed, enter a negative value for that grade. For example,

ENTER GRADE CHANGE? HORN −3, 44

means: replace Horn's second test score with 44.

If the name entered is not present in the name tables, an error message should be printed; Dr. X should then be allowed to retype the name.

Figure 8–16 displays the code used to solve this problem. First the names and respective grades are loaded into the arrays N$, G1, and G2. As these grades are read, their averages are computed and stored in the array A.

Transaction records are then entered one at a time. If the name entered does not exist in the name array (meaning that the FOR/NEXT loop at line 54 goes through its complete cycle), an error message is printed and Dr. X is given a chance to input the correct name. If there is a name match, either one or both scores are changed (lines 68 and 72) and the average is recalculated.

Figure 8–16 A grade change problem.

```
10 REM A GRADE CHANGE PROGRAM
14 REM      S$: ARRAY THAT STORES NAMES
16 REM      G1: ARRAY THAT STORES TEST1 GRADES
18 REM      G2: ARRAY THAT STORES TEST2 GRADES
20 REM      A:  ARRAY THAT STORES AVERAGE OF PAIRS OF GRADES
22 REM      I:  NUMBER OF RECORDS + 1
24 REM      N$: STUDENT NAME FOR WHICH GRADE CHANGE IS DESIRED
26 REM      S1: 1ST GRADE CHANGE (NEGATIVE IF NO CHANGE)
28 REM      S2: 2ND GRADE CHANGE (NEGATIVE IF NO CHANGE)
29 REM
30 DIM S$(90), G1(90), G2(90), A(90)
32 PRINT "PRESENT GRADES ARE"
34 I = 1
36 READ S$(I), G1(I), G2(I)
38 IF S$(I) = "XXX" THEN 48
40    A(I) = (G1(I) + G2(I))/2
42    PRINT S$(I),G1(I),G2(I),A(I)
44    I = I + 1
46    GOTO 36
48 PRINT "ENTER GRADE CHANGES";
50 INPUT N$, S1, S2
52 IF N$ = "FIN" THEN 78
54    FOR K = 1 TO I - 1
56          IF S$(K) = N$ THEN 66
58    NEXT K
60 PRINT "BAD NAME; REENTER NAME"
62 INPUT N$
64 GOTO 54
66 IF S1 < 0 THEN 70
68    G1(K) = S1
70 IF S2 < 0 THEN 74
72    G2(K) = S2
74    A(K) = (G1(K) + G2(K))/2
76 GOTO 48
78 PRINT
80 PRINT "*************************"
82 PRINT "GRADES AFTER CHANGES ARE"
84 FOR K = 1 TO I - 1
86 PRINT S$(K), G1(K), G2(K), A(K)
88 NEXT K
90 DATA BOILLOT, 91, 56
92 DATA GLEASON, 40, 50
94 DATA HORN   , 50, 65
96 DATA MONISH , 70, 70
98 DATA XXX    ,  0,  0
100 END
RUN
PRESENT GRADES ARE
BOILLOT         91          56          73.5
GLEASON         40          50          45
HORN            50          65          57.5
MONISH          70          70          70

ENTER GRADE CHANGES? GLEASON, 77, 60
ENTER GRADE CHANGES? HORN,    -1, 98
ENTER GRADE CHANGES? BULLIT,  40, 36
BAD NAME; REENTER NAME
? BOILLOT
ENTER GRADE CHANGES? FIN,      0, 0

*************************
GRADES AFTER CHANGES ARE
BOILLOT         40          36          38
GLEASON         77          60          68.5
HORN            50          98          74
MONISH          70          70          70
```

Annotations:

- Line 30: Assume fewer than 90 students.
- Line 34: Counts records, including trip.
- Line 36: Read name and two test scores.
- Line 40: Compute the average of the two scores.
- Line 42: Print the input data and the average.
- Line 44: Count the record.
- Line 50: Enter name and grade changes.
- Lines 52–58: Print final roster if no more changes, otherwise find the corresponding name of student in roster. K identifies the array position of the grade to be changed.
- Lines 60–64: If there is no match after the loop has gone through its complete cycle, the user should enter the correct name.
- Lines 66–68: If the first grade is negative, don't change it; otherwise change the first grade to its new value.
- Lines 70–72: If the second grade is negative, don't change it; otherwise change the second grade to its new value.
- Line 74: Compute new average.

8-6-5 Do It Now

1. Modify the program in Figure 8–15 to do the following:
   a. Print random messages if the student's answer is incorrect.
   b. If the student fails to get the right answer after three tries, the computer should print the correct answer and remember those particular exercises. At the conclusion of the session, the student is given another opportunity to try those exercises that he/she failed.
   c. Allow negative numbers in the arithmetic operations, i.e., allow for such combinations as $(-3) + 2$, $(-3) - (-4)$, or $2 + (-3)$.
2. Modify the program in Figure 8–16 so that:
   a. The name of a student could be changed (marriage situation).
   b. A student record could be deleted.
   c. A student record could be added.

8-6-6 String Processing

The following discussion applys *only* to BASIC systems supporting character string arrays. The functions LEFT$, MID$, and RIGHT$ allow you to examine or to extract portions of a string, while the function MID$ also allows you to change one or more characters within a string. Another function (represented by the symbol +) allows you to join or fuse two or more strings together. Finally, the function LEN enables you to count the number of characters within a string.

The RIGHT$, LEFT$, AND MID$ Functions

These functions allow you to access substrings within a particular string.

Example 1:

```
10 PRINT LEFT$("123456",3)
15 PRINT RIGHT$("654321",3)
20 PRINT MID$("123456",3,2)
```

Output

```
123
321
34
```

Example 2:

```
10 A$ = "RECTANGULAR"
15 B$ = MID$(A$,4,3)——————————→ TAN
20 C$ = RIGHT$(LEFT$(A$,6),3)———→ TAN
```

Note that MID$ can always be expressed as a combination of the RIGHT$ and LEFT$ functions.

Example 3:

Such functions may also be used with array entries:

```
10 DIM N$(5)
15 FOR I = 1 TO 5
20      READ N$(I)
30 NEXT I
35 FOR I = 5 TO 1 STEP -1
40      PRINT LEFT$(N$(I),1);
45 NEXT I
50 DATA OKUN,LAURA,LISA,ERIC,HALE
RUN
HELLO
```

The general forms for these functions are:

LEFT$(*string*,*n*)	Examine the first *n* characters of *string*.
RIGHT$(*string*,*n*)	Examine the last *n* characters of *string*.
MID$(*string*,*p*,*n*)	Examine *n* characters starting at position *p*.

where *string* is a string variable or a string constant,
n specifies the number of characters to process, and
p identifies the starting character position for the midportion string.

Note that LEFT$ and RIGHT$ may not appear to the left of the equal sign in a replacement statement, whereas the MID$ function can.

The MID$ function can be used very conveniently to extract substrings from within a particular string. Consider the following commonly carried out procedures:

1. To store the Ith character of A$ into X$, use X$ = MID(A$,I,1).
2. To select the substring of A$ from positions I to J and store it in Z$, use Z$ = MID$(A$,I,J − I + 1).

The MID$ function can also be used to replace characters in a string with other characters; the general form for this is

MID$(*string*,*p*,*n*) = Y$

The characters in *string*, beginning at position *p* are replaced by the first *n* characters in Y$ (or fewer than *n* if the length of Y$ is less than *n*). Note that regardless of the value of *n*, the size of *string* will remain the same, i.e., it cannot become larger than its original size.

Example:

```
10 B$ = "HAPPY  "
12 A$ = "I AM VERY UNHAPPY."
15 MID$(A$,11,7)= B$
20 PRINT A$
RUN
I AM VERY HAPPY  .
```

11th character (arrow points to the U of UNHAPPY)

Replace the first 7 characters starting at UNHAPPY (11th position) with first 7 characters of B$ (HAPPY*bb*).

```
10 B$ = "HAPPY"
RUN
I AM VERY HAPPYPY.
```

Since the length of B$ is only 5 characters, only 5 characters are moved into A$.

```
15 MID$(A$,13,9) = "IMPRESSED"
RUN
I AM VERY UNIMPRES
```

The original length of A$ is 18 characters, and the length cannot be changed; hence if we start at the 13th position of A$, we can only replace 6 characters.

The LEN Function

The length of a particular string can be determined by the LEN function.

Example:

```
10 X$ = "NEW ORLEANS, LA."
15 PRINT LEN(X$)
RUN
16
```

16 ← Number of characters in X$

Concatenation of Strings

To join strings together to form longer strings, you can "add" (concatenate) strings. Recall that strings cannot contain more than 256 characters (the limit may be lower on some systems). The symbol used to denote the concatenation operation is the plus sign (+).

Examples:

1. `A$ = "OVER" + "AND" + "OUT"`

A$

O	V	E	R	A	N	D	O	U	T

2. `R$ = "MR"`
   `N$ = "MRS"`
   `L$ = R$ + " AND " + N$`

L$

M	R		A	N	D		M	R	S

3. `B$ = "4" + "8"`

B$

4	8

4. `P$ = "LONG LIVE AMERICA"`
   `A$ = LEFT$(P$,10) + "FREEDOM"`

A$

L	O	N	G		L	I	V	E		F	R	E	E	D	O	M

5. Concatenation may be used to extract characters; a period in this example.

```
   A$ = "I QUIT. WE QUIT"
T$ = LEFT$(A$,6) + RIGHT$(A$,LEN(A$)-7)
```

T$ = | I | | Q | U | I | T | | W | E | | Q | U | I | T |

Programming Examples

Example 1:

Read a sentence. If the word MOUSE is present in the sentence, replace its first occurrence with the word MOLE. If the word MOUSE is not present, print an appropriate message.

Solution:

Suppose A$ contains the sentence, "THE LITTLE FURRY MOUSE HID IN THE TREE." Assuming MOUSE is not the first word of the sentence, we need to search the 39 characters (LEN(A$)) for the 7-character string | | M | O | U | S | E | |, | | M | O | U | S | E | . |, or any combination of MOUSE followed by a delineator such as a comma or exclamation point. We do not search for | M | O | U | S | E |, since this 5-character sequence could be part of another word (bemoused!). The search process could be carried out as follows:

```
[THE LIT]TLE FURRY MOUSE HID ...     The search starts in position 1.
T[HE LITT]LE FURRY MOUSE HID ...     then moves on to position 2
            .                        then to the third, fourth, fifth, posi-
              .                      tion, and so forth.
THE LITTLE FURRY[ MOUSE ]HID ...     The string is found starting at position
                                     17.
```

Having found the string, we need to create a new string consisting of the left-most 17 characters of A$, followed by the four characters MOLE, followed by the right-most 17 characters of A$, i.e., those at positions 23 through 39:

```
                  17    23              39 i.e., LEN(A$)
                   |     |               |
THE LITTLE FURRY□MOUSE□HID IN THE TREE.
\_______________/   |    \______________/
  17 characters     |     17 characters
        |           |           |
LEFT$(A$,17) + MOLE + RIGHT$(A$,LEN(A$) – 22)
```

When searching for | | M | O | U | S | E | | we should stop 6 characters away from the end of the sentence, i.e., our last chance to pick up | | M | O | U | S | E | . | is at position 33 (since 33 to 39 is 7 characters), hence the search should stop at position 34.

```
T H E   L I T T L E   F U R Y   M O U S E   H I D   I N   T H[E   T R E E .]
                                                              ^           ^
The search should stop at 34, or at LEN (A$) – 6 + 1.―――――――/     position 39
```

The complete code is:

```
10 INPUT A$
15 FOR I = 1 TO LEN(A$) - 6 + 1
20 IF MID$(A$,I,7) = " MOUSE " THEN 40
25 NEXT I
30 PRINT "CLEAR OF RODENTS"
35 STOP
40 A$ = LEFT$(A$,I) + "MOLE" + RIGHT$(A$, LEN(A$) - (I+6) + 1)
45 PRINT A$
50 END
```

6 last remaining characters

At this point other combinations such as " MOUSE," or " MOUSE." could be added.

```
RUN
? THE LITTLE FURRY MOUSE HID IN THE TREE.
THE LITTLE FURRY MOLE HID IN THE TREE.
RUN
? THE LITTLE FURRY MICE HID IN THE TREE.
CLEAR OF RODENTS
```

Note that if MOUSE is found, the index I of the FOR/NEXT loop points to the space character immediately to the left of the M:

I   I+6

THE LITTLE FURRY□MOUSE□HID IN THE TREE.

position 17   LEN(A$) − (I+6) + 1

In some systems with restrictions on size for character strings the CLEAR command may need to be used to allow for more space, for example CLEAR 200 would allow 200 positions for character strings.

Example 2:

Input a sentence and replace every occurrence of the article □A□ with the article THE.

Solution:

In this problem we need to search for the string □A□. A counter I is used to index each character of the sentence (up to LEN(A$) − 2) to determine whether the string □A□ starts at position I. If it does not, I is incremented by 1 and the process is repeated. If the string is found, the left-most I characters of the sentence are preserved. These I characters are then concatenated with the string "THE" and with the remaining right elements of the sentence. In the process, the original sentence grows by two characters. To reflect that change in size, both I and the LENgth of the sentence are incremented by 2.

The complete code is:

```
10 INPUT A$
12 L = LEN(A$) - 2
15 I = 1
20 IF MID$(A$,I,3)<> " A " THEN 40
25    A$ = LEFT$(A$,I) + "THE" + RIGHT$(A$, L-I+1)
30    I = I + 2
35    L = L + 2
40 I = I + 1
45 IF I <= L GOTO 20
50 PRINT A$

RUN
?  A DOG SAW A CAT AND A MOUSE IN A BARN; WHAT A SIGHT AND WHAT A FIGHT!
A DOG SAW THE CAT AND THE MOUSE IN THE BARN; WHAT THE SIGHT AND WHAT THE FIGHT!
```

Example 3:

An input file consists of an unknown number of records, where each record consists of a line of text. Write the code to compute the number of characters and words in the entire text file.

Solution:

Assume no word is hyphenated from one line to the next, and that punctuation characters are followed by one blank space to the right and preceded by non blank characters to the left, i.e., the word DOG could be any one of the following:

DOG.   DOG   DOG?   DOG,   DOG;   DOG!

A word is then a sequence of non-blank contiguous characters. If the word terminates with a punctuation symbol, the punctuation symbol is not counted as a character. One way to proceed is to analyze each character, one at a time, and ask if that character is a non-blank character. If it is a non-blank character, we determine whether the character that follows is a blank. If it is blank, then we have found a word. The program to solve this problem is shown as follows:

```
10 C=0                                  Count of characters
15 W=0                                  Count of words
20 READ A$                              Read a line of text
25      IF A$ = "/" THEN 75             If the end of the file has been reached
30 A$ = A$ + " "                        Add a blank to the string to count the
35 FOR I = 1 TO LEN(A$)                 last word in each line.
40    IF MID$(A$,I,1) = " " THEN 65
45       N$ = MID$(A$,I+1,1)
50       IF N$ = "." OR N$ = "," OR     Don't count the punctuation characters
            N$ = "?" OR N$ = ";" OR
            N$ = "!" GOTO 65
```

```
55           C = C + 1
60           IF N$ = " " THEN W = W + 1
65 NEXT I
70 GOTO 20
75 PRINT "# WORDS =";W, "# CHARACTERS =";C
80 DATA LITTLE JACK HORNER SAT IN A CORNER
85 DATA EATING A CHRISTMAS PIE; HE PUT IN
90 DATA HIS THUMB, AND PULLED OUT A PLUM,
95 DATA AND SAID, WHAT A GOOD BOY AM I!
100 DATA /
105 END
RUN
# WORDS = 29  # CHARACTERS = 101
```

If next character is blank count one more word.

8-6-7 Do It Now

1. Explain why the character A at the beginning of the sentence in the last program (example 2) did not get translated into THE. (*Hint*: Type the following code and analyze the output; to avoid problems, enclose string within quotation marks).

```
10 INPUT X$
15 PRINT X$
RUN
?ƀƀƀƀ THE
```

2. Determine what happens to A$ as a result of the following code:

```
10 INPUT A$
15 N = LEN(A$)
20 FOR I = 1 TO N/2
25     T$ = MID$(A$,I,1)
30     MID$(A$,I,1) = MID$(A$,N-I+1,1)
35     MID$(A$,N-I+1) =T$
40 NEXT I
45 PRINT A$
```

3. Read a sentence and determine the occurrence of the word IS by itself; then determine the occurrence of the characters IS, whether IS is part of a word or not.

4. Read a paragraph of text made up of a few short sentences. Write the code to determine the number of sentences. (Remember: a sentence finishes when a period, an exclamation point, or a question mark is encountered.)

8-6-8 One-Dimensional Character Strings

Many systems do not allow storage of character data in arrays. These systems, however, allow one-dimensional character strings that enable the user to operate on particular characters or subgroups of characters within the string itself. This feature is *not* available to systems supporting character arrays, at least not in the manner described in this section.

A one-dimensional character string can be used by assigning a string to a dimensioned character string variable. The name of a dimensioned character string variable must end with a $ and must be specified in the DIM statement. Lengths for strings can vary from 1 character to 256 characters and must be specified in the DIM statement.

Examples:

`5 DIM N$(30)`	Thirty characters are reserved for the string N$.
`10 LET N$ = "MARC "`	The first five characters of N$ are MARC followed by one blank.
`15 PRINT N$; "SIMS"`	"MARC SIMS" is printed.

The name of the above string is N$; an error would occur if N$(1) were used instead of N$. Even though N$ is dimensioned, it is *not* an array.

Reference to Characters within a String

Individual characters or substrings can be extracted from a string, as follows:

1. The variable A$ refers to the entire string. Its length is the length specified in the DIM statement.
2. The variable A$(I) refers to the set of characters from position I through the last one in the string.
3. The variable A$(I,J) refers to the segment of the string starting at position I up to and including the Jth position.

Consider the following example where the string A$ = 123456789 DOG.

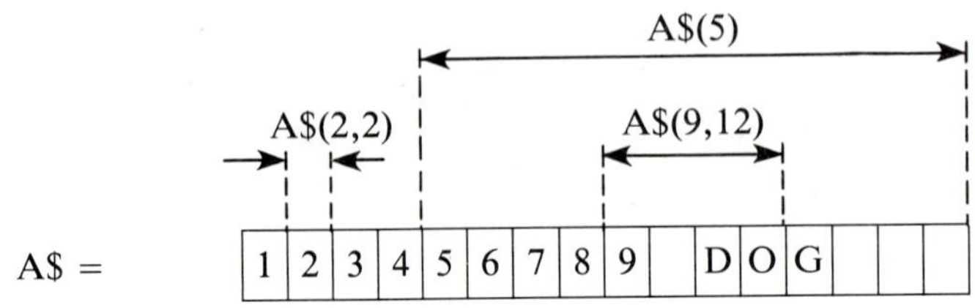


```
10 DIM A$(16)
15 LET A$="123456789 DOG"
20 PRINT A$
25 PRINT A$(5)
30 PRINT A$(9,12)
35 PRINT A$(2,2)
```

```
RUN
123456789 DOG      is printed.
    56789 DOG      is printed.
        9 DO       is printed.
2                  is printed.
```

Subscripts

Characters within a string can be accessed through subscripts. Consider the following example:

```
10 DIM A$(10)
15 A$ = "ABCDEFGHIJ"
20 FOR I = 2 TO 6
25     PRINT A$(I+2),A$(I-1,I+1)
30 NEXT I
RUN
```

Output

```
DEFGHIJ     ABC
EFGHIJ      BCD
FGHIJ       CDE
GHIJ        DEF
HIJ         EFG
```

A$(I + 2)   A$(I − 1,I + 1)

Concatenation of Strings

Different strings can be fused or joined together by using the concatenation operator, which is the comma (,).

Examples:

```
05 DIM A$(5), B$(5), C$(9)
10 LET A$ = "12345"
15 LET B$ = "ABCDE"
20 LET C$ = A$(3),"...",B$(3,5)
24 PRINT C$
25 END
RUN
345...CDE
```

Note concatenation symbol (,)

Comparison of Strings

Strings can be compared to each other as discussed in Section 8-6-2

Examples:

```
50 DIM A$(10), B$(10)
10 LET A$ = "BCDEFG"
15 LET B$ = "36 BCDEFGH"        Note the blank before the letter B.
20 IF A$ > B$ THEN 60           Transfer will occur; since B > 3.
30 IF A$ > B$(4) THEN 70        No transfer, since H > (blank).
40 IF A$(1,4) = B$(4,7) THEN 90 Transfer occurs; the substrings are equal.
```

Programming Examples

Example 1:

The function LEN can be used to determine the number of characters that have been assigned to a particular string. For example, if F$ = "NEW YORK", then LEN(F$) = 8. Consider the following example:

```
10 DIM A$(15)
15 FOR I = 1 TO 5
17 READ A$
20 PRINT A$," HAS ";LEN(A$);"CHARACTERS"
25 NEXT I
30 DATA I
35 DATA AM
40 DATA THE
45 DATA BEST
50 DATA I AM THE BEST
```

Output

```
I              HAS 1 CHARACTER
AM             HAS 2 CHARACTERS
THE            HAS 3 CHARACTERS
BEST           HAS 4 CHARACTERS
I AM THE BEST  HAS 13 CHARACTERS
```

Example 2:

Let us code the introductory section of a conversation between a program and a computer terminal user. The computer introduces itself, asks the user his/her first and last name, and then asks if the user wishes to be called by his/her first or last name.

```
05 DIM T$(31), F$(31), G$(31)
01 PRINT "MY NAME IS ZAN. WHAT'S YOUR FIRST AND LAST NAME"
15 INPUT T$
17 PRINT
20 FOR I = 1 TO LEN(T$)
25   IF T$(I,I) = " " THEN 34          Look for a blank to separate first from
30 NEXT I                              last name.
34 PRINT "WOULD YOU PREFER THAT ";
35 PRINT "I CALL YOU"; T$(1, I);       T$(1,I) is first name.
36 PRINT "OR M.";T$(I + 1, LEN(T$))    T$(I + 1, LEN(T$)) is last name.
40 INPUT F$                            F$ is either M. last name or preferred
45 PRINT "OK";F$                       name of respondent.
```

```
RUN
MY NAME IS ZAN. WHAT'S YOUR FIRST AND LAST NAME
? MICHEL EVANS
WOULD YOU PREFER THAT I CALL YOU MICHEL OR M. EVANS
? M. EVANS
OK M. EVANS
```

8-7 Know Your System Better

8-7-1 Features

The following BASIC commands and functions are available on most BASIC systems. You may wish to check your technical reference manual for more detailed information. Section 8–7–2 is left blank so that you can record your own system's features.

CLEAR This command/instruction sets all numeric variables to 0 and all string variables to the null (empty) string, i.e., there are no characters in the string, not even blanks!

CLEAR 100 All variables are cleared and strings can use up to 100 characters.

As you realize by now, the MID$, LEFT$ and RIGHT$ functions can be used only to manipulate character strings. You might want to manipulate numeric strings (signed numbers) in the same way, i.e., you might want to interchange 2 digits in a number or extract part of a number. To do these things, you would need the following functions:

**STR$** X$ = STR$(numeric expression)

X$ is now a string consisting of the characters present in the numeric expression

Example:

```
10 X = 14.3
15 A$ = STR$(X)
```

The string A$ consists of the characters `" 14.3"`

The leading blank in A$ is to allow for the sign of X.

VAL X = VAL(character string)

If the character string consists of numeric characters with or without the + or − symbols the value for X will be the signed numeric value of the character string; otherwise the value for X will be 0.

Example:

```
10 X = VAL("  -3")
```

X has now the numeric value −3

Notice that the VAL function strips leading blanks.

Examples:

1.
```
10 READ A$              Read an address "1301 NORTH 12TH AVE".
15 X$ = LEFT$(A$,4)     Pick up the number part "1301".
20 Y = VAL(X$)          Y is now the signed number 1301.
25 IF Y > 300 THEN 68   Since Y > 300, transfer is made to line 68.
```

Note that if we had compared X$ with "300", X$ would be less than "300" since "1301" < "300" (1 is less than 3).

2. Suppose X = 1423 and we wish to store the two middle digits in T.

```
10 X = 1423
15 A$ = STR$(X)           A$ = " 1423"
20 B$ = MID$(A$,2,2)      B$ = "42"
25 T = VAL(B$)            T = 42     T now contains the 2 middle digits of X.
```

**INKEY$** INKEY$ allows the user to interact with the computer during the execution of the program. Until now, once RUN was typed, the user could not interrupt the program and tell it to do something (except to terminate execution of the program by pressing a special key).

During execution of a program, the BASIC system always keeps track of the last key pressed by the user. It stores the character corresponding to the key pressed in a special memory location called the *keyhole*. If no key has been pressed, then the key-hold contains the null string, i.e., no characters. The null string in BASIC is identified by two consecutive quotation marks (""). The following action is taken by BASIC when the INKEY$ instruction is encountered in a program:

1. It makes the last character stored in the keyhole available to the user, i.e., the user can store that character (A$ = INKEY$), print it (PRINT INKEY$), compare it (IF INKEY$ ...), and so forth.
2. Then it immediately resets the keyhole to the null string, i.e., the original character is no longer present in INKEY$, i.e., in its place is the null character "".

Example 1:

Try the following code to see a shooting gun effect on your video screen!

```
10 PRINT INKEY$        Print the character in the keyhole
15 GOTO 10             and repeat the process.
RUN
```

While the program is executing, type one character. Since INKEY$ resets the keyhole character to a null string, you will not see a stream of identical characters scrolling on the screen. Instead, the character that you typed will move up from the lower left-hand corner of the screen at a very rapid speed, creating the illusion of a bullet shot from a gun. Let us explain, in slow motion, what happens: The character that was typed after RUN (for example, A) is displayed at the bottom left-hand corner of the screen as a result of the PRINT statement. When the GOTO 10 instruction is executed, the PRINT statement prints a blank line because INKEY$ resets the keyhole character to a null string. Hence the A moves up one line each time statement 10 is executed. If you type other characters or bursts of characters, they will also move up the screen and create an illusion of animation.

Try the above code with: 10 PRINT INKEY$, INKEY$, INKEY$

If line 10 is coded as 10 PRINT INKEY$; (note the semi colon), then the terminal functions as a word processing machine. Every time a key is depressed the corresponding character is displayed on the terminal. Pressing the RETURN/ENTER key causes the cursor to start on a new line while pressing the Backspace key causes the cursor to backspace and erase the character. When no key is pressed, the computer keeps printing the null symbol on the screen, which occupies no space.

Example 2:

Let us write a program to count either up by 1's or down by 1's.

During execution of the program the current counting process can be reversed simply by depressing any key, i.e., if the computer is counting up, you can get it to count down by pressing any key.

`10 K = 0`	Set the counter to 0.
`15 T = 1`	Start counting starting with 1 in ascending order.
`20 IF INKEY$ = "" THEN 30`	If the keyhole contains the null string, keep counting in the same order.
`25 T = -T`	If the user has pressed a key, reverse the counting order.
`30 K = K + T`	Count either up or down depending on whether T is 1 or − 1.
`33 PRINT K;`	Print the count.
`35 GOTO 20`	

After typing RUN, if you have not yet depressed a key, the INKEY$ at line 20 will be null, so line 30 will be executed and 1 will be printed. Since the keyhole is still null, the computer will keep on printing 2,3,4,5, ... until you press a key. At that point INKEY$ will not be null and T will become − 1, which means that the computer will decrement its count from now on. When you press another key, T will become 1 again and the counting up process will resume!

Try the following code to see if your fingers are fast enough to keep the numbers on the screen within the interval − 10 to + 10. If your fingers are very nimble, see if you can keep the numbers in the interval − 5 to + 5 (you will have to type very quickly!).

```
10 I = 1
15 I = I + 1
20 PRINT I
25 IF INKEY$ = "" THEN 15
30 I = I - 1
35 GOTO 25
```

8-7-2 Commands For My System

8-7-3 Do It Now

1. Try and determine what happens at run time if the following code is executed.

```
10 X = 0
20 A$ = INKEY$
30 IF A$ = "1" THEN 60
40 X = X + 1
50 GOTO 20
60 PRINT "X=";X
70 B$ = INKEY$
80 IF B$ = "A" THEN PRINT "STILL SUBTRACTING"
90 X = X - 1
100 IF B$ = "K" THEN 130
110 IF B$ = "S" THEN STOP
120 GOTO 70
130 PRINT "X=";X
140 GOTO 10
```

2. Using a vicious loop, write the code to count from 1 to infinity in steps of 1 and display the count. During execution, the user should be able to type a C to stop, R to continue counting or Q to quit (stop the program).

8-8 Assignments

8-8-1 Test Yourself

1. Which of the following are valid DIM statements? (Assume there are line numbers.)

a. `DIM A(3.2)`

b. `DIM A(1)`

c. `DIM (3*I)`

d. `DIM A(31), DIM B(32)`

e.
```
DIM X(3)
DIM Y(1)
DIM Z(N)
```

2. In terms of memory storage, what is the difference between the three variables X1, X2, and X3, compared to the three variables X(1), X(2), and X(3)?

3. **True or false**
   a. If K = 3 and L = 3, then G(K) = G(L).
   b. If X(I) = X(J), then I = J.
   c. If X(2 + 1) = 4 then it is always true that X(2) + X(1) = 4
   d. If K is the location (position) of the largest value in array X, then X(K) is the largest value.
   e. Given DIM A(20), the instruction READ A will read a value into A(1).
   f. X(A(31)) is a valid subscripted variable.
   g. T(7) = "BOY" is a valid replacement statement.

4. If G is the following array consisting of 5 entries

1.4	3	−4	1.	3.

which of the following are valid statements? If valid, specify the resulting values.

a.
```
L = G(1)
```
b.
```
L = 2
L = G(G(L))
```
c.
```
K = 1
G(K) = G(K) + 1
```
d.
```
K = -2
K = G(K^2-1) + K^2
```
e.
```
L = 2
G(2*L) = "HELLO"
```
f.
```
G(3) = G(2)/G(I)
```

5. Identify the contents of both arrays A and B (size 5) as a result of the code below. Use the following DATA file: DATA 1,2,3,4,5,6,7,8,9,10,11, 12

a.
```
10 FOR I = 1 TO 4
15     READ A(I),A(I+1),B(I)
20 NEXT I
```
b.
```
10 FOR I = 5 TO 1 STEP -1
15     READ A(I)
20 NEXT I
25 FOR J = 1 TO 5 STEP 2
30     READ B(J)
35 NEXT J
```
c.
```
10 FOR I = 1 TO 3
15     READ A(I)
20     FOR J = 1 TO 2
25         READ B(J)
30     NEXT J
35 NEXT I
```

6. Given a table A of size 100, write the code to generate the following output:

a.

A_1	A_2
A_3	A_4
A_5	A_6
.	.
.	.
.	.
A_{99}	A_{100}

b.

A_1	A_{51}
A_2	A_{52}
A_3	A_{53}
.	.
.	.
.	.
A_{50}	A_{100}

c.

1	A_{100}
2	A_{99}
3	A_{98}
.	.
.	.
.	.
100	A_1

d.

A_2
A_4
A_6
.
.
.
A_{100}
$A_1\ A_2\ A_3\ \ldots\ A_9\ A_{10}$
$A_{11}A_{12}A_{13}\ \ldots\ A_{19}A_{20}$
.
.
.
$A_{91}A_{92}A_{93}\ \ldots\ A_{99}A_{100}$

7. Array S contains 100 different employee numbers. Write the code to determine whether T, which is also an employee number, matches any number in array S. Print either of the following messages: "MATCH" or "NO MATCH". Initialize array S with 100 three-digit employee numbers. (Use random number function.)

8. A DATA statement contains at least 51 numbers. Write the code to read the first 20 numbers in array A, the next 30 in array B, and the remainder in array C. Assume that there are no more than 150 numbers and that the last number is 0 and all other numbers are non zero.

9. An input file consists of an unknown number of grades (maximum 100). Write a program to compute the number of grades less than the average. Print all the grades and the count of grades less than the average. Assume there is a negative trip record at the end of the file.

10. Array A (10 elements) contains 10 entries and array B contains 16 elements. The array elements are integers between 1 and 100. Write the code to print the elements that occur in both arrays and the number of identical elements. For example:

A: | 3 | 5 | 3 | 7 | 9 |

B: | 5 | 3 | 7 | 3 | 8 |

Output

3 5 7

11. Load an array A with 20 random integers between 1 and 20. Then write the code to obtain a frequency distribution of the numbers in array A. The output should list the numbers in ascending order and their corresponding frequency, as follows:

NUMBERS	1	3	4	5	10	12	13	14	15	17	18	19
FREQUENCY	1	4	2	1	1	1	2	2	1	2	2	1

12. Determine whether an array that has 10 numbers (not necessarily integers) has any two equal entries.

13. Assume table A consists of 11 entries, the first 10 of which contain numbers arranged in ascending sequence. Read a number X and insert it in its proper position in table A. For example, if X = 23 and table A is

10	20	30	40	50	60	70	80	90	95	

then the new table is

10	20	23	30	34	50	60	70	80	90	95

8-8-2 Exercises

1. Read in a maximum of 15 account numbers and corresponding amounts deposited (each DATA statement will consist of an account number and an amount deposited) and write the code to:
   a. Print all the account numbers of persons who have deposited $50,000 or more.
   b. *Then* print all the account numbers of persons who have deposited between $10,000 and $50,000.

2. a. At the end of each month, members of the U-WATCH-UR-WEIGHT club are weighed in. Each member's name and initial and terminal weights for the month are recorded on a separate DATA statement. The very first DATA statement has the exact number of club members whose weights are recorded on the following DATA statements. Write a program to print each member's name, his/her initial and terminal weights, and weight loss. Also print the average weight loss for the group and the number of members whose weight loss was greater than average. For example, the output might be:

```
                INITIAL  TERMINAL       WEIGHT
NAME            WEIGHT    WEIGHT         LOSS

HUBIT            200        180           20
MARSINI          130        120           10
TODINI           160        154            6

AVERAGE WEIGHT LOSS IS 12 POUNDS
1 MEMBER HAS A WEIGHT LOSS OVER 12 POUNDS
```

   b. Modify the program in part a so that an "*" is printed beside the name of each member whose weight loss was above average. Also print the names of these people in a list.

3. Input a random number between 1 and 10, and let the computer guess it randomly. The computer should not guess the same number twice.

4. An encyclopedia company has hired salespersons (20 at most). The name of each salesperson and the number of encyclopedia sets each has sold are recorded on separate DATA statements. Each salesperson gets paid $90.00 for each set sold, as well as $15.00 extra for each set (and fraction) sold over the average. For example if the average is 5.8 and 8 sets have been sold, the salesperson gets paid a bonus for the 3 sets over the average (2.2 becomes 3). Write a program to produce the names of the salespeople, the number of sets sold, and amount earned. Print the name of the person who has sold a number of sets closest to the average number of sets sold.

5. Klinkon Headquarters has received personnel secrets for the spaceship Renderprize from two of its spies.

The First Spy Reports		*The Second Spy Reports*	
Number	Name	Number	Title
455-30-1980	Kiik	465-29-9136	Engineer
465-29-9136	Skolly	432-98-2316	Navigator
408-32-6166	Spark	446-66-2366	Navigator
432-98-2316	Thekov	433-27-8107	Doctor
492-38-7213	Uhula	455-30-1980	Captain
433-27-8107	Mc Joy	408-32-6166	First Officer
446-66-2366	Lusu	492-38-7213	Communications

As a Klinkon programmer, your job is to program the computer to match up crew member names with their titles. (Star Fleet Command has evidence that when Klinkon programmers make syntax errors, they mysteriously disappear!)

Write the code to produce a list of personnel numbers with the corresponding names and titles:

```
455-30-1980        KIIK        CAPTAIN
465-29-9136        SKOLLY      ENGINEER
     .               .            .
     .               .            .
446-66-2366        LUSU        NAVIGATOR
```

6. An input file consists of many packets of scores, each terminated by a negative number. Write a program to compute the average of each packet and the overall average of all scores. Print the number of all scores below the overall average assume no more than 100 scores altogether; for example:

Input

```
DATA 10,20,30,-4
DATA 30,40,50,60,70,-2
DATA 50,60,70,-4
```

Output

```
SET 1:   10 20 30             AVG = 20
SET 2:   30 40 50 60 70       AVG = 50
SET 3:   50 60 70             AVG = 60
TOTAL SET 10 20 30 30 40 50 60 70 50 60 70 AVG = 44.5
NUMBER OF SCORES BELOW 44.5 = 5
```

7. A table contains 27 numbers that can be either positive or negative. Write a program to print the positive numbers and the negative numbers 4 per line as follows:

```
-14 -12 -34 -56
 -2  -6 -45 -67
        .
        .
        .
-34 -23

12 56 90 21
56 89  6  4
     .
     .
     .
78
```

Don't print the positive numbers if none exist; do the same for the negative numbers.

8. Write the code to produce the following multiplication tables:

1 × 1 = 1	2 × 1 = 2	3 × 1 = 3	4 × 1 = 4	5 × 1 = 5	6 × 1 = 6	7 × 1 = 7	8 × 1 = 8
1 × 2 = 2	2 × 2 = 4	3 × 2 = 6	4 × 2 = 8	5 × 2 = 10	6 × 2 = 12	7 × 2 = 14	8 × 2 = 16
1 × 3 = 3	2 × 3 = 6	3 × 3 = 9	4 × 3 = 12	5 × 3 = 15	6 × 3 = 18	7 × 3 = 21	8 × 3 = 24
1 × 4 = 4	2 × 4 = 8	3 × 4 = 12	4 × 4 = 16	5 × 4 = 20	6 × 4 = 24	7 × 4 = 28	8 × 4 = 32
1 × 5 = 5	2 × 5 = 10	3 × 5 = 15	4 × 5 = 20	5 × 5 = 25	6 × 5 = 30	7 × 5 = 35	8 × 5 = 40
1 × 6 = 6	2 × 6 = 12	3 × 6 = 18	4 × 6 = 24	5 × 6 = 30	6 × 6 = 36	7 × 6 = 42	8 × 6 = 48

9. Using the schedule shown below, write a program to read an adjusted gross income and compute and print the amount of tax owed.

Not over \$3,400	No tax.
Over \$3,400 but not over \$5,500	14% of excess over \$3,400
Over \$5,500 but not over \$7,600	\$294, plus 16% of excess over \$5,500
Over\$7,600 but not over \$11,900.	\$630, plus 18% of excess over \$7,600
Over \$11,900 but not over \$16,000. . . .	\$1,404, plus 21% of excess over \$11,900
Over \$16,000 but not over \$20,200. . . .	\$2,265, plus 24% of excess over \$16,000
Over \$20,200 but not over \$24,600. . . .	\$3,273, plus 28% of excess over \$20,200
Over \$24,600 but not over \$29,900. . . .	\$4,505, plus 32% of excess over \$24,600
Over \$29,900 but not over \$35,200. . . .	\$6,201, plus 37% of excess over \$29,900
Over \$35,200 but not over \$45,800. . . .	\$8,162, plus 43% of excess over \$35,200
Over \$45,800 but not over \$60,000. . . .	\$12,720, plus 49% of excess over \$45,800
Over \$60,000 but not over \$85,600. . . .	\$19,678, plus 54% of excess over \$60,000
Over \$85,600 but not over \$109,400. . . .	\$33,502, plus 59% of excess over \$85,600
Over \$109,400 but not over \$162,400 . . .	\$47,544, plus 64% of excess over \$109,400
Over \$162,400 but not over \$215,400 . . .	\$81,464, plus 68% of excess over \$162,400
Over \$215,400	\$117,504, plus 70% of excess over \$215,400

#10

10. The following integers have been recorded on a DATA statement:

36, 27, 43, 18, 5, 6, 9, 33, 45, 34, 22, 42

Read these numbers into an array and write a program to accomplish the following:

a. Compute the average (mean) of these 12 numbers, rounded to the nearest whole number.

b. Compute the difference between each of these 12 numbers and the mean (subtract the mean from the number) and store each of these deviations in an array.

c. Determine which of the 12 numbers deviates the most from the mean (this corresponds to the deviation having the largest absolute value); print that number (not its deviation).

The output should be as follows:

```
ARRAY     DEVIATION

 36           6
 27          -3
 43          13
  .           .
  .           .
  .           .
 42           8

NUMBER DEVIATING MOST FROM MEAN IS 5
```

11. Professor X records her final grades as follows: The first data item N (N<20) in the record identifies the number of grades for her entire class. N is followed by N grades on the same record. Write a program to produce a grade frequency report. A sample input and output are shown below:

```
DATA 9,  80, 80, 20, 25, 20, 80, 79, 64, 64
```

N < 20 (the first item, 9); N grades (the items that follow)

```
GRADES   COUNT
  20       2
  25       1
  64       2
  79       1
  80       3
```

12. To be admitted to the MENSA club, candidates must score a minimum of 74 points on an intelligence test. Each candidate's name and test score are recorded as shown below. (There are no more than 50 candidates). Write a program to read the input file and produce the following information:

- Two separate paragraph listings of names of successful and unsuccessful candidates. Each line should contain four names.
- Two consecutive vertical listings of names and scores of successful and unsuccessful candidates (one name and corresponding score per line). The input and output will look like:

Input

```
DATA ADAMS,  74
DATA PENSKE, 81
DATA LOUD,   56
DATA MICHEL, 90
DATA LAZY,   48
DATA MILLS,  44
.
.
.
DATA ANTONE, 75
DATA MONISH, 46
```

```
SUCCESSFUL CANDIDATES

ADAMS   PENSKE   MICHEL   SALAAM
JONES   CLARK    WILLS    BROWN
EMMA    BRYARS   ANTONE

UNSUCCESSFUL CANDIDATES

LOUD    LAZY     MILLS    GAMBINO
BOILLOT MONISH

RESULTS NAMES    SCORES

PASSING ADAMS     74
        PENSKE    81
        MICHEL    9Ø
          .
          .
          .
        ANTONE    75

FAILING LOUD      56
        LAZY      48
        MILLS     44
          .
          .
          .
        MONISH    46
```

13. At the Kilpatrick Community College, General Mathematics MS 101 has always been offered in the traditional teacher/lecture format. This year, for the first time, students may take MS 101 using a self-paced approach to instruction through a computer-assisted instructional method (CAI). Because of the novelty of the CAI approach, the mathematics faculty has formulated the following policies concerning grades and tests for those taking MS 101 in the CAI mode.

a. Students may take one, or two, or three tests during the semester.

b. The final score is based on the student's average score, scaled as follows: If the CAI class average (AV) is less than 80 (the standardized average for traditional teacher/lecture form), then the difference 80 − AV should be added to each student's average score; otherwise, the difference AV − 80 is subtracted from each student average. The input data is formatted as follows:

```
DATA ______________, _____, ____, [________], [________]
```

Name: Last, initial — Number of tests taken (1–3) — One, two, or three test scores

Write a program to produce the following score information. For example, the following input data would produce the output data shown:

Input

```
DATA BOILLOT M,1,9Ø.5
DATA HORN L,    2,86,89
DATA GLEASON G,3,6Ø,8Ø,1ØØ
```

Output

```
STUDENT NAME  AVERAGE          SCALED AVERAGE

BOILLOT M.      9Ø.5              84.5
HORN L.         87.5              81.5
GLEASON G.      8Ø.Ø              74.Ø

AVERAGE 86.Ø
```

14. The department of psychology offers a maximum of ten sections of introduction to psychology. Each section contains no more than 25 students. At the end of the semester, final grades for each section are recorded as follows:

Input

```
DATA 3, 6Ø,8Ø,7Ø
DATA 1, 45
DATA 4, 5Ø,6Ø,7Ø,8Ø
  .
  .
  .
```

Number of final grades in each section

Output

```
                                AVERAGE
CLASS 1  6Ø 8Ø 7Ø                 7Ø
CLASS 2  45                       45
CLASS 3  5Ø 6Ø 7Ø 8Ø              65
```

a. Write a program to produce this output.
b. Write a program to produce the following output for averages.

```
CLASS1    CLASS2    CLASS3 ...    CLASS?
  7Ø        45        65            ?
```

Note that there might be fewer than ten classes.

15. a. Input a value for N and draw the following axis graduated in units of 5:

```
If N = 31    ----5----Ø----5----Ø----5----Ø
If N =  7    ----5--
If N =  3    ----
```

b. The Triple Star Corporation has its sales (expressed in millions) for the last 10 years recorded on a DATA statement. These figures lie between 0 and 70 (millions), for example, DATA 13, 22, 19, 30, ... Write a program to produce an output similar to the following:

```
1975
*************
1976
**********************
1977
*******************
1978
******************************
1979
***********************************
198Ø
**************************
1981
***************************************
1982
****************************************
1983
***********************
1984
****************************
+----+----+----+----+----+----+----+----
Ø    5    1Ø   15   2Ø   25   3Ø   35
```

Make sure the program prints the last unit line (+----+----+----) and the gradations 0,5,10,15,.... These gradations should not go beyond the maximum sales figure (1982 salesfigure in the above example).

16. a. Initialize the three following arrays (PART NUMBER, QUANTITY, AND COST/PART) to the values indicated. (Generate these values internally.)

Part Number	*Quantity*	*Cost/Part*
115	50	90
120	60	91
125	70	83
130	80	93
.	.	.
.	.	.
.	.	.
160	140	99

For example, there are 50 of item 115 at a cost of 90 cents each. During the day, sales transactions are recorded on DATA statements as follows:

DATA __________ , __________
Part number Quantity sold

(The transactions can be simulated by a random number generator.)

b. Write a program to read the day's transaction, produce a parts inventory, print a "reorder" message whenever fewer than 20 items are in stock, and discount the price of any part for which there were no sales, by 10% of the original cost (rounded to the nearest penny).
The inventory report, for example, might be drawn as follows:

```
PART                    NUMBER
NUMBER      STOCK        SOLD       COST/PART
 115          40          10           90
 120           0          60           91          **REORDER**
 125          70           0           83            DISCOUNT
 130           5          75           93          **REORDER**
  .            .           .            .
  .            .           .            .
  .            .           .            .
 160          70          70           99
```

c. If a parts number is incorrectly recorded in the transaction data file, generate the same report as in part b with a list of the incorrect part numbers following the inventory report. For example:

```
PART NUMBER        STOCK       NUMBER SOLD        COST/PART
    115              40           10                  90
     .                .            .                   .
     .                .            .                   .
     .                .            .                   .
    160              70           70                  99
117***NO SUCH EXISTING PART. CHECK RECORD***
126***NO SUCH EXISTING PART. CHECK RECORD***
```

d. To prepare for the following day, recreate a new inventory file by deleting all part numbers with exhausted stock and print the new inventory table as follows:

```
PART NUMBER        QUANTITY         COST/PART
    115               40               90  <---- Note absence of part
    125               70               83        number 120.
    130                5               93
     .                 .                .
     .                 .                .
     .                 .                .
    160               70               99
```

e. During the day, a parts salesperson persuades the manager to add three new parts to the current line. These parts have numbers between 100 and 170, different from those already in stock. The manager decides to purchase 300 of each of the new parts. Read three records with new part numbers and corresponding costs, and produce a new inventory table by inserting the new records in their appropriate ascending position in the file:

```
PART NUMBER     QUANTITY     COST/PART
    100            300           60
    115             40           90
    125             70           83
    130              5           93
    132            300           95
     :              :             :
```

Note new inserts.

17. The Meals on Wheels Company operates a fleet of vans used for the delivery of cold foods at various local plants and construction sites. The management is thinking of purchasing a specially built $18,000 van equipped to deliver hot foods. This new addition to the fleet is expected to generate after-tax earnings E_1, E_2, ..., E_6 (as displayed below) over the next six years, at which time the van's resale value will be zero. Projected repair and maintenance costs C_0, C_1, C_2, ..., C_6 over the six years are shown below.

Projected Earnings		*Projected Costs*		
E_1	$2,500	C_0	$18,000	(purchase cost of the van)
E_2	2,500	C_1	1,000	
E_3	3,000	C_2	1,500	
E_4	4,500	C_3	2,000	
E_5	6,000	C_4	2,000	
E_6	6,000	C_5	2,100	
		C_6	2,400	

The decision to purchase the van depends on the benefit/cost ratio (BCR) (grossly speaking, earnings/expenditures) given by the formula

$$\text{BCR} = \frac{E_1(1+i)^6 + E_2(1+i)^5 + \ldots + E_6(1+i)^1}{C_0 + C_1(1+i)^6 + C_2(1+i)^5 + \ldots + C_6(1+i)^1}$$

where i is the rate of investment of earnings by the company. If BCR > 1, then the company should acquire the van. Write a program to determine how high the investment rate (i) would have to be raised to permit the purchase of the vehicle. Write a program to compute the BCR for investment rates starting at 6% and increasing by amounts of 0.1%. The output should be as follows:

```
BENEFIT/COST RATIO          INVESTMENT RATE
        .                        6.0
        .                        6.1
        .                         .
        .                         .
        .                         .
```

Stop when the BCR is greater than 1 and print the following message:

```
PURCHASE OF VAN REQUIRES INVESTMENT RATE OF XX.XX.
```

18. Write a program to read an unknown number of grades ($n < 100$) and calculate the standard deviation of these n grades using the following formula:

$$sd = \sqrt{\frac{(x_1 - x)^2 + (x_2 - x)^2 + (x_3 - x)^2 + \ldots + (x_n - x)^2}{n - 1}}$$

where n = number of grades;
x = average of grades;
$x_1, x_2, x_3 \ldots, x_n$ are the grades.

19. Wrap-around sales averaging. The management at Food Stores, Inc., likes to compare their monthly sales with a running average of their sales for the preceding 11 months. Write a program to read sales data for the preceding 11 months (Jan. to Nov. '83) and read "dummy" sales projections for the next 12 months (Dec. '83 through Nov. '84). Then compute the 11-month running average for Dec. '83 through Nov. '84. The process can be visualized as follows:

Jan.–Nov. 1983											Dec. '83–Nov. '84								Running Average for Preceding 11 Months
J	F	M	A	M	J	J	A	S	O	N	D	J	F	M	A	M	. .	N	
10	11	12	10	11	14	10	11	12	11	12	13								11.27
	11	12	10	11	14	10	11	12	11	12	13	16							11.50
		12	10	11	14	10	11	12	11	12	13	16	11						11.50
			10	11	14	10	11	12	11	12	13	16	11	13					11.63
						.					.								.
						.					.								.
						.					.								.

For the month of December, for example, management will compare the December volume (13) with the running average of the 11 previous months, 11.27 which is (10 + 11 + 12 + 10 + 11 + 14 + 10 + 11 + 12 + 11 + 12)/11.
The output should be similar to:

```
                11-MONTH RUNNING
MONTHS           AVERAGE      MONTH'S SALES

DECEMBER          11.27            13
JANUARY           11.50            16
FEBRUARY          11.50            11
MARCH             11.63            13
   .                .               .
   .                .               .
```

20. For each student in a class, you have one DATA statement with his/her name and 10 test scores. The student's average is based on his/her nine best scores. Write a program to produce an output similar to the following:

```
                GRADE REPORT

NAME: WOODRUFF      AVERAGE = 60
TESTS: 10, 20, 30, 40, 50, 60, 70, 80, 90, 100
NAME: ZIEGLER       AVERAGE = 58.9
TESTS: 100, 50, 60, 40, 35, 65, 80, 20, 30, 70
```

21. The language department at Johns College offers five courses and is now registering students. Each student completes a form with his/her name and one course number. More than one course can be taken by the same student, in which case the student fills out different forms. The list of courses, the maximum enrollment per class, and the room number in which each class meets are described as follows:

Course	*Size*	*Room No.*	*Input*
FRE 110	5	204	`DATA ADAMS, FRE 110`
FRE 120	10	200	`DATA BEVIS, GER 100`
GER 100	6	100	`DATA ADAMS, FRE 120`
SPN 100	10	212	`DATA ADAMS, SPN 100`
SPN 105	15	220	`DATA KERR,  SPN 105`

a. Each record of the input file consists of a student name and a course number. Write a program to read this file and provide the following enrollment information:

```
COURSE      ROOM NO.     ENROLLMENT     MAX ENROLLMENT

FRE 110       204            5                5
FRE 120       200            6               10
   .
   .
   .
SPN 105       220            4               15
```

If a course is filled up, either identify that course by placing an asterisk next to the maximum enrollment figure or list the students who could not enroll.

b. At the conclusion of the enrollment procedure, the department head would like to inquire directly in the data base above to obtain one of the following:

	Query Code	*Data*
a. A list of student names in any particular course:	1	Course number
b. A list of courses taken by a particular student:	2	Student name
c. An actual class size for a particular room:	3	Room number
d. To stop the inquiry process:	4	

For example, the following set of queries would produce the following output (perform input validation on all fields):

inquiries

```
? 1, FRE 12Ø
                    COURSE; FRE 12Ø
                         ADAMS
                         SPRING
                           .
                           .
? 2, ADAMS
                    LIST OF COURSES TAKEN BY ADAMS
                               FRE 11Ø
                               FRE 12Ø
                               SPN 1ØØ
? 3, 2ØØ
                    ** INCORRECT ROOM NUMBER 413 **
? 3, 2ØØ
                    NUMBER STUDENTS IN 2ØØ IS 8
? 4
```

Write a program to input the query information and output the requested information. Another option for inquiries, instead of numerical codes is for the computer to display a menu of inquiries.

22. Systems planning involves estimating development time and projecting costs associated with the completion of a particular task. An example might be planning the construction of a house. A typical list of tasks and a time schedule might be:

Sequence of Events	*Task Description*	*Time in Days*
1	Laying of foundation	15
2	Plumbing installment	12
3	Frame and roof	20
4	Electrical work	7
5	Plastering	4
6	Carpentry	7
7	Landscaping	3

Write a program to produce a bar graph like the following one to represent the duration of each task.

Tasks

```
1    ***************
2                   ************
3                               ********************
4                                                   *******
5                                                          ****
6                                                              *******
7                                                                     ***
     --------------------------------------------------------------------
     ØØØØØØØØØ11111111112222222222333333333344444444445555555555666666666
     12345678901234567890123456789Ø1234567890123456789012345678901234567 8
```

Time duration segments

23. An input file consists of an unknown number of grades in random order. Compute and print the median. The median is the score that divides a distribution of scores into two equal parts. For example,

10, 30, 87, 12	The median is (12 + 30)/2 = 21. (Half are above 21, half are below 21.)
53, 16, 99	The median is 53. (Half are above 53, half are below 53.)

24. Write a program to record in an array P the relative ascending order position of each element of array A. For example, if

array A = | 51 | 20 | 90 | 80 | 100 | then array P = | 2 | 1 | 4 | 3 | 5 |

This means that:

1 is stored in P(2), to indicate that the second element of A (20) is the smallest.
2 is stored in P(1), to indicate that the first element of A (51) is the next-to-smallest.

.
.
.

5 is stored in P(5), to indicate that the fifth element of A (100) is the largest.

The following code would then print the elements of A in ascending numerical sequence

```
5 FOR I = 1 TO 5
6     PRINT A(P(I));
7 NEXT I
```

In what programming situation would the above sort algorithm be preferable to the bubble or mini/max sorts?

25. You work for the National Weather Service. They are going to test changes in wind direction by sending up three balloons on each of five different days. Each of the 15 balloons is assigned a unique identification number (ID) between 100 and 999 inclusive (in no particular order). One balloon is released in the morning, one is released at noon, and one is released in the evening on each of the five days. When the balloons are returned, the ID number, day sent up (1,2,3,4, or 5), the distance traveled will be recorded on one DATA statement per balloon. Write a program to:
    a. Read the data into three separate arrays (ID, day, and distance).
    b. Sort the arrays in ascending order by ID.
    c. Print the sorted arrays, with one ID and corresponding day and distance on each output line.
    d. Find the maximum distance traveled for each day (five maximums); print the ID, day, and maximum distance for each of the five days (print the results for the first day, then the second, third, and so forth).
    e. Find the average distance traveled by balloons released on the *first and fifth days combined.*

    Input: 15 DATA statements (each with an ID, day, and distance traveled)

    Output 15 printed lines of sorted ID's and corresponding days and distances (ID, day, distance)
    5 printed lines of maximum distances for each day (1 thru 5) (ID, day, distance)

1 printed line of the average distance traveled on the first and fifth days

Test Data:						
123	2	143.7		729	2	726.1
269	3	976.4		833	4	433.1
120	1	370.2		621	3	962.4
460	5	980.8		143	4	714.3
111	1	111.3		972	5	320.1
986	4	1,320.6		410	5	820.4
629	3	787.0		511	1	1,240.0
531	2	429.2				

26. The BOISUPP company employs a variable number of salespersons. Records of sales by each salesperson are recorded on DATA statements, which are sorted in ascending order by salesperson number but are not arranged by date. For example, a typical data file might look like this:

```
DATA   JOHN DOE,       111,   Ø11784,   6ØØ.ØØ
DATA   JOHN DOE,       111,   Ø11584,   1ØØ.ØØ
DATA   MARY SMITH,     212,   Ø11584,   15Ø.ØØ
DATA   JAMES BROWN,    314,   Ø11984,    5Ø.ØØ
```

Salesperson name — Salesperson number — Date of sales — Amount of sales

The management wants to print out a monthly sales report to summarize the total sales for each salesperson and the total amount of all sales. Also, a sales-person-of-the-month award will to go the salesperson with highest sales for the month. Entries are to be listed in ascending order by salesperson number. Arrange the output in the following form:

```
SALESPERSON                  DATE OF      SALES       SUBTOTAL
NAME            NUMBER        SALES       AMOUNT        SALES

JOHN DOE          111       Ø1 15 84     15Ø.ØØ
                            Ø1 17 84      5Ø.ØØ        2ØØ.ØØ
MARY SMITH       212        Ø1 15 84     1ØØ.ØØ        1ØØ.ØØ
JAMES BROWN      314        Ø1 19 84     4ØØ.ØØ        4ØØ.ØØ

TOTAL SALES                                            7ØØ.ØØ
**AWARD GOES TO JAMES BROWN**
```

Write a program to read a transaction file and produce a summary report like the one shown. Be sure that you include more than one transaction for some of the salespersons and note that in such a case you print the number of the salesperson only once.

27. Read a three-digit number, N, and store each individual digit of N in three consecutive array locations. For example, if N = 193, then J(3) = 1, J(2) = 9, J(1) = 3. (Hint: Divide N by 100 to get J(3) = 1, then divide N − J(3)*100 (93) by 10 to obtain J(2) = 9, and so on, discarding the fractional digits.)

28. Write a program to compute $n! = (n - 1)*(n - 2)* \ldots *2*1$ for values of n that are so large that the result cannot fit in a single integer memory location. For example, 25! = 15,511,210,043,330,985,984, 000,000. A method to solve the problem is to use an array to store the answer (and partial results) using one memory location in the array per digit. Thus 12! = 479,001,600 would be stored as follows: (see exercise 27).

J(9)	J(8)	J(7)	J(6)	J(5)	J(4)	J(3)	J(2)	J(1)
4	7	9	0	0	1	6	0	0

To compute 13! multiply each memory location by 13 (taking care to move the carries) to obtain:

J(10)	J(9)	J(8)	J(7)	J(6)	J(5)	J(4)	J(3)	J(2)	J(1)
6	2	2	7	0	2	0	8	0	0

29. You may have received personalized form letters like those shown below. Write a program to read sets of names and addresses to produce individualized letters similar to the following:

```
THE COCOZZA'S
6501 S 19 AVE
PENSACOLA                                   AUGUST 12 1984
FLORIDA

DEAR MR AND MRS COCOZZA

ONLY YOU HAVE BEEN SELECTED IN THE PENSACOLA AREA TO APPLY FOR OUR
ONCE IN A LIFETIME SPECIAL ALUMINUM SIDING BARGAIN OF THE YEAR.
THE COCOZZA FAMILY SHOULD INDEED REJOICE IN HAVING THEIR CHARMING
HOME AT 6501 S 19 AVE RESTYLED WITH THE FINEST MATERIAL FROM FLORIDA.

                                            SINCERELY
```

```
THE DELLA TROCES
11 N 123 ST.
AMARILLO                                    JULY 12 1984
TEXAS

DEAR MR AND MRS DELLA TROCE

ONLY YOU HAVE BEEN SELECTED IN THE AMARILLO AREA TO APPLY FOR OUR
ONCE IN A LIFETIME SPECIAL ALUMINUM SIDING BARGAIN OF THE YEAR.
THE DELLA TROCE FAMILY SHOULD INDEED REJOICE IN HAVING THEIR CHARMING
HOME AT 11 N 123 ST. RESTYLED WITH THE FINEST MATERIAL FROM TEXAS.

                                            SINCERELY
```

30. Two sort methods have been presented in chapter 8: the bubble and the mini/max sort. These two sorting techniques are not the most efficient methods, however. An extremely efficient sorting method is the Shell-Metzner sort displayed here in flowchart form. In an article entitled "A Comparison of Sorts" in *Creative Computing,* Volume 2, John Grillo compared the three methods and determined that to sort 100,000 numbers would take 7.1 days, 3.8 days, and 15 minutes for the bubble, mini/max, and Shell-Metzner sort, respectively. To sort 10,000,000 numbers would take 93 years, 50 years, and 2.5 days, respectively! Write a program to sort N numbers using the following flowchart.

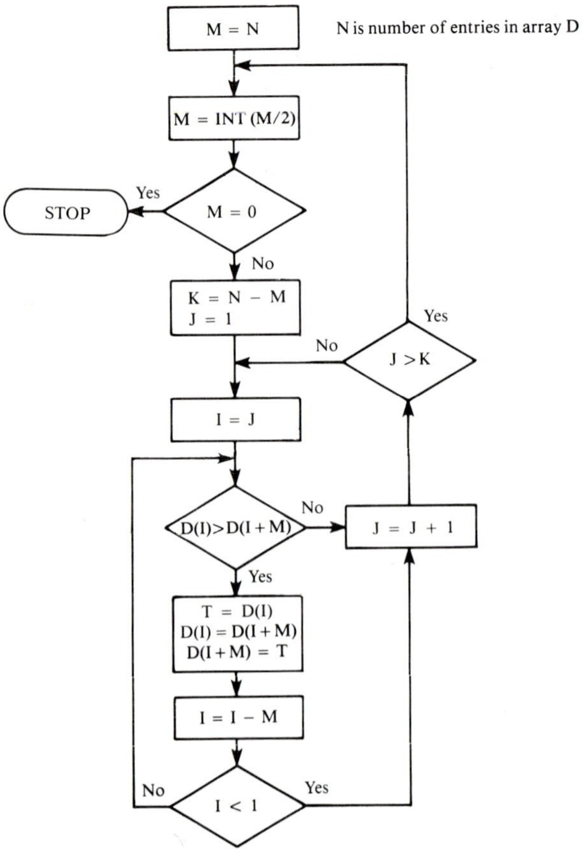

8-8-3 Exercises for BASIC Systems Allowing String Manipulation

1. Read a sentence and print it one word per line.

2. Read a sentence and print the number of vowels, consonants, digits and punctuation marks.

3. To facilitate transmission, words in telegrams are usually separated by slashes (/). Regenerate the original line of a telegraph message by substituting blanks wherever slashes appear.

4. Do the same problem as exercise 3, but compute the cost of the telegram. Each word up to and including the twentieth word costs 15 cents; thereafter, each word costs 12 cents.

5. Addresses in telegrams are transmitted serially. A double slash indicates a new line. Read five such addresses and recreate them as envelope addresses.

   Example: 1301/NORTH12TH/AVE//ATLANTA//GEORGIA/75603//

6. Write a program to convert military time to civilian time.

   Example: 1818 should produce THE TIME IS 18 PAST 6 PM
   1545 should produce THE TIME IS 15 BEFORE 4 PM

7. Write a program to convert civilian time to 24-hour time. Civilian time should contain only the key words P.M. and A.M. The format for the input is

$$\text{DATA hours, minutes, } \left\{ \begin{matrix} \text{“PM”} \\ \text{“AM”} \end{matrix} \right\}$$

   Example: DATA 2,15,PM should produce 1415.

8. Translate dates expressed numerically into the usual month and day and year representation.

   Example: 11/07/84 should produce NOVEMBER 7 1984.

9. Read a word and write it in reverse order; then a sentence in reverse word order.
10. Write a program to determine if a character string accepted as input is a palindrome (See exercise 15.)
11. A very simple method for encoding a message is to substitute each letter of the message with another according to a scheme such as

   letter   A B C D E ... Y Z
   substitute Z Y X W V ... B A

   Write a program to encode a message using this method.

12. Write a program to read a five-letter word and generate all possible two letter combinations using those five letters. Can you avoid duplication of two-letter words?
13. Determine the number of syllables in a word; in a sentence.
14. A palindrome is a sequence of characters that is the same read from left to right as from right to left. For example, 303, 4224 "MOM" and "MADAM, I'M ADAM" are examples of palindromes. Write a program to generate all 2-digit, 3-digit and 4-digit palindromes.
15. Write a program to determine if a number or word accepted as input is a palindrome.
16. Write a program to convert decimal numbers to Roman numerals, employing the usual rules required in Roman numerals. Recall that the basic correspondence between Roman and decimal numerals is:

Roman	*Decimal (Hindu-Arabic)*
M	1000
D	500
C	100
L	50
X	10
V	5
I	1

Test your program with the following:

Decimal	*Expected Roman*	*Decimal*	*Expected Roman*
3	III	49	XLIX
4	IV	50	L
5	V	58	LVIII
7	VII	75	LXXV
9	IX	90	XC
10	X	200	CC
12	XII	350	CCCL
24	XXIV	400	CD
29	XXIX	500	D
38	XXXVIII	900	CM
40	XL	2900	MMCM
44	XLIV		

8-8-4 Exercises Requiring Random Numbers

1. a. In the game of chapter 6 section 6–4, you placed a mole 100 times at position row 3, column 4 of the island and counted the number of times the mole escaped. Now, if the mole were clever, it could remember the route it took the very first time it found the way out, so that from then on it would never drown! Write a program to do just that; i.e., keep track in an array of the sequence of steps leading to a safe exit and reject any sequence of steps leading to drowning. Sooner or later the mole will find a way out; then that path will be recorded in an array and from that point on the mole will always escape.

b. Of course the mole's first path to freedom may not be the shortest way out. Write a program to force the mole to select the shortest escape path out of some 20 escape routes. From then on, the mole should remember that particular path. Print the mole's final exit path using a coordinate system, for example:

(3,4) (3,3) (4,3) ...

row column

2. Write a drill/practice program to randomly generate systems of two equations in two unknowns, accept a solution, and test to see if it is correct. Implement as many of the following optional features as you see fit:

Sign-off procedure.

Statistics produced when a user signs off.

Randomized responses to correct and incorrect answers.

Help in the form of a restatement of the problem or a brief tutorial when a number of incorrect answers to a problem have been given.

A homework assignment produced when a user signs off. The problems might consist of all the problems missed by the user during the session.

The program might start with easy examples and progress to harder problems if the user is successful or remain with easy problems if the user has difficulty. You might be able to identify several levels of difficulty.

Any other feature that you feel would be useful.

8-8-5 Answers to Test Yourself

1. a. Invalid: the decimal point is not allowed.
   b. Valid.
   c. Invalid: expressions cannot be used to declare size of array.
   d. Invalid. However, DIM A(31), B(32) is valid.
   e. Invalid: Z(N) is invalid; size must be a constant.

2. All can hold the same amount of information, but the notion of *order* does not exist for locations X1, X2, and X3. No one can predict what the next variable after X2 is, whereas we know that the item physically next to X(2) in memory is X(3).

3. a. T
   b. F
   c. F
   d. T
   e. F; invalid READ statement.
   f. T
   g. F However, T$(7) = "BOY" is valid for character arrays.

4. a. 1.4
   b. −4
   c. 2.4
   d. 0
   e. Invalid. G is not a character array.
   f. G(I) is undefined; no value is assigned to I.

5. Assume all arrays are initially set to 0's.

   a. Array A:

1	4	7	10	11

   Array B:

3	6	9	12	0

   b. Array A:

5	4	3	2	1

   Array B:

6	0	7	0	8

   c. Array A:

1	4	7	0	0

   Array B:

8	9	0	0	0

6. a.

```
 5 DIM A(1ØØ)
1Ø FOR I = 1 TO 99 STEP 2
2Ø     PRINT A(I), A(I+1)
3Ø NEXT I
```

b.

```
 5 DIM A (1ØØ)
1Ø FOR I = 1 TO 5Ø
2Ø     PRINT A(I), A(I+5Ø)
3Ø NEXT I
```

c.

```
 5 DIM A(1ØØ)
1Ø FOR I = 1 TO 1ØØ
2Ø     PRINT I, A(1Ø1-I)
3Ø NEXT I
```

d.

```
 5 DIM A(1ØØ)
1Ø FOR I = 2 TO 1ØØ STEP 2
2Ø     PRINT TAB (3Ø); A(I)
3Ø NEXT I
4Ø FOR J=Ø TO 9
5Ø   FOR I = 1 TO 1Ø
```

```
60       PRINT A(J*10 + I);
70    NEXT I
80    PRINT
90 NEXT J
```

7.

```
10 DIM S(100)
15 INPUT T
20 FOR I = 1 TO 100
25    S(I) = INT(RND(1)*100+1)
30 NEXT I
35 FOR I = 1 TO 100
40    IF T = S(I) THEN 60
45 NEXT I
50 PRINT "NO MATCH"
55 GO TO 90
60 PRINT "MATCH"
90 END
```

8.

```
10 DATA...
20 DIM A(20), B(30), C(100)
30 FOR I=1 TO 20
40   READ A(I)
50 NEXT I
60 FOR I = 1 TO 30
70   READ B(I)
80 NEXT I
90 FOR I= 1 TO 100
100 REM THE VALUE 0 IS ASSUMED TO BE THE LAST VALUE IN
    THE DATA
110   READ C(I)
120   IF C(I) = 0 THEN 140
130 NEXT I
140 END
```

9.

```
10 DIM G(101)
15 PRINT "GRADES:";
20 S = 0
22 FOR I = 1 TO 101
25 READ G(I)
30 IF G(I) < 0 THEN 46
35    S = S + G(I)
40    PRINT G(I);
45 NEXT I
46 PRINT
50 A = S/(I - 1)
55 C = 0
60 FOR I = 1 TO I-1
65     IF G(I) < A THEN C = C + 1
70 NEXT I
75 PRINT "NO. GRADES LESS AVERAGE ="; C
80 DATA 20,30,40,50,60,-9
```

```
RUN
GRADES: 20  30  40  50  60
NO. GRADES LESS AVERAGE = 2
```

10.
```
10 DIM A(10),B(16),K(100)
15 FOR I = 1 TO 10
20    READ A(I)
25 NEXT I
30 FOR I = 1 TO 16
35    READ B(I)
36 NEXT I
40 FOR I = 1 TO 100
45    K(I) = 0
50 NEXT I
55 FOR I = 1 TO 10
60     FOR J = 1 TO 16
65         IF A(I) = B(J) THEN K(A(I)) = 1
70     NEXT J
75 NEXT I
80 L = 0
85 FOR I = 1 TO 100
90     IF K(I) = 0 THEN 105
95        PRINT I;
100       L = L + 1
105 NEXT I
106 PRINT
110 PRINT "NO. OF EQUAL ITEMS ="; L
115 DATA 0,2,3,3,3,3,3,7,9,0
120 DATA 1,1,2,2,3,3,5,6,6,7,8,8,8,9,10,10

RUN
 2  3  7  9
NO. OF EQUAL ITEMS = 4
```

11.
```
10 DIM A(20), K(20)
15 FOR I = 1 TO 20
20     A(I) = INT(RND(1)*20 + 1)
25     K(I) = 0
30 NEXT I
35 FOR I = 1 TO 20
40     K(A(I)) = K(A(I)) + 1
45 NEXT I
50 PRINT "NUMBERS   ";
55 L = 11
60 FOR I = 1 TO 20
65     IF K(I) = 0 THEN 80
70        PRINT TAB(L);I;
75        L = L + 4
80 NEXT I
85 PRINT
90 PRINT "FREQUENCY";
```

```
 95 L = 11
100 FOR I = 1 TO 20
105     IF K(I) = 0 THEN 120
110        PRINT TAB(L); K(I);
115        L = L + 4
120 NEXT I
125 END

RUN
NUMBERS    1  3  4  5  10  12  13  14  15  17  18  19
FREQUENCY  1  4  2  1  1   1   2   2   1   2   2   1
```

12.
```
10 DIM A(10)
15 FOR I = 1 TO 10
20     READ A(I)
25 NEXT I
30 FOR I = 1 TO 10
35     FOR J = I+1 TO 10
40         IF A(I) = A(J) THEN 65
45     NEXT J
50 NEXT I
55 PRINT "NO EQUAL ENTRIES"
60 STOP
65 PRINT "MATCH EXISTS"
70 DATA 1,2,3,4,5,6,7,8,9,9

RUN
MATCH EXISTS
```

13.
```
 100 DIM A(11)
 200 DATA 2,3,5,6,7,8,9,10,12,14
 300 DATA 4
 400 FOR I=1 TO 10
 500   READ A(I)
 600 NEXT I
 700 READ R
 800 FOR I=1 TO 10
 900   IF A(I) > R THEN 1100
1000 NEXT I
1010 LET A(11) = R
1020 GO TO 1500
1100 FOR J=11 TO I+1 STEP -1
1200   LET A(J) = A(J-1)
1300 NEXT J
1400 LET A(I) = R
1500 FOR I=1 TO 11
1600   PRINT A(I);
1700 NEXT I
1800 END

RUN
2 3 4 5 6 7 8 9 10 12 14
```

9 TWO-DIMENSIONAL ARRAYS AND THE MAT STATEMENTS

9-1 Two-Dimensional Tables

9-1-1 Introduction

Much of the information that we deal with in our everyday lives involves arrangements of data in rows and columns. In a theater, in an airplane, or in a typical classroom, seats are identified by their row and column positions (aisles). Looking up our taxes may mean reading the number at the intersection of an income level row and a number of dependents column. Chess boards and teachers' grade notebooks are other examples of two-dimensional tables or arrays.

Since these row-by-column arrangements are so common in our day-to-day lives, it should come as no surprise that BASIC can handle such geometric arrangements of data. The power of a two-dimensional array lies in its "lookup" procedure, which gives us individual direct access to any entry in the table, without searching through the array entries. By specifying the row and column of an array, we can access the corresponding entry directly. Let us look at an everyday example of a two-dimensional array, the sales tax deduction table shown below, and find the deduction allowed a family with four children and an income of $8,000 to $8,999.

	Income	*Number of Children* 1	2	3	4	5	6
	$0,000.	35.	48.	49.	59.	59.	60.
	$3,000.	44.	58.	61.	71.	73.	75.
	$4,000.	51.	68.	72.	82.	85.	88.
	$5,000.	58.	76.	82.	91.	97.	100.
	$6,000.	64.	84.	91.	100.	107.	112.
	$7,000.	70.	92.	100.	109.	117.	123.
7th entry	$8,000. →	76.	99.	108.	(117.)	127.	133.
	$9,000.	81.	106.	116.	124.	136.	143.
	$10,000.	86.	112.	124.	131.	145.	153.
	$11,000.	91.	118.	132.	138.	154.	163.
	$12,000.	96.	124.	139.	145.	162.	172.
	$13,000.	101.	130.	146.	151.	170.	181.
	$14,000.	106.	136.	153.	157.	178.	190.
	$15,000.	110.	141.	160.	163.	186.	198.
	$16,000.	114.	146.	167.	169.	194.	206.
	$17,000.	118.	151.	173.	175.	201.	214.
	$18,000.	122.	156.	179.	181.	208.	222.
	$19,000.	126.	161.	185.	186.	215.	230.

Once the correct income entry has been pinpointed in the income array (position 7 for $8,000), we look up the figure in the 7th row and 4th column of the table; we use the number of children to identify directly (no IF statements) the proper column of the table. This table is an example of a two-dimensional array consisting of 18 rows and 6 columns. The power behind this type of table is that entries in the table can be successively accessed by varying the row and/or column subscripts.

9-1-2 Problem Example

Mr. Spandex does his daily grocery shopping at four stores (he store-hops for bargains), and he records his daily purchases at the various stores as follows:

		Stores 1	2	3	4	*Explanation*
	1	10	20	10	40	On day 1 he spent \$10 at store 1, \$20 at store 2, \$10 at store 3...
	2	0	15	20	35	On day 2 he spent \$0 at store 1, \$15 at store 2, \$20 at store 3...
Days	3	10	30	0	50	
	4	0	0	40	30	
	5	5	10	60	0	On day 5 he spent \$5 at store 1, \$10 at store 2, \$60 at store 3...

Over the weekend, Mr. Spandex analyzes his grocery expenses by asking himself such questions as:

1. How much did I spend on Monday, on Tuesday, ..., on Friday?
2. How much did I spend for the whole week at store 1, store 2, ..., store 4?
3. On which day did I spend the least? the most?
4. At which store(s) did I spend the least? the most?
5. Which store(s) did I not go to on a particular day?
6. What are my total weekly expenses?
7. What were my expenses for a given day?
8. What was the average amount spent that week at each of the stores?

... the questions go on and on!

Mr. Spandex has a microcomputer at home. He quickly realizes that he needs to store the above table in the memory of the computer and then write the code (manipulate the array) to get the answers to his questions more easily. For example, if the array were called A, Mr. Spandex could type PRINT A(3,4) and the computer would print 50 (day 3, store 4).

In this introductory example, we will help Mr. Spandex do the following:

1. Load his expense table into a 5 by 4 array called A.
2. Print his total expenses for each day.
3. Allow him to print the amount he spent on any given day at any given store.

Loading the Array A

To load the various entries into array A, we first record the entries in row sequence in five DATA statements that simulate the original data arrangement:

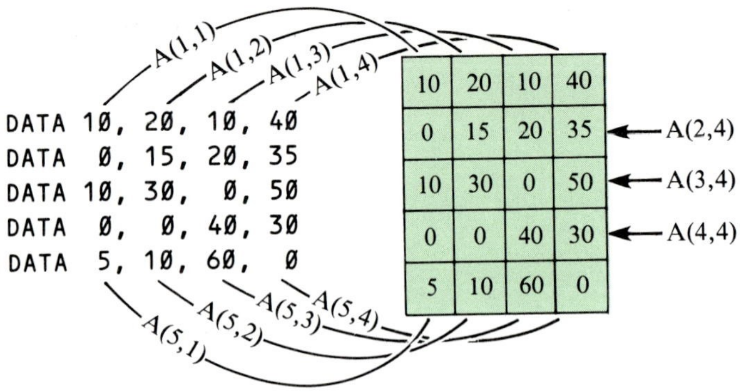

Since the DATA statements give the entries in row fashion, we must also load the array in row fashion, i.e.

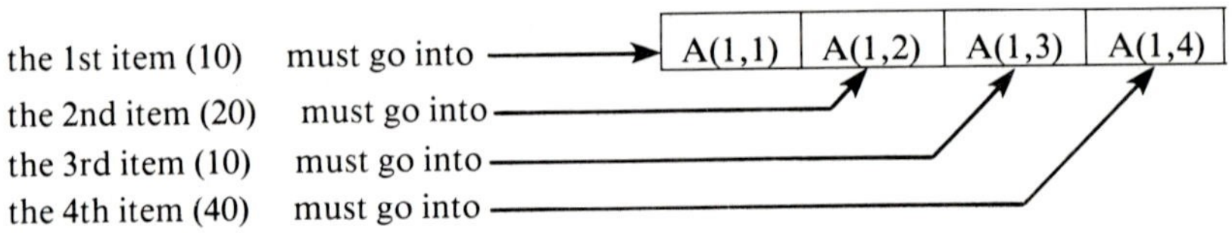

This can be translated into BASIC as

```
1Ø FOR J = 1 TO 4
15     READ A(1,J)        Read in first row.
2Ø NEXT J
```

Likewise, the second DATA row can be stored into the second row of A with the following statements:

```
25 FOR J = 1 TO 4
3Ø     READ A(2,J)        Read in second row.
35 NEXT J
```

The same process could be repeated for the 3rd, 4th and 5th DATA statements, but a simpler method would be to use a variable row index:

```
FOR J = 1 TO 4
    READ A(I,J)        where I would be 1 the 1st time, 2 the 2nd time,
NEXT J                                   3 the 3rd time, ...
```

Hence, we can use a nested loop where the outer loop index I freezes the row to a particular value while an inner loop index J runs from 1 to 4:

```
1Ø DIM A(5,4)              Reserve an array with 5 rows and 4 columns.
15 FOR I = 1 TO 5          I controls the number of rows.
2Ø     FOR J = 1 TO 4      J controls the number of columns.
25         READ A(I,J)     Read the items into their slots in the array.
3Ø     NEXT J
35 NEXT I
```

Printing The Total Daily Expenses

Computing the daily total expense means adding the elements of a particular row. Since each row can be thought of as a one-dimensional array, we have the familiar problem of accumulating the elements of a one-dimensional array. For example, to compute the sum of the first row, we could write

```
S = A(1,1) + A(1,2) + A(1,3) + A(1,4)    or    S = Ø
                                               FOR J = 1 TO 4
     (varying column index)                        S = S + A(1,J)
                                               NEXT J
```

Since the same process needs to be repeated for the remaining rows 2 through 5, we let the row index I vary from 1 to 5:

```
4Ø FOR I = 1 TO 5          Process 5 days.
45     S = Ø               Initialize the accumulator for total daily expenses to 0.
5Ø     FOR J = 1 TO 4      Each row consists of 4 column entries (stores).
55         S = S + A(I,J)  Add these 4 column entries for a given row to compute
6Ø     NEXT J              the total expenses for the particular day.
65     PRINT S             Print each day's total expenses.
7Ø NEXT I
```

Interactive Communication between Mr. Spandex and the Computer

To enable Mr. Spandex to determine a purchase amount for a given day and store, we add the following code:

```
75 PRINT "ENTER DAY AND STORE. TO STOP ENTER Ø,Ø"
8Ø INPUT D,S
85 PRINT A(D,S)        Print the expense corresponding to day D and store S.
9Ø GO TO 75
```

The entire program is shown in Figure 9–1.

■ **Figure 9–1** A grocery analysis problem.

```
10 REM GROCERY SHOPPING ANALYSIS
12 REM DATA ANALYSIS
14 REM       A: ARRAY CONTAINING WEEKLY EXPENSES
16 REM       S: USED TO ACCUMULATE TOTAL DAILY EXPENSES
18 REM       D: IDENTIFIES A PARTICULAR DAY
20 REM       S: IDENTIFIES A PARTICULAR STORE
22 REM
24 DIM A(5,4)                  Reserve an array with 5 rows and 4 columns.
26 FOR I = 1 TO 5            }
28     FOR J = 1 TO 4        }
30         READ A(I,J)       }  Load the array into memory.
32     NEXT J                }
34 NEXT I                    }
36 FOR I = 1 TO 5               Process 5 days.
38     S = 0                    Set expense total to 0.
40     FOR J = 1 TO 4           Add expenses at the 4 stores
42         S = S + A(I,J)       for a given day I.
44     NEXT J
46     PRINT "TOTAL DAILY EXPENSES FOR DAY"; I; "WERE"; S
48 NEXT I
50 PRINT
52 PRINT "ENTER DAY, STORE"  Allow interaction between the user and the computer.
54 INPUT D, S
55 IF D = 0 THEN 70
56 PRINT "YOU SPENT"; A(D,S); "DOLLARS ON DAY";D;"AT STORE "; S
58 GOTO 52
60 DATA 10, 20, 10, 40       }  Day 1's expenses at 4 stores.
62 DATA  0, 15, 20, 35       }        .
64 DATA 10, 30,  0, 50       }        .
66 DATA  0,  0, 40, 30       }        .
68 DATA  5, 10, 60,  0       }  Day 5's expenses at 4 stores.
70 END

RUN
TOTAL DAILY EXPENSES FOR DAY 1 WERE 80
TOTAL DAILY EXPENSES FOR DAY 2 WERE 70
TOTAL DAILY EXPENSES FOR DAY 3 WERE 90
TOTAL DAILY EXPENSES FOR DAY 4 WERE 70
TOTAL DAILY EXPENSES FOR DAY 5 WERE 75

ENTER DAY, STORE
? 1,3
YOU SPENT 10 DOLLARS ON DAY 1 AT STORE 3
ENTER DAY, STORE
? 3,4
YOU SPENT 50 DOLLARS ON DAY 3 AT STORE 4
ENTER DAY, STORE
?0,0
```

9-1-3 Do It Now

1. Could the printing of the day's total purchases have been taken care of while loading the array into memory?
2. Write the code to enable Mr. Spandex to print the total daily expenses for any given day through interactive communication.
3. Write the code to enable Mr. Spandex to print the list of expenses for any given day (interactive communication).

Answers

1. Yes, as follows:

```
26 S = Ø
3Ø FOR I = 1 TO 5
32      FOR J = 1 TO 4
34          READ A(I,J)
36          S = S + A(I,J)
38      NEXT J
4Ø      PRINT "TOTAL DAILY EXPENSES="; S
42 NEXT I
5Ø PRINT
52 PRINT "ENTER DAY, STORE"
```

2.

```
36 INPUT D
38 S = Ø
4Ø FOR J = 1 TO 4
42      S = S + A(D,J)
44 NEXT J
46 PRINT "TOTAL EXPENSES FOR SAY"; D; "IS"; S
```

3.

```
7Ø PRINT "ENTER DAY"
72 INPUT D
74 FOR I = 1 TO 4
76      PRINT A(D,I);
78 NEXT I
```

9-2 BASIC Statements

9-2-1 Two-Dimensional Arrays

In Chapter 8 we discussed one-dimensional or *linear* arrays; only one subscript is needed to address elements of a linear array. For two-dimensional tables, we address a particular array element by specifying first the row and then the column. Thus, the element in the second row and third column of array A is addressed as A(2,3). In general, A(I,J) refers to the element found in the Ith row and Jth column of array A.

Note the comma separating the two subscripts. Figure 9–2 displays a 3 by 3 array. Analyze the subscripts carefully.

Figure 9–2 A two-dimensional array.

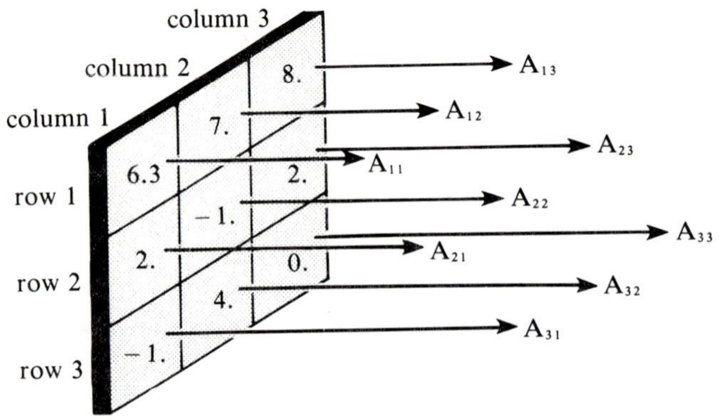

9-2-2 The DIM Statement

The general form of the DIM statement is:

> *line number* DIM *variable* (*row limit*, *column limit*) [,...]

where *variable* is the name of the array, the *row limit* is a positive integer constant specifying the maximum number of rows, and the *column limit* is a positive integer constant specifying the maximum number of columns.

Any number of two- or one-dimensional arrays can be specified in a DIM statement. For example, the statement DIM B(6,8), C(10), I(10,25) reserves 48 memory locations for the array B, 10 memory locations for array C, and 250 locations for array I. Any reference to the variable name B or I must include two subscripts. For example, the statement LET B(I) = 0 is invalid, since it includes only one subscript.

The row subscript value used in a reference to a two-dimensional array must be between 1 (in many systems 0 is permitted) and the row limit specified in the DIM statement. A similar restriction applies to the column subscript. For example, given the size of the array A defined by DIM A(3,5), the references A(1,1), A(2,4), and A(3,5) are valid, whereas A(4,1) and A(3,6) are invalid, since one or more of the subscripts are outside the allowable subscript range.

Subscript expressions for two-dimensional arrays behave the same way as they do for one-dimensional arrays. The following references to a two-dimensional array are valid

T(3*K,I+2)	If K = 1.4 and I = −1,	then we have T(4,1).
B(10/L,J*2)	If L = 3 and J = 0,	then we have B(3,0).
C(ABS(X),RND(4))	If X = −3 and RND(4) = 2,	then we have C(3,2).

In these examples, the subscript expressions are first evaluated and then truncated to their integer values. Note that functions *can* be part of subscript expressions.

9-2-3 Do It Now

Use the following arrays to answer questions 1 through 3.

A

1	−2	.5	3
3	0	0	−1
2	1	5	6
3	1	0	1

B

10	5
0	6
−1	.5

1. What is the value of

a. A(3,4)

b. A(2,3) + B(1,2)

c. A(3,2) * A(4,3)

d. B(2,1) + B(2,2)

e. 1/2*A(4,4) + B(3,1)

2. List the variable names (not the values) for the following:

a. the diagonal elements of A

b. the 2nd row of B

c. the 3rd column of A

3. If I = 2, J = 4, specify the values that will be printed:

a.
```
PRINT A(J,I)
```

b.
```
PRINT B(I + 1,2)
```

c.
```
S = Ø
FOR K = 2 TO 4
    S = S + A(I,K)
NEXT K
PRINT S
```

d.
```
FOR L = 1 TO 4
    M = 5 - L
PRINT A(M,J)
NEXT L
```

e.
```
FOR L = 1 TO 2
    PRINT B(L,L)
NEXT L
```

Answers

1. a. 6; b. 5; c. 0; d. 6; e. −0.5

2. a. A(1,1), A(2,2), A(3,3), A(4,4)
   b. B(2,1), B(2,2)
   c. A(1,3), A(2,3), A(3,3), A(4,3)

3. a. 1 b. 0.5 c. −1 d. 1, 6, −1, 3 e. 10, 6

9-2-4 Processing Two-Dimensional Arrays

Two-dimensional arrays can be processed in essentially the same way as one-dimensional arrays, except that another subscript must be used. Generally, two loops will be needed: one to control the rows and one to control the columns. The order of these loops (which one is the inner one) is usually immaterial, since a table can be processed in row fashion or in column fashion. Some examples of common procedures follow.

Example 1: Initializing all elements of an array to 0.

```
1Ø DIM A(1Ø,6),B(1Ø,6)
15 FOR I = 1 TO 1Ø
2Ø     FOR J = 1 TO 6
25         A(I,J) = Ø
3Ø         B(I,J) = Ø
35     NEXT J
4Ø NEXT I
```

The elements are zeroed out in row fashion.

```
1Ø DIM A(1Ø,6),B(1Ø,6)
15 FOR J = 1 TO 6
2Ø     FOR I = 1 TO 1Ø
25         A(I,J) = Ø
3Ø         B(I,J) = Ø
35     NEXT I
4Ø NEXT J
```

The elements are zeroed out in column fashion.

Example 2: Array Addition

Given the arrays A and B,

A =

1	2	3
2	1	4

B =

−1	2	0
1	3	4

we can add these two arrays to obtain another array C such that each element of C is equal to the sum of the corresponding entries of A and B, i.e.

$$C = \begin{array}{ccc} 1 + (-1) & 2 + 2 & 3 + 0 \\ 2 + 1 & 1 + 3 & 4 + 4 \end{array} \quad \text{or} \quad C = \begin{array}{|c|c|c|} \hline 0 & 4 & 3 \\ \hline 3 & 4 & 8 \\ \hline \end{array}$$

In general, C(I,J) = A(I,J) + B(I,J) as I goes from 1 through 2, and as J goes from 1 to 3:

```
1Ø FOR J = 1 TO 3
15     FOR I = 1 TO 2
2Ø         C(I,J)=A(I,J)+B(I,J)
25     NEXT I
3Ø NEXT J
```

or

```
1Ø FOR J = 1 TO 3
15    FOR I = 1 TO 2
2Ø       C(I,J) = A(I,J)+B(I,J)
25    NEXT I
3Ø NEXT J
```

Example 3: Array Search

Suppose we are to identify the row and column position of the largest number in array A. To start the search process, we assume the largest number is at row R = 1 and column C = 1. We then compare A(R,C) with the entries of the array, first checking each elements in row 1, then row 2, and so forth. Whenever we find an entry larger than A(R,C), we reset R and C to the row and column position of the larger number just found.

```
1Ø DIM A(10,15)
15 R = 1
2Ø C = 1
25 FOR I = 1 TO 1Ø
3Ø     FOR J = 1 TO 15
35         IF A(R,C) >= A(I,J) THEN 5Ø
4Ø             R = I
45             C = J
5Ø     NEXT J
15 NEXT I
```

Assume the largest number is at row R = 1 and column C = 1 (subject to later change, of course).

Keep searching if A(R,C) is still largest.

Since A(R,C) is no longer the largest, but A(I,J) is, reset R and C to the current location of the largest number.

Example 4: Row Summation and Column Interchange

Let us write the code to:

1. Add all the entries of the Nth row of array A (size 10 by 17). N will be accepted from input.
2. Interchange column 3 with column 17.

The row sum to be calculated is S = A(N,1) + A(N,2) + A(N,3) + ... + A(N,16) + A(N,17). Hence the row index is fixed to N, while the column index varies from 1 to 17.

The interchange procedure can be accomplished by successively moving each element of column 3 into a temporary location T, then moving the corresponding element of column 17 into the vacated column 3 position, and finally moving the saved value in T into the appropriate position in column 17. (If no temporary location T were used, the elements of column 3 would be destroyed by the statement A(I,3) = A(I,17) as I ranges from 1 to 10.) The code to perform the row summation and column interchange is:

```
1Ø DIM A(1Ø,17)
4Ø INPUT N
45 LET S = Ø
5Ø FOR J = 1 TO 17
55    LET S = S + A(N,J)
6Ø NEXT J
65 FOR I = 1 TO 1Ø
7Ø    LET T = A(I,3)
75    LET A(I,3) = A(I,17)
8Ø    LET A(I,17) = T
85 NEXT I
```

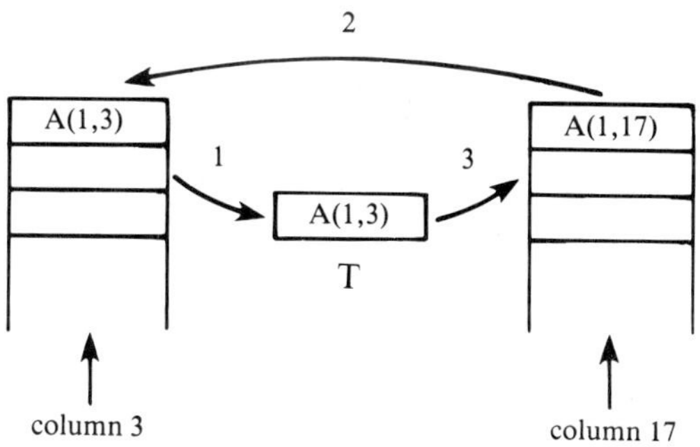

Example 5: Row Summation

Given the array A, shown below, we would like to compute the sum of the elements of the 1st row and store that sum in S(1), compute the sum of the elements of the 2nd row and store it in S(2), ...:

A →

1	4	7
2	5	8
3	6	9

S(1) = 1 + 4 + 7

S(2) = 2 + 5 + 8

S(3) = 3 + 6 + 9

There are two methods that can be used.

Row Method:

The sum of each row can be computed by fixing the row index I of A to 1 and varying the column index from 1 to 3, then repeating the same process for I equal to 2 and 3. Assume array S has been initialized to zeroes.

```
10 FOR I = 1 TO 3
15     FOR J = 1 TO 3
20         S(I)=S(I)+A(I,J)
25     NEXT J
30 NEXT I
```

I=1 $S_1 = 1 + 4 + 7 = 12$

I=2 $S_2 = 2 + 5 + 8 = 15$

I=3 $S_3 = 3 + 6 + 9 = 18$

Column Method:

The same results can be obtained, in a less apparent way, if we interchange lines 10 and 15 as follows:

```
10 FOR J = 1 TO 3
15     FOR I = 1 TO 3
20     S(I) = S(I) + A(I,J)
25     NEXT I
30 NEXT J
```

J = 1: $\begin{cases} S_1 = A_{11} \\ S_2 = A_{21} \\ S_3 = A_{31} \end{cases}$ J = 2: $\begin{cases} S_1 = A_{11} + A_{12} \\ S_2 = A_{21} + A_{22} \\ S_3 = A_{31} + A_{32} \end{cases}$ J = 3: $\begin{cases} S_1 = A_{11} + A_{12} + A_{13} \\ S_2 = A_{21} + A_{22} + A_{23} \\ S_3 = A_{31} + A_{32} + A_{33} \end{cases}$

9-2-5 Do It Now

1. What will be the values stored in array X after each of the following?

a.
```
10 DIM X(3,4)
20 FOR I = 1 TO 3
30    FOR J = 1 TO 4
40       X(I,J) = I*J
50    NEXT J
60 NEXT I
```

b.
```
10 DIM X(3,4)
20 LET L = 1
30 FOR I = 1 TO 3
40    FOR J = 1 TO 4
50       X(I,J) = L
60       LET L = L + 1
70    NEXT J
80 NEXT I
```

2. If A is a table of size 10 by 6, write a program to initialize the first column of A with 1's, the second column with 2's, the third column with 3's, ..., and column 6 with 6's.

3. Write the basic code to load a 10 by 10 array with 100 random numbers, *then* compute the average of all the entries of the array.

4. Given an array A(5,7), write the code to input a value for C and print the largest value in column C of the array.

5. Write the code to compute the sum of the elements of the first and the sum of the second diagonals of array A(6,6). These diagonals are defined as follows:

first diagonal

second diagonal

Answers

1. a.

X =

1	2	3	4
2	4	6	8
3	6	9	12

b.

X =

1	2	3	4
5	6	7	8
9	10	11	12

2.

```
12 DIM A(10,6)
14 FOR J = 1 TO 6
16       FOR I = 1 TO 10
18             A(I,J) = J
22       NEXT I
24 PRINT
26 NEXT J
```

3.

```
42 DIM A(10,10)
44 FOR I = 1 TO 10
46       FOR J = 1 TO 10
48             A(I,J) = RND
50       NEXT J
52 NEXT I
54 S = 0
56 FOR I = 1 TO 10
58       FOR J = 1 TO 10
60             S = S + A(I,J)
62       NEXT J
64 NEXT I
66 PRINT S/100
```

4.

```
28 DIM A(5,7)
30 INPUT C
32 L = A(1,C)
34 FOR I = 2 TO 5
36       IF L < A(I,C) THEN L = A(I,C)
38 NEXT I
40 PRINT L
```

5.
```
70 DIM A(6,6)
72 D1 = 0
74 D2 = 0
76 FOR I = 1 TO 6
78      D1 = D1 + A(I,I)
82      D2 = D2 + A(I,7-I)
86 NEXT I
```

9-2-6 Input and Output of Two-Dimensional Arrays

Input of Arrays

Arrays can be loaded into memory through either the INPUT or the READ statement.

Example 1:

Suppose the table shown below is to be loaded into array A, while preserving the same geometrical arrangement (3 rows and 5 columns). You can type the entries in either row or column fashion:

TABLE

1	2	3	4	5
6	7	8	9	0
9	8	7	6	5

Row input

```
 5 DATA 1,2,3,4,5
10 DATA 6,7,8,9,0
15 DATA 9,8,7,6,5
20 REM LOAD ROW-WISE
25 FOR I = 1 TO 3
30    FOR J = 1 TO 5
35       READ A(I,J)
40    NEXT J
45 NEXT I
```

Data is read in row fashion.

Read sequence:
$A_{11}, A_{12}, \ldots, A_{15}, A_{21}, A_{22}, \ldots$

Column input

```
 5 DATA 1,6,9
10 DATA 2,7,8
15 DATA 3,8,7
20 DATA 4,9,6,5,0,5
25 FOR K = 1 TO 5
30    FOR L = 1 TO 3
35       READ A(L,K)
40    NEXT L
45 NEXT K
```

Data is read in row fashion.

Read sequence:
$A_{11}, A_{21}, A_{31}, A_{12}, A_{22}, A_{32}, \ldots$

Example 2:

Professor X's grade roster contains the information shown below, which he has typed on DATA statements. There are at most 100 records. Let us write the code to read this data file into the three arrays NAME, NUMBER and GRADES, shown as follows:

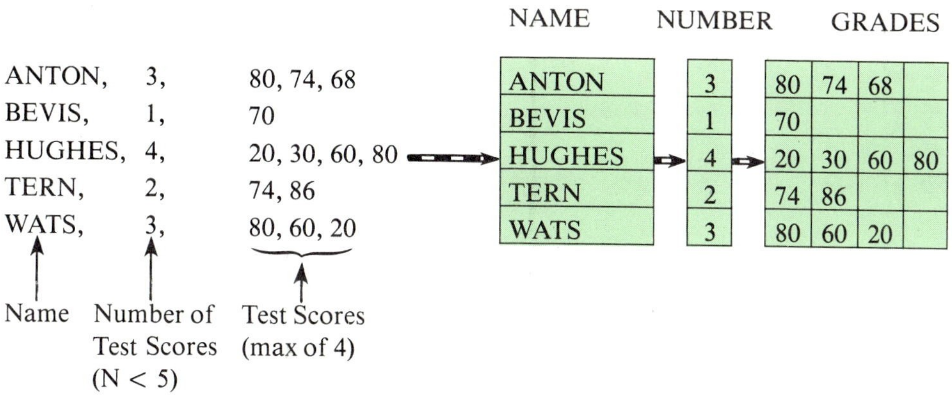


```
10 DIM N$(101),T(100,4),B(101)
12 FOR I = 1 TO 101
14   READ N$(I), B(I)
16   IF N$(I) = "X" THEN 26
18   FOR J = 1 TO B(I)
20      READ T(I,J)
22   NEXT J
24 NEXT I
26 N = I - 1
```

We use 101 instead of 100 locations so that if there are exactly 100 records the trip N$(101) will still be read. Read a name and corresponding number of tests. The name "X" terminates the input file.

Read the student's test scores.

N represents the total number of students.

Output of Arrays

Example 1:

After having stored the table of grocery expenses in memory (see section 9-1-2), Mr. Spandex wants to write the code to obtain the following output:

```
          STORE 1     STORE 2     STORE 3     STORE 4

DAY 1       10          20          10          40
DAY 2        0          15          20          35
DAY 3       10          30           0          50
DAY 4        0           0          40          30
DAY 5        5          10          60           0
```

Two FOR/NEXT loops are needed to print the four numeric entries per line, as shown in Figure 9-3. To simplify the PRINT statement at line 50, the TAB feature is used to print the four entries at positions 11, 24, 37, and 50 (13 * J − 2, as J goes from 1 to 4).

■ **Figure 9–3** Output of two-dimensional array.

```
10 DIM A(5,4)
26 FOR I = 1 TO 5
28     FOR J = 1 TO 4
30         READ A(I,J)                    Load array into memory.
32     NEXT J
34 NEXT I
36 FOR I = 1 TO 4
38   PRINT TAB(13*I - 3); "STORE"; I;     Adjust captions on the output.
40 NEXT I
42 PRINT
43 PRINT
44 FOR I = 1 TO 5
46   PRINT "DAY"; I;
48   FOR J = 1 TO 4
50     PRINT TAB(13*J - 2); A(I,J);       Place entries under captions.
52   NEXT J
54   PRINT
56 NEXT I
58 DATA 10, 20, 10, 40
60 DATA  0, 15, 20, 35
62 DATA 10, 30,  0, 50                    Mr. Spandex's grocery expenses.
64 DATA  0,  0, 40, 30
66 DATA  5, 10, 60,  0
68 END
RUN
          STORE 1      STORE 2      STORE 3      STORE 4

DAY 1      10           20           10           40
DAY 2      0            15           20           35
DAY 3      10           30           0            50
DAY 4      0            0            40           30
DAY 5      5            10           60           0
```

Example 2:

In example 2 of the preceding section, we wrote the code to load Professor X's grade roster in table T(101,5). Let's write the code to print out the table of grades according to the following design:

```
NAME      TESTS   TEST 1   TEST 2   TEST 3   TEST 4

ANTON       3       80       74       68
BEVIS       1       70
HUGHES      4       20       30       60       80
TERN        2       74       86
WATS        3       80       60       20
```

Lines 40 through 52 of Figure 9–4 contain the code to print this report. The name is printed in the outer loop at line 42, while the number of test scores B(I), and the scores of student I are printed at line 46 in the inner loop. Note that index J of the inner loop (line 44) ranges from 1 to B(I).

Figure 9–4 A two-dimensional array output problem.

```
10 DIM N$(101),T(100,4),B(101)   We use 101 locations so the trip N$(101) will still be read
12 FOR I = 1 TO 101               even if there are exactly 100 records.
14    READ N$(I), B(I)            Read a name and corresponding number of tests.
16    IF N$(I) = "X" THEN 26
18    FOR J = 1 TO B(I)
20       READ T(I,J)              Read the student's test scores starting at J + 1,
22    NEXT J                      since T(I,1) is the number of scores.
24 NEXT I
26 N = I - 1                      N represents the total number of students.
28 PRINT "NAME";TAB(9);"TESTS  ";  Start printing the output captions.
30 FOR I = 1 TO 4
32    PRINT TAB(13*I+9); "TEST";I;  Finish printing output captions.
34 NEXT I
36 PRINT
38 PRINT
40 FOR I = 1 TO N                 Process N student records.
42     PRINT N$(I);               Print name of student.
44     FOR J = 1 TO B(I)          Print the number of test scores and
46       PRINT   TAB(13*J-3);B(I);T(I,J);  the scores themselves.
48     NEXT J
50 PRINT
52 NEXT I
54 DATA ANTON,  3, 80, 74, 68
56 DATA BEVIS,  1, 70
58 DATA HUGHES, 4, 20, 30, 60, 80
60 DATA TERN,   2, 74, 86
62 DATA WATS,   3, 80, 60, 20
64 DATA X,0
66 END
```

RUN

NAME	TESTS	TEST 1	TEST 2	TEST 3	TEST 4
ANTON	3	80	74	68	
BEVIS	1	70			
HUGHES	4	20	30	60	80
TERN	2	74	86		
WATS	3	80	60	20	

9-2-7 Do It Now

1. Modify the program of Figure 9–3 to obtain the following output:

	STORE 1	STORE 2	STORE 3	STORE 4
DAY 1	1Ø	2Ø	1Ø	4Ø
DAY 2	Ø	15	2Ø	35
DAY 3	1Ø	3Ø	Ø	5Ø
DAY 4	Ø	Ø	4Ø	3Ø
DAY 5	5	1Ø	6Ø	Ø
AVERAGE	5	15	26	31

2. Modify the program of Figure 9–4 to obtain the following output:

NAME	TESTS	TEST 1	TEST 2	TEST 3	TEST 4	AVERAGE
ANTON	3	8Ø	74	68		74
BEVIS	1	7Ø				7Ø
HUGHES	4	2Ø	3Ø	6Ø	8Ø	47.5
TERN	2	74	86			8Ø
WATS	3	8Ø	6Ø	2Ø		53.3
AVERAGE		64.8	62.5	49.3	8Ø	

Answers

1. Insert the following code:

```
11 DIM S(4)
12 FOR I = 1 to 4
14     S(I) = Ø
16 NEXT I
31 S(J) = S(J) + A(I,J)
```

and insert the following instructions between lines 56 and 58:

```
PRINT "AVERAGE";
FOR J = 1 TO 4
    PRINT TAB(13*J-2);S(J)/5;
NEXT J
```

2. Insert at line 11: DIM S(100),C(4) where S is for the row average, and C for the column average.

Initialize arrays S and C to 0's.
Initialize array T to negative numbers (all entries).
Insert at line 21: S(I) = S(I) + T(I,J) to compute sum of rows.
Insert at line 23: S(I) = S(I)/B(I) to compute row averages.
Insert at line 49: PRINT TAB(70);S(I).
Starting at line 53 or thereafter: compute the average of each column, as follows:

```
1ØØ PRINT "AVERAGE";
11Ø FOR J=1 TO 4
12Ø    L = Ø
```

```
130    FOR I = 1 TO N
140       IF T(I,J) < 0 THEN 170
150          L = L + 1
160          C(J) = C(J) + T(I,J)
170     NEXT I
180     PRINT TAB(13*J+10);C(J)/L;
190 NEXT J
200 END
```

9-3 Programming Examples

9-3-1 A Frequency Distribution

Data regarding the smoking habits of students at a university have been gathered. Each record contains a student's class (1 = freshman, 2 = sophomore, 3 = junior, 4 = senior, 5 = graduate) and a code representing the student's smoking habits (1 = doesn't smoke, 2 = one pack or less a day, 3 = more than one pack a day). We want to write a program to generate a frequency table displaying the frequency of students' smoking habits by class.

Understanding the Problem

This problem essentially deals with counting, i.e., we need to count how many freshmen do not smoke, how many freshmen smoke one pack or less a day, how many freshmen smoke in excess of one pack, and so forth. Altogether we need 15 counters (five student classifications and three habits). One simple way to solve the problem manually is to draw a table with five rows and three columns and proceed as follows:

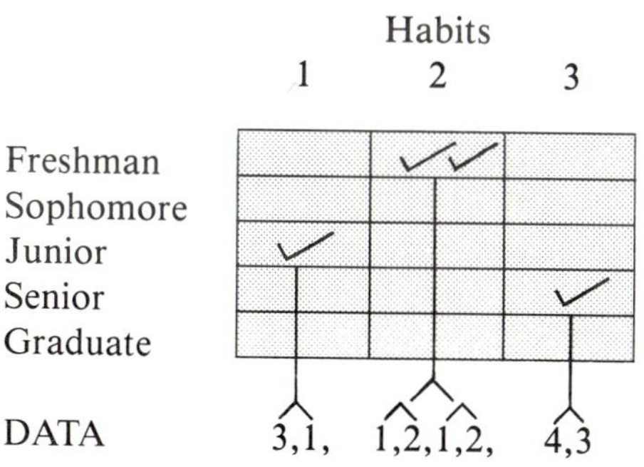

We read the first record, say 3,1 (3 = junior, 1 = doesn't smoke). We then place a check mark in the box at row 3 and column 1. We read the next record, say 1,2 and check the corresponding box. We repeat the process until we run out of records, then we add up the checks in each box.

The table shown here reflects the various counts (frequencies) obtained by processing the four data records given.

To solve this problem on a computer, we can simulate the manual counting process by creating a two-dimensional array K (five rows and three columns), where each entry serves as a counter. Initially, these counters are all set to 0, and every time we read a pair of numbers (class and habit codes), we add 1 to the corresponding array entry. For example, if class = 1 and habit = 2, we add 1 to K (class, habit) which is K (1,2). When all data have been read, K(I,J) will reflect the count of type I students with smoking habit J.

Output Design

Let us use a tabular design to identify the various classifications and habits, using words for student classifications instead of numeric codes. A typical layout could be:

	DONT SMOKE	1 PACK OR LESS	MORE THAN 1
FRESHMAN	Ø	3	Ø
SOPHOMORE	1	1	1
JUNIOR	1	1	Ø
SENIOR	2	1	Ø
GRADUATE	Ø	Ø	2

Data Dictionary

The following variables are needed:

K : K is a two-dimensional array of size 5 by 3; five rows for the five student classifications, and three columns for the three smoking habits. This array consists of 15 entries that are used as counters. K(I,J) identifies the count of class I students with smoking habit J.

N$: N$ is a one-dimensional array of size 5. To simplify the output process, the words FRESHMAN, SOPHOMORE, and so forth, will be read into N$(1), N$(2), ... and then written out as N$(I) as I varies from 1 to 5.

C and S : These two variables are used by the READ statement to read the student's classification code (1–5) and smoking habits (1–3).

Program Development

This program is very similar to the frequency distribution problem of section 8–4–4. The classification code and the smoking code are used to designate which counter is to be incremented. When we read C and S, we know we need to add 1 to the counter K(C,S), since K(C,S) identifies a student with classification C and smoking habit S. Hence, the two statements

```
READ C,S
K(C,S) = K(C,S) + 1
```

are at the heart of the program.

Initially we set all entries of array K to 0. We then use the classification and smoking codes as subscripts of the array K to update the frequency count. For example, if the codes 5 and 3 are read, the number 1 is added to K(5,3) to count another graduate student smoking one or more pack. The code to solve this problem is shown in Figure 9–5.

9-3-2 Airline Reservation Problem

You have been asked to write an on-line reservation system for a small commuter airline company. Each plane can carry up to 20 passengers, distributed along 5 rows with 4 seats per row. The counter agent is to ask each passenger his/her row and seat preference. If the seat requested is available, the agent should reserve that seat. In the event the seat is already taken, the agent is to assign the first available seat starting with row 1, row 2, ..., up to row 5. A message should appear on the screen as soon as the seating capacity has been reached. When all passenger requests have been taken care of, the program should print the seating arrangement, i.e., show the remaining available seats.

Figure 9–5 A frequency distribution using a two-dimensional array.

```
10 REM TWO-DIMENSIONAL FREQUENCY DISTRIBUTION
12 REM DATA DICTIONARY
14 REM K:  ARRAY USED AS COUNTERS. SIZE IS 5 BY 3
16 REM N$: ARRAY CONTAINING STUDENT CLASSIFICATION. SIZE IS 5
18 REM C:  STUDENT CLASSIFICATION CODE (1=F; 2=S; 3=J; 4=S; 5=G)
20 REM S:  SMOKING HABIT (1 = NO SMOKE; 2 = 1 PACK OR LESS; 3 = MORE THAN 1)
22 DIM K(5,3), N$(5)
24 FOR I = 1 TO 5
26     READ N$(I)                  Read student classification words.
28     FOR J = 1 TO 3
30         K(I,J) = 0              Initialize the 15 counters to 0.
32     NEXT J
34 NEXT I
36 READ C, S                       Read a classification code and a smoking habit
38 IF C = 0 THEN 44
40     K(C,S) = K(C,S) + 1         Update corresponding counter; for example, if
42     GOTO 36                     C=2 and S=3 then K(2,3) = K(2,3) + 1.
44 PRINT
46 PRINT TAB(11);"DONT SMOKE";TAB(24);"1 PACK OR LESS";TAB(40);"MORE THAN 1"
48 FOR I = 1 TO 5
50     PRINT N$(I), K(I,1), K(I,2), K(I,3)     Print the counters
52 NEXT I
54 DATA FRESHMAN, SOPHOMORE, JUNIOR, SENIOR, GRADUATE
56 DATA 3,1, 1,2, 3,2, 1,2, 5,3, 1,2, 5,3, 2,2, 2,3, 4,1, 4,1, 4,2, 2,1, 0,0
58 END

RUN

               DONT SMOKE    1 PACK OR LESS    MORE THAN 1
FRESHMAN           0               3               0
SOPHOMORE          1               1               1
JUNIOR             1               1               0
SENIOR             2               1               0
GRADUATE           0               0               2
```

Understanding the Problem

We will represent the plane's seating configuration with a 5 by 4 array P. Initially, these 20 seats are set to 0 to indicate nonreserved seats. Thus P(3,4) = 0 means that seat number 4 in row 3 is empty. When a particular seat is reserved, we set the corresponding array entry to 1. Thus if row 4 seat 4 has been reserved, we set P(4,4) to 1. If there are fewer than 20 passengers, the agent enters a special code to terminate the reservation process and the computer prints a seating arrangement of the plane. Seat preferences are accepted by the agent through the INPUT statement. The following diagram illustrates the reservation process.

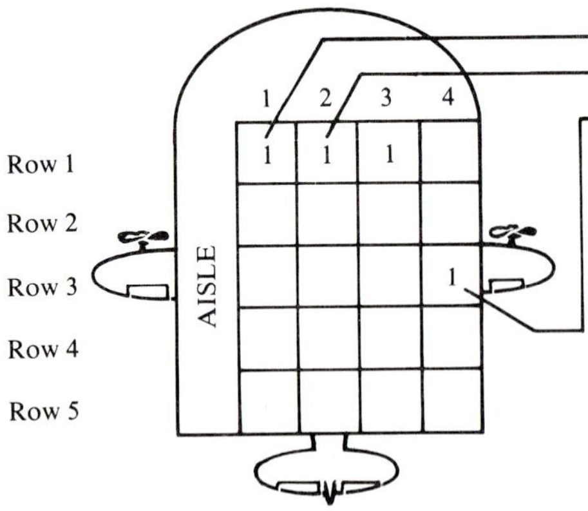


```
INPUT ROW,SEAT ? 1,1
INPUT ROW,SEAT ? 1,1
INPUT ROW,SEAT ? 3,4
INPUT ROW,SEAT ? 3,4
```

Note that the second request of seat 1 at row 1 is already taken, hence we assign the next available seat which is at row 1 seat 2 according to the scheme explained above.

Output Design

Since passenger requests will be accepted through the INPUT statement, both the INPUT data and the final seating arrangements, will be displayed on the output:

Input Information

```
ENTER ROW THEN SEAT? 1,2
ENTER ROW THEN SEAT? 2,3
ENTER ROW THEN SEAT? 1,2
ENTER ROW THEN SEAT? 4,1
ENTER ROW THEN SEAT? 4,4
ENTER ROW THEN SEAT? 5,1
ENTER ROW THEN SEAT? Ø,Ø
```

Final Seating Arrangement

```
ROW 1      1  1  Ø  Ø
ROW 2      Ø  Ø  1  Ø
ROW 3      Ø  Ø  Ø  Ø
ROW 4      1  Ø  Ø  1
ROW 5      1  Ø  Ø  Ø
```

Data Dictionary

The following variables are needed for this problem:

P : P is an array consisting of 5 rows and 4 columns (for the 4 seats). Initially, each array entry is 0; as seats are reserved, corresponding entries are set to 1.

R and S : R is the row preference of the passenger, and S is his/her seat preference. These two variables are used in the input statement INPUT R,S to accept the passenger's request.

Program Development

In a problem like this one, a verbal outline may be preferable to pseudo code or flowchart:

Main Procedure

Zero out all elements of array P.
Input a seat request (R,S).
If there are no more passengers (R = 0, S = 0), transfer to TERMINATE procedure.
If seat is not taken, reserve it, count it, and go back to input another seat request; otherwise go through SEARCH procedure.

Search Procedure

Start the search for an available seat at position 1,1.
If the seat is available, reserve it, and go back to input a seat request; otherwise keep searching in row fashion starting with row 1.
If all the seats are taken, print a message and terminate.

Terminate Procedure

Print the seating arrangement.
Stop.

The code to solve this problem is shown in Figure 9-6.

Testing

The program in Figure 9-6 should be tested on each of the three distinct paths illustrated by the following DATA statements:

1. `DATA 1,1, 3,1, 5,1`	All requests are distinct (all are available).
2. `DATA 1,1, 1,1, 1,1, 3,1`	Some of the seats are already reserved.
3. `DATA 1,1, ..., 1,1`	Twenty seat requests force message "PLANE IS FULL" to be displayed.

9-3-3 Do It Now

Suppose the airline's policy on seating arrangements was as follows: If a seat is already taken, give the passenger the first available seat in the requested row; if this is not possible, move back a row (toward the tail of the airplane) and continue in this way to the last row, then move up to the 1st row, 2nd row, and so forth. Modify the program to use this policy.

■ **Figure 9–6** An airline reservation problem.

```
1Ø REM AIRPLANE SEATING RESERVATION
12 REM DATA DICTIONARY
14 REM       P: ARRAY DISPLAYING PLANE SEATING ARRANGEMENT
18 REM       R: PASSENGER'S ROW REQUEST
2Ø REM       S: PASSENGER'S SEAT PREFERENCE
22 DIM P(5,4)
26 FOR I = 1 TO 5
28     FOR J = 1 TO 4
3Ø         P(I,J) = Ø                      Initialize all seats to 0.
32     NEXT J
34 NEXT I
36 PRINT "ENTER ROW THEN SEAT";
37 INPUT R, S                              Accept passenger seat requests.
38 IF R = Ø THEN 67                        Are there any more passengers?
4Ø    IF P(R,S) = 1 THEN 48                If seat is taken, go to line 48 to assign first available seat.
42       P(R,S) = 1                        If seat available, reserve it.
46       GOTO 36                           Go accept new passenger seat requests.
48 FOR I = 1 TO 5                          Start checking for available seats, working
5Ø     FOR J = 1 TO 4                      from row 1 through row 5.
52         IF P(I,J) = 1 THEN 6Ø
54            P(I,J) = 1                   If seat is available, reserve it.
58           GOTO 36                       Go to the next customer's requests.
6Ø        NEXT J                           If the loop exits through the NEXT I statement,
62 NEXT I                                  then all seats are taken and plane is full.
64 PRINT "PLANE IS FULL; TERMINATE RESERVATION"
66 GOTO 84
67 PRINT,,"FINAL SEATING ARRANGEMENT"  0,0 terminates the reservation process.
68 PRINT
7Ø     FOR I = 1 TO 5
72         PRINT ,,"ROW"; I,
74         FOR J = 1 TO 4
76             PRINT P(I,J);               Print plane's seating arrangement.
78         NEXT J
8Ø         PRINT
82     NEXT I
84 END
RUN
ENTER ROW THEN SEAT? 1,2
ENTER ROW THEN SEAT? 2,3
ENTER ROW THEN SEAT? 1,2
ENTER ROW THEN SEAT? 4,1
ENTER ROW THEN SEAT? 4,4
ENTER ROW THEN SEAT? 5,1
ENTER ROW THEN SEAT? Ø,Ø

                         FINAL SEATING ARRANGEMENT

                         ROW 1          1  1  Ø  Ø
                         ROW 2          Ø  Ø  1  Ø
                         ROW 3          Ø  Ø  Ø  Ø
                         ROW 4          1  Ø  Ø  1
                         ROW 5          1  Ø  Ø  Ø
```

9-3-4 A Bar Graph

The daily volume of a major stock exchange is given in millions of shares for the three weeks starting July 8:

JULY 8		JULY 15		JULY 22	
VOLUME TRANSACTION	WORKDAY	VOLUME TRANSACTION	WORKDAY	VOLUME TRANSACTION	WORKDAY
5	1	5	1	3	1
7	2	3	2	2	2
8	3	5	3	1	3
9	4	4	4	2	4
7	5	2	5	4	5

Write a program to produce a bar graph like the one shown below for the 15 workdays starting July 8.

```
Volume

9             *
8          *  *
7       *  *  *  *
6       *  *  *  *
5    *  *  *  *  *  *     *
4    *  *  *  *  *  *     *  *                 *
3    *  *  *  *  *  *  *  *  *     *           *
2    *  *  *  *  *  *  *  *  *  *  *  *     *  *
1    *  *  *  *  *  *  *  *  *  *  *  *  *  *  *
     1_ 2_ 3_ 4_ 5_ 1_ 2_ 3_ 4_ 5_ 1_ 2_ 3_ 4_ 5__> Days
```

Understanding the Problem

For this problem we need to use an array G$ consisting of at least 9 rows (for the maximum volume of sales during the 15-day period) and 15 columns (for the 15 days). Initially, we set the array G$ to blanks. (If your system does not support alphanumeric arrays, use array G and initialize G to 0's.) We then read the transaction volume for the first day of the first week—it is 5, which means that we must insert 5 asterisks in the 1st column of G$. We then proceed with the next transaction volume (7) and insert 7 asterisks in the second column. The same steps are carried out up to the 15th day, where we insert 4 asterisks in the elements G$(1,15), G$(2,15), G$(3,15), and G$(4,15). The process can be visualized as follows:

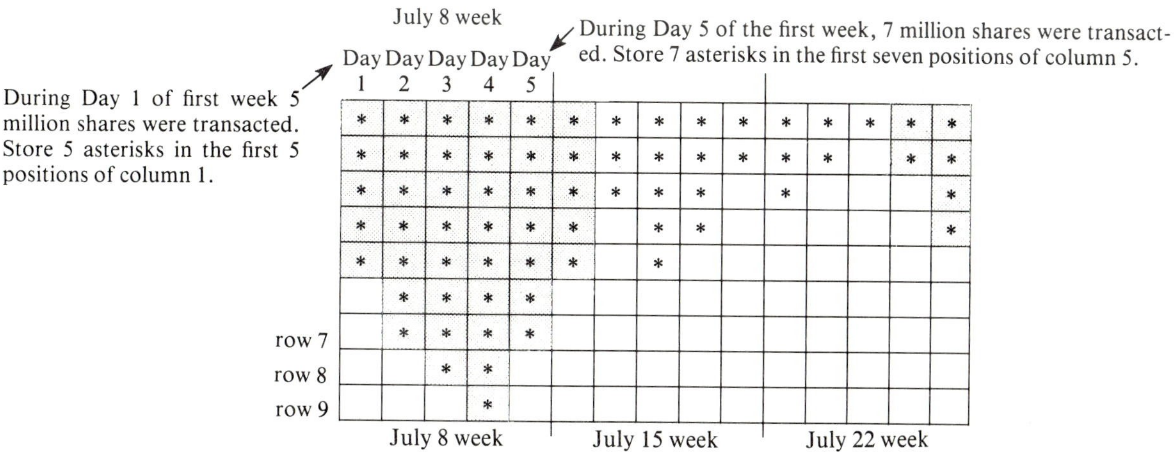

In the diagram on the previous page, the bar graph peaks down rather than up. We want to turn it upside down, i.e., rotate it 180°, as follows:

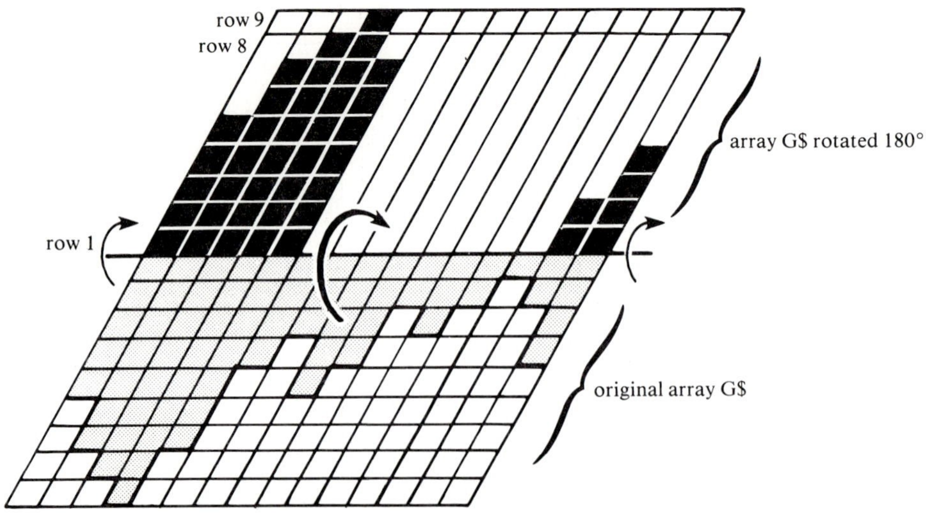

This rotation can be achieved by printing the bottom of the array first, i.e., printing row 9 on the first line, row 8 on the second line, and so forth.

Data Dictionary

The following variables are needed:

G$: G$ is a 9 by 15 array. Each column of that array will be filled with an appropriate number of asterisks to reflect, graphically, the transaction volume for a particular day. If alphanumeric arrays are not available on your system, replace the asterisk with the number 1 and replace the blank character with 0.

V : V represents the volume of a particular day's transaction. This value represents the number of asterisks that we must store in a particular column of array G$.

I and J : I and J represent the variables used to identify the graduations on each axis (volume and day).

Program Development

The problem can be broken down into the following tasks:

1. Initialize array G$(9,15) with blank characters.
2. Read the number of transactions for the 1st day and call it V.
   Store V asterisks in the 1st column of G$.
   Then read the number of transactions for the 2nd day, call it V.
   Store V asterisks in the 2nd column of G$.
   Keep repeating these steps for days 3, 4, ..., up to 15.
3. Print the array G$, starting with row 10, row 9, ..., to row 1.
4. Print the graduations for the day axis, i.e. 1,2,3,4,5,1,2,3,4,5,1,2,3,4,5.

■ **Figure 9–7** A bar graph.

```
10 REM TWO-DIMENSIONAL BAR GRAPH
11 REM DATA DICTIONARY
12 REM      G$: EACH OF THE 15 COLUMNS DEPICTS A DAY'S TRANSACTION VOLUME
13 REM      V:  REPRESENTS A DAY'S TRANSACTION VOLUME
14 REM      I:  REPRESENTS THE VERTICAL GRADUATIONS OF GRAPH
15 REM      J:  REPRESENTS THE HORIZONTAL GRADUATIONS ALONG AXIS
17 REM
18 DIM G$(9,15)
20 FOR I = 1 TO 9
25     FOR J = 1 TO 15
30         G$(I,J) = "   "
35     NEXT J
40 NEXT I
45 FOR J = 1 TO 15
50     READ V
55     FOR I = 1 TO V
60         G$(I,J) = " * "
65     NEXT I
70 NEXT J
75 FOR I = 9 TO 1 STEP -1
80     PRINT I; TAB(4);
85     FOR J = 1 TO 15
90         PRINT G$(I,J);
95     NEXT J
97  PRINT
100 NEXT I
101 PRINT
105 PRINT TAB(4);
110 FOR I = 1 TO 3
115     FOR J = 1 TO 5
120         PRINT J;
125     NEXT J
130 NEXT I
135 DATA 5, 7, 8, 9, 7
140 DATA 5, 3, 5, 4, 2
145 DATA 3, 2, 1, 2, 4
150 END
```

Lines 30–40: Blank out array G$. Each array element is 3 characters so that the "bars" of asterisks on the output are well aligned with the numeric graduations.

Line 45: Process 15 columns.

Lines 50–60: Read the number of transactions for a day and represent it by storing an equal number of asterisks in a particular column.

Line 75: Print the array starting with the bottom row.

Lines 80–85: Print vertical graduation first, followed by the 9th row of G, then the 8th row, and so forth.

Line 120: Print the horizontal graduations 1 through 15.

Line 135: First week's daily transactions.

Line 140: Second week's daily transactions.

Line 145: Third week's daily transactions.

```
RUN
9       *
8     * *
7   * * * *
6   * * * *
5 * * * * * *   *
4 * * * * * *   * *           *
3 * * * * * * * * *   *       *
2 * * * * * * * * * * * *   * *
1 * * * * * * * * * * * * * * *

  1 2 3 4 5 1 2 3 4 5 1 2 3 4 5
```

The BASIC code to solve this problem is shown in Figure 9-7.
It is also possible to print the bar graph using solid bars instead of asterisks:

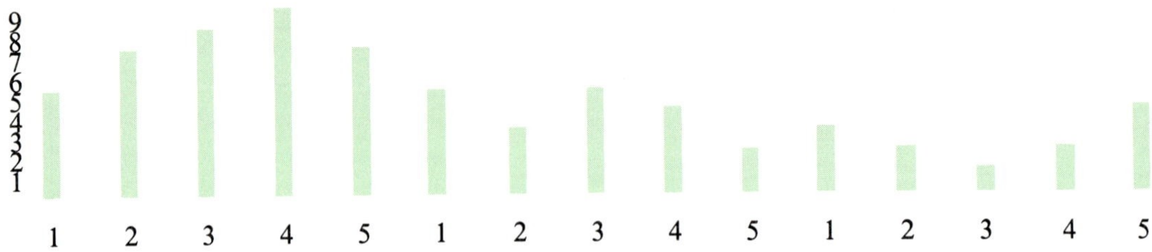

To do this, change line 60 to: G$(I,J) = "   " + CHR$(239) + "   "
where CHR$(239) = ■ (this numeric code may differ from printer to printer).
Also the line feed may have to be set to 1/2 advance, as was done in the above display. This can be done by inserting LPRINT CHR$(X) at line 19 (X is your printer code for ½ line advance; see your printer reference manual for the value of X).

9-3-5 Do It Now

Change the code of Figure 9-7 to print the same bar graph in the following form:

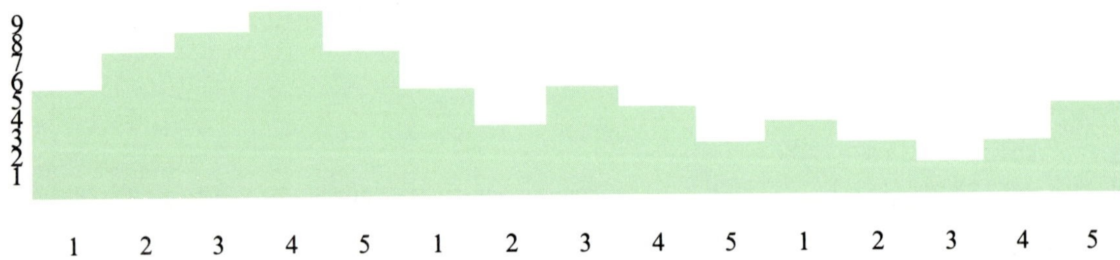

Answer

Change line 60 to: G$(I,J) = CHR$(239) + CHR$(239) + CHR$(239). Note again that the graphic symbol ■ will differ from one printer model to the next. To draw this display on a video screen on an IBM PC computer change 239 to 219; on a TRS-80 model 2 change 239 to 155. For other systems, look up the video graphic code for ■ in the reference manual.

9-3-6 A Warehouse Stock Problem

You own six warehouses across the country, each of which can stock five particular items. The stock quantities for each of the five items in each warehouse are recorded in a data file like the one shown below. Write a program to read the data into a two-dimensional array to produce the output shown on the next page.

Identify on the output any item that is out of stock (stock is 0) in three or more warehouses. Also print the warehouses and item numbers where the stock is below 10. When listing those item numbers with stock level less than 10, note that commas separate each item—the list should terminate with an item number, not a comma.

Output

```
                      ITEMS            TOTALS
              1    2    3    4    5

WAREHOUSE 1  21    6   23   12   58      120
WAREHOUSE 2  44   22   33   44   55      198
WAREHOUSE 3  74    0    0    6   89      169
WAREHOUSE 4   9    0   22   33   55      119
WAREHOUSE 5  45    0    0   11   65      121
WAREHOUSE 6  55    0    0    6    3       64

TOTALS      248   28   78  112  325

ITEM 2 HAS 0 STOCK IN 3 OR MORE WAREHOUSES
ITEM 3 HAS 0 STOCK IN 3 OR MORE WAREHOUSES

WAREHOUSE   ITEM NUMBER (STOCK BELOW 10)
    1         2
    3         2,3,4
    4         1,2
    5         2,3
    6         2,3,4,5
```

Items 2, 3 and 4 have stock below 10 in warehouse 3.

Input

```
DATA 21,06,23,12,58
DATA 44,22,33,44,55
DATA 74,00,00,06,89
DATA 09,00,22,33,55
DATA 45,00,00,11,65
DATA 55,00,00,06,03
```

Warehouse 1, 2, 3, 4, 5, 6

Item 1 quantity

Item 4 quantity

Item 5 quantity

Understanding the Problem

The problem consists of four parts:

1. Computing the sum of each row of the array.
2. Computing the sum of each column of the array.
3. Searching each column to determine whether it has 3 or more 0 entries.
4. Searching each row to find entries that are less than 10.

The last part is probably the more interesting part of the problem as it requires us to look at a row and identify in that row the column number of any array element less than 10. We need to print the column number (item number), not the column entry (quantity). Separating the output items with commas requires a little more attention, however. We cannot use the statement PRINT J;"," every time we find an entry less than 10 in column J, since a comma would appear to the right of the last item number, i.e., we cannot have:

```
WAREHOUSE   ITEM NUMBER
    3         2, 3, 4,
```

No trailing comma is allowed after the last item number.

We could avoid this problem by printing the comma and *then* the item number, but then a comma would precede the first number:

```
WAREHOUSE    ITEM NUMBER
    3        , 2, 3, 4
```

There should be no comma before the first item.

We will solve this problem by simply printing the item number using the statement PRINT J the first time we encounter an item number whose stock is less than 10; then for all other item numbers we will use the statement PRINT ",";J .

Data Dictionary

The following variables are needed to solve this problem:

W(6,5) : This array will contain the various stock quantities for each of the 5 items in each of the 6 warehouses.

We will make the output design easier by using the PRINT USING statement. We could obtain the same output layout with the TAB statement at the expense of a little more work. The character strings for the PRINT USING statements are A$, B$, C$, and D$.

C(5) : This optional array allows us to compute the sums of each column as the data is read into the array, so that the column totals can be printed as soon as the array W has been loaded.

K : The variable K is used in the third part of the problem to count the number of entries that are less than 10 in a particular column. In the fourth part of the problem, K is used as a switch or flag: When K is 0, transfer will be made to the statement PRINT J, but when K = 1, transfer will be made to PRINT ",";J to ensure that a comma will separate each item number in the list of item numbers.

Program Development

Let us analyze the program shown in Figure 9–8. Initially, the array C is set to 0's. The array C is used to compute the five sums of the five columns of array W. As each DATA statement is read, we accumulate the sums of each row (line 225) and we also accumulate partial column totals (line 230). Each row and the sum of its entries are then printed (line 240). When the entire array has been printed, we print the column totals (line 255).

In the third part of the problem, we examine each column (line 265) and search for entries that are 0. If there are 3 or more zero entries in a particular column, we print the column number (item number) and the message. K is used to count each occurrence of a zero entry (line 295.) If K is less than 3, no message is printed.

In the fourth part of the problem, we analyze each row and print the item numbers whose stock level is below 10. The variable K is used as a flag. Initially K is set to 0 (line 325) and tested for zero value at line 336; if it is 0, the item number is printed without a comma (line 339) and K is reset to 1. The next time we find an item number whose quantity is below 10, a comma will be printed before the item number (line 337) since K is now nonzero.

Figure 9–8 A warehouse stock problem.

```
100 REM WAREHOUSE STOCK PROBLEM
105 REM DATA DICTIONARY
110 REM       W: 6 WAREHOUSES EACH STOCKING 5 DIFFERENT ITEMS: 6 BY 5 ARRAY
115 REM       B$ AND C$ ARE USED TO PRINT THE HEADERS
120 REM       A$ AND D$ ARE USED TO PRINT THE VARIOUS OUTPUT LINES
125 REM       S: ACCUMULATES THE SUM OF EACH ROW OF ARRAY W
130 REM       C: ARRAY USED TO ACCUMULATE THE SUMS OF EACH COLUMNS
135 REM       K: COUNTS NUMBER OF ITEMS WITH Ø STOCK IN ANY PARTICULAR WAREHOUSE
140 REM       K: IS A FLAG USED TO DECIDE IF A COMMA IS TO BE PRINTED OR NOT
145 REM
150 DIM W(6,5), C(5)
155 C$ = "                          ITEMS           TOTALS      "
160 B$ = "                 1    2    3    4    5               "
165 A$ = "WAREHOUSE #     ##   ##   ##   ##   ##      ###       "
170 D$ = "TOTALS         ###  ###  ###  ###  ###                "
175 PRINT C$
180 PRINT B$
185 PRINT
190 FOR  I = 1 TO 5
195      C(I) = Ø
200 NEXT I
205 FOR I = 1 TO 6
210     S = Ø
215     FOR J = 1 TO 5
220         READ W(I,J)
225         S = S + W(I,J)
230         C(J) = C(J) + W(I,J)
235     NEXT J
240 PRINT USING A$; I,W(I,1),W(I,2),W(I,3),W(I,4),W(I,5),S
245 NEXT I
250 PRINT
255 PRINT USING D$;C(1),C(2),C(3),C(4),C(5)
260 PRINT
265 FOR J = 1 TO 5
270     K = Ø
275     FOR  I = 1 TO 6
280          IF W(I,J) <> Ø THEN 290
285             K = K + 1
290     NEXT I
295     IF K < 3 THEN 305
300        PRINT "ITEM";J;"HAS Ø STOCK IN 3 OR MORE WAREHOUSES"
305 NEXT J
310 PRINT
315 PRINT "WAREHOUSE","ITEM NUMBER (STOCK BELOW 1Ø)"
320 FOR I = 1 TO 6
325   K = Ø
330   FOR J = 1 TO 5
335     IF W(I,J) >= 1Ø THEN 35Ø
336        IF K = Ø THEN 339
337           PRINT ","; J;
338           GOTO 34Ø
339           PRINT TAB(4);I,J;
340        K = 1
350   NEXT J
380 NEXT I
385 DATA 21,Ø6,23,12,58
390 DATA 44,22,33,44,55
395 DATA 74,ØØ,ØØ,Ø6,89
400 DATA Ø9,ØØ,22,33,55
405 DATA 45,ØØ,ØØ,11,65
410 DATA 55,ØØ,ØØ,Ø6,Ø3
415 END
```

```
                                ITEMS               TOTALS
                  1     2     3     4     5

WAREHOUSE 1      21     6    23    12    58        12Ø
WAREHOUSE 2      44    22    33    44    55        198
WAREHOUSE 3      74     Ø     Ø     6    89        169
WAREHOUSE 4       9     Ø    22    33    55        119
WAREHOUSE 5      45     Ø     Ø    11    65        121
WAREHOUSE 6      55     Ø     Ø     6     3         64

TOTALS          248    28    78   112   325

ITEM 2 HAS Ø STOCK IN 3 OR MORE WAREHOUSES
ITEM 3 HAS Ø STOCK IN 3 OR MORE WAREHOUSES

WAREHOUSE       ITEM NUMBER (STOCK BELOW 1Ø)
    1           2
    3           2 , 3 , 4
    4           1 , 2
    5           2 , 3
    6           2 , 3 , 4 , 5
```

9-3-7 Do It Now

Modify the program in Figure 9–8 so that no array is used to store the various column totals.

Answer

Delete lines 190 through 200, 230, and 255, and add the following code:

```
251 PRINT "TOTALS",
252 FOR J = 1 TO 5
253     T = Ø
254     FOR I = 1 TO 6
255         T = T + W(I,J)
256     NEXT I
257     PRINT T;
258 NEXT J
259 PRINT
```

9-4 Matrices

Not all BASIC systems support matrix operations. Also, some details of the matrix statements differ among the systems that do support matrix operations. The reader is advised to read the documentation for his/her system carefully before attempting programs using the matrix statements described in this section.

9-4-1 Definition

A matrix is a rectangular arrangement of objects in row and column fashion. A chessboard is an example of a matrix. In this chapter, we will define a matrix as a rectangular array of numbers. Matrices play an important role in nearly all areas of science, where they are subject to various types of operations and manipulation.

9-4-2 A Matrix Case Study

Mr. Fish is a microcomputer salesman, and the entire Fish family (10 children) has access to a microcomputer installed in the Fishes' living room. Mrs. Fish has just completed an introductory course in principles of management, and as a result of her brief exposure to computers in that course, she has decided to "computer watch" her food expenditures. Mrs. Fish feeds her family store-bought sandwiches: hamburgers, hot dogs, and tacos. At the end of the week, Mrs. Fish has tabulated the family's daily consumption of delicacies as follows:

	MON	TUES	WED	THURS	FRI	SAT	SUN
Hamburgers	32	30	28	25	23	24	28
Hot dogs	12	14	16	17	20	25	20
Tacos	18	20	22	24	22	25	30

She has now kept track of her food expenses for two weeks in this fashion and would like a computer printout sheet of the two corresponding "consumption" tables. Initially, she writes programs with and without matrices, as shown in Figure 9–9.

Figure 9–9 Matrix input/output.

ARRAY INPUT/OUTPUT WITHOUT MAT STATEMENT

```
100 REM WITHOUT MATRICES
150 DIM F1(3,7)
200 DIM F2(3,7)
250 FOR I = 1 TO 3
300   FOR J = 1 TO 7
350      READ F1(I,J)
400      PRINT F1(I,J);
450   NEXT J
500   PRINT
550 NEXT I
600 PRINT
650 FOR I = 1 TO 3
700   FOR J = 1 TO 7
750      READ F2(I,J)
800      PRINT F2(I,J);
850   NEXT J
900   PRINT
950 NEXT I
1000 REM FIRST WEEK DATA
1050 DATA 32, 30, 28, 25, 23, 24, 28
1100 DATA 12, 14, 16, 17, 20, 25, 20
1150 DATA 18, 20, 22, 24, 22, 25, 30
1200 REM SECOND WEEK DATA
1250 DATA 30, 28, 33, 27, 25, 26, 23
1300 DATA 15, 17, 14, 20, 21, 27, 25
1350 DATA 20, 21, 25, 19, 18, 27, 33
1450 END
```

ARRAY INPUT/OUTPUT WITH MAT STATEMENTS

```
100 REM WITH MATRICES
150 DIM F1(3,7)      Consumption table for first week.
200 DIM F2(3,7)      Consumption table for second week.
350 MAT READ F1      Read first weekly table.
400 MAT PRINT F1     Print first weekly table.
750 MAT READ F2      Read second weekly table.
800 MAT PRINT F2     Print second weekly table.
1000 REM FIRST WEEK DATA
1050 DATA 32, 30, 28, 25, 23, 24, 28
1100 DATA 12, 14, 16, 17, 20, 25, 20
1150 DATA 18, 20, 22, 24, 22, 25, 30
1200 REM SECOND WEEK DATA
1250 DATA 30, 28, 33, 27, 25, 26, 23
1300 DATA 15, 17, 14, 20, 21, 27, 25
1350 DATA 20, 21, 25, 19, 18, 27, 33
1450 END
```

Output: Weekly Consumption Tables

Table F1	32	30	28	25	23	24	28
	12	14	16	17	20	25	20
	18	20	22	24	22	25	30
Table F2	30	28	33	27	25	26	23
	15	17	14	20	21	27	25
	20	21	25	19	18	27	33

Mrs. Fish would now like to print an up-to-date table reflecting the accumulated daily consumption (sum of both tables) and an average consumption table for the last two weeks (each entry in the accumulated table is divided by 2). She adds the code shown in Figure 9–10 to the existing program.

Analyzing her new "average" table consumption, Mrs. Fish becomes concerned about excessive calorie intake. She decides that her family should cut its consumption by 10%, so she adds the code to adjust each entry by 10% and print the resulting "calorie-adjusted" table (Figure 9–11), so that she can see what a more desirable consumption level would be.

Mrs. Fish now becomes concerned about costs. She recalls that hamburgers cost 50 cents, hot dogs 35 cents, and tacos 55 cents. She decides to compute the daily cost associated with last week's food purchases. To simplify her calculations, she rearranges the weekly consumption table in column form as shown on next page:

Figure 9–10 Matrix addition and scalar multiplication.

ARRAY OPERATIONS WITHOUT MAT STATEMENTS

```
210 REM F IS THE SUM OF F1 + F2
220 DIM F(3,7)
952 FOR I = 1 TO 3
954    FOR J = 1 TO 7
956       LET F(I,J) = F1(I,J) + F2(I,J)
958       PRINT F(I,J);
960    NEXT J
962    PRINT
964 NEXT I
966 FOR I = 1 TO 3
968    FOR J = 1 TO 7
970       LET F(I,J) = F(I,J)/2
972       REM F IS THE AVERAGE TABLE
974       PRINT F(I,J);
976    NEXT J
978    PRINT
980 NEXT I
```

ARRAY OPERATIONS WITH MAT STATEMENTS

```
210 REM F IS THE SUM OF F1 + F2
220 DIM F(3,7)

956 MAT F = F1 + F2      Add both arrays.
958 MAT PRINT F          Print the result (sum
                         of the two arrays).

970 MAT F = (.5)*F       Multiply each
                         entry by 0.5.
974 MAT PRINT F          Print resulting
                         array.
```

Output

Sum of two tables F = F1 + F2

```
62 58 61 52 48 50 51
27 31 30 37 41 52 45
38 41 47 43 40 52 63
```

Average of two tables F = (F1 + F2)/2

```
31    29    30.5 26    24    25    25.5
13.5 15.5 15    18.5 20.5 26    22.5
19    20.5 23.5 21.5 20    26    31.5
```

DAYS	HAM-BURGERS	HOT DOGS	TACOS
1	30	15	20
2	28	17	21
3	33	15	25
4	27	20	19
5	25	21	18
6	26	27	27
7	23	25	33

$$\text{daily cost} = 30 \times 0.5 + 15 \times 0.35 + 20 \times 0.55 = 31.25$$

$$\text{daily cost} = 28 \times 0.5 + 17 \times 0.35 + 21 \times 0.55 = 31.5$$

.
.
.

(↑ Cost of hamburgers, ↑ Cost of hot dogs, ↑ Cost of tacos)

She has computed the first two days' cost by hand and decides to add the code to her existing program to complete the problem. She first tries to multiply with arrays but soon can't extricate herself from the many loops. She then recalls how matrices can be used to do the job: multiply the preceding 7-row, 3-column consumption table by the cost matrix (.50,.35,.55). She writes the code shown in Figure 9–12.

The daily costs (array Z) for the second week as shown in Figure 9–12 seems a little high to Mrs. Fish. As a meticulous housewife and manager, she has kept her daily food bills for the last week. The daily store receipts don't quite match the computerized list of daily costs shown in Figure 9–12. Her store receipts show the amounts given in Figure 9–13 (taxes excluded).

Figure 9–11 Matrix subtraction and scalar multiplication.

ARRAY OPERATIONS WITHOUT MAT STATEMENTS

```
225 REM L IS THE CALORIE ADJUSTED TABLE


23Ø DIM L(3,7)
982 FOR I = 1 TO 3
984   FOR J = 1 TO 7
986     LET L(I,J) = F(I,J) - .1*F(I,J)
988     PRINT L(I,J);
99Ø   NEXT J
992   PRINT
994 NEXT I
```

ARRAY OPERATIONS WITH MAT STATEMENT

```
225 REM L IS THE CALORIE
226 REM ADJUSTED TABLE
23Ø DIM L(3,7)

986 MAT L = (.1)*F
988 MAT L = F - L
99Ø MAT PRINT L
```

Output

Adjusted table L

27.9	26.1	27.45	23.4	21.6	22.5	22.95
12.15	13.95	13.5	16.65	18.45	23.4	2Ø.25
17.1	18.45	21.15	19.35	18	23.4	28.35

■ **Figure 9–12** Matrix transpose and matrix multiplication.

```
 234 REM FINDING THE DAILY COST
 235 DIM T(7,3)                    Second weekly consumption table rearranged.
 240 DIM C(3,1)                    Cost array of sandwiches according to Mrs.
                                   Fish's recollections.
 245 DIM Z(7,1)                    Array to show daily costs of sandwich purchases.
1355 MAT T = TRN(F2)               Make the rows of array F2 become the columns of T.
1360 MAT PRINT T                   Print rearranged array.
1365 MAT READ C                    Read in the cost array.
1370 MAT Z = T*C                   Find the daily costs for seven days.
1375 MAT PRINT Z                   Print the costs.
1380 DATA .50, .35, .55            Cost of sandwiches.
```

Output

```
30    15    20  }
28    17    21  }
33    14    25  }  This array T is the second week's daily consumption
27    20    19  }  table F2, rearranged (transposed). The columns of T
25    21    18  }  are just the rows of F2.
26    27    27  }
23    25    33  }

31.25           }  Sandwich costs for first day of second week.
31.5            }  Sandwich costs for second day of second week.
35.15           }  .
30.95           }  .       Array Z
29.75           }  .
37.3            }
38.4            }
```

■ **Figure 9–13** Store receipts for second week.

DAY	STORE RECEIPTS
1	31.00
2	31.00
3	34.85
4	30.35
5	29.05
6	35.90
7	36.65

Mrs. Fish attributes the difference in costs to the fact that she wasn't entirely sure about the cost of each sandwich when she wrote the program shown in Figure 9–12. She could call up the store and inquire about the cost of each sandwich, but she decides to do some double-checking by calculating the cost per sandwich herself. She knows the number of sandwiches bought each day, and she knows what the store charged for the sandwiches each day. So she writes the following sets of equations:

30 hamburgers + 15 hot dogs + 20 tacos = 31.00
28 hamburgers + 17 hot dogs + 21 tacos = 31.00
33 hamburgers + 14 hot dogs + 25 tacos = 34.85

⋮

23 hamburgers + 25 hot dogs + 33 tacos = 36.65

Mrs. Fish tries to write a program without matrices to solve this problem, but simply can't do it. From her course in management, she recalls how to solve a system of equations using matrices. Mrs. Fish figures she needs only any three of these equations to determine the cost per sandwich. She arbitrarily selects the first three equations and rewrites them in a less cumbersome way:

$$30X + 15Y + 20Z = 31.00$$
$$28X + 17Y + 21Z = 31.00$$
$$33X + 14Y + 25Z = 34.85$$

X, Y and Z represent the unit cost of hamburgers, hot dogs, and tacos to be computed

She gives a name to the matrix of coefficients of the variables (unknowns).

$$T = \begin{pmatrix} 30 & 15 & 20 \\ 28 & 17 & 21 \\ 33 & 14 & 25 \end{pmatrix} \qquad R = \begin{pmatrix} X \\ Y \\ Z \end{pmatrix} \qquad Z = \begin{pmatrix} 31 \\ 31 \\ 34.85 \end{pmatrix}$$

Matrix of coefficients — Result array — Purchases for first three days

She now solves the system of equations using the program shown in Figure 9–14.

Mrs. Fish calls the store and finds out that hamburgers cost 55 cents, hot dogs 30 cents, and tacos 50 cents. She is satisfied that these figures match the figures she obtained with her program (Figure 9–14).

Figure 9–14 Determining the cost of each sandwich.

```
 246 REM DETERMINING COST PER ITEM
 247 DIM I1(3,3), T(3,3)      Array I1 is used to compute the inverse of the coefficient matrix.
 249 DIM R(3,1), Z(3,1)       Result array will show costs of the three sandwiches.
1385 MAT READ T               Read the first three rows of the matrix of coefficients.
1387 MAT READ Z               Read the first three daily costs.
1389 MAT I1 = INV(T)          Compute the inverse of the matrix of coefficients T.
1391 MAT R = I1*Z             Compute cost of each of the three items.
1393 MAT PRINT R              Print out results.
1395 DATA 30, 15, 20 )
1396 DATA 28, 17, 21 }        Matrix of coefficents T.
1397 DATA 33, 14, 25 )
1398 DATA 31, 31, 34.85       Matrix Z.

             ( .54999999993   Cost of hamburgers
Matrix R =  {  .30000000003   Cost of hot dogs
             ( 0.5            Cost of tacos
```

9-4-3 Matrix Statements

Figure 9–15 displays the thirteen matrix statements that are available on many BASIC systems with matrix features.

Figure 9–15 BASIC operations on matrices.

OPERATION	*BASIC STATEMENTS*		*COMMENTS*
Dimension	`DIM A(3,3),B(3,3),C(3,3)`		Establish matrix sizes

Input/Output	`MAT READ A,B`
	`MAT INPUT A,B`
	`MAT PRINT A,B`
		$A=\begin{pmatrix}1 & 2 & -3\\ -4 & 5 & 6\\ 7 & 8 & 9\end{pmatrix}$	$B=\begin{pmatrix}14 & -1 & 3\\ 4 & -1 & 2\\ 1 & 2 & -3\end{pmatrix}$

Replacement	`MAT C = A`	$C=\begin{pmatrix}1 & 2 & -3\\ -4 & 5 & 6\\ 7 & 8 & 9\end{pmatrix}$	
Addition	`MAT C = A + B`	$C=\begin{pmatrix}1 & 2 & -3\\ -4 & 5 & 6\\ 7 & 8 & 9\end{pmatrix}+\begin{pmatrix}14 & -1 & 3\\ 4 & -1 & 2\\ 1 & 2 & -3\end{pmatrix}=\begin{pmatrix}15 & 1 & 0\\ 0 & 4 & 8\\ 8 & 10 & 6\end{pmatrix}$	
Subtraction	`MAT C = A - B`	$C=\begin{pmatrix}1 & 2 & -3\\ -4 & 5 & 6\\ 7 & 8 & 9\end{pmatrix}-\begin{pmatrix}14 & -1 & 3\\ 4 & -1 & 2\\ 1 & 2 & -3\end{pmatrix}=\begin{pmatrix}-13 & 3 & -6\\ -8 & 6 & 4\\ 6 & 6 & 12\end{pmatrix}$	
Scalar multiplication	`MAT C = (3)*A`	$C=3\begin{pmatrix}1 & 2 & -3\\ -4 & 5 & 6\\ 7 & 8 & 9\end{pmatrix}=\begin{pmatrix}3 & 6 & -9\\ -12 & 15 & 18\\ 21 & 24 & 27\end{pmatrix}$	
Multiplication	`MAT C = A*B`	$C=\begin{pmatrix}1 & 2 & -3\\ -4 & 5 & 6\\ 7 & 8 & 9\end{pmatrix}*\begin{pmatrix}14 & -1 & 3\\ 4 & -1 & 2\\ 1 & 2 & -3\end{pmatrix}=\begin{pmatrix}19 & -9 & 16\\ -30 & 11 & -20\\ 139 & 3 & 10\end{pmatrix}$	
Replace by constant 0	`MAT C = ZER`	$C=\begin{pmatrix}0 & 0 & 0\\ 0 & 0 & 0\\ 0 & 0 & 0\end{pmatrix}$	All entries of the matrix are set to zero.
Replace by constant 1	`MAT C = CON`	$C=\begin{pmatrix}1 & 1 & 1\\ 1 & 1 & 1\\ 1 & 1 & 1\end{pmatrix}$	All entries are set to one (1).
Identity	`MAT C = IDN`	$C=\begin{pmatrix}1 & 0 & 0\\ 0 & 1 & 0\\ 0 & 0 & 1\end{pmatrix}$	C is set to the identity matrix: 1's down the main diagonal and 0's elsewhere.
Transpose	`MAT C = TRN(A)`	$C=\begin{pmatrix}1 & -4 & 7\\ 2 & 5 & 8\\ -3 & 6 & 9\end{pmatrix}$	C is the transpose of matrix A: the rows of C are equal to the columns of A.
Inverse	`MAT C = INV(B)`	$C=\begin{pmatrix}1 & -3 & -1\\ -14 & 45 & 16\\ -9 & 29 & 10\end{pmatrix}$	C is the inverse of B; that is, C*B = B*C = I, where I is the identity matrix.

9-4-4 Matrix Input/Output

The general form for matrix input/output statements is

$$\textit{line number}\quad \text{MAT} \begin{Bmatrix} \text{READ} \\ \text{PRINT} \\ \text{INPUT} \end{Bmatrix} \textit{list of matrices}$$

where MAT is a required key word and the operation to be performed is specified by choosing one of the key words READ, PRINT, or INPUT. The *list of matrices* is a list of variable names separated by commas. Each variable *must* be dimensioned. No undimensioned variable names or constants may appear in the list of matrices.

Examples:

`5 MAT READ X,Y,Z1`	Valid if X,Y,Z1 appear in DIM statement.
`10 MAT PRINT X1,Y1`	Valid if X1,Y1 appear in DIM statement.
`15 MAT INPUT A`	The matrix A will be entered. A must appear in a DIM statement.

Note that the instruction MAT PRINT "MATRIX A", A is invalid because it contains literal characters. The matrix input/output statements allow the programmer to load or print one- or two-dimensional arrays without indexing the array. Thus the BASIC code can be greatly simplified.

Matrices are read into memory or printed out in row order. The number of elements (entries) to be read/printed per row and the number of rows to be read/printed are taken from the size declaration of the matrix in the DIM statement. Figure 9–16 shows the code to read and print two matrices of unequal sizes. X has two rows and two columns, and Y has two rows and three columns.

When the MAT PRINT statement is used, each new matrix is printed on a new line starting in the leftmost zone. Each entry occupies one zone. If there are more row entries than there are zones on the line, two or more lines of output may be required for one matrix row (see Figure 9–17). Automatic single spacing is provided for each matrix row, and double spacing is used to separate matrices.

A blank PRINT statement following a MAT PRINT statement is generally recommended, otherwise subsequent lines of nonmatrix output will be continued on the last row of the matrix output.

To provide for more compact matrix output, a semicolon (;) should follow the matrix for which compact output is desired (see Figure 9–18).

■ **Figure 9–16** Example of matrix input/output.

```
Ø5 DIM X(2,2),Y(2,3)
1Ø MAT READ X,Y
15 MAT PRINT X,Y
2Ø DATA 11,22,33,44
25 DATA 15,17,13
3Ø DATA 12,2Ø,4Ø
35 END

RUN

11          22
33          44

15          17          13
12          2Ø          4Ø
```

Note: All X and Y matrix elements could have been typed in just one DATA statement.

Matrix X

Matrix Y

■ **Figure 9–17** Example of MAT PRINT statement.

```
Ø5 DIM X(1,7)
1Ø MAT READ X
15 MAT PRINT X
2Ø DATA 1,2,3,4,5,6,7

RUN

1           2           3           4           5
6           7
```

The seven entries will not fit on one line of output.

■ **Figure 9–18** Compact matrix output.

```
Ø5 DIM X(2,2),Y(2,3)
1Ø MAT READ X,Y
15 MAT PRINT X;Y;
2Ø DATA 11,22,33,44
25 DATA 15,17,13
3Ø DATA 12,2Ø,4Ø
35 END

RUN

11 22
33 44

15 17 13
12 2Ø 4Ø
```

Note the semicolons.

Matrix X written in compact form.

Matrix Y written in compact form.

When using the MAT INPUT statement, the system will generally respond with a ?. The user should then enter one entire matrix row, separating the entries with commas and pressing the RETURN key at the end of each row. On some systems, if the user types fewer or more entries than there are in a matrix row (as specified in the DIM statement), the system will respond with an error message. The user then needs to retype the exact number of entries for that row. See Figure 9–19. On some other systems, it is possible to enter the entire matrix data on just one line.

Figure 9–19 MAT INPUT example.

```
05 DIM X(2,2),Y(2,3)
10 MAT READ X,Y
15 MAT PRINT X,Y
35 END

RUN

? 11,22                     } Matrix X entered.
? 33,44
? 2E14, 1.98, -7.6E-3       } Matrix Y entered.
? 1E-3, 25,    32.4

11         22
33         44

2E+14      1.98     -7.6E-03
1E-03        25     32.4
```

9-4-5 Matrix Operations

BASIC can perform the following elementary matrix operations:

Replacement	MAT C = X	Set matrix C equal to matrix X.
Addition/subtraction	MAT C = X ± Y	Set C to sum or difference of X and Y.
Scalar Multiplication	MAT C = (expression)*X	Note the use of the parentheses around the expression.
Multiplication	MAT C = X*Y	C is set to the product of X and Y.

All of these matrix operations require that the matrix operands be *conformable*. Matrices must be equal in size for addition and subtraction. To multiply X*Y, the number of columns of X must equal the number of rows of Y (the mechanics of matrix multiplication are explained in question 5 of section 9–6).

Only *one* matrix operation is allowed on the right side of the equal sign.

Examples:

`5 MAT C = (2)X + Y`	Invalid: two matrix operations.
`6 MAT C = X - Y + Z`	Invalid: two matrix operations.
`7 MAT C = -X`	Invalid use of scalar multiplication.

In matrix multiplication, the same matrix may not appear on both sides of the matrix statement.

Examples:

`5 MAT X = X * X`	X is on both sides—invalid for multiplication.
`6 MAT C = C + X`	C is on both sides—valid for addition/subtraction.

9-4-6 Matrix Functions

In addition to the aforementioned matrix operations, BASIC conveniently allows the user to initialize matrices to elementary matrix configurations and to determine the transpose and the inverse of a given matrix. The following functions are provided:

`MAT C = ZER` — All entries of C are set to 0's. The size of C is defined in the DIM statement. C need not be square.

`MAT C = CON` — All entries of C are set to 1's. The size of C is defined in the DIM statement.

`MAT C = IDN` — C is set to the identity matrix: 1's down the main diagonal and 0's elsewhere. If C is not square, the main diagonal of 1's will start in the lower right-hand corner of the matrix.

Example:

$$\begin{pmatrix} 0 & 1 & 0 & 0 \\ 0 & 0 & 1 & 0 \\ 0 & 0 & 0 & 1 \end{pmatrix}$$

`MAT C = TRN(X)` — The matrix C becomes the matrix X where all symmetric entries across the main diagonal have been interchanged (each row has been replaced by its corresponding column).

Example:

If $X = \begin{pmatrix} 1 & 2 \\ 4 & 5 \\ 7 & 8 \end{pmatrix}$

then $TRN(X) = \begin{pmatrix} 1 & 4 & 7 \\ 2 & 5 & 8 \end{pmatrix}$

`MAT C = INV(X)` C becomes the inverse matrix of X. The inverse of X is that matrix C is such that C*X = X*C = I, where I is the identity matrix.

Example:

$$\text{If} \quad X = \begin{pmatrix} 1 & 2 & -3 \\ 4 & -1 & 2 \\ 14 & -1 & 3 \end{pmatrix}$$

$$\text{then} \quad \text{INV}(X) = \begin{pmatrix} -1 & -3 & 1 \\ 16 & 45 & -14 \\ 10 & 29 & -9 \end{pmatrix}$$

The INV function can only be applied to a square matrix. The inverse of a matrix is only defined for square matrices; yet not all square matrices have inverses. The INV routine will print an appropriate message if no inverse exists.

9-4-7 Do It Now

If your system supports matrix operations, determine the differences between the standard described in this section and your BASIC system for each of the following:

1. MAT READ
2. MAT PRINT
3. MAT INPUT
4. MAT replacement statement
5. Arithmetic operations on matrices
6. MAT functions:
   a. ZER
   b. CON
   c. IDN
   d. TRN
   e. INV
7. Other statements and functions

9-5 Solving a System of Equations

Solve the following system of equations using matrix operations:

$$\begin{aligned} x + y + 2z + 3w &= 2 \\ 12x + 23y + 45z + 5w &= 3 \\ -9x + 67y + 56z + 23w &= 4 \\ 2x + 3y + 5z - 34w &= 5 \end{aligned}$$

The system of equations can be written in matrix form as

$$\begin{pmatrix} 1 & 1 & 2 & 3 \\ 12 & 23 & 45 & 5 \\ -9 & 67 & 56 & 23 \\ 2 & 3 & 5 & -34 \end{pmatrix} * \begin{pmatrix} x \\ y \\ z \\ w \end{pmatrix} = \begin{pmatrix} 2 \\ 3 \\ 4 \\ 5 \end{pmatrix}$$

Let A be the 4×4 matrix consisting of the coefficients of the variables (unknowns). Let X be the 4×1 matrix of variables x, y, z, w. Let B be the 4×1 matrix of constants (2,3,4,5). Then the preceding matrix equation becomes $A \cdot X = B$. By multiplying both sides of the equation by the inverse A^{-1}, if it exists, we obtain

$$A^{-1} \cdot A \cdot X = A^{-1} \cdot B \quad \text{or} \quad I \cdot X = A^{-1} \cdot B \quad \text{or} \quad X = A^{-1} \cdot B$$

B is known; A^{-1} can be calculated since A is given; hence the column matrix X can be easily computed. Figure 9–20 displays the program to solve any square system of equations up to size 10. Note the redimensioning of the matrix A at statement number 35 to allow the user to enter his/her specific system of equations.

9-6 You Might Want to Know

1. Once I have processed an array with a MAT statement, can I still process that array without using MAT statements?

   Answer: Yes. Suppose M is a 3 by 4 matrix containing scores and we wish to determine the highest score in row 3 and print all scores in the second column. The following code could be used.

```
 5 DIM M(3,4)
10 DATA 1,2,3,4,5,9,7,6,5,4,1,3
15 MAT READ M                          Read matrix.
20 LET L = M(3,1)                      Initialize L to first score in row 3.
25 FOR J = 2 TO 4
30    IF L >= M(3,J) THEN 40
35    LET L = M(3,J)                   L is largest score in row 3.
40 NEXT J
45 FOR I = 1 TO 3
50    PRINT M(I,2);                    Print elements of second column.
60 NEXT I
```

2. In the *list of matrices* in a MAT PRINT statement, can I make use of both the comma and the semicolon, as follows?

```
 5 DIM A(2,3), B(2,2), C(2,2)
10 MAT READ A,B,C
15 MAT PRINT A;B,C                     Note semicolon and comma.
20 DATA 1,2,3,4,5,6
25 DATA 11,22,33,44
30 DATA 99,88,77,66
```

■ **Figure 9–20** Solution to system of linear equations using matrix inverse.

```
Ø2 REM SOLVING A SYSTEM OF EQUATIONS
Ø5 DIM A(1Ø,1Ø),B(1Ø,1)
1Ø DIM C(1Ø,1Ø),X(1Ø,1)
15 PRINT "WHAT IS THE SIZE OF THE SYSTEM OF EQUATIONS..."
2Ø PRINT "SIZE SHOULD BE LESS THAN 11"
25 INPUT N
26 REM THE PROGRAM MAY SOLVE SYSTEMS OF VARIOUS SIZES (UP TO 1Ø)
27 PRINT
3Ø PRINT "ENTER MATRIX OF COEFFICIENTS ROW-WISE"
35 MAT INPUT A(N,N)
36 REM THE MATRICES ARE NOW REDIMENSIONED TO USER SPECIFICATION
37 PRINT
4Ø PRINT "ENTER MATRIX OF CONSTANTS"
45 MAT INPUT B(N,1)
46 MAT C = ZER(N,N)        May be required to redimension matrix C.
5Ø MAT C = INV(A)
51 MAT X = ZER(N,1)        May be required to redimension matrix X.
55 MAT X = C*B
57 PRINT
6Ø PRINT "THE MATRIX OF COEFFICIENTS IS"
65 MAT PRINT A;
7Ø PRINT "MATRIX OF CONSTANTS IS"
75 MAT PRINT B
8Ø PRINT "THE SOLUTIONS TO THE EQUATIONS ARE IN COLUMN FORM"
85 MAT PRINT X
99 END

RUN
WHAT IS THE SIZE OF THE SYSTEM OF EQUATIONS...
SIZE SHOULD BE LESS THAN 11
? 4
ENTER MATRIX OF COEFFICIENTS ROW-WISE
? 1,1,2,3
? 12,23,45,5
? -9,67,56,23
? 2,3,5,-34
ENTER MATRIX OF CONSTANTS
? 2
? 3
? 4
? 5
THE MATRIX OF COEFFICIENTS IS
 1        1        2        3
12       23       45        5
-9       67       56       23
 2        3        5      -34
THE MATRIX OF CONSTANTS IS
2
3
4
5
THE SOLUTIONS TO THE EQUATIONS ARE IN COLUMN FORM
 4.23996            result for x
 2.65938            result for y
-2.42111            result for z
-1.9Ø416E - Ø2      result for w
```

Answer: Yes. This code would yield

```
1  2  3          Matrix A in compact form.
4  5  6

  11              22   }
  33              44   }
                       }  Matrices B and C in zone form.
  99              88   }
  77              66   }
```

3. Can I use MAT statements on arrays that have only one index in the DIM statement?

   Answer: On most systems, you can. The following, for example, is valid:

```
 5 DIM A(5)             Only one index in the DIM statement.
10 MAT A = ZER          Zero out matrix and print it.
15 MAT PRINT A
```

4. Once a matrix has been dimensioned to a certain size, is it possible to change its size at run time?

   Answer: Matrices must be dimensioned before MAT statements can be used. Since the MAT statements make use of the stated sizes of the matrices in the DIM statement, one might think that once a matrix has been dimensioned one can no longer use that same matrix to store matrices of different sizes. Sometimes it may be more efficient or convenient to reuse the same matrix X to read or process matrices of varying sizes. This can be accomplished by redimensioning the matrix at execution time. Redimensioning is valid as long as the dimensions of the new matrices *do not* exceed the dimension of the original matrix stated in the DIM statement. Figure 9–21 shows how the two matrices X and Y can be redimensioned by stating the new dimensions in the MAT READ statement.

Figure 9–21 Input of redimensioned matrix.

```
05 DIM X(2,2), Y(2,3)
10 MAT READ X(1,2),Y(2,2)        Both matrices X and Y have been
                                 redimensioned.
15 MAT PRINT X,Y                 Note the absence of dimensions in the
                                 PRINT statement.
20 DATA 11,22,33,44,55,65
35 DATA 55,65,75,84,90,95
40 END
RUN
11        22   } Matrix X

33        44   }
55        65   } Matrix Y
```

Figure 9–22 shows how matrices can be redimensioned using variable subscripts. The same matrices X and Y will be used to compute C = X + Y with X and Y varying from 3 × 3 to 1 × 1. Note the use of the RESTORE statement, which forces any READ statement to start at the beginning of the DATA statement. Once a matrix A has been redimensioned, any reference to that matrix A, such as in MAT READ A, implies the most recently redimensioned size.

Figure 9–22 Redimensioning matrices using variable subscripts.

```
05 DIM X(3,3),Y(3,3),C(3,3)
10 MAT C = ZER                   Zero out matrix C.
15 FOR I = 3 TO 1 STEP -1
20   MAT READ X(I,I),Y(I,I)
25   RESTORE                     The next READ will start at the beginning of
                                 the DATA list.
30   MAT C = X + Y               Note how C is automatically redimensioned to
                                 the successive sizes of matrices X and Y by the
                                 statement MAT C = X + Y. In some systems,
35   MAT PRINT X;Y;C             it may be necessary to redimension C before
40 NEXT I                        calculating the sum. A statement such as
50 DATA 1,2,3,4,5,6,7,8,9        29 MAT C = ZER(I,I) could be used.
60 DATA 11,22,33,44,55,66
70 DATA 77,88,99

RUN
1   2   3  }
4   5   6  }                     Matrix X
7   8   9  }

11  22  33 }
44  55  66 }                     Matrix Y
77  88  99 }

12        24        36   }
48        60        72   }       Matrix X + Y
84        96        108  }

1   2  }
3   4  }                         Matrix X

5   6  }
                                 Matrix Y
7   8  }

6   8  }
                                 Matrix X + Y
10  12 }

1 }                              Matrix X
2 }                              Matrix Y
3 }                              Matrix X + Y
```

5. How is matrix multiplication performed?

Answer: To multiply two matrices A X B together, A and B must be conformable, that is, the number of columns of A must equal the number of rows of B. For example,

$$\begin{pmatrix} a_{11}\ a_{12}\ a_{13} \\ a_{21}\ a_{22}\ a_{23} \end{pmatrix} \cdot \begin{pmatrix} b_{11}\ b_{12} \\ b_{21}\ b_{22} \\ b_{31}\ b_{32} \end{pmatrix} = \begin{pmatrix} a_{11}b_{11} + a_{12}b_{21} + a_{13}b_{31} & a_{11}b_{12} + a_{12}b_{22} + a_{13}b_{32} \\ a_{21}b_{11} + a_{22}b_{21} + a_{23}b_{31} & a_{21}b_{12} + a_{22}b_{22} + a_{23}b_{32} \end{pmatrix}$$

If A is $m \times n$ (m rows, n columns) and B is $n \times q$ then the product matrix $C = A \times B$ is of size $m \times q$.

6. Which matrix statements can be used to redimension matrices?

Answer: Only the following matrix statements can be redimension matrices:

MAT {READ | INPUT} *dimensioned variable (expression₁, expression₂)* [,...]

MAT *dimensioned variable* = {ZER | IDN | CON} *(expression₁, expression₂)*

where *expression*₁ and *expression*₂ become, respectively, the number of rows and the number of columns of the redimensioned matrix.

Examples:

`MAT C = CON(A+B, 4*3)`	Initializes matrix C with A + B rows and 12 columns to 1's.
`MAT C = ZER(3,5)`	Zero out a 3 × 5 matrix.
`MAT PRINT X(3,5)`	Invalid: PRINT cannot redimension matrices.
`MAT READ X(3,3),Y(2,2)`	More than one matrix can be redimensioned in a MAT READ statement.

9-7 Assignments

9-7-1 Test Yourself

1. Load arrays A, B, and C with the following (generate numbers internally):

A

1	2	3	4
5	6	7	8
9	10	11	12

B

10	20	30	40
50	60	70	80
90	100	110	120

C

500

Write the code to print the following array arrangements (given the above arrays):

a.

1	2	3	4	...	11	12	10	20	30	40	...	110	120	500

b.

1	2	3	4	10	20	30	40	500
5	6	7	8	50	60	70	80	500
9	10	11	12	90	100	110	120	500

c.

1	5	9	500	10	50	90
2	6	10	500	20	60	100
3	7	11	500	30	70	110
4	8	12	500	40	80	120

d.

1	10	2	20	3	30	4	40
5	50	6	60	7	70	8	80
9	90	10	100	11	110	12	120

e.

1	10	5	50	9	90	2	20	6	60	10	100
3	30	7	70	11	110	4	40	8	80	12	120

2. Data is recorded on records (DATA statements) as follows. Generate the input statements to load the arrays in the order shown:

a.
DATA $a_{11},a_{21},a_{31},a_{41}$
DATA $a_{12},a_{22},a_{32},a_{42}$
DATA $a_{13},a_{32},a_{33},a_{43}$

b.
DATA a_{11},a_{12},a_{13}
DATA a_{14},a_{15},a_{16}
DATA $b_1,\ b_2,b_3,b_4,b_5,b_6$

c.
DATA $a_{11},b_{11},a_{21},b_{21}$
DATA $a_{31},b_{31},a_{41},b_{41}$
DATA $a_{51},b_{51},a_{61},b_{61}$

d.
DATA $a_{11},b_{11},a_{21},b_{12}$
DATA $a_{31},b_{13},a_{41},b_{14}$
DATA $a_{51},b_{15},a_{61},b_{16}$

e.
DATA $a_{11},a_{12},a_{13},b_{11},b_{12}$
DATA $a_{21},a_{22},a_{23},b_{21},b_{22}$
. .
. .
DATA $a_{91},a_{92},a_{93},b_{91},b_{92}$

f.
DATA $a_{11},a_{12},\ldots,a_{19}$
DATA $a_{21},a_{22},\ldots,a_{29}$
. .
. .
DATA $a_{81},a_{82},\ldots,a_{89}$
DATA $b_{11},b_{21},b_{31},b_{41}$
DATA $b_{12},b_{22},b_{32},b_{42}$

3. Using the random number generator routine, write the code to store random numbers in an array F of size 40 × 17. Then store the rows of the array F sequentially into a one-dimensional array G of size 680 (40 × 17) as follows:

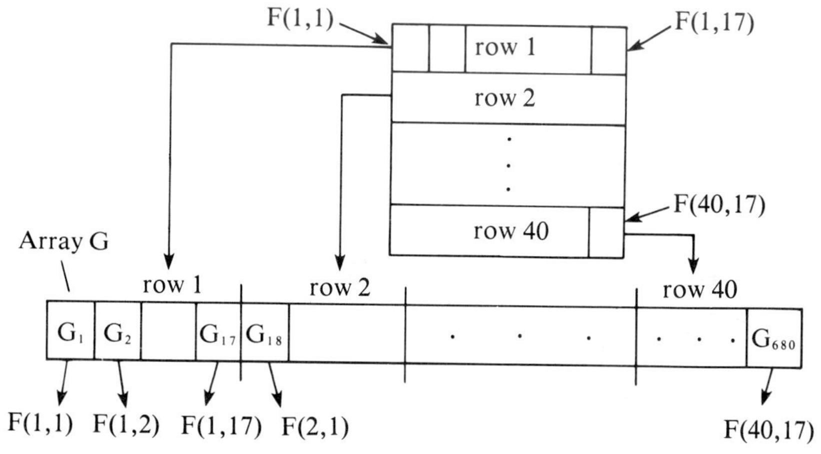

4. An array A of size 5 × 5 is to be read from five DATA statements, with five entries (one row) per DATA statement. Write the BASIC code to
   a. Read in the array and write it out in row form (one row per line), then print each column on one line, i.e., A_{11}, A_{21}, A_{31}, A_{41}, A_{51} on one line, then A_{12} A_{22},...,A_{52} on the second line, and so forth.
   b. Calculate the sum of the elements in the third row.
   c. Find the largest value in the first column.
   d. Create a linear array B consisting of five elements initialized to zero. Calculate the sum of each column of A, and store the result in the corresponding column position of B.
   e. Add the corresponding elements of rows 2 and 3 of the array A, and store the results in row 3; that is, A(3,1) = A(3,1) + A(2,1), and so forth.
   f. Interchange column 3 and column 4.
   g. Compute the sum of the entries of the secondary diagonal and determine the largest entry of that diagonal. (The secondary diagonal consists of elements A_{15}, A_{24}, A_{33}, A_{42}, A_{51})
   h. Print the largest element of the array A and its position in the array (row, column).

5. Read in two arrays C and D of size 5 × 5, given the following input description:

DATA	1,2,3,4,5,	1,2,3,6,8,	4,5,6,7,8,	4,5,6,7,6, ...
	Row 1 of C	Row 1 of D	Row 2 of C	Row 2 of D

9-7-2 Exercises

1. An array A has size 4 by 9. Write the code to interchange the first column with the ninth column, the second column with the eighth column, and so forth.

2. Each record in a file consists of six data items: a student number, and five test scores. There are at most 100 records.

```
DATA   111,      10, 20, 30, 40, 50
  .
  .
DATA   222,      10, 10, 70, 60, 40
```

Student number (222) — Five test scores (10, 10, 70, 60, 40)

Read the data into a two-dimensional table. For example, A(3,I), with I ranging from 1 to 5, represents the *third* student's test scores. Compute the average score for each student and the average score on each test. The format for the output is:

NUMBER	TEST 1	TEST 2	TEST 3	TEST 4	TEST 5	AVERAGE
111	10	20	30	40	50	30.0
222	10	10	70	60	40	38.0
AVERAGE/TEST	10	15	50	50	45	

Test your program with at least five of your own data records.

3. The personnel department of a small insurance company maintains a payroll file for its seven insurance representatives, who work in different states. Each employee's record contains (among other information) the following data:

EMPLOYEE NUMBER	*HOURS WORKED*	*RATE OF PAY*	*STATE TAX*
111222	45	10.00	.05

Generate seven DATA statements using the same format (one for each representative) and initialize an array A(7,4) with your data base. Then write the code to:

a. Compute and print each employee's pay before and after tax.
b. Compute the total payroll for the firm before the state tax is witheld.
c. Give a $1,000 bonus to the employee with lowest hourly rate who has worked the most hours, if such an employee exists.

The output should be similar to

```
EMPLOYEE     HOURS     RATE OF    GROSS    STATE    NET
 NUMBER     WORKED       PAY       PAY      TAX     PAY
 111222       45        1Ø.ØØ    475.ØØ     .Ø5    451.25
   .          .           .        .         .       .
   .          .           .        .         .       .
   .          .           .        .         .       .
COMPANY PAYROLL = XXXX.XX
BONUS OF $1,ØØØ GOES TO NUMBER XXXXXX WHO WORKED
XX HOURS AT XX.XX PER HOUR.
```

4. A small airplane has a seating capacity of five rows with three seats per row. Seat reservations are handled by a computer. Seat preferences for each passenger are entered on DATA statements with the name of the passenger, the row, and the seat number on the DATA statement. If a requested seat is vacant, reserve the seat for the passenger and print his/her name and seat number. If the requested seat is already taken, assign seats in row fashion, starting with leftmost seat in row 1 and moving to the end of the row before starting with the second row, and so forth. Print the passenger's name and his/her assigned seat and row. Print a message if the plane is fully loaded. For example, given the following data, the output should be as follows:

```
DATA GOLD      , 3,1
DATA MANUEL    , 3,1
DATA HORN      , 5,2
DATA GLEASON   , 5,2
DATA BARDOT    , 1,2
DATA MOORE     , 1,3
```

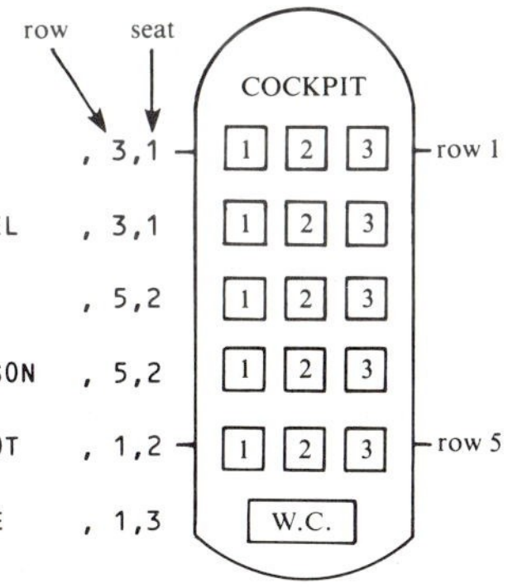


```
NAME        ROW   SEAT
GOLD         3     1
MANUEL       1     1
HORN         5     2
GLEASON      1     2
BARDOT       1     3
MOORE        2     1
```

Then print the plane's seating arrangement by name, in rows, starting with row 1. Use sequence of minus symbols to identify unoccupied seats.

```
1 MANUEL   GLEASON   BARDOT
2 MOORE    ------    ------
3 GOLD     ------    ------
4 ------   ------    ------
5 ------   HORN      ------
```

5. Your itemized deduction for general sales tax paid can be estimated from tables like the one shown here. To use the tables:

Step 1—Figure your total available income.

Step 2—Count the number of exemptions for you and your family.

Step 3 A—If your total available income is not over $40,000, find the income line for your state on the tables and read across to find the amount of sales tax for your family size.

Step 3 B—If your income is over $40,000, but not over $100,000, find the deduction listed on the income line "$38,001–$40,000" for your family size and state. For each $5,000 (or part of $5,000) of income over $40,000, increase the deduction by the amount listed for the line "$40,001–$100,000."

Step 3 C—If your income is over $100,000, your sales tax deduction is limited to the deduction for income of $100,000. To figure your sales tax deduction, use Step 3 B but don't go over $100,000.

Income	*Family size*					
	1	2	3	4	5	Over 5
$1– $8,000	93	115	122	131	142	160
$8,001–$10,000.	109	132	142	153	165	185
$10,001–$12,000	124	147	161	173	187	208
$12,001–$14,000	138	161	178	191	206	228
$14,001–$16,000	152	174	194	209	225	248
$16,001–$18,000	164	186	210	226	242	266
$18,001–$20,000	176	197	225	242	259	284
$20,001–$22,000	188	208	239	257	275	301
$22,001–$24,000	199	218	253	271	290	317
$24,001–$26,000	210	228	266	285	305	332
$26,001–$28,000	221	238	279	299	320	347
$28,001–$30,000	231	247	291	313	334	362
$30,001–$32,000	241	256	303	326	347	376
$32,001–$34,000	251	265	315	338	360	390
$34,001–$36,000	261	274	327	350	373	403
$36,001–$38,000	271	282	338	362	386	416
$38,001–$40,000	280	290	349	374	399	429
$40,001–$100,000 . . . . (See Step 3B)	14	15	17	19	20	21

Assume that the table given here is appropriate for your state. Write a program that will input an income and determine and print the corresponding sales tax deduction.

6. At the end of every semester, Dr. Landrum, head of the Business Data Systems department, likes to check grade reports of the department's freshman class (100 students at most). Each student's final grades in three subject areas are entered on DATA statements, one DATA statement per student; for example:

```
10    DATA    SMITH  ,   58  ,   78  ,   44
                ↑          ↑       ↑       ↑
        Student Name       |  Business Law |
                     Accounting I      Principles of
                                       Management
```

Enter in an array N$ all student names and enter each student's grades into a corresponding two-dimensional array G. For example, G(3,2) represents the third student's score in Business Law.

Write a program for Dr. Landrum to

a. Compute the average score of each student across all disciplines.
b. Compute the freshman average score for each subject, i.e., for accounting I, business law, and principles of management.
c. Provide a list of all students whose three final scores are all above the freshman average test scores in each of the three subjects.

d. Award a prize to student(s) with highest scores in principles of management. Print the name(s) of the recipient(s).
e. If any student obtains the three highest scores in the three subject areas, award a scholarship to that student.

The output should be similar to the following report:

```
                     SEMESTER END REPORT
               ACCT. I      LAW         MANAGEMENT    AVERAGE
HORNET          40          50             60            50
BOILLOT         50          90             40            60
SMITHEN         20          60             10            30

CLASS AVERAGE   36.7        66.7           36.7
STUDENT NAMES WHOSE 3 TESTS EXCEED THE 3 CLASS AVERAGES
                       BOILLOT

MANAGEMENT AWARD GOES TO HORNET
SCHOLARSHIP IS AWARDED TO NO ONE
```

7. Read into an array named W$ eight of each of the following: pronouns, verbs, adverbs, adjectives, nouns, and articles (repeated if necessary) and store their corresponding numerical word codes (1 = pronoun, 2 = verb, 3 = adverb, and so forth) in an integer array called K. For example:

```
DATA HORRIBLE,4,  MONKEY,5,  THE,6,  THEY, 1
DATA EATS     2,  VERY,  3,  A,  6,  A,     6
  .           .   .          .       .
  .           .   .          .       .
  .           .   .          .       .
DATA DOLL,    5,  DREAMS,2,  AN, 6,  LUCID,4
```

} 48 words

As a result of the read operation, two arrays, W$ and K, would appear as follows:

W$	HORRIBLE	MONKEY	THE	THEY	EATS	VERY	...	DOLL	DREAMS	AN	LUCID

K	4	5	6	1	2	3	...	5	2	6	4
	K(1)	K(2)									K(48)

a. Write a program to search the word code array and print out all the words of the word array using the following format:

```
PRONOUNS  VERBS  ADVERBS  ADJECTIVES  NOUNS   ARTICLES
  HE      EATS    VERY     HORRIBLE   MONKEY    THE
  .        .       .          .         .        .
  .        .       .          .         .        .
  .        .       .          .         .        A
                                       DOLL      A
```

b. Using the random-number generator routine to extract entries from the 48-word array (not from the six sorted word arrays), construct two English sentences to fit the following grammatical structure:

Article noun verb adjective. Pronoun verb article adverb adjective noun.

For example, the following sentences might be generated:

```
THE BOY IS TALL. HE IS A VERY BEAUTIFUL MONKEY.
```

Analyze the selected numerical codes to keep rejecting words until they satisfy the desired grammatical structure. [*Hint*: You might want to store the numerical word codes for the sentence in an array where NUM(1) = 6, NUM (2) = 5,NUM(3) = 2,...,NUM(10) = 5 and compare NUM(I) with KODE(J), where I varies from 1 to 10 and J is a random number between 1 and 48.]

8. Grid analysis is a marketing strategy technique used to examine product-related needs of customers. The following market grid for apartments was developed in Dallas to help builders better understand needs (dotted squares) of customers:

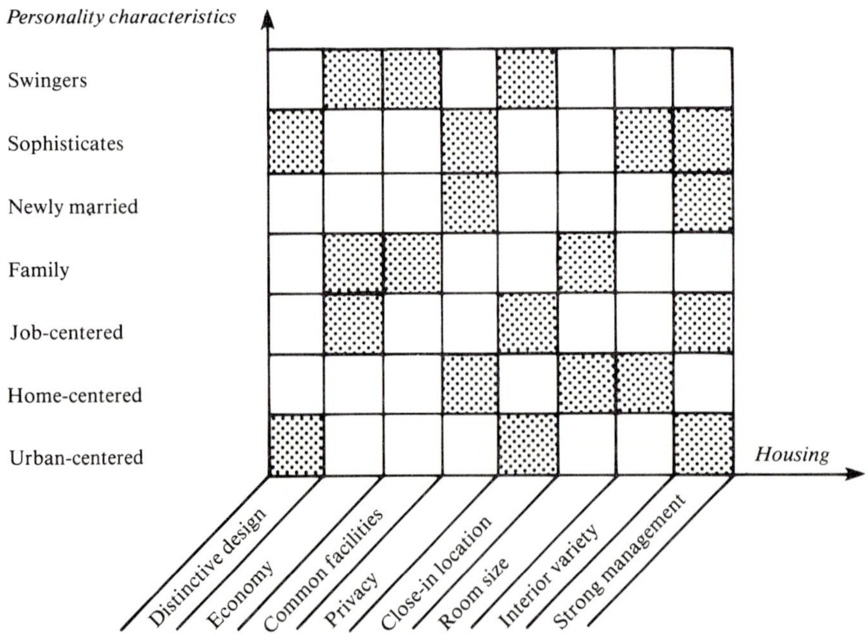

Write a program to read the data shown (using any code you wish) into an array to perform the following functions:

a. Accept one personality characteristic from input and list corresponding housing needs. For example,

```
INPUT PERSONALITY CHARACTERISTIC
? FAMILY
FOR FAMILY CHARACTERISTICS THE FOLLOWING NEEDS ARE:

      1 ECONOMY
      2 COMMON FACILITIES
      3 ROOM SIZE
```

b. Accept one housing need from input and list personality characteristics sharing that need. Use the same format for input/output as in part a above.
c. Accept one housing need from input and list the personality characteristics that do *not* require that need.
d. Accept a pair of personality characteristics and list its corresponding needs. For example, newly wed, urban-centered: distinctive design, privacy, close-in location, strong management.

9. You are tabulating returns from a primary election in which five candidates were running for office: Aiken, Andover, Hilary, Martin, and Watson. Each vote is recorded on one record with two entries per record. The first entry is a number identifying the party of the voter (1 = Democrat, 2 = Republican, 3 = Independent). The second entry identifies the name of the candidate.

a. Write a program to determine the total number of votes obtained by each candidate. If a candidate obtains more than 5 votes from any party, print the number of votes from that party and the party. For example:

```
CANDIDATE    TOTAL VOTES     PARTY        NUMBER OF VOTES

AIKEN              4

WATSON                      DEMOCRAT                6
WATSON            21        INDEPENDENT            1Ø

ANDOVER            8

HILARY            14        INDEPENDENT            1Ø

MARTIN                      DEMOCRAT                6
MARTIN                      REPUBLICAN              6
MARTIN            2Ø        INDEPENDENT             8
```

Note for example that Watson must have received 5 votes from the Republican party; the name of the party is not printed, however, since he did not obtain at least 6 votes in that party.

b. Specify the candidates who obtained votes from each of the three parties. For the example given above the output would be:

```
WATSON
MARTIN
```

c. Identify candidates who were elected by one or more democrats, by one or more republicans, etc. Given the above input the output could be as follows:

```
DEMOCRAT:      AIKEN ANDOVER MARTIN WATSON
REPUBLICAN:    MARTIN HILARY WATSON
INDEPENDENT:   ANDOVER HILARY MARTIN WATSON
```

10. A large computer company decided some years ago to make a study on whether there was any relationship between the major of a college student and his/her success in the computer field. Four hundred graduates were selected as follows: 70 in mathematics, 156 in engineering, and 174 in liberal arts. At the end of the company training period, overall scores revealed the following:

	Performance		
	Excellent	*Fair*	*Unsatisfactory*
Mathematics	37	23	10
Liberal arts	56	76	42
Engineering	25	64	67

The formula used to determine whether a major is a significant factor in success is:

$$x = \tfrac{1}{4} \sum_{j=1}^{3} \sum_{i=1}^{3} (f_{ij} - e_{ij})^2 = \tfrac{1}{4} [(f_{11} - e_{11})^2 + (f_{12} - e_{12})^2 + (f_{13} - e_{13})^2$$
$$+ (f_{21} - e_{21})^2 + \ldots + (f_{33} - e_{33})^2]$$

where

$$f_{ij} \text{ is } \frac{(\text{sum of row } i)\cdot(\text{sum of column } j).}{\text{sum of all entries of performance array}}$$

For example, $f_{23} = \dfrac{(56 + 76 + 42)\cdot(10 + 42 + 67)}{400}$

e_{ij} is number of students at row i and column j. For example, $e_{23} = 42$.

Write a program to read the given numbers in an array and determine whether or not there is a relationship between "major" and future success. If $x > 9.588$, the relationship exists; otherwise, it does not.

11. The region shown below is a two-dimensional model of a section of a nuclear reactor. The point marked S is the source of particles that are free to travel one mesh step in any direction with equal probability. Points marked A are centers of absorption, and any particle reaching such a point is considered to have been absorbed. Points marked R are reflectors and return a particle to the point from which it came, taking a total of two steps in the process. Points marked E indicate that a particle has escaped through the absorbing medium. Blank points are scattering centers from which the particle moves one mesh step in any direction with equal probability. Motion can be in the horizontal or vertical direction only. The source is to be considered a normal mesh point.

```
  E E E E E E E
E . . . . . . . A A A
  A . . . A . . . . . A
R . . . . . . . . . . . A
R . . . A . . . A . . . A E E A A
R . . . . . . . . . . . . . . . . A
R . . . . . . . . . . . . . . . . . A A A
R . . . . . . . . . . . . . . . . . . . . E
R . . . . . . . . . . . . . . . . . . . . E
R . . . . . . . . . . . . . . . . . . . . E
R . S . . . A . . . A . . . . . . . . . . E
R . . . . . . . . . . . . . . . . . . . . E
R . . . . . . . . . . . . . . . . . . . . E
R . . . . . . . . . . . . . . . . . . . . E
R . . . . . . . . . . . . . . . . . . . . E
R . . . . . . . . . . . . . . . . . A A A
R . . . . . . . A A A . . . . . . E
R . . . . A . . . . . . E A E E A
  E E A A   E A E E E E
```

Write a program which starts individual particles one at a time from point S and follows them one at a time to their escape or absorption.

a. Run 500 particles; keep track of each particle in an array that records the number of steps taken and whether the particle was absorbed or escaped. Terminate any particles remaining in the reactor after 500 moves and count them. Such particles are neither absorbed nor escaped.
b. Print out the percentage of particles that escaped and that were absorbed.
c. Print out the number of particles that escaped versus the number of steps taken (so many escaped on the fifth step, so many escaped on the sixth step, and so forth). Do the same for the particles that have been absorbed.
d. Print how many particles escaped through the rightmost points. The output should be similar to:

```
PERCENTAGE ESCAPED                        XXX.XX
PERCENTAGE ABSORBED                       XXX.XX
ESCAPES THROUGH RIGHTMOST POINTS            XX
PARTICLES REMAINING AFTER 5ØØ MOVES         XX

NO.STEPS            ABSORBED               ESCAPED
    4                  2                     Ø
    8                  5                     Ø
   1Ø                  Ø                     5
   96                  Ø                    22
    .                  .                     .
    .                  .                     .
    .                  .                     .
  126                 24                     Ø
    .                  .                     .
    .                  .                     .
  5ØØ                  Ø                     1
```

12. An input file contains at most 100 records. Each record contains a student name the number of optional tests the student took that semester (N) and the test scores themselves (see the sample input below). Students may take only the final if they want to, or both the second test and the final, or the first two tests and the final. The tests are recorded in the input record in the following order: Final, test-2, and test-1.

First read the input data into three arrays (name, scores, and number of tests) but do not accumulate or compute anything during this initial reading phase. After the scores have been read into the two-dimensional table G, process the data. First, list the names, the scores, and the test averages of all students who took three tests. Provide a similar list for those students who took two tests and then for those who took one test. Finally, print the class average for the three tests. A sample output is shown below.

No grades other than the scores read from the input record should be stored in the grade array i.e., unused elements of G should not be initialized to 0's or to any other values.

Sample input

```
DATA GAYMAL    N, 2,  59,67
DATA SYMMES    L, 3,  91,65,87
DATA GAELID    W, 1   67
DATA ANTONINA  T, 1,  95
DATA JONES     A, 1,  78
DATA CHAMID    S, 2,  99,87
DATA ANDROS    K, 3,  29,38,64
DATA TELEAIKEN G, 3,  65,1ØØ,5Ø
DATA GLZSINSKI Y, 1,  76
```

Number of tests — Final — test2 — test1

Sample Output

NAME		TEST 1	TEST 2	FINAL	AVERAGE
SYMMES	L	87	65	91	81.Ø
ANDROS	K	64	38	29	43.7
TELEAIKEN	G	5Ø	1ØØ	65	71.7
GAYMAL	N		67	59	63.Ø
CHAMID	S		87	99	93.Ø
GAELID	W			67	67.Ø
ANTONINA	T			95	95.Ø
JONES	A			78	78.Ø
GLZSINSKI	Y			76	76.Ø

Array G

59	67	
91	65	87
67		
95		
78		
99	87	
29	38	64
65	100	50
76		

Array N

2
3
1
1
1
2
3
3
1

13. The world is at war, and the only hope to conquer the enemy is to destroy its command post. Army intelligence agents have intercepted a chart (see diagram that follows) of an area in the Mohave desert, showing exactly where the enemy command post is located. This chart divides a certain region of the desert into areas of square yards. Each square yard on the chart is identified by two numbers. The first number represents its north-south position on the chart and the second number represents its east-west position on the chart. The chart has a total of ten yards running north to south and a total of ten yards running east to west. The top of the chart is north and the bottom is south (rows), while the left side of the chart is west and the right side is east (columns). (For example, area (1,1) on the chart is the area in the upper left corner and (10,10) is the area on the lower right corner; area (3,4) means the third area down and the fourth area to the right.) To fully protect the enemy's command post, explosive land mines are planted in every square yard around the post except for a *single* path so that men and supplies can move in and out. Any person that steps on any portion of the square yard with a mine will be blown up. Using the provided chart you are to follow the path free from mines and destroy the enemy command post, being careful not to step on any areas with mines. Initialize a two-dimensional array with ones for the squares in the gray area and zeroes for the path free of mines (light area).

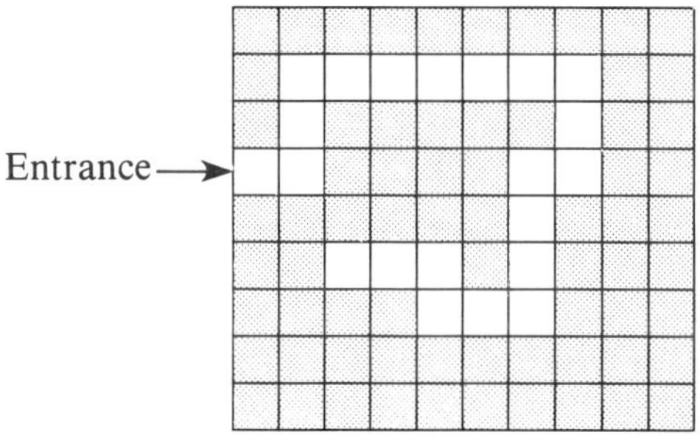

Output:

a. Print out the map of zeroes and ones using an attractive format.
b. Once all the data is read, you are to follow the path that must be taken to safely reach the command post and print out the two integer identification numbers for each area you travel through (including the area where you start and end). The following assumptions must be made:
   (1) The path starts at (4,1).
   (2) You cannot go back and retrace your steps.
   (3) When the path ends and you can go no further (mines are all around you) you have reached the command post and are not to try to travel any further!
   (4) You can travel only north, south, east, or west (not diagonally).
c. Once you have found the correct path, you radio the path coordinates to your second in command who is to follow your footsteps directly to the command post, without testing for mines. To ensure that he obeys, you order him to replace all 0's of the clear path by 3's and to print the region once safe at the command post.

14. A matrix is a rectangular array of numbers. Addition and multiplication of matrices is illustrated in the following examples:

Addition

$$\begin{pmatrix} a_{11}a_{12}a_{13} \\ a_{21}a_{22}a_{23} \end{pmatrix} + \begin{pmatrix} b_{11}b_{12}b_{13} \\ b_{21}b_{22}b_{23} \end{pmatrix} = \begin{pmatrix} a_{11} + b_{11} & a_{12} + b_{12} & a_{13} + b_{13} \\ a_{21} + b_{21} & a_{22} + b_{22} & a_{23} + b_{23} \end{pmatrix}$$

Multiplication

$$\begin{pmatrix} a_{11}a_{12}a_{13} \\ a_{21}a_{22}a_{23} \end{pmatrix} \cdot \begin{pmatrix} b_{11}b_{12} \\ b_{21}b_{22} \\ b_{31}b_{32} \end{pmatrix} = \begin{pmatrix} a_{11}\cdot b_{11} + a_{12}\cdot b_{21} + a_{13}\cdot b_{31} & a_{11}\cdot b_{12} + a_{12}\cdot b_{22} + a_{13}\cdot b_{32} \\ a_{21}\cdot b_{11} + a_{22}\cdot b_{21} + a_{23}\cdot b_{31} & a_{21}\cdot b_{12} + a_{22}\cdot b_{22} + a_{23}\cdot b_{32} \end{pmatrix}$$

In general, if A is $m \times n$ (m rows and n columns) and B is $n \times q$, then the product matrix C = A·B is of size $m \times q$. The entry c_{ij} of the product matrix can be computed by multiplying the ith row of A by the jth column of B as follows:

jth column

$$i\text{th row } a_{i1}a_{i2}\cdots a_{in} \quad \begin{pmatrix} b_{1j} \\ b_{2j} \\ \vdots \\ b_{nj} \end{pmatrix} = a_{i1}\cdot b_{1j} + a_{i2}\cdot b_{2j} + \cdots + a_{in}\cdot b_{nj} = c_{ij}$$

Note: To multiply two matrices, A and B, the number of columns in A must equal the number of rows in B. Such matrices are *conformable*.

a. Write a program to read two 4×3 matrices and compute their sum and difference (for subtraction, corresponding entries are subtracted).
b. Write a program to read a 3×3 matrix A and a 3×3 matrix B. Compute $A \cdot B$ and $(A + B)\cdot(A - B)$.
c. Write a program to input N and compute A^N where A is a matrix that has been read in.

$$A^N = \underbrace{A \cdot A \cdot \ldots A}_{N \text{ matrices}}$$

d. Read in a square matrix A and print out its transpose A^T (the rows of A^T are equal to the columns of A; row i of A^T = column i of A).

15. The XYZ Company manufactures four products: P1, P2, P3, and P4. Each of these products must undergo some type of operation on five different machines: A, B, C, D, and E. The time (in units of hours) required for each of these products on each of the five machines is shown below:

	A	B	C	D	E
P1	0.2	0.2	0.1	0.58	0.15
P2	0.26	0.1	0.13	0.61	0.3
P3	0.5	0.21	0.56	0.45	0.27
P4	0.6	0.17	1.3	0.25	0.31

For example, product P1 requires 0.2 hour on machine A, 0.2 hour on machine B, 0.1 hour on machine C, and so on.

a. The XYZ Company has been requested to fill an order for 356 of product P1, 257 of product P2, 1,058 of product P3, and 756 of product P4. Write a program to determine the total number of hours that *each* machine will be used. [*Hint*: Express the above table as a 4 x 5 matrix; express the order as a 1×4 matrix, and multiply both matrices. You do not need to know about matrices to solve this problem, however!]
b. The XYZ company is renting the five machines A, B, C, D, E from a tooling company. The hourly rental cost for each machine is:

Machines	A	B	C	D	E
Rental cost/hour	\$10.00	\$5.75	\$3.50	\$10.00	\$5.76

Write a program to compute the total rental expense for all machines. [*Hint*: Express rental costs as a 1 x 5 matrix and multiply by matrix result of part a. This problem can be solved without matrices, however.]

9-7-3 Exercises Suited for Matrix Operations

1. Write a program to verify that the following are true (choose any conformable matrices X, Y, and Z):
   a. $(X+Y)Z = X \cdot Z + Y \cdot Z$
   b. $(X \cdot Y)Z = X \cdot (Y \cdot Z)$
   c. $X \cdot X^{-1} = X^{-1} \cdot X = I$ (assuming X has an inverse)
2. Let us refer to A' (read as A prime) as the transpose of matrix A. Write a program to demonstrate that
$$(A')^{-1} = (A^{-1})'$$
for a square matrix of five rows (assuming that matrix has an inverse).
3. An $n \times n$ matrix A is said to be *symmetric* if and only if A = A'. Write a program to demonstrate that
   a. $A \cdot A'$ is symmetric and
   b. $A + A'$ is symmetric.
4. A *strictly triangular* matrix is a square matrix with all entries on and below the main diagonal equal to zero. Write a program to demonstrate that if A is such a 4×4 matrix, then $A^4 = A \cdot A \cdot A \cdot A$ is the zero matrix. (In general, A^n = zero matrix if A is an $n \times n$ strictly triangular matrix).
5. Write a program to verify that $DET(A \cdot B) = DET(A) \cdot DET(B)$ where A and B are square matrices and DET refers to the determinant of the matrix.
6. Write a program to verify that the determinant of a triangular matrix is equal to the product of its diagonal elements; choose a square matrix of size 4.
7. An iterative method for computing the inverse of a matrix A is given by
$$A^{-1} = I + B + B^2 + B^3 + B^4 + \ldots,$$
where $B = I - A$ (I is the identity matrix). Compute the inverse of
$$A = \begin{pmatrix} 1/2 & 1 & 0 \\ 0 & 2/3 & 0 \\ -1/2 & -1 & 2/3 \end{pmatrix}$$
Stop at B^{10} in the expansion for A^{-1}. Check the result by computing $A^{-1}*A$. This method is valid only if the eigen values of A are less than 1 in absolute value.
8. The trace of a matrix is defined as the sum of its diagonal elements. Let A be a 5 by 5 matrix and B be a 5 by 5 matrix. Write a program to verify that $tr(A \cdot B) = tr(B \cdot A)$ and $tr(A + B) = tr(A) + tr(B)$.
9. A method for computing the inverse of any matrix on a computer is as follows: Let A be an $n \times n$ matrix ($n \geq 1$). Then
$$A^{-1} = -\frac{1}{c_n}(A^{n-1} + c_1A^{n-2} + c_2A^{n-3} + \cdots + c_{n-1}I)$$

where the c's are all constants defined as

$$c_1 = -\text{tr}(A) \text{ (See exercise 8 for the definition of the trace.)}$$
$$c_2 = -1/2(c_1\text{tr}(A) + \text{tr}(A^2))$$
$$c_3 = -1/3(c_2\text{tr}(A) + c_1\text{tr}(A^2) + \text{tr}(A^3))$$
$$\vdots$$
$$c_n = -1/n(c_{n-1}\text{tr}(A) + c_{n-2}\text{tr}(A^2) + \cdots + c_1\text{tr}(A^{n-1}) + \text{tr}(A^n))$$

Write a program to compute the inverse of a 5×5 matrix A and check that it is indeed the inverse by verifying that $A \cdot A^{-1} = I$.

For example, the inverse of a 2×2 matrix X is $X^{-1} = -\frac{1}{c_2}(X + c_1 I)$ where $c_2 = -1/2(c_1\text{tr}(X) + \text{tr}(X^2))$ and $c_1 = -\text{tr}(X)$.

9-7-4 Projects

1. *A Digital Data Noise-Elimination Problem.*
A common problem in the collection of digital data via telecommunications is the phenomenon of noise—momentary fluctuations in the signal. When the data being transmitted represents an image (for example, pictures transmitted by satellites and space vehicles), noise results in obviously invalid random black, white, and gray spots when the image is reconverted to visual form. At least some of the noise can be eliminated by examining the image in digital form prior to converting it to visual form and replacing noise elements with an estimate of the correct signal. Noise elements can be found by examining the difference between each element and the elements surrounding it. Noise elements generally differ drastically from the surrounding elements, for example, a white element surrounded by black elements or a black element surrounding by white. An estimate of the correct signal can be made by replacing the noise element by the average of the surrounding elements.

Write a program to eliminate noise from a digitized image stored in a 30×30 array. Each element of the array represents one "spot" in the image and stores a value from 0 to 9. Zero (0) represents white; 9 represents black; the values between 0 and 9 represent shades of gray. An element can be assumed to be a noise element if it differs in absolute value by 4 or more from five of its surrounding elements. For example, consider the element A(3,3) in the array below:

There are eight elements surrounding A(3,3); the relevant differences are:

$|7 - 3| = 4$
$|6 - 3| = 3$
$|9 - 3| = 6$
$|9 - 3| = 6$
$|2 - 3| = 1$
$|8 - 3| = 5$
$|8 - 3| = 5$
$|1 - 3| = 2$

Array A→

7	2	1	2	5
6	7	6	9	7
8	9	3	2	2
7	8	8	1	2
5	6	7	1	7

Five of the differences are greater than or equal to 4, hence the element may be classified as a noise element. Noise elements should be replaced by the average of the surrounding elements; in this case

$$A(3,3) = \frac{7 + 6 + 9 + 9 + 2 + 8 + 8 + 1}{8} = 6$$

2. *A Digital Image Enhancement.*
Another problem in the analysis of images in digitized form is that objects are sometimes difficult to recognize because of insufficient contrast between the object and its background. One method that can be used to enhance digital images is to reduce the number of distinct shades of gray from the number represented in the initial signal (ten in the preceding problem) to a lesser number such as five (black, white, and three shades of gray), three (black, white, and gray), or even two (black and white). This process is somewhat like increasing the contrast on a black and white television set. With increased contrast, some detail is lost but the remaining images are more prominent.

Write a program to enchance contrast in a 30 × 30 digitized image described in exercise 1. Perform three enhancements: translate the image from the original ten different values to five (low contrast), three (medium contrast,) and two (high contrast) different values using the following table of transformations:

Original value	Low contrast	Medium contrast	High contrast
0	0	0	0
1	0	0	0
2	2	0	0
3	2	4	0
4	4	4	0
5	4	4	9
6	6	4	9
7	6	9	9
8	8	9	9
9	8	9	9

For example, if the original image appears as

7	6	9
9	6	2
8	8	1

the transformations would yield the following results:

Low contrast

6	6	8
8	6	2
8	8	0

Medium contrast

9	4	9
9	4	0
9	9	0

High contrast

9	9	9
9	9	0
9	9	0

9-7-5 Answers to Test Yourself

1.

```
10 DIM A(3,4),B(3,4)
15 LET K=1
20 FOR I=1 TO 3
30   FOR J=1 TO 4
40      LET A(I,J)=K
50      LET B(I,J)=10*A(I,J)
55      LET K=K+1
60   NEXT J
70 NEXT I
80 LET C=500
```

a.

```
100 FOR I=1 TO 3
200   FOR J=1 TO 4
300      PRINT A(I,J);
400   NEXT J
500 NEXT I
600 FOR I=1 TO 3
700   FOR J=1 TO 4
800      PRINT B(I,J);
900   NEXT J
1000 NEXT I
1100 PRINT C
```

Output

```
1 2 3 4 5 6 7 8 9 10 11 12 10 20 30 40 50 60 70 80 90 100 110 120 500
```

b.

```
12 FOR I=1 TO 3
13   FOR J=1 TO 4
14      PRINT A(I,J);
15   NEXT J
16   FOR J=1 TO 4
17      PRINT B(I,J);
18   NEXT J
19   PRINT C
20 NEXT I
```

Output

```
1 2 3 4 10 20 30 40 500
5 6 7 8 50 60 70 80 500
9 10 11 12 90 100 110 120 500
```

c.

```
21 FOR J=1 TO 4
22   FOR I = 1 TO 3
23      PRINT A(I,J);
24   NEXT I
25   PRINT C;
26   FOR I=1 TO 3
27      PRINT B(I,J);
28   NEXT I
29   PRINT
30 NEXT J
```

Output

```
1 5 9 500 10 50 90
2 6 10 500 20 60 100
3 7 11 500 30 70 110
4 8 12 500 40 80 120
```

d.

```
31 FOR I=1 TO 3
32   FOR J=1 TO 4
33      PRINT A(I,J);B(I,J);
34   NEXT J
35   PRINT
36 NEXT I
```

Output

```
1 10 2 20 3 30 4 40
5 50 6 60 7 70 8 80
9 90 10 100 11 110 12 120
```

e.

```
37 FOR K=2 TO 4 STEP 2
38   FOR J=K-1 TO K
39      FOR I=1 TO 3
40         PRINT A(I,J);B(I,J);
41      NEXT I
42   NEXT J
43   PRINT
44 NEXT K
45 END
```

Output

```
1 10 5 50 9 90 2 20 6 60 10 100
3 30 7 70 11 110 4 40 8 80 12 120
```

2. a.

```
10 DIM A(4,3)
50 DATA 1,2,3,4,5,6,7,8,9,10,11,12
```

```
100 FOR J=1 TO 3
200   FOR I=1 TO 4
300      READ A(I,J)
400   NEXT I
500 NEXT J
550 MAT PRINT A
600 END
```

Output

```
1   5    9
2   6   10
3   7   11
4   8   12
```

b.

```
100 DIM A(1,6),B(6)
200 DATA 1,2,3,4,5,6,1,2,3,4,5,6
300 FOR J=1 TO 6
400   READ A(1,J)
500 NEXT J
600 FOR I=1 TO 6
700   READ B(I)
800 NEXT I
900 MAT PRINT A;B
1000 END
```

Output

```
1 2 3 4 5 6
1         2         3         4         5
6
```

c.

```
100 DIM A(6,1),B(6,1)
200 DATA 1,1,2,2,3,3,4,4,5,5,6,6
300 FOR I=1 TO 6
400   READ A(I,1),B(I,1)
500 NEXT I
600 MAT PRINT A;B;
700 END
```

Output

```
1
3
4
5
6
1
2
3
4
5
6
```

d.

```
100 DIM A(6,1),B(1,6)
200 DATA 1,1,2,2,3,3,4,4,5,5,6,6
300 FOR I = 1 TO 6
400   READ A(I,1),B(1,I)
500 NEXT I
600 MAT PRINT A;B;
700 END
```

Output

```
1
2
3
4
5
6
1 2 3 4 5 6
```

e.

```
100 DIM A(9,3),B(9,2)
200 DATA 1,1,1,1,1,2,2,2,2,2,3,3,3,3,3
300 DATA 4,4,4,4,4,5,5,5,5,5,6,6,6,6,6
350 DATA 7,7,7,7,7,8,8,8,8,8,9,9,9,9,9
400 FOR I=1 TO 9
500   FOR J=1 TO 3
600      READ A(I,J)
700   NEXT J
800   FOR J=1 TO 2
```

output for part e

Output

```
1 1 1
2 2 2
3 3 3
4 4 4
5 5 5
6 6 6
7 7 7
8 8 8
9 9 9

1 1
2 2
3 3
4 4
5 5
6 6
7 7
8 8
9 9
```

```
 900       READ B(I,J)
1000    NEXT J
1100 NEXT I
1200 MAT PRINT A;B;
1300 END
```

f.

```
 100 DIM A(8,9),B(4,2)
 200 DATA 1,1,1,1,1,1,1,1,1,2,2,2,2,2,2,2,2,2,
           3,3,3,3,3,3,3,3,3,4,4,4,4,4,4,4,4,4
 300 DATA 5,5,5,5,5,5,5,5,5,6,6,6,6,6,6,6,6,6,
 350 DATA 7,7,7,7,7,7,7,7,7,8,8,8,8,8,8,8,8,8
 400 DATA 1,2,3,4,5,6,7,8
 500 FOR I=1 TO 8
 600    FOR J=1 TO 9
 700       READ A(I,J)
 800    NEXT J
 900 NEXT I
1000 FOR J=1 TO 2
1100    FOR I=1 TO 4
1200       READ B(I,J)
1300    NEXT I
1400 NEXT J
1500 MAT PRINT A;B;
1600 END
```

Output

```
1 1 1 1 1 1 1 1 1
2 2 2 2 2 2 2 2 2
3 3 3 3 3 3 3 3 3
4 4 4 4 4 4 4 4 4
5 5 5 5 5 5 5 5 5
6 6 6 6 6 6 6 6 6
7 7 7 7 7 7 7 7 7
8 8 8 8 8 8 8 8 8

1 5
2 6
3 7
4 8
```

3.

```
10 DIM F(40,17), G(680)
15 FOR I = 1 TO 40
20    FOR J = 1 TO 17
25       F(I,J)=RND(100)
30    NEXT J
35 NEXT I
40 K=1
45 FOR I = 1 TO 40
50    FOR J = 1 TO 17
55       G(K)= F(I,J)
60    NEXT J
65 NEXT I
```

4. a.

```
 10 REM EXERCISE 4A
 20 DIM A(5,5)
 30 DATA 1,2,3,4,5
 40 DATA 6,7,8,9,10
 50 DATA 11,12,13,14,15
 60 DATA 16,17,18,19,20
 70 DATA 21,22,23,24,25
 80 FOR I=1 TO 5
 90    FOR J=1 TO 5
100       READ A(I,J)
110    NEXT J
120 NEXT I
130 FOR I=1 TO 5
140    FOR J=1 TO 5
```

Output

```
1  2  3  4  5
6  7  8  9  10
11 12 13 14 15
16 17 18 19 20
21 22 23 24 25
**************
1  2  3  4  5
6  7  8  9  10
11 12 13 14 15
16 17 18 19 20
21 22 23 24 25
```

```
150      PRINT A(I,J);
160    NEXT J
170    PRINT
180 NEXT I
185 PRINT "**************"
190 REM ALTERNATE SOLUTION TO 4A
200 RESTORE
210 MAT READ A
220 MAT PRINT A;
```

For second part of exercise interchange I and J at lines 130, 140, 160 and 180.

b.
```
230 REM EXERCISE 4B
240 LET S=0
250 FOR J=1 TO 5
260   LET S=S+A(3,J)
270 NEXT J
280 PRINT "SUM OF 3RD ROW=";S
```

Output

```
SUM OF 3RD ROW = 65
```

c.
```
300 REM EXERCISE 4C
310 LET L=A(1,1)
320 FOR I=2 TO 5
330   IF A(I,1)>L THEN LET L=A(I,1)
340 NEXT I
350 PRINT "LARGEST VALUE IN FIRST COLUMN IS"; L
360 PRINT
```

Output

```
LARGEST VALUE IN FIRST COLUMN IS 21
```

d.
```
370 REM EXERCISE 4D
380 DIM B(5)
390 FOR I=1 TO 5
400   LET B(I) = 0
410 NEXT I
420 FOR I=1 TO 5
430   FOR J=1 TO 5
440      LET B(J)=B(J)+A(I,J)
450   NEXT J
460 NEXT I
470 PRINT "SUM OF COLUMNS"
475 MAT PRINT B;
```

Output

```
SUM OF COLUMNS
55 60 65 70 75
```

e.
```
480 REM EXERCISE 4E
490 PRINT "OLD CONTENT OF A"
500 MAT PRINT A;
510 FOR I=1 TO 5
520   LET A(3,I)=A(3,I)+A(2,I)
530 NEXT I
540 PRINT "NEW CONTENT OF A"
550 MAT PRINT A;
```

Output

```
OLD CONTENT OF A
1  2  3  4  5
6  7  8  9  10
11 12 13 14 15
16 17 18 19 20
21 22 23 24 25

NEW CONTENT OF A
1  2  3  4  5
6  7  8  9  10
17 19 21 23 25
16 17 18 19 20
21 22 23 24 25
```

f.
```
560 REM EXERCISE 4F
570 PRINT "OLD CONTENT OF A"
580 MAT PRINT A;
590 FOR I=1 TO 5
600   LET H=A(I,3)
610   LET A(I,3)=A(I,4)
620   LET A(I,4)=H
630 NEXT I
640 PRINT "NEW CONTENT OF A"
650 MAT PRINT A;
```

Output

```
OLD CONTENT OF A
1  2  3  4  5
6  7  8  9  10
17 19 21 23 25
16 17 18 19 20
21 22 23 24 25

NEW CONTENT OF A
1  2  4  3  5
6  7  9  8  10
17 19 23 21 25
16 17 19 18 20
21 22 24 23 25
```

g.
```
740 REM EXERCISE 4G
750 LET S2=0
752 LET L=A(1,5)
760 FOR I=1 TO 5
770   LET S2=S2+A(I,6-I)
775   IF A(I,6-I) > L THEN L = A(I,6-I)
780 NEXT I
790 PRINT "SUM OF SECOND DIAGONAL"; S2
795 PRINT "LARGEST VALUE IS"; L
```

Output

```
SUM OF SECOND DIAGONAL 74
LARGEST VALUE IS 23
```

h.
```
920 REM EXERCISE 4H
930 REM R REPRESENTS ROW POSITION OF LARGEST ELEMENT
940 REM C REPRESENTS COLUMN POSITION OF LARGEST ELEMENT
950 LET R=1
960 LET C=1
970 FOR I=1 TO 5
980   FOR J=1 TO 5
990     IF A(I,J)<=A(R,C) THEN 1020
1000     LET R=I
1010     LET C=J
1020   NEXT J
1030 NEXT I
1040 PRINT "LOCATION OF LARGEST ELEMENT IS ROW";R;
     "COLUMN";C
1050 END
```

Output

```
LOCATION OF LARGEST ELEMENT IS ROW 3 COLUMN 5
```

5.
```
10 DIM C(5,5),D(5,5)
15 FOR I = 1 TO 5
20   FOR J = 1 TO 5
25     READ C(I,J)
30   NEXT J
35   FOR J = 1 TO 5
40     READ D(I,J)
45   NEXT J
50 NEXT I
```

10 SUBROUTINES AND FUNCTIONS

10-1 Subroutines

Subroutines are powerful, convenient, and some times necessary programming tools to help you better structure, document, code, test, and debug your programs.

10-1-1 Program Structure: Modularity

One way to improve the structure of a program is to decompose the original problem or task to be solved into independent subtasks and then execute these subtasks in a predefined sequence. In the process, each subtask is clearly identified and documented, and the order in which these subtasks are to be executed is determined. Such a well-organized plan results in code that is easier to write, follow, test, and debug and easier for others to read.

Another advantage of a well-organized program is that you will find yourself using the GOTO statement less frequently. This in itself is very important, since the undisciplined use of the GOTO statement can often give rise to the "spaghetti code syndrome," which makes it very difficult for the program reader to remember where in the program he/she comes from and where he/she is going! M. Dijkstra, who played a critical role in the formulation and early development of structured program design, was an outspoken critic of the GOTO statement and felt that it should be abolished from all higher level programming languages! Nevertheless, the GOTO statement lives on in BASIC. Subroutines, however, minimize the need for its use and, in so doing, improve the clarity and readability of the resulting code.

Decomposing a problem into smaller pieces (modules) allows you to focus more easily on a particular piece of the problem without worrying about the overall problem. The tasks become easier to solve and are more manageable since each performs a very specific function. Typically, you can code each module independently of the others and even test and debug each module separately. Once all modules are working properly, you can link them together by writing the coordinating code (generally called the root segment or the main code). The coordinating code activates the various modules in a predetermined sequence. Consider Figure 10–1, which illustrates these principles. Note that the resulting program consists of 5 modules: the coordinating module and the four modules A, B, C, and D. It is, of course, conceivable that a particular module itself might be broken down into other modules.

By breaking down a problem into independent modules, a programmer in charge of a very complex problem can easily assign various members of a team the responsibility for developing one or more modules. Such modules can be run and tested independently of one another. [Making one change in one module is a very local intervention that does not require an understanding of all other modules. In contrast, making one change in a nonmodular program held together by myriads of GOTO statements not only requires an understanding of the whole program but can also have dramatic repercussions throughout the program, producing masses of error messages as well as unwanted output!] When all the modules are complete, they can be joined together to form a whole, which can then be tested. In BASIC these modules are referred to as *subroutines*.

■ **Figure 10–1** Program decomposition.

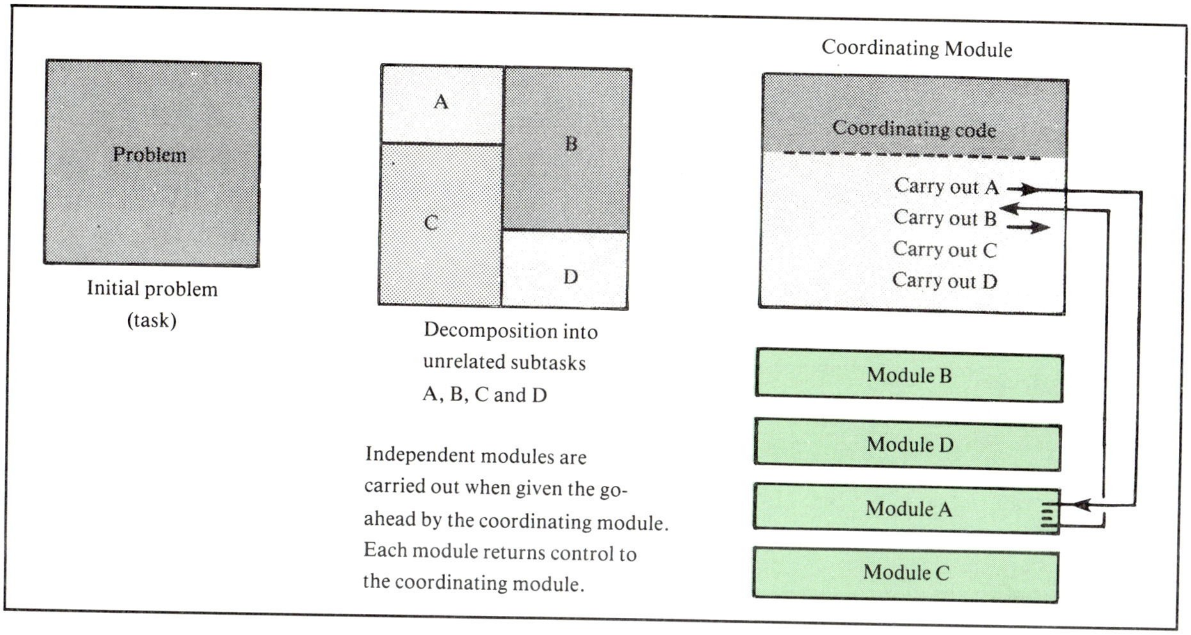

■ **Figure 10–2** A structured diagram.

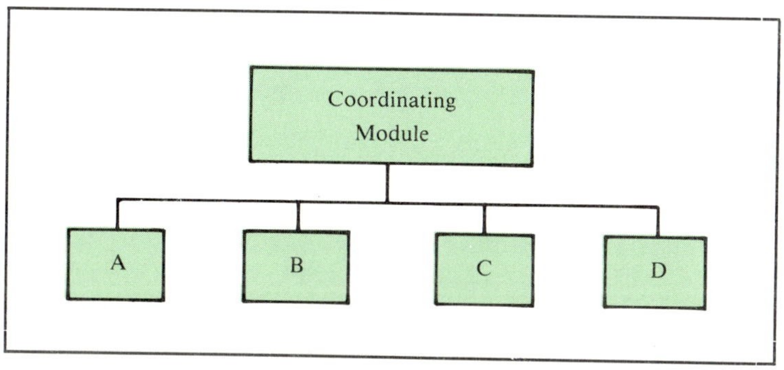

In this modular environment, each module can be respecified as a sequence of smaller modules describing what is to be done at increasing levels of detail. This technique of expanding a program plan into one or more levels of detailed subplans is sometimes referred to as *top-down* design, where the structure of the program is presented as a hierarchy of tasks. A useful tool to illustrate module relationships and hierarchies is a hierarchy chart, sometimes called a structured diagram. Figure 10–2 shows a hierarchy chart for the program of Figure 10–1.

10-1-2 Do It Now

Assume module B of Figure 10–2 required module X, which required module P. Also assume that module C required 2 different modules, Y and Z. Draw the corresponding structured diagram.

Answer

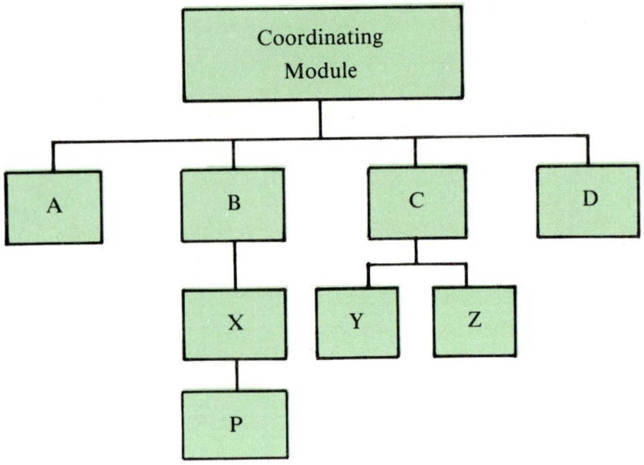

10-1-3 The GOSUB Statement

BASIC activates subroutines by means of the GOSUB statement. The GOSUB instruction specifies a target line, for example, GOSUB 300, where 300 is a line number, and transfer is then made to that line number. Thus GOSUB behaves very much like a GOTO or IF/THEN statement. All instructions starting at the target line to the RETURN statement (end of subroutine) are carried out. The RETURN statement returns control to the instruction that physically follows the GOSUB statement. The subroutine is the code segment that starts at the line designated by the GOSUB statement and ends with the RETURN statement.

Examples:

```
10 GOSUB 40
15 .
   .
   .
40 PRINT "HELLO"
45 RETURN
```

One module

```
05 INPUT X
10 GOSUB 80
15 .
   .
   .
80 IF X > 0 THEN 95
85 PRINT "NEGATIVE"
90 GOTO 98
95 PRINT "POSITIVE"
98 RETURN
```

One module

We will illustrate program modularity and explain the use of the GOSUB statement in the problem in section 10–1–4. The program itself may seem somewhat unrealistic in the sense that it could have been written without subroutines. However, it illustrates the concepts discussed in this section: program documentation (readability), program structure, program modification, and program testing, where each subroutine is an independent module that performs a specific task.

10-1-4 Program Modularity: An Extreme Example

You have been assigned team leader of a group of four programmers (A, B, C, and D) and your task is to solve the following problem:

An input file consists of an unknown number of records. Each record consists of a meal cost and a meal code (1 = breakfast, 2 = lunch, 3 = dinner). Write a program to print the count of dinner meals and the maximum dinner cost. An error message should be printed if a meal code is not 1, 2, or 3. The input and output are shown in Figure 10-3.

You realize that the problem can be broken down very easily into four parts that are completely independent of one another. Hence, you assign these four tasks to the four programmers as follows:

1. Programmer A will be responsible for writing the headings and column captions.
2. Programmer B will take care of the validation problem, i.e., making sure that the codes read are valid.
3. Programmer C will find the maximum dinner cost as well as the number of dinner meals served that day.
4. Programmer D will print the final results—the maximum dinner cost and the number of dinner meals.

You are essentially subcontracting tasks to four individuals. As team leader, you are responsible for coordinating these tasks in a main program so that the integrated

Figure 10-3 Program output.

Input

```
DATA  5.75, 1
DATA  2.89, 3
DATA 10.67, 2
DATA  6.33, 4
DATA  4.56, 3
```

```
         ELITE RESTAURANT

MEAL COST       MEAL CODE

  5.75            1
  2.89            3
 10.67            2
  6.33            4   **INVALID CODE
  4.56            3

MAXIMUM DINNER COST 4.56
NUMBER OF DINNERS IS 2
```

code works satisfactorily. Having delegated these responsibilities to your team members, you now diagram the sequence of coding activities, as shown in Figure 10-4.

Figure 10-4 Main program segment identifying various modules.

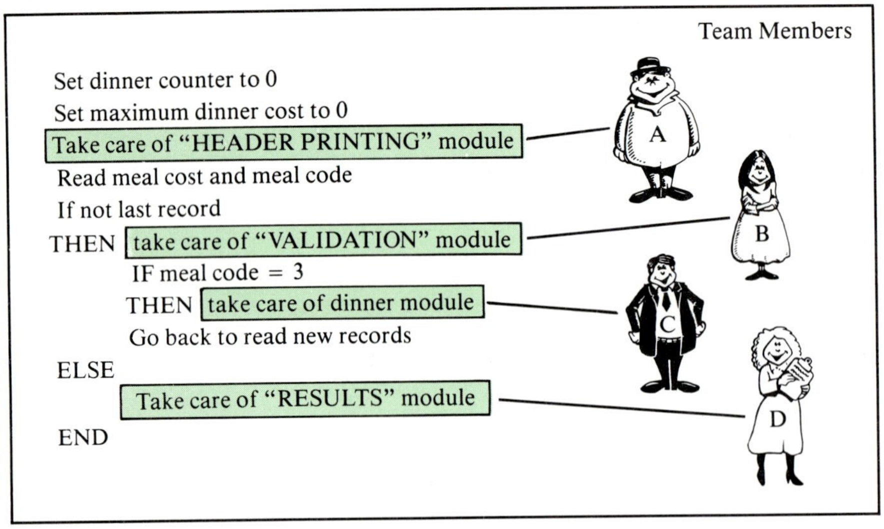

So that each programmer understands exactly what kind of data he/she will work with, you specify the following:

1. To programmer A you say: "Write the code to generate the headers shown in the report of Figure 10-3."
2. To programmer B you say: "Every time I pass control to you, the variable K should contain either a 1 or a 2 or a 3. If K is one of these numbers, let me know about it by setting F to 0. If, on the other hand, K is not one of these three numbers, then set F to 1. I will then decide what to do, based on whether F is 1 or 0."
3. To programmer C you say: "Every time the variable C gets to you, it is a dinner cost. Keep track of the maximum dinner cost in M (assume M is initially 0) and keep track of the number of dinners in variable D (assume D is initially 0)."
4. To programmer D you say: "M represents a dinner cost, and D represents the total number of dinners. Print these two numbers according to the layout of the report in Figure 10-3."

At this point, your team goes to work and you receive their resulting code as follows:

Programmer A:

```
10 PRINT TAB(5); "ELITE RESTAURANT"
15 PRINT
20 PRINT TAB(3); "MEAL COST", "MEAL CODE"
25 PRINT
30 RETURN            (This means "Back to you now!")
```

Programmer B:

```
10 F = 0
15 IF K = 1 THEN 40
20 IF K = 2 THEN 40
25 IF K = 3 THEN 40
30    F = 1
40 RETURN
```

Programmer C:

```
10 IF M >= C THEN 20
15    M = C
20 D = D + 1
25 RETURN
```

Programmer D:

```
10 PRINT "MAXIMUM DINNER COST"; M
20 PRINT "NUMBER OF DINNERS IS"; D
25 RETURN
```

You then use these modules in your coordinating program by using the BASIC instruction GOSUB to link these different modules, as shown in the program of Figure 10–5. Note that the modules are not placed in the program in any particular sequence. The module at line 345 is carried out, for example, until the RETURN at line 365 is encountered, at which time control is passed to the statement following the GOSUB (line 140).

10-1-5 Do It Now

Could the input data validation module itself have printed the "invalid code" error message?

Answer

Yes. However if this were the case, the program would no longer be "properly" structured. Exit from a module should always be made through the RETURN statement, meaning that if line 330 had been replaced with the statements 330 and 332:

```
.
.
330 PRINT C, K; "**INVALID CODE"
332 GOTO 150        Location 150 is outside subroutine
335 RETURN
```

the module would no longer be self-contained, i.e., it would no longer function as an independent module since the GOTO statement at line 332 specifies a line number that is outside the module. The return is *now* fixed to line 150, which makes the subroutine useless in terms of being called from different locations in the program, i.e., the statement READ C, K would always have to be coded at line 150 in order for the validation module to work properly.

10-1-6 Generalized Procedures and Subroutines

Another reason for using a subroutine is to execute a coding segment more than once from various points in a program. For example, suppose you need to sort two arrays, array A at the start of a program and another array B at the end of the program. It

Figure 10-5 A modularized program.

```
100 REM PROGRAM MODULARITY
105 REM MAIN PROGRAM SEGMENT
110 REM DATA DICTIONARY
115 REM       D: USED TO COUNT NUMBER OF DINNERS
120 REM       M: MAXIMUM DINNER COST. INITIALLY SET TO 0
125 REM       C: USED TO READ THE COSTS OF MEALS
130 REM       K: MEAL CODE (1=BREAKFAST; 2=LUNCH; 3=DINNER)
135 GOSUB 345
140 D = 0
145 M = 0
150 READ C, K
155 IF C < 0 THEN 200
160    GOSUB 310
165    IF F = 0 THEN 180
170       PRINT C, K; " **INVALID CODE"
175       GOTO 150
180       PRINT C, K
185       IF K <> 3 THEN 150
190          GOSUB 250
195          GOTO 150
200 GOSUB 230
205 STOP
210 REM OUTPUT MODULE
215 REM DATA DICTIONARY
220 REM       D: USED TO COUNT NUMBER OF DINNERS
225 REM       M: MAXIMUM DINNER COST. INITIALLY SET TO 0
230 PRINT
235 PRINT "MAXIMUM DINNER COST" ; M
240 PRINT "NUMBER OF DINNERS IS"; D
245 RETURN
250 REM SEARCH FOR MAXIMUM DINNER COST MODULE
255 REM DATA DICTIONARY
260 REM       D: USED TO COUNT NUMBER OF DINNERS
265 REM       M: MAXIMUM DINNER COST. INITIALLY SET TO 0
270 IF M > C THEN 280
275    M = C
280 D = D + 1
285 RETURN
290 REM INPUT DATA VALIDATION MODULE
295 REM DATA DICTIONARY
300 REM       F: IF VALID CODE SET F TO 0 OTHERWISE SET F TO 1
305 REM       K: MEAL CODE (1=BREAKFAST; 2=LUNCH; 3=DINNER)
310 F = 0
315 IF K = 1 THEN 335
320 IF K = 2 THEN 335
325 IF K = 3 THEN 335
330    F = 1
335 RETURN
340 REM HEADER PRINT MODULE
345 PRINT TAB(5); "ELITE RESTAURANT"
350 PRINT
355 PRINT "MEAL COST", "MEAL CODE"
360 PRINT
365 RETURN
370 DATA   5.75, 1
375 DATA   2.89, 3
380 DATA  10.67, 2
385 DATA   6.33, 4
390 DATA   4.56, 3
395 DATA  -4.00, 0
400 END
```

would be wasteful of your time and energy to write all the sorting code at the beginning of the program and then rewrite essentially the same code at the end of the program. The sorting procedure itself is independent of any specific array, so it should be possible to write the code to sort any type of one-dimensional array. Other than the names of the array and the number of items to be sorted, the codes to sort A and B should be the same. In that respect, subroutines are extremely convenient because they allow us to code generalized procedures that are data-independent, and this, in turn, means that code duplication can be avoided, the program is shorter, the potential for errors is less, and the programmer has become more efficient.

To illustrate the concept of a generalized procedure, consider the following example:

Suppose an array A contains 20 numbers and suppose that at three variable points in your program you have to print out the numbers of array A as follows:

1. 3 numbers per line at the beginning of the program
2. 4 numbers per line in the middle of the program
3. 6 numbers per line at the very end of the program.

If you did not know of the existence of subroutines, you might write the code as follows:

Beginning:

```
48 K = 0
50 FOR I = 1 TO 20
52     PRINT A(I);
54     K = K + 1
56     IF K <> 3 THEN 62
58         PRINT
60         K = 0
62 NEXT I
.
.
.
```

Output
(3 numbers per line)

```
10  20  30
40  50  60
70  80  90
11  22  33
44  55  66
77  88  99
 0  12
```

Middle:

```
70 K = 0
72 FOR I = 1 TO 20
74     PRINT A(I);
76     K = K + 1
78     IF K <> 4 THEN 84
80         PRINT
82         K = 0
84 NEXT I
.
.
.
```

(4 numbers per line)

```
10  20  30  40
50  60  70  80
90  11  22  33
44  55  66  77
88  99   0  12
```

End:

```
92 K = 0
93 FOR I = 1 TO 20
94     PRINT A(I);
95     K = K + 1
96     IF K <> 6 THEN 99
97     PRINT
98     K = 0
99 NEXT I
```

(6 numbers per line)

```
10  20  30  40  50  60
70  80  90  11  22  33
44  55  66  77  88  99
 0  12
```

With subroutines, the previous code can be rewritten as:

```
48 L = 3                Go and print 3 numbers/line.
50 GOSUB 85
.
.
60 L = 4                Go and print 4 numbers/line.
62 GOSUB 85
.
.
70 L = 6                Go and print 6 number/line.
72 GOSUB 85
.
.
85 K = 0
87 FOR I = 1 TO 20
89     PRINT A(I);
91     K = K + 1
93     IF K <> L THEN 98
95         PRINT
97         K = 0
98 NEXT I
99 RETURN
```

Note that lines 85 through 99 will be executed three separate times. The only variable that changes for each execution is L, which is set to the desired value just before the GOSUB instructions at lines 50, 62, and 72 are executed. Note also that this subroutine can be called and executed from any point in the program. The return from the subroutine will always be made to the instruction following the GOSUB 85 that was just executed. The subroutine should be a totally independent segment of code, i.e., nowhere in the subroutine code should there by any instructions that transfer out of the subroutine to any specific line numbers in the program.

Consider the following invalidly written subroutine (assume GOSUB 80):

```
80 K = 0
.
.
85 IF X < 0 GOTO 38
.
.
91 GOTO 150
.
.
99 RETURN
```

This code would be useless since the subroutine code itself is not self-contained, i.e., lines 85 and 91 transfer to specific line numbers outside the subroutine. This means that this code could not be called from more than one point in the program, since it would always return to the same location (line 38 or 150). Also, every time you made a change in your program or changed line 38 or 150, you would have to change lines 85 and 91 in the subroutine. Finally, how would someone contracted to write this subroutine know where to branch back into your main program before your main program was written?

10-1-7 A Complete Example

Final scores have been computed for students enrolled in business management sections at a large university. Each section has two sets of DATA statements: The first DATA statement identifies the class section number and the number of students in that class. The second DATA statement in the set contains the scores for that section. The trip record contains the word "SECTION" and a negative number. For example,

```
DATA "SECTION 58", 3 <—Number of scores
DATA 5Ø, 6Ø 4Ø <———— List of scores for section 58; in this case, 3
DATA "SECTION 59", 4
DATA 6Ø, 4Ø 8Ø, 6Ø
DATA "SECTION" ,  -3 <— trip record
```

Write a program to accomplish the following:

1. Compute the score average for each section and for the combined sections and list the scores for each section and for the combined sections.
2. Print the number of scores above the average in each section and in the combined sections.

Use a subroutine to compute the number of scores over the average and another subroutine to print the results from parts 1 and 2. Given the sample input shown above, the output should be similar to the following:

```
         SECTION 58

             5Ø
             6Ø
             4Ø

NO. SCORES OVER AVERAGE IS 1
CLASS AVERAGE IS 5Ø
----------------------------
         SECTION 59

             6Ø
             4Ø
             8Ø
             6Ø

NO. SCORES OVER AVERAGE IS 1
CLASS AVERAGE IS 6Ø
----------------------------
        COMBINED LIST

             5Ø
             6Ø
             4Ø
             6Ø
             4Ø
             8Ø
             6Ø

NO. SCORES OVER AVERAGE IS 4
CLASS AVERAGE IS 55.71429
```

Figure 10–6 A complete subroutine example.

```
100 REM SUBROUTINE EXAMPLE
110 REM       G1: ARRAY STORES ONE SET OF SCORES AT A TIME
115 REM       G:  ARRAY STORES ALL COMBINED SCORES
120 REM       H$: STORES SECTION NUMBER
121 REM       N:  NUMBER OF SCORES IN SECTION
125 REM       S:  ACCUMULATES SCORES OF ARRAY G1 AND THEN OF ARRAY G
130 REM       J:  COUNTS SCORES IN ALL SECTIONS
135 REM       A:  STORES THE AVERAGE
136 REM       K:  NUMBER OF SCORES ABOVE AVERAGE
140 REM
145 DIM G1(100), G(1000)             G1 stores one set of scores at a time.
150 J = 0                            J counts all the scores.
160     S = 0
165     READ H$, N                   Read section number and number of scores.
167     IF N < 0 THEN 235
170     PRINT TAB(10); H$            Print section number.
175     PRINT
180     FOR I = 1 TO N               Process N scores.
185         READ G1(I)               Read scores from one section.
190         PRINT TAB(13); G1(I)
195         S = S + G1(I)            Accumulate the scores.
200         J = J + 1                Count all scores
205         G(J) = G1(I)             Keep a record of all scores in array G.
210     NEXT I
215     A = S/N                      Compute the average.
220     GOSUB 305                    Go and compute the number of scores over average A.
225     GOSUB 350                    Print results: K = number of scores over average
230     GOTO 160                     and A = score average.
235 PRINT TAB(10); "COMBINED LIST"
240 PRINT
245 S = 0                            Get ready to accumulate combined scores.
250 FOR I = 1 TO J                   Altogether there are J scores.
255     G1(I) = G(I)                 Store all grades in G1, since the subroutine uses G1.
260     S = S + G(I)                 Accumulate sum of all scores.
265     PRINT TAB(13); G(I)          Print these scores.
270 NEXT I
275 A = S/J                          Compute average of combined scores.
280 N = J                            Since N is used by the subroutine, set N equal to J.
285 GOSUB 305                        Count scores over average.
290 GOSUB 350                        Print results for combined sections.
295 STOP
305 REM THIS SUBROUTINE COMPUTES THE NUMBER OF SCORES OVER THE AVERAGE
310 REM DATA DICTIONARY
315 REM       K: COUNTS NUMBER OF SCORES OVER THE AVERAGE
320 K = 0
325 FOR I = 1 TO N                   Subroutine processes N scores in array G1.
330     IF G1(I) <= A THEN 340
335         K = K + 1                If the score is greater than A, count it.
340 NEXT I
345 RETURN                           Return is first made to 225, then to 290
350 REM THIS SUBROUTINE PRINTS THE SUMMARY RESULTS FOR EACH SECTION
355 PRINT
360 PRINT "NO. SCORES OVER AVERAGE IS"; K
365 PRINT "CLASS AVERAGE IS";A
370 PRINT "------------------------------"
375 RETURN
380 DATA "SECTION 58", 3     }       scores for section 58
385 DATA 50,60,40            }
390 DATA "SECTION 59", 4     }       scores for section 59
395 DATA 60, 40, 80, 60      }
400 DATA "SECTION",-3
405 END
```

The program to solve this problem is shown in Figure 10–6. Note the use of the GOSUB statements at lines 220, 225, 285, and 290. The program can be thought of as consisting of three independent program segments:

1. The main program (line numbers 100–295), which reads the grades into arrays G and G1, computes the average A, and coordinates the use of the two subroutines.
2. A subroutine at line 305, which processes N grades and stores the number of scores above the average in the variable K.
3. Another subroutine at line 355, which prints out the summary results (lines 355-375).

Note that the subroutine to determine the number of scores above the average always processes N scores in an array always called G1 and always refers to the variable A as the score average. These three variables G1, N, and A are referred to as the *dummy arguments* of the subroutine. It is very important that the program using this subroutine initialize these arguments to their desired values before transferring to the subroutine. This is done in the program of Figure 10–6, as follows:

1. Just before the first call to the subroutine starting at 305, G1 is used to store the scores of section 58, N is 3, and A is 50. Return from the subroutine is made to statement 225.
2. Just before the second call to the subroutine starting at 305, G1 is used to store the scores of section 59, N is 4, and A is 60.
3. Just before the third call to the subroutine (line 285), G1 is used to store the combined scores of both sections (which were stored in array G—see line 255) and N is set to J (total number of scores) at line 280. Return is made to line 290.
4. In the second subroutine at 350, the dummy arguments are K and A, which are initialized at three different times to their respective values by the calling program. The average A is computed twice at statement 215 and once at 275, while K is computed three times by the subroutine starting at 320 (there are three calls to the subroutine).

The structured diagram or hierarchical chart for the program in Figure 10–6 consists of three modules, as follows:

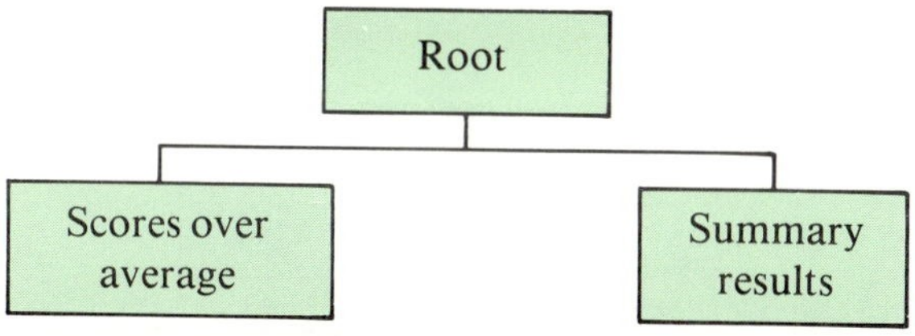

10-2 The GOSUB and RETURN Statements

The general form and structure of the GOSUB and RETURN statements are as follows:

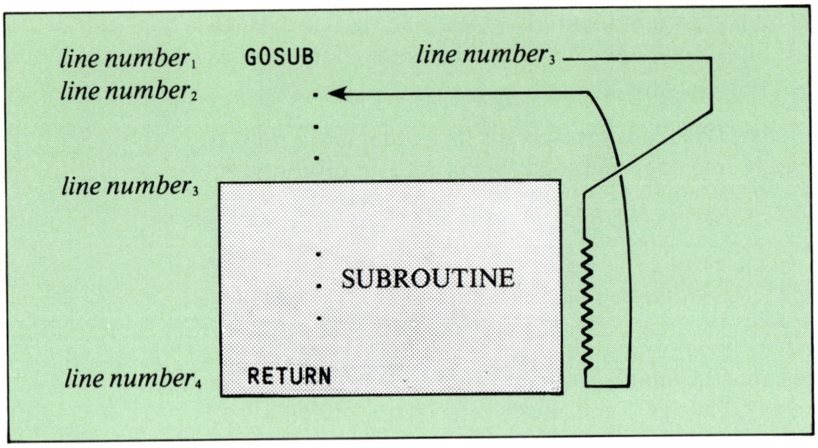

where

GOSUB	is the BASIC key word that allows transfer to the subroutine.
line number$_3$	is the line number identifying the start of the subroutine.
line number$_4$	identifies the end of the subroutine. There may be more than one RETURN statement in a subroutine.
line number$_2$	Upon RETURN from the subroutine, control is passed to *line number*$_2$.
RETURN	is a BASIC key word that should always be the last instruction executed by the subroutine. This statement causes transfer to *line number*$_2$.

All subroutines should logically terminate with the RETURN statement. The physical location of the subroutine within the program is not important. Generally subroutines are placed after the coordinating module (main code).

The distinguishing feature of the subroutine is that, at its conclusion, it returns to a variable point in the program, i.e., a point determined by GOSUB statement that called the subroutine.

Example 1: Pay Calculation with One Subroutine

```
05 REM N$,H,R: NAME,HOURS,RATE
10 READ N$,H,R
15 GOSUB 30
20 PRINT "PAY=";P
25 STOP
30 IF H <= 40 THEN 45
35    P = R * 1.5 * (H-40) + 40*R
40    GOTO 50
45    P = H * R
50    RETURN
```

Structured Diagram

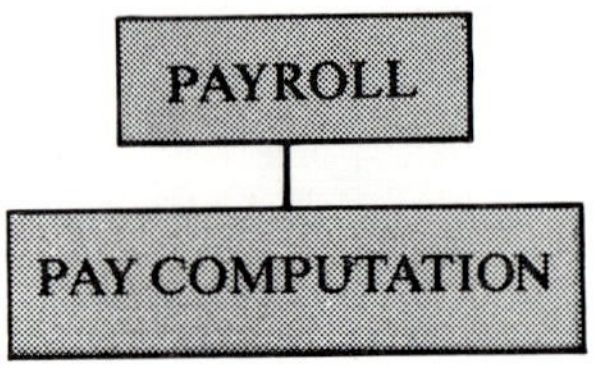

Example 2: Pay Calculation with Two Subroutines

```
Ø5 REM N$,H,R: NAME,HOURS,RATE
1Ø READ N$,H,R
15 IF R < Ø THEN 35
2Ø GOSUB 4Ø
25 PRINT "PAY=";P
3Ø GOTO 1Ø
35 STOP
4Ø IF H > 4Ø THEN 65
5Ø P = H * R
6Ø GOTO 7Ø
65 GOSUB 8Ø
7Ø RETURN
8Ø V = (H-4Ø) * 1.5 * R
85 P = 4Ø * R + V
9Ø RETURN
```

Overtime subroutine (lines 8Ø–9Ø)

Structured Diagram

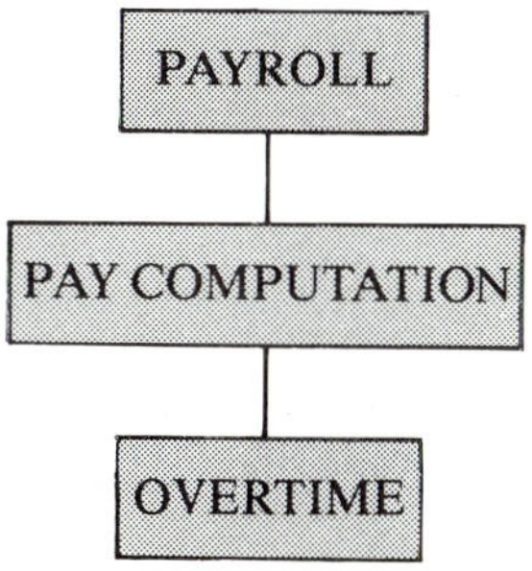

It is important that a subroutine not be executed except by a GOSUB statement. If transfer is made into a subroutine by a means other than a GOSUB statement, the transfer that will be made by the RETURN statement is unpredictable.

10-2-1 Do It Now

1. In Example 2 in the preceding section, what would happen if (a) we replaced line 40 by IF H > 40 THEN 80 ? (b) we replaced line 40 by IF H > 40 THEN GOSUB 80?
2. Add a subroutine to the code in Example 2 to perform the input data validation, i.e., check that H is less than 100 and R is less than 300. Also, draw the corresponding structured diagram.
3. Write a subroutine to compute the sums of corresponding elements of one dimensional arrays A and B, placing the results in the corresponding positions of array C (C(1) = A(1) + B(1) etc.) Assume N represents the number of array elements to be processed for A, B, and C.
4. Write a subroutine to print a row of N asterisks. Then write a program using this subroutine to produce a horizontal bar graph of the various values contained in array X of size 10.
5. Write a BASIC subroutine to calculate the approximate number of days between two dates: M1, D1, Y1 and M2, D2, Y2 where M, D and Y refer to month, day and year. [*Hint*: There are an average of 365.25 days in each year and an average of 30.4 days in each month; express both quantities in days.]

Answers

1. a. There would be a logical error since line 90 transfers us to line 25.
   b. Logical error: return would be made to line 50.

2. Insert the following code:

```
16 GOSUB 92
17 IF K = 0 THEN 20
18 PRINT "INVALID HOURS OR RATE"
19 GOTO 10
20
.
.
92 K = 0
93 IF H >= 100 THEN K = 1
94 IF R >= 300 THEN K = 1
95 RETURN
```

Structured Diagram

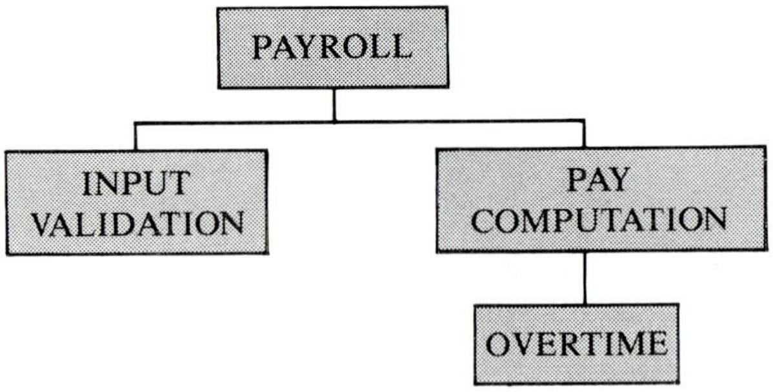

3.

```
1000 FOR I = 1 TO N
1010   LET C(I) = A(I) + B(I)
1020 NEXT I
1030 RETURN
```

4.

```
 10 DIM X(10)
 20 FOR I = 1 TO 10
 30   INPUT X(I)
 40 NEXT I
 50 FOR I = 1 TO 10
 60   PRINT I, X(I);
 65   LET N = X(I)
 70   GOSUB 100
 80 NEXT I
 90 STOP
100 FOR J = 1 TO N
110   PRINT "*";
120 NEXT J
130 PRINT
140 RETURN
150 END
```

5.

```
1000 LET J1 = 365.25*Y1 + (M1-1)*30.4 + D1
1010 LET J2 = 365.25*Y2 + (M2-1)*30.4 + D2
1020 IF J1 > J2 THEN LET D = J1 - J2
1030 IF J1 < J2 THEN LET D = J2 - J1
1040 RETURN
```

10-3 Programming Examples

10-3-1 Sorting with Subroutines

The Department of Management Science has received the final scores obtained by their students in the various sections of introduction to management. The input file consists of various class records where each record consists of the section number and the section's scores. A negative value terminates the list of scores, while the trip value "***" terminates the input file. A sample input file might be:

```
DATA MNGM 1Ø2,    3Ø,2Ø,6Ø,-4 ←-----Trip code for scores
DATA MNGM 1Ø3,    1Ø,4Ø,-2
DATA MNGM 1Ø4,    1Ø,9Ø,2Ø,8Ø,-6
DATA ***←-------------------Trip code for input file
```

Write a program for the department to sort the scores in ascending order for each class, and to produce one list of sorted scores consisting of all scores from all sections.

Since the code for sorting is fairly long and the program needs the sorting procedure performed several times, we will use a subroutine to perform the sorting. Also, since the program will print several score arrays, we will write another subroutine for the output functions. The output should be similar to the following:

```
MNGM 1Ø2          2Ø  3Ø  6Ø
MNGM 1Ø3          1Ø  4Ø
MNGM 1Ø4          1Ø  2Ø  8Ø  9Ø
COMBINED SCORES   1Ø  1Ø  2Ø  2Ø  3Ø  4Ø  6Ø  8Ø  9Ø
```

A program to solve this problem is shown in Figure 10–7.

10-3-2 On-Line Inquiry System

The Furniture Company has stock in three different warehouses. The controller dispatcher needs to know at any given time the number of items in any of the three warehouses; he may also need to know the number of any particular item in any warehouse. Initially the stock of items in all warehouses is as follows:

	WAREHOUSE 1	WAREHOUSE 2	WAREHOUSE 3
Desks	123	44	76
Chairs	789	234	12
Beds	67	456	90

The controller has at his fingertips a terminal where he can inquire about a particular item. For example, when he types "BEDS" the system furnishes him with the number

■ **Figure 10–7** A subroutine sort example.

```
10 REM A MODULARIZED SORTING PROGRAM
14 REM      T:  ARRAY TO STORE ALL SCORES
16 REM      G:  ARRAY TO SUCCESSIVELY CONTAIN SECTIONS' SCORES
18 REM      H$: CONTAINS COURSE CAPTION DESCRIPTION
20 REM      K:  COUNTS ALL SCORES
22 REM      N:  COUNTS SCORES IN EACH SECTION, SUCCESSIVELY
23 REM
24 DIM T(50), G(50)
26 K = 1                        K counts all scores.
28 READ H$                      Read course caption.
30 IF H$ = "***" THEN 52        Check for end of input file.
32    N = 0                     N counts number of scores in each section.
34    READ T(K)                 Read a score.
36    IF T(K) < 0 THEN 46       If end of section, go and sort scores.
38          N = N + 1           Keep track of number of scores in section.
40          G(N) = T(K)         Store score in array G needed by sort subroutine.
42          K = K + 1           Keep track of all scores.
44          GOTO 34
46    GOSUB 88                  Go and sort scores of a particular section.
48    GOSUB 70                  Go and print course name and corresponding scores.
50    GOTO 28                   Keep reading the input file.
52 FOR I = 1 TO K-1             Transfer all scores to array G before transferring
54     G(I) = T(I)              to the subroutine, which
56 NEXT I                       expects scores to be in array G.
58 H$ = "COMBINED SCORES"       H$ and N must be reinitialized before transferring
60 N = K - 1                    to the subroutine to print the course number
62 GOSUB 88                     and the sorted scores.
64 GOSUB 70                     Go print results for each section and for
66 STOP                         combined sections.
67 REM
68 REM SUBROUTINE TO PRINT COURSE NUMBER AND SCORES
70 PRINT H$; TAB(20);
72 FOR I = 1 TO N
74     PRINT G(I);              Print the sorted scores
76 NEXT I
78 PRINT
80 RETURN
82 REM SUBROUTINE SORTS N ELEMENTS IN ASCENDING ORDER
86 REM       Q: TEMPORARY LOCATION FOR INTERCHANGE
87 REM
88 FOR I = 1 TO N - 1
90     FOR J = 1 TO N - I
92         IF G(J)  <=G(J+1) THEN 100
94            Q      = G(J)
96            G(J)   = G(J+1)
98            G(J+1) = Q
100    NEXT J
102 NEXT I
104 RETURN
108 DATA MNGM 102, 30,20,60,-4
110 DATA MNGM 103, 40,10,-2
112 DATA MNGM 104, 10,90,20,80,-6
114 DATA ***
116 END
RUN
MNGM 102             20  30  60
MNGM 103             10  40
MNGM 104             10  20  80  90
COMBINED SCORES      10  10  20  20  30  40  60  80  90
```

of beds at the three warehouses. He can also type a warehouse number to list all items at that warehouse. The program allows communications like the following between the dispatcher and the data base:

```
ENTER REQUEST
?BEDS
                WAREHOUSE1   WAREHOUSE2   WAREHOUSE3
BEDS                67          456           90         TOTAL 613
ENTER REQUEST
?WAREHOUSE3
                   DESKS        CHAIRS         BEDS
WAREHOUSE3          76            12           90         TOTAL 178
ENTER REQUEST
?CHAIRS
               WAREHOUSE1    WAREHOUSE2    WAREHOUSE3
CHAIRS             789           234            12        TOTAL 1035
ENTER REQUEST
?
```

The program to respond to these inquiries is shown in Figure 10–8.

10-4 You Might Want to Know

1. Must all references to a subroutine be made to the same initial statement?

   Answer: No. A subroutine can be entered at any point. For example, consider the following code:

```
10 GOSUB 200
.
.
40 GOSUB 220
.
.
200 LET X=X+1  <---  Note the entry points to the subroutine.
210 GO TO 230
220 LET X=X-1  <---
230 PRINT X
240 RETURN
```

2. Does it matter where in the program a subroutine is placed?

   Answer: No, but it is important that the routine not be executed except by a GOSUB statement.

■ **Figure 10–8** An on-line inquiry problem.

```
10 REM ON-LINE INQUIRY PROBLEM
20 REM      A$: CONTAINS WORDS: BEDS, CHAIRS...OR WAREHOUSE1, WAREHOUSE2,...
30 REM      F$: CONTAINS WORDS: DESKS, CHAIRS, AND BEDS
40 REM      G$: CONTAINS WORDS: WAREHOUSE1, WAREHOUSE2, AND WAREHOUSE3
50 REM      P:  ALLOWS SUBROUTINE TO PROCESS A ROW OR COLUMN OF ARRAY V(3,3)
60 REM      V:  CONTAINS INVENTORY OF THE 3 WAREHOUSES: 2-DIMENSIONAL
70 REM      R$: CONTAINS WAREHOUSE OR FURNITURE ITEM REQUEST
80 DIM F$(3), G$(3), A$(3), P(3), V(3,3)
90 FOR I = 1 TO 3
100     FOR J = 1 TO 3
110         READ V(I,J)
120     NEXT J
130 NEXT I
140 FOR I = 1 TO 3
150     READ F$(I), G$(I)
160 NEXT I
```

array V(3,3)

	1	2	3
Desks	123	44	76
Chairs	789	234	12
Beds	67	456	90

```
180 PRINT "ENTER REQUEST"          Enter warehouse or furniture request.
190 INPUT R$
200 GOSUB 380                      Find out which row or column of V to work with.
210 IF F = 0 GOTO 300              List furniture items at a particular warehouse.
220     IF F = 1 THEN 250          List stock at each warehouse for item request.
230         PRINT "INVALID REQUEST"
240         GOTO 180               If improper request, try again.
250     FOR I = 1 TO 3             Initialize A$ with words WAREHOUSE1, WAREHOUSE2,
260         A$(I) = G$(I)          WAREHOUSE 3.
270         P(I)  = V(K,I)         Initialize P with elements of row K of array V.
280     NEXT I
290     GOTO 340                   Transfer to the subroutines.
300 FOR I = 1 TO 3
310     A$(I) = F$(I)              Initialize A$ with words DESKS, CHAIRS, BEDS.
320     P(I)  = V(I,K)             Set P to entries of column K of array V.
330 NEXT I
340 GOSUB 500                      Print the 3 captions of items or warehouses.
350 GOSUB 570                      Print the stock level underneath the captions.
360 GOTO 180
370 REM SUBROUTINE
380 FOR I = 1 TO 3                 This subroutine returns in K the row or
390     IF F$(I) = R$ THEN 460     column number of array V associated with
400     IF G$(I) = R$ THEN 440     the request entered. For example, if BEDS is
410 NEXT I                         entered, K = 3; if WAREHOUSE2 is entered K = 2.
420 F = -1                         F is a flag that is set to -1 if request is invalid.
430 GOTO 480
440 F = 0                          F is set to 0 if warehouse information is requested.
450 GOTO 470
460 F = 1                          F is set to 1 if a furniture item is requested.
470 K = I                          K points to either a row or a column of V.
480 RETURN
490 REM SUBROUTINE
500 PRINT TAB(15);                 Print captions; either the three furniture items
510 FOR I = 1 TO 3                 or the three WAREHOUSE captions.
520     PRINT  A$(I),
530 NEXT I
540 PRINT
550 RETURN
560 REM SUBROUTINE
570 PRINT R$,                      This subroutine prints the request and
580 S = 0                          the corresponding stock level entries.
590 FOR I = 1 TO 3
600     S = S + P(I)
610     PRINT P(I),
620 NEXT I
630 PRINT "TOTAL"; S               Print the total stock for item or for warehouse
640 RETURN
660 DATA 123,44,76,789,234,12,67,456,90       warehouse inventory
670 DATA DESKS,WAREHOUSE1,CHAIRS,WAREHOUSE2,BEDS,WAREHOUSE3
690 END
RUN
ENTER REQUEST
? BEDS
                WAREHOUSE1      WAREHOUSE2      WAREHOUSE3
BEDS             67              456             90              TOTAL 613
ENTER REQUEST
? WAREHOUSE3
                DESKS           CHAIRS          BEDS
WAREHOUSE3       76              12              90              TOTAL 178
```

3. What statements can be used in a subroutine?

Answer: Any BASIC statement can be used in a subroutine.

4. Can a subroutine call another subroutine?

Answer: Yes.

5. Can a subroutine call itself?

Answer: Yes, in some versions of BASIC, but this programming technique (called *recursion*) is outside the scope of this text.

6. Can a subroutine return to another GOSUB statement?

Answer: Yes.

7. What happens if you transfer to a REM statement with a GOSUB?

Answer: Control is passed to the next executable statement after the REM; hence it is a perfectly valid practice.

10-5 User-Defined Functions

10-5-1 The DEF Statement

The DEF (*def*inition) statement is used to define a programmer-written function. It allows the user to define a function just once in a program and then use that same function with different arguments wherever needed in the program. The DEF statement is nonexecutable and hence (like the DATA statement) may be placed anywhere in the program. It is generally placed at the "top" of the program along with the DIM statements, and it should be placed before the first statement that uses the function. The general form of the DEF statement is

line number DEF *name(dummy argument list) = expression*

where DEF is a BASIC key word

name is the function name

dummy argument list is a list of one or more nonsubscripted variables that will assume the values of the actual arguments when the function is referred to (the dummy arguments illustrate the way the actual arguments will be used to produce a functional value).

expression is any arithmetic expression.

The *name* that can be given to a programmer-defined function is restricted to FNA, FNB, FNC, FND, ..., FNY, FNZ.

The dummy arguments of the function should always appear in the expression on the right-hand side of the equal sign, for example,

```
10 DEF FNB(X)=(X+2)/(X-2) + X^2
20 LET A = 4

30 PRINT FNB(A)
```

$$B(x) = \frac{x+2}{x-2} + x^2$$

The result printed would be 19.

Note that the dummy arguments in the DEF statement take on no real values. Their only purpose is to show the way in which the function value is produced. In fact, it is possible to have a dummy argument with the same name as another "regular" variable in a program, as in:

```
10 F = 212
20 DEF FNA(F) = 5/9*(F-32)
30 PRINT F                212 is printed.     The value of F is not changed by line 20.
40 PRINT FNA(F)           100 is printed.
50 PRINT FNA(32)            0 is printed.
```

All user functions can even be defined using the same argument, and the expression in the DEF statement can contain function names other than the one being defined, as in:

```
10 DEF FNS(X) = (3.14*X)/180
20 DEF FNR(X) = SIN(FNS(X))

30 LET Y = 90
40 PRINT Y, FNS(Y),FNR(Y)
```

FNS(X) converts x degrees into radians.
FNR(X) computes sin (x) with x in degrees.
FNR(90) = SIN (FNS(90)) = $\sin(\pi/2) = 1$
Y = 90
FNS(90) = $\pi/2$
FNR(90) = $\sin(\pi/2) = 1$

In most systems, more than one dummy argument can be used:

```
10 DEF FNA(A,B,C) = (A+B+C)/3        Computes average of 3 numbers.
15 INPUT X,Y,Z
20 PRINT FNA(X,Y,Z)                  Prints the average of X, Y, and Z.
```

In addition to the dummy arguments, the expression on the right side of the DEF statement may contain other variables that are used in the program:

```
10 LET A = 2
20 LET B = 3
30 LET C = 4
40 DEF FNC(X)=A*X^2 + B*X + C
50 LET Z = FNC(2)
```

$C(x) = ax^2 + bx + c$
$Z = 2 \cdot 4 + 3 \cdot 2 + 4 = 18$

The argument of a function FNA can also be a function, even FNA itself:

```
10 DEF FNA(X) = X^2
15 PRINT FNA(FNA(2))
```

The number 16 will be printed (X = 2).

However, recursive definitions of functions are *not* allowed in the DEF statement:

```
10 DEF FNA(X) = FNA(X) + C
```

This is invalid.

Functions can be nested, as in the following example:

```
10 DEF FNA(X) = ABS(X)
20 DEF FNB(Y) = (FNA(Y))^2
30 DEF FNC(Z) = LOG(FNB(Z))/10
```

$A(x) = |x|$

$B(y) = |y|^2$

$C(z) = \frac{\log|z|^2}{10}$

Most BASIC systems allow a depth of four functions.

When referencing user-defined functions, subscripted variables or expressions can be used in the *argument* (line 30).

```
10 DEF FNA(Z)=(Z + 2)/(Z - 2)
15 LET B(3) = 4
20 LET Z = 2
30 LET X = FNA(B(3) + Z)
```

$F(z) = \frac{z + 2}{z - 2}$

$x = \frac{B(3) + z + 2}{B(3) + z - 2} = \frac{8}{4} = 2$

Function definitions must be limited to one line of code. If longer definitions are necessary, subroutines must be used.

To illustrate the simplicity and convenience of the DEF statement, consider the problem of determining the date for Easter Sunday. The date for any Easter Sunday can be computed as follows (let Y be the year for which Easter Sunday will be computed:

Let A be the remainder of the division of Y by 19.
Let B be the remainder of the division of Y by 4.
Let C be the remainder of the division of Y by 7.
Let D be the remainder of the division of (19A + 24) by 30.
Let E be the remainder of the division of (2B + 4C + 6D + 5) by 7.

The date for Easter Sunday is March (22 + D + E), which can also give us a date in April.

Let us write a program to input a year Y and compute that year's Easter date. The problem requires computing the remainder of a division five times, so it would be very helpful to define a remainder function. In general, the remainder R of the division of Y by X can be calculated through the statement R = Y − X * INT(Y/X). Hence we will define the remainder function as follows:

DEF FNR(X) = Y − X * INT(Y/X) where FNR(X) is the remainder of Y/X. For example the remainder of 18 divided by 5 is 3. We can make the definition more general by defining the remainder function in terms of two arguments: FNR(Y,X) = Y − X * INT(Y/X).

The program in Figure 10–9 solves this problem using the remainder function.

10-5-2 Do It Now

1. Write a function FND which computes the approximate difference between two dates M1, D1, Y1 and M2, D2, Y2. See exercise 5 section 10–2–1.
2. Write a function FNR which rounds a value Q to the nearest hundredth.

3. Write a function FNX which computes the remainder after dividing argument X by Y.

4. Write a function FNH to compute the length of the hypotenuse of a right triangle, given sides A and B. ($H^2 = A^2 + B^2$)

Answers

1.
```
10 DEF FNJ(M,D,Y) = 365.25*Y + (M-1)*30.4 + D
20 DEF FND(M1,D1,Y1,M2,D2,Y2) = ABS(FNJ(M1,D1,Y1) - FNJ(M2,D2,Y2))
```

2.
```
10 DEF FNR(Q) = INT((Q + .005)*100)/100
```

3.
```
10 DEF FNX(X,Y) = X -INT(X/Y)*Y
```

4.
```
10 DEF FNH(A,B) = SQR(A^2 + B^2)
```

Figure 10–9 An Easter date computation.

```
 10 DEF FNR(X) = Y - X*INT(Y/X)       Define the remainder function.
 20 INPUT Y                           Y is the year.
 25 IF Y < 0 THEN 160
 30 LET A = FNR(19)
 40 LET B = FNR(4)
 50 LET C = FNR(7)
 60 LET Y = 19*A + 24                 Reset the value of Y to compute D.
 70 LET D = FNR(30)
 80 LET Y = 2*B + 4*C + 6*D + 5       Reset value of Y to compute E.
 90 LET E = FNR(7)
100 LET R = 22 + D + E
110 IF R <= 31 THEN 140               Is Easter in March or April?
120     PRINT "EASTER SUNDAY IS APRIL"; R - 31
130     GO TO 20
140 PRINT "EASTER SUNDAY IS MARCH";R
150 GO TO 20
160 END

RUN
? 1979 EASTER SUNDAY IS APRIL 15
? 1980 EASTER SUNDAY IS APRIL 6
? 2000 EASTER SUNDAY IS APRIL 23
? 2050 EASTER SUNDAY IS APRIL 10
? 10000 EASTER SUNDAY IS APRIL 12
? 1 EASTER SUNDAY IS APRIL 9
? 1978 EASTER SUNDAY IS MARCH 26
? 0
```

10-5-3 Graph Plotting

Let us write a program to graph the function $y = \dfrac{x^2}{5} + 1$ in the first quadrant for values of x ranging from 1 to 7 in steps of 1. Before we write the program let us get a general idea about how we might proceed. Graphing the function means plotting various points that belong on the curve of the function and then joining these points together. We pick various values of x (such as 1, 2, 3,...,7) then we determine the corresponding values for y and plot those points, as follows:

x	y
1	1.2
2	1.8
3	2.8
4	4.2
5	6
6	8.2
7	10.8

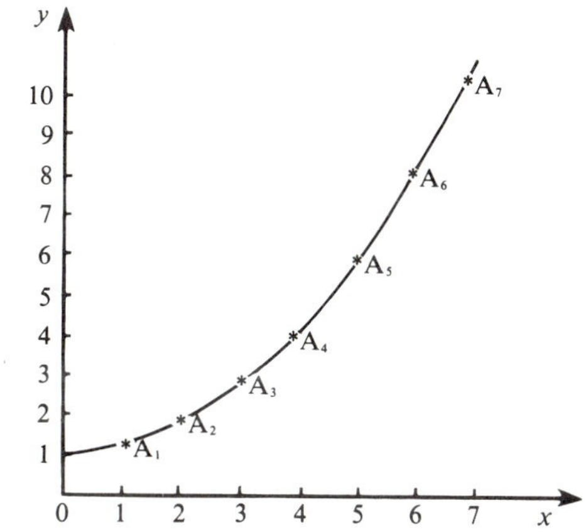

It is a little more difficult to print this graph using a computer because of the vertical movement of the printer paper (the paper moves up in increments of one line). Thus it is difficult to print A_1 first and then print A_2 since the computer would print A_2 on the line below A_1. You might ask, "Why not print A_7, then A_6, on down through to A_1 to keep the points moving down the page. We could use incremental values of y equal to 10, 9, 8,..., 1 and compute the corresponding values of x using the formula $x = \sqrt{5y - 1}$ instead of $y = x^2/5 + 1$." This, of course, would work in this particular case, but what if we wanted to graph the function $y = x^4 - 16x^3 + 2x^2 - 1$? How would you compute x in terms of y?

The approach we will take is to use the vertical axis as the x axis so that each new line corresponds to a unit increment of x. The horizontal axis will be the y axis. For each value of x, we will print a graphic symbol y units away from the x axis. The graph of the function will then appear as:

x	y	*y rounded*
1	1.2	1
2	1.8	2
3	2.8	3
4	4.2	4
5	6	6
6	8.2	8
7	10.8	11

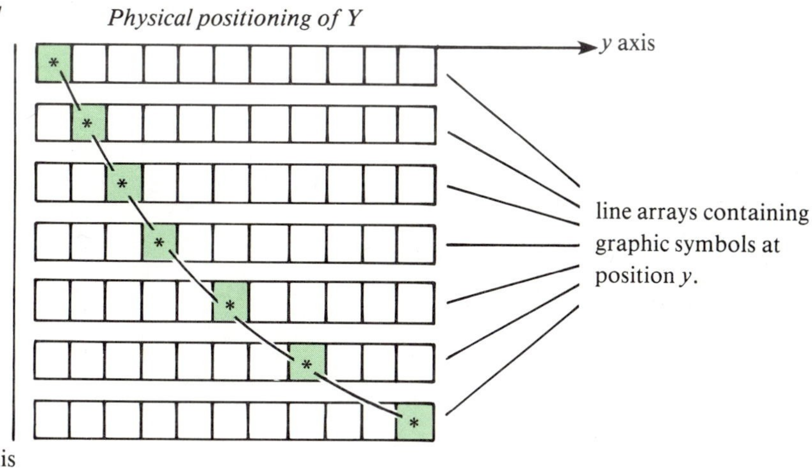

From this example, the graphing process becomes more evident. We use an array to print one horizontal line at a time. The line array is initially set to blanks. For a given value of x, the corresponding value of the function y is computed and a graphic symbol such as "*" is inserted at position y in the line array. The array (line) is then printed, and the same process is repeated for the different values of x. In essence you can visualize *any* graph on your printer as follows:

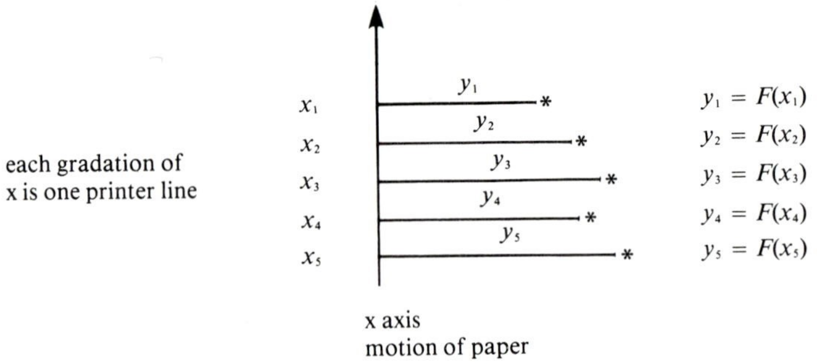

Figure 10–10 Plotting a graph.

```
10 REM PLOTTING Y = X^2/5 + 1 WITH ARRAYS
12 DIM N$(11)                         N$(11) is the line array that prints the graphic symbol *
15 PRINT " X"; "    Y"                on each line.
17 PRINT
22      FOR J = 1 TO 11
23           N$(J) = " "              Blank out line array.
24      NEXT J
25 FOR X = 1 TO 7
26      Y = X^2/5 + 1                 Compute Y value.
27      PRINT X; Y,,
30      N$(Y) = "*"                   Insert * at position Y of line array.
35      FOR J = 1 TO 11
36           PRINT N$(J);             Print out each line with graphic symbol.
37      NEXT J
38      N$(Y) = " "                   Line array is now blank.
39      PRINT
40 NEXT X
45 END

RUN
 X   Y

 1  1.2
 2  1.8
 3  2.8
 4  4.2
 5  6
 6  8.2
 7  10.8
```

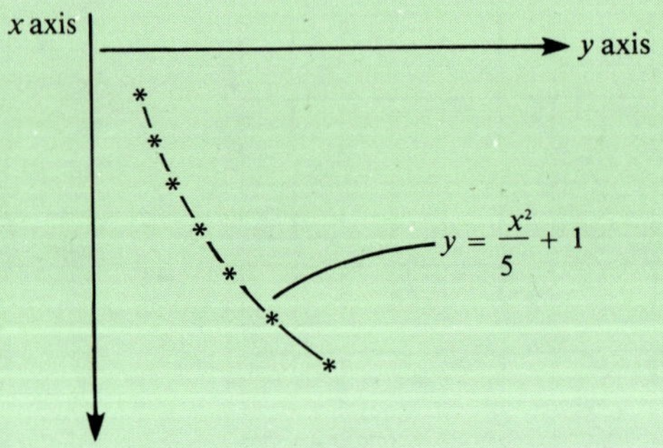

Care must be exercised if y is negative. In this case, an appropriate constant should be added to all values of y; this causes the graph to be shifted to the right on the output line, but the shape of the graph is preserved. Also, if the changes in the magnitude of y are fractional, y should be scaled (multiplied by a constant); for example, if for $x = 2$ the value of y is 1.3, and if for $x = 3$ the value of y is 1.4, you might want to multiply y by 10 to obtain 13 and 14; then the graphic symbol on the first line will be one position to the left of the graphic symbol on the second line, otherwise the graph might be represented by a vertical straight line!

The code to graph the function $y = \frac{x^2}{5} + 1$ is shown in Figure 10–10.

This graphing technique can be used only if your BASIC permits you to store graphic symbols (alphanumeric data) in arrays. A very similar approach that does not require arrays is to place the graphic symbol in its y position on the line by using a TAB expression that is a function of y. The code to plot

$$y = \frac{x^2}{5} + 1 \text{ using this method is:}$$

```
10 REM PLOTTING Y = X^2/5 + 1 WITHOUT ARRAYS
15 PRINT " X", "  Y"
17 PRINT
20 FOR X = 1 TO 7
25      Y = X^2/5 + 1                Compute Y value.
30      PRINT X, Y;
35      PRINT TAB(30 + Y);"*"        Place asterisk at Y position on line.
40 NEXT X
45 END
```

```
RUN
X               Y
1               1.2
2               1.8
3               2.8
4               4.2
5               6
6               8.2
7               10.8
```

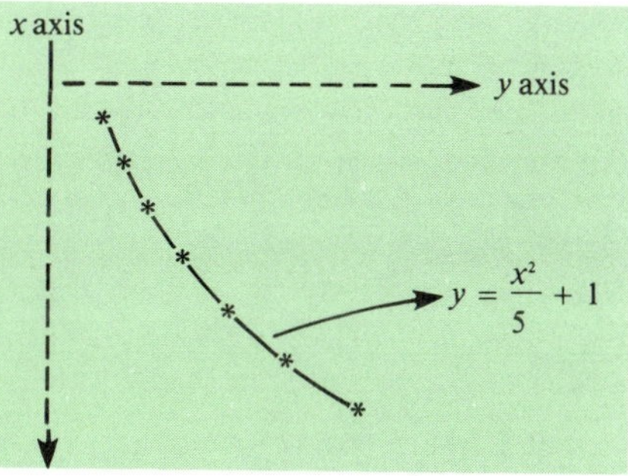

10-5-4 Do It Now

System analysts at the XYZ Company have computed the revenue function associated with the manufacture and marketing of a new company product. A cost function was also projected for that product. The functions are given as follows:

Revenue function $y = 15xe^{-x/3}$ where $e = 2.718\ldots$

Cost function $y = \frac{x^3}{16} - \frac{x^2}{2} + \frac{7x}{4} + 4$

The analysts want to determine the break-even points, i.e., the values of x which will cause the revenue to equal the cost. Mathematically, this means solving the equation

$$15xe^{-x/3} = \frac{x^3}{16} - \frac{x^2}{2} + \frac{7x}{4} + 4$$

Since this type of equation is not easily solved, the analysts decide to graph the two curves to determine whether they intersect or not. If they intersect, the point(s) of intersection will be the break-even values. You have been hired by the analysts to graph both functions. Use the two methods described in the graph plotting section, i.e., the one using arrays and the one using the TAB function.

Answers

Figure 10–11 illustrates the plotting process using the TAB function.

Figure 10–11 Break-even analysis.

```
 5 REM BREAK-EVEN ANALYSIS
10 PRINT "REVENUE";TAB(9);"COST"
15 DEF FNA(X)=INT((((X-8)*X+28)*X+64)/16)        Cost function.
20 DEF FNB(Z)=INT(15*Z*EXP(-Z/3))                Revenue function.
25 FOR X = 0 TO 12
30     LET C = FNA(X)
35     LET R = FNB(X)
40     PRINT R;TAB(9);C;
45     LET K = 22 + R + .5
50     LET L = 22 + C + .5
55     IF C < R GO TO 70
60         PRINT TAB(K);"R";TAB(L);"C"
65         GOTO 75
70         PRINT TAB(L);"C";TAB(K);"R"
75 NEXT X
80 END
```

If the cost C is less than the revenue R, plot first the cost and then the revenue; otherwise, plot the revenue first and then the cost. In either case, both graphic symbols will be on same line.

```
RUN
REVENUE COST
 0        4
10        5
15        6
16        6
15        7
14        8
12       10
10       13
 8       18
 6       24
 5       34
 4       45
 3       61
```

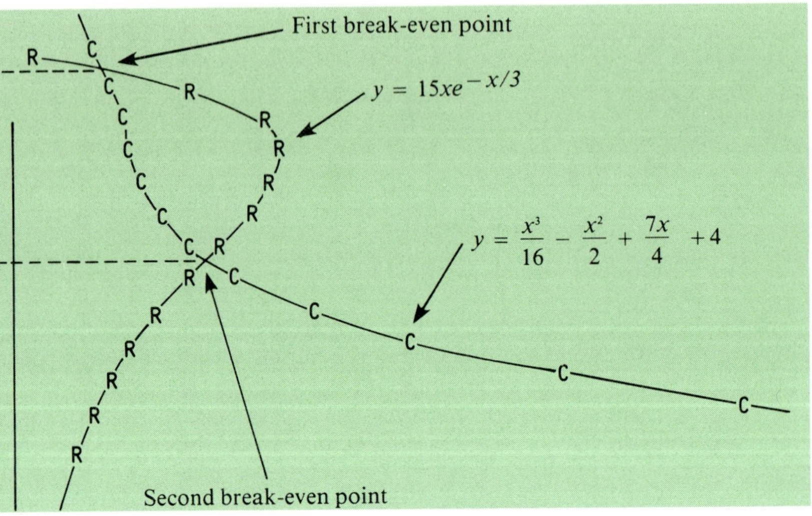

The following program plots the same functions using arrays:

```
10 DIM N$(50)
15 PRINT "REVENUE";TAB(9);"COST"
20   FOR J=0 TO 50
25     LET N$(J)=" "        Blank out line.
30   NEXT J
30   FOR X = 0 TO 12
35   LET C=INT((((X-8)*X+28)*X+64)/16)
40   LET R =INT(15*X*EXP(-X/3))
50   LET N$(C)="C"          Insert graphic symbols.
55   LET N$(R)="R"
60   PRINT TAB(2);R;TAB(9);C;TAB(16)
65   FOR J=0 TO 50
70     PRINT N$(J);         Print the line.
75   NEXT J
80   LET N$(C)=" "          Blank out array.
85   LET N$(R)=" "
90   PRINT
90 NEXT X
99 END
```

10-6 Assignments

10-6-1 Test Yourself

1. True or False?

a. Functions make use of dummy-arguments; subroutines do not.
b. Functions and subroutines can help avoid duplication of programming effort.
c. The RETURN statement is used in functions but not in subroutines.
d. Names for functions follow the same convention as other variable names.
e. ABC is a valid programmer-defined function name.
f. Subroutines may have only one entry point.
g. The RETURN statement causes control to return to the statement that follows the GOSUB statement.
h. If a program enters a subroutine other than by a GOSUB statement, the results are unpredictable.
i. Modularization within a program is to be avoided, since it has an adverse effect on program readability.
j. Certain BASIC statements cannot be used in a subroutine.
k. In some cases, subroutines do not need RETURN statements.
l. Subroutines can always be coded in such a way that they only have one RETURN statement.

m. The STOP statement generally should not be used in a subroutine.
n. Subscripted variables may not be used as arguments in the definition of a user-defined function.
o. An error message will be printed by BASIC if the RETURN statement is omitted in a subroutine.

2. Translate each of the following into BASIC:
   a. generate a random number in the range 1 to 100
   b. $y = |\sqrt{a} - \sqrt{b}|$
   c. $\ln(e^x - e^{-x})$
   d. $\sin^2(x^2)$
   e. $\cot(x)$ (recall that $\cot(x) = \dfrac{1}{\tan(x)}$)

3. Write a BASIC subroutine to compute the cost of postage P for a first class letter weighing X ounces. Postage costs 20 cents for the first ounce and 17 cents for each additional ounce or part thereof.

10-6-2 Exercises

1. Each DATA statement consists of an employee name, a number of hours worked, and a rate of pay. Write a main program to read the DATA statements, and write a subroutine to compute each employee's pay. Hours over 40 are paid at time and a half the regular rate. Use another subroutine to perform the input data validation. The rate of pay should not exceed $50.00 per hour, and the hours worked should be no more than 80. The main program should write the error messages if there are errors; there could be two error messages if both the rate and the hours exceed their maximums. The printout should list the employee name, number of hours, rate of pay, and pay.

2. A salesman is assigned a commission on the following basis:

SALE	*COMMISSION*
$0 -$ 499.00	1%
500– 5000	5%
over 5000	8%

   Write a main program to read sales and use a subroutine to compute the commission.

3. Each DATA statement contains a student's name and 10 test scores. The student is allowed to drop his/her lowest score to figure his/her average. Use a subroutine to find the sum of each students scores and another subroutine to find his/her minimum score. The main program should compute the "best" average. Print each student's name and average.

4. a. Write a subroutine to accept a number between 1 and 10 and return the corresponding word. For example, 3 would yield THREE.
   b. Accept a number between 20 and 99 and return the corresponding words. For example, 25 would yield TWENTY FIVE.

5. The coordinates of three ships are accepted as input. Write a program to print the distances between each ship. If x_1 and y_1, and x_2 and y_2 are the coordinates of any two ships, the formula to compute the distance separating them is

$$d = \sqrt{|x_1 - x_2|^2 + |y_1 - y_2|^2}$$

where $|x_1 - x_2|$ means the absolute value of $x_1 - x_2$. Use GOSUB to compute d.

6. You are the personnel director of a large company, and for every person you place in a job, you enter the following two entries on a DATA statement:
   Sex code (2 = male, 1 = female)
   First year's starting salary

   Write a program using different subroutines to determine each of the following:
   a. Total number of males placed in jobs.
   b. Total amount of salaries paid the first year to females.
   c. Maximum salary paid to males.
   d. Average salary paid to females.

7. Write a program to enter a number with five fractional digits. Write four user-defined functions to round the number to 0, 1, 2, and 3 fractional digits. Print the rounded values on one line. Then try to solve the problem with just one function.

8. On the first DATA statement, we have entered the answers (1, 2, 3, 4) to a multiple choice test of 10 questions. On the second DATA statement, we have entered the number of students taking the test. Each following DATA statement consists of a student's name and 10 answers to the 10 questions. Write a main program to determine the percentage of correct answers for each student, and write a subroutine to determine the grade (90–100 = A, 80–89 = B, 60–79 = C, below 60 = D). Another subroutine should print the output: student name, the letter grade, and percentage. Given the following input, the output should be as follows:

Correct answers to the 10 questions

```
DATA 1,1,2,3,1,4,2,4,3,3
DATA 3 <---number of students
DATA JONES, 1,1,2,3,1,4,2,4,3,3
DATA SATO,  1,1,2,3,1,1,1,3,2,4
DATA LAKY,  4,1,2,3,1,4,2,4,3,2
```

```
NAME   GRADE  PERCENTAGE

JONES    A       100
SATO     D        50
LAKY     B        80
```

9. Each record of an input file consists of a name of a city and the average daily temperature for that city. For example:

```
DATA  MOBILE,17,   MADISON,-3,  PARIS,0,    NEW YORK,33
DATA  TAMPA,65,    TUCSON,48,   WAUSAU,-5,  SEATTLE,0
```

Write a program to produce an output similar to the following:

```
ABOVE ZERO:    MOBILE     NEW YORK    TAMPA
               TUCSON

AT ZERO:        PARIS      SEATTLE

BELOW ZERO:     MADISON    WAUSAU
```

Use a subroutine for the output functions. Note that only three city names are printed per line.

10. a. Array A contains N elements. Write a subroutine to perform a sequence check on the elements of A. If the array is in ascending sequence, return the value of 1; otherwise return value 0.
    b. Repeat part (a) for an array A where it is not known whether the elements are in descending or ascending order. Assume the first two numbers are in sequence.

11. Professor X determines her students' final grades by the following computerized method: If the average of their six weeks', 12 weeks', and final scores is higher than their final score, that average score becomes their semester grade; otherwise their score on the final becomes their semester grade. The semester grade is either a *pass* (if the resulting score exceeds 70) or a *fail*. Professor X would also like to determine the average of the 6 weeks' scores, the average of the 12 weeks' scores, the average of the final scores, and the resulting grade for the entire class based on these three average scores. For example, given the input shown below, the program should produce the following output:

Input

```
DATA  DOE, 5Ø, 6Ø, 69
DATA  BAT, 8Ø, 8Ø, 68
DATA  MOT, 2Ø, 31, 73
```

Name — 6 weeks — 12 weeks — final

Output

NAME	T6	T12	FINAL	SCORE	GRADE
DOE	5Ø	6Ø	69	69	FAIL
BAT	8Ø	8Ø	68	76	PASS
MOT	2Ø	31	73	73	PASS
CLASS	5Ø	57	7Ø	7Ø	FAIL

Write one subroutine to compute each student's (or the class') best score combination and another subroutine to determine the letter grade (PASS or FAIL). The main program should perform all input and output functions.

12. Dr. D teaches two BASIC classes. Array F1 contains the final scores of class 1, while array F2 contains the final scores of class 2. To ensure fairness in both classes, Dr. D assigns final scores as follows:

    If the average of class 1 is less than the average of class 2, all class 1 students get 5% of their class average added to their scores.

    If the average of class 2 is less than the average of class 1, all class 2 students get 5% of their class average added to their scores.

    Write a program to carry out the following, in the sequence shown:

    1. Read the scores in arrays F1 and F2 and print both sets of scores.
    2. Write a subroutine to compute the average score for arrays F1 and F2.
    3. Write a subroutine to compute the 5% bonus and add the bonus to each score; print the adjusted scores and the bonus.

Given the following input file, the output should be as follows:

Input

```
DATA  60, 70, 80, 90, 50, 60, 70, 80, 80, 60  ←Class 1 scores
DATA  10, 20, 30, 40, 50, 60, 70, 80  ←Class 2 scores
```

```
FINAL1    60  70  80  90  50  60  70  80  80  60
FINAL2    10  20  30  40  50  60  70  80
AVERAGE 1 = 70
AVERAGE 2 = 45
BONUS = 2.3
ADJUSTED SCORES:  12.3  22.3  32.3  42.3  52.3  62.3  72.3  82.3
```

13. Use the DEF statement to compute the square root of 43, using the formula:

$$x = \frac{1}{2}(x + \frac{43}{x}) \quad \text{starting with } x = 1 \text{ until } |x^2 - 43| < 0.01.$$

Start with $x = 1$ to get a new value for x, and use that new value in the formula to get a newer value. Proceed in this fashion until the refined value x is such that

$$|x^2 - 43| < 0.01$$

14. The number e can be defined as the limit of $\left(\frac{n+1}{n}\right)^n$ as n tends to infinity:

$$e = \lim_{n \to \infty} \left(\frac{n+1}{n}\right)^n$$

Using this definition of e write a program to determine n so that:

$$\left| e - \left(\frac{n+1}{n}\right)^n \right| < 0.001$$

Use the function EXP for e.

15. Write a program to show that as n gets larger and larger, the following expressions converge to one limit. Can you guess at the limits from your printouts?

a. $\frac{n^2 + 1}{n + 1}$ b. $\frac{\log(n)}{n}$ c. $n \cdot \log\left(1 + \frac{1}{n}\right)$

16. Write a program to determine the limits of the following expressions as x approaches 0. (Let x range from 1° to 0.1° in steps of 0.1°.)

a. $\frac{\sin(x)}{x}$

b. $\frac{\tan(x)}{x}$

c. $\frac{\tan(2x)}{\sin(7x)}$

d. $\frac{x \cdot \sin(x)}{1 - \cos(x)}$

e. $\frac{15t}{\tan(6t)}$

Recall that x must be expressed in radians.

17. Using the exponential function EXP(X), compute EXP(1). (The value of e to nine places is 2.71828182.) Can you obtain a better approximation than EXP(1) by using the following series definition?

$$e^x = 1 + \frac{x}{1!} + \frac{x^2}{2!} + \frac{x^3}{3!} + \ldots + \frac{x^n}{n!} + \ldots$$

How many terms of the series do you need to improve on EXP(1)?

18. A company has 10 delivery trucks. It uses a two-dimensional coordinate scheme to keep track of the location of each truck:

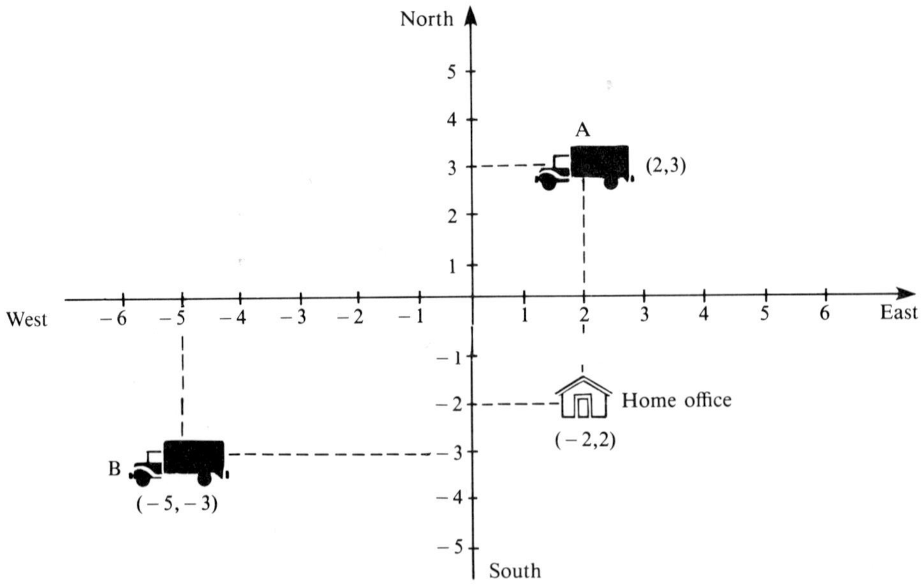

a. Write a program to read 10 truck coordinates and determine which truck is closest to the home office. Write one subroutine to compute the distances separating each truck from the home office and another subroutine to determine the least distance. The main program should print the location of the closest truck and its ID number.

b. Set up the program so that the user can enter updated coordinated for some of the trucks and identify truck closest to the home office at any given time.

19. Write a program to generalize the on-line inquiry system of Section 10–3–2 to allow the manager to keep track of supply and exit shipments. The manager should be able to type in commands similar to the following to mean:

Chairs, −36,1	Ship out 36 chairs from warehouse 1.
Beds,57,2	Supply warehouse 2 with an additional 57 beds.

The inventory should be updated automatically and a warning message printed whenever any furniture stock item falls below 40% of beginning inventory.

20. The Stayfirm Company accounting system keeps sales records for each salesperson on a day-to-day basis. This data is transcribed on DATA statements as follows:

```
        SALESMAN NAME        DATE OF SALE    AMOUNT OF SALE
DATA     SMITH JOHN     ,     Ø11583     ,      1ØØ.ØØ
DATA     SMITH JOHN     ,     Ø11383     ,       5Ø.ØØ
DATA     GRANT CARY     ,     Ø12783     ,       1Ø.ØØ
DATA     SMITH JOHN     ,     Ø12783     ,      15Ø.ØØ
DATA     GRANT CARY     ,     Ø12783     ,      19Ø.ØØ
DATA     HOLBERT SUE    ,     Ø11383     ,      1ØØ.ØØ
```

Note that the transactions are not arranged alphabetically by salesperson name. Also note that the dates are not sorted in ascending order. (Assume the dates cover only a 30-day period starting with the first day of the month to the thirtieth day of that month.)

Write a program using a sort subroutine to produce a monthly sales report summarizing total sales and total sales for each salesperson. Entries in the report must be listed by salesperson name in alphabetical order, and these in turn must be sorted by date of sales. For example, given the preceding data the output should be as follows:

```
SALESPERSON    DATE OF SALE   SALE AMOUNT   TOTAL AMOUNT

GRANT CARY       Ø12683         19Ø.ØØ
GRANT CARY       Ø12783          1Ø.ØØ
                                              2ØØ.ØØ
HOLBERT SUE      Ø11383         1ØØ.ØØ
                                              1ØØ.ØØ
SMITH JOHN       Ø11383          5Ø.ØØ
SMITH JOHN       Ø11583         1ØØ.ØØ
SMITH JOHN       Ø12783         15Ø.ØØ
                                              3ØØ.ØØ
                            TOTAL-SALES       6ØØ.ØØ
```

21. The following table illustrates the dimensions of some U.S. companies, in thousands of dollars:

COMPANY	*ASSETS*	*SALES*	*MARKET VALUE*	*NET PROFIT*
Citicom	64,281,504	4,843,838	4,085,923	401,352
Celanex	1,910,000	2,123,000	685,511	69,000
Bendil	1,653,600	2,965,500	941,945	104,700
American Corp	991,586	2,315,470	116,641	– 46,340
Telextron	1,808,479	3,381,075	1,045,840	112,807

Write a program to read the company names in array N$ and the other associated data in a two-dimensional array A(5,4). Entries should be read by rows. For example, N$(3) and A(3,1), A(3,2), A(3,3), A(3,4) describe the financial characteristics of the Bendil Corporation. The program should sort and print the names of the various companies by ascending asset value, then by sales, then by market value, and then by net profit. Additionally, names of companies with highest assets, sales, market value, and net profit should be listed. Use subroutines for sorting and for determining highest values.

22. Dr. X has unusual grading practices. He assigns random grades (1–100) to his class of *N* students (where *N* is accepted from input). Each student gets three random test scores for three tests. Write a program to compute the average grade of each student and the average of the entire class. The results should be tabulated in page form as follows: (15 students per page).

```
                                                                PAGE 1
                    STUDENT
                    NUMBER    SCORE 1   SCORE 2   SCORE 3   AVERAGE
                       1        2Ø        3Ø        4Ø        3Ø
                       2        2Ø        8Ø        2Ø        4Ø
                       .        .         .         .         .
                       .        .         .         .         .
                      15        1         Ø         98        33
2 blank lines   {
1 dotted line --> ---------------------------------------------------
                                                                PAGE 2
2 blank lines   {
                    STUDENT
                    NUMBER    SCORE 1   SCORE 2   SCORE 3   AVERAGE
1 blank line
                      16        5Ø        6Ø        7Ø        6Ø
                      17        .         .         .         .
                       .        .         .         .         .
                       .        .         .         .         .
                      3Ø
2 blank lines   {
1 dotted line --> ---------------------------------------------------
                                                                PAGE 3
2 blank lines   {
                    STUDENT
                    NUMBER    SCORE 1   SCORE 2   SCORE 3   AVERAGE
                       .        .         .         .         .
                       .        .         .         .         .
```

A subroutine should be used to simulate automatic ejection to the top of a new page to provide for a page number, headings, and a demarcation line to be used by Dr. X. to cut each page and bind them in booklet form. The average class grade should be printed all by itself on a new numbered page. Would you expect the class average grade to be close to 50?

23. Mr. Mathis has taken out a loan for $18,750 at 16.5%. His payments are to be quarterly (every three months). He can manage quarterly payments anywhere between $900 to $1,500 but would prefer to keep them as close to $900 as possible.

He would also like to stick to a 10-year repayment schedule. Write a program to determine his minimum quarterly payments (*Hint:* Vary his quarterly payments from \$900 to \$1,500 and analyze the term T (duration) of the loan, given by the formula

$$T = -\frac{\log\left(1 - \dfrac{P \cdot i}{N \cdot R}\right)}{\log\left(1 + \dfrac{i}{N}\right)} \cdot \frac{1}{N}$$

where T = duration of payments in years
P = principal
i = annual interest rate
N = number of payments per year
R = amount of payments

Use the DEF function to compute T as a function of R.)

24. There are five sections of a financial management course FI 550. For each of these sections, we have entered on separate DATA statements the section number and the number of students who enrolled in that section during preregistration (two entries per DATA statement). Following these five DATA statements, we have other DATA statements for students wishing to add FI 550. These student DATA statements contain two entries: a name and the section number the student wants to add. The maximum number of students in sections 1 through 5 is 13, 15, 17, 9, and 8, respectively (enter in an array). Write a program using subroutines to process these student DATA statements. If a request for a section cannot be filled, print out the student name and the section requested. At the conclusion of the program, print out each section number and the updated enrollment. For example, given the following input, the output should be as follows:

Input

Pre-registration

```
DATA 100, 13
DATA 110, 14
DATA 105, 10
DATA 121, 9
DATA 107, 5
```

Late registration

```
DATA JOE, 100
DATA SUE, 110
DATA CLO, 107
DATA FLO, 100
DATA MIK, 110
```

Output

```
        SECTIONS CLOSED

SECTION 100
     JOE
     FLO
SECTION 110
     MIK

         UPDATED FILE
  SECTION       ENROLLMENT

     100            13
     110            15
     105            10
     121             9
     107             6
```

25. Systems of two equations in two unknowns, such as

$$a_1x + b_1y = c_1$$
$$a_2x + b_2y = c_2$$

can be solved by using Cramer's rule:

$$x = \frac{\begin{vmatrix} c_1 & b_1 \\ c_2 & b_2 \end{vmatrix}}{\begin{vmatrix} a_1 & b_1 \\ a_2 & b_2 \end{vmatrix}} \qquad y = \frac{\begin{vmatrix} a_1 & c_1 \\ a_2 & c_2 \end{vmatrix}}{\begin{vmatrix} a_1 & b_1 \\ a_2 & a_2 \end{vmatrix}}$$

where, in general, the determinant $\begin{vmatrix} a & b \\ c & d \end{vmatrix} = a \cdot d - c \cdot b$

Write a program to enter sets of values for a_1,b_1,c_1,a_2,b_2,c_2 and determine the solution using a subroutine to calculate each determinant.

26. The president of the XSTAR Company realizes that the company's present accounting procedures are too slow, too inefficient, and not sufficiently accurate to deal with the company's increasing annual processing volume. Plans have been made to replace manual accounting operations with a wholly computerized system. The current total operating costs (in dollars) for the manual system volume is given by $y = x + .5$ (where y is the dollar cost and x the annual processing volume). Projected total computerized cost is given by the formula $y = .75x + 2$. The anticipated annual processing volume will be close to four units.

Write a program to

a. Determine graphically whether the president's decision to switch to a computerized system is economically sound (graph both lines).
b. Determine graphically the break-even point (the annual volume of processing that would justify the president's plan for changing method of operation).

Realizing that an annual volume of processing of four units is not sufficient to warrant such a change in operations, a compromise is effected. The new operational procedures will involve both manual and computer operations. The cost attached to such a new system is given by $y = .445x + 1.5$.

Write a program to

c. Determine graphically whether such a system would be economically beneficial to the company.
d. Determine graphically the break-even point for the total computerized system versus the computer-manual plan.

27. The Toystar Corporation is marketing a new toy. Expected revenues are approximated by the function $y = 2 + x^2/4$. Costs associated with the production and the sales of the toy are defined by the function $y = 3\sqrt{x}$. Write a program to determine graphically the break-even point for the production of the new toy.

28. Write a program to graph the total profit function of the example in Exercise 27. The total profit function is defined as the difference between the cost and revenue functions; that is, $T(x) = |R(x) - C(x)|$, where R, C, and T are respectively the revenue, the cost, and the total profit functions. In the case of Exercise 27 identify on the total profit graph the point at which profit is maximum.

29. Sometimes it is helpful to expand or contract a graph. Scale factors are used for this purpose. Rewrite the break-even analysis program of Figure 10–11 to change both graphs by using the functions

$$y = n\,(15xe^{-x/3}) \quad \text{and} \quad y = n\left(\frac{x^3}{16} - \frac{x^2}{2} + \frac{7x}{4} + 4\right)$$

where n is a scale factor accepted from input. If $n = 1$, the graph should be identical to the one depicted in Figure 10–11. If $n = 10$, the graph should be steeper and if $n = .5$ the graph should be wider (more elongated). Try various scale factors.

30. Write a program to plot a circle. [*Hint:* The equation of a circle of radius r centered on the y axis passing through the orgin is

$$(y - r)^2 + x^2 = r^2 \quad \text{or} \quad y = \pm\sqrt{r^2 - x^2} + r$$

Plot both branches by adding 0.5 to the y positive branch and -0.5 to the y negative branch. User $r = 4.5$ initially.]

10-6-3 Exercises Requiring Random Numbers

1. As a promotional gimmick, every patron of the Circle K gas station gets a lucky card with three numbers on it ranging between 10 and 10,000. The station manager then draws at random a number between 1 and 10,000. If any of the customer numbers matches the one drawn by the manager, the customer gets a dollar amount equal to 1/10 of the lucky number. Write a program to read 10 customer lucky cards and determine the dollar amount of any lucky win. For example, if the lucky card contains the numbers 50, 100, and 200 and the manager draws the number 50, the customer wins 5 dollars. Use a subroutine to determine lucky wins.

2. Verify that all 13 possible values of INT(RND(0)*13) or RND(13) occur with approximately equal frequency. Generate several thousand values and construct a frequency distribution plot.

3. You are dealt 13 cards. These are entered on one DATA statement as follows: 2 of spades to the ace of spades are identified by the numbers 1 to 13; 2 to ace of hearts by the numbers 14–26; 2 to ace of diamonds by 27–39; and 2 to ace of clubs by 40–52.

   a. Use the RND function to deal your hand. Determine the number of kings you have and print their suit.

b. Can you write the code to print your hand as follows?

Clubs	1, 10, 12	
Diamonds	5, 7, 9, 13	
Hearts	10, 11, 12, 13	Not necessarily in any order.
Spaces	11, 9	

c. Print your hand with the words ACE, KING, QUEEN, and JACK spelled out, rather than their corresponding numerical codes.

d. Write the code to determine your best poker hand from the hand dealt in part a.

4. a. Write separate subroutines to print each of the following geometric symbols:

b. Write a main program to generate primitive art artificially (through random number generator routine) by printing the preceding geometric symbols vertically in random fashion (assign the numbers 1–5 to the five symbols). For example:

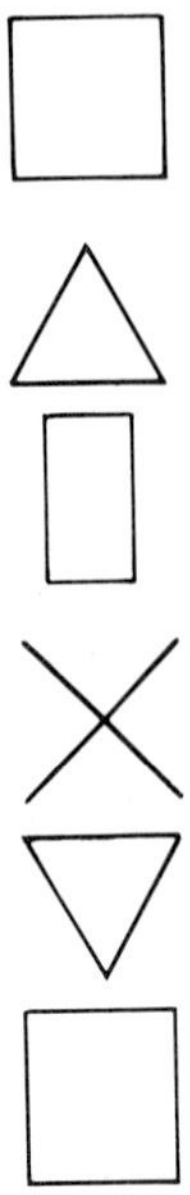

5. Write a program to play the game of Chinese War. Assume that there are 25 sticks in a pile. Players take turns removing 1, 2, 3, or 4 sticks from the pile. The player who is forced to take the last stick loses.

10-6-4 Projects

1. LUXURMART is an exclusive clothing store where Luxurmart members are required to maintain \$1,000 in their accounts at all times. Members charge all purchases on Luxur credit cards. Write a main program to create a master member file consisting of member names with an initial \$1,500 credit for all members.

   Some members frequently return merchandise that must be credited to their accounts; others may purchase items and cause their credit to fall below \$1,000, in which case a message is to be printed requesting the member to write a check for an amount bringing his/her credit back to \$1,000. In some cases, a member name may not be on the master file, and an appropriate message should be printed.

   Write a subroutine to update each customer's account. Transaction records contain member names and dollar amounts for credit or debit. The subroutine tells the main program whether a message is to be printed. The main program performs all output functions and should produce an updated member file after all transaction records have been processed. For example, input and output data are shown as follows:

Input

MASTER FILE

```
HOWARD      1500
NIARCO      1500
PELLON      1500
ROCKER      1500
```

TRANSACTION FILE

```
PELLON       106
MOCKER       500
NIARCO       -10
HOWARD      -600
NIARCO        -5
```

Output

```
**NO MATCHING NAME FOR MOCKER**
-- HOWARD MUST PAY 100 NOW --

      UPDATED MASTER FILE

         HOWARD     900
         NIARCO    1485
         PELLON    1606
         ROCKER    1500
```

2. Repeat the preceding exercise, with the following variation:

   To simplify and minimize transcription errors, tag numbers, instead of dollar amounts, are recorded on transaction records for items purchased or returned. A "D" or a "C" signifies debit and credit, respectively. For example:

HOWARD	9 D	means debit HOWARD's account by whatever item 9 costs.
NIARCO	10 C	means credit NIARCO's account by the value of item 10.

   Create a table of costs for the different items. For example:

ITEM TAG	*COST*
1	44.50
2	100.75
3	94.50
.	.
.	.
.	.
10	46.00

3. Write a check program to accept a name, a date, and a dollar amount (not to exceed $999.99) and transcribe this information numerically and in words on a computer-produced check as follows:

```
NAME? ARIPE CAYENNO
DATE (MM,DD,YY)? 11,18,84
AMOUNT? 104.98
```

2385

ARIBA GIVEAWAY
4206 GABRIELLA DR.
PENSACOLA, FLORIDA 32503 NOVEMBER 18 19 84

PAY TO THE ORDER OF ARIPE CAYENNO $ 104.98

ONE HUNDRED FOUR AND 98/100 DOLLARS

FIRSTAMFED BANK

4. Plot the graph of the sine function for values of x ranging between 0 and 7.

5. An interesting method of encoding data is to load a message to be encoded into a two-dimensional array and then interchange rows and interchange columns a number of times. The resultant sequence of characters is the encoded message. In order to decode the message, the sequence of steps used in the encoding process is followed in reverse order. For example, consider the message "I HAVE BUT ONE LIFE TO GIVE FOR MY COUNTRY". Let us load the message into a 6×7 array:

I		H	A	V	E	
B	U	T		O	N	E
	L	I	F	E		T
O		G	I	V	E	
F	O	R		M	Y	
C	O	U	N	T	R	Y

Now consider the following encoding process:

Interchange row 1 and row 3

	L	I	F	E		T
B	U	T		O	N	E
I		H	A	V	E	
O		G	I	V	E	
F	O	R		M	Y	
C	O	U	N	T	R	Y

Interchange column 2 and column 5

	E	I	F	L		T
B	O	T		U	N	E
I	V	H	A		E	
O	V	G	I		E	
F	M	R		O	Y	
C	T	U	N	O	R	Y

Interchange row 4 and 6

	E	I	F	L	T	
B	O	T		U	N	E
I	V	H	A		E	
C	T	U	N	O	R	Y
F	M	R		O	Y	
O	V	G	I		E	

Interchange column 1 and column 5

L	E	I	F			T
U	O	T		B	N	E
	V	H	A	I	E	
O	T	U	N	C	R	Y
O	M	R		F	Y	
	U	G	I	O	E	

The resulting string is "LEIF TUOT BNE VHAIE OTUNCRYOMR FY UGIOE ." To decode the message, the encoding process is reversed; i.e., the encoded message would be loaded into a 6 X 7 array and then the following interchanges would be performed:

columns 1 and 5
rows 4 and 6
columns 2 and 5
rows 1 and 3

Write subroutines to perform the column and row interchange operations; then write a program to encode and decode messages.

10-6-5 Answers to Self Test

1.

a. F	b. T	c. F
d. F	e. F	f. F
g. T	h. T	i. F
j. F	k. F	l. T
m. T	n. T	o. T

2.

a. `10 X = INT(RND(0)*100) + 1` or on some systems X = RND (100)

b. `10 LET Y = ABS(SQR(A) - SQR(B))`

c. `LOG(EXP(X) - EXP(-X))`

d. `(SIN(X^2))^2`

e. `1/TAN(X)`

3.

```
1000 IF X <= 1 THEN 1040
1010      LET Z = INT(X + .99999) - 1
1020      LET P = .2 + .17*Z
1030      RETURN
1040 LET P = .2
1050 RETURN
```

11 SEQUENTIAL FILE PROCESSING

11-1 Introduction

Most versions of BASIC contain features for processing and storing data in external files on disk or magnetic tape. Unfortunately, the ANSI specifications for minimal BASIC do not contain any standards for file processing statements, so the details of these statements vary from one version of BASIC to another. A comparison of the file processing statements for several common BASIC systems is shown in section 11-5. The examples in this chapter use the statements for the IBM Personal Computer and the Radio Shack TRS-80 Model II and Model III microcomputing systems. Although the details differ somewhat among different BASICs, the concepts and problem-solving techniques illustrated in this chapter apply to all BASICs that have file processing capabilities.

This chapter discusses sequential file processing using hard magnetic disks or flexible diskettes for storage. File access methods other than sequential access are *not* discussed in this chapter because these methods differ so greatly from one computing system to another, but most systems support random access files that use the GET and PUT statements.

11-1-1 File Concepts

Many applications of computers, particularly those used in business data processing, require the storage and processing of large amounts of data. Typically there is too much data to store in memory at one time, or data must be retained for later processing; therefore external storage for the data is utilized. The very earliest computers used punched cards and magnetic tapes for external storage of data; later computers utilized magnetic disks. Time-sharing systems today usually permit users to store data files on disk for subsequent processing. Microcomputing systems usually have one or more floppy disk drives or a cassette tape drive that can be used for data storage.

Data is organized into *records* containing related data items. Groups of related records constitute a *file*. For example, a personnel file might contain one record for each employee in a company. Each record would be composed of such data items as the employee name, social security number, position code, pay rate, number of dependents, and so on. For convenience in processing, the data items in each record are stored in the same order.

Some files may contain records that have no order relationship between them. A file containing sales records, for example, may contain records in the order in which the sales were made; one record is essentially unrelated to its successor and predecessor. Other files are organized so that they can be accessed easily to process the data they contain. A data item designated as the *record key* is used as the basis for organizing the file. For a personnel file, the employee social security number might be the record key (see Figure 11-1). The file might then be organized sequentially, randomly, or in some other schemes. Using sequential organization, records are placed in the file in order by record keys. Each record has a record key value larger than that of its predecessor. A file that is organized sequentially is usually processed sequentially. A program processes each record in turn, starting with the first record in the file. Other types of file organizations give the user the ability to access records on demand by specifying the record number, thus making it possible to process any specified record without processing other records in the file.

Regardless of the type of file organization and the device used for storage, certain tasks are commonly performed in a file-processing environment. Initially, the file must be created and stored on the external storage device. Various programs are then required to add records to the file, delete records from the file, merge the contents of two files, change data items on individual records in the file, and generate reports based on data contained in the file.

Figure 11-1 Employee file example.

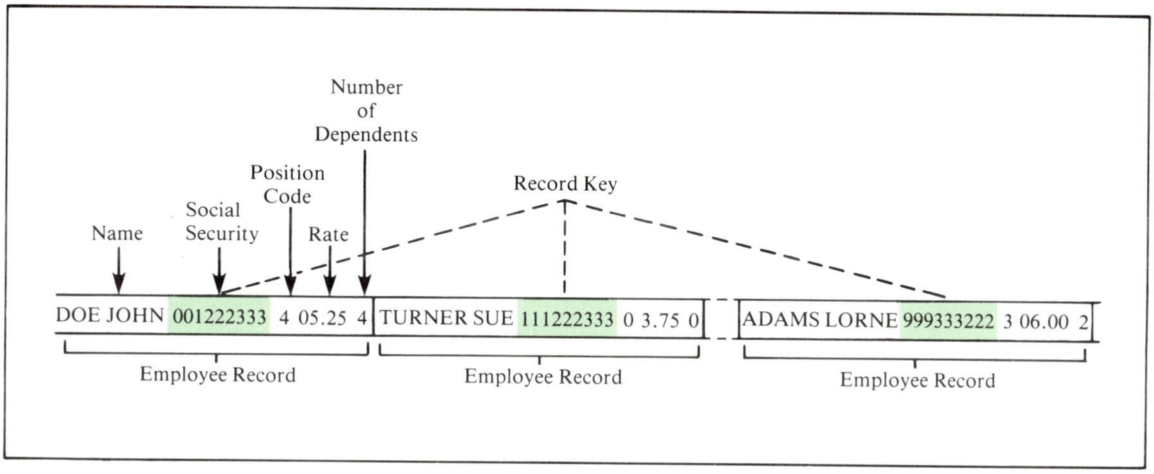

11-1-2 Some Facts about Files

The only files we have talked about up to this point are the input DATA files that are physically present in the BASIC programs we write; READ statements typically read and process information typed on these DATA statements.

Many times, though, we would like to create an input file that is *not* stored within a BASIC program itself, but which can be read and processed by different BASIC programs. Such an input file would be stored on disk and would consist of a sequence of records with no DATA statements and no line numbers. A file stored on disk might appear as:

Such a file could be read by any number of BASIC programs. The input file and the BASIC program reading that input file would be two separate physical entities stored on two different areas of the disk. The files would be stored on the disk under different names. In the same way we use the SAVE command to give a BASIC program a name, we use the OPEN instruction to give our data file a name and the PRINT instruction to write (to store) our data file on disk.

One very important reason why we need the capability to store independent data files on disk is to allow our own BASIC programs to create and store their own output files on disk. So far, none of the programs we have written have produced output files on any output device except the printer or the video screen! But what would we do in the case of a program that is supposed to update a particular inventory file (master file) on a daily basis? What do we do with today's updated file that we need to update again tomorrow? Listing the updated file on the printer or screen does not help the next day's updating process! A file processing system gives us the ability to store the updated inventory (new master file) on a disk so that it can be used as our new master file for tomorrow's date (see Figure 11–3). Today's output becomes tomorrow's input, and this sequence of steps can be repeated day after day.

11-1-3 Practical Considerations: A Quick Overview of BASIC File Statements

Consider the file creation program shown in Figure 11–2. This program can be used on the IBM Personal Computer or on the Radio Shack computers to create a disk file containing numeric and alphanumeric records. The same program then reads the disk file that it just created from the disk. Let us look carefully at some of the important file processing statements. (Before running the program in Figure 11–2 on a TRS-80 Model II, the user should type BASIC – F:1 instead of BASIC; this sets up the system

Figure 11–2 Creating a disk file and reading from a disk file.

```
10 OPEN "O",1,"DATA"
15 X = 1.2
20 Y = -4.3
25 Z = 100
30 PRINT #1, X; Y; Z
35 A$ = "WE"
40 B$ = "AM"
45 C$ = "US"
50 PRINT #1,A$; ","; B$; ","; C$
55 PRINT #1,"HE IS"; ","; Z; ","; "YEARS OLD"
60 CLOSE 1
65 OPEN "I", 3, "DATA"
70 INPUT #3, X,Y,Z,R$,S$,T$,X$,A,Y$
75 PRINT X, Y, Z
80 PRINT R$, S$, T$
85 PRINT X$, A, Y$
90 CLOSE 3
95 END
```

Lines 10–25: Prepare to create and store a data file on disk under the name "DATA". "O" stands for output and 1 is an ID number for the file.

Line 30: Write the values contained in X, Y, and Z on the disk file.

Lines 50–60: On that same file (#1), write the string of characters contained in A$, B$, and C$. Then write the characters "HE IS" followed by Z and the string "YEARS OLD". Close the file.

Line 65: Make the file that we just created available as an input file ("I"). This time we will refer to this file as file 3. (We could have used 1 just as well.)

Lines 70–95: Line 70 reads all the information that we stored in the file, and lines 75, 80, and 85 print the data that was read from the disk file.

```
RUN
 1.2            -4.3            100
WE              AM              US
HE IS            100            YEARS OLD
```

Figure 11–3 The file processing system cycle.

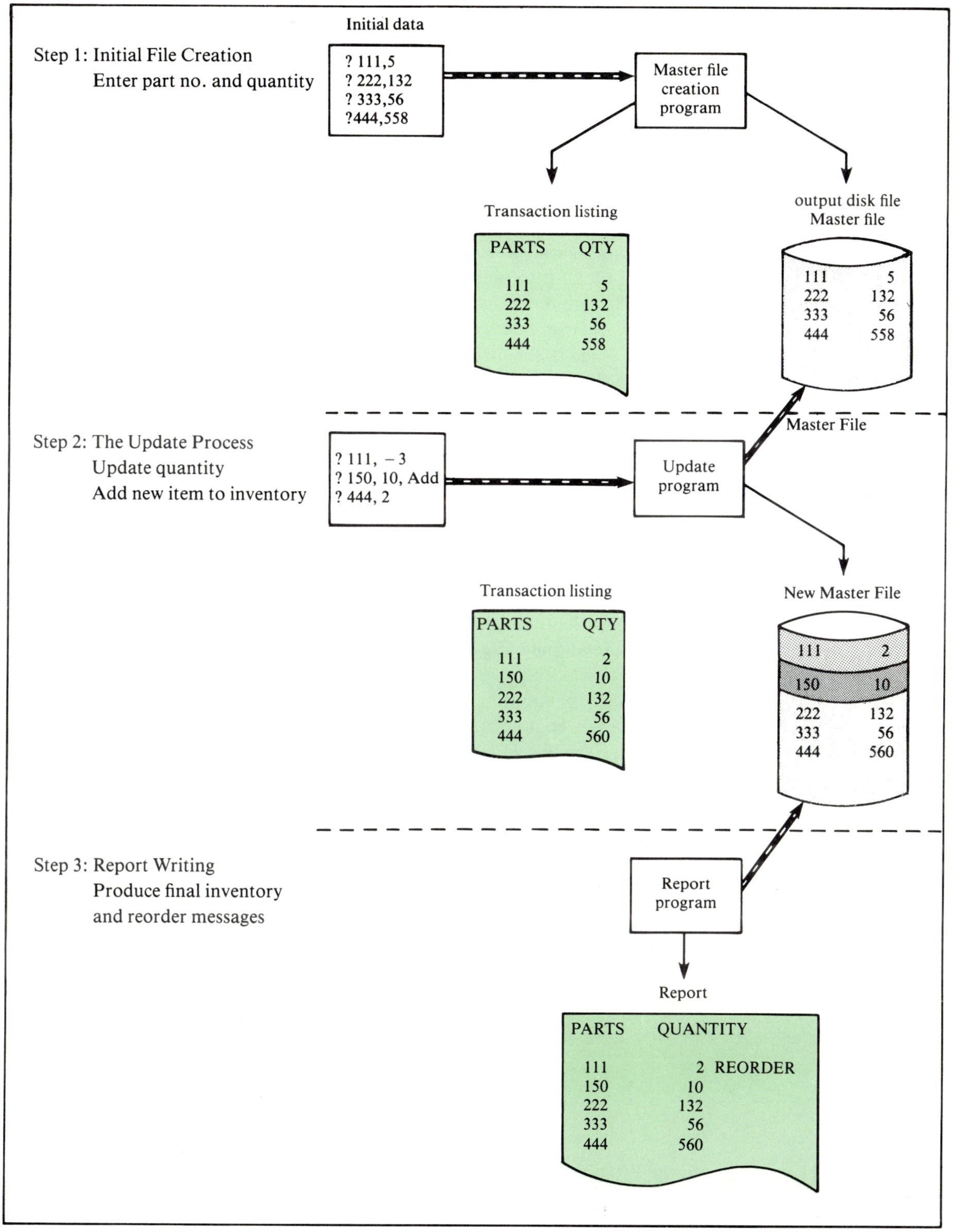

for one file. If four files are needed, type BASIC –F:4. On the IBM PC, three files are automatically allocated when you type BASIC; if you need to work with four files, type BASIC /F:4 instead of BASIC.)

Line 10:

The OPEN instruction informs BASIC that the current program will be working with a disk file.
The "O" field specifies that an **O**utput file will be created and will be written onto a disk.
The number 1 gives a numeric label to the output file that we will work with. (We could have used the number 2 or 3 instead.) These file numbers are used by the BASIC instructions PRINT#, INPUT# and CLOSE to identify which file is to be processed in the event that the program works with more than one file.
The user chosen name DATA is given by the user and will be used by the system for cataloging purposes, i.e., this file will be listed in the directory as DATA in much the same way SAVE "PROG1" causes PROG1 to be listed in the directory for a BASIC program. Note that the file name can specify a particular disk drive, for example

`"DATA"`	specifies drive A on IBM and drive 0 on TRS-80.
`"DATA :1"`	specifies drive 1 on TRS-80.
`"B: DATA"`	specifies drive B for IBM system.

Line 30:

The PRINT #1 instruction will write out three numeric items in file 1 on the disk. The semicolons in X;Y;Z mean that on the disk the three numeric items will be close together (separated from one another by at least one blank). A comma could also have been used: PRINT #1,X,Y,Z—this would mean that more disk space would be required to record these three items, since each would be written in a different zone. Note that PRINT #1,X;Y,Z could also have been used. In general, it is a good idea to use a semicolon between numeric entries, since this will save space on the disk.

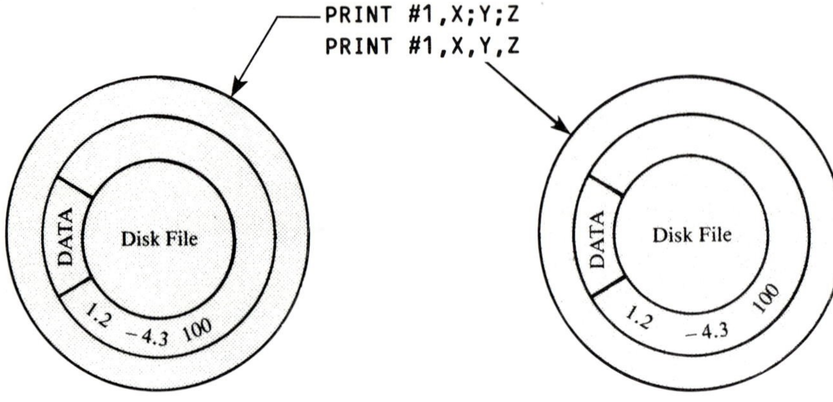

Line 50:

This instruction is very similar to the PRINT statement at line 30, except that a comma in quotation marks must separate each alphanumeric item. If you had written PRINT #1,A$;B$;C$, the string WEAMUS would have been written on disk as one record. The "," must be used to separate the items.

On the IBM PC, the instructions WRITE # automatically provides the "," to delimit the fields, i.e., WRITE #1,A$,B$,C$ is equivalent to PRINT #1,A$;",";B$;",";C$. This instruction is not available on the TRS-80 models.

Line 55:

Any alphanumeric item to be written on disk must be separated by "," from the next item, whether that item is numeric or alphanumeric. Hence "," is used between "HE IS" and Z.

Line 60:

The CLOSE 1 instruction makes sure that the output file is written onto the disk and makes file 1 unavailable to the user until that file is reopened. It also causes an end-of-file marker to be written on that file; this can then be used by the EOF BASIC instruction to detect an end-of-file condition, so trip records are no longer needed!

Line 65:

The OPEN instruction makes the disk file DATA available to the program as an **I**nput file ("I"). In this mode, the program can only read the file; it cannot add or change records.
The number 3 gives the input file a numeric identity that is later used by the INPUT and the CLOSE instructions. Any other positive integer could have been used instead of 3.

Line 70:

The instruction INPUT# (*not* READ#) is used to read data from disk files. In this particular case, nine items are read from the disk in the same sequence that they were written. These items should be separated from one another by a comma(s).

Line 90:

The CLOSE 3 instruction makes file 3 unavailable to the program (for the time being).

11-1-4 Program Example

Mr. X wishes to maintain data regarding the number of parts on hand at his company's warehouse. The company has just taken inventory, so the number of parts on hand at the present time is known. This data is to be entered into the computer system and retained in a file. The BASIC program shown in Figure 11-4 is used to create this file, which will be stored under the name "INVEN". Files stored on disk must always be named so that the operating system can provide access to the file. The OPEN statement (line 90) declares the mode of the file ("I" means input, "O" means output), assigns it an arbitrary file number or *buffer* number (3 in this case), and gives the name of the file ("INVEN"). A *buffer* is a temporary storage area. Records are read into and written from buffers. Each file to be processed by the program is assigned a different buffer, numbers 1, 2, 3, and so forth. Subsequent input/output statements reference the buffer assigned to the file in the OPEN statement (see line 200).

Note that the file "INVEN" is organized sequentially with the part number as the key field. This organization will facilitate the work of other programs that will process the file.

■ **Figure 11–4** File creation program.

```
10 REM THIS PROGRAM IS USED TO CREATE A PARTS INVENTORY FILE
20 REM
30 REM THE OPEN STATEMENT IS USED TO DECLARE
40 REM     ┌────THE MODE OF THE FILE (INPUT, OUTPUT, ETC.)
50 REM     │   ┌─THE FILE NUMBER USED BY THE PRINT AND INPUT
60 REM     │   │      STATEMENTS TO REFER TO THIS FILE
70         │   │    THE NAME OF THE FILE
80 REM     ↓   ↓    ↓
90 OPEN "O",3,"INVEN"         "O" means that we are creating an output file.
100 REM                       The 3 will be used in the PRINT statement.
105 REM                       The file will be stored on the disk with name INVEN.
110 PRINT "ENTER PART NUMBER, QUANTITY"
120 INPUT P,Q
130 REM
140 REM A PART NUMBER OF 999999 IS USED TO SIGNIFY END OF INPUT
150 REM
160 IF P = 999999 THEN 300
170 REM
180 REM THE PRINT # STATEMENT IS USED TO WRITE A RECORD ON THE
190 REM FILE WHICH WILL BE STORED ON THE DISK
200 PRINT #3, P;Q
250 GO TO 100
300 REM
310 REM THE CLOSE STATEMENT IS USED TO TERMINATE PROCESSING
320 REM OF THE FILE
330 REM
340 CLOSE 3
350 END
READY
RUN
ENTER PART NUMBER,QUANTITY
? 6,3
ENTER PART NUMBER,QUANTITY
? 12,42
ENTER PART NUMBER,QUANTITY
? 35,7
ENTER PART NUMBER,QUANTITY
? 40,0
ENTER PART NUMBER,QUANTITY
? 55,9
ENTER PART NUMBER,QUANTITY
? 999999,0
```

Later, as parts are used from the inventory or added to the inventory, it will be necessary to update the data recorded in this file. A second program, shown in Figure 11-5, could be used for this purpose. In this program the OPEN statement (line 36)

Figure 11-5 File update program (part 1 of 2 parts).

```
 10 REM THIS PROGRAM IS USED TO UPDATE THE FILE INVEN
 20 DIM P(100), Q(100)
 30 REM THE CONTENT OF THE FILE IS LOADED INTO THE ARRAYS P AND Q
 35 REM THE FILE IS OPENED AS AN INPUT FILE
 36 OPEN "I", 1, "INVEN"
 40 FOR I=1 TO 100
 50 REM
 60 REM THE EOF FUNCTION DETERMINES IF THERE IS MORE DATA IN THE FILE
 80 REM
 90 IF EOF(1) THEN 230      (If it is the end of the file, transfer to line 230.)
100 REM THE INPUT# STATEMENT IS USED TO READ DATA FROM THE FILE
105 REM M = THE NUMBER OF RECORDS IN THE FILE
106 LET M=I
110 INPUT#1, P(I),Q(I)
120 NEXT I
200 REM
210 REM WHEN ALL DATA HAS BEEN READ THE FILE IS CLOSED
220 REM
230 CLOSE 1
240 REM
250 REM CHANGES TO THE FILE ARE ACCEPTED IN THE FORM
260 REM PART NUMBER, CHANGE
270 REM THE END OF CHANGES IS SIGNIFIED BY ENTERING
280 REM A PART NUMBER = 999999
290 REM
300 PRINT "ENTER PART NUMBER, CHANGE"
310 INPUT N,C
320 IF N=999999 THEN 500
330 REM PROGRAM ATTEMPTS TO LOCATE PART NUMBER
340 FOR K=1 TO M
350    IF P(K) = N THEN 400
360 NEXT K
370 REM ROUTINE USED WHEN PART NUMBER IS NOT FOUND
380 PRINT "INVALID PART NUMBER"
390 GO TO 300
400 REM ROUTINE USED WHEN PART NUMBER IS FOUND
410 LET Q(K)=Q(K) + C
420 PRINT "NUMBER ON HAND IS NOW"; Q(K)
430 GO TO 300
500 REM
510 REM ROUTINE USED WHEN ALL CHANGES HAVE BEEN ENTERED
520 PRINT "DO YOU WISH CHANGES TO BECOME PERMANENT"
530 INPUT A$
540 IF A$ <> "YES" THEN 700
550 REM
560 REM ROUTINE USED TO PLACE CONTENT OF ARRAYS P AND Q IN THE FILE
580 REM
590 OPEN "0", 1, "INVEN"      (Switch file to output status with same name.)
600 FOR K= 1 to M
610 PRINT#1,P(K);Q(K)
620 NEXT K
630 CLOSE 1
700 END
```

Figure 11–5 File update program (part 2 of 2 parts).

```
RUN
ENTER PART NUMBER, CHANGE
? 40,5
NUMBER OF HAND IS NOW 5
ENTER PART NUMBER,CHANGE
? 6,-1
NUMBER ON HAND IS NOW 2
ENTER PART NUMBER,CHANGE
? 42,7
INVALID PART NUMBER
ENTER PART NUMBER,CHANGE
? 55,-3
NUMBER ON HAND IS NOW 6
ENTER PART NUMBER,CHANGE
? 999999,0
DO YOU WISH CHANGES TO BECOME PERMANENT
? YES
```

Figure 11–6 File listing program.

```
 10 REM THIS PROGRAM LISTS THE CONTENT OF THE FILE
 30 PRINT "ENTER NAME OF THE FILE"
 40 INPUT F$
 50 OPEN "I",1,F$
 55 PRINT "CONTENT OF ";F$
 56 PRINT "***************************************"
 60 PRINT "PART NUMBER", "QUANTITY ON HAND"
 61 IF EOF (1) THEN 150
 62      INPUT#1,P,Q
 70      PRINT P,Q
 80      GO TO 61
150 PRINT "***************************************"
160 CLOSE 1
170 END
RUN
ENTER NAME OF THE FILE
? INVEN
CONTENT OF INVEN
***************************************
PART NUMBER    QUANTITY ON HAND
     6               2
    12              42
    35               7
    40               5
    55               6
***************************************
```

specifies that the file will be an input file ("I" means input) assigned to buffer number 1. (Remember, the choice of a buffer number is arbitrary, but within a given program all subsequent references must adhere to the choice made in the OPEN statement.)

Finally, a program will be required to list the content of the file in order to determine how many parts are available, how many should be ordered, and so forth. The program shown in Figure 11-6 is used for this purpose.

Figure 11-7 shows a system flowchart for the inventory maintenance system. A system flowchart shows the relationship of data files and programs in a data processing system. The flowlines in a system flowchart show the flow of data between files and programs.

11-1-5 Do It Now

1. Note that, in the update program of Figure 11-5, the original master file INVEN is destroyed while it is being updated. This could become a real problem if for some particular reason (such as power failure, disk failure, or disk drive failure), the update process is aborted; then the master file INVEN would be totally lost! In general, it is an excellent idea to make a back-up copy of the master file, not just because of potential hardware problems, but also in the event that transactions for the update prove to be incorrect. Preservation of a master file can be accomplished in many ways. One way is to make a back-up copy of INVEN before the update process. Another way is to write the updated file on a different disk file (INVEN1 instead of INVEN). Using the latter method, modify the program of Figure 11-5 to store the updated file on INVEN1.

Figure 11-7 System flowchart for inventory program.

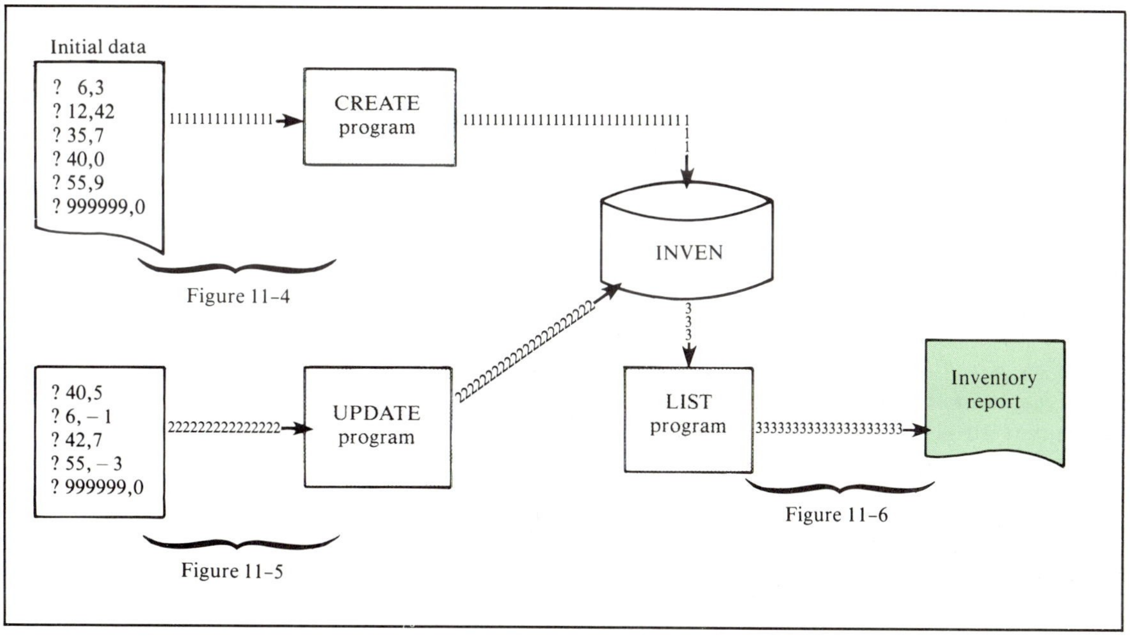

2. What external data storage facilities are available for your system?
3. If you are using shared facilities, is it necessary to obtain permission to store files on external storage for your system? If so, how is this permission obtained?
4. What limitations are placed on the amount of data you may store on external files?

Answers

1. Change line 590 of Figure 11–5 to: 590 OPEN "O",1,"INVEN1"

11-2 BASIC Statements

Since BASIC file processing statements vary so much from one BASIC to another, section 11–2–6 is left blank for the file processing statements of your particular BASIC.

11-2-1 The OPEN and CLOSE Statements

The OPEN statement is required to initiate the processing of a file. The general form of the OPEN statement for the TRS-80 Models II and III and the IBM Personal Computer is

line number OPEN *mode, file number, file name*

where

mode can be: "I" to make the file an **I**nput file, i.e., to read from a disk file.
"O" to make the file an **O**utput file, i.e., to create a disk file.

file number or *buffer* — is any integer number from 1 to 15. This number is used by the PRINT# and INPUT# instructions to differentiate among files if more than one file is referred to in the program.

file name — is the name of the file; it can also specify the disk drive where the file is located.

The *mode* and *file name* can be specified as literals (enclosed in quotes) or as string variables. The *file number* can be specified as any numeric expression. The *file number* declared in the OPEN statement is used by other input/output statements to refer to that file. Any existing file opened as an output file ("O") will be destroyed!

Note that *file number* must be an integer that may not exceed X where X is the number of files that *you* specified when you typed BASIC −F:X (TRS-80) or BASIC /F:X (IBM). If for example you typed BASIC −F:4, then you may not use 5 through 15 as a file number.

The IBM PC allows an alternate form of the OPEN statement:

$$\text{OPEN } \textit{file name} \text{ FOR } \begin{Bmatrix} \text{INPUT} \\ \text{OUTPUT} \\ \text{APPEND} \end{Bmatrix} \text{ AS [\#] } \textit{file number}$$

where INPUT and OUTPUT have the same meaning as "I" and "O" in the previous general form of the OPEN statement. The option APPEND means that the file is positioned to the end of the file when the file is opened. If the file does not already exist, then the file is treated just like OUTPUT. This feature is very convenient for adding to a file; otherwise an entirely new output file would have to be created. The TRS-80 Model III also offers the same feature as APPEND with the mode E (Extend) feature (see example 3).

Example 1

```
30 OPEN "I", 4, "DATAFILE"
```

The file "DATAFILE" is opened as an input file, implying that data will be read from the file. File number 4 is assigned to the file. The file number established in the OPEN statement must be used in subsequent statements which refer to the file (e.g., INPUT #4 and CLOSE 4).

Example 2

```
20 INPUT G$                    Assume you entered O.
30 LET F$ = "DATAFILE"
40 OPEN G$, 2, F$
```

The file named in F$ ("DATAFILE" in this example) is opened as an output file. File number 2 is assigned to the file. Data will be placed in the file beginning with the first record. If the file exists, the new data records will replace the old ones. If the file does not exist, it will be created.

Example 3

```
50 OPEN "E", 10, "PARTS"              TRS-80 Model III
50 OPEN "PARTS" FOR APPEND AS #10     IBM PC
```

The file "PARTS" is opened in the extend mode. If the file does not exist, records will be written on the file beginning with the first record. If the file does exist, records written on the file will be added to the file after the last existing record. Note that the extend mode can be used to add records only to unorganized files, since the key field value is not considered when records are placed in the file.

Files that have been processed should be closed at some point in the execution of a BASIC program. A file that has been closed can be reopened in the same program and processing will start at the first record of that file (unless E or APPEND have been specified). The general form of the CLOSE statement is

line number CLOSE [*file number* [, file number] ...]

Example 1

`10 CLOSE`	All files in use are closed
`15 CLOSE 1`	Close file number 1
`20 CLOSE 1,2,3`	Close file numbers 1, 2 and 3

Example 2

`10 OPEN "O",1, "TEST"`	Create an output file "TEST"
.	
.	
`60 CLOSE 1`	Close output file "TEST"
`65 OPEN "I", 3, "TEST"`	Reopen file "TEST" as an input file and use file number 3 to process "TEST".
.	
.	

11-2-2 The INPUT# Statement

The INPUT# statement is used to read data items from records in an external file. The general form of the statement is

line number INPUT# *file number*, *list of variables*

where *file number* is the buffer associated with the file in the OPEN statement, and *list of variables* consists of a string of variables separated by commas.

The INPUT# statement causes data items to be read from a disk file and stored in the listed variables in the same way that data is read and transferred by the INPUT statement. The file must, of course, be opened in input mode before the INPUT# statement can be executed.

Example

```
20 OPEN "I", 4, "PURCHASE"
30 INPUT#4,A$,B,C
```

Suppose the next record in the file "PURCHASE" contains the data

SPEAKERS	6.30	29.56

The value contained in A$ would be "SPEAKERS". The value of B would be 6.3. The value of C would be 29.56.

11-2-3 The EOF Function

The EOF (end of file) function enables the program to determine if more data records are contained on a data file. The general form of the EOF function reference is

> EOF (*file number*)

where the *file number* is the number specified in the OPEN statement.

The EOF function is a logical function. It has value "true" if end-of-file has been reached and there are no more records on the file for processing; otherwise it has value "false."

Example

```
60 OPEN "I", 4, "DATAFILE"
.
.
100 IF EOF(4) THEN 200
110     INPUT#4,A,B,C
.
.
190     GO TO 100
200...
.
.
```

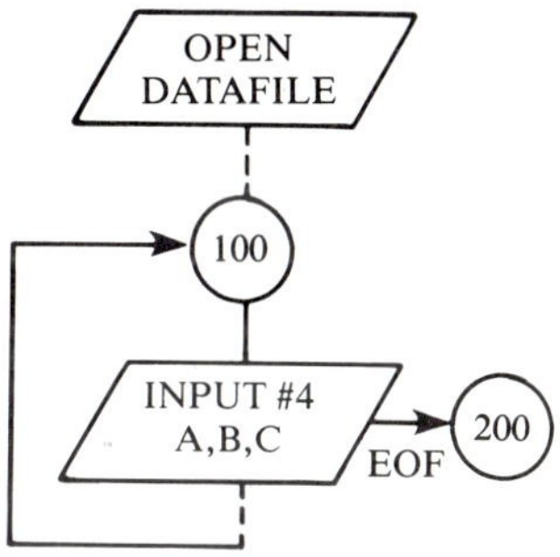

In this example, if there is more data on file 4 at statement 100, the value of EOF(4) will be false, resulting in the execution of the INPUT # statement at line 110. On the other hand, if end-of-file has been reached, the value of EOF(4) will be true, resulting in execution of line 200. Statements at lines 100 and 110 taken together are equivalent to the flowchart block:

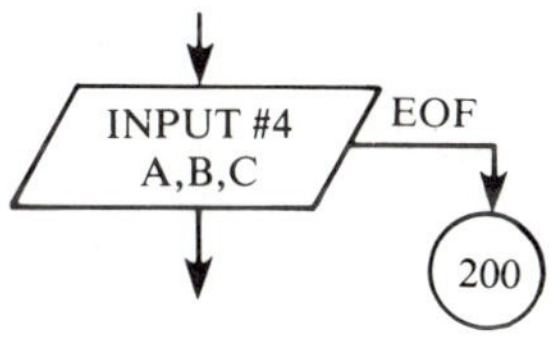

It is important to check for end-of-file *prior* to each INPUT from an external file. An attempt to read more data than is contained on the file will result in an error message and immediate termination of the execution of the program.

11-2-4 The PRINT# Statement

The PRINT# statement is used to write records on an external file. The general form of the statement is

> *line number* PRINT# *file number, list of items*
> *line number* PRINT# *file number*, USING "image"; *list of items*

The file number is the number associated with the file in the OPEN statement.

The PRINT # statement causes values of data items, expressions, and/or literals contained in the *list of items* to be written onto a record in the file in much the same way as the PRINT statement writes output on the user's screen/printer. If the list of items consists solely of numeric items, commas or semi colons are used to separate the items. Semi colons result in compact spacing on the disk, whereas commas result in zone spacing (wasteful of disk space). If any two consecutive items are alphanumeric, or alphanumeric and numeric, a comma within quotation marks must separate the items in addition to the comma/semi colon delimiters.

Examples

`10 PRINT#1, A;3.1;X`	Compact spacing; numeric items
`15 PRINT#2, A,B, X+3`	Zone spacing; numeric items
`20 PRINT#3, A$; ","; B$`	Alphanumeric items
`25 PRINT#4, A$; ","; "AMOUNT"`	Alphanumeric items
`30 PRINT#5, A$; ","; 3.1;",";"SUM"`	If the data written is read by line 35
`35 INPUT#5, D$,X,A$`	then D$ = A$; X = 3.1 and A$ = "SUM"
`40 PRINT#5, USING "$$##.#";32.36`	If the data written is read by
`45 INPUT#5, A$`	line 45 then A$ = b$32.4

11-2-5 Do It Now

1. What is the equivalent of the OPEN statement for your system? (See Figure 11-16 to begin.)
2. What is the equivalent of the INPUT # statement for your system?
3. What is the equivalent of the PRINT # statement for your system?
4. Does your system require a CLOSE statement? If so, what is its syntax?
5. Does your system have an end-of-file detection statement? If so, what is its syntax?
6. Use the answers to questions 1–5 above to modify the programs of Figures 11-4, 11-5, and 11-6 to run on your system.
7. Identify the values printed by line 90.

```
10 OPEN "O",1,"LOT"
20 PRINT#1,3,4.1; "DOG"
30 A$ = "MAN"
40 X = -3
50 PRINT#1,A$;",","DOG";",";2*X + 1
60 CLOSE 1
70 OPEN "I",3,"LOT"
80 INPUT #3,A,B,C$,D$,E$,F
90 PRINT A,B,C$,D$,E$,F
```

Answers

7. 3, 4.1, DOG, MAN, DOG, −5

11-2-6 MY SYSTEM IS DIFFERENT

This section is left blank for you to write any different system commands that your system uses. You may also want to list the various steps that are required to start a session with your system.

11-3 Programming Examples

The programs in this section will illustrate a very simple data processing system for a payroll application. Two files will be created: a master file containing one record for each employee on the payroll, and a data file containing one record for each employee to be paid during a pay period. Programs are given to create, list, and update the master file, to create and list the data file, and to process both files to produce a payroll report.

11-3-1 The Master File Utility Program

The program shown in Figure 11–8 is a general purpose program to create, list, and perform limited updating of the employee master file. Each record in the file contains

employee identification, name, pay rate.

The key field is the employee identification number.

The execution of the program of Figure 11–8 for sample data is shown in Figure 11–9. Note that the program is *menu driven*, i.e. the user selects the desired option of the program at the beginning of the session (see lines 50–130). The program-defined codes are:

I	to secure a listing of the master file
O	to create a master file
E or APPEND	to extend the master file, i.e., add records to the file
Q	to terminate the session

Note that extending the file can only result in records being added to the end of the file. It *cannot* be used to insert records into the middle of the file. Note also that it is the responsibility of the user to enter the records in proper sequence. The program will not reorder the records to produce a file with key field values in ascending sequence. If the user enters data records in improper sequence, other programs that process the file thus created will not operate properly.

11-3-2 Do It Now

Modify the program of Figure 11–8 to produce an error message during the listing of the file if the file contains a record with key field value smaller than or equal to the key field value of the preceding record (file not in ascending key order).

■ **Figure 11–8** Master file utility program.

```
 10 REM GENERAL PURPOSE FILE UTILITY PROGRAM
 20 REM
 30 REM DISPLAY MENU
 50 PRINT "ENTER FUNCTION DESIRED"
 60 PRINT "TO LIST FILE ENTER        I          "
 70 PRINT "TO CREATE FILE ENTER      O          "
 80 PRINT "TO EXTEND FILE ENTER      E OR APPEND"
 85 PRINT "TO TERMINATE ENTER        Q          "
 90 INPUT F$
100 IF F$ = "I" THEN 200
110 IF F$ = "O" OR F$ = "E" THEN 300
115 IF F$ = "Q" THEN 700
120 PRINT F$;" IS AN INVALID FUNCTION CODE"
130 GO TO 50
200 REM
201 REM ROUTINE FOR LISTING FILE
202 REM
203 PRINT "ENTER NAME OF FILE TO BE LISTED"
210 INPUT L$
220 OPEN F$, 2, L$
225 PRINT "LISTING OF FILE "; L$
230 FOR I=1 TO 45
240    PRINT "#";
250 NEXT I
255 PRINT
260 PRINT "ID NUMBER", "NAME", "HOURLY WAGE"
270 IF EOF (2) THEN 290
280       INPUT#2,I,N$,H     Read the I.D., name, and number of hours.
282       PRINT I,N$,H
285       GO TO 270
290 FOR I = 1 TO 45
295    PRINT "#";
296 NEXT I
297 PRINT
298 CLOSE 2
299 GO TO 10
300 REM
310 REM ROUTINE FOR CREATING OR EXTENDING THE FILE
320 REM
330 PRINT "ENTER NAME OF FILE"
340 INPUT L$
350 OPEN F$,2,L$
360 PRINT "ENTER ID NUMBER, NAME,HOURLY WAGE"
362 PRINT "TO STOP ENTER 0,0,0"
370 INPUT I, N$, H
375 IF I = 0 AND N$ = "0" AND H = 0 THEN 400
380    PRINT#2, I; ","; N$;",";H     Write the I.D., the name, and number of hours.
390    GO TO 360
400 CLOSE 2
410 GO TO 10
700 END
```

■ **Figure 11-9** Sample execution of master file utility program. (part 1 of 2 parts).

```
ENTER FUNCTION DESIRED
TO LIST ENTER         I
TO CREATE FILE ENTER  O
TO EXTEND FILE ENTER  E OR APPEND
TO TERMINATE ENTER    Q
? O
ENTER NAME OF FILE
? MASTERDATA
ENTER ID NUMBER, NAME,HOURLY WAGE
TO STOP ENTER Ø,Ø,Ø
? 111111,JOHN DOE,4.2
ENTER ID NUMBER, NAME,HOURLY WAGE
TO STOP ENTER Ø,Ø,Ø
? 222222,MARY SMITH,6
ENTER ID NUMBER, NAME,HOURLY WAGE
TO STOP ENTER Ø,Ø,Ø
? 333333,JAMES BROWN,5
ENTER ID NUMBER, NAME,HOURLY WAGE
TO STOP ENTER Ø,Ø,Ø
? 444444,SALLY MAE,3.5
ENTER ID NUMBER, NAME,HOURLY WAGE
TO STOP ENTER Ø,Ø,Ø
? 555555,SAM SMITH,7.9
ENTER ID NUMBER, NAME,HOURLY WAGE
TO STOP ENTER Ø,Ø,Ø
? Ø,Ø,Ø
ENTER FUNCTION DESIRED
TO LIST ENTER         I
TO CREATE FILE ENTER  O
TO EXTEND FILE ENTER  E OR APPEND
TO TERMINATE ENTER    Q
? I
ENTER NAME OF FILE TO BE LISTED
? MASTERDATA
LISTING OF FILE MASTERDATA
##############################################
ID NUMBER         NAME           HOURLY WAGE
 111111         JOHN DOE          4.2
 222222         MARY SMITH        6
 333333         JAMES BROWN       5
 444444         SALLY MAE         3.5
 555555         SAM SMITH         7.9
##############################################
```

■ **Figure 11–9** Sample execution of master file utility program. (part 2 of 2 parts).

```
ENTER FUNCTION DESIRED
TO LIST ENTER          I
TO CREATE FILE ENTER  O
TO EXTEND FILE ENTER  E OR APPEND
TO TERMINATE ENTER    Q
? E
ENTER NAME OF FILE
? MASTERDATA
ENTER ID NUMBER, NAME,HOURLY WAGE
TO STOP ENTER Ø,Ø,Ø
? 666666,JOE JONES,4
ENTER ID NUMBER, NAME,HOURLY WAGE
TO STOP ENTER Ø,Ø,Ø
? Ø,Ø,Ø
ENTER FUNCTION DESIRED
TO LIST ENTER          I
TO CREATE FILE ENTER  O
TO EXTEND FILE ENTER  E OR APPEND
TO TERMINATE ENTER    Q
? I
ENTER NAME OF FILE TO BE LISTED
? MASTERDATA
LISTING OF FILE MASTERDATA
#############################################
ID NUMBER          NAME             HOURLY WAGE
 111111          JOHN DOE            4.2
 222222          MARY SMITH          6
 333333          JAMES BROWN         5
 444444          SALLY MAE           3.5
 555555          SAM SMITH           7.9
 666666          JOE JONES           4
#############################################
ENTER FUNCTION DESIRED
TO LIST ENTER          I
TO CREATE FILE ENTER  O
TO EXTEND FILE ENTER  E OR APPEND
TO TERMINATE ENTER    Q
? Q
```

Answer

Delete lines 270–285.
Insert the following:

```
261 INPUT#2, I, N$, H
262 PRINT I, N$, H
263 LET I1 = I
264 IF EOF(2) THEN 29Ø
265 INPUT#2, I, N$, H
266 IF I <= I1 THEN 27Ø
267 LET I1 = I
268 PRINT I, N$, H
269 GO TO 264
27Ø LET I1 = I
27Ø PRINT I, N$, H, "OUT OF SEQUENCE"
272 GO TO 264
```

11-3-3 Adding New Records to the Master File

The program shown in Figure 11–10 is used to add new records to the master file. Execution of the program for sample data is shown in Figure 11–11. The algorithm used by the program of Figure 11–10 can be summarized as follows:

1. Create (lines 95–150) a work file (WORKFILE) containing all new records to be added to the existing file (MASTERDATA) specified by the INPUT F$ at line 200.
2. Input first record from existing file and work file (lines 270–280).
3. If all records in existing file have been processed
   go to step 4 (line 325)
   else
   if existing key < work file key (line 330)
   place record from existing file onto new file
   input another record from existing file
   (lines 400–495)
   go to step 3
   else
   if existing key > work file key (line 340)
   place work file record onto new file
   input another record from work file
   go to step 3
   else
   write error message
   place work file record onto new file
   input next record from work file (lines 350–370)
   go to step 3.
4. Generate listing of new file (lines 600–735).

■ **Figure 11–10** Merge program (part 1 of 2 parts).

```
10 REM THIS PROGRAM MERGES NEW RECORDS INTO AN EXISTING FILE
60 REM
70 REM USER ENTERS NEW DATA IN ASCENDING SEQUENCE
80 REM PROGRAM STORES THE NEW DATA TEMPORARILY IN A FILE
90 REM
95 OPEN "0", 3, "WORKFILE"
100 PRINT "ENTER ID NUMBER, NAME, HOURLY WAGE"
101 PRINT "ENTER 0,0,0 TO STOP"
110 INPUT I, N$, H              Create file of records to be merged.
115 IF I=0 AND N$ = "0" AND H = 0 THEN 150
120    PRINT#3,I;",",N$;",";H
130    GO TO 100
150 CLOSE 3
160 REM
170 REM PROGRAM WILL MERGE NEW RECORDS INTO EXISTING FILE
180 REM
190 PRINT "ENTER NAME OF EXISTING FILE"
200 INPUT F$
210 OPEN "I",2,F$               Old master file.
220 OPEN "I",3,"WORKFILE"       File made up of records to be added.
230 OPEN "O",1,"NEWFILE"        New master file.
240 REM
250 REM INPUT FIRST RECORD FROM EXISTING FILE AND WORKFILE
260 REM
270 INPUT#2,I,N$,E              Read master file record.
280 INPUT#3,I1,N1$,E1           Read record to be merged.
290 REM
300 REM PLACE RECORDS IN NEWFILE UNTIL ENDS OF EXISTING
310 REM FILE AND WORKFILE ARE REACHED
320 REM
321 REM LARGE VALUE IN KEY FIELD INDICATES END OF FILE
322 REM HAS BEEN REACHED
325 IF I = 999999 AND I1 = 999999 THEN 600
326   REM
330   IF I < I1 THEN 400
340   IF I > I1 THEN 500
350     REM KEY FIELDS ARE EQUAL IS AN ERROR CONDITION
351     REM GET NEW RECORD FROM WORKFILE
352     REM
360     PRINT I1, N1$,E1 "ERROR: RECORD ALREADY EXISTS"
370     GO TO 500
400   REM
410   REM PLACE RECORD FROM EXISTING FILE INTO NEW FILE
420   REM
430   PRINT#1,I;",";N$;",";E
440   REM
450   REM INPUT RECORD FROM EXISTING FILE
470   IF EOF(2) THEN 490
480     INPUT#2,I,N$,E
485   GO TO 320
490   LET I=999999
495   GO TO 320
```

One condition in line 325 is satisfied. From now on I1 is always less than I, and the remaining records of the work file are added to the new file.

■ **Figure 11-10** Merge program (part 2 of 2 parts).

```
500   REM
510   REM PLACE RECORD FROM WORKFILE INTO NEW FILE
511   REM
512   PRINT#1,I1;",";N1$;",";E1
513   REM
514   REM INPUT NEXT RECORD FROM WORK FILE
520   REM
530   IF EOF(3) THEN 540
535     INPUT#3,I1,N1$,E1
539     GO TO 320
540   LET I1=999999
550   GO TO 320
600 REM
610 REM END OF BOTH FILES HAS BEEN REACHED
620 REM
630 CLOSE 1,2,3
640 REM
650 REM GENERATE LISTING OF NEWFILE
660 REM
670 PRINT "CONTENT OF NEWFILE IS AS FOLLOWS"
680 OPEN "I",1,"NEWFILE"
685 IF EOF(1) THEN 720
690   INPUT#1,I,N$,H
700   PRINT I,N$,H
710   GO TO 685
720 REM MAKE CHANGE PERMANENT IF USER DESIRES
730 REM
735 CLOSE 1
740 PRINT "DO YOU WISH CHANGES TO BECOME PERMANENT"
750 INPUT A$
760 IF A$ = "YES" THEN 800
770 IF A$ = "NO" THEN STOP
780 GO TO 740
800 REM
810 REM COPY NEWFILE INTO EXISTING FILE
820 REM
830 OPEN "I",1,"NEWFILE"
840 OPEN "O",2,F$
850 IF EOF(1) THEN 900
860   INPUT#1,I,N$,E
870   PRINT#2,I;",";N$;",";E
880   GO TO 850
900 CLOSE 1,2
910 PRINT "CHANGES ARE NOW PERMANENT"
920 END
```

The end of the records to be merged is reached. From now on I will always be less than I1, and the remaining records of the old master file are added to the new file.

5. If user wishes to have changes become permanent (lines 740–760)
   copy new files into master file and stop (lines 800–920)
   else
      stop (line 770).

Note that the program of Figure 11–10 places a large value (999999) in the key field variable when end-of-file is reached on either the work file or existing file (see lines 470–495, 530–550). This enables the program to continue ordinary processing in step 3 of the above algorithm without treating end-of-file conditions on either of the input files with special logic. If end-of-file is reached on the existing file before end-of-file on the work file, the value of the existing key will be 999999, which will be larger than all other work file key field values. This will force the remaining work file records to be placed onto the new file. A similar procedure occurs with the existing file records if end-of-file is encountered on the work file before end-of-file on the existing file.

This technique is extremely useful for processing of multiple sequential files in one program.

Figure 11–11 Sample execution of merge program.

```
ENTER ID NUMBER, NAME, HOURLY WAGE
ENTER 0,0,0 TO STOP
? 100000,JOE ABLE,6.8
ENTER ID NUMBER, NAME, HOURLY WAGE
ENTER 0,0,0 TO STOP
? 333333,AMY BROWN,7
ENTER ID NUMBER, NAME, HOURLY WAGE
ENTER 0,0,0 TO STOP
? 600000,RED JAMES,4
ENTER ID NUMBER, NAME, HOURLY WAGE
ENTER 0,0,0 TO STOP
? 0,0,0
ENTER NAME OF EXISTING FILE
? MASTERDATA
 333333          AMY BROWN       7 ERROR: RECORD ALREADY EXISTS
CONTENT OF NEWFILE IS AS FOLLOWS
 100000          JOE ABLE        6.8
 111111          JOHN DOE        4.2
 222222          MARY SMITH      6
 333333          AMY BROWN       7
 444444          SALLY MAE       3.5
 555555          SAM SMITH       7.9
 600000          RED JAMES       4
 666666          JOE JONES       4
DO YOU WISH CHANGES TO BECOME PERMANENT
? YES
CHANGES ARE NOW PERMANENT
```

Creation of file to be merged. This file is then merged with those records in MASTER DATA file.

11-3-4 Do It Now

What would happen in the execution of the program of Figure 11–10 if records in the work file were not in ascending sequence? How could the program be modified to take care of this problem?

Answer

Records from the work file will be inserted into the new file in an inappropriate sequence. The problem can be solved by performing a sequence check on the work file similar to that shown in Section 11–3–3. If a sequence error is found in the work file the program would not attempt to merge the two files.

11-3-5 The Data File Utility Program

Figure 11–12 contains a program used to create, extend, or list the data file containing the hours worked for employees to be paid during a pay period. Each record contains an employee identification and the number of hours worked. Execution of the program for sample data is shown in Figure 11–13. The program of Figure 11–12 is menu driven and is basically similar in logic to the program of Figure 11–10 used for similar operations on the master file.

11-3-6 The Pay Report Program

The program shown in Figure 11–14 with sample execution is used to process the master file (containing employee identification numbers, names, and pay rates) and the data file (containing employee identification numbers and hours worked) to produce a report showing gross pay. The procedure used can be summarized as follows:

1. Open master file and data file (lines 50–120).
2. Input first record in each file (lines 140–170).
3. If end-of-file has been reached on both files close files and stop (line 179).

```
   else
           if master key = data key (line 180)
              compute gross pay
              print line of report
              input next record from data file
              go to step 3
              (lines 300–399)
   else
           if master key < data key (line 190)
              input next record from master file
              go to step 3
              (lines 400–460)
   else
              print error message
              input next record from data file
              go to step 3
              (lines 200–240).
```

Note the use of large values (999999) in the key field to indicate that end-of-file has been reached on one or the other of the files. As in the program of Figure 11–10, this technique enables the processing loop (in step 3 of the above algorithm) to continue in a natural fashion until the end of both files is reached.

Figure 11–12 Data file utility program.

```
 10 REM THIS PROGRAM IS A UTILITY PROGRAM TO CREATE, LIST
 20 REM OR ADD TO A DATA FILE WITH TWO NUMERIC FIELDS
 30 REM
 40 REM DISPLAY MENU
 50 REM
 60 PRINT "ENTER FUNCTION CODE"
 70 PRINT "TO LIST ENTER             I            "
 80 PRINT "TO CREATE FILE ENTER      O            "
 85 PRINT "TO EXTEND FILE ENTER      E OR APPEND"
 86 PRINT "TO TERMINATE ENTER        Q            "
 90 INPUT M$
100 IF M$ = "O" OR M$ = "E" THEN 300
110   IF M$ = "I" THEN 200
115     IF M$ = "Q" THEN 400
120       PRINT "INVALID FUNCTION CODE"
130     GO TO 60
200   REM
210   REM FILE LISTING ROUTINE
220   REM
221   PRINT "ENTER FILE NAME"
222   INPUT F$
225   OPEN M$,1,F$
230   FOR I=1 TO 30
240       PRINT "*";
250   NEXT I
260   PRINT
261   PRINT "ID NUMBER","HOURS WORKED"
270   IF EOF(1) THEN 292
280     INPUT#1,N,A
290     PRINT N,A
291     GO TO 270
292   CLOSE 1
293   FOR I=1 TO 30
294     PRINT "*";
295   NEXT I
296   PRINT
299   GO TO 60
300 REM
310 REM FILE CREATION,EXTENSION ROUTINE
320 REM
330 PRINT "ENTER NAME OF FILE"
340 INPUT F$
350 OPEN M$,1,F$
360 PRINT "ENTER ID, HOURS"
361 PRINT "ENTER 0,0 TO TERMINATE"
370 INPUT N,H
372 IF N=0 AND H=0 THEN 395
380   PRINT#1,N;H
390   GO TO 360
395 CLOSE 1
399 GO TO 60
400 END
```

■ **Figure 11–13** Sample execution of data file utility program.

```
ENTER FUNCTION CODE
TO LIST ENTER          I          "
TO CREATE FILE ENTER   0          "
TO EXTEND FILE ENTER   E OR APPEND"
TO TERMINATE ENTER     Q          "
? 0
ENTER NAME OF FILE
? HOURS
ENTER ID,HOURS
ENTER Ø,Ø TO TERMINATE
? 111111,3Ø
ENTER ID,HOURS
ENTER Ø,Ø TO TERMINATE
? 222222,4Ø
ENTER ID,HOURS
ENTER Ø,Ø TO TERMINATE
? 3ØØØØØ,5Ø
ENTER ID,HOURS
ENTER Ø,Ø TO TERMINATE
? 444444,42
ENTER ID,HOURS
ENTER Ø,Ø TO TERMINATE
? Ø,Ø
ENTER FUNCTION CODE
TO LIST ENTER          I          "
TO CREATE FILE ENTER   0          "
TO EXTEND FILE ENTER   E OR APPEND"
TO TERMINATE ENTER     Q          "
? I
ENTER FILE NAME
? HOURS
******************************
ID NUMBER       HOURS WORKED
 111111          3Ø
 222222          4Ø
 3ØØØØØ          5Ø
 444444          42
******************************
ENTER FUNCTION CODE
TO LIST ENTER          I          "
TO CREATE FILE ENTER   0          "
TO EXTEND FILE ENTER   E OR APPEND"
TO TERMINATE ENTER     Q          "
? Q
```

Figure 11–14 Pay report program.

```
 10 REM THIS PROGRAM PROCESSES THE MASTER FILE AND
 20 REM HOURS FILE TO PRODUCE A GROSS PAY REPORT
 40 REM
 50 PRINT "ENTER NAME OF MASTER FILE"
 60 INPUT M$
 70 PRINT "ENTER NAME OF HOURS FILE"
 80 INPUT H$
 90 PRINT "MASTER FILE IS ";M$
100 PRINT "HOURS FILE IS ";H$
110 OPEN "I",1,M$
120 OPEN "I",2,H$
130 REM
140 REM INPUT FIRST RECORD FROM EACH FILE
150 REM
160 INPUT#1,I,N$,R
170 INPUT#2,I1,H
175 REM
176 REM CONTINUE PROCESSING UNTIL END OF BOTH FILES
177 REM SIGNIFIED BY LARGE VALUE IN KEY FIELDS
178 REM
179 IF I=999999 AND I1=999999 THEN 500
180   IF I=I1 THEN 300
190     IF I < I1 THEN 400
200     REM
210     REM NO MATCH
230     PRINT "NO MATCHING RECORD IN MASTER FILE ";I1
240     GO TO 350
300   REM
310   REM RECORDS MATCH
330   LET G=H*R
340   PRINT I;TAB(10);N$;TAB(20);R;TAB(25);H;TAB(32);G
350   REM
360   REM INPUT NEXT HOURS RECORD
370   REM
380   IF EOF(2) THEN 390
385     INPUT#2,I1,H
386     GO TO 175
390   LET I1 = 999999
399   GO TO 175
400   REM
410   REM INPUT NEXT MASTER RECORD
420   REM
430   IF EOF(1) THEN 450
440     INPUT#1,I,N$,R
445     GO TO 175
450   LET I = 999999
460   GO TO 175
500 CLOSE 1,2
510 END
RUN
ENTER NAME OF MASTER FILE
? MASTERDATA
ENTER NAME OF HOURS FILE
? HOURS
MASTER FILE IS MASTERDATA
HOURS IN FILE IS HOURS
 111111      JOHN DOE   4.2   30   126
 222222      MARY SMITH 6     40   240
NO MATCHING RECORD IN MASTER FILE 300000
 444444      SALLY MAE  3.5   42   147
```

11-3-7 Do It Now

1. How will the program of Figure 11–14 handle out-of-sequence records in the data file?
2. How will the program of Figure 11–14 handle records from the data file with duplicate key field values?

Answers

1. An error message will be written.
2. Duplicate lines in the report will be produced.

11-4 Data Files Created through BASIC

A file can be created using the BASIC operating system in much the same way a BASIC program is entered. Each line must begin with a line number and end by pressing the ENTER key. The line number can serve as a data item in the file (it might be an identification number for some entity in the file) or it may bear no relation to the data items in the file. When the file is read by BASIC program, the line number participates as a data item. If the line number corresponds to an identification number of some sort, this causes no difficulty; if the line number has no meaning in the program, instructions must still be included to read the line number as a data item (although the program must not process the line number in any way). This procedure offers several advantages over using a BASIC program to create and update data files.

1. The BASIC operating system can be used to create the file; no special file creation program needs to be written.
2. The BASIC command LIST can be used to produce a listing of the file; no special file listing program is necessary.
3. The BASIC system automatically arranges the file into ascending sequence by line number; no sorting of the file is required.
4. The BASIC system can be used to add lines to the file and delete lines from the file; no special update program is required.

On the other hand, there are some disadvantages to this technique:

1. The line number participates as a data item. Each line written onto a file must begin with a line number, even when the file is the output of a BASIC program; otherwise, the file cannot be processed by the BASIC command LIST.
2. No headings or other identifying information is produced by the LIST command; only the data listed.

3. If the key field value is longer than the permissible line number (for example, 5 digits on the TRS-80 III), the key field value cannot be used as the line number. This makes "automatic" updating via the BASIC system more difficult.

One special word of warning is in order for users of the TRS-80 Models II and III and IBM PC who wish to utilize this technique: when a file that will subsequently be processed by a BASIC program is SAVEd, the records must not be in compressed format. The SAVE command required is:

SAVE *"file name"*,A

The character "A" causes the program or data file to be saved in ASCII format; this means that such programs or data files can then be read by a BASIC program.

Files SAVEd by the usual SAVE command have their records in compressed format and cannot be processed by a BASIC program.

11-4-1 Do It Now

In your system, is it possible for a BASIC program to process a file created under the BASIC file creation/editing system? If so, what procedures and special considerations are applicable?

Figure 11-15 Comparison of file processing statements.

	TRS-80 III, II	Burroughs (large systems)	Apple Soft	IBM personal	DEC
Open files	OPEN	FILE #	PRINT D$;"OPEN"...	OPEN	OPEN
Input statement	INPUT #	INPUT # READ #	PRINT D#;"READ"... then INPUT	INPUT #	INPUT #
Output statement	PRINT #	PRINT # WRITE #	PRINT D$;"WRITE"... then PRINT	PRINT # WRITE #	PRINT # WRITE #
End-of-file detection	EOF function	NODATA #	ON ERR/GO TO	EOF function	ON ERR/GO TO
Close files	CLOSE	RESET #	PRINT D$;"CLOSE"	CLOSE	CLOSE #
NOTES			D$ = ""(nullstring)		

11-5 File Handling on Other BASIC Systems

The table in Figure 11-15 gives an abbreviated comparison of how file processing statements are implemented on a variety of common BASIC systems. However there is no substitute for the manual provided with each system, and the reader is strongly encouraged to refer to this document for his/her system before attempting to write programs requiring file manipulation.

11-6 Assignments

11-6-1 Test Yourself

1. A group of related data items is called a __________.
2. A data file is composed of many __________.
3. The purpose of a record key is __________.
4. Files are usually organized in __________ sequence.
5. The purpose of opening a file is __________.
6. The purpose of closing a file is __________.
7. End-of-file is reached when __________.
8. Placing a large value in the record key when end-of-file is reached enables a program to __________.
9. When a data file can be created via the BASIC system, the line number is usually utilized as __________.
10. A list of options presented to a program user is called a __________.
11. Suppose the file INVEN in the example of Section 11-1-2 cannot be contained in memory. Design a procedure to determine quantity on hand for part numbers accepted from input.
12. In the example of Figure 11-10, suppose the new items are not in sorted sequence. Add logic to perform the sort.
13. Write a procedure to delete items from the master file created in the program of Figure 11-12.
14. Write a procedure to process changes in name and hourly wage for the master file in the program of Figure 11-12.

11-6-2 Programming Assignments

1. Write programs for the Widget Manufacturing Company's sales information system. A sales file is to be created with records in the following format:

   salesperson number, amount of sale

   A master file must also be created with records in the format:

   salesperson number, name, amount of sales to date

   Programs are needed to:
   a. create the files,
   b. update the master file from data in the sales file, and
   c. produce a report summarizing sales by salesperson.

2. Dr. X teaches an introduction to computers course to fifteen or so students. Three equally weighted tests are given in the course. A file is created for the class; each record consists of a student's name followed by the student's grade. Records are sorted by name in alphabetical order. Each time a test is given, the file is updated to reflect the total score (sum of grades) obtained by each student so far. At the end of the semester, Dr. X computes the average of the three scores and assigns letter grades as follows:

90 and above	A	60–69	D
80–90	B	Below 60	F
70–79	C		

   a. Write a program to create a class file for Dr. X. Initially the students' scores are all zero.
   b. Simulate three sets of test scores for the fifteen students; update the class file three times.
   c. Produce a listing of names with their corresponding averages and letter grades.
   d. Write a program to input a student's name and print out that student's total test score so far.

3. In exercise 2 above, make necessary changes to the student's record and to the program to allow for the following message to be printed out when assigning the letter grade for each student: "Cannot determine student's final grade. Student did not take all three tests."

4. A bank maintains its accounts mater file with items in the following format:

   account number, name, present balance

   Checks must be processed against the master file. Write a program that accepts information about checks to be processed as input and updates the master file. Note that checks can be presented in any order, so that some sorting will be required before updating the file. Also note that more than one check may be processed against an account. What type of error conditions must be encountered? If your system supports random access binary files, this problem can be greatly simplified.

5. Rewrite the airline reservation problem of Exercise 4, Section 9-7-2, to allow maintenance of passenger reservation information files.

6. The Grand Order of Beavers bills its members for dues on a monthly basis. The Vice Exalted Flat Tail has been performing this task by hand, but since a computer system has become available, he feels that the billing could be made more efficient by using a computerized system. Design and implement a system to maintain membership rolls and produce bills and associated reports. Payments should be processed in small batches as they are received. Include a feature for dropping members if their dues are in arrears by three months or more.

7. At the end of the semester, students' final grades are recorded in a file called GRADE-ROSTER-FILE. The file is organized sequentially using each student's social security number as a key. Identical social security numbers occur in groups, i.e., each group identifies a particular student's grades in each course taken by the student. An example of GRADE-ROSTER-FILE is as follows:

GRADE-ROSTER-FILE

	Social Security	Name	Course Number		Grade	Date
Student 1	111222333	GLEASON JIM	NG	1ØØ	A	Ø61281
	111222333	GLEASON JIM	HES	1Ø2	B	Ø61281
	111222333	GLEASON JIM	BY1	1Ø4	C	Ø61281
	111222333	GLEASON JIM	BY2	1Ø6	D	Ø61281
	111222333	GLEASON JIM	PSY	1Ø8	F	Ø61281
Student 2	212356553	WOLFE MONA	PSY	1Ø8	B	Ø61281
	212356553	WOLFE MONA	BY2	1Ø6	A	Ø61281
.						
.						

The Registrar's office also has a list of student names organized sequentially by social security key on a disk file called STUDENT-ADMISSION-FILE. Each disk record, in addition to the student's name and social security number, contains the student's current cumulative hours and cumulative grade point, as well as the student's major field of study and classification. An example of STUDENT-ADMISSION-FILE is:

STUDENT-ADMISSION-FILE

	Name	Social Security	Major	Class	Cum. hours	Cum. points
Student 1	GLEASON JIM	111222333	NURSING	SENIOR	1ØØ	3455
Student 2	WOLFE MONA	212356553	HOME EC.	SOPH	Ø3Ø	Ø65Ø
.						
.						

3 credits A = 3×4 = 12 cum. pts.
2 credits B = 2×3 = 6 cum. pts.
4 credits F = 4×0 = 0 cum. pts.

Total credits = 9 Cum. pts. = 18

Since each record of the GRADE-ROSTER-FILE neither indicates the number of credits associated with the particular course nor the verbal description of the course, a file called COURSE-CATALOG-FILE is used as a course identification directory to look up the number of credits for a particular course (3-digit course number) and the corresponding verbal description. An example of such a file is shown below:

COURSE-CATALOG-FILE

```
100|NURSING II        |4——►Course number 100 is Nursing II and
102|EL. NUTRITION     |3   it is a 4-credit course.
104|MICROBIOLOGY      |3
106|MICROBIOLOGY LAB  |1
108|GEN. PSYCHOLOGY   |3
```

Let us write a program that will:

1. Read the GRADE-ROSTER-FILE and print each of the student's end-of-semester grade reports.
2. Compute the student's grade point average for the semester, as well as his cumulative grade point average.
3. Print the semester total hours, as well as the cumulative hours.
4. Update the student admission file to reflect updated entries for both the cumulative points and cumulative hours.

An example of a student's end-of-semester grade report is shown as follows:

```
FIELD STUDY  CLASS   STUDENT NAME          DATE       SS. NUMBER
NURSING      SENIOR  GLEASON JIM         06 12 81     111222333
*****************************************************************
COURSE       NUMBER  DESCRIPTION       HOURS  GRADE  POINTS    GPA
*************CUMULATIVE TOTALS         100           345.5
NG           100     NURSING II          4      A     16.0
HES          102     EL. NUTRITION       3      B      9.0
BY1          104     MICROBIOLOGY        3      C      6.0
BY2          106     MICROBIOLOGY LA     1      D      1.0
PSY          108     GEN. PSYCHOLOGY     3      F      0.0
*****************************************************************
                     SEMESTER TOTALS   14             32.0  2.285
                     CUM.      TOTALS 114            377.5  3.311
```

The interaction or the relationship between the various transaction files and the master file is shown below. This figure illustrates the way in which data is captured from the various files to produce a complete end-of-semester grade report.

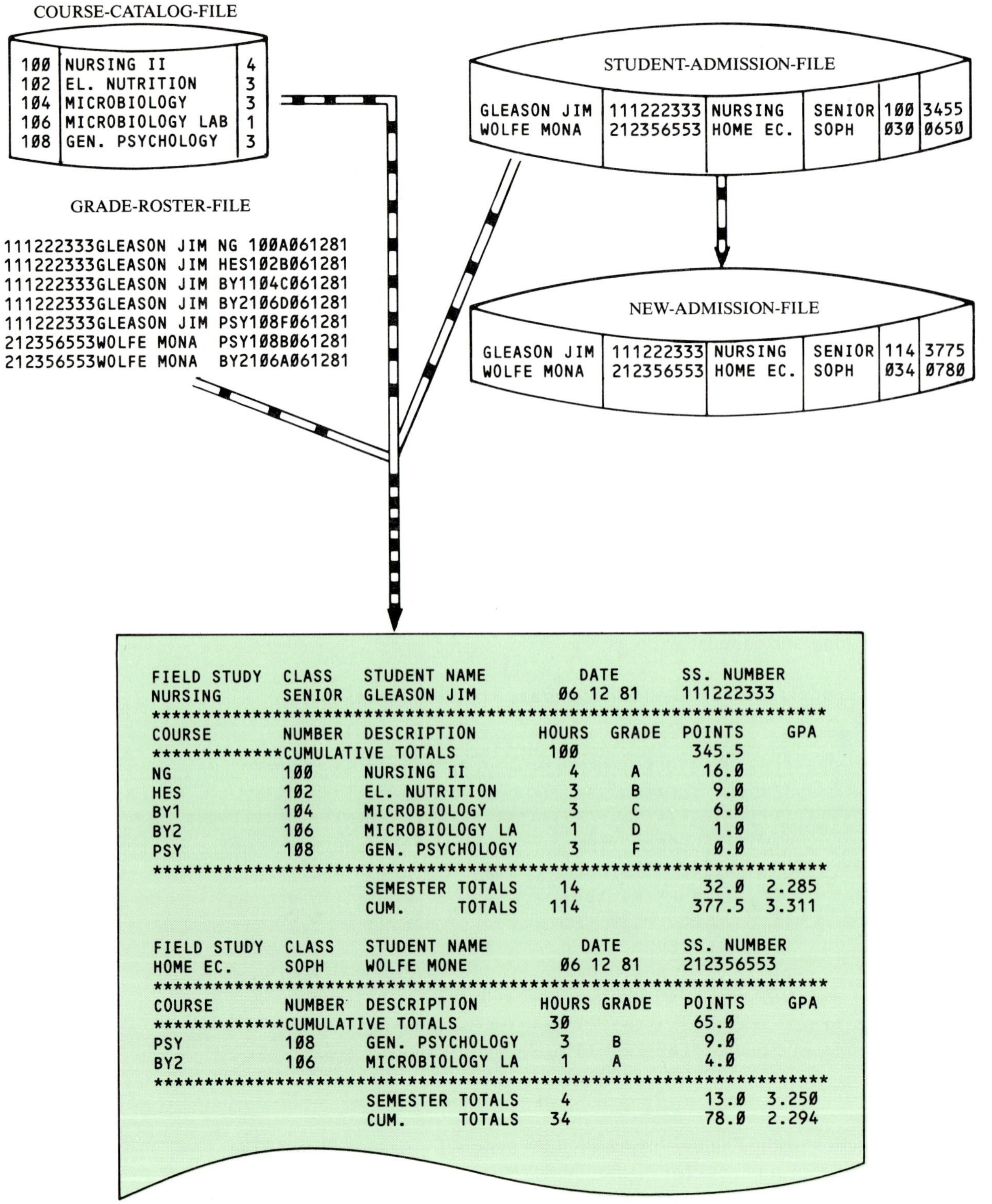
COURSE-CATALOG-FILE
100 NURSING II 4
102 EL. NUTRITION 3
104 MICROBIOLOGY 3
106 MICROBIOLOGY LAB 1
108 GEN. PSYCHOLOGY 3
STUDENT-ADMISSION-FILE
GLEASON JIM 111222333 NURSING SENIOR 100 3455
WOLFE MONA 212356553 HOME EC. SOPH 030 0650
GRADE-ROSTER-FILE
111222333GLEASON JIM NG 100A061281
111222333GLEASON JIM HES102B061281
111222333GLEASON JIM BY1104C061281
111222333GLEASON JIM BY2106D061281
111222333GLEASON JIM PSY108F061281
212356553WOLFE MONA PSY108B061281
212356553WOLFE MONA BY2106A061281
NEW-ADMISSION-FILE
GLEASON JIM 111222333 NURSING SENIOR 114 3775
WOLFE MONA 212356553 HOME EC. SOPH 034 0780
FIELD STUDY CLASS STUDENT NAME DATE SS. NUMBER
NURSING SENIOR GLEASON JIM 06 12 81 111222333
****
COURSE NUMBER DESCRIPTION HOURS GRADE POINTS GPA
**************CUMULATIVE TOTALS 100 345.5
NG 100 NURSING II 4 A 16.0
HES 102 EL. NUTRITION 3 B 9.0
BY1 104 MICROBIOLOGY 3 C 6.0
BY2 106 MICROBIOLOGY LA 1 D 1.0
PSY 108 GEN. PSYCHOLOGY 3 F 0.0
****
SEMESTER TOTALS 14 32.0 2.285
CUM. TOTALS 114 377.5 3.311
FIELD STUDY CLASS STUDENT NAME DATE SS. NUMBER
HOME EC. SOPH WOLFE MONE 06 12 81 212356553
****
COURSE NUMBER DESCRIPTION HOURS GRADE POINTS GPA
*************CUMULATIVE TOTALS 30 65.0
PSY 108 GEN. PSYCHOLOGY 3 B 9.0
BY2 106 MICROBIOLOGY LA 1 A 4.0
****
SEMESTER TOTALS 4 13.0 3.250
CUM. TOTALS 34 78.0 2.294

8. In the program of exercise 7, which produced the end-of-semester grade report, include the code to change a student name in STUDENT-ADMISSION-FILE whenever the following situation arises: Matching social security numbers in GRADE-ROSTER-FILE and STUDENT-ADMISSION-FILE do not identify the same student name. This could happen, for instance, if during the semester a name change occurred as a result of marriage, etc.

9. The problem example of exercise 7 dealt with end-of-semester grade report/transcript, which did not include error checking. Rewrite the program to take care of the following situations:

a. A social security number in GRADE-ROSTER-FILE has no corresponding match in STUDENT-ADMISSION-FILE. In such a case, print an appropriate error message identifying the name of the student not listed in the STUDENT-ADMISSION-FILE.

b. A course number in the GRADE-ROSTER-FILE has been incorrectly typed and is not found in the course directory. Type an appropriate message and abort the report for the particular student. Note that in such a case successive social security numbers may still belong to the current group of social security numbers identifying the particular student. Such records should be flushed out before continuing with the next different student record(s).

c. The grade specified in the GRADE-ROSTER-FILE is incorrectly recorded; i.e., the grade is neither F, D, C, B or A. Abort current report and continue with the next report.

10. Dr. Teach keeps his student's grades on diskettes on his own microcomputer system. He has already entered into his master file the following information on each student: name, two test scores and two blank entries for the final average and the corresponding letter grade. Dr. Teach's input file might be similar to:

Name	Test1	Test2	Average	Grade
.				
DOE J	80	90	?	?
HILL K	60	62	?	?
.				
.				

A	= 90 or above
B+	= 85–89
B	= 80–84
C+	= 75–79
C	= 60–74
D	= 50–59
F	= below 50

Dr. Teach is now ready to write a program to compute each student's final score and corresponding letter grade. He realizes that in some cases, either or both test scores may have to be changed. Some students have withdrawn from his class and want their name deleted from his master file. Write a program to:

a. Create a class file arranged alphabetically by student name. Each record should contain a name, two test scores and two initial blank fields for the final average and the letter grade.

b. Create a transaction file consisting of change records. Such records can cause deletion of certain records or changes in either one or both test scores. Use change codes of your choice (continued on next page).

c. Print an updated grade roster file listing the names of the students as well as their scores and letter grade. Identify transaction names that do not have corresponding matches in the master file.

The master file, transaction file and output can be visualized as follows:

Master file

```
DOE JOE     50  70
LIKE SALLY  80  90
TASS MIKE   65  75
TURAN LEO   80  70
```

Transaction file

```
DOE JOE     DELETE
LIKE SALLY  CHANGE  1  70
TASS MIKE   CHANGE  1  80
TURAN LEO   CHANGE  2  80
TURAN LEO   CHANGE  1  60
AMIGO LUIS  CHANGE  1  60
```

Output

```
NAME          T1  T2  AVG  GRADE

LIKE SALLY    70  90  80     B
TASS MIKE     80  70  75     C+
TURAN LEO     60  80  70     C
NO MATCH FOR AMIGO
```

11. WKNE station's meteorologist has access to a master file containing weather data on most of the cities that lie within a 50-mile radius of the WKNE broadcasting station. Each record contains the name of the city and its record high and low temperatures for each of the past 20 years. The master file records have the following layout:

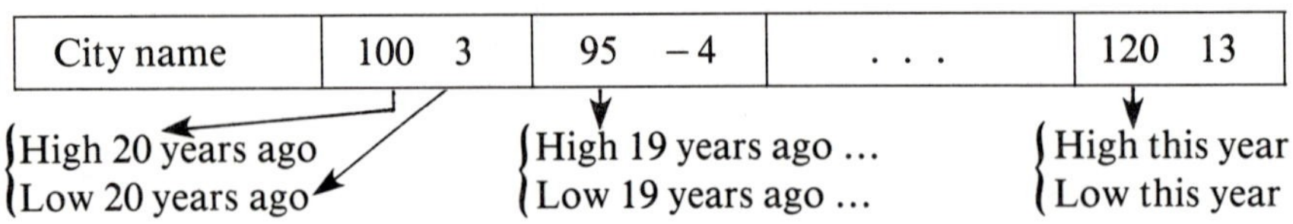

a. Write a program to read a data file where each record contains the name of a city and the corresponding high and low temperatures for the day. Such records are as follows:

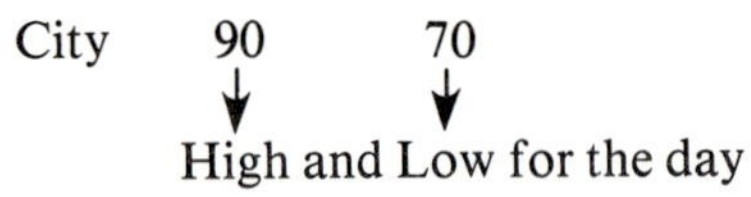

The program should list the temperature (high and low) of the day for each city and indicate whether any temperature records were broken during the day. A typical listing might be:

```
CITY         HIGH  LOW

ATMORE        98   70
BEULAH        95   68   PREVIOUS RECORD HI WAS 94 IN 1971
CHUMUCKLA     92   65   PREVIOUS RECORD LO WAS 66 IN 1979
MILTON        98   62
MARYESTHER   100   58   PREVIOUS RECORD HI WAS 98 IN 1965
                        PREVIOUS RECORD LO WAS 60 IN 1974

PACE          94   71
```

Make sure to update the master file if any record temperatures are broken; i.e., change the records in the master file to identify new highs or lows.

b. Design an on-line inquiry system which allows the meteorologist to perform the following functions:

(1) Key in a city name and a year and list the high and low for that city and year.

(2) Key in a city name and identify the year of its record high and low of the last 20 years. Print the city, year and record high and low.

(3) Key in a year and identify the city (cities) with record high and low for that year.

(4) Produce a listing arranged in year sequence order, identifying the record high and low for each city during the year. Over the 20-year period the output might be as follows:

YEAR	CITIES	HI	LO
1962	ATMORE	94	15
	BEULAH	91	21
	CHUMUCKLA	96	16
	MILTON	89	23
	MARYESTHER	9Ø	2Ø
	PACE	94	9
1963	ATMORE	98	1Ø
	BEULAH	94	16
	CHUMUCKLA	89	14
	.		
	.		
1982	ATMORE	91	1Ø
	BEULAH	9Ø	12
	.		
	.		
	PACE	99	2Ø

12. The Furniture Company has stock in three different warehouses. The controller/dispatcher needs to know at any given time the number of particular furniture items at any of the three warehouses. He may also need to know the number (quantity) of each particular item at a warehouse. Initially, the stock of items in all warehouses is as follows:

	WAREHOUSE 1	WAREHOUSE 2	WAREHOUSE 3
DESKS	123	44	76
CHAIRS	789	234	12
BEDS	67	456	9Ø

The controller has at his fingertips a terminal where he can inquire about a particular item. For example, when he types "BEDS," the system furnishes him with the number of beds at the three warehouses.

a. Write a program to allow the following communications between the dispatcher and the data base:

```
ENTER REQUEST
BEDS
                WAREHOUSE1    WAREHOUSE2    WAREHOUSE3
BEDS                67           456            9Ø        TOTAL 613

ENTER REQUEST
WAREHOUSE3
                   DESKS         CHAIRS          BEDS
WAREHOUSE3          76           12              9Ø        TOTAL 178

ENTER REQUEST
CHAIRS
               WAREHOUSE1    WAREHOUSE2    WAREHOUSE3
CHAIRS              789          236           12         TOTAL 1Ø35

ENTER REQUEST
```

Note that the message "ENTER REQUEST" is printed after each request has been satisfied. If the dispatcher enters an invalid request, the system should print an appropriate error message to force him to renew his request.

b. How would you design a program to update such a master file? Do so.

13. The PAYROLL-FILE at Tricity College consists of records containing the following information:

a. Employee social security number.
b. A federal tax coefficient that is applied to gross pay to determine pay period federal taxes.
c. A year-to-date gross pay.
d. A year-to-date federal tax.
e. A year-to-date social security tax.
f. A year-to-date net pay.

Create a disk payroll file for the Tricity College personnel department and a transaction file consisting of records containing an employee social security number and an employee pay period gross pay.

(1) Write a program to update PAYROLL-FILE with TRANSACTION-FILE and print each employee's check and check stub, as follows:

```
TRICITY COLLEGE
DATE  4/16/82

PAY TO  DOE  JON     $***668.84

------------------------------------------
CHECK DATE  4/16/82
SOCIAL SECURITY     NAME
109-84-8224         JON  DOE

GROSS PAY      FED. TAX     FICA   NET PAY
1,008.77         272.85     67.08  668.84

Y-T-D          Y-T-D        Y-T-D  Y-T-D
GROSS PAY      FED. TAX     FICA   NET PAY
8,070.16       2,246.90     536.64 3,057.90
------------------------------------------

TRICITY COLLEGE
DATE  4/16/82

PAY TO  CHARMS  LINDA      $**1,664.48

------------------------------------------
CHECK DATE  4/16/82
SOCIAL SECURITY     NAME
304-12-3334         LINDA  CHARMS
      .          .            .       .
      .          .            .       .
------------------------------------------
```

(2) Using tables, try to complete the above paychecks by writing out the pay amount in words, as in:

```
TRICITY COLLEGE
DATE  4/16/82

PAY TO      DOE  JON          $***668.84
            -------------
SIX HUNDRED AND SIXTY-EIGHT AND 84/100
```

14. The Chique Boutique is an exclusive ladies' fashion store where the Chique Boutique members are required to maintain at least \$1,000 in their accounts at all times. Members charge purchases on Chique Boutique credit cards. Write a program to create a master file consisting of customer numbers, customer names and an initial balance of over \$1,500 for each member.

Members may return merchandise, in which case their account is credited appropriately. In some cases, purchases may cause the member's credit to fall below \$1,000, in which case a notice is sent to the member requesting that a check be written to bring back the member's credit to at least $1,000.

A TRANSACTION-FILE for the month consists of various purchase records sorted by ascending customer numbers. Such records include a customer number, an item description and a date of purchase. Individual customer transactions, if more than one, occur in groups.

a. Write a program to update the master file and produce a monthly customer invoice similar to the following:

```
CHIQUE BOUTIQUE
ACCT NO: 1215
DATE 02/05/82                    DATE       BALANCE      PURCHASES
                                            10,000.00
***JOVANT BOOTS               01/20/82        360.00
   ENSEMBLE LINGERIE          01/23/82                     550.75
   FLEURETTE FOUNDATION       01/25/82                     145.25
   PENDANT 20 KT.             01/27/82                   2,600.00
                                            ---------   --------
                                             7,064.00   3,296.00
```

Note that *** is a credit entry (return).

```
CHIQUE BOUTIQUE
ACCT NO: 1315
DATE 02/05/82                    DATE       BALANCE      PURCHASES
                                             2,000.00
 NEGLIGEE EXQUIS              01/15/82                     600.00
 PEIGNOIR BROCADE             01/20/82                     400.00
 ILUNA ESSENCE 6 OZ. FL.      01/23/82                     300.00
                                            ---------   --------
PLEASE REMIT MINIMUM OF $300.00                700.00   1,300.00
```

b. The Chique Boutique sales department would like to produce the following monthly sales activity report by ascending customer account number:

```
MONTHLY SALES REPORT: APRIL 1982

ACCOUNT NO.   TOTAL SALES   CUSTOMER BALANCE
   1215         3,296.00        7,064.00
   1315         1,300.00          700.00
   1446        10,432.00        5,600.00
              ___________     __________
               15,028.00       13,364.00
```

Write the code to generate such a report.

c. The internal auditor would like to obtain a sales summary report for each day of the month as follows:

SUMMARY DAILY SALES

DATE	SALES
Ø1/Ø1/82	23,452.ØØ
Ø1/Ø2/82	13,452.ØØ
Ø1/Ø3/82	33,4ØØ.7Ø
.	.
.	.
	.

d. The auditor would also like to obtain a summary of daily sales by items, as follows:

DETAILED DAILY SALES

DATE	ITEMS	SALES	TOTALS
Ø1/Ø1/82			
	112	344.ØØ	
	2Ø9	246.ØØ	
	321	41Ø.ØØ	
	4ØØ	22,452.ØØ	
			23,452.ØØ
Ø1/Ø2/82			
	112	344.ØØ	
	216	1Ø,ØØØ.ØØ	
	312	3,1Ø8.ØØ	
			13,452.ØØ
.	.	.	.
.	.	.	.

14. The Tricity College library staff is thinking about using computers to assist them in dealing with the high volume of book transactions. For the purpose of this exercise, four types of transactions are considered:

a. Books checked in.
b. Books checked out.
c. New books put into circulation.
d. Old books withdrawn from circulation.

Books have an 8-digit numeric code identification, the last two digits of which indicate a multicopy identification number:

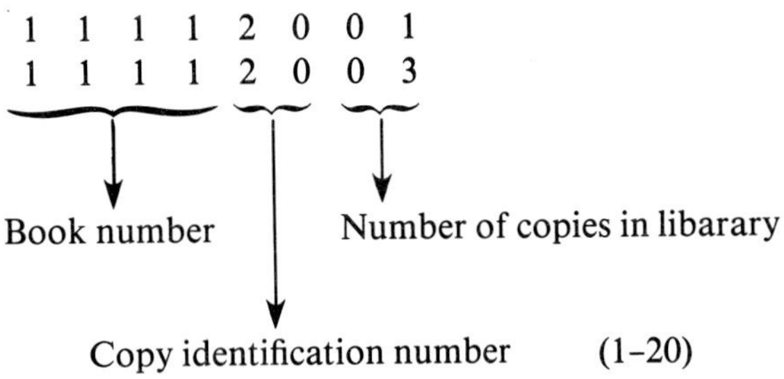

The library clerks manually deal with four types of files:

a. The CHECK-IN-OUT-FILE.

This file consists of a daily list of books that have been checked either in or out. The record layout for each file is as follows:

Item	Nature
1	Book number identification
2	Disposition code (1 = check in, 2 = check out)
3	Julian date (025 means Jan. 25, 365 is Dec. 31)
4	Patron's identity (1 = faculty, 2 = student)
5	Patron's telephone number

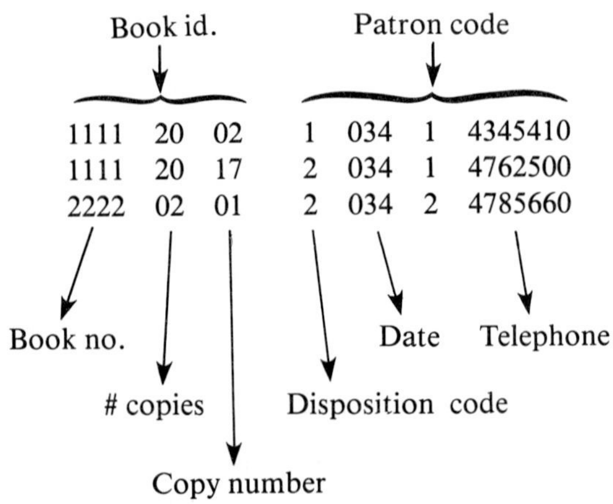

b. The NEW-BOOK-FILE.

This file consists of books that do not exist in the master file. Such books have been either purchased or donated. The record layout for such file records is:

Item	Nature
1	Book number identification
2	Year of edition
3	Disposition status (1 = available, 2 = reserve)
4	Author
5	Acquisition code (1 = purchased, 2 = donation)

c. The DELETE-FILE.

Transaction records in this file allow the librarian to delete books from the master file or to change the status field of a particular book. The record layout for such file records is:

All 1130 books are deleted from the inventory.

Item	Nature		
1	Book number identification	1 1 3 0	1
2	Change code { 1 = delete, 2 = make status available, 3 = make status reserve }	1 4 0 0	2

All 1400 books are now changed to available status, i.e., however many there were.

d. The MASTER-FILE.

All records in the master file have the following layout:

Item	Nature
1	Book identification number
2	Author
3	Edition Year
4	Status disposition (1 = on loan, 2 = on shelf)
5	Date loaned (0 if book is not loaned)
6	Patron's identity (1 = faculty, 2 = student, 3 = on the shelf)
7	Acquisition code (1 = purchased, 2 = donation)
8	Reserve status (1 = available, 2 = reserve)
9	Patron's telephone number

Write a program to perform the following tasks:

(1) Create the above four files and store them on disk. Assume the records are arranged sequentially according to the 8-digit book identification number.

(2) Print the four disk files.

(3) a. Assume that all disk file records are in sequence and that all transaction records are valid; i.e., transaction keys have all corresponding matching keys in the master file. Update MASTER-FILE with CHECK-IN-OUT-FILE.

b. Print a listing of the updated file.

c. Print a list of telephone numbers of patrons who possess overdue books. A book is overdue if it has been kept 30 days or more. A fine of 10 cents a day is charged for each day over 30 days. Such a report should indicate the telephone number, the number of days overdue, the original checkout day, and the corresponding fine in dollars and cents. No fines are listed for faculty members. Books that have not been returned after a 100-day overdue period are considered stolen. Flag such books on the output to allow the librarian to charge the patron for the cost of the book plus the 100-day fine. (These books will be deleted in part 6 of this exercise by their inclusion in the DELETE-FILE.)

d. List each book identification number of MASTER-FILE and summarize for each volume the number of copies in or out (on the shelf or on loan). The report should be similar to:

```
BOOK IDENTIFICATION        IN      OUT
     1111 2Ø Ø3
     1111 2Ø Ø8
     1111 2Ø 17
                            3       17
     2ØØØ 18 Ø2
     2ØØØ 18 12
          .                 2       16
          .
          .
```

e. Determine the percentage of books currently held by faculty and the percentage of books currently held by the students.

(4) a. Update the current MASTER-FILE with NEW-BOOK-FILE; i.e., merge the two files. It is understood that no book in NEW-BOOK-FILE exists in the current MASTER-FILE. (See part 7 for additions of books that currently exist in the master file.) Print an updated inventory listing.

b. During the update pass (i.e., without reprocessing the master file), keep track of all the book identification numbers that have been donated so as to print a list of such titles at the conclusion of the update process.

(5) a. Identify any author who has written two or more different books. Specify the author and corresponding list of books.

b. Produce a list of books arranged by ascending author order.

(6) a. Update MASTER-FILE with DELETE-FILE.

b. Print the list of books that have been deleted (all such books are assumed to be currently on the shelf). Remember, there may be more than one of the same title.

c. Any book that has not been returned after 100 days from checkout date is considered stolen, and hence should be deleted and brought to the attention of the librarian by means of an appropriate message.

d. Print the updated file.

(7) On many occasions, the library purchases additional copies of existing books. Design a system to allow the librarian to add these books to the master file. Such purchases of new books can give rise to the following situations: Either the new books purchased need to be added to similar copies already on the shelf, in which case the quantity of existing books on hand needs to be changed; or the books to be added are newer editions, in which case all books with edition year less than new edition must be taken out of circulation, i.e., deleted. If this is the case, the librarian would like to obtain a list of all such books that are to be deleted, so that these entries can be added to the DELETE file of part 6 of this problem. Write the code to take care of the above possibilities.

11-6-3 Answers to Test Yourself

1. record.
2. records.
3. facilitate retrieval of data records in a file.

4. ascending.
5. to enable the operating system to locate the file and make it ready for processing.
6. to enable the operating system to make its information about the file permanent so that other programs can process the data.
7. there are no more records in the file.
8. use one loop to process all data contained in multiple files without the incorporation of special logic to handle end-of-file situations.
9. the record key.
10. menu.
11. 1. Input part number
    2. Open master file
    3. If end of master file
            move large value to master part number
        else
            input record from master file
    4. If part number = master part number
            print quantity on hand
            close master file
            go to step 1
        else
            if part number < master part number
                go to step 3
        else
            print error message
            close master file
            go to step 1.
12. Replace lines 95–150 with the following:

```
 95 DIM D(100),M$(100),R(100)
 96 FOR J = 1 TO 100
 97 INPUT D(J),M$(J),R(J)
 98 IF D(J) = 0 AND M$(J) = "0" AND R(J) = 0 THEN 101
 99 M = J
100 NEXT J
101 FOR J = M-1 TO 1 STEP -1
102 FOR K = 1 TO J
103    IF D(K) <= D(K+1) THEN 113
104       T = D(K)
105       D(K) = D(K+1)
106       D(K+1) = T
107       T$ = M$(K)
108       M$(K) = M$(K+1)
109       M$(K+1) = T$
110       T = R(K)
111       R(K) = R(K+1)
112       R(K+1) = T
113  NEXT K
114 NEXT J
115 OPEN "O",3,"WORKFILE"
116 FOR J = 1 TO M
117  PRINT#3,D(J); ",";M$(J); ",";R(J)
118 NEXT J
119 CLOSE 3
```

13.

```
1. Create a file containing deletions
2. Open master file, deletion file, work file
3. If end of master file
        move large value to master id
     else
        input master file record
4. If end of deletion file
        move large value to deletion id
     else
        input deletion file record.
5. If master id = large value and deletion id = large value
        go to step 8
6. If master id = deletion id
        go to step 3
     else
        if master id < deletion id
        print master record data on work file
        go to step 7
     else
        print error message
        go to step 4
7. If end of master file
        move large value to master id
     else
        input master file record
     go to step 5
8. Close files
9. Copy content of work file into master file
```

14.

```
1. Create change file containing all changes to be made
2. Open change file, master file, and work file
3. If end of change file
        move large value to change id
     else
        input change file record
4. If end of master file
        move large value to master id
     else
        input master file record
5. If master id = large value and change id = large value
        go to step 7
     else
        if master id < change id
        print master-record on workfile
        go to step 4
     else
        if master id change id
        go to step 6
     else
        print change record on work file
        go to step 3
```

6. Print error message
   if end of change file
      move larger value to change id
   else
      input change file record
   go to step 5
7. Close files
8. Copy content of work file into master file

INDEX